Handbook of Research on Thrust Technologies' Effect on Image Processing

Binay Kumar Pandey
Department of Information Technology, College of Technology, Govind Ballabh Pant University of Agriculture and Technology, India

Digvijay Pandey
Department of Technical Education, Government of Uttar Pradesh, India

Rohit Anand
G.B. Pant DSEU Okhla-1 Campus, India & Government of NCT of Delhi, New Delhi, India

Deepak S. Mane
Performance Engineering Lab, Tata Research, Development, and Design Center, Australia

Vinay Kumar Nassa
Rajarambapu Institute of Technology, India

IGI Global
PUBLISHER of TIMELY KNOWLEDGE

A volume in the Advances in Computational Intelligence and Robotics (ACIR) Book Series

Published in the United States of America by
IGI Global
Engineering Science Reference (an imprint of IGI Global)
701 E. Chocolate Avenue
Hershey PA, USA 17033
Tel: 717-533-8845
Fax: 717-533-8661
E-mail: cust@igi-global.com
Web site: http://www.igi-global.com

Library of Congress Cataloging-in-Publication Data

Names: Pandey, Binay Kumar, 1983- editor. | Pandey, Digvijay, editor. |
    Anand, Rohit, editor. | Mane, Deepak S., 1977- editor. | Nassa, Vinay
    Kumar, editor.
Title: Handbook of research on thrust technologies' effect on image processing
    / edited by Binay Kumar Pandey, Digvijay Pandey, Rohit Anand, Deepak S. Mane,
    and Vinay Kumar Nassa.
Description: Hershey, PA : Information Science Reference, [2023] | Includes
    bibliographical references and index. | Summary: "This book is a useful
    resource for researchers to grow their interest and understanding in the
    burgeoning fields of image processing. The entire book serves as a
    manual for researchers and industry experts who want to learn about the
    latest trends and optimization methods and how to watermark photographs
    to increase privacy and security. The strengths of security in the areas
    of Cloud, IoT, and Android are strengthened by the multidisciplinary
    approaches to image processing. It examines several case studies,
    suggests new methods, and handles some more recent security issues.
    Along with 2D and 3D imaging approaches, this book will also cover cloud
    computing, the Internet of Things, digital watermarking, neural
    networks, feature identification, and optimization."-- Provided by
    publisher.
Identifiers: LCCN 2022062289 (print) | LCCN 2022062290 (ebook) | ISBN
    9781668486184 (h/c) | ISBN 9781668486207 (ebook)
Subjects: LCSH: Image processing--Digital techniques--Technological
    innovations.
Classification: LCC TA1637 .T477 2023 (print) | LCC TA1637 (ebook) | DDC
    006.4/2--dc23/eng/20230126
LC record available at https://lccn.loc.gov/2022062289
LC ebook record available at https://lccn.loc.gov/2022062290

This book is published in the IGI Global book series Advances in Computational Intelligence and Robotics (ACIR) (ISSN: 2327-0411; eISSN: 2327-042X)

British Cataloguing in Publication Data
A Cataloguing in Publication record for this book is available from the British Library.

For electronic access to this publication, please contact: eresources@igi-global.com.

Advances in Computational Intelligence and Robotics (ACIR) Book Series

Ivan Giannoccaro
University of Salento, Italy

ISSN:2327-0411
EISSN:2327-042X

MISSION

While intelligence is traditionally a term applied to humans and human cognition, technology has progressed in such a way to allow for the development of intelligent systems able to simulate many human traits. With this new era of simulated and artificial intelligence, much research is needed in order to continue to advance the field and also to evaluate the ethical and societal concerns of the existence of artificial life and machine learning.

The **Advances in Computational Intelligence and Robotics (ACIR) Book Series** encourages scholarly discourse on all topics pertaining to evolutionary computing, artificial life, computational intelligence, machine learning, and robotics. ACIR presents the latest research being conducted on diverse topics in intelligence technologies with the goal of advancing knowledge and applications in this rapidly evolving field.

COVERAGE

- Pattern Recognition
- Computational Intelligence
- Fuzzy Systems
- Robotics
- Heuristics
- Algorithmic Learning
- Artificial Life
- Cognitive Informatics
- Computational Logic
- Adaptive and Complex Systems

IGI Global is currently accepting manuscripts for publication within this series. To submit a proposal for a volume in this series, please contact our Acquisition Editors at Acquisitions@igi-global.com or visit: http://www.igi-global.com/publish/.

Titles in this Series

For a list of additional titles in this series, please visit: www.igi-global.com/book-series

Stochastic Processes and Their Applications in Artificial Intelligence
Christo Ananth (Samarkand State University, Uzbekistan) N. Anbazhagan (Alagappa University, India) and Mark Goh (National University of Singapore, Singapore)
Engineering Science Reference • copyright 2023 • 220pp • H/C (ISBN: 9781668476796) • US $270.00 (our price)

Handbook of Research on Deep Learning Techniques for Cloud-Based Industrial IoT
P. Swarnalatha (Department of Information Security, School of Computer Science and Engineering, Vellore Institute of Technology, India) and S. Prabu (Department Banking Technology, Pondicherry University, India)
Engineering Science Reference • copyright 2023 • 432pp • H/C (ISBN: 9781668480984) • US $335.00 (our price)

Handbook of Research on AI-Based Technologies and Applications in the Era of the Metaverse
Alex Khang (Global Research Institute of Technology and Engineering, USA) Vrushank Shah (Institute of Technology and Engineering, Indus University, India) and Sita Rani (Department of Computer Science and Engineering, Guru Nanak Dev Engineering College, India)
Engineering Science Reference • copyright 2023 • 517pp • H/C (ISBN: 9781668488515) • US $345.00 (our price)

Advanced Interdisciplinary Applications of Machine Learning Python Libraries for Data Science
Soly Mathew Biju (University of Wollongong, UAE) Ashutosh Mishra (Yonsei University, South Korea) and Manoj Kumar (University of Wollongong, UAE)
Engineering Science Reference • copyright 2023 • 300pp • H/C (ISBN: 9781668486962) • US $275.00 (our price)

Predicting Pregnancy Complications Through Artificial Intelligence and Machine Learning
D. Satish Kumar (Nehru Institute of Engineering and Technology , India) and P. ManiIarasan (Nehru Institute of Engineering and Technology, India)
Medical Information Science Reference • copyright 2023 • 350pp • H/C (ISBN: 9781668489741) • US $350.00 (our price)

Effective AI, Blockchain, and E-Governance Applications for Knowledge Discovery and Management
Rajeev Kumar (Infrastructure University Kuala Lumpur (IUKL), Malaysia) Abu Bakar Abdul Hamid (Infrastructure University Kuala Lumpur (IUKL), Malaysia) and Noor Inayah Binti Ya'akub (Infrastructure University Kuala Lumpur (IUKL), Malaysia)
Engineering Science Reference • copyright 2023 • 330pp • H/C (ISBN: 9781668491515) • US $270.00 (our price)

Recent Developments in Machine and Human Intelligence

701 East Chocolate Avenue, Hershey, PA 17033, USA
Tel: 717-533-8845 x100 • Fax: 717-533-8661
E-Mail: cust@igi-global.com • www.igi-global.com

List of Contributors

Table of Contents

Detailed Table of Contents

Chapter 1

    Rajneesh Talwar, Chitkara University, India
    Manvinder Sharma, Malla Reddy Engineering College and Management Sciences,
        Hyderabad, India
    Harjinder Singh, Punjabi University, Patiala, India
    Prem Sagar, Malla Reddy Engineering College and Management Sciences, Hyderabad,
        India

Image processing has become an important tool in medical applications, with the ability to extract and analyze information from medical images. This chapter provides an overview of various image processing approaches used in medical applications, including deep learning algorithms, segmentation techniques, and a combination of both. The authors also discuss several studies on brain tumor detection, cancer detection, and X-ray analysis using image processing techniques. The studies demonstrate the potential of image processing techniques to significantly improve the accuracy and speed of disease detection, allowing for earlier diagnosis and treatment. Image processing techniques can also assist in treatment planning and lead to more informed diagnoses and treatment decisions. Continued research in this area will undoubtedly lead to even more advanced and sophisticated approaches to image processing, further enhancing the ability of healthcare professionals to diagnose and treat a wide range of medical conditions.

Chapter 2

    Binay Kumar Pandey, Department of Information Technology, Govind Ballabh Pant
        University of Agriculture and Technology, Pantnagar, India
    Poonam Devi, Chaudhary Devi Lal University, Sirsa, India
    A. Shaji George, Business System Department, Almarai Company, Saudi Arabia
    Vinay Kumar Nassa, Rajarambapu Institute of Technology, India
    Pankaj Dadheech, Swami Keshvanand Institute of Technology, Management, and
        Gramothan, India
    Blessy Thankachan, School of Computer Applications, JECRC University, India
    Pawan Kumar Patidar, Swami Keshvanand Institute of Technology, Management, and
        Gramothan, India
    Sanwta Ram Dogiwal, Swami Keshvanand Institute of Technology, Management, and
        Gramothan, India

This chapter provides an analysis of the various kinds of distracting noise that can be seen in degraded complex images, such as those found in newspapers, blogs, and websites. A complicated image that had been deteriorated as a result of noise such as salt and pepper noise, random valued impulse noise, speckle noise, and Gaussian noise, amongst others, was the result. There is an extraordinarily high demand for saving the text that can be read from complicated images that have been degraded into a form that can be read by computers for later use.

Sampangirama Reddy B. R., School of Sciences, Jain University (Deemed), India
Ashendra Kumar Saxena, Teerthanker Mahaveer University, India
Binay Kumar Pandey, Department of Information Technology, Govind Ballabh Pant University of Agriculture and Technology, India
Sachin Gupta, Sanskriti University, India
Shashikala Gurpur, Symbiosis Law School, Symbiosis International University (Deemed), Pune, India
Sukhvinder Singh Dari, Symbiosis Law School, Symbiosis International University (Deemed), Pune, India
Dharmesh Dhabliya, Symbiosis Law School, Symbiosis International University (Deemed), Pune, India

Taking into account the uses of ML in the field of vision, many practical vision systems' first processing stages include enhancing or reconstructing images. The goal of these tools is to enhance the quality of photos and give accurate data for making decisions based on appearance. In this research study, the authors examine three distinct types of neural networks: convolutional networks, residual networks, and generative countermeasure networks. There is a proposal for a model structure of a scalable supplementary generation network as part of a network that enhances evidence images as a generative countermeasure. The authors present the objective loss function definition, as well as the periodic consistency loss and the periodic perceptual consistency loss analysis. An in-depth solution framework for picture layering is offered once the problem's core aspects are explained. This approach implements multitasking with the help of adaptive feature learning, this provides a strong theoretical guarantee.

Ismayel Gollapudi, Malla Reddy Engineering College and Management Sciences, India
Kallol Bhaumik, Malla Reddy Engineering College and Management Sciences, India
Digvijay Pandey, Department of Technical Education(U.P), A.P.J. Abdul Kalam University, India
Juttu Suresh, Malla Reddy Engineering College and Management Sciences, India
K. V. Ganesh, Malla Reddy Engineering College and Management Sciences, India
Uday Kumar Kanike, Georgia State University, USA

The development of autonomous electric vehicles has gained significant attention due to their potential to reduce carbon emissions and improve road safety. Image processing has become an important tool in the development of these vehicles, enabling them to detect and respond to objects and obstacles in their environment. In this review paper, we explore the use of image processing in electric vehicles and driverless cars, with a focus on the various techniques proposed by authors. The comparison of the performance and effectiveness of different approaches, including deep learning, computer vision, and sensor fusion, in detecting and recognizing objects in the environment. Our review highlights the advantages and limitations of each technique and their potential for future development in the field of electric vehicles. Overall, image processing has shown to be a promising solution for the development of safe and efficient autonomous electric vehicles.

S. Balasubramani, Department of CSE, KL University (Deemed), Vaddeswaram, India
Renjith P. N., School of Computer Science and Engineering, Vellore Institute of Technology, Chennai, India
K. Ramesh, Department of Computer Science and Engineering, Sri Krishna College of Engineering and Technology, India
A. S. Hovan George, Tbilisi State Medical University, Georgia
A. Shaji George, Business System Department, Almarai Company, Saudi Arabia
Aakifa Shahul, SRM Medical College, Kattankulathur, India

The healthcare industry is one of the world's fastest growing, and the impact of artificial intelligence (AI) is already being felt. AI is changing the way healthcare is delivered, from reducing administrative processes to offering individualized patient care. AI is predicted to have a significant impact on healthcare in the next years. Its possible applications range from bettering patient care and outcomes to lowering healthcare expenses. Diagnostics is one area where AI has the potential to have a substantial effect. AI-powered diagnostic technologies have the potential to transform how diseases are discovered and treated. AI-based diagnostic tools can find patterns and connections in big data sets that the human eye may miss. AI can also be utilized to create patient-specific treatment strategies.

Chapter 6

Sampath Boopathi, Muthayammal Engineering College, India
Binay Kumar Pandey, College of Technology, Govind Ballabh Pant University of Agriculture and Technology, India
Digvijay Pandey, Department of Technical Education, India

AI has had a substantial influence on image processing, allowing cutting-edge methods and uses. The foundations of image processing are covered in this chapter, along with representation, formats, enhancement methods, and filtering. It digs into methods for machine learning, neural networks, optimization strategies, digital watermarking, picture security, cloud computing, image augmentation, and data pretreatment methods. The impact of cloud computing on platforms, performance, privacy, and security are also covered. The chapter's consideration of future trends and applications emphasises the substantial contributions that AI has made to image processing as well as the ethical and societal ramifications of this technology.

Shalini Ninoria, College of Computing Sciences and I.T., Teerthanker Mahaveer University, Moradabad, India
Ramakant Upadhyay, Sanskriti University, Mathura, India
Reena Susan Philip, School of Sciences, Jain University (Deemed), India
Richa Dwivedi, Symbiosis Law School, Symbiosis International University (Deemed), India
Gabriela Micheal, Symbiosis Law School, Symbiosis International University (Deemed), India
Ankur Gupta, Vaish College of Engineering, Rohtak, India
Sudha Mishra, J.K. Institute of Engineering, India

Artificial intelligence system has been frequently used for crime prevention. Image and video analytics are playing significant role during such operation. However it has become quite challenging to implement over IoT environment, with the development of artificial intelligence where the discipline of research and analysis has entered a new age. The use of video analytics, a branch of artificial intelligence that is undergoing fast advancement, is supporting law enforcement agencies in significantly reducing crime rates. Video Analytics examines video footage using algorithms to categorize a wide variety of object types and distinguish certain behaviors or activities in order to deliver real-time alerts and insights to customers. Traditional CCTV cameras are so yesterday. But there is need to reduce the time consumption and space consumption during image analytic and video analytics operations. Present work is focusing on performance enhancement during image and video analytics.

D. Devasena, Sri Ramakrishna Engineering College, India
Y. Dharshan, Sri Ramakrishna Engineering College, India
S. Vivek, Mechmet Engineers, India
B. Sharmila, Sri Ramakrishna Engineering College, India

Quality is the keyword for Industry Revolution 4.0, as industries have moved from product based to customer-based manufacturing. People have started moving towards the quality rather than the cost of the product. The automobile section is deemed to be a major manufacturing sector as multiple components required for assembling final product. Bearing is a major component in the engine to operate the piston. The inspection of component done 100% manually where time is high, in turn delay in dispatch. A proposed automated machine vision system (MVS) is used to identify missing operations, also detect scratches in surface of the component. The algorithm is developed using LabVIEW, in which detection-based algorithm is implemented to detect the missing operations in the component. An artificial intelligent (AI) based algorithm is proposed for detecting the scratches that occurred due to the manufacturing process/ mishandling of component. The implemented algorithm has shown better results compared with the manual process, as inspection time has reduced, and the number of components inspected has increased.

In order to address the issues posed by emerging technologies like IoT, IP, and AI, the legislation governing information technology in India is undergoing a period of fast development (AI). Since these technologies are able to gather, share, and analyse massive quantities of data, regulations arc necessary to safeguard individuals' right to privacy about such data. Companies and organizations need to have a full awareness of the legal framework around IoT/IoE, image processing, and AI in order to guarantee that they are in compliance with the laws that have been enacted. Companies and organisations may assist in guaranteeing that they are employing these technologies in a legally responsible way by using legal knowledge gained through understanding the legal consequences of using these technologies. It has been observed that there are several applications of IT law in India on IoT/ IoE. Present research work is considering the role of image processing in IoT environment.

This chapter explores the role of AI and machine learning (ML) in image processing, focusing on their applications. It covers AI techniques like supervised learning, unsupervised learning, reinforcement learning, and deep learning. AI techniques include rule-based systems, expert systems, fuzzy logic, and genetic algorithms. Machine learning techniques include SVM, decision trees, random forests, K-means clustering, and PCA. Deep learning techniques like CNN, RNN, and GANs are used in tasks like object recognition, classification, and segmentation. The chapter emphasizes the impact of AI and ML on accuracy, efficiency, and decision-making. It also discusses evaluation metrics and performance analysis, emphasizing the importance of selecting appropriate metrics and techniques. The chapter also addresses ethical considerations, such as fairness, privacy, transparency, and human-AI collaboration.

A deep learning approach is gaining popularity day by day in image data classification. The process of classification of graphical data considering training network is managed by conventional neural network. Such types of networks allow automatic classification by making use of CNN approach. But the issues that are faced during forensic investigation are slow in performance and lack accuracy. The major objective of work is to consider the CNN approach that is processing graphic data in order to perform cyber forensic investigation.

An image plays a vital role in today's environment. An image is a visual representation of anything that can be used in the future for recollecting or memorizing that scene. This visual representation is created by recording the scene through an optical device like a camera or mobile phone. The image fusion process helps integrate relevant data of the different images in a process into a single image. Image fusion applications are wide in range, and so is the fusion technique. In general, pixel, feature, and decision-based techniques for picture fusion are characterised. This study's main thrust is the application and comparison of two approaches to the image fusion process: PCA (principal component analysis) and CNN (convolutional neural network).The study implemented a practical approach to MATLAB. The result of the study is that CNN is much more favorable in terms of image quality and clarity but less favorable in terms of time and cost.

Vishnu Venkatesh N., School of Sciences, Jain University (Deemed), India

Priyank Singhal, College of Computing Sciences and I.T., Teerthanker Mahaveer University, Moradabad, India

Digvijay Pandey, Department of Technical Education, A.P.J. Abdul Kalam Technical University, Lucknow, India

Meenakshi Sharma, Sanskriti University, Mathura, India

Rupal Rautdesai, Symbiosis Law School, Symbiosis International University (Deemed), India

Deepti Nahush Khubalkar, Symbiosis Law School, Symbiosis International University (Deemed), India

Ankur Gupta, Vaish College of Engineering, Rohtak, India

The present research is focused on crime forecasting and CNN has been used for image classification in order to categorize crime events. However, there are different classification mechanisms used in conventional research work. But CNN is playing a significant role in identification and prediction of crime. The major issues during CNN based classification are time consumption and accuracy. However, proposed research has resolved issue of time consumption by reducing image size by applying the RGB2GRAY model, and images are resized before training operation. Simulation results conclude that the proposed work provides a scalable and reliable approach for crime forecasting.

Shahanawaj Ahamad, University of Hail, Saudi Arabia

Vivek Veeraiah, Adichunchanagiri University, India

J. V. N. Ramesh, Koneru Lakshmaiah Education Foundation, India

R. Rajadevi, Kongu Engineering College, India

Reeja S. R. (3c24e765-ddec-44be-a352-9c454dfd3acf, VIT-AP University, India

Sabyasachi Pramanik, Haldia Institute of Technology, India

Ankur Gupta, Vaish College of Engineering, India

The time is now for deep learning (DL)-dependent analysis of healthcare images to move from the realm of exploratory research projects to that of translational ones, and eventually into clinical practise. This process has been sped up by developments in data availability, DL methods, and computer power over the last decade. As a result of this experience, the authors now know more about the potential benefits and drawbacks of incorporating DL into clinical treatment, two factors that, in the authors' opinion, will propel progress in this area over the next several years. The most significant of these difficulties are the widespread need of strength of commonly utilized DL training approaches to various pervasive pathological properties of healthcare images and storages, the need of an properly digitised environment in hospitals, and the need of sufficient open datasets on which DL approaches may be trained and tested.

K. Manju, Sona College of Technology, India
R. Anand, Department of ECE, Sri Eshwar College of Engineering, Coimbatore, India
Binay Kumar Pandey, Department of Information Technology, Govind Ballabh Pant
    University of Agriculture and Technology, Pantnagar, India
Vinay Kumar Nassa, Rajarambapu Institute of Technology, India
Aakifa Shahul, SRM Medical College, Kattankulathur, India
A. S. Hovan George, Tbilisi State Medical University, Georgia
Sanwta Ram Dogiwal, Swami Keshvanand Institute of Technology, Management, and
    Gramothan, India

In order to find the glaucoma in an early stage with the help of optical coherence tomography (OCT) using deep learning and extracting the features of glaucoma, the authors are able to classify the four types of glaucoma such as CNV, DME, DRUSEN, and the normal ones with perfect accuracy by training this dataset. This dataset contained 968 images and 242 images of each type the authors trained their model by using CNN algorithm, and has greater accuracy of when compared to the determination of glaucoma using support vector machine image. The authors have good architecture constructed for the determination. They pre-trained their deep learning model in order to obtain the initial representation. The proposed system gives out 95.4% accuracy level of sensitivity, specificity, and classification. A large increase in the volume of the cup, a larger cup diameter, and a thickened lip of the neuroretina rim suggest glaucoma. These regions correspond anatomically to currently used clinical markers for glaucoma diagnosis.

T. Shanthi, Sona College of Technology, Salem, India
R. Anand, Sri Eshwar College of Engineering, Coimbatore, India
Binay Kumar Pandey, Department of Information Technology, Govind Ballabh Pant
    University of Agriculture and Technology, Pantnagar, India
Vinay Kumar Nassa, Rajarambapu Institute of Technology, India
Aakifa Shahul, SRM Medical College, Kattankulathur, India
A. S. Hovan George, Tbilisi State Medical University, Georgia
Pankaj Dadheech, Swami Keshvanand Institute of Technology, Management, and
    Gramothan, India

Diabetic Retinopathy (DR) affects people who have diabetes mellitus for a long period (20 years). It is one of the most common causes of preventable blindness in the world. If not detected early, this may cause irreversible damage to the patient's vision. One of the signs and serious DR anomalies are exudates, so these lesions must be properly detected and treated as soon as possible. To address this problem, the authors propose a novel method that focuses on the detection and classification of Exudateas Hard and soft in retinal fundus images using deep learning. Initially, the authors collected the retinal fundus images from the IDRID dataset, and after labeling the exudate with the annotation tool, the YOLOV3 is trained with specific parameters according to the classes. Then the custom detector detects the exudate and classifies it into hard and soft exudate.

Chapter 17

S. Dhamodaran, Sathyabama Institute of Science and Technology, India
Shahanawaj Ahamad, University of Hail, Saudi Arabia
J. V. N. Ramesh, Koneru Lakshmaiah Education Foundation, India
S. Sathappan, Bharathi Institute of Technology, India
Arpit Namdev, University Institute of Technology RGPV, India
Reshma Ramakant Kanse, Bharati Vidyapeeth (Deemed), India
Sabyasachi Pramanik, Haldia Institute of Technology, India

One of the new and difficult study fields in the contemporary environment is the idea of smart cities. The cities are bordered by woods, farmland, or open spaces where fires might break out, endangering human lives and wiping out many resources. This chapter uses the idea of sensor networks and UAV technology to develop an early fire detection system that will help eliminate fire incidents. The suggested design uses sensors to track environmental factors and uses sensors and IoT applications to analyze the data. The suggested fire detection system combines cloud computing, UAVs, and wireless sensor technologies. The suggested fire detection system additionally incorporates certain image processing methods to more accurately and efficiently identify the fire occurrence. Rules are also developed in order to increase the genuine detection rate. The suggested fire detection system's simulation results are contrasted with those of several current techniques.

Chapter 18

S. Dhamodaran, Sathyabama Institute of Science and Technology, India
Shahanawaj Ahamad, University of Hail, Saudi Arabia
J. V. N. Ramesh, Koneru Lakshmaiah Education Foundation, India
G. Muthugurunathan, Madanapalle Institute of Technology and Science, India
K. Manikandan, Vellore Institute of Technology, India
Sabyasachi Pramanik, Haldia Institute of Technology, India
Digvijay Pandey, Department of Technical Education, Government of Uttar Pradesh, India

The leading and suitable techniques for examining and assessing the microstructure of things are nowadays high-resolution optical microscopy and imaging approaches. Manfred Von Ardenne developed scanning electron microscopy (SEM), a kind of surface microscopy, in the 1930s. SEM employs electron behaviour to produce 3D pictures of entities that provide knowledge about their topology, morphology, and constitution. This method has been discovered to have uses throughout the previous several decades in a variety of commercial and industrial arena, forensic analysis, and ordinary studies in science and business. An effective tool for seeing and characterising hybrid organic and inorganic substances and surfaces is the scanning electron microscope.

Chapter 19

Sonali Dash, Chandigarh University, India

Priyadarsan Parida, GIET University, India

Vinay Kumar Nassa, Rajarambapu Institute of Technology, India

A. Shaji George, Business System Department, Almarai Company, Saudi Arabia

Aakifa Shahul, SRM Medical College, Kattankulathur, India

A. S. Hovan George, Tbilisi State Medical University, Georgia

A series of illnesses known as glaucoma harm the optic nerve in the eye. Glaucoma can cause lifelong blindness or vision loss if it is not addressed. Because glaucoma frequently has no symptoms in its early stages, it is particularly difficult. If symptoms start to show up, it might be too late to stop blindness. There are numerous ways to identify glaucoma, including tonometry, which measures the pressure inside the eye, ophthalmoscopy, which looks at the optic nerve's form and color, and perimeter, which measures the entire field of vision. However, because of the fact that each person's glaucoma is unique, these procedures do not allow for the detection of all forms of glaucoma. A visual assessment technique that can identify glaucoma is cup-to-disc ratio. By image processing methods like binarization the cup-to-disc ratio is calculated in this project and utilized to assess the glaucomatous status of an eye using super pixel classification.

Chapter 20

Vivek Veeraiah, Adichunchanagiri University, India

Dolly John Shiju, R.D. Memorial College of Nursing, India

J.V.N. Ramesh, Koneru Lakshmaiah Education Foundation, India

Ganesh Kumar R., CHRIST University (Deemed), India

Sabyasachi Pramanik, Haldia Institute of Technology, India

Digvijay Pandey, Department of Technical Education, Government of Uttar Pradesh, India

Ankur Gupta, Vaish College of Engineering, Rohtak, India

Technology has been fundamental in defining, advancing, and reinventing medical practises, equipment, and drugs during the last century. Although cloud computing is quite a newer concept, it is now one of the most often discussed issues in academic and therapeutic contexts. Many academics and healthcare persons are focused in providing vast, conveniently obtainable, and reconstruct assets like virtual frameworks, platforms, and implementations having lesser business expenditures. As they need enough assets to operate, store, share, and utilise huge quantity of healthcare data, specialists in the field of medicine are transferring their operations in the cloud. Major issues about the application of cutting-edge cloud computing in medical imaging are covered in this chapter. The research also takes into account the ethical and security concerns related to cloud computing.

Chapter 21

Santosh Walke, College of Engineering, National University of Science and Technology, Muscat, Oman

Manoj Mandake, Bharati Vidyapeeth College of Engineering, India

Ravi W. Tapre, Datta Meghe College of Engineering, India

Makarand Naniwadekar, Savitribai Phule Pune University, India

Chetan Thakar, Savitribai Phule Pune University, India

Sandhya Dilip Jadhav, Bharati Vidyapeeth College of Engineering, India

This chapter gives a thorough overview of image processing's uses and potential in industrial chemical engineering. Image processing can provide precise and in-depth information about chemical processes, products, and its significance in this field is highlighted. The foundations of image processing are covered in this chapter, including image formation and acquisition, image preprocessing, feature extraction, and selection. The applications of image-based process monitoring and control, image analysis for product quality control, and the newest developments and difficulties in machine learning in image-based chemical engineering are also covered. The section on machine learning in image-based chemical engineering gives a general overview of machine learning methods and how they are used in the field of chemical engineering. The chapter's discussion of image processing's limitations in chemical engineering, as well as current trends and future research prospects, come to close.

Chapter 22

    R. Manivannan, Stanley College of Engineering and Technology for Women, India
    Y. V. S. S. Pragathi, Stanley College of Engineering and Technology for Women, India
    Uday Kumar Kanike, Georgia State University, USA

The integration of image processing methods with IoT devices in healthcare has revolutionized patient health checking procedures, enabling continuous monitoring, automated image analysis, and personalized treatments. This improves diagnostic precision, prompt action, and favorable patient outcomes. Wearable health trackers and medical equipment collect real-time vital sign data, enabling informed judgments. IoT device integration also enables remote access, virtual consultations, and follow-ups, boosting patient engagement and treatment compliance. However, issues like data security, interoperability, and infrastructure must be resolved for successful deployment. Future directions include advancements in 6G networks, AI integration, augmented reality, and data fusion methods.

Chapter 23

    Manvinder Sharma, Malla Reddy Engineering College and Management Sciences,
        Hyderabad, India
    Sudhakara Reddy Saripalli, Malla Reddy Engineering College and Management Sciences,
        Hyderabad, India
    Anuj Kumar Gupta, Chandigarh Group of Colleges, Landran, India
    Rajneesh Talwar, Chitkara University, India
    Pankaj Dadheech, Computer Science and Engineering, Swami Keshvanand Institute of
        Technology, Management, and Gramothan, India
    Uday Kumar Kanike, Georgia State University, USA

The primary form of transportation is roads. But because of the high volume of traffic on the roads and other environmental conditions, regular maintenance is required. This maintenance is frequently neglected as it is impossible to watch over every location, or just out of ignorance. Potholes are created as a result, which increases traffic and increases the likelihood of accidents. However, there are many methods/systems available which can be used to detect potholes using various image processing methods. The accuracy of these systems is highly affected in rainy weather. In this chapter, a system is designed to detect pothole during rainy season effectively. This system also collects the location of potholes, which can be further provided to authorities for maintenance work. The proposed system can be used for driverless cars.

   Shawni Dutta, Department of Computer Science, The Bhawanipur Education Society
      College, Kolkata, India
   Utsab Mukherjee, Department of Computer Science, The Bhawanipur Education Society
      College, Kolkata, India
   Digvijay Pandey, Department of Technical Education, Institute of Engineering and
      Technology, Lucknow, India

A new hype known as the novel coronavirus has consumed many human lives over the past few years. Consequently, the continued pandemic crisis will necessitate the use of an automated system. The computerised system should be able to provide constant monitoring of different domains of the COVID-19 disease. This study has concentrated on heterogeneous fields of COVID-19 including suspected-infected-recovered-deceased count analysis, impact of lockdown, different health habits responsible for this disease, analysis perforation patterns of lungs due to COVID-19, vaccination intake, and progress investigation. The literature included in this study has been investigated in terms of their prediction efficiency and possible improvements. Due to the exhaustive discourse of current COVID-19 based literature, the study is able to provide a comprehensive knowledge of the ongoing research trends. A concrete future perspective regarding each of the aforementioned domains has been included in the conclusion section which can effectively assist in finding the shortcomings of the existing research.

   K. N. Anantha Subramanya Iyer, Jain University (Deemed), India
   S. Mahalakshmi, Jain University (Deemed), India
   S. Hemanth Kumar, Jain University (Deemed), India
   Anitha Nallasivam, Jain University (Deemed), India
   C. Selvaraj, Dhaanish Ahmed College of Engineering, Chennai, India

The future directions and current trends of warehouse management using image processing techniques are thoroughly reviewed in this chapter. The chapter starts off with a summary of warehouse management and the function of image processing methods in analyzing and deciphering images from warehouse environments. It also discusses the benefits and drawbacks of popular image processing methods. The following section of the essay looks at current developments in image processing-based warehouse management, including the methods employed and the advantages of this approach. The potential for combining image processing with other cutting-edge technologies is also investigated, including cloud computing and the internet of things (IoT). The conclusion of the chapter discusses the opportunities and challenges of applying image processing techniques to warehouse management.

Chapter 26

Rajesh Gupta, Sanskriti University, Mathura, India

Manashree Mane, School of Sciences, Jain University (Deemed), India

Shambhu Bhardwaj, College of Computing Sciences and I.T., Teerthanker Mahaveer University, Moradabad, India

Ujwal Nandekar, Symbiosis Law School, Symbiosis International University (Deemed), India

Ahmar Afaq, Symbiosis Law School, Symbiosis International University (Deemed), India

Dharmesh Dhabliya, Symbiosis Law School, Symbiosis International University (Deemed), India

Binay Kumar Pandey, Department of Information Technology, Govind Ballabh Pant University of Agriculture and Technology, Pantnagar, India

Use of artificial intelligence for image processing to aid digital forensics is a controversial topic. Some people believe that AI can be very helpful in this field, while others are concerned about the potential misuse of AI technology. There are a few key legislative challenges that need to be addressed before AI can be widely used for image processing in digital forensics. First, there is the issue of data privacy. If images processed by AI contain personal data, then there are risks that this data could be mishandled or misused. There are also concerns that AI could be used to create false or misleading evidence. Another key challenge is ensuring that AI systems are transparent and accountable. If an AI system makes a mistake, it should be possible to understand why it made that mistake and how to avoid similar mistakes in the future. AI has the potential to revolutionize digital forensics, but there are still some important challenges that need to be addressed before it can be widely used.

Chapter 27

Sabyasachi Samanta, Haldia Institute of Technology, India

Priyatosh Jana, Haldia Institute of Technology, India

Abhijit Sarkar, Haldia Institute of Technology, India

Soumen Ghosh, Haldia Institute of Technology, India

Visual cryptography is an excellent cryptographic method by which the visual information is encrypted and decrypted with or without using of computer systems depending on the human visual system. In visual cryptography techniques, the carrier (with secret information) is divided into multiple shares, in particular any one of which does not reveal any knowledge about the secret information. In this chapter, a newly color component-based visual cryptographic technique, i.e., image share formation for image and video, has been introduced. As video is a sequential amalgamation of image frames, the same has also been implemented for video. In this time, the method supports the {k, n} threshold framework. Out of n transparencies, using k number of shares, the reformation is possible. Using the image, shares data may be embedded to different shares using steganography or watermarking techniques. Furthermore, some suitable comparisons also have been performed to measure the newly developed technique.

The integration of image processing techniques in marketing has rapidly increased in recent years, and their implications for marketing management are becoming more significant. The chapter highlights the various types of image processing techniques used in marketing, including image segmentation, image filtering, and image recognition. The review also discusses the applications of these techniques in marketing, including product classification, branding, advertising, and customer experience management. Additionally, the review identifies the implications of image processing techniques for marketing management. The chapter also examines the limitations of image processing techniques in marketing. Finally, the chapter concludes by providing suggestions for further research, including the need for more studies on the effectiveness of image processing techniques in marketing and development of new frameworks to integrate image processing techniques in marketing management.

Preface

Welcome to *Handbook of Research on Thrust Technologies' Effect on Image Processing*. In this reference book, we delve into the fascinating world of image processing and explore its wide-ranging applications and the technologies that drive its advancements. The field of image processing has witnessed remarkable growth in recent years, finding utility in diverse domains such as remote sensing, space exploration, industrial operations, medical diagnostics, and military strategies.

In this edition, we bring together the expertise of Digvijay Pandey, Deepak S. Mane, Binay Kumar Pandey, and A. Shaji George to provide valuable insights into image processing and its integration with cutting-edge technologies. Our goal is to equip researchers, academicians, and industry professionals with a comprehensive resource that explores the latest trends, optimization techniques, and security considerations in image processing.

The book commences by addressing fundamental concepts, including scanning methods, statistical analysis, and the extraction of accurate picture values for image analysis. We then embark on an exploration of emerging imaging systems, spanning chemical, optical, thermal, medicinal, and molecular imaging. We showcase the profound impact of thrust technologies on image processing, paving the way for future satellite applications built on a foundation of in-depth imaging research.

Our focus extends beyond traditional 2D and 3D imaging approaches. We delve into the realms of cloud computing, the Internet of Things (IoT), digital watermarking, neural networks, feature identification, and optimization. By providing a holistic view of these interconnected areas, we empower our readers to harness the synergies between image processing and multidisciplinary fields such as security, Android development, and IoT applications.

Throughout the book, we present real-world case studies, propose innovative methodologies, and tackle pressing security challenges. The integration of machine learning and deep learning techniques in biomedical imaging offers immense potential in healthcare industries, a topic that we explore in detail. We encourage researchers to leverage the discussed modern and innovative approaches to further expand the boundaries of image processing.

The chapters in this book cover a range of essential topics, including image augmentation, compression, restoration, and segmentation. We delve into the exciting realm of artificial intelligence and its application in image analytics. Advanced machine learning and deep learning methodologies are explored in the context of image processing. We investigate the intersection of image processing and IoT, examining its implications for security and privacy. Furthermore, we delve into the challenges and privacy issues that arise in the domain of image processing, while also exploring the impact of cloud computing on image-related operations. Optimization models and digital watermarking techniques in image processing are also addressed, alongside the role of neural networks and pattern recognition.

As editors, our aim is to foster a comprehensive understanding of image processing and its manifold applications. We hope this book serves as a valuable manual for researchers and industry experts alike, empowering them to stay at the forefront of this rapidly evolving field. By disseminating knowledge, we contribute to the collective growth of image processing, enabling the development of more efficient, secure, and innovative solutions.

We extend our gratitude to all the contributors who have shared their expertise and insights, making this revised edition a truly collaborative endeavor. We hope that readers find this book both informative and inspiring, encouraging them to embark on new explorations and advancements in image processing.

CHAPTER OVERVIEW

Chapter 1: A Comparative Analysis on Image Processing Based Algorithms and Approaches in Healthcare

In this chapter, Rajneesh Talwar, Manvinder Sharma, Harjinder Singh, and Prem Sagar present a comprehensive overview of the diverse image processing approaches utilized in medical applications. The authors highlight the significance of image processing as a valuable tool for extracting and analyzing information from medical images, paving the way for improved healthcare outcomes.

The chapter begins by exploring various image processing algorithms, with a specific focus on deep learning techniques. Deep learning algorithms have shown tremendous potential in medical imaging, enabling precise segmentation and accurate analysis of medical data. The authors delve into the intricacies of these algorithms and discuss their effectiveness in different medical applications.

Furthermore, the chapter delves into the combination of image processing and segmentation techniques, demonstrating their combined power in detecting and diagnosing medical conditions. The authors examine studies that have utilized image processing to detect brain tumors, identify cancerous cells, and analyze X-ray images. These studies showcase how image processing techniques can significantly enhance the speed and accuracy of disease detection, leading to earlier diagnosis and more timely treatment interventions.

Importantly, the authors emphasize that image processing techniques not only aid in disease detection but also contribute to treatment planning and decision-making. By leveraging the insights gained from image processing, healthcare professionals can make more informed diagnoses and tailor treatment approaches to individual patients' needs.

Throughout the chapter, the authors emphasize the potential for further advancements in image processing techniques in the healthcare domain. They highlight the importance of ongoing research and development efforts, which are poised to yield even more sophisticated approaches to image processing. These advancements will undoubtedly enhance the capabilities of healthcare professionals, enabling them to diagnose and treat a broader range of medical conditions with greater precision and effectiveness.

Chapter 1 provides a solid foundation for understanding the role of image processing in healthcare applications. It serves as a valuable resource for researchers, medical professionals, and technologists seeking to explore the potential of image processing in improving diagnostics, treatment planning, and patient outcomes in the field of healthcare.

Chapter 2: Review on Different Types of Disturbing Noise for Degraded Complex Images

In this chapter, Binay Pandey, Poonam Devi, A. Shaji George, Vinay Kumar Nassa, Pankaj Dadheech, Blessy Thankachan, Pawan Kumar Patidar, and Sanwta Ram Dogiwal present a comprehensive review of the various types of disturbing noise that can be encountered in degraded complex images. These images often originate from sources such as newspapers, blogs, and websites. The authors shed light on the challenges posed by noise in complex images and explore techniques to mitigate its impact.

The chapter focuses on the analysis of different types of noise that can degrade complex images. Examples of noise covered include salt and pepper noise, random valued impulse noise, speckle noise, and Gaussian noise, among others. By examining each type of noise, the authors provide valuable insights into their characteristics and the challenges they present in image processing tasks.

The authors highlight the importance of preserving the textual information contained within complex images that have been degraded by noise. Such preservation is crucial for enabling subsequent computer-based analysis and utilization of the text. By developing techniques to effectively address the noise-related degradation in complex images, researchers can enhance the accessibility and usability of the textual content embedded within them.

Throughout the chapter, the authors explore existing methods and algorithms used to mitigate the impact of noise on complex images. They discuss the strengths and limitations of each approach, shedding light on their applicability in different scenarios. The insights provided in this review enable readers to make informed decisions about the most suitable noise reduction techniques for specific image processing tasks.

The chapter concludes by emphasizing the ongoing demand for effective noise reduction strategies in complex images. With the exponential growth of digital media and the increasing reliance on computer-based analysis, the ability to accurately extract and utilize textual information from degraded images is of paramount importance.

Chapter 2 serves as a valuable reference for researchers, image processing practitioners, and professionals working with complex image data. It equips readers with a comprehensive understanding of the various types of disturbing noise encountered in complex images and provides insights into the techniques and algorithms employed to mitigate their impact. By addressing this critical aspect of image processing, the chapter contributes to the advancement of methods for extracting meaningful information from degraded complex images.

Chapter 3: Machine Learning Application for Evidence Image Enhancement

In Chapter 3, Sampangirama Reddy B R, Ashendra Kumar Saxena, Binay Kumar Pandey, Sachin Gupta, Dr. Shashikala Gurpur, Sukhvinder Singh Dari, and Dharmesh Dhabliya delve into the realm of machine learning and its application in enhancing evidence images. The chapter focuses on the utilization of machine learning algorithms to improve the quality and accuracy of images, enabling better decision-making based on visual information.

The authors begin by emphasizing the widespread use of machine learning in vision systems, particularly in the initial stages of image processing. These systems aim to enhance and reconstruct images, ultimately providing high-quality visuals that facilitate informed decision-making.

Within this research study, the authors explore three distinct types of neural networks: convolutional networks, residual networks, and generative countermeasure networks. Each network type plays a unique role in enhancing evidence images and serves as a valuable tool in the image enhancement process. Specifically, the authors propose a model structure for a scalable supplementary generation network that functions as a generative countermeasure, augmenting the quality and fidelity of evidence images.

The chapter delves into the technical aspects of this model structure, presenting the definition of the objective loss function. The authors analyze the periodic consistency loss and the periodic perceptual consistency loss, shedding light on their importance in maintaining image quality and perceptual accuracy throughout the enhancement process.

Furthermore, the authors offer an in-depth solution framework for picture layering, which serves as a comprehensive approach to address the core aspects of the problem. This framework incorporates multitasking with adaptive feature learning, providing a robust theoretical foundation and guarantee for the effectiveness of the proposed approach.

Chapter 3 presents a significant contribution to the field of image enhancement by leveraging machine learning techniques. It provides researchers, practitioners, and professionals with valuable insights into the application of neural networks for enhancing evidence images. The proposed model structure and solution framework offer practical methodologies for enhancing image quality, enabling accurate analysis, and supporting decision-making processes.

By bridging the gap between machine learning and image enhancement, this chapter promotes the development of advanced techniques in evidence image processing. It stimulates further research in the field, ultimately enhancing the capabilities of vision systems and facilitating the extraction of meaningful information from evidence images.

Chapter 4: A Comprehensive Review on Algorithms of Image Processing for Autonomous and Electric Vehicles

In Chapter 4, Ismayel Gollapudi, Kallol Bhaumik, Digvijay Pandey, Juttu Suresh, and K.V. Ganesh provide a comprehensive review of the algorithms used in image processing for autonomous and electric vehicles. The chapter focuses on the application of image processing techniques to enhance the capabilities of these vehicles, enabling them to detect and respond to objects and obstacles in their surroundings.

The authors highlight the growing importance of autonomous electric vehicles in reducing carbon emissions and improving road safety. Image processing plays a crucial role in the development of these vehicles by enabling them to perceive and interpret the visual information from their environment. By analyzing images captured by cameras and other sensors, autonomous vehicles can make informed decisions and navigate safely.

Within this review paper, the authors explore the various techniques proposed by researchers in the field of image processing for electric and autonomous vehicles. They delve into the performance and effectiveness of different approaches, including deep learning, computer vision, and sensor fusion. The comparison of these techniques allows for a comprehensive evaluation of their strengths, weaknesses, and suitability for different scenarios.

The chapter emphasizes the advantages and limitations of each image processing technique in detecting and recognizing objects in the vehicle's environment. Deep learning algorithms have shown promising results in object detection and classification, while computer vision techniques provide robust image analysis capabilities. Sensor fusion approaches, which combine information from multiple sensors, enhance the reliability and accuracy of object detection systems.

Through their review, the authors shed light on the potential of image processing algorithms to contribute to the development of safe and efficient autonomous electric vehicles. They discuss the ongoing advancements in the field and highlight the areas that require further research and development.

Chapter 4 serves as a valuable resource for researchers, engineers, and professionals working in the domain of autonomous and electric vehicles. It provides a comprehensive overview of the image processing algorithms utilized in these vehicles and offers insights into their performance, effectiveness, and potential for future advancements. By leveraging image processing techniques, the chapter contributes to the development of intelligent vehicles that can navigate complex environments and ensure the safety of passengers and pedestrians alike.

Chapter 5: A Detailed Analysis of Many Different Artificial Intelligence-Based Healthcare Systems

In Chapter 5, Balasubramani S, Renjith P N, Ramesh K, A.S. Hovan George, A. Shaji George, and Aakifa Shahul provide a detailed analysis of various artificial intelligence (AI)-based healthcare systems. The chapter focuses on the transformative impact of AI in the healthcare industry, highlighting its potential to revolutionize healthcare delivery, improve patient care, and reduce costs.

The authors begin by acknowledging the rapid growth of the healthcare industry and the profound influence of AI within it. They explore the wide-ranging applications of AI in healthcare, from streamlining administrative processes to delivering personalized patient care. AI is poised to play a pivotal role in shaping the future of healthcare, and its potential impact is expected to be substantial in the coming years.

The chapter emphasizes the potential of AI in diagnostics, an area where AI-powered technologies have the capacity to revolutionize disease detection and treatment. AI-based diagnostic tools have the ability to analyze vast amounts of data and identify patterns and connections that may elude human observation. By leveraging AI, healthcare professionals can improve the accuracy and efficiency of diagnostics, leading to earlier detection and personalized treatment strategies.

Furthermore, the authors highlight the role of AI in creating patient-specific treatment plans. AI algorithms can analyze patient data, including medical records, genetics, and lifestyle factors, to develop tailored treatment strategies that optimize patient outcomes. This personalized approach has the potential to enhance the effectiveness and efficiency of healthcare interventions.

Through their detailed analysis, the authors provide insights into the diverse AI-based healthcare systems currently in use. They explore the technologies, algorithms, and methodologies employed in these systems, shedding light on their strengths, limitations, and potential impact on healthcare delivery.

Chapter 5 serves as a valuable resource for healthcare professionals, researchers, and policymakers seeking to understand and leverage the potential of AI in healthcare. By providing a comprehensive analysis of AI-based healthcare systems, the chapter contributes to the advancement of intelligent healthcare solutions that improve patient care, outcomes, and cost-effectiveness.

Chapter 6: Advances in Artificial Intelligence for Image Processing – Techniques, Applications, and Optimization

In Chapter 6, Sampath Boopathi, Binay Kumar Pandey, and Digvijay Pandey present a comprehensive overview of the advancements in artificial intelligence (AI) for image processing. The chapter explores a wide range of techniques, applications, and optimization strategies that have emerged as a result of the integration of AI into image processing.

The authors emphasize the significant impact of AI on image processing, enabling the development of cutting-edge methods and applications. The chapter begins by covering the foundations of image processing, including image representation, formats, enhancement methods, and filtering techniques. This provides readers with a solid understanding of the fundamental principles that underpin image processing.

The chapter delves into the utilization of machine learning and neural networks in image processing. These techniques enable the extraction of valuable insights and patterns from images, leading to enhanced analysis and interpretation. The authors also explore optimization strategies, which play a crucial role in improving the efficiency and effectiveness of image processing algorithms.

Furthermore, the chapter investigates the application of AI in digital watermarking, ensuring the security and authenticity of images. It explores techniques for securing and protecting images, addressing the challenges associated with image privacy and security in the era of AI-driven image processing.

Cloud computing is another area of focus in this chapter, as it has had a profound impact on image processing platforms. The authors examine the implications of cloud computing on performance, privacy, and security, shedding light on its benefits and considerations in the context of image processing.

The chapter also highlights the importance of image augmentation and data preprocessing techniques, which contribute to the enhancement and refinement of image datasets. These techniques enable researchers and practitioners to create more diverse and representative datasets for training AI models.

Throughout the chapter, the authors consider future trends and applications in AI for image processing. They emphasize the substantial contributions that AI has made to the field, while also addressing the ethical and societal implications of this technology.

Chapter 6 serves as a comprehensive guide for researchers, practitioners, and professionals working in the field of image processing. It showcases the advancements in AI techniques, applications, and optimization strategies, providing insights into the potential of AI to revolutionize image processing. By exploring the intersection of AI and image processing, the chapter promotes the development of innovative solutions that enhance image analysis, security, and overall performance.

Chapter 7: AI and Crime Prevention With Image and Video Analytics Using IoT

In Chapter 7, Shalini Ninoria, Ramakant Upadhyay, Reena Susan Philip, Richa Dwivedi, Gabriela Micheal, Ankur Gupta, and Sudha Mishra explore the utilization of artificial intelligence (AI) and image and video analytics for crime prevention, particularly in the context of an Internet of Things (IoT) environment. The chapter addresses the challenges of implementing AI in IoT systems and focuses on enhancing the performance of image and video analytics for effective crime prevention.

The authors highlight the frequent use of AI systems in crime prevention, wherein image and video analytics play a significant role. However, implementing such systems in an IoT environment poses challenges due to the complexity and dynamic nature of IoT systems. The chapter discusses the evolving field of AI research and analysis and its integration with IoT for crime prevention purposes.

Video analytics, a branch of AI, has witnessed rapid advancements and is proving to be instrumental in supporting law enforcement agencies in reducing crime rates. By leveraging algorithms, video analytics enables the categorization of objects and the identification of specific behaviors or activities in video footage. Real-time alerts and insights derived from video analytics empower law enforcement agencies to respond swiftly and effectively to potential threats.

The chapter acknowledges the traditional use of closed-circuit television (CCTV) cameras but highlights the need to reduce time and space consumption during image and video analytics operations. The authors emphasize the importance of enhancing the performance of these analytics processes to ensure efficient crime prevention.

The present work focuses on performance enhancement in image and video analytics for crime prevention. By addressing the challenges specific to IoT environments, the authors propose strategies to optimize image and video analytics operations. These strategies aim to improve the efficiency and effectiveness of crime prevention efforts by leveraging AI and IoT technologies.

Chapter 7 serves as a valuable resource for researchers, law enforcement agencies, and professionals involved in crime prevention and surveillance. By exploring the integration of AI, image and video analytics, and IoT, the chapter contributes to the advancement of systems and methodologies for efficient crime prevention. The insights provided empower stakeholders to leverage the potential of AI and analytics in enhancing public safety and security.

Chapter 8: AI-Based Quality Inspection of Industrial Products

In Chapter 8, Devasena D., Dharshan Y., Vivek S., and Sharmila B. focus on the application of artificial intelligence (AI) in the quality inspection of industrial products. The chapter highlights the importance of quality in the context of Industry 4.0, where customer-oriented manufacturing has become the norm, shifting the focus from cost to quality.

The authors specifically address the automobile manufacturing sector, which relies on multiple components for the assembly of the final product. One crucial component in the engine is the bearing, which plays a significant role in operating the piston. Manual inspection of these components is a time-consuming process, leading to delays in dispatch.

To address this challenge, the authors propose an automated machine vision system (MVS) for quality inspection. The MVS utilizes AI-based algorithms to identify missing operations and detect surface scratches on the components. The algorithm is developed using LabVIEW, a graphical programming platform.

The detection-based algorithm implemented in the MVS enables the identification of missing operations in the components. Additionally, an AI-based algorithm is employed to detect scratches that may occur during the manufacturing process or due to mishandling of the components. These algorithms enhance the efficiency and accuracy of the inspection process.

The chapter highlights the superior performance of the implemented AI-based quality inspection system compared to the manual process. The inspection time is significantly reduced, allowing for faster inspection and increased throughput. The system also ensures a higher number of components are inspected, thereby enhancing the overall quality control process.

Chapter 8 serves as a valuable resource for industrial professionals, researchers, and quality control practitioners involved in the manufacturing sector. By leveraging AI in quality inspection, the chapter contributes to the advancement of industrial processes, enabling higher quality standards and improved

customer satisfaction. The insights provided in this chapter demonstrate the benefits of AI-based automation in streamlining inspection processes, reducing costs, and enhancing productivity.

Chapter 9: Application of Information Technology Law in India on IoT/IoE With Image Processing

In Chapter 9, Ramesh Chandra Tripathi, Poonam Gupta, Rohit Anand, R Jayashankar, Aparajita Mohanty, Gabriela Michael, and Dharmesh Dhabliya explore the application of information technology (IT) law in India concerning the use of Internet of Things (IoT), Internet of Everything (IoE), and image processing technologies. The chapter highlights the evolving legal framework in India to address the challenges posed by these emerging technologies.

As IoT, IP, and AI technologies continue to gather, share, and analyze vast amounts of data, regu-
lations are crucial to protect individuals' right to privacy regarding their data. The Indian legislation governing information technology is undergoing rapid development to address the legal implications and safeguards required for these technologies. It is essential for companies and organizations to have a thorough understanding of the legal framework surrounding IoT/IoE, image processing, and AI to ensure compliance with the enacted laws.

The chapter emphasizes the importance of legal awareness in employing these technologies responsibly and ethically. By gaining knowledge of the legal consequences associated with the use of IoT/IoE, image processing, and AI, companies and organizations can ensure that they adhere to the legal requirements and protect individuals' privacy rights.

The authors observe that there are numerous applications of IT law in India related to IoT/IoE. These applications pertain to various aspects such as data privacy, security, intellectual property rights, and consumer protection. By exploring the legal implications specific to IoT/IoE, the chapter provides valuable insights into the legal considerations that organizations must navigate in the Indian context.

The present research work specifically focuses on the role of image processing in IoT environments. By addressing the legal aspects associated with image processing in the context of IoT, the chapter contributes to a comprehensive understanding of the legal landscape surrounding these technologies.

Chapter 9 serves as a valuable resource for legal professionals, policymakers, researchers, and organizations operating in the IoT/IoE and image processing domains. It highlights the importance of compliance with IT laws in India and provides guidance on navigating the legal framework to ensure responsible and lawful use of these technologies. The insights provided contribute to the development of ethical practices and regulatory frameworks, fostering a secure and privacy-conscious environment for IoT/IoE and image processing applications.

Chapter 10: Applications of Artificial Intelligence and Machine Learning Techniques in Image Processing

In Chapter 10, Sampath Boopathi and Dr. Uday Kanike delve into the applications of artificial intel-
ligence (AI) and machine learning (ML) techniques in image processing. The chapter explores various AI and ML techniques, highlighting their role in image processing tasks and their impact on accuracy, efficiency, and decision-making.

The authors begin by discussing different AI techniques, including supervised learning, unsupervised learning, reinforcement learning, and deep learning. Supervised learning enables the training of models using labeled data, while unsupervised learning techniques uncover patterns and structures in unlabeled data. Reinforcement learning involves learning through interactions with an environment, and deep learning techniques, such as convolutional neural networks (CNN), recurrent neural networks (RNN), and generative adversarial networks (GANs), enable advanced image processing tasks like object recognition, classification, and segmentation.

Machine learning techniques are also explored in the chapter, including support vector machines (SVM), decision trees, random forests, K-means clustering, and principal component analysis (PCA). These techniques play a crucial role in analyzing and extracting meaningful information from image data.

The chapter emphasizes the importance of evaluation metrics and performance analysis in assessing the effectiveness of AI and ML techniques in image processing. It highlights the significance of selecting appropriate metrics to measure the performance and quality of image processing algorithms, ensuring that they align with the specific goals and requirements of the application.

Ethical considerations in AI and ML applications are also addressed, including fairness, privacy, transparency, and human-AI collaboration. As AI and ML techniques are increasingly integrated into image processing systems, it is essential to consider ethical implications and ensure that these technologies are used responsibly and with the utmost consideration for privacy, fairness, and transparency.

Chapter 10 serves as a valuable resource for researchers, practitioners, and professionals working in the field of image processing. It provides insights into the diverse applications of AI and ML techniques, enabling readers to understand their potential and select appropriate techniques for specific image processing tasks. The chapter also highlights the ethical considerations associated with AI and ML, fostering a responsible and ethical approach to image processing in various domains.

Chapter 11: CNN Based Deep Learning Approach Over Image Data for Cyber Forensic Investigation

In Chapter 11, Aishwary Awasthi, Priyanksha Das, Rupal Gupta, Raj Varma, Shilpa Sharma, Ankur Gupta, and Huma Khan focus on the application of convolutional neural network (CNN) based deep learning approach for cyber forensic investigation involving image data. The chapter addresses the challenges faced in forensic investigations, such as performance speed and accuracy, and proposes a CNN-based solution to overcome these issues.

The authors highlight the growing popularity of deep learning approaches, particularly CNN, in image data classification. Traditional neural networks have been used for classification tasks, but CNNs provide automatic classification capabilities by leveraging their ability to process graphical data effectively.

However, in the context of cyber forensic investigation, there are challenges in terms of performance speed and accuracy. The authors aim to address these challenges by considering a CNN-based deep learning approach that specifically focuses on processing graphic data for cyber forensic investigations.

By utilizing CNNs, the proposed approach offers improved performance and accuracy in classifying image data, enhancing the effectiveness of cyber forensic investigations. The chapter explores the implementation and utilization of CNNs for image classification tasks in the forensic context.

Chapter 11 serves as a valuable resource for researchers, practitioners, and professionals involved in cyber forensic investigations. It highlights the potential of CNN-based deep learning approaches in analyzing image data, aiding in the identification and classification of digital evidence.

By employing CNNs in cyber forensic investigations, investigators can enhance the speed and accuracy of their analyses, ultimately improving the efficiency and effectiveness of the investigation process. The insights provided in this chapter contribute to the advancement of forensic techniques and methodologies, enabling more accurate and reliable identification and analysis of digital evidence in the context of cybercrimes.

Overall, Chapter 11 offers a specialized focus on the utilization of CNN-based deep learning approaches for cyber forensic investigations involving image data, demonstrating the potential for advancements in this critical field.

Chapter 12: Comparison of the Theoretical and Statistical Effects of the PCA and CNN Image Fusion Approaches

In Chapter 12, Ashi Agarwal, Binay Kumar Pandey, Poonam Devi, Sunil Kumar, Mukundan Appadurai Paramashivan, Ritesh Agarwal, and Pankaj Dadheech explore and compare the effects of two image fusion approaches: PCA (Principal Component Analysis) and CNN (Convolutional Neural Network). The chapter focuses on the theoretical and statistical aspects of these approaches, highlighting their impact on image fusion results.

The authors emphasize the importance of images in today's environment as visual representations that hold significant value for recollection and memorization. Image fusion, the process of integrating relevant data from different images into a single image, plays a crucial role in various applications. The fusion techniques employed can vary, including pixel, feature, and decision-based methods.

The main objective of this study is to compare the application and effectiveness of two image fusion approaches: PCA and CNN. PCA is a widely used statistical technique that analyzes the covariance structure of a dataset to identify principal components, while CNN is a deep learning-based approach that learns hierarchical features from input images.

The study implements a practical approach using MATLAB to evaluate and compare the two approaches. The results of the study indicate that CNN offers advantages in terms of image quality and clarity. However, it is less favorable in terms of time and cost compared to PCA. The chapter provides insights into the trade-offs between the two approaches, allowing practitioners to make informed decisions based on their specific requirements.

Chapter 12 serves as a valuable resource for researchers, practitioners, and professionals involved in image fusion applications. By comparing the theoretical and statistical effects of PCA and CNN, the chapter provides a deeper understanding of the strengths and limitations of each approach. This understanding enables practitioners to select the most suitable technique based on their priorities, whether it is image quality, processing time, or resource utilization.

Overall, the chapter contributes to the advancement of image fusion methodologies by highlighting the benefits and trade-offs of PCA and CNN approaches. It encourages further research and exploration of image fusion techniques, fostering the development of efficient and effective methods for integrating and analyzing visual data.

Chapter 13: Crime Forecasting Using Historical Crime Location Using CNN-Based Image Classification Mechanism

In Chapter 13, Vishnu Venkatesh N, Priyank Singhal, Digvijay Pandey, Meenakshi Sharma, Dr. Rupal Rautdesai, Deepti Khubalkar, and Ankur Gupta focus on crime forecasting using historical crime location data. The chapter explores the application of Convolutional Neural Network (CNN) for image classification to categorize crime events based on historical crime data.

The authors highlight the significance of CNN in identifying and predicting crime events. While various classification mechanisms have been used in conventional research, CNN has proven to be an effective tool in this context. However, there are challenges related to time consumption and accuracy in CNN-based classification.

To address the time consumption issue, the proposed research employs an approach that reduces the image size by applying the RGB2GRAY model and resizing the images before the training operation. By optimizing the image data, the proposed approach aims to enhance the efficiency and scalability of crime forecasting.

The simulation results presented in the chapter demonstrate that the proposed approach provides a scalable and reliable method for crime forecasting. By utilizing CNN-based image classification on historical crime location data, the research contributes to the development of effective crime prediction models.

Chapter 13 serves as a valuable resource for researchers, practitioners, and professionals involved in crime forecasting and law enforcement. The utilization of CNN in crime prediction offers the potential for more accurate and proactive approaches to crime prevention and control.

By analyzing historical crime location data and employing CNN-based image classification, law enforcement agencies can gain insights into crime patterns and trends, allowing them to allocate resources effectively and implement targeted preventive measures.

The chapter highlights the benefits of incorporating deep learning techniques, such as CNN, into crime forecasting, emphasizing the potential for improved accuracy and efficiency in crime prevention efforts. The research presented encourages further exploration and refinement of CNN-based crime forecasting models, ultimately enhancing public safety and security.

Overall, Chapter 13 contributes to advancing the field of crime forecasting by utilizing CNN-based image classification mechanisms and demonstrating their effectiveness in analyzing historical crime location data.

Chapter 14: Deep Learning-Based Cancer Detection Technique

In Chapter 14, Shahanawaj Ahamad, Vivek Veeraiah, J.V.N. Ramesh, R. Rajadevi, Reeja S R, Sabyasachi Pramanik, and Ankur Gupta explore the application of deep learning (DL) techniques in the detection of cancer. The chapter emphasizes the need for the transition from exploratory research projects to translational and clinical practice in healthcare image analysis using DL.

Advancements in data availability, DL methods, and computational power over the past decade have accelerated the process of incorporating DL into clinical treatment. Through their experience, the authors have gained insights into the potential benefits and drawbacks of integrating DL into clinical practice, which they believe will drive progress in this field in the coming years.

The chapter highlights several challenges that need to be addressed for the successful implementation of DL-based cancer detection techniques. One of the significant challenges is the need to adapt DL training approaches to account for the diverse pathological characteristics present in healthcare images and data. The authors also point out the requirement for properly digitized environments in hospitals to facilitate DL implementation. Additionally, the availability of sufficient open datasets for training and testing DL approaches is crucial for their effectiveness.

By leveraging DL techniques, the proposed cancer detection technique aims to enhance the accuracy and efficiency of cancer diagnosis. DL models can analyze healthcare images to identify patterns and anomalies associated with cancer, assisting medical professionals in making timely and accurate diagnoses.

Chapter 14 serves as a valuable resource for researchers, healthcare practitioners, and professionals involved in cancer detection and diagnosis. It sheds light on the potential of DL in transforming clinical practice and emphasizes the need to address the challenges associated with implementing DL in healthcare settings.

The insights provided in this chapter encourage further research and development in DL-based cancer detection techniques. As DL continues to evolve and datasets become more readily available, the integration of DL into clinical practice holds the promise of improving cancer detection rates, enhancing treatment outcomes, and ultimately benefiting patient care.

Overall, Chapter 14 contributes to advancing the field of cancer detection by highlighting the significance of DL techniques and the challenges that need to be overcome for their successful implementation in clinical practice.

Chapter 15: Determination of Early Onset Glaucoma Using OCT Image

In Chapter 15, Manju K, Anand R, Binay Pandey, Vinay Kumar Nassa, Aakifa Shahul, A.S. Hovan George, Hareesha Bharadwaj, and Sanwta Ram Dogiwal focus on the use of Optical Coherence Tomography (OCT) images for the early detection of glaucoma. The chapter explores the application of deep learning techniques, specifically Convolutional Neural Networks (CNN), to extract glaucoma features and classify different types of glaucoma, including CNV, DME, DRUSEN, and normal cases.

The authors highlight the significance of early detection in glaucoma to enable timely intervention and prevent further vision loss. By utilizing OCT images and deep learning algorithms, the proposed system achieves high accuracy in classifying glaucoma cases. The dataset used for training consists of 968 images, with 242 images for each glaucoma type.

The CNN algorithm is employed to train the model and extract features that are indicative of glaucoma. The accuracy achieved by the proposed system surpasses that of the support vector machine (SVM) image-based approach for glaucoma determination. The authors have designed a robust architecture for the determination process and have utilized pre-training of the deep learning model to obtain initial representations.

The results of the study demonstrate a high level of accuracy, with a sensitivity and specificity rate of 95.4% and a successful classification of glaucoma cases. The identification of significant anatomical markers, such as an increase in cup volume, larger cup diameter, and thickened lip of the neuroretinal rim, aligns with existing clinical markers used for glaucoma diagnosis.

In comparison to feature-based machine learning algorithms, the proposed deep learning method exhibits superior performance in glaucoma determination. The chapter highlights the potential of using

OCT images and deep learning techniques to enhance the accuracy and efficiency of early glaucoma detection.

Chapter 15 serves as a valuable resource for researchers, ophthalmologists, and professionals involved in the field of glaucoma diagnosis. The insights provided contribute to the advancement of glaucoma detection methodologies, emphasizing the potential of deep learning approaches for early onset glaucoma identification.

Overall, the chapter showcases the successful application of deep learning techniques, specifically CNN, in determining early onset glaucoma using OCT images. The research findings contribute to improving glaucoma diagnosis accuracy, enabling early intervention, and ultimately improving patient outcomes in the management of this vision-threatening condition.

Chapter 16: Exudate Detection in Fundus Images Using Deep Learning Algorithms

In Chapter 16, T Shanthi, Anand R, Binay Pandey, Vinay Kumar Nassa, Aakifa Shahul, A.S. Hovan George, and Pankaj Dadheech address the detection and classification of exudates in retinal fundus images using deep learning algorithms. The objective of the study is to detect exudates, which are one of the significant signs of Diabetic Retinopathy (DR), a leading cause of preventable blindness worldwide.

The authors emphasize the importance of early detection of DR to prevent irreversible damage to a patient's vision. Exudates are lesions that require prompt identification and treatment. To address this challenge, the proposed method utilizes deep learning techniques to detect and classify exudates as either hard or soft in retinal fundus images.

The study utilizes the IDRID dataset, which contains retinal fundus images, and annotates the exudates using an annotation tool. The YOLOV3 deep learning algorithm is trained with specific parameters based on the exudate classes. A custom detector is then employed to detect the exudates and classify them into hard and soft categories.

By leveraging deep learning algorithms, the proposed method aims to enhance the accuracy and efficiency of exudate detection in retinal fundus images. Early identification of exudates facilitates timely intervention and treatment for patients with DR.

Chapter 16 serves as a valuable resource for researchers, ophthalmologists, and professionals involved in the field of DR diagnosis and management. The insights provided contribute to the advancement of deep learning-based methodologies for the detection and classification of exudates, enabling early intervention and improving patient outcomes in the management of DR.

Overall, the chapter highlights the successful application of deep learning algorithms in exudate detection using retinal fundus images. The research findings showcase the potential of deep learning approaches in improving the accuracy and efficiency of DR diagnosis, ultimately leading to better patient care and prevention of vision loss caused by this condition.

Chapter 17: Fire Detection System Utilizing an Aggregate Technique in UAV and Cloud Computing

In Chapter 17, Dhamodaran S, Shahanawaj Ahamad, J.V.N. Ramesh, S. Sathappan, Arpit Namdev, Reshma Ramakant Kanse, and Sabyasachi Pramanik explore the development of an early fire detection system using an aggregate technique that combines UAV (Unmanned Aerial Vehicle) and cloud computing. The chapter addresses the challenges posed by the risk of fires in areas surrounding cities, such as forests, farmland, and open spaces, which can endanger lives and cause significant damage.

The authors propose a design that leverages sensor networks, UAV technology, and cloud computing to create an effective fire detection system. Environmental factors are monitored using sensors, and the collected data is analyzed using IoT applications. By integrating cloud computing, UAVs, and wireless sensor technologies, the proposed system aims to enhance early detection and response to fire incidents.

To improve the accuracy and efficiency of fire detection, the system incorporates image processing techniques. These techniques allow for more precise identification of fire occurrences. Additionally, rules are developed to enhance the genuine detection rate, reducing false positives.

The simulation results of the suggested fire detection system are compared with several existing techniques, demonstrating its effectiveness and superiority. The chapter highlights the potential of the proposed system to significantly contribute to fire prevention and mitigation efforts in smart cities and areas prone to fires.

Chapter 17 serves as a valuable resource for researchers, professionals, and practitioners involved in fire safety and smart city development. The insights provided contribute to the advancement of fire detection systems by incorporating UAV technology, cloud computing, and image processing techniques.

Overall, the chapter showcases the potential of utilizing an aggregate technique in UAV and cloud computing to develop an early fire detection system. The research findings highlight the importance of early detection and response to minimize the impact of fire incidents, safeguard human lives, and preserve valuable resources in fire-prone environments.

Chapter 18: Food Quality Assessment Using Image Processing Technique

In Chapter 18, Dhamodaran S, Shahanawaj Ahamad, J.V.N. Ramesh, G. Muthugurunathan, Manikandan K, Sabyasachi Pramanik, and Digvijay Pandey explore the application of image processing techniques for food quality assessment. The chapter highlights the significance of high-resolution optical microscopy and imaging approaches in examining and assessing the microstructure of food items.

The authors discuss the development of scanning electron microscopy (SEM) by Manfred Von Ardenne in the 1930s. SEM is a surface microscopy technique that utilizes electron behavior to generate 3D images of objects, providing insights into their topology, morphology, and composition. Over the past several decades, SEM has found applications in various industries, forensic analysis, and scientific research.

The scanning electron microscope serves as an effective tool for visualizing and characterizing both organic and inorganic substances and surfaces. In the context of food quality assessment, image processing techniques can be employed to analyze and evaluate the microstructure of food samples. These techniques enable researchers and professionals to gain insights into the quality, composition, and characteristics of food products.

By leveraging image processing techniques, the proposed approach aims to enhance food quality assessment, enabling better understanding and control of the microstructure of food items. This, in turn, contributes to improving food safety, optimizing production processes, and ensuring consumer satisfaction.

Chapter 18 serves as a valuable resource for researchers, professionals, and practitioners involved in the field of food quality assessment. The insights provided contribute to the advancement of image processing techniques for analyzing and evaluating the microstructure of food items.

Overall, the chapter highlights the significance of image processing techniques, particularly SEM, in assessing food quality. The research findings showcase the potential of these techniques in enhancing our understanding of food microstructure and improving overall food safety and quality control measures.

Chapter 19: Glaucoma Assessment Using Super Pixel Classification

In Chapter 19, Sonali Dash, Priyadarsan Parida, Vinay Kumar Nassa, A.Shaji George, Aakifa Shahul, and A.S. Hovan George focus on glaucoma assessment using super pixel classification. Glaucoma is a group of eye diseases that can cause damage to the optic nerve and, if left untreated, can lead to lifelong blindness or vision loss. Early detection of glaucoma is challenging as it often presents no symptoms in its early stages, making it difficult to intervene before irreversible vision loss occurs.

The chapter discusses various methods used to identify glaucoma, such as tonometry for measuring intraocular pressure, ophthalmoscopy for examining the optic nerve's structure and color, and perimeter for measuring the entire visual field. However, due to the unique nature of each person's glaucoma, these methods may not detect all forms of the disease effectively.

The proposed approach in this project involves utilizing image processing techniques, specifically super pixel classification, to calculate the cup-to-disc ratio, a visual assessment technique for glaucoma. By applying binarization methods, the cup-to-disc ratio is determined, and this ratio is then used to assess the glaucomatous status of an eye.

By leveraging super pixel classification and image processing techniques, the proposed approach aims to improve the accuracy and efficiency of glaucoma assessment. The chapter highlights the potential of using these methods to enhance early detection and intervention, ultimately preventing or minimizing vision loss associated with glaucoma.

Chapter 19 serves as a valuable resource for researchers, ophthalmologists, and professionals involved in glaucoma assessment and diagnosis. The insights provided contribute to the advancement of image processing techniques in the field of glaucoma assessment and emphasize the importance of early detection for better management and preservation of vision.

Overall, the chapter showcases the potential of super pixel classification and image processing techniques in glaucoma assessment. The research findings contribute to improving the accuracy and effectiveness of glaucoma diagnosis, enabling timely intervention and improving patient outcomes in the management of this sight-threatening condition.

Chapter 20: Healthcare Cloud Services in Image Processing

In Chapter 20, Vivek Veeraiah, Dolly John Shiju, J.V.N. Ramesh, Ganesh Kumar R, Sabyasachi Pramanik, Digvijay Pandey, and Ankur Gupta delve into the utilization of cloud computing in healthcare, particularly in the context of image processing. Over the past century, technology has played a pivotal role in shaping and advancing medical practices, equipment, and pharmaceuticals. Cloud computing, although a relatively newer concept, has emerged as a prominent topic in both academic and healthcare domains.

Healthcare professionals and researchers recognize the need for extensive, easily accessible, and scalable resources to handle the vast amount of healthcare data, including medical images. Cloud computing offers a solution by providing virtual frameworks, platforms, and infrastructure with lower operational costs. The chapter explores the adoption of cloud computing in the field of medicine, focusing on the application of cutting-edge cloud services in medical imaging.

The authors address key issues and considerations related to implementing cloud computing in medical imaging, including data management, storage, sharing, and utilization. They highlight the benefits of cloud services, such as scalability and cost-effectiveness, in facilitating image processing tasks. Additionally, the chapter examines ethical and security concerns associated with cloud computing in the healthcare domain, emphasizing the importance of data privacy and regulatory compliance.

By leveraging cloud services, healthcare professionals can enhance their image processing capabilities, streamline workflows, and access resources more efficiently. The chapter provides insights into the potential of cloud computing in improving the accessibility, availability, and utilization of healthcare data and image processing tools.

Chapter 20 serves as a valuable resource for researchers, healthcare practitioners, and professionals involved in the field of healthcare informatics and medical imaging. The insights provided contribute to a deeper understanding of the benefits, challenges, and ethical considerations associated with utilizing cloud services for image processing in healthcare.

Overall, the chapter highlights the increasing importance of cloud computing in healthcare, particularly in the context of image processing. The research findings emphasize the potential of cloud services to revolutionize medical imaging practices by enabling scalable and cost-effective solutions while addressing privacy and security concerns.

Chapter 21: Image Processing in Industrial Chemical Engineering Trends and Applications

In Chapter 21, Santosh Walke, Manoj Mandake, Ravi Tapre, Makarand Naniwadekar, Chetan Thakar, and Sandhya Jadhav provide a comprehensive overview of the applications and potential of image processing in industrial chemical engineering. The chapter highlights the significance of image processing in providing precise and detailed information about chemical processes and products.

The chapter covers the fundamental concepts of image processing, including image formation and acquisition, image preprocessing, and feature extraction and selection. These foundational topics lay the groundwork for understanding the applications of image processing in industrial chemical engineering.

The authors explore various applications of image processing in this field, such as image-based process monitoring and control, where images are used to monitor and regulate chemical processes. They also discuss image analysis for product quality control, where image processing techniques are employed to ensure the quality and consistency of chemical products.

The chapter further delves into the latest developments and challenges in machine learning for image-based chemical engineering. It provides an overview of machine learning methods and how they are applied in the field of chemical engineering, enhancing the capabilities of image processing techniques.

Additionally, the chapter addresses the limitations of image processing in the context of chemical engineering and discusses current trends and future research prospects. It offers insights into the ongoing advancements and areas of focus for further exploration and innovation in image processing for industrial chemical engineering applications.

Chapter 21 serves as a valuable resource for researchers, professionals, and practitioners in the field of industrial chemical engineering. The insights provided contribute to a deeper understanding of the potential of image processing in this domain and highlight the advancements and challenges associated with its application.

Overall, the chapter emphasizes the significance of image processing in industrial chemical engineering, showcasing its diverse applications and potential for process monitoring, quality control, and product analysis. The research findings provide a foundation for further exploration and utilization of image processing techniques in this field.

Chapter 22: Integration of Image Processing and IoT for Enhanced Patient Health Checking – A Case Study

In Chapter 22, R Manivannan, Y.V.S.S. Pragathi, and Uday Kanike explore the integration of image processing techniques with IoT (Internet of Things) devices in healthcare, focusing on enhanced patient health checking. This integration has revolutionized the way patient health is monitored, analyzed, and treated, leading to improved diagnostic accuracy, timely interventions, and better patient outcomes.

The chapter highlights the role of wearable health trackers and medical equipment connected to IoT devices in collecting real-time vital sign data. This continuous monitoring enables healthcare professionals to make informed decisions based on the captured data. The integration of image processing methods with IoT allows for automated image analysis, which further enhances the diagnostic process and provides valuable insights into patient health.

By leveraging IoT devices, remote access to patient data becomes possible, enabling virtual consultations and follow-ups. This not only improves patient engagement but also facilitates timely interventions and reduces the need for physical visits. The chapter emphasizes the benefits of personalized treatments enabled by the integration of image processing and IoT, as healthcare professionals can tailor interventions based on real-time data and analysis.

However, the chapter acknowledges the challenges associated with this integration, including data security, interoperability, and infrastructure requirements. These issues must be addressed to ensure the successful deployment and widespread adoption of image processing and IoT in healthcare settings.

The authors also discuss future directions and emerging trends in this field. Advancements in 6G networks, the integration of artificial intelligence (AI) techniques, augmented reality, and data fusion methods are identified as areas of potential growth and development. These advancements have the potential to further enhance the integration of image processing and IoT, leading to more advanced and comprehensive healthcare solutions.

Chapter 22 presents a case study that demonstrates the practical implementation and benefits of integrating image processing and IoT in patient health checking. It serves as a valuable resource for researchers, healthcare professionals, and practitioners interested in leveraging these technologies for improved patient care.

Overall, the chapter showcases the transformative potential of integrating image processing and IoT in healthcare, enabling enhanced patient health monitoring, personalized treatments, and remote access to healthcare services. The research findings contribute to the growing body of knowledge in this field and highlight future directions for advancements and improvements.

Chapter 23: Real-Time Pothole Detection During Rainy Weather Using Dashboard Camera for Driverless Cars

In Chapter 23, Manvinder Sharma, Sudhakara Saripalli, Anuj Gupta, Rajneesh Talwar, Pankaj Dadheech, and Dr. Uday Kumar Kanike address the crucial issue of pothole detection on roads, particularly during rainy weather conditions, using dashboard cameras for driverless cars. Roads serve as a primary mode of transportation, and regular maintenance is essential to ensure safety and smooth traffic flow. However, monitoring every location for potholes is impractical, often resulting in neglected maintenance and increased risks for accidents and traffic congestion.

Various image processing methods have been developed to detect potholes, but their accuracy can be significantly affected during rainy seasons. This chapter presents a system specifically designed to effectively detect potholes during rainy weather conditions. By leveraging dashboard cameras installed in driverless cars, real-time pothole detection becomes possible, enabling timely actions to be taken to address the issue.

The proposed system not only detects potholes but also collects their location data, which can be shared with relevant authorities for maintenance work. This contributes to a proactive approach in maintaining road infrastructure and ensuring the safety of both autonomous vehicles and other road users.

The chapter highlights the importance of accurate pothole detection, especially during rainy weather, as the visibility of potholes may be compromised. By utilizing image processing techniques and the capabilities of dashboard cameras, the system offers a practical solution for real-time pothole detection, even in challenging weather conditions.

The authors emphasize the applicability of this system in driverless cars, where proactive measures to avoid potholes can be implemented, leading to improved safety and reduced vehicle damage. The integration of pothole detection with driverless car technology opens up possibilities for automated responses, such as route adjustment or alerting nearby vehicles.

Chapter 23 serves as a valuable resource for researchers, engineers, and professionals working in the field of autonomous vehicles, transportation infrastructure, and image processing. The research findings provide insights into the development of practical solutions for pothole detection, especially during rainy weather, contributing to safer and more efficient road networks.

Overall, the chapter addresses the critical issue of pothole detection in rainy weather conditions, specifically focusing on its applicability in driverless cars. The proposed system showcases the potential of utilizing dashboard cameras and image processing techniques to enhance road maintenance and improve road safety for both autonomous vehicles and human drivers.

Chapter 24: Recent Trends of Addressing COVID-19 Disease by AI/ML

In Chapter 24, Shawni Dutta, Utsab Mukherjee, and Digvijay Pandey explore the recent trends in addressing the COVID-19 disease using AI/ML (Artificial Intelligence/Machine Learning) techniques. The COVID-19 pandemic has significantly impacted human lives worldwide, necessitating the development of automated systems that can provide continuous monitoring and analysis across various domains related to the disease.

This study focuses on heterogeneous fields of COVID-19, including the analysis of suspected, infected, recovered, and deceased cases, the impact of lockdown measures, identification of health habits contributing to the disease, analysis of lung perforation patterns caused by COVID-19, and investigation of vaccination intake and progress. The literature relevant to these domains has been thoroughly examined, considering their prediction efficiency and potential for improvement.

By reviewing the existing research trends, this chapter provides a comprehensive understanding of the ongoing efforts in combating COVID-19 using AI/ML. The authors analyze the effectiveness of different approaches and methodologies employed in addressing various aspects of the disease. This critical evaluation helps identify the strengths and weaknesses of existing research and highlights areas for further improvement.

The chapter concludes with a concrete future perspective, offering insights into each of the afore-mentioned domains. These perspectives aim to guide researchers and practitioners in identifying the shortcomings of current research and directing their efforts towards filling those gaps. By leveraging AI/ML techniques, researchers can contribute to more effective and efficient approaches for managing and combating COVID-19.

Chapter 24 serves as a valuable resource for individuals interested in the intersection of AI/ML and COVID-19 research. The comprehensive overview of recent trends and the critical analysis of existing literature provide readers with a deeper understanding of the ongoing efforts in addressing the COVID-19 pandemic. The chapter's insights can inform the development of innovative solutions and contribute to the collective fight against this global health crisis.

Overall, Chapter 24 sheds light on the application of AI/ML techniques in addressing various aspects of the COVID-19 disease. It underscores the importance of leveraging advanced technologies to enhance monitoring, prediction, and response strategies, ultimately contributing to the global efforts in mitigating the impact of the pandemic.

Chapter 25: Revolutionizing Warehouse Management With Image Processing – A Review of Current Trends and Future Directions

In Chapter 25, Anantha Subramanya Iyer K N, Mahalakshmi S, Hemanth Kumar S, Anitha Nallasivam, and C Selvaraj provide a comprehensive review of the current trends and future directions in warehouse management through the application of image processing techniques. The chapter begins by providing an overview of warehouse management and the role of image processing methods in analyzing and interpreting images captured within warehouse environments. The benefits and limitations of popular image processing techniques are also discussed.

The subsequent section of the chapter focuses on the current advancements in warehouse manage-ment that are based on image processing. It explores the various methods employed in this approach and highlights the advantages it offers in terms of enhancing warehouse operations. Furthermore, the chapter delves into the potential for integrating image processing with other cutting-edge technologies, such as cloud computing and the Internet of Things (IoT). This exploration uncovers the possibilities for further optimizing warehouse management processes through the synergy of these technologies.

The concluding part of the chapter presents an assessment of the opportunities and challenges associ-ated with the implementation of image processing techniques in warehouse management. It underscores the potential for image processing to revolutionize various aspects of warehouse operations, including inventory management, product tracking, and quality control. However, it also acknowledges the chal-lenges that need to be addressed, such as data privacy and security concerns, algorithm accuracy, and system integration complexities.

Chapter 25 serves as a valuable resource for individuals involved in warehouse management, logistics, and supply chain operations. It offers a comprehensive review of the current state of image processing applications in this field and provides insights into the future directions of research and development. The chapter's exploration of the potential synergies between image processing and other emerging tech-nologies opens up new avenues for enhancing warehouse management practices.

Overall, Chapter 25 sheds light on the transformative potential of image processing techniques in revolutionizing warehouse management. By leveraging the power of image analysis and interpretation, organizations can optimize their operations, improve efficiency, and enhance overall productivity. The chapter's review of current trends and future directions paves the way for further advancements in this field and inspires innovative approaches to warehouse management.

Chapter 26: Use of Artificial Intelligence for Image Processing to Aid Digital Forensics – Legislative Challenges

In Chapter 26, Rajesh Gupta, Manashree Mane, Shambhu Bhardwaj, Ujwal Nandekar, Ahmar Afaq, Dharmesh Dhabliya, and Binay Pandey delve into the use of artificial intelligence (AI) for image processing in digital forensics and highlight the legislative challenges associated with its implementation. The chapter presents a balanced perspective, considering both the potential benefits of AI in digital forensics and the concerns surrounding its misuse.

The authors begin by acknowledging the divided opinions on the topic, with proponents recognizing the potential of AI to greatly assist in digital forensics, while others express concerns about its ethical implications and the potential for false or misleading evidence. The legislative challenges that need to be addressed are identified as key considerations for the responsible deployment of AI in image processing for digital forensics.

Data privacy emerges as a crucial legislative challenge in the context of AI-based image processing. As personal data may be present in the images processed by AI systems, there is a risk of mishandling or misuse of this sensitive information. The chapter emphasizes the need for robust data protection measures and legislative frameworks to ensure the privacy rights of individuals while leveraging AI technology in digital forensics.

Another important legislative challenge highlighted is the need for transparency and accountability in AI systems used for image processing. If an AI system produces erroneous or misleading results, it is essential to understand the reasons behind these outcomes and learn from them to avoid similar mistakes in the future. Legislative measures can play a crucial role in establishing standards and requirements for AI systems, promoting transparency, and ensuring the responsible use of AI in digital forensics.

The chapter emphasizes that while AI holds significant potential to revolutionize digital forensics, it is vital to address the legislative challenges to ensure its ethical and responsible implementation. By establishing comprehensive regulations and guidelines, the risks associated with data privacy, the creation of false evidence, and the lack of transparency can be mitigated.

Chapter 26 serves as a valuable resource for policymakers, legal professionals, and digital forensics experts involved in shaping legislative frameworks around the use of AI for image processing in digital forensics. It highlights the importance of striking the right balance between leveraging AI's capabilities and safeguarding individual rights and the integrity of forensic investigations.

In conclusion, Chapter 26 sheds light on the legislative challenges that must be addressed to effectively utilize AI for image processing in digital forensics. By addressing concerns related to data privacy, transparency, and accountability, society can harness the benefits of AI while ensuring the responsible and ethical use of this technology in the field of digital forensics.

Chapter 27: Visual Cryptographic Shares Using Color Component

In Chapter 27, Sabyasachi Samanta, Priyatosh Jana, Abhijit Sarkar, and Soumen Ghosh explore the concept of visual cryptography, a cryptographic method that encrypts and decrypts visual information without relying on computer systems. The authors introduce a new technique based on color components for visual cryptographic shares, specifically focusing on image and video data.

Visual cryptography involves dividing a carrier containing secret information into multiple shares, with each individual share revealing no knowledge about the original secret information. In this paper, the authors propose a color component-based approach for generating visual cryptographic shares for both images and videos. Since videos consist of sequential image frames, the proposed method extends to video data as well. The technique follows a {k, n} threshold framework, where the reformation of the original information is possible using k out of n shares.

The chapter highlights that the proposed method allows for the embedding of data into different shares using steganography or watermarking techniques, offering additional possibilities for information hiding and retrieval. The authors also conduct comparative analyses to assess the effectiveness and performance of the newly developed technique.

By leveraging color components and employing visual cryptographic shares, the proposed method offers a novel approach to secure information transmission and storage. The use of visual cryptography enhances data confidentiality, as the secret information remains hidden in the shares, and human visual perception is employed for decryption.

Chapter 27 provides valuable insights into the application of color component-based visual cryptographic shares, expanding the possibilities for secure communication and data protection. The research contributes to the field of visual cryptography and offers a basis for further exploration and refinement of this technique.

Overall, Chapter 27 serves as a comprehensive reference for researchers and practitioners interested in visual cryptography, color component-based encryption, and the application of these techniques in image and video data security. The chapter's findings and comparisons provide a solid foundation for future research and advancements in visual cryptographic methods.

Chapter 28: Visualizing the Future of Marketing – A Review of Image Processing Techniques and Their Implications for Marketing Management

In Chapter 28, Ganesh Waghmare, Nishant Tyagi, and Anshuman Magar provide a comprehensive review of the integration of image processing techniques in marketing and its implications for marketing management. The chapter explores various image processing techniques used in marketing and their applications in different marketing activities.

The authors begin by discussing the types of image processing techniques employed in marketing, including image segmentation, image filtering, and image recognition. These techniques allow marketers to analyze and manipulate images to extract valuable insights and enhance marketing strategies. The chapter delves into the specific applications of these techniques in marketing, such as product classification, branding, advertising, and customer experience management. By leveraging image processing techniques, marketers can improve visual content, personalize marketing campaigns, and create more engaging customer experiences.

l

The chapter also highlights the implications of image processing techniques for marketing management. It emphasizes the need for marketers to understand and leverage the power of visual content in today's digital age. Image processing techniques provide opportunities for marketers to gather meaningful data, gain insights into consumer preferences, and tailor marketing efforts accordingly. Effective utilization of these techniques can lead to improved targeting, higher customer engagement, and increased brand visibility.

While discussing the applications and implications of image processing techniques, the chapter also addresses their limitations in marketing. Challenges related to data quality, privacy concerns, and algorithmic biases are discussed, highlighting the need for ethical considerations and responsible use of image processing techniques in marketing practices.

The chapter concludes by outlining areas for future research. It emphasizes the importance of conducting empirical studies to evaluate the effectiveness of image processing techniques in marketing outcomes. The authors also suggest the development of new frameworks and models that integrate image processing techniques into marketing management practices.

Chapter 28 serves as a valuable resource for marketers, researchers, and marketing managers interested in understanding the potential of image processing techniques in marketing. The comprehensive review of techniques, applications, and implications provides insights into the future of visual marketing and the role of image processing in shaping marketing strategies. The chapter encourages further exploration and investigation in this evolving field, facilitating the advancement of marketing practices in an increasingly visual-driven marketplace.

IN SUMMARY

In conclusion, this edited reference book serves as a comprehensive and authoritative resource in the field of image processing. The chapters presented in this book cover a wide range of topics, showcasing the diverse applications, techniques, and advancements in image processing across various domains. From healthcare to industrial engineering, from digital forensics to marketing management, the book provides valuable insights and in-depth analyses of the integration of image processing methods.

The chapters, written by leading experts in their respective fields, offer a deep understanding of the theoretical foundations, practical implementations, and future directions of image processing. The research presented in this book highlights the significant contributions of image processing in addressing complex challenges and improving various industries and domains.

Throughout the book, readers will find a wealth of knowledge on state-of-the-art algorithms, machine learning approaches, deep learning models, and innovative applications of image processing techniques. The chapters provide detailed explanations, comparative analyses, and case studies, allowing readers to grasp the intricacies and potential of image processing methods.

Furthermore, this book also sheds light on the ethical considerations, legislative challenges, and potential risks associated with the use of image processing technologies. It emphasizes the importance of responsible and transparent practices to ensure the ethical and legal use of these techniques in various applications.

As the editor(s) of this book, we are immensely grateful to the authors for their valuable contributions and expertise. Their rigorous research and insightful perspectives have enriched this compilation, making it a valuable reference for researchers, professionals, and students working in the field of image processing.

We hope that this edited reference book will inspire further research, innovation, and collaboration in the field of image processing. It is our belief that the knowledge shared within these pages will contribute to the advancement of image processing techniques, leading to new breakthroughs and transformative applications in diverse domains.

Finally, we express our gratitude to the readers for their interest in this book. We sincerely hope that the chapters presented here will broaden their understanding, spark new ideas, and inspire them to explore the fascinating world of image processing.

Binay Kumar Pandey
Department of Information Technology, College of Technology, Govind Ballabh Pant University of Agriculture and Technology, India

Digvijay Pandey
Department of Technical Education, Government of Uttar Pradesh, India

Rohit Anand
G.B. Pant DSEU Okhla-1 Campus, India & Government of NCT of Delhi, New Delhi, India

Deepak S. Mane
Performance Engineering Lab, Tata Research, Development, and Design Center, Australia

Vinay Kumar Nassa
Rajarambapu Institute of Technology, India

Chapter 1
A Comparative Analysis on Image Processing–Based Algorithms and Approaches in Healthcare

Rajneesh Talwar
https://orcid.org/0000-0002-2109-8858
Chitkara University, India

Manvinder Sharma
https://orcid.org/0000-0001-9158-0466
Malla Reddy Engineering College and Management Sciences, Hyderabad, India

Harjinder Singh
Punjabi University, Patiala, India

Prem Sagar
Malla Reddy Engineering College and Management Sciences, Hyderabad, India

ABSTRACT

Image processing has become an important tool in medical applications, with the ability to extract and analyze information from medical images. This chapter provides an overview of various image processing approaches used in medical applications, including deep learning algorithms, segmentation techniques, and a combination of both. The authors also discuss several studies on brain tumor detection, cancer detection, and X-ray analysis using image processing techniques. The studies demonstrate the potential of image processing techniques to significantly improve the accuracy and speed of disease detection, allowing for earlier diagnosis and treatment. Image processing techniques can also assist in treatment planning and lead to more informed diagnoses and treatment decisions. Continued research in this area will undoubtedly lead to even more advanced and sophisticated approaches to image processing, further enhancing the ability of healthcare professionals to diagnose and treat a wide range of medical conditions.

DOI: 10.4018/978-1-6684-8618-4.ch001

1. INTRODUCTION

Image processing has transformed the field of healthcare by providing accurate, efficient, and non-invasive diagnosis and treatment options. Medical imaging plays a crucial role in patient care, and image processing techniques have significantly improved the quality of medical images and their interpretation. In this article, we will discuss the applications of image processing in healthcare and their impact on patient care. Image processing has had a significant impact on the field of healthcare, providing clinicians with advanced tools for diagnosis and treatment planning. In the past, medical imaging was primarily limited to traditional modalities such as X-ray and CT scans. Duncan, James S et al. (2019) . However, with the advent of image processing techniques, these images can now be enhanced and analyzed with greater accuracy and precision, providing clinicians with more detailed information about a patient's condition. Gupta, Akhil et.al (2021)] Figure 1 shows various applications of image processing in healthcare.

One of the most significant applications of image processing in healthcare is in the diagnosis of cancer. Medical imaging plays a critical role in cancer diagnosis, and image processing techniques can improve the accuracy of cancer detection and diagnosis. Image processing techniques could improve the detection of breast cancer on mammograms, reducing the number of false positives and false negatives. Yap, M. H. et. al (2015) Image processing techniques are to analyze CT scans of lung cancer patients and found that this approach could predict treatment outcomes and survival rates. L., Cheng et. al (2020) Figure 2 shows steps involved for detecting cancer using image processing.

Image processing techniques are also used in treatment planning for cancer and other diseases. For example, radiation therapy relies on accurate imaging to target tumors while minimizing damage to healthy tissue. Image processing techniques can be used to create 3D models of organs and structures,

Figure 1. Applications of Image processing in healthcare

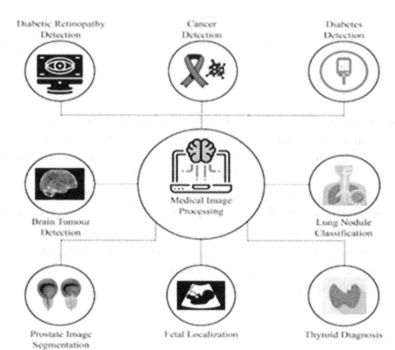

Figure 2. Detection of cancer using image processing

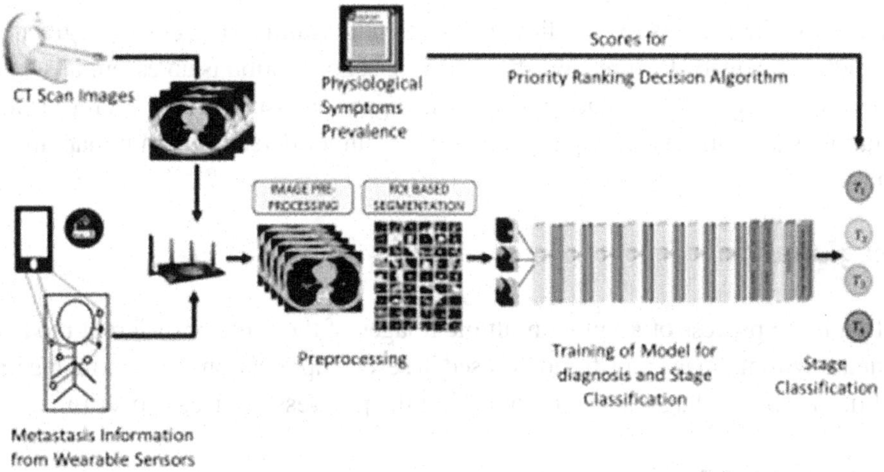

allowing radiation oncologists to precisely plan and deliver radiation therapy. Image processing techniques to develop a personalized treatment planning approach for cervical cancer patients, improving treatment outcomes and reducing side effects. Zhang, Duoer et.al (2022)

In addition to cancer diagnosis and treatment planning, image processing techniques are also used in the diagnosis and management of neurological disorders. For example, MRI scans are used to diagnose and monitor conditions such as multiple sclerosis and Alzheimer's disease. Image processing techniques can be used to analyze these images and identify structural and functional changes in the brain that may indicate disease progression. Image processing techniques were used to analyze MRI scans of Alzheimer's disease patients and found that this approach could predict disease progression with high accuracy. Lanjewar, Madhusudan G. et.al (2022)

Image processing techniques are also used in the development of new diagnostic and therapeutic approaches. For example, researchers are exploring the use of machine learning algorithms to analyze medical images and identify biomarkers for disease diagnosis and treatment response. A study used machine learning techniques to analyze MRI scans of glioblastoma patients and identified biomarkers that could predict treatment response and survival rates. Macyszyn, Luke et.al (2015).

2. PROCESS FOR EXTRACTION OF DISEASE USING IMAGING

2.1 Image Acquisition

Image processing starts with image acquisition, which involves capturing images of the patient's body using various imaging modalities such as X-ray, CT, MRI, ultrasound, and PET. Image processing techniques can enhance the quality of these images by removing noise, artifacts, and other imperfections that can affect the accuracy of diagnosis.

2.2 Image Segmentation

Image segmentation is the process of dividing an image into multiple regions or segments based on certain criteria such as intensity, texture, and shape. Image segmentation is an essential step in medical image processing as it allows for the isolation of specific organs or tissues of interest for further analysis. Image segmentation is used in several applications such as tumor detection, brain mapping, and blood vessel segmentation.

2.3 Image Registration

Image registration is the process of aligning multiple images of the same or different modalities into a common coordinate system. Image registration is used in several applications such as fusing images from multiple modalities for better diagnosis and monitoring the progress of disease over time.

2.4 Image Classification

Image classification is the process of assigning a label or a class to an image based on certain features such as texture, shape, and intensity. Image classification is used in several applications such as disease diagnosis, tumor detection, and tissue classification.

2.5 Image Enhancement

Image enhancement is the process of improving the quality of an image by removing noise, sharpening edges, and enhancing contrast. Image enhancement is used in several applications such as improving the clarity of X-ray images, enhancing the visibility of blood vessels in angiograms, and improving the contrast of CT scans.

2.6 Image Reconstruction

Image reconstruction is the process of creating a three-dimensional image from multiple two-dimensional images. Image reconstruction is used in several applications such as creating 3D models of organs, tissues, and structures for better diagnosis and treatment planning.

2.7 Image Analysis

Image analysis involves extracting quantitative information from medical images using various techniques such as machine learning, computer vision, and statistical analysis. Image analysis is used in several applications such as identifying biomarkers for disease diagnosis, predicting disease progression, and monitoring treatment response.

3. LITERATURE REVIEW ON DIFFERENT TECHNIQUES FOR MEDICAL IMAGE PROCESSING

There are numerous approaches to image processing in medical applications that have been proposed by various authors. In this essay, we will discuss some of the commonly used approaches and their applications in medical imaging.

3.1 Wavelet-Based Techniques

Wavelet-based techniques have been widely used for image processing in medical applications due to their ability to analyze signals at multiple resolutions. Wavelet transforms decompose an image into a set of wavelet coefficients at different scales and orientations. These coefficients can be used to extract features such as edges, texture, and shape. Wavelet-based techniques have been used for various medical applications such as denoising, segmentation, and registration. Kaur, Navpreet et. al (2017) .

For instance, a study proposed a wavelet-based approach for denoising and segmentation of magnetic resonance (MR) images of the brain. The proposed approach employed a wavelet thresholding technique for denoising the MR images and a region-growing algorithm for segmenting the brain tissue. The experimental results showed that the proposed approach achieved superior performance compared to other state-of-the-art approaches. Alexander, M. E et.al (2000) .

3.2 Deep Learning-Based Techniques

Deep learning has gained significant attention in recent years for image processing in medical applications due to its ability to automatically learn features from data. Convolutional neural networks (CNNs) are one of the most popular deep learning-based techniques used in medical image processing (Pandey, D., et al.(2021)). CNNs consist of multiple layers of convolutional and pooling operations that extract features from images. These features can be used for various tasks such as segmentation, classification, and detection (Sharma, Manvinder et.al (2022)).

For example, a study proposed a CNN-based approach for the detection of skin cancer using dermoscopy images. The proposed approach employed a deep residual network for feature extraction and a fully connected layer for classification. The experimental results showed that the proposed approach achieved superior performance compared to dermatologists in the detection of skin cancer (Garg, Rishu et. al (2021)) .

3.3 Morphological Techniques

Morphological techniques are a class of image processing techniques that are based on the mathematical morphology theory. Morphological techniques operate on the shape and structure of images to extract features such as edges, boundaries, and shape (Pandey, B. K., et al.(2021)). Morphological techniques have been widely used in medical applications such as segmentation and classification (Juang, Li-Hong, et. al (2011)).

For instance, a study proposed a morphological approach for the segmentation of breast lesions in mammography images. The proposed approach employed a combination of morphological operations such as erosion, dilation, and opening for the extraction of the lesion region (Sharma, Manvinder et.al

(2021)). The experimental results showed that the proposed approach achieved superior performance compared to other state-of-the-art approaches. Lilei, Huijie Sun et. al (2021) .

3.4 Level Set-Based Techniques

Level set-based techniques are a class of image processing techniques that use a level set function to represent the boundaries of objects in images. Level set-based techniques have been widely used for various medical applications such as segmentation, tracking, and registration(Shi, Yonggang et. al (2008)) .

A study proposed a level set-based approach for the segmentation of the optic disc in retinal images. The proposed approach employed a level set function to represent the boundary of the optic disc and a gradient vector flow field for the evolution of the level set function. The experimental results showed that the proposed approach achieved superior performance compared to other state-of-the-art approaches. Wong, D. W. K et. al (2008) .

3.5 Fuzzy-Based Techniques

Fuzzy-based techniques are a class of image processing techniques that use fuzzy logic to handle uncertainty and imprecision in images. Fuzzy-based techniques have been widely used in medical applications such as segmentation, classification, and diagnosis(Raju, G. et. al (2014)).

For instance, a study proposed a fuzzy-based approach for the segmentation of brain tumors in MRI images. The proposed approach employed a fuzzy c-means clustering algorithm for the segmentation of the tumor region. The experimental results(Mathur, Neha et. al (2018))

The performance and accuracy of each technique depend on the specific application and the type of image data (Lelisho, M. E.,.et al. (2023))Wavelet-based techniques have high computational efficiency and are good at denoising and segmentation, making them suitable for applications such as MRI analysis. Deep learning-based techniques have high accuracy and can learn complex features, making them suitable for tasks such as segmentation, classification, and detection (Sennan, S.,et al. (2022)). Morphological-based techniques have high accuracy in segmentation and are good at handling small objects, making them suitable for applications such as tumor detection (Pandey, B. K.,et al. (2022)). Level set-based techniques have high accuracy and can handle complex shape variations, making them suitable for tasks

Table 1. Comparison of various techniques used

Technique	Performance	Accuracy	Application
Wavelet-based	High computational efficiency, good at denoising	High accuracy in segmentation	Denoising, Segmentation, Registration
Deep learning-based	High accuracy, can learn complex features	High accuracy in segmentation, classification, and detection	Segmentation, Classification, Detection
Morphological-based	High accuracy in segmentation, good at handling small objects	High accuracy in segmentation and classification	Segmentation, Classification
Level set-based	High accuracy, can handle complex shape variations	High accuracy in segmentation and tracking	Segmentation, Tracking, Registration
Fuzzy-based	Good at handling uncertainty and imprecision	High accuracy in segmentation and classification	Segmentation, Classification, Diagnosis

such as segmentation and tracking of organs. Fuzzy-based techniques are good at handling uncertainty and imprecision, making them suitable for applications such as segmentation, classification, and diagnosis.

4. COMPARATIVE ANALYSIS FOR VARIOUS MEDICAL IMAGING APPROACHES

4.1 For Brain Tumor Detection

There have been several studies on brain tumor detection using image processing techniques. In this section, we will compare some of the work done by different authors in this area.

One approach used by researchers is the use of machine learning algorithms for tumor detection. In a study, the authors used a machine learning algorithm called a probabilistic neural network (PNN) to detect brain tumors from MRI scans. The results showed that the PNN approach had a high accuracy of 94.7% for tumor detection(Varuna Shree, N. et. al (2018)) .

Another study used a deep learning algorithm called a convolutional neural network (CNN) for brain tumor detection. The authors trained the CNN on MRI scans and achieved an accuracy of 91.9% for tumor detection(Ghassemi, Navid et. al (2020)) .

In addition to machine learning algorithms, other researchers have used image processing techniques such as segmentation for brain tumor detection. Segmentation involves separating the tumor from the surrounding brain tissue. A study used a segmentation algorithm called region growing for brain tumor detection from MRI scans. The authors achieved an accuracy of 93.75% using this approach(Latif, Ghazanfar et. al (2018)) .

Another study used a segmentation algorithm called the level set method for brain tumor detection from MRI scans. The authors achieved an accuracy of 89.3% using this approach(Gull, Sahar et. al (2021)) .

Some researchers have also used a combination of machine learning and segmentation techniques for brain tumor detection. For example, a study used a combination of a CNN and a segmentation algorithm called the k-means algorithm for brain tumor detection from MRI scans. The authors achieved an accuracy of 96.5% using this approach(Biswas, A. et. al (2021)) .

Table 2. Summary of the various approaches used by different authors for brain tumor detection using image processing techniques

Approach	Accuracy
Probabilistic neural network (PNN)	94.7%
Convolutional neural network (CNN)	91.9%
Segmentation (region growing)	93.75%
Segmentation (level set method)	89.3%
CNN + Segmentation (k-means algorithm)	96.5%

4.2 For Cancer Detection

One approach used by researchers is the use of machine learning algorithms for cancer detection. A study used a machine learning algorithm called a support vector machine (SVM) for breast cancer detection from mammography images. The authors achieved an accuracy of 88.2% using this approach (Sharma, Ayush et. al (2017)) .

Another study used a deep learning algorithm called a CNN for lung cancer detection from CT scans. The authors achieved an AUC of 0.94 for cancer detection using this approach (Cengil, Emine et. al (2018)) .

In addition to machine learning algorithms, other researchers have used image processing techniques such as segmentation for cancer detection. A study used a segmentation algorithm called active contour models for breast cancer detection from mammography images. The authors achieved an accuracy of 86.5% using this approach (Malathi, M. et. al (2021)) .

Another study used a segmentation algorithm called the GrabCut algorithm for lung cancer detection from CT scans. The authors achieved an accuracy of 86.5% using this approach(Zhang, Shengchao et. al (2018)) .

Some researchers have also used a combination of machine learning and segmentation techniques for cancer detection. For example, a study used a combination of a CNN and a segmentation algorithm called the U-Net for lung cancer detection from CT scans. The authors achieved an AUC of 0.91 using this approach(Protonotarios, Nicholas E. et. al (2022)) .

Table 3. Summary of the various approaches used by different authors for cancer detection using image processing techniques

Approach	Accuracy/AUC
SVM	88.2%
CNN	AUC of 0.94
Segmentation (active contour models)	86.5%
Segmentation (GrabCut algorithm)	86.5%
CNN + Segmentation (U-Net)	AUC of 0.91

4.3 For X-Ray/CT Scan Analysis

X-rays are widely used in medical imaging for the diagnosis and monitoring of various conditions. Image processing techniques can be used to enhance and analyze X-ray images for better visualization and diagnosis. In this section, we will compare some of the work done by different authors for X-ray analysis using image processing techniques.

One approach used by researchers is the use of deep learning algorithms for X-ray analysis. A study used a deep learning algorithm called a CNN for the detection of 14 different diseases from chest X-ray images. The authors achieved an accuracy of up to 83.1% using this approach (Rahman, Tawsifur et. al (2020)).

Table 4. Summary of the various approaches used by different authors for X-ray analysis using image processing techniques

Approach	Accuracy/AUC
CNN	Up to 83.1%
Capsule Network	83.2%
Segmentation (active contour models)	85.4%
Segmentation (Watershed algorithm)	Up to 92%
CNN + Segmentation (Mask R-CNN)	AUC of 0.81

Another study used a deep learning algorithm called a capsule network for the detection of lung nodules from CT scans. The authors achieved an accuracy of 83.2% using this approach (Afshar, Parnian et. al (2021)).

In addition to deep learning algorithms, other researchers have used image processing techniques such as segmentation for X-ray analysis. A study used a segmentation algorithm called active contour models for the detection of lung nodules from CT scans. The authors achieved an accuracy of 85.4% using this approach(Keshani, Mohsen et. al (2013)) .

Another study used a segmentation algorithm called the Watershed algorithm for the detection of bone fractures from X-ray images. The authors achieved an accuracy of up to 92% using this approach (Bagaria, Rinisha et. al (2021)) .

Some researchers have also used a combination of machine learning and segmentation techniques for X-ray analysis. A study used a combination of a CNN and a segmentation algorithm called the Mask R-CNN for the detection of lung nodules from CT scans. The authors achieved an AUC of 0.81 using this approach (Yan, Huanlan et. al (2019)) .

5. APPLICATIONS OF IMAGE PROCESSING IN HEALTHCARE

Image processing techniques are used to diagnose several diseases such as cancer, heart disease, and neurological disorders. Medical images such as X-ray, CT, MRI, and PET scans are used to detect abnormalities in the body, and image processing techniques are used to enhance the quality of these images for accurate diagnosis. Image processing techniques are used to plan and monitor the progress of treatment for several diseases. For example, image processing techniques are used to create 3D models of organs and structures for better treatment planning in radiation therapy, surgery, and interventional procedures (Pandey, D., et al.(2021)).

Image processing techniques are used in drug development to identify and quantify the effects of drugs on the body. Medical imaging is used to monitor the response of the body to the drug, and image processing techniques are used to analyze the images and extract quantitative information. Image processing techniques are used in medical research to study the structure and function of organs, tissues, and cells. Image analysis techniques are used to identify biomarkers for disease diagnosis and treatment response, and to develop new diagnostic and therapeutic approaches (Zargar, S. A.,et al.(2021)).

6. CONCLUSION

Image processing has proven to be a powerful tool in medical applications, providing significant benefits to healthcare professionals and patients alike. The ability to extract and analyze information from medical images has greatly improved the accuracy of disease detection and diagnosis, as well as the overall quality of patient care. This article has compared various image processing approaches used in medical applications, including deep learning algorithms, segmentation techniques, and a combination of both. We have also highlighted some of the work done by different authors in the areas of brain tumor detection, cancer detection, and X-ray analysis using image processing techniques. The studies on brain tumor detection have shown that image processing techniques can significantly improve the accuracy and speed of tumor detection, allowing for earlier diagnosis and treatment. Similarly, the studies on cancer detection have demonstrated the potential of image processing techniques to identify cancerous tissues with high accuracy and to assist in treatment planning. In X-ray analysis, image processing techniques have been used to detect lung nodules, bone fractures, and other abnormalities with high accuracy, helping healthcare professionals to make more informed diagnoses and treatment decisions. Overall, image processing techniques have the potential to revolutionize the field of medical imaging and improve the quality of patient care. Continued research in this area will undoubtedly lead to even more advanced and sophisticated approaches to image processing, further enhancing the ability of healthcare professionals to diagnose and treat a wide range of medical conditions.

REFERENCES

Afshar, P., Naderkhani, F., Oikonomou, A., Rafiee, M. J., Mohammadi, A., & Plataniotis, K. N. (2021). MIXCAPS: A capsule network-based mixture of experts for lung nodule malignancy prediction. *Pattern Recognition*, *116*, 107942. doi:10.1016/j.patcog.2021.107942

Alexander, M. E., Baumgartner, R., Summers, A. R., Windischberger, C., Klarhoefer, M., Moser, E., & Somorjai, R. L. (2000). A wavelet-based method for improving signal-to-noise ratio and contrast in MR images. *Magnetic Resonance Imaging*, *18*(2), 169–180. doi:10.1016/S0730-725X(99)00128-9 PMID:10722977

Babu, S. Z. D., Pandey, D., & Sheik, I. (2020). Acts Of COVID19. *International Journal of Advanced Engineering*, *3*, 2457–0397.

Bagaria, R., Wadhwani, S., & Wadhwani, A. K. (2021). A wavelet transform and neural network based segmentation & classification system for bone fracture detection. *Optik (Stuttgart)*, *236*, 166687. doi:10.1016/j.ijleo.2021.166687

Biswas, A., & Islam, M. S. "ANN-Based Brain Tumor Classification: Performance Analysis Using K-Means and FCM Clustering With Various Training Functions." In Explainable Artificial Intelligence for Smart Cities, pp. 83-102. CRC Press, 2021. doi:10.1201/9781003172772-6

Cengil, E., & Cinar, A. (2018). A deep learning based approach to lung cancer identification. In *2018 International Conference on Artificial Intelligence and Data Processing (IDAP)*, (pp. 1-5). IEEE. 10.1109/IDAP.2018.8620723

Duncan, J. S., Insana, M. F., & Ayache, N. (2019). Biomedical imaging and analysis in the age of big data and deep learning [scanning the issue]. *Proceedings of the IEEE, 108*(1), 3–10. doi:10.1109/JPROC.2019.2956422

Garg, R., Maheshwari, S., & Shukla, A. (2021). Decision support system for detection and classification of skin cancer using CNN. In *Innovations in Computational Intelligence and Computer Vision: Proceedings of ICICV 2020*, (pp. 578-586). Springer Singapore. 10.1007/978-981-15-6067-5_65

Ghassemi, N., Shoeibi, A., & Rouhani, M. (2020). Deep neural network with generative adversarial networks pre-training for brain tumor classification based on MR images. *Biomedical Signal Processing and Control, 57*, 101678. doi:10.1016/j.bspc.2019.101678

Gull, S., & Akbar, S. (2021). *Artificial intelligence in brain tumor detection through MRI scans: Advancements and challenges*. Artificial Intelligence and Internet of Things. doi:10.1201/9781003097204-10

Gupta, A., Anand, R., Pandey, D., Sindhwani, N., Wairya, S., Pandey, B. K., & Sharma, M. (2021). Prediction of breast cancer using extremely randomized clustering forests (ERCF) technique: Prediction of breast cancer. [IJDST]. *International Journal of Distributed Systems and Technologies, 12*(4), 1–15. doi:10.4018/IJDST.287859

Gupta, A. K., Sharma, M., Sharma, A., & Menon, V. (2022). A study on SARS-CoV-2 (COVID-19) and machine learning based approach to detect COVID-19 through X-ray images. *International Journal of Image and Graphics, 22*(03), 2140010. doi:10.1142/S0219467821400106

Juang, L.-H., & Wu, M.-N. (2011). Psoriasis image identification using k-means clustering with morphological processing. *Measurement, 44*(5), 895–905. doi:10.1016/j.measurement.2011.02.006

Kaur, N., & Sharma, M. (2017). Brain tumor detection using self-adaptive K-means clustering. In *2017 International Conference on Energy, Communication, Data Analytics and Soft Computing (ICECDS)*, (pp. 1861-1865). IEEE. 10.1109/ICECDS.2017.8389771

Keshani, M., Azimifar, Z., Tajeripour, F., & Boostani, R. (2013). Lung nodule segmentation and recognition using SVM classifier and active contour modeling: A complete intelligent system. *Computers in Biology and Medicine, 43*(4), 287–300. doi:10.1016/j.compbiomed.2012.12.004 PMID:23369568

Kumar Pandey, B., Pandey, D., Nassa, V. K., Ahmad, T., Singh, C., George, A. S., & Wakchaure, M. A. (2021). Encryption and steganography-based text extraction in IoT using the EWCTS optimizer. *Imaging Science Journal, 69*(1-4), 38–56. doi:10.1080/13682199.2022.2146885

Lanjewar, M. G., Parab, J. S., & Shaikh, A. Y. (2022). Development of framework by combining CNN with KNN to detect Alzheimer's disease using MRI images. *Multimedia Tools and Applications, 82*(8), 12699–12717. doi:10.100711042-022-13935-4

Latif, G., Iskandar, D. N. F. A., Alghazo, J., & Jaffar, A. (2018). Improving brain MR image classification for tumor segmentation using phase congruency. *Current Medical Imaging, 14*(6), 914–922. doi:10.2174/1573405614666180402150218

Lelisho, M. E., Pandey, D., Alemu, B. D., Pandey, B. K., & Tareke, S. A. (2023). The negative impact of social media during COVID-19 pandemic. *Trends in Psychology*, *31*(1), 123–142. doi:10.100743076-022-00192-5

Li, L., Cheng, Z., Zhang, X., & Gu, Y. (2020). Radiomics analysis of CT images for prediction of chemotherapy response and survival in patients with advanced non-small cell lung cancer. *Medical Science Monitor*, *26*, e922451.

Macyszyn, L., Akbari, H., Pisapia, J. M., Da, X., Attiah, M., Pigrish, V., Bi, Y., Pal, S., Davuluri, R. V., Roccograndi, L., Dahmane, N., Martinez-Lage, M., Biros, G., Wolf, R. L., Bilello, M., O'Rourke, D. M., & Davatzikos, C. (2015). Imaging patterns predict patient survival and molecular subtype in glioblastoma via machine learning techniques. *Neuro-Oncology*, *18*(3), 417–425. doi:10.1093/neuonc/nov127 PMID:26188015

Malathi, M., Sinthia, P., Farzana, F., & Aloy Anuja Mary, G. (2021). Breast cancer detection using active contour and classification by deep belief network. *Materials Today: Proceedings*, *45*, 2721–2724. doi:10.1016/j.matpr.2020.11.551

Mathur, N., Meena, Y. K., Mathur, S., & Mathur, D. (2018). *Detection of brain tumor in MRI image through fuzzy-based approach*. High-Resolution Neuroimaging-Basic Physical Principles and Clinical Applications. doi:10.5772/intechopen.71485

Pandey, D., Islam, T., & Malik, M. A. (2021). Novel coronavirus disease (SARS-COV-2): an overview. *Asian Journal of Advances in Medical Science*, 39-43.

Pandey, D., Aswari, A., Taufiqurakman, M., Khalim, A., & Azahrah, F. F. (2021). System of education changes due to Covid-19 pandemic. *Asian Journal of Advances in Research*, 168-173.

Pandey, B. K., Pandey, D., Wairya, S., & Agarwal, G. (2021). An advanced morphological component analysis, steganography, and deep learning-based system to transmit secure textual data. [IJDAI]. *International Journal of Distributed Artificial Intelligence*, *13*(2), 40–62. doi:10.4018/IJDAI.2021070104

Pandey, B. K., Pandey, D., Wairya, S., Agarwal, G., Dadeech, P., Dogiwal, S. R., & Pramanik, S. (2022). Application of integrated steganography and image compressing techniques for confidential information transmission. *Cyber Security and Network Security*, 169-191.

Pandey, B. K., Pandey, D., Wairya, S., Agarwal, G., Dadeech, P., Dogiwal, S. R., & Pramanik, S. (2022). Application of integrated steganography and image compressing techniques for confidential information transmission. *Cyber Security and Network Security*, 169-191.

Pandey, B. K., Pandey, D., Wariya, S., & Agarwal, G. (2021). A deep neural network-based approach for extracting textual images from deteriorate images. *EAI Endorsed Transactions on Industrial Networks and Intelligent Systems*, *8*(28), e3–e3. doi:10.4108/eai.17-9-2021.170961

Pandey, B. K., Pandey, D., Wariya, S., Aggarwal, G., & Rastogi, R. (2021). Deep learning and particle swarm optimisation-based techniques for visually impaired humans' text recognition and identification. *Augmented Human Research*, *6*(1), 1–14. doi:10.100741133-021-00051-5

Pandey, D., Islam, T., Magray, J. A., Gulzar, A., & Zargar, S. A. (2021). Use of statistical analysis to monitor novel coronavirus-19 cases in Jammu and Kashmir, India. *European Journal of Biological Research*, *11*(3), 274–282.

Pandey, D., Nassa, V. K., Jhamb, A., Mahto, D., Pandey, B. K., George, A. H., & Bandyopadhyay, S. K. (2021). An integration of keyless encryption, steganography, and artificial intelligence for the secure transmission of stego images. In *Multidisciplinary approach to modern digital steganography* (pp. 211–234). IGI Global. doi:10.4018/978-1-7998-7160-6.ch010

Pandey, D., Wairya, S., Pradhan, B., & Wangmo. (2022). Understanding COVID-19 response by twitter users: A text analysis approach. *Heliyon*, *8*(8), e09994. doi:10.1016/j.heliyon.2022.e09994 PMID:35873536

Protonotarios, N. E., Katsamenis, I., Sykiotis, S., Dikaios, N., Kastis, G. A., Chatziioannou, S. N., Metaxas, M., Doulamis, N., & Doulamis, A. (2022). A few-shot U-Net deep learning model for lung cancer lesion segmentation via PET/CT imaging. *Biomedical Physics & Engineering Express*, *8*(2), 025019. doi:10.1088/2057-1976/ac53bd PMID:35144242

Rahman, T., & Muhammad, E. H. (2020). Transfer learning with deep convolutional neural network (CNN) for pneumonia detection using chest X-ray. *Applied Sciences (Basel, Switzerland)*, *10*(9), 3233. doi:10.3390/app10093233

Raju, G., & Madhu, S. (2014). A fast and efficient color image enhancement method based on fuzzy-logic and histogram. *AEÜ. International Journal of Electronics and Communications*, *68*(3), 237–243. doi:10.1016/j.aeue.2013.08.015

Sennan, S., Pandey, D., Alotaibi, Y., & Alghamdi, S. (2022). A Novel Convolutional Neural Networks Based Spinach Classification and Recognition System. *Computers, Materials & Continua*, *73*(1), 343–361. doi:10.32604/cmc.2022.028334

Sharma, A., Kulshrestha, S., & Daniel, S. (2017). Machine learning approaches for breast cancer diagnosis and prognosis. In *2017 International conference on soft computing and its engineering applications (icSoftComp)*, (pp. 1-5). IEEE. 10.1109/ICSOFTCOMP.2017.8280082

Sharma, M., Pandey, D., Khosla, D., Goyal, S., Pandey, B. K., & Gupta, A. K. (2022). Design of a GaN-Based Flip Chip Light Emitting Diode (FC-LED) with Au Bumps & Thermal Analysis with Different Sizes and Adhesive Materials for Performance Considerations. *Silicon*, *14*(12), 7109–7120. doi:10.100712633-021-01457-x

Sharma, M., Sharma, B., Gupta, A. K., Khosla, D., Goyal, S., & Pandey, D. (2021). A study and novel AI/ML-based framework to detect COVID-19 virus using smartphone embedded sensors. In *Sustainability Measures for COVID-19 Pandemic* (pp. 59–74). Springer Nature Singapore. doi:10.1007/978-981-16-3227-3_4

Sharma, M., & Singh, H. (2022). Contactless Methods for Respiration Monitoring and Design of SIW-LWA for Real-Time Respiratory Rate Monitoring. *Journal of the Institution of Electronics and Telecommunication Engineers*, 1–11. doi:10.1080/03772063.2022.2069167

Shi, Y., & Karl, W. C. (2008). A real-time algorithm for the approximation of level-set-based curve evolution. *IEEE Transactions on Image Processing*, *17*(5), 645–656. doi:10.1109/TIP.2008.920737 PMID:18390371

Sun, L., Sun, H., Wang, J., Wu, S., Zhao, Y., & Xu, Y. (2021). Breast mass detection in mammography based on image template matching and CNN. *Sensors (Basel)*, *21*(8), 2855. doi:10.339021082855 PMID:33919623

Varuna Shree, N., & Kumar, T. N. R. (2018). Identification and classification of brain tumor MRI images with feature extraction using DWT and probabilistic neural network. *Brain Informatics*, *5*(1), 23–30. doi:10.100740708-017-0075-5 PMID:29313301

Wong, D. W. K., Liu, J., Lim, J. H., Jia, X., Yin, F., Li, H., & Wong, T. Y. (2008). Level-set based automatic cup-to-disc ratio determination using retinal fundus images in ARGALI. In *2008 30th annual international conference of the IEEE engineering in medicine and biology society*, (pp. 2266-2269). IEEE. 10.1109/IEMBS.2008.4649648

Yan, H., Lu, H., Ye, M., Yan, K., Xu, Y., & Jin, Q. (2019). Improved mask R-CNN for lung nodule segmentation. In *2019 10th International Conference on Information Technology in Medicine and Education (ITME)*, (pp. 137-141). IEEE. 10.1109/ITME.2019.00041

Yap, M. H., Pons, G., Marti, J., & Ganau, S. (2015). Automated detection of breast cancer in mammograms using cascaded deep learning neural networks. In *International Conference on Medical Image Computing and Computer-Assisted Intervention* (pp. 632-640). Springer.

Zargar, S. A., Islam, T., Rehman, I. U., & Pandey, D. (2021). Use of cluster analysis to monitor novel corona virus (Covid-19) infections In India. *Asian Journal of Advances in Medical Science*, 32-38.

Zhang, D., Yuan, Z., Hu, P., & Yang, Y. (2022). Automatic treatment planning for cervical cancer radiation therapy using direct three-dimensional patient anatomy match. *Journal of Applied Clinical Medical Physics*, *23*(8), e13649. doi:10.1002/acm2.13649 PMID:35635799

Zhang, S., Zhao, Y., & Bai, P. (2018). Object localization improved grabcut for lung parenchyma segmentation. *Procedia Computer Science*, *131*, 1311–1317. doi:10.1016/j.procs.2018.04.330

Chapter 2
Review on Different Types of Disturbing Noise for Degraded Complex Image

Binay Kumar Pandey
https://orcid.org/0000-0002-4041-1213
Department of Information Technology, Govind Ballabh Pant University of Agriculture and Technology, Pantnagar, India

Poonam Devi
https://orcid.org/0000-0002-3656-0654
Chaudhary Devi Lal University, Sirsa, India

A. Shaji George
https://orcid.org/0000-0002-8677-3682
Business System Department, Almarai Company, Saudi Arabia

Vinay Kumar Nassa
https://orcid.org/0000-0002-9606-7570
Rajarambapu Institute of Technology, India

Pankaj Dadheech
https://orcid.org/0000-0001-5783-1989
Swami Keshvanand Institute of Technology, Management, and Gramothan, India

Blessy Thankachan
School of Computer Applications, JECRC University, India

Pawan Kumar Patidar
https://orcid.org/0009-0008-8115-9094
Swami Keshvanand Institute of Technology, Management, and Gramothan, India

Sanwta Ram Dogiwal
https://orcid.org/0000-0002-4524-002X
Swami Keshvanand Institute of Technology, Management, and Gramothan, India

ABSTRACT

This chapter provides an analysis of the various kinds of distracting noise that can be seen in degraded complex images, such as those found in newspapers, blogs, and websites. A complicated image that had been deteriorated as a result of noise such as salt and pepper noise, random valued impulse noise, speckle noise, and Gaussian noise, amongst others, was the result. There is an extraordinarily high demand for saving the text that can be read from complicated images that have been degraded into a form that can be read by computers for later use.

DOI: 10.4018/978-1-6684-8618-4.ch002

INTRODUCTION

There are many practical advancements that are of significant interest in the field of picture denoising, and these advancements call for a consistent and ongoing evaluation of the relevant noise theory. As a result of this, a large number of scholars have conducted literature reviews on both practical and theoretical aspects of the topic.

Noise in imaging systems expresses itself throughout the phases of picture acquisition, coding, transmission, and processing, and this is a problem that has been addressed in every study to far. This noise degrades the quality of the signals carrying the primary information in audio and visual media. Researchers are left wondering things like how much of the original signal was lost, whether or if the signal can be recovered, and what kind of noise model is associated with the noisy image(Kumar Pandey, B et al. (2022)).

Theoretical and practical principles of entitl noises included in digital photos, however, will occasionally necessitate reinforcement learning. In this section, we will examine various noise models in an effort to provide an answer to all of these issues.

The statistical notions from noise theory have served as the foundation for this article's literature review. To begin, we will discuss noise and the role that noise plays in visual distortion. A random signal is what we call noise. It is put to use in the process of wiping out the majority of the image's information. Image processing is plagued by one of its most frustrating issues: image distortion. Noise types that are crucial in the case of digital photographs include Gaussian noise, Poisson noise, Speckle noise, Salt and Pepper noise, and many more. photographs can become damaged as a result of these and other types of noise. Image-capturing devices, such as cameras, may have introduced these noises due to imperfections or inaccuracies in the devices themselves, such as misaligned lenses, weak focal length, scattering, and other potentially damaging conditions that may be present in the atmosphere (Pandey, D., et al. (2023)). This means that studying noise and noise models in great detail is an essential part of the image denoising process. This allows for the best possible noise model to be chosen by the image denoising system.

Noise Model

In digital images, noise conveys information that is not wanted. The presence of noise results in undesired effects such as artefacts, false edges, unseen lines, corners, blurred objects, and disrupted background scenes.

In order to mitigate these unintended impacts, it is necessary to get knowledge of noise models in advance of further processing. Noise in digital signals can originate from a wide variety of different sources, including Charge Coupled Device (CCD) and Complementary Metal Oxide Semiconductor (CMOS) sensors. Analysis of noise models that is timely, comprehensive, and quantitative has been accomplished, at least in part, with the help of the points spreading function (PSF) and the modulation transfer function (MTF). Histograms and probability density functions (PDFs) can also be utilised in the process of designing and characterising noise models. In this article, we will talk about a few noise models, as well as the several sorts and categories that digital photographs can fall into (Lelisho, M. E., et al.(2022)).

Noise for Degraded Complex Image

The deteriorated complex image was impacted by a variety of types of noise, including Brownian Noise (also known as Fractal Noise), Rayleigh Noise, Gamma Noise, Poisson-Gaussian Noise, salt and pepper noise, random valued impulse noise, speckle noise, Gaussian noise, and Structured Noise, amongst others, as will be illustrated in the following section. Without an adequate comprehension of the noise model, it is extremely challenging to eliminate noise from complicated images (Jayapoorani, S., et al.(2023)).

Basic Classification of Noise

Noise is a random variation that can occur in digital photographs and can lead to varied intensity values of individual pixels rather than the actual pixel values.

Noise not only diminishes image quality but also has the potential to cause the loss of important information that was previously hidden in photos. An effect of noise on an image is a change in the picture elements or the values of its pixels, which can lead to a shift in colour or brightness. The process of acquiring or transmitting a digital image typically involves the addition of noise to the image.

The quality of image sensors can be affected by a number of different aspects, such as the weather conditions that prevail at the time a picture is being acquired, in addition to the quality of the sensor itself. Due to electromagnetic interference in the channel, digital images suffer quality loss both during the process (Pandey, D., et al.(2019)) of their capture and while they are being transmitted.

Because environmental disturbances, insufficient light levels, the image sensor, and interference in the transmission channel are the primary contributors to noise in digital images, we can assume that the noise model is spatially invariant, which means that it is not dependent on spatial location.

A noisy image can be modelled by an equation as follows:

$$g(x, y) = f(x, y) + \cdot (x, y) \tag{1}$$

Where, f(x, y) = Original image

η (x, y) = Noise added to the original image

g (x, y) = Resulting image with noise

Figure 1. Image degradation model

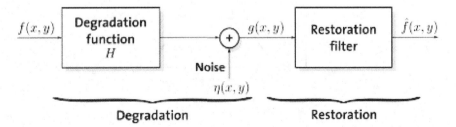

There are numerous types of noise in image processing that affects the image invarious manners. Some of the most common types of noise are explained as follows:

Gaussian Noise

This noise is most prevalent in photos during the process of their capture. It has a cumulative effect in the wild. Normal distribution, often known as the Gaussian distribution, is equivalent to its Probability Density Function (PDF), which describes the distribution of its data. Since it can be produced by amplifiers as well as detectors, some people refer to it as electronic noise (Meslie, Y., Enbeyle, W., (2021)). The most common reason for employing these noise models is due to their workability in both the spatial and frequency domains.

The following equation can be used to define the probability density function (PDF) of a Gaussian random variable:

$$p(z) = \frac{1}{\sqrt{2\pi\sigma^2}} e^{-\frac{(z-\bar{z})^2}{2\sigma^2}} \tag{2}$$

Where, z = Intensity

$\bar{z}$ = Mean value of z

Figure 2. PDF of Gaussian noise

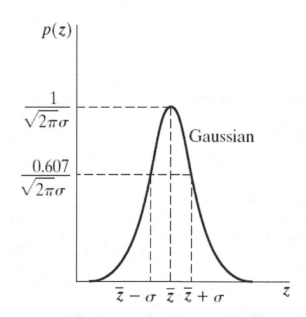

σ = Standard deviation

$σ^2$ =Variance of z

Speckle Noise

This particular kind of noise has a multiplicative effect on its surroundings. It's possible that speckle noise will look the same as Gaussian noise in an image. The gamma distribution can be found in the probability density function of this thing (Madhumathy, P., et al. (2022)).

Impulse Noise

Because the noise causes black dots to appear in bright regions and white dots to appear in dark regions, it is also known as salt and pepper noise. This is because black dots appear in bright regions. The majority of this noise is produced during the process of gearbox or conversion. The typical pixel value for salt noise in a picture with 8 bits is 255, while the value for pepper noise is 0. The following is an example of the PDF for the Impulse noise (Pandey, B. K., et al.(2023)):

$$p(z) = \begin{cases} P_a & for & z = a \\ P_b & for & z = b \\ 0 & otherwise \end{cases} \qquad (3)$$

Figure 3. PDF of impulse noise

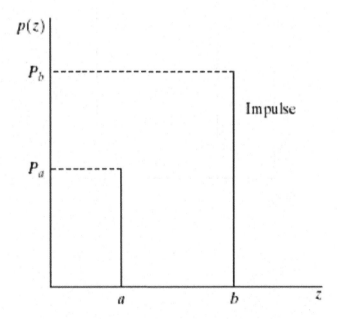

Uniform Noise

Because it is produced by assigning discrete values to the individual pixel values that make up a sensed image, uniform noise is also referred to by the name quantization noise.It has a distribution that is typically uniform. The probability density function, or PDF, of uniform noise or quantization noise is as follows (Bruntha, P. M., et al.(2022)):

$$p(z) = \begin{cases} \dfrac{1}{b-a} & if \quad a \leq z \leq b \\ 0 & otherwise \end{cases} \tag{4}$$

The mean and variance of uniform noise are given as follows:

$$\mu = \frac{a+b}{2} \quad and \quad \sigma^2 = \frac{(b-a)^2}{12}$$

Figure 4. PDF of uniform noise

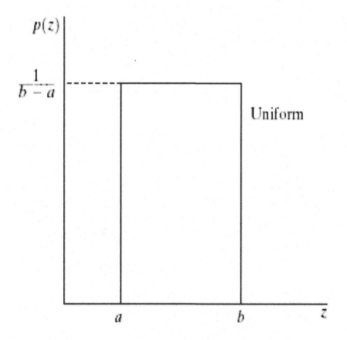

Brownian Noise (Fractal Noise)

There are several types of coloured noise, some of which are Brownian noise, pink noise, flicker noise, and 1/f noise. The power spectral density of Brownian noise is proportional to the square of the frequency over an octave; in other words, the noise's power is distributed as follows: it falls on the 14th component at a rate of 6 dB per octave. Brownian motion results in the generation of brownian noise. Brownian motion is characterised by the unforced motion of particles that are suspended in fluid. Brownian noise can also be created by using white noise as the input. On the other hand, this noise is generated by a stochastic mechanism that is not stationary. This method conforms to the standard (Pandey, D., et al. (2022)) operating procedure. In statistical terms, the phenomenon known as fractal noise refers to fractional Brownian noise. Natural processes create fractal noise.

Periodic Noise

This noise is caused by various forms of electronic interference, most notably in the power signal during image acquisition. This noise, when amplified to multiples of a certain frequency, possesses distinctive qualities, such as being spatially dependent and having a nature that is sinusoidal. It manifests itself as conjugate spots when seen in the frequency domain. This can be easily remedied by employing either a band reject filter or notch filter with a short passband (Pandey, D., et al.(2022)).

White Noise

The basic characteristic of noise is referred to as its power. The level of power in white noise is constant throughout its spectrum. The power of the noise is equivalent to the power of the power spectral density function. It isn't entirely correct to suggest that white noise and Gaussian noise are typically interchangeable. White noise prevents correlation from occurring because each pixel's value is unique in comparison to those of its neighbours. Because of this, there is no auto-correlation in the data (Hasan, A., et al.(2021)). As a consequence of this, white noise tends to alter the pixel values of a picture in a constructive manner.

Effect of Noise on Digital Image

The effect of various kinds of noise such as Gaussian noise, salt and peppernoise, speckle noise, uniform noise etc. on the uncorrupted image is demonstrated in Figure 5.

Image Filtering Techniques

In digital image processing, one of the most important challenges is to restore the original image while removing any noise that may have been introduced. Consequently, a number of different filtering strategies can be implemented in order to improve the overall image quality by removing various kinds of noise. By utilising a number of different filters, we are able to keep the picture's characteristics while simultaneously enhancing the image's overall quality. Filters are one-of-a-kind tools that take an image as their input, transform it through the application of an algorithm, and then return it to the user in a modified form that has less or no effect of noise (Pandey, D., et al.(2021)).

Figure 5. Image affected by various types of noise
i) Original image (without noise) ii) Gaussian noise iii) Salt and pepper or impulse noise iv) Speckle noise

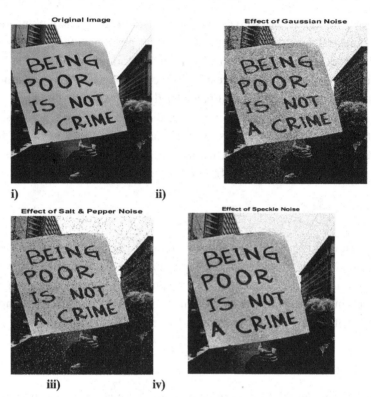

In the world of image processing, removing noise from photographs is an extremely important step. There are a few different approaches of taking noise out of an image. The most important quality of a good image de-noising model is that it should be able to remove all noise from images while also restoring the edges. This is the case for any excellent image de-noising model (Kumar, M. S., et al. (2021)). In the past, linear filters were used to remove noise from photographs; however, linear filters have a poor track record when it comes to addressing non-additive disturbances. In the presence of nonlinearities or a statistical system that is not Gaussian, the performance of linear filters is also not as good as it could be. The linear filters are commonly employed because of the rapid processing action they provide, however they are not great at maintaining edges in the image. On the other hand, non-linear filters are able to preserve the text boundaries, but they are not appropriate for quick processing (Pandey, D. et al. (2020)).

In image processing, removing noise from images is a very crucial step because it is very helpful for image analysis. This makes removing noise from photos a very important component. The process of removing noise from an image can be accomplished in a variety of ways; however, the perfect filter will not only be able to remove all of the noise from a complicated image but will also restore each and every detail that was present in the original image. Image filters can generally be broken down into three categories: the adaptive filter, the order statistics filter, and the averaging filter. Linear and non-linear filtering techniques are the most popular types of filters, and they are both employed extensively in the process of image de-noising. While the output of a non-linear filtering technique is non-linear, the output of a linear filtering technique is linear. Linear filtering techniques produce linear outputs. The

Mean Filter is a specialised kind of linear spatial filter that takes a noisy pixel value and replaces it with the average of the values of its nearby pixels. The following is a discussion of the picture filters that are used in image de-noising procedures the most frequently.

CONCLUSION

Throughout the course of this article, we have discussed the many distinct types of noise that are able to manifest themselves in images as a result of the process of image acquisition or transmission. Deleted some light on the reasons of these noises as well as the principal sources of those noises. Also deleted some light on the causes of these noises. It is possible for noise to appear in photographs at any point during the process of taking the photographs or while they are being transferred. The noise model serves as a good illustration of this phenomenon. As a result of this, the examination of noise models is a component of image processing that is of the utmost significance. On the other hand, one of the most important steps in the process of picture processing is known as image denoising. If we do not have prior knowledge of the noise model, we will be unable to develop and implement any denoising algorithms.

Because of this, we will be discussing and presenting a range of noise models that are available in digital photos during the course of this essay.

We addressed the issue that noise models can be identified with the help of their location of origin in this section. The probability density function is also used in the construction of noise models. The mean, variance, and the majority of grey levels in digital images are used as inputs in these models. We have great hopes that this work will serve as a helpful resource not just for image processing specialists with years of expertise but also for those who are just beginning their careers in the field.

It is vital to have some background knowledge on the many different types of noise that were responsible for the image's degradation in order to select the de-noising procedure that is most suited to meet your needs. Therefore, when determining which method, if any, should be utilised in the process of de-noising the image that contains noise, the behaviour of the noise should be taken into consideration. This study presents the fundamental de-noising techniques in addition to the fundamental noise models. Both sets of information may be found here. This study comes to the conclusion that there are a lot of noise models for complicated photos. On the other hand, there are also a lot of things that may happen in future researches for the aim of reaching the largest accuracy and quality in the image filtering methods. There is a need for additional research to be carried out in order to locate the most effective solution and establish the most desirable outcome in this field.

REFERENCES

Bruntha, P. M., Dhanasekar, S., Hepsiba, D., Sagayam, K. M., Neebha, T. M., Pandey, D., & Pandey, B. K. (2022). Application of switching median filter with L 2 norm-based auto-tuning function for removing random valued impulse noise. *Aerospace Systems*, 1-7.

Hasan, A., Pandey, D., & Khan, A. (2021). Application of EEG Time-Varying Networks in the Evaluation of Dynamic Functional Brain Networks. *Augmented Human Research*, 6(1), 1–8. doi:10.100741133-021-00046-2

Jayapoorani, S., Pandey, D., Sasirekha, N. S., Anand, R., & Pandey, B. K. (2023). Systolic optimized adaptive filter architecture designs for ECG noise cancellation by Vertex-5. *Aerospace Systems*, *6*(1), 163–173. doi:10.100742401-022-00177-3

Kumar, M. S., Sankar, S., Nassa, V. K., Pandey, D., Pandey, B. K., & Enbeyle, W. (2021). Innovation and creativity for data mining using computational statistics. In *Methodologies and Applications of Computational Statistics for Machine Intelligence* (pp. 223–240). IGI Global. doi:10.4018/978-1-7998-7701-1.ch012

Kumar Pandey, B., Pandey, D., Nassa, V. K., Ahmad, T., Singh, C., George, A. S., & Wakchaure, M. A. (2022). Encryption and steganography-based text extraction in IoT using the EWCTS optimizer. *Imaging Science Journal*, 1–19.

Lelisho, M. E., Pandey, D., Alemu, B. D., Pandey, B. K., & Tareke, S. A. (2022). The Negative Impact of Social Media during COVID-19 Pandemic. *Trends in Psychology*, *31*(1), 1–20. doi:10.100743076-022-00192-5

Madhumathy, P., & Pandey, D. (2022). Deep learning based photo acoustic imaging for non-invasive imaging. *Multimedia Tools and Applications*, *81*(5), 7501–7518. doi:10.100711042-022-11903-6

Meslie, Y., Enbeyle, W., Pandey, B. K., Pramanik, S., Pandey, D., Dadeech, P., & Saini, A. (2021). Machine intelligence-based trend analysis of COVID-19 for total daily confirmed cases in Asia and Africa. In *Methodologies and Applications of Computational Statistics for Machine Intelligence* (pp. 164–185). IGI Global. doi:10.4018/978-1-7998-7701-1.ch009

Pandey, B. K., Pandey, D., Gupta, A., Nassa, V. K., Dadheech, P., & George, A. S. (2023). Secret Data Transmission Using Advanced Morphological Component Analysis and Steganography. In *Role of Data-Intensive Distributed Computing Systems in Designing Data Solutions* (pp. 21–44). Springer International Publishing. doi:10.1007/978-3-031-15542-0_2

Pandey, D., George, S., Aremu, B., Wariya, S., & Pandey, B. K. (2021). *Critical Review on Integration of Encryption*. Steganography, IOT and Artificial Intelligence for the Secure Transmission of Stego Images.

Pandey, D., & Pandey, B. K. (2022). An Efficient Deep Neural Network with Adaptive Galactic Swarm Optimization for Complex Image Text Extraction. In *Process Mining Techniques for Pattern Recognition* (pp. 121–137). CRC Press. doi:10.1201/9781003169550-10

Pandey, D., Pandey, B. K., & Wariya, S. (2019). Study of various types noise and text extraction algorithms for degraded complex image. *Journal of Emerging Technologies and Innovative Research*, *6*(6), 234–247.

Pandey, D., Pandey, B. K., & Wariya, S. (2020). An approach to text extraction from complex degraded scene. *IJCBS*, *1*(2), 4–10.

Pandey, D., & Wairya, S. (2023). An optimization of target classification tracking and mathematical modelling for control of autopilot. *Imaging Science Journal*, 1–16.

Pandey, D., Wairya, S., Sharma, M., Gupta, A. K., Kakkar, R., & Pandey, B. K. (2022). An approach for object tracking, categorization, and autopilot guidance for passive homing missiles. *Aerospace Systems*, 1-14.

Chapter 3
Machine Learning Application for Evidence Image Enhancement

Sampangirama Reddy B. R.

School of Sciences, Jain University (Deemed), India

Ashendra Kumar Saxena

Teerthanker Mahaveer University, India

Binay Kumar Pandey

iD https://orcid.org/0000-0002-4041-1213

Department of Information Technology, Govind Ballabh Pant University of Agriculture and Technology, India

Sachin Gupta

Sanskriti University, India

Shashikala Gurpur

Symbiosis Law School, Symbiosis International University (Deemed), Pune, India

Sukhvinder Singh Dari

Symbiosis Law School, Symbiosis International University (Deemed), Pune, India

Dharmesh Dhabliya

Symbiosis Law School, Symbiosis International University (Deemed), Pune, India

ABSTRACT

Taking into account the uses of ML in the field of vision, many practical vision systems' first processing stages include enhancing or reconstructing images. The goal of these tools is to enhance the quality of photos and give accurate data for making decisions based on appearance. In this research study, the authors examine three distinct types of neural networks: convolutional networks, residual networks, and generative countermeasure networks. There is a proposal for a model structure of a scalable supplementary generation network as part of a network that enhances evidence images as a generative countermeasure. The authors present the objective loss function definition, as well as the periodic consistency loss and the periodic perceptual consistency loss analysis. An in-depth solution framework for picture layering is offered once the problem's core aspects are explained. This approach implements multitasking with the help of adaptive feature learning, this provides a strong theoretical guarantee.

DOI: 10.4018/978-1-6684-8618-4.ch003

1. INTRODUCTION

Images have become an integral part of contemporary life due to the wealth of information they hold & the vital role they play in the dissemination of that information. Image-based target categorization and identification are only two examples of the many computer vision-related applications that are continually appearing because of the fast growth of deep learning technology (Babu, S.Z.D., et al, 2022). While smartphone cameras continue to improve in quality, the one employed for this study has obvious drawbacks. The environmental effect is frequently the reason why the camera's acquired photos don't fulfill the standards of this study (Nassa V. K., 2021). It's up to the computer to fix the broken scene back to normal. All too often, photographs in need of restoration suffer from artifacts like noise or insufficient detail (Bhattacharya, S., et al, 2021). Images are the primary way in which a vision system gathers data; nevertheless, low-quality photos gathered without the necessary information input may reduce the efficiency and precision of a computer vision system (Dushyant, K., et al, 2022). Thus, the method of enhancement processing for damaged photos warrants special attention. Models are selected by incorporating them into some different deep-learning models. Compute an average estimate by adding together the findings of all of the predictors. If the individual models are robust, then the combined impact of using widely varied network topologies and technologies will be more reliable. Contrarily, you may perform experiments backward and forward as well. The network model is reset at the start of each training session, and the final weight converges to a new value every time. The algorithm's limited generalization power may be circumvented by repeatedly using this procedure to construct several network models & afterward combining prediction results from these models. (Gupta, A., et al, 2019)

1.1 Machine Learning

A field of AI and computer science focused on modeling human learning with the use of data and algorithms is called ML. (Gupta, N., et al, 2020)

. To learn anything new, one may use one of four primary routes: supervised, unsupervised, semi-supervised, or reinforcement learning. Data scientists' algorithm selection is informed by the nature of the information they're trying to forecast. (Jain, V., 2022) The study of machine learning (ML) focuses on developing and improving systems that can "learn," or use available data to get better results in a given context. It is often included under AI. ML algorithms use example data to build a model from which they may draw conclusions and make decisions without being explicitly trained. (Jin, L., et al, 2021) The term "training data" describes these examples. In areas such as medicine, EF, VR, agriculture, and CV, when it is difficult or impossible to construct classical algorithms to carry out the necessary tasks, ML algorithms are used. (Kaushik, D., 2021) Yet, some types of ML have close ties to computational statistics, which is focused on making predictions with the use of computers. The study of mathematical optimization has given the field of machine learning access to new resources, theoretical frameworks, and application domains. (Kaushik, K., 2021) Data mining is closely connected to the field of computer science, and it focuses on exploratory data analysis using unsupervised learning. Several types of ML use information and NN in ways that are theoretically similar to the way the human brain operates. ML, which uses statistical methods to anticipate outcomes, goes by the name predictive analytics when applied to business issues. (Maglietta, R., 2022)

CNN, which stands for "Convolutional Neural Network," is the most widely used and successful model for classifying pictures. (Mandal, D., 2022) The method is based on deep learning techniques, in which a computer is taught to recognize faces by seeing and mimicking human ones. After the system has been trained on certain characteristics of human faces, it will begin to recognize those traits wherever they appear in a picture. (Monga, V., 2021) The quality of the network model will suffer if the original data set is insufficient for training the model. To enhance a picture is to apply some processing to the source image to increase the size of the data set, which in turn may boost the model's accuracy.

- The scale-invariant feature transform (SIFT) approach for mapping features.
- The RANSAC algorithm, for registering images is based on a random sampling of their data.
- Picture Classification using Neural Networks.
- Convolutional neural networks for image categorization (CNNs)

1.2 Image Enhancement

To improve the quality of a digital picture for viewing or analysis, a procedure known as "image augmentation" is carried out. Noise may be reduced, edges can be sharpened, and shadows can be illuminated to draw attention to what's important in a picture. (Niu, K., 2021) To make a picture better serve a certain purpose, such as making it more aesthetically acceptable to humans, image enhancement is performed. (Oh, J. G., 2022) Most picture enhancement methods are improvised with little thought given to how the original image degraded. Images may be enhanced in many different ways. EE and SF are some of the most often used techniques. After correcting for geometric and radiometric flaws, in the resulting image, any further attempts at improvement are made. (Pandey, B. K., et al, 2022) Histogram equalization is a widely used technique for improving images (HE). The goal of this technique is to improve the quality of photos and to provide a more accurate portrayal of various visual content.

1.3 Role of Machine Learning in Image Enhancement

The rapid adoption of image recognition systems is occurring in many sectors, including security, healthcare, education, fintech, manufacturing, telecom, utilities, and military, all to improve visual data processing and analysis speeds, accuracy, and efficiency. Retinex algorithm's picture-enhancing details are best at a tiny scale, but the situation as a whole is terrible in this setting. (Pathania, V., et al, 2022) In a scenario with a lot of haze, the Retinex algorithm works well. The enhancing impact is weak at larger scales, but the color accuracy of the picture improves. (Shukla A., 2021) CNN excels in deep learning image identification due to its distinctive method of operation. To apply creative filters, tune a picture for optimum quality, or enhance certain image features to improve quality for computer vision tasks, Nowadays, DNN is only one example of an ML Model used in cutting-edge IP techniques. IR is a technique for identifying and classifying things inside an image based on how those objects are often seen by people looking at those same images. (Sreekanth, N., 2022)

1.4 Limitation of Existing Research

Existing imaging hardware has constraints that make it difficult to capture high-quality photos in the natural world (Sungheetha, A., 2021). This is compounded by the fact that different kinds of weather may harm the equipment used to take such images. The study reveals that the camera's rejected light is used as an image source. At night or in low light, however, the amount of light reflected back to the sensor is reduced, resulting in a significant loss of scene information. (Sangeetha, A., 2021) All three of the aforementioned situations share the issue of poor quality collected natural photos as a result of environmental conditions, hence this work is dedicated to the topic of how to increase the quality of these images (Talukdar, V., 2022). If you want to teach a deep neural network anything, you may utilize either training data or test data. (Valikhani, A., 2021) The results of computer vision tasks performed on these images or movies with obvious qualities and aesthetics have been rather promising. (Veeraiah V., 2022) Images and films with a high feature density, high contrast, and high visibility are used in image recognition & other types of computer vision testing. A wide range of application problems, such as image smoothing and denoising, ID, and high dynamic range tone mapping (Verma, A., 2021), fall under the umbrella of the E problems of image enhancement and reconstruction. When the input picture is a poor one, both attempt to improve it visually. Image enhancement, on the other hand, isn't concerned with preserving the picture's "authentic" look; rather, it emphasizes particular details and information that are relevant to the task at hand, while downplaying or eliminating those that aren't, to produce an end result that is highly expressive and characterized by obvious qualities and a wealth of useful data. (Xiao, H., et al, 2021)

2. LITERATURE REVIEW

There have been several researches in the area of machine learning and image processing. The present paper is considering these research works and discusses the methodology applied in conventional research work. Considering this research it would be easy to trace the issues and challenges in the implication of machine learning and image processing in relevant areas.

Anusha, K et al. (2023) focused on DL-based fingerprint image enhancement for forensic investigations. Fingerprint identification has found widespread usage in a variety of business contexts. Suspects' inadvertent perspiration or oily fingerprints are a major source of latent fingerprints. These traces are often obscured and invisible to the human eye. These forensic fingerprint scans are crucial in solving complex crimes. The quality of the latent prints is poor; they are blurry and distorted by background noise. To make a high-quality print from a latent picture, image enhancement is required. In this paper, we offer a fully automated latent fingerprint recognition system that uses a CNN as part of a DL method to address these problems.

A. Sungheetha, et al.(2021) provided work on input processing for human-machine Interaction in 3D Picture Processing Using ML. Human-robot interaction provides some useful services in a wide range of real-world contexts (HRI). To aid in the identification of objects via the use of digital visualization in robotic systems, the notion of convergence of a 3D picture into a plane-based projection was used. The convergence process leads to recognition problems due to the incorrect identification of projections in different planes. Input processing approach depending on projection technique may help lower these recognition error rates. By viewing the input picture projected in all dimensions, the conjoining indices may be determined. To expedite computation and enhance recognition accuracy, an ML approach was applied. To divide the intersection without using joined indices, a labeled analysis was used. Finding the potential dimension projections where the indices don't correlate is a good way to avoid making mistakes. Inputs are labeled and associated with similar inputs for later use, which makes it impossible to match indices and deviations across planes. The suggested model was tested and shown to be accurate on error, complexity, time, and recognition ratio criteria.

A. Valikhani et al.(2021) looked at ML and IP methods, and the roughness of concrete surfaces was evaluated using inexpensive cameras. A new index as a function of aggregate proportional area to surface area was developed to distinguish coarse aggregate from cement paste in the first application process. Computer vision and ML techniques such as data augmentation & transfer learning are used in the second method to classify new images in light of known examples. Both of these implementations were linked to a conventional technique for 3D laser scanning of blasted concrete. Eventually, both approaches were put to the test and validated using an entirely new collection of photos of sandblasted surfaces. The results demonstrate that both approaches were capable of producing estimates of the concrete surface roughness with accuracies greater than 93%.

H. Xiao, et al.(2021) looked at the methods for registering 3D medical images was reviewed, with an emphasis on those that use deep learning. This study aimed to outline the last five years' worth of work on deep learning-based 3D image registration, highlighting both the successes and failures of the field thus far. ROI, picture modality, supervision technique, and registration assessment criteria were used to conduct a statistical analysis of the pooled investigations. Researchers separated the experiments into three groups: those that used deep iterative registration, those that used supervised registration, and those that used unsupervised registration. A comprehensive analysis is performed on the research, with special emphasis on the contributions that each study made. After reviewing each research type and evaluating its benefits, drawbacks, and trends, a summary was provided. In last, they talk about the problems that affect every group and suggest areas for further study.

J. G. Oh, et al.(2022) introduced hybrid DL using loss functions with mixed norms to enhance low-light photos. This study introduces a novel method for enhancing dark photos using a deep-learning network with mixed-norm loss functions. A decomposition net, an illumination-enhancement net, and a chroma net were all used to create this hybrid network. To take advantage of the relationship between red, green, and blue channels throughout the training and restoration processes, RGB is converted to YCbCr. For a less noisy and more accurate feature map, the illuminance was utilized to train the reflectance, which should subsequently be detached from the luminance. The lighting is improved while halo artifacts are reduced with the aid of the decomposition net and its associated illumination enhancement net. The chroma-net may also be used independently to limit variations in hue. Taking into consideration reflectance, illumination, and chroma quality, a mixed-norm loss function is designed and used during training for each network to increase stability and decrease blurring in the reconstructed image. The experimental results demonstrate the superiority of the proposed method over the best existing DL algorithms.

K. Niu, et al.(2021) reviewed two-channel DL-based picture restoration for night vision. The photos acquired after night vision restoration have a high quality and a positive visual impression. Average PSNR and SSIM values for the reconstructed infrared night vision image obtained by the FMRB-based deep learning network were 3.56 dB and 0.091 2 higher than those for the image obtained by the SRCNN reconstruction algorithm, while those for the enhanced low-light-level night vision image obtained by the FMRB based DL network were 3. (MSRCR). The experimental findings demonstrate that the resolution of the reconstructed picture was definitely increased, the brightness of the enhanced image was also greatly improved, and the visual impact of the fusion image created from the aforementioned images was better when utilizing the suggested approach. The night vision pictures are successfully restored by the suggested technique.

L. Jin, et al.(2021) enhanced the SSD-based DL method for picture processing. Most of the items in remote sensing photos were tiny in size, and they were packed in tightly. CNN's convolution layer also lacks sufficient context information, which results in subpar identification performance when applied to remote sensing images. Aiming to improve detection accuracy while keeping real-time detection speed, this study presents an effective object identification approach for ship detection in remote sensing photos based on improved SSD. We start by integrating a feature fusion module into shallow feature layers to enhance the feature extraction capacity of small objects. Then, we implement an attention mechanism by splicing a Squeeze-and-Excitation Network (SE) module into each of the feature layers. The average detection rate for SSDD was found to be 31 frames per second, while the mAP was found to be 94.41%. In terms of detection accuracy, our improved technique surpasses SSD and other representative object identification methods.

L. Yan, et al.(2021) did research on generative adversarial networks with enhanced network performance for improved picture quality. The suggested technique begins by feeding the picture into the generator through the enhancement network, which then produces an identical image in the new space; secondly, the enhancement network is used to further improve the generated image, the generator was trained using a loss function that was minimized to compare the generated image with the original; and third, the discriminator was trained using the generated image as a comparison target. Using two picture datasets (DPED and LOL), they used the suggested method and compared it to both conventional image-enhancing techniques and a DL approach. Our experimental results reveal that our suggested network enhances pictures in a way that was successful in boosting low-light images, as measured by the PNSR and SSIM.

Mhatre, A et al. (2023) reviewed the deep learning in conjunction with image enhancement techniques for automatic license plate reading has been developed. Both frameworks might benefit from our proposed picture-enhancing methods, which they also offer. The system includes components for both the detection & recognition of license plates. During the detecting stage, a picture of the vehicle is captured using a digital camera. The license plate is then extracted from the larger picture using Alexnet & MobileNetV2 framework. After the number plate number area was cropped off, the low-resolution picture was "super res" to make it high quality. The convolutional layer of a CNN was combined with a super-resolution method to bring back the high quality of the original image's pixels. They use a bounding box technique to identify individual characters in a number plate number. During the recognition phase, features were retrieved and tagged via the CNN method.

P. Zhang, et al.(2022) focused on the deep learning-powered technique for improving picture quality. In this research study, they focus on the CNN, RNN, & generative countermeasure network. An expandable supplementary generation network was presented as part of a model framework for enhancing rain fog images using generative countermeasures. In addition to defining the objective loss function, they also provide evaluations of the periodic consistency loss and the periodic perceptual consistency loss. The underlying challenge of layering images was analyzed, and a model for addressing it was presented. Using adaptive feature learning, this method can multitask with high theoretical assurance. Other than improving the performance of computer vision programs, reading this essay will also improve your visual experience. Better definition, more texture details, and less noise may be achieved in low-light images with the use of image-enhancing technologies.

R. Maglietta, et al.(2022) introduced a comprehensive Analysis of ML and IP Techniques for Picture Identification of Cetaceans. Following the guidelines of the Preferred Reporting Items for Systematic Reviews and Meta-Analyses statement, they conducted a systematic evaluation of machine learning and statistical methodologies for cetacean picture identification systems. This article summarizes the growing attention given to the topic and the many different intelligent systems that have been introduced in recent years. There were still some unanswered concerns, however, better-automated techniques for picture-identifying cetaceans should be developed.

R. Zhang, et al.(2021) provided work on ReLLIE uses deep RL to improve low-light images in a way that is unique to each user. The reward is derived from a set of meticulously crafted non-reference loss functions, and the network's weight is kept low so that it can estimate the curves for lighting a low-light image input. As ReLLIE learns a policy as opposed to translating images one-to-one, it can accommodate a wide range of low-light measurements and provide highly tailored improved outputs via repeated policy applications. In addition, a plug-and-play denoiser makes it simple for ReLLIE to improve photos with hybrid corruptions, such as noise, in the real world. Comprehensive trials on a wide range of benchmarks show that ReLLIE outperforms state-of-the-art approaches, proving its value.

S. Bhattacharya, et al.(2021) examined the state of DL and medical IP in light of the recent coronavirus (COVID-19) epidemic. First, they provide a review of the literature on the topic of deep learning for COVID-19 medical IP, focusing on the most recent & significant findings. Secondly, they summarize the DL field and its recent healthcare applications. After that, three case studies from China, Korea, and Canada are shown as examples of how deep learning has been used for COVID-19 medical IP. Lastly, they highlight some problems and difficulties associated with DL implementations for COVID-19 medical IP, which were anticipated to motivate more research into containing the epidemic and averting the catastrophe, ultimately leading to smart, healthy communities.

V. Monga, et al.(2021) looked at the algorithm: DL that can be read like a book in signal and IP. In several practical signal & IP issues, Using DNN, researchers can achieve breakthroughs in performance that were previously impossible. Notwithstanding these breakthroughs, deep networks' black-box nature, i.e. a lack of interpretability and the need for exceedingly huge training sets, offers barriers to their future development and practical implementation.

3. PROPOSED RESEARCH METHODOLOGY

The methodology lays out in great detail the procedures and techniques that are going to be used for the intended work. Bringing attention to the stages that come after is essential to the growth and enhancement of the algorithm. The following explanations apply to each of these terms:

Figure 1. Research methodology

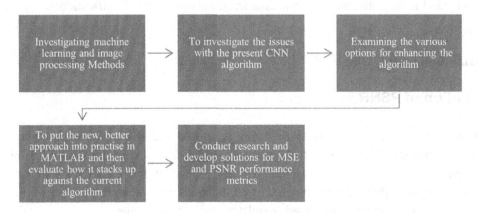

Calculating other performance measures, such as PSNR and MSE, will also be done to evaluate the effectiveness of the proposed approach. To put the suggested method for picture enhancement into action, MATLAB is the programming environment of choice. The software program known as MATLAB is used for numerical calculation and visualization. A matrix is the most straightforward structure for storing information. In MATLAB, an image is handled the same way as a matrix. MATLAB is a piece of software that comes as a bundle that has a development environment as well as a programming language that is both simple enough for beginners to understand. Moreover, it has powerful graphical capabilities and can manage matrices as well as matrix operations. The following are the methods that may be taken to improve picture resolution:

Figure 2. Steps for improving image enhancement

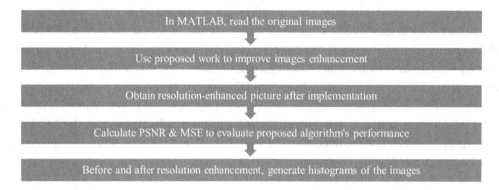

4. PROPOSED WORK

Images have been taken into consideration throughout this study project to achieve picture improvement. In the work that has been suggested, the picture is scaled down during the preprocessing step, and then twenty distinct thresholds are applied across the image while it is being enhanced. After that, the PSNR and MSE of these pictures are both computed. These determined PSNR and MSE values are then sent to the ACO optimizer to get the best possible PSNR and MSE values. After getting noise eliminated image training and testing are made in a machine learning system for classification.

5. RESULT AND DISCUSSION

5.1 Simulation of PSNR

At the preprocessing stage of the work that is being suggested, the image will be blown up. Following that, 10 different thresholds are applied to the picture as it is being changed into an image enhancement. PSNR of these photographs is then calculated after that. After that, the predicted PSNR values are sent to the ACO optimizer so that they may be used to get the highest possible PSNR. One of the options for enhancing images that might be considered correlates to the PSNR value.

Figure 3. Proposed work

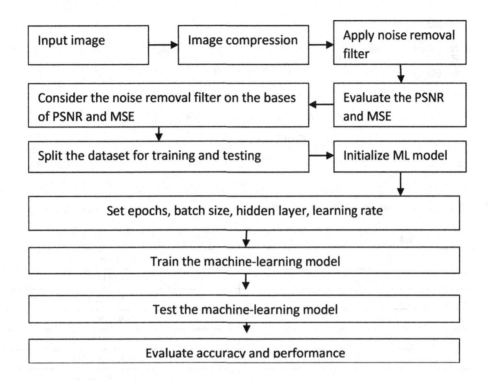

Table 1. PSNR for images at different thresholds

Configuration	PSNR
1	63.82544269
2	70.08694679
3	64.94577528
4	63.95329544
5	63.5491357
6	60.29370496
7	61.89764548
8	64.08110071
9	70.04746522
10	64.14161697

5.2 Simulation of MSE

During the preliminary processing of the planned work, the image is magnified. The picture is then processed via 10 separate thresholds as part of its transformation into an Image Enhancement. MSE of these images is calculated afterward. The ACO optimizer receives these predicted MSE values and uses

Figure 4. PSNR for images

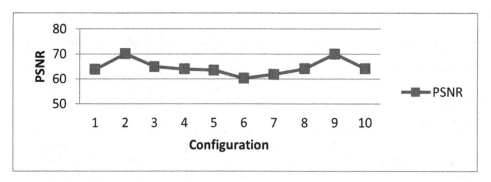

Table 2. PSNR for images at different thresholds

Configuration	MSE
1	94.63917567
2	94.23579181
3	94.8694836
4	94.4603176
5	94.73433432
6	94.66363911
7	94.18064359
8	94.52952803
9	94.78582931
10	94.81964325

Figure 5. 13 MSE for images

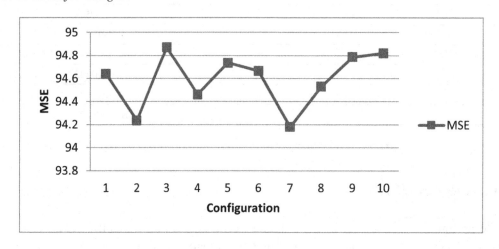

them to try to get the lowest possible MSE. Image Enhancement has an option that may be considered that is similar to MSE.

5.3 Simulation of Accuracy After Machine Learning

During machine learning, 10 epochs are considered. The accuracy gets increase at each epoch. Table 3 is presenting an increment in accuracy at each epoch.

Table 3. Simulation of accuracy after machine learning

Epochs	Accuracy
1	88.68%
2	89.04%
3	90.40%
4	91.42%
5	92.33%
6	93.83%
7	94.55%
8	95.87%
9	96.54%
10	97.96%

Figure 6. Simulation of accuracy after machine learning

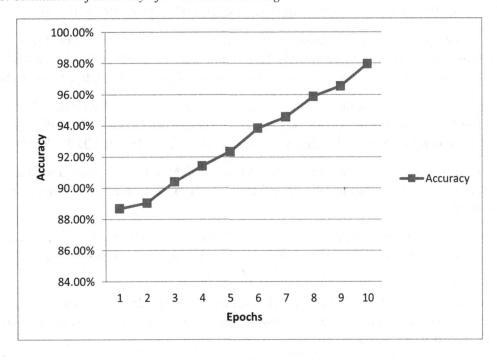

6. CONCLUSION AND FUTURE SCOPE

Image-enhancing techniques have found their way into more and more practical uses as image-processing technology and intelligent robots have advanced. It is accelerated progress in image-enhancement study thanks to machine learning's quick rise. Using an objective function, machine learning continually adds more complicated features to a system to increase its learning ability, all to improve the quality of the provided picture. Adjusting contrast so that picture information may be viewed clearly is key to improving images captured in dim light. The machine's recognition accuracy may be improved by expanding the feature information. This method improves the network's performance by using a hybrid attention mechanism that combines spatial attention & channel attention to extract features, producing high-contrast, noise-free color images. There are still some issues to be further investigated in this work, but overall, the results of the experimental study create a closed loop that achieves a virtuous cycle, which will facilitate later picture improvement. For instance, while creating, transmitting, storing, recording, and displaying photographs, it's sometimes important to fix any damage or distortion that occurs along the way. When restoring a picture, it's important to figure out how it degraded in the first place so that you may apply the opposite technique to it. They need to be rounded out in further studies.

REFERENCES

Anusha, K., & Siva Kumar, P. V. (2023, January). Fingerprint Image Enhancement for Crime Detection Using Deep Learning. In *Proceedings of the International Conference on Cognitive and Intelligent Computing: ICCIC 2021,* (pp. 257-268). Springer Nature Singapore. 10.1007/978-981-19-2358-6_25

Babu, S. Z. D. (2022). The analysation of Big Data in Smart Healthcare. In M. Gupta, S. Ghatak, A. Gupta, & A. L. Mukherjee (Eds.), *Artificial Intelligence on Medical Data. Lecture Notes in Computational Vision and Biomechanics* (Vol. 37). Springer. doi:10.1007/978-981-19-0151-5_21

Bansal, R., Gupta, A., Singh, R., & Nassa, V. K. (2021).Role and Impact of Digital Technologies in E-Learning amidst COVID-19 Pandemic. *2021 Fourth International Conference on Computational Intelligence and Communication Technologies (CCICT),* pp. 194-202.10.1109/CCICT53244.2021.00046

Bhattacharya, S., Reddy Maddikunta, P. K., Pham, Q. V., Gadekallu, T. R., & Krishnan, S. (2020, November). Deep learning and medical image processing for coronavirus (COVID-19) pandemic: A survey. *Sustainable Cities and Society*, *65*, 102589. doi:10.1016/j.scs.2020.102589 PMID:33169099

Gupta, A. (2019). Script classification at the word level for a Multilingual Document. *International Journal of Advanced Science and Technology*, *28*(20), 1247–1252. http://sersc.org/journals/index.php/IJAST/article/view/3835

Gupta, N., Khosravy, M., Patel, N., Dey, N., Gupta, S., Darbari, H., & Crespo, R. G. (2020). Economic data analytic AI technique on IoT edge devices for health monitoring of agriculture machines. *Applied Intelligence*, *50*(11), 3990–4016. doi:10.100710489-020-01744-x

Hai, J., Xuan, Z., Yang, R., Hao, Y., Zou, F., Lin, F., & Han, S. (2023). R2rnet: Low-light image enhancement via real-low to real-normal network. *Journal of Visual Communication and Image Representation*, *90*, 103712. doi:10.1016/j.jvcir.2022.103712

Jain, V., Beram, S. M., Talukdar, V., Patil, T., Dhabliya, D., & Gupta, A. (2022). Accuracy Enhancement in Machine Learning During Blockchain-Based Transaction Classification. *Seventh International Conference on Parallel, Distributed and Grid Computing (PDGC)*. IEEE. 10.1109/PDGC56933.2022.10053213

Jin, L., & Liu, G., (2021). An approach to image processing of deep learning based on improved SSD.

Kaushik, K., Garg, M., Gupta, A., & Pramanik, S. (2021). Application of Machine Learning and Deep Learning in Cyber security: An Innovative Approach. in M. Ghonge, S. Pramanik, R. Mangrulkar and D. N. Le, (eds.) Cybersecurity and Digital Forensics: Challenges and Future Trends. Wiley.

Kumar, M. S., Sankar, S., Nassa, V. K., Pandey, D., Pandey, B. K., & Enbeyle, W. (2021). Innovation and creativity for data mining using computational statistics. In *Methodologies and Applications of Computational Statistics for Machine Intelligence* (pp. 223–240). IGI Global. doi:10.4018/978-1-7998-7701-1.ch012

Kumar Pandey, B., Pandey, D., Nassa, V. K., Ahmad, T., Singh, C., George, A. S., & Wakchaure, M. A. (2022). Encryption and steganography-based text extraction in IoT using the EWCTS optimizer. *Imaging Science Journal*, 1–19.

Lelisho, M. E., Pandey, D., Alemu, B. D., Pandey, B. K., & Tareke, S. A. (2022). The Negative Impact of Social Media during COVID-19 Pandemic. *Trends in Psychology*, *31*(1), 1–20. doi:10.100743076-022-00192-5

Liu, X., Ma, W., Ma, X., & Wang, J. (2023). LAE-Net: A locally-adaptive embedding network for low-light image enhancement. *Pattern Recognition*, *133*, 109039. doi:10.1016/j.patcog.2022.109039

Maglietta, R., Carlucci, R., Fanizza, C., & Dimauro, G. (2022). Machine Learning and Image Processing Methods for Cetacean Photo Identification: A Systematic Review. *IEEE Access : Practical Innovations, Open Solutions*, *10*(July), 80195–80207. doi:10.1109/ACCESS.2022.3195218

Mhatre, A., & Sharma, P. (2023). Deep Learning Approach for Vehicle Number Plate Recognition System with Image Enhancement Technique. *International Journal of Intelligent Systems and Applications in Engineering*, *11*(1s), 251–262.

Monga, V., Li, Y., & Eldar, Y. C. (2021). Algorithm Unrolling. *IEEE Signal Processing Magazine*, *38*(March), 18–44. doi:10.1109/MSP.2020.3016905

Niu, K., Chen, Y., & Shen, J. (2021). Dual-channel night vision image restoration method based on deep learning. Computer Applications, vol. 41, no. 6, p. 10, doi:10.339022186904

Oh, J. G., & Hong, M. C. (2022). Low-Light Image Enhancement Using Hybrid Deep-Learning and Mixed-Norm Loss Functions. Sensors (Basel), 22(18), 6904. doi:10.3390/s22186904

Pandey, B. K. (2022). Effective and Secure Transmission of Health Information Using Advanced Morphological Component Analysis and Image Hiding. In M. Gupta, S. Ghatak, A. Gupta, & A. L. Mukherjee (Eds.), *Artificial Intelligence on Medical Data. Lecture Notes in Computational Vision and Biomechanics* (Vol. 37). Springer. doi:10.1007/978-981-19-0151-5_19

Pathania, V. (2022). A Database Application for Monitoring COVID-19 in India. In M. Gupta, S. Ghatak, A. Gupta, & A. L. Mukherjee (Eds.), *Artificial Intelligence on Medical Data. Lecture Notes in Computational Vision and Biomechanics* (Vol. 37). Springer. doi:10.1007/978-981-19-0151-5_23

Sungheetha, A. (2021). 3D Image Processing using Machine Learning based Input Processing for Man-Machine Interaction. *Journal of Innovative Image Processing*, *3*(1), 1–6. doi:10.36548/jiip.2021.1.001

Talukdar, V., Dhabliya, D., Kumar, B., Talukdar, S. B., Ahamad, S., & Gupta, A. (2022) Suspicious Activity Detection and Classification in IoT Environment Using Machine Learning Approach. *Seventh International Conference on Parallel, Distributed and Grid Computing (PDGC)*, Solan, Himachal Pradesh, India. 10.1109/PDGC56933.2022.10053312

Valikhani, A., Jaberi Jahromi, A., Pouyanfar, S., Mantawy, I. M., & Azizinamini, A. (2021). Machine learning and image processing approaches for estimating concrete surface roughness using basic cameras. *Computer-Aided Civil and Infrastructure Engineering*, *36*(2), 213–226. doi:10.1111/mice.12605

Veeraiah, V., Ahamad, G. P. S., Talukdar, S. B., Gupta, A., & Talukdar, V. (2022) Enhancement of Meta Verse Capabilities by IoT Integration. *2022 2nd International Conference on Advance Computing and Innovative Technologies in Engineering (ICACITE)*, (pp. 1493-1498). 10.1109/ICACITE53722.2022.9823766

Xiao, H., Xinzhi, T., Liu, C., Li, T., Ren, G., Yang, R., Shen, D., & Cai, J. (2021). A review of deep learning-based three-dimensional medical image registration methods. *Quantitative Imaging in Medicine and Surgery*, *11*(12), 11. doi:10.21037/qims-21-175 PMID:34888197

Yan, L., Fu, J., Wang, C., Ye, Z., Chen, H., & Ling, H. (2021). Enhanced network optimized generative adversarial network for image enhancement. *Multimedia Tools and Applications*, *80*(9), 14363–14381. doi:10.100711042-020-10310-z

Zhang, P. (2022). Image Enhancement Method Based on Deep Learning. *Mathematical Problems in Engineering*, *2022*, 1–9. Advance online publication. doi:10.1155/2022/6797367 PMID:35781947

Zhang, R., Guo, L., Huang, S., & Wen, B. (2021)ReLLIE: Deep reinforcement learning for customized low-light image enhancement. In *Proceedings of the 29th ACM international conference on multimedia*, (pp. 2429-2437). IEEE. 10.1145/3474085.3475410

Chapter 4
A Comprehensive Review on Algorithms of Image Processing for Autonomous and Electric Vehicles

Ismayel Gollapudi

Malla Reddy Engineering College and Management Sciences, India

Kallol Bhaumik

 https://orcid.org/0000-0003-2469-1937

Malla Reddy Engineering College and Management Sciences, India

Digvijay Pandey

 https://orcid.org/0000-0003-0353-174X

Department of Technical Education(U.P), A.P.J. Abdul Kalam University, India

Juttu Suresh

Malla Reddy Engineering College and Management Sciences, India

K. V. Ganesh

Malla Reddy Engineering College and Management Sciences, India

Uday Kumar Kanike

 https://orcid.org/0000-0002-8792-5721

Georgia State University, USA

ABSTRACT

The development of autonomous electric vehicles has gained significant attention due to their potential to reduce carbon emissions and improve road safety. Image processing has become an important tool in the development of these vehicles, enabling them to detect and respond to objects and obstacles in their environment. In this review paper, we explore the use of image processing in electric vehicles and driverless cars, with a focus on the various techniques proposed by authors. The comparison of the performance and effectiveness of different approaches, including deep learning, computer vision, and sensor fusion, in detecting and recognizing objects in the environment. Our review highlights the advantages and limitations of each technique and their potential for future development in the field of electric vehicles. Overall, image processing has shown to be a promising solution for the development of safe and efficient autonomous electric vehicles.

DOI: 10.4018/978-1-6684-8618-4.ch004

1. INTRODUCTION

Image processing is critical for autonomous driving in both electric vehicles and driverless automobiles. Image processing algorithms can extract meaningful information about the vehicle's environment and make educated judgements about its motions and interactions with other objects by utilizing various sensors such as cameras, LiDAR, and radar. [1] Object detection algorithms can identify and track various objects such as other vehicles, pedestrians, and obstacles, allowing the vehicle to make appropriate decisions about its speed and direction of travel. Lane detection algorithms can detect and track road markings, helping the vehicle to stay within its lane and maintain safe distances from other vehicles. [2] Figure 1 shows vehicle controlled by image processing

Figure 1. Vehicle controlled by image processing

Traffic sign recognition algorithms can identify and interpret road signs, enabling the vehicle to understand speed limits, stop signs, and other traffic signals. These algorithms can also help the vehicle to adjust its speed and trajectory accordingly. [3]

Real-time processing algorithms are particularly important for autonomous driving, as they must operate quickly and efficiently in order to make decisions in real-time. This requires sophisticated algorithms and powerful computing hardware, but the results can be significant, enabling safer and more efficient driving in a range of conditions. Figure 2 shows real-time processing using input image. [4-5]

Overall, image processing is a critical component of autonomous driving systems in both electric vehicles and driverless cars, and it will continue to play an important role as these technologies evolve and become more widespread. By improving the accuracy and reliability of object detection, lane detection, and other key functions, image processing algorithms will help to bring us closer to a future of safer, more efficient, and more convenient transportation.

Figure 2. Real time control using image processing algorithms

The use of multiple sensors such as cameras, LiDAR, and radar can provide a comprehensive and accurate view of the vehicle's surroundings, enabling it to make informed decisions about its movements and interactions with the environment. [6] Each sensor type has its own strengths and weaknesses, and combining them can provide a more robust and reliable system for electric vehicles.

Cameras are useful for providing high-resolution images of the environment, allowing for detailed object detection, recognition, and tracking. They are also relatively inexpensive and widely available, making them a popular choice for many autonomous vehicle applications. However, cameras can be limited by poor visibility in adverse weather conditions, and they can struggle to detect certain types of objects such as low-contrast or reflective surfaces.

LiDAR, on the other hand, uses laser beams to create a 3D map of the environment, providing accurate distance and depth measurements. [7-8] This makes it ideal for detecting and tracking objects in complex and dynamic environments, such as urban areas or construction sites. However, LiDAR sensors can be expensive and are often larger and more cumbersome than cameras or radar sensors.

Radar sensors use radio waves to detect objects in the environment, making them useful for detecting objects at longer distances or in adverse weather conditions. They are also relatively low-cost and can be easily integrated into existing vehicle systems. However, radar sensors can struggle to detect certain types of objects such as small or low-reflectivity objects.

By combining these sensors, electric vehicles can benefit from the strengths of each technology while minimizing their weaknesses. For example, cameras can be used to provide detailed object detection and recognition, while LiDAR and radar sensors can be used for distance measurements and object tracking. [9] This can provide a more robust and reliable system for autonomous driving, improving safety and efficiency on the road.

2. IMAGE PROCESSING BASED ALGORITHMS FOR ELECTRIC VEHICLE CONTROL

2.1 Object Detection

Object detection is one of the most commonly used approaches in image processing for electrical vehicles. Object detection is a crucial task in autonomous driving. It involves identifying objects on the road such as vehicles, pedestrians, and traffic signs. There are various deep learning-based object detection algorithms such as YOLO (You Only Look Once) and Faster R-CNN (Region-based Convolutional Neural Networks) that have been used for object detection in electric vehicles and driverless cars. Figure 3 shows algorithm steps for object detection.

Figure 3. Steps for object detection

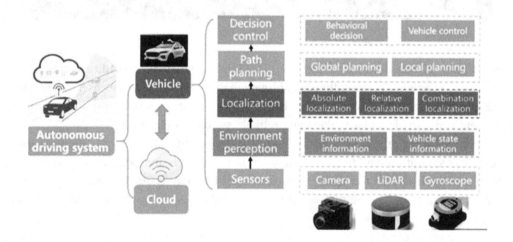

YOLO is a real-time object detection algorithm that can detect objects in an image in a single pass. YOLO divides the input image into a grid and predicts bounding boxes and class probabilities for each grid cell. This makes YOLO very fast and efficient. YOLO has been used for pedestrian detection in electric vehicles and driverless cars. [10]

Faster R-CNN is a two-stage object detection algorithm that first proposes regions of interest (RoIs) and then classifies them into different object categories. Faster R-CNN is slower than YOLO but is more accurate. Faster R-CNN has been used for object detection in electric vehicles and driverless cars. [11]

2.2 Lane Detection

Lane detection is another important task in autonomous driving. It involves detecting lane markings on the road and determining the vehicle's position within the lane. There are various image processing-based algorithms that have been used for lane detection in electric vehicles and driverless cars such as Hough transform, Canny edge detection, and Sobel edge detection. Figure 4 shows algorithm steps for lane detection.

Figure 4. Algorithm steps for lane detection

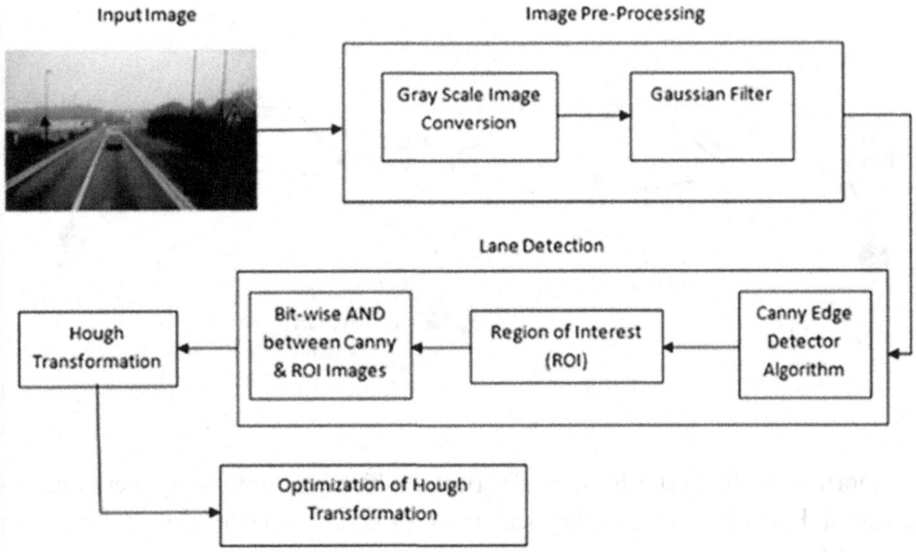

Hough transform is a popular algorithm used for detecting lines in an image. It works by converting the image space into a parameter space and detecting lines as peaks in the parameter space. Hough transform has been used for lane detection in electric vehicles and driverless cars.[12]

Canny edge detection is another popular algorithm used for detecting edges in an image. Canny edge detection works by convolving the image with a Gaussian filter to reduce noise and then detecting edges using a gradient-based algorithm. Canny edge detection has been used for lane detection in electric vehicles and driverless cars. [13]

Sobel edge detection is a simple edge detection algorithm that works by computing the gradient magnitude of the image. Sobel edge detection has been used for lane detection in electric vehicles and driverless cars [14]

2.3 Traffic Sign Recognition

Traffic sign recognition involves detecting and recognizing traffic signs in real-time to assist the vehicle in obeying traffic laws. Some of the commonly used techniques for traffic sign recognition include deep learning-based approaches such as convolutional neural networks (CNNs) and recurrent neural networks (RNNs). [15-17] Figure 5. Algorithm for traffic sign recognition

2.4 Pedestrian Detection

Pedestrian detection is another critical task in autonomous driving, as it involves detecting pedestrians on the road and avoiding collisions with them. There are various deep learning-based pedestrian detection algorithms that have been used for pedestrian detection in electric vehicles and driverless cars. [18]

Figure 5. Algorithm for traffic sign recognition

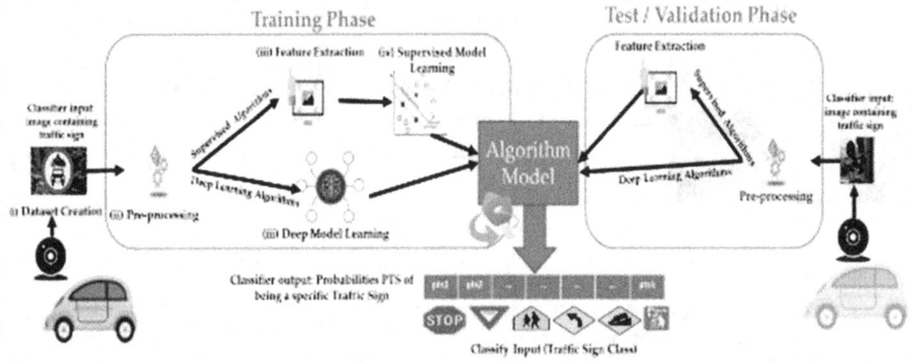

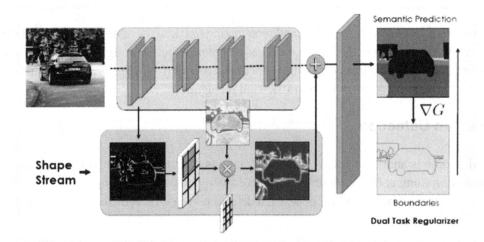

One such algorithm is the Faster R-CNN algorithm, which was previously mentioned as an object detection algorithm. Faster R-CNN has also been used for pedestrian detection in electric vehicles and driverless cars. [19]

Another popular pedestrian detection algorithm is the Single Shot MultiBox Detector (SSD) algorithm. SSD is a real-time object detection algorithm that can detect objects in an image in a single pass. SSD has been used for pedestrian detection in electric vehicles and driverless cars. [20]

2.5 Semantic Segmentation

Semantic segmentation is the task of assigning a semantic label to every pixel in an image. Semantic segmentation is used to identify and classify every pixel in an image, which helps the autonomous vehicle to understand the scene in more detail. There are various deep learning-based semantic segmentation algorithms such as Fully Convolutional Networks (FCN), U-Net, and SegNet that have been used for

Figure 6. Semantic segmentation using image processing

semantic segmentation in electric vehicles and driverless cars. Figure 6 shows semantic segmentation using image processing.

FCN is a popular semantic segmentation algorithm that works by using a fully convolutional neural network to generate pixel-wise predictions. FCN has been used for semantic segmentation in electric vehicles and driverless cars. [21]

2.5 Real-Time Processing

Real-time processing is essential in image processing for electrical vehicles, as it enables the vehicle to make fast and accurate decisions based on the information obtained from the camera sensors. [22] Techniques used for real-time processing include parallel processing, multi-threading, and optimized algorithms. Table 1 shows the comparison of various approaches.

Table 1. Performance comparison of various approaches used for electric vehicle and driverless cars

Approach	Techniques	Accuracy	Computational Cost	Performance
Object detection	Faster R-CNN, YOLO, SSD	Faster R-CNN: high, YOLO: medium, SSD: low	Faster R-CNN: high, YOLO: medium, SSD: low	Faster R-CNN: slower, YOLO: faster, SSD: fastest
Lane detection	Hough transform, Canny edge detection, Sobel edge detection	Hough transform: high, Sobel: medium, Canny: low	Hough transform: high, Sobel: medium, Canny: low	Hough transform: slower, Sobel: moderate, Canny: faster
Traffic sign recognition	CNN-based approaches such as CNNs and RNNs	CNNs: high, RNNs: medium	CNNs: high, RNNs: medium	CNNs: slower, RNNs: faster
Pedestrian detection	Haar cascades, HOG descriptors, CNN-based approaches	Haar cascades: low, HOG: medium, CNNs: high	Haar cascades: low, HOG: high, CNNs: highest	Haar cascades: faster, HOG: slower, CNNs: slowest
Real-time processing	Parallel processing, multi-threading, optimized algorithms	Dependent on the specific implementation	Dependent on the specific implementation	Dependent on the specific implementation

3. LITERATURE REVIEW

3.1 Various Approaches Under Object Detection

3.1.1 YOLO (You Only Look Once) Algorithm

The YOLO algorithm is a popular real-time object detection algorithm that can detect objects in an image in a single pass. [23] YOLO divides the input image into a grid and predicts bounding boxes and class probabilities for each grid cell. The YOLO algorithm has been used for pedestrian detection in electric vehicles and driverless cars.[24]

3.1.2 Faster R-CNN (Region-Based Convolutional Neural Networks) Algorithm

The Faster R-CNN algorithm is a two-stage object detection algorithm that first proposes regions of interest (RoIs) and then classifies them into different object categories. The Faster R-CNN algorithm is slower than YOLO but is more accurate. The Faster R-CNN algorithm has been used for object detection in electric vehicles and driverless cars. [25-26]

3.1.3 RetinaNet

The RetinaNet algorithm is another popular object detection algorithm that is based on the Feature Pyramid Network (FPN) architecture. RetinaNet addresses the issue of class imbalance in object detection by introducing a novel focal loss function. RetinaNet has been used for object detection in electric vehicles and driverless cars. [27-28]

3.1.4 SSD (Single Shot MultiBox Detector) Algorithm

The SSD algorithm is a real-time object detection algorithm that can detect objects in an image in a single pass. SSD uses a single neural network to predict bounding boxes and class probabilities for each object. The SSD algorithm has been used for object detection in electric vehicles and driverless cars. [29-30]

3.1.5 Mask R-CNN Algorithm

The Mask R-CNN algorithm is an extension of the Faster R-CNN algorithm that adds a mask prediction branch to the network, which can be used for instance segmentation. The Mask R-CNN algorithm has been used for object detection and instance segmentation in electric vehicles and driverless cars. [31-33] Table 2 shows comparison.

Table 2. Comparison of various algorithms for object detection

Algorithm	Frames Per Second (FPS)	Mean Average Precision (mAP)
YOLOv3	62	57.9
Faster R-CNN	5	73.2
RetinaNet	17	39.1
SSD	46	74.3
Mask R-CNN	5	62.3

3.2 Various Approaches Under Lane Detection

3.2.1 Hough Transform Algorithm

The Hough Transform algorithm is a classic lane detection algorithm that works by detecting lines in an image. In the case of lane detection, Hough Transform can detect the edges of the lane markings and then apply a line fitting algorithm to obtain the lane lines. The Hough Transform algorithm has been used for lane detection in electric vehicles. [34-35]

3.2.2 Canny Edge Detection Algorithm

The Canny Edge Detection algorithm is a classic edge detection algorithm that can be used for lane detection in electric vehicles. Canny Edge Detection detects edges in an image by identifying areas with a high rate of change in pixel intensity. Once the edges are detected, they can be further processed to extract the lane markings. [36]

3.2.3 Sobel Edge Detection Algorithm

The Sobel Edge Detection algorithm is another classic edge detection algorithm that can be used for lane detection in electric vehicles. Sobel Edge Detection works by detecting edges in an image by analyzing the intensity gradients of the pixels in the image. [37-38]

3.2.4 Hough-Lines P Algorithm

The Hough-Lines P algorithm is an extension of the Hough Transform algorithm that can detect lines in an image more accurately. The Hough-Lines P algorithm is capable of detecting lines with gaps and can also detect curved lines. The Hough-Lines P algorithm has been used for lane detection in electric vehicles. [39-40]

3.2.5 Deep Learning Based Algorithm

Deep Learning-based algorithms have gained popularity in recent years for lane detection in electric vehicles. These algorithms use Convolutional Neural Networks (CNNs) to extract features from the input image and then use these features to detect the lane markings. Deep Learning-based algorithms can achieve high accuracy and are capable of detecting complex lane markings. [41-43] Table 3 shows performance comparison of various lane detection algorithms.

Table 3. Performance comparison of lane detection algorithms

Algorithm	FPS	Accuracy
Hough Transform	20	Moderate
Canny Edge Detect	45	Moderate
Sobel Edge Detect	50	Moderate
Hough-Lines P Detect	20	High
Deep Learning Based Detect	30	Very High

3.3 Approaches Under Pedestrian Detection

3.3.1 Haar Cascade Classifier

The Haar Cascade Classifier algorithm is a classic object detection algorithm that works by training a classifier on positive and negative samples of an object. In the case of pedestrian detection, Haar Cascade Classifier can detect the edges and shapes of pedestrians and then apply a machine learning algorithm to classify the detected objects as pedestrians. The Haar Cascade Classifier algorithm has been used for pedestrian detection in electric vehicles. [44]

3.3.2 Histogram of Oriented Gradients (HOG) with Support Vector Machine (SVM)

The HOG with SVM algorithm is another classic object detection algorithm that works by extracting features from the image using the Histogram of Oriented Gradients (HOG) technique. The extracted features are then fed into a Support Vector Machine (SVM) classifier to classify the detected objects. The IIOG with SVM algorithm has been used for pedestrian detection in electric vehicles. [45]

3.3.3 Deep Learning Based Algorithm

Deep Learning-based algorithms have gained popularity in recent years for pedestrian detection in electric vehicles. These algorithms use Convolutional Neural Networks (CNNs) to extract features from the input image and then use these features to detect pedestrians. Deep Learning-based algorithms can achieve high accuracy and are capable of detecting complex pedestrian features.[46] Table 4 shows performance comparison of various pedestrian detection algorithms.

Table 4. Performance comparison of various pedestrian detection algorithms

Algorithm	FPS	Accuracy
Haar Cascade Classifier	10	Moderate
HOG with SVM Pedestrian Detect	20	High
Deep Learning Based Pedestrian Detect	30	Very High

3.4 Approaches Under Traffic Light Recognition

3.4.1 Template Matching

Template Matching is a basic method used for traffic sign recognition that involves matching an image of a traffic sign with a pre-defined template image of the traffic sign. This approach is simple to implement but can be less accurate and sensitive to changes in lighting conditions and orientation. [47]

3.4.2 Neural Network-Based Algorithms

Neural Network-based algorithms are increasingly popular for traffic sign recognition in electric vehicles. These algorithms use Convolutional Neural Networks (CNNs) to extract features from traffic sign images and classify them based on a set of predefined traffic signs. Neural Network-based algorithms can achieve high accuracy and can be trained to recognize a wide range of traffic signs. [48]

3.4.3 Cascade Classifier

Cascade Classifier is a classic object detection algorithm used for traffic sign recognition in electric vehicles. This algorithm works by training a classifier on positive and negative samples of a traffic sign. The classifier can then detect the edges and shapes of the traffic sign and classify it based on a set of predefined traffic signs.[49] Table 5 shows comparison of various traffic light recognition algorithms

Table 5. Comparison of various traffic light recognition algorithms

Algorithm	FPS	Accuracy
Template Matching	60+	Low
CNN-based Traffic Sign Recognition	15-30	High
Cascade Classifier	30+	Moderate

3.5 Various Approaches Under Real Time Detection

3.5.1 Haar Cascade Classifier

Haar Cascade Classifier is a popular object detection algorithm used for real-time processing in electric vehicles. This algorithm works by scanning an image at different scales and detecting objects based on predefined features. Haar Cascade Classifier is fast and can detect objects in real-time, but it may not be as accurate as more complex algorithms. [50]

3.5.2 YOLO (You Only Look Once)

YOLO is a deep learning-based object detection algorithm used for real-time processing in electric vehicles. This algorithm works by dividing an image into a grid and predicting bounding boxes and class probabilities for each grid cell. YOLO is very fast and accurate and can detect multiple objects in a single pass, making it suitable for real-time applications. [51-52]

3.5.3 SSD (Single Shot Detector)

SSD is another deep learning-based object detection algorithm used for real-time processing in electric vehicles. This algorithm works by predicting bounding boxes and class probabilities for each feature map in a single pass. SSD is very fast and accurate and can detect multiple objects in a single pass,

Table 6. Performance comparison of real time detection algorithms

Algorithm	FPS	Accuracy
Haar Cascade Classifier	30+	Moderate
YOLO	45+	High
SSD	40+	High

Table 7. Performance metrics for various image processing based algorithms used for electric vehicle and driverless cars

Algorithm	Performance	Accuracy	Cost	Advantages	Disadvantages	Applications
Haar Cascade Classifier	Fast	Moderate	Low	- Easy to implement	- Low accuracy compared to more complex algorithms	Object detection
YOLO (You Only Look Once)	Very fast	High	High	- Can detect multiple objects in a single pass - High accuracy - Works well in real-time	- High cost due to the use of deep learning algorithms	Object detection, lane detection, pedestrian detection, traffic sign recognition, and other image recognition tasks
SSD (Single Shot Detector)	Fast	High	High	- Can detect multiple objects in a single pass - High accuracy - Works well in real-time	- High cost due to the use of deep learning algorithms	Object detection, lane detection, pedestrian detection, traffic sign recognition, and other image recognition tasks
Faster R-CNN	Moderate to fast	High	High	- High accuracy	- Slower than some other algorithms	Object detection
Mask R-CNN	Moderate to slow	High	Very high	- Can detect and segment objects - High accuracy	- High cost due to the use of deep learning algorithms - Slow compared to some other algorithms	Object detection, lane detection, pedestrian detection, traffic sign recognition, and other image recognition tasks
Hough Transform	Slow	High	Low to moderate	- High accuracy	- Slow compared to some other algorithms	Lane detection
Semantic Segmentation	Moderate to slow	High	Very high	- Can segment an image into regions that correspond to different classes of objects - High accuracy	- High cost due to the use of deep learning algorithms - Slow compared to some other algorithms	Lane detection, pedestrian detection, and other image recognition tasks
Deep Learning-Based	Moderate to very fast	High	High to very high	- High accuracy - Can detect complex features of the environment	- High cost due to the use of deep learning algorithms - Requires a lot of computing power and data for training	Object detection, lane detection, pedestrian detection, traffic sign recognition, and other image recognition tasks

making it suitable for real-time applications. [53] Table 6 shows performance comparison of real time detection algorithms.

Table 7 shows performance metrics of various image processing based algorithms used for electric vehicle and driverless cars, advantages, disadvantages and applications.

Deep learning-based algorithms like YOLO, SSD, and Mask R-CNN have the highest accuracy, but are also the most expensive. Haar Cascade Classifier and Hough Transform are less accurate, but also less expensive and easier to implement.

4. CONCLUSION

Image processing has become a key technology in the development of electric vehicles and driverless cars. With the increasing demand for autonomous driving, image processing plays a critical role in ensuring the safety and reliability of such systems. This review paper aims to provide an overview of the current state of image processing techniques used in electric vehicles and driverless cars, as well as recent advances and future trends in this field.The various algorithms are studied for various application and compared. One of the most common applications of image processing in electric vehicles and driverless cars is object detection and recognition. The use of cameras, LiDAR, and radar sensors can provide a 360-degree view of the environment around the vehicle, which can be analyzed using image processing techniques to detect and recognize objects such as other vehicles, pedestrians, traffic signs, and traffic lights. This information can then be used to make decisions and control the vehicle accordingly.

REFERENCES

Abu-Jassar, T., Mohammad, Y., Al-Sharo, Y., Lyashenko, V., & Sotnik, S. (2021). Some Features of Classifiers Implementation for Object Recognition in Specialized Computer systems. *TEM Journal*, *10*(4), 1645.

Alokasi, H., & Ahmad, M. B. (2022). Deep Learning-Based Frameworks for Semantic Segmentation of Road Scenes. *Electronics (Basel)*, *11*(12), 1884. doi:10.3390/electronics11121884

Badrinarayanan, V., Kendall, A., & Cipolla, R. (2017). Segnet: A deep convolutional encoder-decoder architecture for image segmentation. *IEEE Transactions on Pattern Analysis and Machine Intelligence*, *39*(12), 2481–2495. doi:10.1109/TPAMI.2016.2644615 PMID:28060704

Boukerch, A., & Belaroussi, R. (2019). Lane detection and tracking for autonomous driving applications: A comprehensive review. *Journal of Intelligent Transport Systems*, *23*(5), 441–462.

Bouti, A., Mahraz, M. A., Riffi, J., & Tairi, H. (2020). Med AdnaneMahraz, Jamal Riffi, and Hamid Tairi. "A robust system for road sign detection and classification using LeNet architecture based on convolutional neural network.". *Soft Computing*, *24*(9), 6721–6733. doi:10.100700500-019-04307-6

Chandan, G. (2018). Ayush Jain, and Harsh Jain. "Real time object detection and tracking using Deep Learning and OpenCV. In *2018 International Conference on inventive research in computing applications (ICIRCA)*, (pp. 1305-1308). IEEE. 10.1109/ICIRCA.2018.8597266

Dalal, N., & Triggs, B. (2005). Histograms of oriented gradients for human detection. In *Proceedings of the IEEE conference on computer vision and pattern recognition* (pp. 886-893). IEEE. 10.1109/CVPR.2005.177

De la Escalera, A., Armingol, J. M., & Mata, M. (2003). Traffic sign recognition and analysis for intelligent vehicles. *Image and Vision Computing*, *21*(3), 247–258. doi:10.1016/S0262-8856(02)00156-7

Fan, C., & Ren, Y. (2010). Study on the edge detection algorithms of road image. In *2010 Third International Symposium on Information Processing*, (pp. 217-220). IEEE.

Gao, H., Cheng, B., Wang, J., Li, K., Zhao, J., & Li, D. (2018). Object classification using CNN-based fusion of vision and LIDAR in autonomous vehicle environment. *IEEE Transactions on Industrial Informatics*, *14*(9), 4224–4231. doi:10.1109/TII.2018.2822828

Gupta, A. K., Sharma, M., Sharma, A., & Menon, V. (2022). A study on SARS-CoV-2 (COVID-19) and machine learning based approach to detect COVID-19 through X-ray images. *International Journal of Image and Graphics*, *22*(03), 2140010. doi:10.1142/S0219467821400106

Gupta, A. K., Sharma, M., Singh, S., & Palta, P. (2020). *A Modified Blind Deconvolution Algorithm for Deblurring of Colored Images*. Advances in Computational Intelligence Techniques. doi:10.1007/978-981-15-2620-6_10

Hague, T., Marchant, J. A., & Tillett, N. D. (2000). Ground based sensing systems for autonomous agricultural vehicles. *Computers and Electronics in Agriculture*, *25*(1-2), 11–28. doi:10.1016/S0168-1699(99)00053-8

Iftikhar, S., Zhang, Z., Asim, M., Muthanna, A., Koucheryavy, A., & Abd El-Latif, A. A. (2022). Deep Learning-Based Pedestrian Detection in Autonomous Vehicles: Substantial Issues and Challenges. *Electronics (Basel)*, *11*(21), 3551. doi:10.3390/electronics11213551

Kaur, N., & Sharma, M. (2017). Brain tumor detection using self-adaptive K-means clustering. In *2017 International Conference on Energy, Communication, Data Analytics and Soft Computing (ICECDS)*, (pp. 1861-1865). IEEE. 10.1109/ICECDS.2017.8389771

Kaur, S. P., & Sharma, M. (2015). Radially optimized zone-divided energy-aware wireless sensor networks (WSN) protocol using BA (bat algorithm). *Journal of the Institution of Electronics and Telecommunication Engineers*, *61*(2), 170–179. doi:10.1080/03772063.2014.999833

Khan, M. A.-M., Haque, M. F., Hasan, K. R., Alajmani, S. H., Baz, M., Masud, M., & Nahid, A.-A. (2022). LLDNet: A Lightweight Lane Detection Approach for Autonomous Cars Using Deep Learning. *Sensors (Basel)*, *22*(15), 5595. doi:10.339022155595 PMID:35898103

Khan, M. A.-M., Haque, M. F., Hasan, K. R., Alajmani, S. H., Baz, M., Masud, M., & Nahid, A.-A. (2022). LLDNet: A Lightweight Lane Detection Approach for Autonomous Cars Using Deep Learning. *Sensors (Basel)*, *22*(15), 5595. doi:10.339022155595 PMID:35898103

Kumar, A. (2019). SS Sai Satyanarayana Reddy, and Vivek Kulkarni. "An object detection technique for blind people in real-time using deep neural network. In *2019 Fifth International Conference on Image Information Processing (ICIIP)*, (pp. 292-297). IEEE. 10.1109/ICIIP47207.2019.8985965

Li, J., & Zhang, Y. (2013). Learning surf cascade for fast and accurate object detection. In *Proceedings of the IEEE conference on computer vision and pattern recognition*, (pp. 3468-3475). IEEE. 10.1109/CVPR.2013.445

Li, Q., & Li, X. (2021). A review of pedestrian detection for autonomous vehicles. *IEEE Access : Practical Innovations, Open Solutions, 9*, 54332–54350.

Long, J., Shelhamer, E., & Darrell, T. (2015). Fully convolutional networks for semantic segmentation. In *Proceedings of the IEEE conference on computer vision and pattern recognition* (pp. 3431-3440). IEEE.

Malinovskiy, Y., Wu, Y.-J., & Wang, Y. (2009). Video-based vehicle detection and tracking using spatiotemporal maps. *Transportation Research Record: Journal of the Transportation Research Board, 2121*(1), 81–89. doi:10.3141/2121-09

Malmir, S., & Shalchian, M. (2019). Design and FPGA implementation of dual-stage lane detection, based on Hough transform and localized stripe features. *Microprocessors and Microsystems, 64*, 12–22. doi:10.1016/j.micpro.2018.10.003

McCall, J. C., & Trivedi, M. M. (2006). Video-based lane estimation and tracking for driver assistance: Survey, system, and evaluation. *IEEE Transactions on Intelligent Transportation Systems, 7*(1), 20–37. doi:10.1109/TITS.2006.869595

Moghadam, P. Wijesoma, W., & Feng, D. (2008). Improving path planning and mapping based on stereo vision and lidar. In *2008 10th International Conference on Control, Automation, Robotics and Vision*, (pp. 384-389). IEEE.

Nabati, R., & Qi, H. (2019). Rrpn: Radar region proposal network for object detection in autonomous vehicles. In *2019 IEEE International Conference on Image Processing (ICIP)*, (pp. 3093-3097). IEEE. 10.1109/ICIP.2019.8803392

Ni, J., Chen, Y., Chen, Y., Zhu, J., Ali, D., & Cao, W. (2020). A survey on theories and applications for self-driving cars based on deep learning methods. *Applied Sciences (Basel, Switzerland), 10*(8), 2749. doi:10.3390/app10082749

Redmon, J., Divvala, S., Girshick, R., & Farhadi, A. (2016). You only look once: Unified, real-time object detection. In *Proceedings of the IEEE conference on computer vision and pattern recognition* (pp. 779-788). 10.1109/CVPR.2016.91

Ren, S., He, K., Girshick, R., & Sun, J. (2015). Faster R-CNN: Towards real-time object detection with region proposal networks. In Advances in neural information processing systems (pp. 91-99).

Ronneberger, O., Fischer, P., & Brox, T. (2015). U-net: Convolutional networks for biomedical image segmentation. In *International Conference on Medical image computing and computer-assisted intervention* (pp. 234-241). Springer, Cham. 10.1007/978-3-319-24574-4_28

Ruta, A., Li, Y., & Liu, X. (2010). Real-time traffic sign recognition from video by class-specific discriminative features. *Pattern Recognition, 43*(1), 416–430. doi:10.1016/j.patcog.2009.05.018

Shangzheng, L. (2019). A traffic sign image recognition and classification approach based on convolutional neural network. In *2019 11th International Conference on Measuring Technology and Mechatronics Automation (ICMTMA)*, (pp. 408-411). IEEE. 10.1109/ICMTMA.2019.00096

Sharma, M., & Gupta, A. K. (2021). An algorithm for target detection, identification, tracking and estimation of motion for passive homing missile autopilot guidance. In *Mobile Radio Communications and 5G Networks: Proceedings of MRCN 2020*, (pp. 57-71). Springer Singapore. 10.1007/978-981-15-7130-5_5

Sharma, M., Pandey, D., Palta, P., & Pandey, B. K. (2022). Design and power dissipation consideration of PFAL CMOS V/S conventional CMOS based 2: 1 multiplexer and full adder. *Silicon*, *14*(8), 4401–4410. doi:10.100712633-021-01221-1

Sharma, M., Sharma, B., Gupta, A. K., & Khosla, D. (2021). A study and novel AI/ML-based framework to detect COVID-19 virus using smartphone embedded sensors. In *Sustainability Measures for COVID-19 Pandemic* (pp. 59–74). Springer Nature Singapore. doi:10.1007/978-981-16-3227-3_4

Sharma, M., Sharma, B., Gupta, A. K., & Pandey, D. (2023). Recent developments of image processing to improve explosive detection methodologies and spectroscopic imaging techniques for explosive and drug detection. *Multimedia Tools and Applications*, *82*(5), 6849–6865. doi:10.100711042-022-13578-5

Sharma, M., & Singh, H. (2022). Contactless Methods for Respiration Monitoring and Design of SIW-LWA for Real-Time Respiratory Rate Monitoring. *Journal of the Institution of Electronics and Telecommunication Engineers*, 1–11. doi:10.1080/03772063.2022.2069167

Sharma, M., Singh, H., & Pandey, D. (2022). Parametric Considerations and Dielectric Materials Impacts on the Performance of 10 GHzSIW-LWA for Respiration Monitoring. *Journal of Electronic Materials*, *51*(5), 2131–2141. doi:10.100711664-022-09482-1

Sharma, M., Singh, H., Singh, S., & Gupta, A. (2020). A novel approach of object detection using point feature matching technique for colored images. In *Proceedings of ICRIC 2019: Recent Innovations in Computing*, (pp. 561-576). Springer International Publishing. 10.1007/978-3-030-29407-6_40

Shi, W., Alawieh, M. B., Li, X., & Yu, H. (2017). Algorithm and hardware implementation for visual perception system in autonomous vehicle: A survey. *Integration (Amsterdam)*, *59*, 148–156. doi:10.1016/j.vlsi.2017.07.007

Singh, S., Singla, B., Sharma, M., Goyal, S., & Sabo, A. (2020). Comprehensive Study on Internet of Things (IoT) and Design Considerations of Various Microstrip Patch Antennas for IoT Applications. In *Mobile Radio Communications and 5G Networks: Proceedings of MRCN 2020*, (pp. 19-30). Springer Singapore.

Sun, Y., Wu, N., Tateno, S., & Ogai, H. (2012). Development of driving support system for electric vehicle by using image processing technology. In *2012 12th International Conference on Control, Automation and Systems*, (pp. 1965-1968). IEEE.

Varghese, J. Z., & Boone, R. G. (2015). Overview of autonomous vehicle sensors and systems. In *International Conference on Operations Excellence and Service Engineering*, (pp. 178-191). IEEE.

Vinh, T. Q., & Nguyen, T. N. A. (2020). Real-time face mask detector using YOLOv3 algorithm and Haar cascade classifier. In 2020 international conference on advanced computing and applications (ACOMP), (pp. 146-149). IEEE. doi:10.1109/ACOMP50827.2020.00029

Viola, P., & Jones, M. J. (2004). Robust real-time face detection. *International Journal of Computer Vision*, *57*(2), 137–154. doi:10.1023/B:VISI.0000013087.49260.fb

Xu, Y., Li, D., Xie, Q., Wu, Q., & Wang, J. (2021). Automatic defect detection and segmentation of tunnel surface using modified Mask R-CNN. *Measurement*, *178*, 109316. doi:10.1016/j.measurement.2021.109316

Yue, X., Li, H., Shimizu, M., Kawamura, S., & Meng, L. (2022). YOLO-GD: A deep learning-based object detection algorithm for empty-dish recycling robots. *Machines*, *10*(5), 294. doi:10.3390/machines10050294

Yue, X., Li, H., Shimizu, M., Kawamura, S., & Meng, L. (2022). Deep learning-based real-time object detection for empty-dish recycling robot. In *2022 13th Asian Control Conference (ASCC)*, (pp. 2177-2182). IEEE. 10.23919/ASCC56756.2022.9828060

Zhang, X., Zhu, S., & Tann, J. (2016). A review of recent advances in lane detection and departure warning system. In *International Conference on Intelligent Transportation* (pp. 107-118). Springer, Cham.

Zhang, X., & Zhu, X. (2019). Autonomous path tracking control of intelligent electric vehicles based on lane detection and optimal preview method. *Expert Systems with Applications*, *121*, 38–48. doi:10.1016/j.eswa.2018.12.005

Zhao, G., Ge, W., & Yu, Y. (2021). GraphFPN: Graph feature pyramid network for object detection." In *Proceedings of the IEEE/CVF international conference on computer vision*, (pp. 2763-2772). IEEE. 10.1109/ICCV48922.2021.00276

Zhao, K., Kang, J., Jung, J., & Sohn, G. (2018). Building extraction from satellite images using mask R-CNN with building boundary regularization. In *Proceedings of the IEEE conference on computer vision and pattern recognition workshops*, (pp. 247-251).

Chapter 5
A Detailed Analysis of Many Different Artificial Intelligence-Based Healthcare Systems

S. Balasubramani
Department of CSE, KL University (Deemed), Vaddeswaram, India

Renjith P. N.
School of Computer Science and Engineering, Vellore Institute of Technology, Chennai, India

K. Ramesh
Department of Computer Science and Engineering, Sri Krishna College of Engineering and Technology, India

A. S. Hovan George
Tbilisi State Medical University, Georgia

A. Shaji George
https://orcid.org/0000-0002-8677-3682
Business System Department, Almarai Company, Saudi Arabia

Aakifa Shahul
SRM Medical College, Kattankulathur, India

ABSTRACT

The healthcare industry is one of the world's fastest growing, and the impact of artificial intelligence (AI) is already being felt. AI is changing the way healthcare is delivered, from reducing administrative processes to offering individualized patient care. AI is predicted to have a significant impact on healthcare in the next years. Its possible applications range from bettering patient care and outcomes to lowering healthcare expenses. Diagnostics is one area where AI has the potential to have a substantial effect. AI-powered diagnostic technologies have the potential to transform how diseases are discovered and treated. AI-based diagnostic tools can find patterns and connections in big data sets that the human eye may miss. AI can also be utilized to create patient-specific treatment strategies.

DOI: 10.4018/978-1-6684-8618-4.ch005

Figure 1. Representation of model of medical internet of things

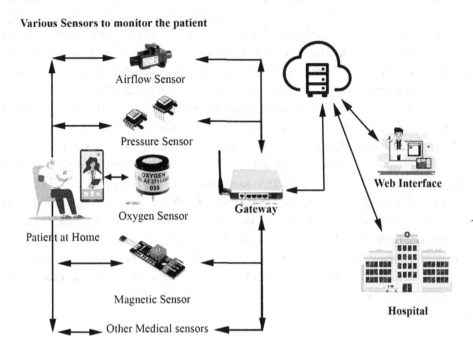

INTRODUCTION

The healthcare industry has the opportunity for significant transformation through the application of Artificial Intelligence (AI), which can improve patient outcomes, reduce expenses, and enhance operational efficiency (DJ, B. J et.al., 2022). Several AI-based healthcare systems have been created to handle many areas of healthcare delivery, including diagnosis, treatment planning, and drug development (Zheng, L., 2022).

Artificial Intelligence (AI) in healthcare shows great promise, particularly in the field of medical diagnosis. Through the use of AI-based diagnostic algorithms, medical imaging like X-rays and CT scans can be analyzed to assist doctors in accurately identifying various diseases and conditions (Hilmizen, N et al., 2020). These algorithms, employing deep learning techniques, analyze images to identify patterns indicative of specific illnesses. Studies have demonstrated the reliability of such systems, which exhibit high sensitivity and specificity in diagnosing diseases like lung cancer and breast cancer. Moreover, AI diagnostic systems can also predict the progression of diseases, facilitating early detection and treatment planning (Chang, K. C et al., 2021). Additionally, AI finds application in treatment planning, as illustrated in Figure 1, which showcases a model of the Internet of Medical Things. On the basis of a patient's medical history, symptoms, and test findings, AI-based solutions have been developed to aid physicians in designing individualized treatment programmes. These systems examine data using machine learning techniques and find patterns that are suggestive of particular situations. These algorithms can accurately identify the optimal therapy options for patients with illnesses such as heart disease and diabetes, according to studies (Bernardini et al., 2021). In addition, the AI-based treatment planning system can be used to track the patient's development and modify the treatment plan accordingly. Moreover, AI has been utilized to increase the effectiveness of drug discovery. The development of AI-based algorithms to aid researchers in finding prospective medication candidates and forecasting their efficacy has occurred. These systems evaluate vast quantities of data on the molecular structure of medications, their interactions with the body, and their adverse effects using machine learning techniques. These systems can reliably estimate the efficacy of drug candidates and identify probable negative effects, allowing researers to create more effective and safer medications (Ghimire et al., 2020).

In the healthcare industry, AI-based healthcare solutions have showed considerable potential for improving patient outcomes, decreasing costs, and enhancing efficiency. These systems were designed to handle various facets of healthcare delivery, including diagnosis, treatment planning, and drug discovery (Firouz et al., 2021). Research have demonstrated that these systems are capable of properly identifying diseases, predicting the most effective treatments, and identifying promising drug candidates. However, it is equally essential to remember that AI-based systems should be used in conjunction with human expertise and should be continuously checked and assessed to guarantee that they produce accurate and trustworthy results. Using AI-based healthcare solutions can be advantageous for improving patient outcomes, decreasing expenses, and increasing industry efficiency. It is essential to stress, however, that the outcomes of AI-based systems must be confirmed by human specialists, and the systems must be continuously monitored and assessed to guarantee they produce accurate and dependable results (Balasubramani et al., 2022).

LITERATURE REVIEW

The way we monitor and control our health has been changed by Artificial Intelligence (AI). From identifying and diagnosing diseases to forecasting future health outcomes, AI-based health care systems can deliver more precise and timely data than conventional systems. This article examines the present state of AI-based health care systems, including their development, implementation, and impact on healthcare (Mamun et al., 2022). Medical pictures, such as CT and MRI scans, can be analyzed by AI-based systems in order to identify disease symptoms. A common use of AI in medical imaging is the identification of lung cancer, for instance (Wang et al., 2019). AI-based systems may be taught to analyses CT scans and identify lung nodules, a common indicator of lung cancer. These technologies can also categories nodules as benign or malignant, hence reducing the number of needless biopsies and enhancing patient outcomes.

Other ailments, such as diabetes and cardiovascular disease, can also be detected and diagnosed using AI-powered devices. For instance, AI-based systems can be trained to evaluate retinal pictures and detect symptoms of diabetic retinopathy (Weigand et al., 2016), a diabetic condition that can lead to blindness. These technologies can also be used to evaluate ECG and other cardiac data in order to detect heart disease symptoms such as arrhythmias and heart failure. These systems can also be used to forecast the side effects of medications, hence reducing the time and expense associated with drug development.

A further advantage of AI-based health monitoring systems is their capacity to assess vast quantities of data and forecast future health outcomes (Inibhunu et al., 2021). For instance, ML systems can be trained to forecast the risk that a patient would get a particular disease based on their medical history, genetic data, and other data. This can aid in the identification of high-risk patients and the implementation of preventative actions to lower the possibility of disease development. Notwithstanding its potential benefits, the development and implementation of AI-based health monitoring systems present a number of obstacles. To train machine learning (ML) algorithms, massive quantities of high-quality data are required. This information must be representative of the population, diversified, and error- and omission-free. In addition, data privacy and informed permission must be considered while collecting and utilizing this information. (He Y et al., 2020) AI-based diagnostic systems in radiology and to identify key areas for future research. According to the study, AI-based diagnostic solutions must enhance the precision, effectiveness, and cost-effectiveness of radiology. These investigations analyzed medical imaging such as CT scans, MRI scans, and X-rays utilizing machine learning, deep learning, and other AI approaches. Studies evaluating the performance of AI-based systems in various applications, such as the identification of lung cancer, cardiac disease, and bone fractures, were also included.

The study concluded that AI-based diagnostic systems have the potential to enhance radiology's precision, efficiency, and cost-effectiveness. For instance, AI-based systems can be trained to evaluate medical images and identify symptoms of disease, such as lung nodules, so reducing the frequency of unnecessary biopsies and enhancing patient outcomes. They also discovered that AI-based algorithms can be used to categories nodules as benign or malignant, hence reducing the number of unnecessary biopsies and enhancing patient outcomes (Imaizumi, H et al., 2017). The objective of is to assess the present state of AI-based medical imaging systems and their performance in diverse applications. These studies analyzed medical pictures such as CT scans, MRI scans, and X-rays using machine learning, deep learning, and other artificial intelligence approaches. In addition, they investigated the performance of AI-based systems in various applications, such as lung cancer diagnosis, diabetic retinopathy, and bone fractures. The study discovered that AI-based solutions have the potential to enhance the precision and efficacy of medical imaging. For instance, AI-based systems can be taught to analyses CT scans and identify lung nodules, which are a common indicator of lung cancer. These technologies can also categories nodules as benign or malignant, hence reducing the frequency of needless biopsies and enhancing patient outcomes (Nilashi et al., 2017). In addition, the authors discovered that AI-based systems can be used to scan retinal pictures and detect indicators of diabetic retinopathy, a potentially blinding complication of diabetes. This can enhance the precision and effectiveness of diabetic retinopathy diagnosis and treatment. However, the authors also observed that the research and deployment of AI present a number of obstacles.

AI has the ability to increase the accuracy, efficiency, and cost-effectiveness of healthcare, according to the study. For instance, AI-based systems can be used to evaluate medical pictures and detect disease indicators, such as lung nodules, thereby reducing the frequency of unnecessary biopsies and enhancing patient outcomes (Swapna et al., 2018). In addition, AI-based systems can be used to evaluate massive volumes of medical data and forecast future health outcomes, such as the risk that a patient would get a particular disease. This enables the identification of patients at high risk and the implementation of preventative actions to lower the possibility of illness development. However, the authors also stress that the research and deployment of AI in healthcare face a number of obstacles. The necessity for enormous amounts of high-quality data to train AI systems is one of the major obstacles. This information must be representative of the population, diversified, and error- and omission-free. In addition, data privacy and informed permission must be considered while collecting and utilizing this information. In addition, the authors note that there are ethical and legal issues related with the use of AI in healthcare, such as the possibility of bias and discrimination in the development and deployment of AI-based systems. Suzuki, K. (2017), presents a detailed assessment of the current state of artificial intelligence in healthcare, stressing its potential benefits and problems. Future research should focus on the establishment of standardized criteria and methodologies for evaluating AI-based healthcare systems, as well as tackling the ethical and legal challenges connected with the use of AI in healthcare.

AI in Healthcare

The application of Artificial Intelligence (AI) in different areas, including healthcare, is accelerating. The healthcare industry is one of the most data-intensive industries, making it a potential application area for artificial intelligence (Liberati et al., 2009). AI has the potential to improve healthcare by enhancing the precision and effectiveness of medical diagnosis, therapies, and drug discovery. In this section, we will examine the current state of artificial intelligence in healthcare, its potential benefits, and the obstacles that must be overcome.

Medical imaging is one of the most important uses of AI in healthcare. Medical pictures, such as CT and MRI scans, can be analyzed by AI-based systems in order to identify disease symptoms. A common use of AI in medical imaging is the diagnosis of lung cancer, for instance. Fig.2. Basic Arduino-based health monitoring system block diagram. AI-based systems may be taught to analyses CT scans and identify lung nodules, a common indicator of lung cancer. These methods can also categories nodules as benign or malignant, so reducing the frequency of needless biopsies and enhancing patient outcomes. A further application of AI in healthcare is drug discovery and development [38]. AI-based systems can be used to evaluate enormous volumes of data, such as genetic and molecular data, in order to find possible therapeutic targets for a number of diseases. These systems can also be used to forecast the probable negative effects of medications, hence reducing the time and expense associated with drug development.

AI-based systems can also be used to detect and diagnose various ailments, including diabetes and cardiovascular disease. For instance, AI-based systems can be trained to evaluate retinal pictures and detect indications of diabetic retinopathy, a potentially blinding consequence of diabetes. These devices can also be used to evaluate ECG and other cardiac data in order to detect heart disease symptoms such

Figure 2. Block diagram of basic Arduino based health monitoring system

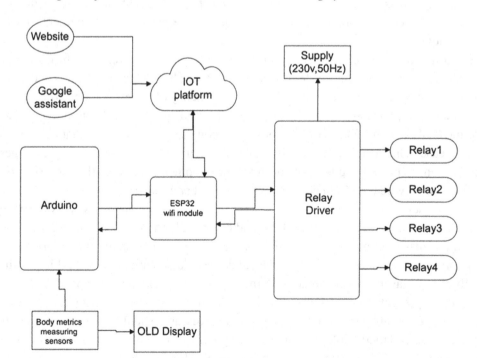

as arrhythmias and heart failure. In addition to its diagnostic skills, AI can enhance the efficiency of healthcare delivery by automating repetitive tasks.

Artificial Intelligence in Healthcare

Medical imaging is one of the primary uses of machine learning in healthcare. Medical pictures, such as CT and MRI scans, can be analyzed by machine learning algorithms in order to identify disease symptoms (Chen et al., 2017). For instance, lung cancer diagnosis is a common application of machine learning in medical imaging. It is possible to train machine learning algorithms to evaluate CT scans and identify the existence of lung nodules, a common indicator of lung cancer (Tran et al., 2022). These algorithms can also be used to categories nodules as benign or malignant, so reducing unnecessary biopsies and improving patient outcomes. Drug research and development is a further application of machine learning in the healthcare industry. Large volumes of data, such as genetic and molecular data, can be analyzed using machine learning algorithms to identify possible therapeutic targets for a range of disorders. These algorithms can also be used to forecast the probable negative effects of medications, hence reducing the time and costs associated with drug development (Karatekin et al., 2019).

Deep Learning in Healthcare

Deep learning (DL) is a subset of machine learning and artificial intelligence that analyses and learns from data using deep neural networks (Liang et al., 2014). Deep learning is being applied to a variety of healthcare applications, such as medical imaging, drug development, and precision medicine. For example, lung cancer diagnosis is a common application of deep learning in medical imaging. DL algorithms may be trained to evaluate CT scans and detect lung nodules, a typical indicator of lung cancer (Kumar et al., 2021). These algorithms can also be used to categories nodules as benign or malignant, so reducing unnecessary biopsies and improving patient outcomes. Drug research and development is a second application of deep learning in the healthcare industry. Large volumes of data, such as genetic and molecular data, can be analyzed using DL algorithms to find prospective therapeutic targets for a range of disorders (24. Muhammad et al., 2020). These algorithms can also be used to forecast the potential negative effects of medications, hence reducing the time and expense associated with drug development.

In addition to diabetes and heart disease, deep learning algorithms can also be used to detect and diagnose other diseases, such as cancer. Deep learning algorithms can be trained to examine retinal images and detect indicators of diabetic retinopathy, a potentially blinding consequence of diabetes. These algorithms can also be used to evaluate ECG and other cardiac data in order to detect heart disease symptoms such as arrhythmias and heart failure Mittal, P. (2023). Deep learning has also been implemented in the field of natural language processing, which enables the study of electronic health records (EHR) by extracting crucial information from unstructured data such as physician's notes, lab reports, and discharge summaries. This can enable more accurate diagnoses and more efficient treatment approaches.

Yet, the research and deployment of deep learning in healthcare present a number of obstacles. The necessity for vast quantities of high-quality data to train DL algorithms is one of the most significant obstacles. These data must be representative of the population, diversified, and error-free (Subiksha, K. P., 2018). In addition, data privacy and informed permission must be considered while collecting and utilizing this information. Moreover, the interpretability of DL models is problematic, as it might be challenging to comprehend how the model arrived at a particular conclusion.

Deep learning has the potential to improve healthcare by enhancing the precision and efficacy of medical diagnosis, therapies, and drug discovery. Yet, it is essential to solve the obstacles associated with the development and application of deep learning in healthcare, such as the need for vast quantities of high-quality data and the interpretability of DL models.

Performance Evaluation of AI in Healthcare

It is essential to evaluate the performance of artificial intelligence (AI) in healthcare to ensure that AI-based systems are accurate, dependable, and safe for clinical application. It entails evaluating the performance of AI-based systems using a variety of metrics and techniques, including as precision, sensitivity, specificity, and area under the receiver operating characteristic curve (AUC-ROC). This section discusses the significance of AI performance evaluation in healthcare, the metrics and methods used to evaluate AI-based systems, and the difficulties involved with AI performance evaluation in healthcare.

In healthcare AI, performance evaluation is essential since it allows us to analyses the efficacy and safety of AI-based systems. It helps to verify that AI-based systems used in clinical practice are accurate, trustworthy, and safe (Dol et al., 2021). It also aids in identifying areas for improvement and developing strategies to solve any identified problems. Several metrics and approaches are used to evaluate the performance of AI-based healthcare systems. Among these are precision, sensitivity, specificity, and AUC-ROC. Accuracy indicates the frequency with which an AI-based system properly anticipates the outcome. Sensitivity represents the frequency with which an AI-based system accurately recognizes affirmative cases. Specificity is the frequency with which an AI-based system accurately recognizes negative cases. AUC-ROC is a measure of a system's capacity to differentiate between positive and negative situations.

In addition to these criteria, numerous approaches exist for measuring the performance of AI-based healthcare systems. Cross-validation and hold-out procedures are included. Cross-validation is a technique for assessing the effectiveness of an AI-based system that divides the data into training and test sets. The hold-out strategy entails conserving a portion of the data for testing and using the remainder for training (Han et al., 2007). There are also a number of obstacles involved with evaluating the performance of AI in healthcare. The need for vast amounts of high-quality data to train and test AI-based systems is one of the greatest obstacles. This information must be representative of the population, diversified, and error- and omission-free.

Medical Imaging and AI

Medical imaging is the process of producing visual representations of the interior of the body for the purposes of clinical investigation and medical intervention. Artificial intelligence (AI) is increasingly being applied to medical imaging to improve diagnostic precision, therapeutic efficacy, and cost-effectiveness. In this section, we discuss the current level of AI in medical imaging, its prospective benefits, and the obstacles that must be overcome.

One of the most important uses of AI in medical imaging is disease detection. AI-based systems, such as convolutional neural networks (CNNs), can be trained to evaluate medical pictures, such as CT and MRI scans, in order to identify illness indicators. A frequent use of AI in medical imaging is the identification of lung cancer, for instance (Ju L et al., 2022). AI-based systems may be taught to analyses CT scans and identify lung nodules, a common indicator of lung cancer. These methods can also categories nodules as benign or malignant, so reducing the frequency of needless biopsies and enhancing patient outcomes.

The field of picture segmentation is another use of AI in medical imaging. Image segmentation is the process of dividing an image into distinct parts, or segments, depending on specific attributes. Medical pictures, such as MRI scans, can be segmented by AI-powered algorithms to identify specific features, such as cancers or blood vessels. This can increase the diagnostic and treatment planning accuracy. AI can also be used to increase medical imaging efficiency. For instance, AI-based solutions can be used to automate picture processing, hence reducing the time and expense associated with diagnosis and treatment. In addition, AI-based systems can be utilized to enhance the image quality of medical images, for instance by reducing noise or enhancing contrast (Kim et al., 2022).

AI-Based Diagnostic Systems

AI-based diagnostic systems are computer programmes that analyses medical data, such as medical imaging and electronic health records (EHRs) and generate predictions about a patient's diagnosis or therapy using artificial intelligence (AI) techniques. These technologies have the potential to enhance the precision, effectiveness, and cost-efficiency of medical diagnostics. The current status of AI-based diagnostic systems, their potential advantages, and the obstacles that must be overcome.

The capacity of AI-based diagnostic systems to increase the accuracy of medical diagnosis is one of its primary advantages. AI-based systems can be programmed to evaluate medical pictures, such as CT and MRI scans, and identify illness indicators, such as tumors and lesions. They can also be used to categories these symptoms as benign or malignant, hence reducing the number of needless biopsies and enhancing patient outcomes. In addition, AI-based systems can be used to evaluate vast amounts of medical data, such as EHRs, in order to forecast a patient's diagnosis or therapy. The capacity of AI-based diagnostic systems to improve the efficiency of medical diagnosis is another advantage (Huang et al., 2022). The automation of image analysis using AI-based systems can minimize the time and cost of diagnosis and treatment. In addition, AI-based systems can be used to enhance the image quality of medical photographs, for instance by eliminating noise or enhancing contrast.

Moreover, AI-based diagnostic tools are employed to enhance the treatment of chronic diseases. For instance, AI-based systems can be used to evaluate data from wearable devices such as activity trackers and forecast the chance of a patient developing a chronic ailment such as diabetes or cardiovascular disease.

AI in Drug Discovery and Development

The application of artificial intelligence tools in drug discovery and development. This may involve the use of AI for target discovery, lead identification and optimization, and drug design and development. The analysis of vast amounts of data is one of the most important ways in which AI is used in drug discovery. For instance, machine learning techniques can be applied to genomics data in order to find prospective therapeutic targets. Similarly, (Jiang et al., 2021) artificial intelligence can be used to examine chemical libraries in order to uncover prospective therapeutic candidates.

Simulation of drug-protein interactions is another area where AI is being employed in drug discovery. This may involve employing AI to forecast the binding affinity of a small molecule to a protein target as well as the potential off-target effects of a therapeutic candidate. In addition to these uses, AI is also applied in the development of pharmaceuticals (Wu C et al., 2022). AI can be used to analyses clinical trial data in order to discover potential adverse effects of medications and subpopulations that may respond differently to a specific drug. The application of artificial intelligence in drug research and development has the potential to dramatically accelerate the process of discovering and creating novel medications. It is essential to emphasize, however, that AI is still in its infancy in this subject, and there is still much work to be done to fully fulfil its promise. The requirement for vast amounts of high-quality data is one of the greatest obstacles to the application of AI in drug research and development. This can contain information regarding the structure and function of proteins and the chemical characteristics of tiny molecules. In addition, robust and accurate algorithms that can successfully interpret these data are required.

The requirement for collaboration amongst experts in several domains, such as computational biology, chemistry, and medicine, is an additional obstacle. As the field of AI in drug discovery and development continues to evolve, academics and practitioners will need to collaborate to develop new approaches and tools that may be utilized to expedite the discovery and development of novel medications. AI has the ability to alter the drug research and development process by providing novel methods for data analysis and identifying new therapeutic candidates (Gillani et al., 2022). The use of AI in this field is an interesting area of research that has the potential to have a big impact on human health, despite the fact that there are still numerous obstacles to overcome.

AI in Precision Medicine

AI in precision medicine is the creation of tailored treatment plans. This can involve utilizing AI to forecast which treatment will be most beneficial for a certain patient and to identify probable negative effects associated with a given treatment (Goodyear O et al., 1990). AI is often utilized in clinical trials to identify patient subpopulations that may respond differentially to a given medication. This can involve employing AI to identify individuals at high risk for experiencing specific adverse effects, as well as patients most likely to respond to a given medication. The application of AI in precision medicine has the potential to substantially enhance patient outcomes. It is crucial to emphasize, however, that AI is still in its infancy in this field, and there is still much work to be done to fully fulfil its promise.

The requirement for vast amounts of high-quality patient data is one of the greatest obstacles to the application of AI in precision medicine. This can include genetic and lifestyle and environment information about the patient. In addition, robust and accurate algorithms that can successfully interpret these data are required. Another obstacle is the requirement for collaboration between professionals from many domains, such as computer science, statistics, and medicine. As the field of AI in precision medicine continues to evolve, academics and practitioners will need to collaborate to develop new methodologies and tools that may be used to enhance patient outcomes (Aljaaf et al., 2015). AI has the potential to change precision medicine by introducing novel methods for analyzing patient data and identifying novel treatment techniques. The use of AI in this field is an interesting area of research that has the potential to have a big impact on human health, despite the fact that there are still numerous obstacles to overcome.

AI in Clinical Decision Support

AI in clinical decision support refers to the application of artificial intelligence tools to aid healthcare workers in making educated patient care decisions. This may involve the use of AI for tasks like diagnosis, therapy planning, and patient monitoring. The analysis of patient data is one of the most prominent

AI applications in clinical decision support. For instance, machine learning algorithms can be used to examine patient data in order to uncover patterns and trends that can be utilized to forecast patient outcomes. Similarly, AI can be used to examine patient data to uncover potentially valuable biomarkers for the diagnosis and treatment of specific diseases.

The creation of clinical decision support systems is another application of AI in clinical decision assistance (CDSS). These systems may incorporate the use of artificial intelligence to give clinicians with real-time advice for diagnosis and therapy, as well as alerts for potential problems or adverse occurrences. AI is also employed in the creation of computer-assisted diagnostic (CAD) systems. These systems may employ AI to evaluate medical pictures, such as X-rays and CT scans, in order to detect probable anomalies. The use of AI in clinical decision support has the potential to substantially enhance patient outcomes. It is essential to emphasize, however, that AI is still in its infancy in this subject, and there is still much work to be done to fully fulfil its promise. The necessity for huge quantities of high-quality patient data is one of the primary obstacles to the application of AI in clinical decision assistance (Fitriyani et al., 2020) This can include genetic and lifestyle and environment information about the patient. In addition, robust and accurate algorithms that can successfully interpret these data are required. Another obstacle is the requirement for collaboration between professionals from many domains, such as computer science, statistics, and medicine. As the field of AI in clinical decision support continues to evolve, academics and practitioners will need to collaborate to develop new methodologies and tools that may be utilized to improve patient outcomes. AI has the potential to change clinical decision support by giving new ways to examine patient data and by providing real-time diagnosis and treatment suggestions. The use of AI in this field is an interesting area of research that has the potential to have a big impact on human health, despite the fact that there are still numerous obstacles to overcome.

AI in Electronic Health Records

AI in electronic health records (EHR) refers to the application of artificial intelligence techniques to aid in the management, analysis, and use of electronic health records. This may involve the use of AI for data entry, data extraction, and data analysis (Beierle et al., 2017). The use of natural language processing (NLP) techniques to extract structured data from unstructured text in clinical notes is a fundamental AI application in EHR. This may involve gathering patient demographics, diagnoses, prescriptions, and lab results, which can then be utilized to automatically populate EHR fields. Another application of AI in EHR is the creation of clinical decision support systems (CDSS). These systems may incorporate the use of artificial intelligence to give clinicians with real-time advice for diagnosis and therapy, as well as alerts for potential problems or adverse occurrences. By integrating EHR data, these systems are also able to give patients with individualized suggestions based on their medical history and present condition (Murray et al., 2019).

EHR systems are also utilizing AI to improve data quality, data security, and data privacy. For instance, AI-based systems can be used to discover and repair errors in EHR data, detect and prevent unwanted access to EHR data, and protect the privacy of patient data by employing advanced encryption and anonymization techniques. The integration of AI in EHR has the potential to dramatically enhance the quality, efficiency, and safety of electronic health records. Figure 3 depicts the operation of ML-based threat identification prediction. It is essential to emphasize, however, that AI is still in its infancy in this subject, and there is still much work to be done to fully fulfil its promise. The requirement for voluminous, high-quality, and standardized patient data (Abdar et al., 2022) is one of the greatest obstacles to

Figure 3. Represents working of ML based prediction for threat identification

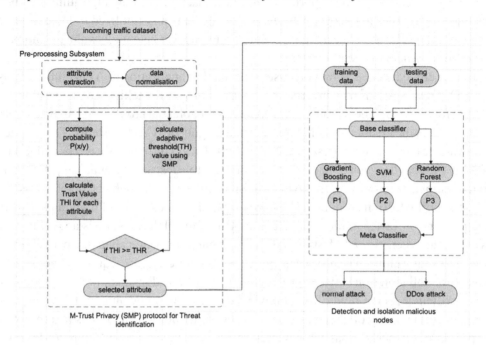

the application of AI in EHR. This can include genetic and lifestyle and environment information about the patient. In addition, powerful and accurate algorithms that can efficiently evaluate these data, as well as adequate governance and legislation to assure data security and patient privacy, are required.

The necessity for collaboration between professionals from other domains, such as computer science, medicine, and healthcare legislation, is an additional obstacle. As the field of AI in EHR continues to evolve, it will be crucial for researchers and practitioners to collaborate on the development of new methodologies and tools to enhance the management, analysis, and utilization of electronic health data. AI has the potential to change electronic health records by introducing novel techniques for extracting, analyzing, and utilizing patient data. The use of AI in this industry is an attractive area of research with the potential to dramatically improve healthcare quality, efficiency, and security, despite the fact that there are still numerous problems to be addressed.

RESEARCH DIRECTION

There are several research directions that are currently being pursued in the field of AI-based healthcare systems. These include:

Personalized Medicine

Using AI for personalized medicine is one of the primary research directions for AI-based healthcare systems. This includes the use of AI to evaluate vast volumes of patient data in order to uncover patterns and trends that may be used to forecast patient outcomes and build individualized treatment regimens. Customized medicine is an approach to treatment that takes into consideration the genetic, environmental, and behavioral differences between individuals. In AI-based healthcare, personalized medicine is achieved by analyzing vast volumes of patient data to uncover patterns and trends that may be used to forecast patient outcomes and build individualized treatment regimens. In customized medicine, genomics data processing is one of the primary applications of artificial intelligence. For instance, machine learning algorithms can be used to evaluate genomic data in order to detect genetic changes that may be linked to a specific disease. This information can then be used to forecast whether people are at a high risk for getting a certain disease and to build disease-specific preventative and treatment methods. The study of electronic health record (EHR) data is another area where AI is being applied in customized medicine. This may involve employing AI to find patterns and trends in patient data that may be utilized to forecast patient outcomes and build individualized treatment regimens. For instance, AI can be used to evaluate patient data to determine which patients are most likely to respond to a certain medication and to identify probable negative effects associated with that treatment. In addition to these uses, AI is also utilized to create individualized treatment regimens.

Predictive Analytics

The use of AI in healthcare predictive analytics is another area of study. This involves the use of AI to predict patient outcomes, such as the probability of getting specific diseases, as well as the efficacy of certain treatments. In AI-based healthcare, predictive analytics refers to the application of AI tools to evaluate patient data and forecast future health outcomes. This may involve estimating the risk of developing particular diseases, the efficacy of certain treatment options, and the probability of hospital readmissions.

Moreover, AI is employed to forecast the probability of hospital readmissions. This may involve employing AI to assess patient data, including as test results, medical history, and discharge information, in order to estimate the likelihood of a patient being readmitted to the hospital within a specified time frame. This data can then be utilized to develop measures to reduce hospital readmission rates. In addition to these uses, AI is also being utilized to enhance the efficacy and quality of healthcare organizations. For instance, AI can be used to estimate workforce requirements, uncover system inefficiencies, and optimize resource allocation. However, although predictive analytics has the potential to greatly improve healthcare outcomes, it is vital to guarantee that the predictions generated by AI-based systems are accurate and trustworthy, as well as to examine the ethical and legal consequences of utilizing these systems. The rapidly expanding field of predictive analytics in AI-based healthcare has the potential to greatly enhance patient outcomes. By analyzing patient data with AI, healthcare companies can anticipate future health outcomes and devise focused preventive and therapeutic measures. However, it is essential to guarantee that the predictions provided by these systems are accurate and trustworthy, as well as to address the ethical and legal consequences of their use.

Digital Health

Given the rising prevalence of mobile and wearable devices in healthcare, there is a growing interest in the application of AI to the development of digital health solutions. This involves employing AI to evaluate data from these devices in order to uncover patterns and trends that may be leveraged to enhance patient outcomes.

The use of natural language processing (NLP) tools to extract structured data from unstructured text in clinical notes is another significant research field. This may involve gathering patient data, diagnoses, prescriptions, and lab results, which can subsequently be utilized to automatically populate EHR fields. Lack of transparency and explain ability of AI-based systems is one of the most significant obstacles to the application of AI in healthcare. Research is required to develop ways for evaluating and explaining the decisions made by AI-based systems and to ensure that these systems are transparent, trustworthy, and accountable.

Assuring the confidentiality and privacy of patient data is a vital feature of AI-based healthcare systems. There is a rising need for research in this field to develop new methods and technologies to protect patient data and ensure compliance of AI-based systems with applicable legislation and guidelines. These are some of the most active research directions in the field of AI-based healthcare systems, and as the field continues to expand, it is possible that additional research directions may arise.

CONCLUSION

In recent years, there has been an increasing interest in the application of artificial intelligence within the healthcare industry. This has led to the creation of numerous AI-based healthcare systems, including computer-aided diagnostic (CAD) systems, clinical decision support systems (CDSS), and electronic health record (EHR) systems. These systems have the potential to substantially enhance the quality, efficiency, and accessibility of healthcare services. Before these systems can be extensively used, it is necessary to evaluate their performance to determine their efficacy and pinpoint areas for improvement.

The diagnosis accuracy of AI-based healthcare systems is a crucial part of evaluating their effectiveness. This may involve utilizing measurements like as sensitivity, specificity, and area under the receiver operating characteristic curve (AUC) to evaluate the system's capacity to effectively diagnose a certain condition. In the case of CAD systems, for instance, the diagnostic accuracy of the system can be determined by comparing the system's results with those of human specialists.

Evaluation of the system's ability to give clinical decision support is an additional crucial part of performance evaluation. This may involve evaluating the system's capacity to deliver meaningful and timely suggestions for diagnosis and treatment, as well as its capacity to provide alerts for potential problems or adverse occurrences. It may also involve an evaluation of the system's capacity to customize recommendations depending on the patient's medical history and present condition. In addition to these factors, the performance of AI-based healthcare systems can also be measured by its usability and user acceptance. This can involve analyzing the system's usability and the level of satisfaction among healthcare professionals who employ the system. It may also involve assessing the system's capacity to integrate with existing healthcare systems and to grow to meet the needs of large healthcare organizations. Lack of a consistent set of measurements and evaluation methodologies is a significant obstacle in evaluating the success of AI-based healthcare systems. Each system is unique, and the selection of assessment metrics and methodologies will depend on the system's particular objectives and requirements. In addition, it is essential to address the ethical and legal consequences of employing AI in healthcare, such as patient privacy and data security, and to verify that the system complies with applicable legislation and guidelines.

The performance evaluation of AI-based healthcare systems is a crucial step in establishing their efficacy and discovering development opportunities. This includes evaluating the diagnostic accuracy, clinical decision support, usability, and user acceptance of the system, as well as its ethical and legal consequences. The choice of metrics and techniques for assessment will rely on the system's specific objectives and requirements, and it is essential to ensure that the system complies with applicable legislation and guidelines. Although AI-based healthcare systems have the potential to transform healthcare, it is essential to analyses their performance in order to determine their efficacy and suggest areas for development.

REFERENCES:

Abdar, M., Khosravi, A., Islam, S. M. S., Acharya, U. R., & Vasilakos, A. V. (2022). The need for quantification of uncertainty in artificial intelligence for clinical data analysis: Increasing the level of trust in the decision-making process. *IEEE Systems, Man, and Cybernetics Magazine, 8*(3), 28–40. doi:10.1109/MSMC.2022.3150144

Aljaaf, A. J., Al-Jumeily, D., Hussain, A. J., Fergus, P., Al-Jumaily, M., & Abdel-Aziz, K. (2015, July). Toward an optimal use of artificial intelligence techniques within a clinical decision support system. In *2015 Science and Information Conference (SAI)* (pp. 548-554). IEEE. 10.1109/SAI.2015.7237196

Balasubramani, S., Sudhakar, A., Kalyan, C., & Satwik, M. S. (2022, February). Analysis and Prediction of COVID-19 Cases Using Machine Learning Algorithms. In *International Conference on Computing, Communication, Electrical and Biomedical Systems* (pp. 405-414). Cham: Springer International Publishing. 10.1007/978-3-030-86165-0_34

Beierle, C., Sader, B., Eichhorn, C., Kern-Isberner, G., Meyer, R. G., & Nietzke, M. (2017, June). On the ontological modelling of co-medication and drug interactions in medical cancer therapy regimens for a clinical decision support system. In *2017 IEEE 30th International Symposium on Computer-Based Medical Systems (CBMS)* (pp. 105-110). IEEE. 10.1109/CBMS.2017.102

Bernardini, M., Romeo, L., Mancini, A., & Frontoni, E. (2021). A Clinical Decision Support System to Stratify the Temporal Risk of Diabetic Retinopathy. *IEEE Access : Practical Innovations, Open Solutions, 9*, 151864–151872. doi:10.1109/ACCESS.2021.3127274

Chen, M., Hao, Y., Hwang, K., Wang, L., & Wang, L. (2017). Disease prediction by machine learning over big data from healthcare communities. *IEEE Access : Practical Innovations, Open Solutions, 5*, 8869–8879. doi:10.1109/ACCESS.2017.2694446

DJ. B. J., Rajan, S. S., Vibinanth, R., Pamela, D., & Manimegalai, P. (2022, April). I-Doc–A Cloud Based Data Management System For Health Care. In *2022 6th International Conference on Devices, Circuits and Systems (ICDCS)* (pp. 85-88). IEEE.

Dol, M., & Geetha, A. (2021, August). A learning transition from machine learning to deep learning: A survey. In *2021 International Conference on Emerging Techniques in Computational Intelligence (ICETCI)* (pp. 89-94). IEEE. 10.1109/ICETCI51973.2021.9574066

Firouzi, F., Farahani, B., Daneshmand, M., Grise, K., Song, J., Saracco, R., Wang, L. L., Lo, K., Angelov, P., Soares, E., Loh, P.-S., Talebpour, Z., Moradi, R., Goodarzi, M., Ashraf, H., Talebpour, M., Talebpour, A., Romeo, L., Das, R., & Luo, A. (2021). Harnessing the power of smart and connected health to tackle COVID-19: IoT, AI, robotics, and blockchain for a better world. *IEEE Internet of Things Journal, 8*(16), 12826–12846. doi:10.1109/JIOT.2021.3073904 PMID:35782886

Fitriyani, N. L., Syafrudin, M., Alfian, G., & Rhee, J. (2020). HDPM: An effective heart disease prediction model for a clinical decision support system. *IEEE Access : Practical Innovations, Open Solutions, 8*, 133034–133050. doi:10.1109/ACCESS.2020.3010511

Ghimire, A., Thapa, S., Jha, A. K., Kumar, A., Kumar, A., & Adhikari, S. (2020, November). AI and IoT solutions for tackling COVID-19 pandemic. In *2020 4th International Conference on Electronics, Communication and Aerospace Technology (ICECA)* (pp. 1083-1092). IEEE.

Gillani, I. S., Shahzad, M., Mobin, A., Munawar, M. R., Awan, M. U., & Asif, M. (2022, September). Explainable AI in Drug Sensitivity Prediction on Cancer Cell Lines. In *2022 International Conference on Emerging Trends in Smart Technologies (ICETST)* (pp. 1-5). IEEE. 10.1109/ICETST55735.2022.9922931

Goodyear, O. M., Shamsolmaali, A., Hobsley, M., & Scurr, J. (1990, April). Decision support and the medical data environment: an example from breast surgery. In *IET Colloquium on AI in Medical Decision Making* (pp. 6-1). IET.

Han, X., & Fischl, B. (2007). Atlas renormalization for improved brain MR image segmentation across scanner platforms. *IEEE Transactions on Medical Imaging, 26*(4), 479–486. doi:10.1109/TMI.2007.893282 PMID:17427735

He, Y., Luo, C., Camacho, R. S., Wang, K., & Zhang, H. (2020, September). AI-Based Security Attack Pathway for Cardiac Medical Diagnosis Systems (CMDS). In 2020 [IEEE.]. *Computers in Cardiology*, 1–4.

Hilmizen, N., Bustamam, A., & Sarwinda, D. (2020, December). The multimodal deep learning for diagnosing COVID-19 pneumonia from chest CT-scan and X-ray images. In *2020 3rd international seminar on research of information technology and intelligent systems (ISRITI)* (pp. 26-31). IEEE.

Chang, K. C., Huang, J. W., & Wu, Y. F. (2021, September). Design of e-health system for heart rate and lung sound monitoring with AI-based analysis. In *2021 IEEE International Conference on Consumer Electronics-Taiwan (ICCE-TW)* (pp. 1-2). IEEE.

Huang, B., Ye, Y., Xu, Z., Cai, Z., He, Y., Zhong, Z., Liu, L., Chen, X., Chen, H., & Huang, B. (2021). 3D lightweight network for simultaneous registration and segmentation of organs-at-risk in CT images of head and neck cancer. *IEEE Transactions on Medical Imaging, 41*(4), 951–964. doi:10.1109/TMI.2021.3128408 PMID:34784272

Imaizumi, H., Watanabe, A., Hirano, H., Takemura, M., Kashiwagi, H., & Monobe, S. (2017, June). Hippocra: Doctor-to-doctor teledermatology consultation service towards future ai-based diagnosis system in japan. In *2017 IEEE International Conference on Consumer Electronics-Taiwan (ICCE-TW)* (pp. 51-52). IEEE. 10.1109/ICCE-China.2017.7990990

Inibhunu, C., McGregor, C., & Pugh, J. E. V. (2021, December). An alert notification subsystem for ai based clinical decision support: A protoype in nicu. In *2021 IEEE International Conference on Big Data (Big Data)* (pp. 3511-3518). IEEE. 10.1109/BigData52589.2021.9671579

Jiang, X., Xu, C., Guo, Q., & Zhu, H. (2021, October). AI-aided Data Mining in Gut Microbiome: The Road to Precision Medicine. In *2021 14th International Congress on Image and Signal Processing, BioMedical Engineering and Informatics (CISP-BMEI)*. (pp. 1-5). IEEE.

Ju, L., Wang, X., Wang, L., Mahapatra, D., Zhao, X., Zhou, Q., Liu, T., & Ge, Z. (2022). Improving medical images classification with label noise using dual-uncertainty estimation. *IEEE Transactions on Medical Imaging*, *41*(6), 1533–1546. doi:10.1109/TMI.2022.3141425 PMID:34995185

Karatekin, T., Sancak, S., Celik, G., Topcuoglu, S., Karatekin, G., Kirci, P., & Okatan, A. (2019, August). Interpretable machine learning in healthcare through generalized additive model with pairwise interactions (GA2M): Predicting severe retinopathy of prematurity. In *2019 International Conference on Deep Learning and Machine Learning in Emerging Applications (Deep-ML)* (pp. 61-66). IEEE.

Kim, B., & Lee, E. (2022, October). Medical artificial intelligence framework for the development of medical imaging artificial intelligence devices. In *2022 13th International Conference on Information and Communication Technology Convergence (ICTC)* (pp. 2210-2212). IEEE. 10.1109/ICTC55196.2022.9952625

Kumar, Y., Gupta, S., & Gupta, A. (2021, November). Study of machine and deep learning classifications for IOT enabled healthcare devices. In *2021 International Conference on Technological Advancements and Innovations (ICTAI)* (pp. 212-217). IEEE. 10.1109/ICTAI53825.2021.9673437

Liang, Z., Zhang, G., Huang, J. X., & Hu, Q. V. (2014, November). Deep learning for healthcare decision making with EMRs. In *2014 IEEE International Conference on Bioinformatics and Biomedicine (BIBM)* (pp. 556-559). IEEE. 10.1109/BIBM.2014.6999219

Liberati, A., Altman, D. G., Tetzlaff, J., Mulrow, C., Gøtzsche, P. C., Ioannidis, J. P., & Moher, D. (2009). The PRISMA statement for reporting systematic reviews and meta-analyses of studies that evaluate health care interventions: Explanation and elaboration. *Annals of Internal Medicine*, *151*(4), W-65. doi:10.7326/0003-4819-151-4-200908180-00136 PMID:19622512

Mamun, M., Farjana, A., Al Mamun, M., & Ahammed, M. S. (2022, June). Lung cancer prediction model using ensemble learning techniques and a systematic review analysis. In *2022 IEEE World AI IoT Congress (AIIoT)* (pp. 187-193). IEEE. 10.1109/AIIoT54504.2022.9817326

Mittal, P. (2023). Fusion of Machine Learning and Blockchain Techniques in IoT-based Smart Healthcare Systems. In *Deep Learning for Healthcare Decision Making* (pp. 245–266). River Publishers.

Muhammad, K., Khan, S., Del Ser, J., & De Albuquerque, V. H. C. (2020). Deep learning for multigrade brain tumor classification in smart healthcare systems: A prospective survey. *IEEE Transactions on Neural Networks and Learning Systems*, *32*(2), 507–522. doi:10.1109/TNNLS.2020.2995800 PMID:32603291

Murray, M., Macedo, M., & Glynn, C. (2019, November). Delivering health intelligence for healthcare services. In *2019 First International Conference on Digital Data Processing (DDP)* (pp. 88-91). IEEE. 10.1109/DDP.2019.00026

Nilashi, M., Ibrahim, O., Ahmadi, H., & Shahmoradi, L. (2017). A knowledge-based system for breast cancer classification using fuzzy logic method. *Telematics and Informatics, 34*(4), 133–144. doi:10.1016/j.tele.2017.01.007

Subiksha, K. P. (2018, December). Improvement in analyzing healthcare systems using deep learning architecture. In *2018 4th International Conference on Computing Communication and Automation (ICCCA)* (pp. 1-4). IEEE. 10.1109/CCAA.2018.8777545

Suzuki, K. (2017). Overview of deep learning in medical imaging. *Radiological Physics and Technology, 10*(3), 257–273. doi:10.100712194-017-0406-5 PMID:28689314

Swapna, G., Vinayakumar, R., & Soman, K. P. (2018). Diabetes detection using deep learning algorithms. *ICT express, 4*(4), 243-246.

Tran, N. D. T., Leung, C. K., Madill, E. W., & Binh, P. T. (2022, June). A deep learning based predictive model for healthcare analytics. In *2022 IEEE 10th International Conference on Healthcare Informatics (ICHI)* (pp. 547-549). IEEE.

Wang, X., Chen, H., Gan, C., Lin, H., Dou, Q., Tsougenis, E., Huang, Q., Cai, M., & Heng, P. A. (2019). Weakly supervised deep learning for whole slide lung cancer image analysis. *IEEE Transactions on Cybernetics, 50*(9), 3950–3962. doi:10.1109/TCYB.2019.2935141 PMID:31484154

Weigand, K., Witte, R., Moukabary, T., Chinyere, I., Lancaster, J., Pierce, M. K., Goldman, S., & Juneman, E. (2016). In vivo electrophysiological study of induced ventricular tachycardia in intact rat model of chronic ischemic heart failure. *IEEE Transactions on Biomedical Engineering, 64*(6), 1393–1399. doi:10.1109/TBME.2016.2605578 PMID:27608446

Wu, C. T., Wang, S. M., Su, Y. E., Hsieh, T. T., Chen, P. C., Cheng, Y. C., Tseng, T.-W., Chang, W.-S., Su, C.-S., Kuo, L.-C., Chien, J.-Y., & Lai, F. (2022). A Precision Health Service for Chronic Diseases: Development and Cohort Study Using Wearable Device, Machine Learning, and Deep Learning. *IEEE Journal of Translational Engineering in Health and Medicine, 10*, 1–14. doi:10.1109/JTEHM.2022.3207825 PMID:36199984

Zheng, L., Guo, S., & Kawanishi, M. (2022). Magnetically Controlled Multifunctional Capsule Robot for Dual-Drug Delivery. *IEEE Systems Journal, 16*(4), 6413–6424. doi:10.1109/JSYST.2022.3145869

Chapter 6
Advances in Artificial Intelligence for Image Processing:
Techniques, Applications, and Optimization

Sampath Boopathi
 https://orcid.org/0000-0002-2065-6539
Muthayammal Engineering College, India

Binay Kumar Pandey
 https://orcid.org/0000-0002-4041-1213
College of Technology, Govind Ballabh Pant University of Agriculture and Technology, India

Digvijay Pandey
 https://orcid.org/0000-0003-0353-174X
Department of Technical Education, India

ABSTRACT

AI has had a substantial influence on image processing, allowing cutting-edge methods and uses. The foundations of image processing are covered in this chapter, along with representation, formats, enhancement methods, and filtering. It digs into methods for machine learning, neural networks, optimization strategies, digital watermarking, picture security, cloud computing, image augmentation, and data pretreatment methods. The impact of cloud computing on platforms, performance, privacy, and security are also covered. The chapter's consideration of future trends and applications emphasises the substantial contributions that AI has made to image processing as well as the ethical and societal ramifications of this technology.

DOI: 10.4018/978-1-6684-8618-4.ch006

INTRODUCTION

AI has a huge influence on image processing by providing cutting-edge techniques and applications. The basics of image processing, representation, formats, enhancement techniques, filtering, machine learning, neural networks, optimization techniques, digital watermarking, picture security, cloud computing, image augmentation, and data pretreatment are covered in this chapter. It also talks about how platforms, performance, privacy, and security are affected by cloud computing. Future developments and applications will demonstrate the important advances AI has achieved in image processing while simultaneously tackling moral and societal issues(Anitha et al., 2023; Reddy et al., 2023). An important development in image processing is deep learning, a subfield of AI that makes use of artificial neural networks. Convolutional Neural Networks (CNNs) have demonstrated effectiveness in a variety of tasks, including segmentation, object recognition, and image categorization. These deep learning architectures achieve excellent generalisation and accuracy levels by extracting key features from raw visual input(Alam et al., 2022).

A generator and discriminator neural network are combined to create GANs, which are AI image processing methods. They have important uses in a variety of fields, including healthcare, where they enhance diagnostic accuracy, early sickness detection, and customised treatment plans. In dermatology, pathology, and radiology, AI has also excelled in identifying abnormalities, diseases, and medical professionals. Robots are now able to recognise and evaluate visual information like humans thanks to AI in image processing(Janardhana, Anushkannan, et al., 2023; Jeevanantham et al., 2023; Selvakumar et al., 2023). AI algorithms are used by autonomous vehicles for safe navigation, and surveillance systems monitor activity and boost safety. The entertainment industry has benefited from AI's expansion of creativity by making content production, video editing, and special effects possible. In order to increase the efficacy and efficiency of algorithms, optimization is essential in AI image processing. Optimizing the training and inference procedures is crucial as the complexity of deep learning models rises. Deep neural network training is accelerated by methods including parallel computing, distributed learning, and hardware acceleration, enabling the deployment of real-time applications on devices with limited resources(Letourneau-Guillon et al., 2020; Malik et al., 2018).

The utilisation of computational resources like memory and energy efficiently is necessary for improved AI algorithms for processing images. Model compression techniques like pruning, quantization, and knowledge distillation reduce the size of deep learning models and the amount of compute required without significantly reducing performance. The deployment of AI-powered image processing apps on a variety of platforms, including edge devices and cloud-based infrastructure, is made possible by these optimization approaches(Khokhar et al., 2015).

AI has had a big influence on image processing thanks to cutting-edge methods like deep learning, CNNs, and GANs. These methods allow for the creation of hierarchical representations from data, which makes them advantageous for usage in fields including surveillance, self-driving cars, healthcare, and transportation. AI image processing techniques have improved, allowing for real-time applications and deployment on limited devices(A. Mohanty, Jothi, et al., 2023; Rahamathunnisa et al., 2023; Samikannu et al., 2023). This article will highlight recent developments and their effects on the area of image processing by concentrating on particular approaches, applications, and optimization techniques. The creation of intelligent systems that can carry out activities that need human intelligence is known as artificial intelligence (AI). It combines computer vision, natural language processing, and machine learning. Innovations in deep learning architectures, neural networks, and machine learning algorithms have propelled the development of AI(Baduge et al., 2022). AI has uses in a number of industries, including entertainment, banking, healthcare, and transportation. This summary offers a strong framework for comprehending the importance of AI in image processing. In fields like computer vision, medical imaging, and digital media, image processing is essential(Boopathi, Arigela, et al., 2023; A. Mohanty, Venkateswaran, et al., 2023; Senthil et al., 2023). AI significantly contributes to the automation of processes like photo processing, producing results that are quicker and more accurate(Anitha et al., 2023; Babu et al., 2023; Boopathi, Arigela, et al., 2023; Jeevanantham et al., 2023; Subha et al., 2023). Accuracy enhancements, efficiency improvements, and the capacity for handling big datasets are all advantages. Autonomous cars, facial recognition software, and image analysis in medicine are examples of practical uses. These examples show how much AI has affected image processing(Sun et al., 2019).

The chapter focuses on artificial intelligence (AI) methods and their usage in image processing, including computer vision methods, deep learning frameworks, and machine learning algorithms. It emphasises current developments and new patterns, including explainable AI, transfer learning, and GANs. Potential difficulties are also discussed in the chapter, including data privacy, interpretability, and moral issues(Babu et al., 2023; Boopathi, Khare, et al., 2023; Vennila et al., 2023). It also looks at potential study areas and future approaches, giving readers a comprehensive overview of AI in image processing that covers both present state-of-the-art methods and foreseeable futures. This thorough analysis of AI in image processing gives readers a good knowledge of its background, goals, and focus areas. They are better equipped to explore AI-based image processing and its many applications with this expertise(Abduljabbar et al., 2019).

FUNDAMENTALS OF IMAGE PROCESSING

Basics of Digital Images

Digital pictures, which are discrete representations of visual information in pixels, require an understanding of image processing. The number of pixels in the grid determines resolution, with higher resolutions offering more information. Grayscale and colour digital pictures are often used, with grayscale images having a single channel for intensity or brightness levels and colour photos having three channels for colour intensity. These channels are combined to provide a depiction in full colour(Bagheri et al., 2019).

Image Representation and Formats

There are several file formats that may be used to encode and save images, each having its own features and methods of compression. The popular file types include JPEG, PNG, BMP, and GIF. JPEG is a lossy format for natural photos that achieves excellent compression ratios by choosing which information to keep and which to delete. PNG is a lossless format used for transparency or fine detail preservation that supports both grayscale and colour pictures(Wang et al., 2020). In Windows systems, BMP is a straightforward uncompressed picture format that stores data as a series of pixels without compression. Using LZW compression, the GIF format is compressed and ideal for basic visuals and colour schemes. By storing several photos in a single file, it facilitates animation.

Image Enhancement Techniques

By adjusting a picture's attributes including brightness, contrast, sharpness, and colour balance, image enhancement techniques seek to increase the visual quality of a given image. These methods draw attention to crucial details, reduce noise, and improve the image's overall attractiveness. A typical method for improving contrast that makes use of the whole dynamic range of the image is histogram equalisation. By emphasising high-frequency components, image sharpening methods like unsharp masking and Laplacian sharpening filters improve edges and details. By adjusting colour balance and saturation, colour correction ensures that colours seem natural and consistent on various devices and in a variety of lighting situations(Berg et al., 2019). Image enhancement requires noise reduction, especially when there is little light or when the sensor sensitivity is high. Gaussian and median filters, for instance, smooth out noise while keeping crucial visual information.

Image Filtering and Restoration

For photos to be of higher quality and be useful for analysis or display, artefacts, blur, and distortions must be removed using image filtering and restoration procedures. By convolutional filtering a picture with a preset kernel, linear filters, such as Gaussian and mean filters, blur and smooth images. Non-linear filters that maintain edges and fine features while lowering noise include median and bilateral filters. Deblurring techniques estimate and reverse the blurring process to restore sharpness and clarity. They are used to treat problems like motion blur or defocus blur. Effective image processing requires a thorough understanding of digital picture principles, representation formats, and image augmentation and filtering methods. These fundamental ideas offer a strong framework for investigating sophisticated methods and applications in AI-driven image processing(Kan, 2017).

MACHINE LEARNING FOR IMAGE ANALYSIS

Introduction to Machine Learning

A critical area of artificial intelligence called machine learning (ML) creates algorithms and models that can recognise patterns and take wise judgments without explicit programming. A model is trained on a dataset that has been labelled, where input data (pictures) is linked to matching output labels (classifications or annotations). In order to generalise and make predictions on data that has not yet been observed, the model learns underlying patterns and relationships in the training data(Harikaran et al., 2023; Koshariya et al., 2023; Subha et al., 2023; Vanitha et al., 2023). ML algorithms may be divided into three categories: reinforcement learning, unsupervised learning, and supervised learning(Madabhushi & Lee, 2016).

Supervised Learning Algorithms for Image Classification

Models are trained using labelled examples in the supervised learning paradigm of machine learning, which is utilised for image classification problems. SVMs, decision trees, and random forests are a few examples of algorithms that learn decision boundaries in feature space to divide various classes. Convolutional neural networks (CNNs), in particular, have transformed picture categorization by processing grid-like input data and detecting regional patterns as well as global structures. On difficult image classification tasks, CNN architectures like AlexNet, VGGNet, and ResNet have shown state-of-the-art results(Abduljabbar et al., 2019).

Unsupervised Learning Techniques for Image Clustering

In unlabeled training data, latent patterns or structures are uncovered using unsupervised learning approaches. Unsupervised learning methods are frequently employed in image analysis to cluster comparable pictures based on visual similarity. Data is divided into groups using clustering techniques like k-means, hierarchical clustering, and Gaussian mixture models, where photos inside a cluster are more similar to one another than those in other clusters(Boopathi, 2023a; Janardhana, Singh, et al., 2023; Kavitha et al., 2023; Sathish et al., 2023). Without depending on predetermined labels or annotations, these methods facilitate the exploration and organisation of enormous picture collections.

Deep Learning Approaches for Image Recognition

Picture identification problems including object detection, image segmentation, and facial recognition have been transformed by deep learning. In these challenging challenges, deep neural networks have excelled by learning hierarchical representations from unprocessed visual input. R-CNN, YOLO, and SD are a few object identification algorithms that can locate and categorise various things in a picture. Fully Convolutional Networks (FCNs) and U-Net architectures are used in image segmentation techniques to divide pictures into semantically significant sections(Boopathi, Siva Kumar, et al., 2023; Boopathi, Venkatesan, et al., 2023; Gowri et al., 2023; Yupapin et al., 2023). Face recognition software learns discriminative representations of faces for precise face detection, recognition, and attribute analysis. Deep learning models are used to identify and validate persons based on facial traits. Learning similarity metrics for face recognition is aided by methods such as Siamese networks and deep metric learning.

Transfer Learning in Image Processing

Transfer learning is a method that uses pretraining on one task or dataset to transfer information to another task or dataset that is linked to the first. Due to the availability of extensive pretraining datasets like ImageNet, it is essential in image processing. Deep learning models that have already been trained, such as those on ImageNet, are capable of learning detailed visual representations from tagged photos and may be used as a base for a variety of image processing applications. Transfer learning enables faster convergence and enhanced performance on target tasks by reusing and optimising these models. Feature extraction, where the convolutional layers of the pretrained model are employed as fixed feature extractors, and fine-tuning, where both convolutional and classifier layers are tweaked on the target task, are two ways to implement transfer learning. As a result, the model may take use of the general information gathered during pretraining while also adapting to the target task's unique properties(Berg et al., 2019; Kan, 2017).

Finally, by enabling image categorization, grouping, identification, and other difficult tasks, machine learning techniques have significantly enhanced image analysis tasks. These techniques consist of deep learning, unsupervised learning, and supervised learning. Transfer learning has improved performance on specific image processing applications by utilising pretrained models.

NEURAL NETWORKS IN IMAGE PROCESSING

The applications of neural networks in image processing are shown in Figure 1.

Basics of Neural Networks

Modern image processing and analysis need neural networks, which were inspired by the structure and operation of the human brain. These computational models are made up of artificial neurons that are linked to one another and carry out calculations and generate results. The artificial neuron, which performs a nonlinear transformation on a weighted sum of inputs, is the fundamental component of a neural network(Boopathi, 2023b; Harikaran et al., 2023; Jeevanantham et al., 2023; Rahamathunnisa et al., 2023). With the help of training, neural networks may learn intricate mappings between inputs and outputs, empowering them to anticipate the future and carry out tasks like image analysis(Baduge et al., 2022; Madabhushi & Lee, 2016; Sun et al., 2019).

Convolutional Neural Networks (CNN) for Image Analysis

By using spatial linkages and local patterns in pictures, CNNs revolutionise image analysis. They are made up of convolutional layers, pooling layers, and fully linked layers and are designed for input data with a grid-like structure. Convolutional layers capture regional patterns like edges, corners, and textures by using filters or kernels to extract features at various spatial positions.

By downsampling the features' spatial dimensions, pooling layers aid in the extraction of the most pertinent data while lowering the computing burden. Max and average pooling are two common pooling procedures. Each layer's neurons are linked by fully connected layers, which allow a network to learn high-level representations and generate predictions. Large labelled datasets are used to train CNNs, while backpropagation and gradient descent are used to maximise performance. Using the learnt network, tasks like image

Recurrent Neural Networks (RNN) for Image Sequence Analysis

Recurrent neural networks (RNNs) are useful for applications like video analysis, captioning, and picture descriptions because they are excellent for evaluating visual sequences and time-series data. RNNs may preserve data from earlier inputs thanks to connections that create loops. In order to capture temporal relationships and context in sequential data, the recurrent unit maintains an internal state that is modified based on input and prior state. RNNs have the ability to process a sequence of pictures and create output at each stage or to process the full sequence and then provide a final output. For the vanishing gradient issue and long-term dependencies, popular alternatives include Long Short-Term Memory (LSTM) and Gated Recurrent Unit (GRU)(Egmont-Petersen et al., 2002; Zhao et al., 2015).

Figure 1. Neural networks in image processing

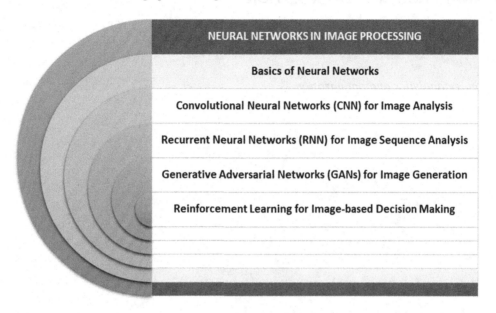

Generative Adversarial Networks (GANs) for Image Generation

Neural networks called Generative Adversarial Networks (GANs) are employed to create brand-new pictures or alter old ones. They are made up of a discriminator network and a generator network that can discriminate between created and genuine pictures while learning to create realistic images. While the discriminator seeks to accurately identify pictures, the generator and discriminator networks compete to create indistinguishable images during training(Boopathi, 2022a, 2022b; A. Mohanty, Jothi, et al., 2023; Samikannu et al., 2023). The generator strives to produce more realistic pictures as a result of this competitive process. In picture creation tasks such creating realistic faces, original artwork, high-resolution photos, image-to-image translation, and style transfer, GANs have shown amazing results(Mehdy et al., 2017).

Reinforcement Learning for Image-Based Decision Making

In order to optimise reward signals, agents might make decisions or conduct actions in an environment using the reinforcement learning (RL) paradigm. It is used in situations where agents must make decisions based on pictures or video frames in order to comprehend and interact with their surroundings. These inputs are processed by convolutional neural networks, which subsequently extract pertinent information that can be utilised to decide or control activities. Successful applications of this strategy include robotic control, autonomous driving, and game play(Ranganath et al., 1995). With CNNs excelling at extracting spatial information from pictures, RNNs for evaluating image sequences, and Generative Adversarial Networks (GANs) revolutionising image production, neural networks have considerably enhanced image processing and analysis. Reinforcement Learning (RL) promotes innovation in the area of image processing by enabling image-based decision-making in dynamic contexts.

IMAGE ANALYTICS AND OPTIMIZATION

Image Analytics and Optimization processes are illustrated in Figure 2.

Figure 2. Image analytics and optimization

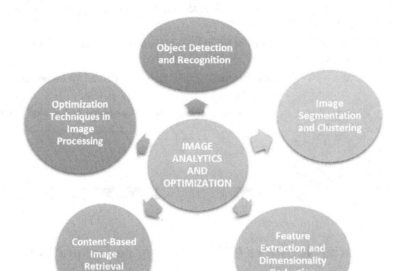

Object Detection and Recognition

Identifying and categorising things of interest within a picture is the focus of the critical image analytics tasks of object detection and recognition. In order to acquire discriminative features from labelled training data, machine learning algorithms like CNNs are frequently utilised. These characteristics may subsequently be used to find and identify objects in fresh photos. Region-based Convolutional Neural Networks (R-CNN), Faster R-CNN, and You Only Look Once are a few examples of object identification frameworks (YOLO). Assigning class labels to the objects in an image is the process of object recognition. Deep learning models, such as CNNs, are very good at learning and identifying objects from visual data because they can capture both low-level visual features and high-level semantic representations, leading to robust and accurate object recognition(Letourneau-Guillon et al., 2020; Mikołajczyk et al., 2018; Naranjo-Torres et al., 2020).

Image Segmentation and Clustering

Techniques for picture segmentation and clustering divide images into useful sections based on visual similarity. With the use of methods like thresholding, region-growing, and graph-based segmentation, pictures are divided into coherent sections. Semantic segmentation has demonstrated promising results using deep learning techniques like FCNs and U-Net. Image clustering uses methods like k-means, hierarchical clustering, and spectral clustering to group similar photos together without the need of labels. Images can be grouped according to meaningful representations that can be learned using unsupervised learning approaches, such as deep clustering algorithms(Li et al., 2018).

Feature Extraction and Dimensionality Reduction

The most useful and discriminative characteristics of pictures are captured using feature extraction and dimensionality reduction algorithms, which also try to simplify the data. Raw picture data is converted into representative features, such as texture descriptors, colour histograms, or SIFT features, through the process of feature extraction. Using both low-level and high-level characteristics, deep learning techniques like CNNs learn hierarchical representations from unstructured data. Techniques for reducing dimensionality while keeping crucial information include Principal Component Analysis (PCA), t-distributed Stochastic Neighbor Embedding (t-SNE), and autoencoders. These methods get rid of elements that are unnecessary or redundant, increase computational effectiveness, and make it easier to visualise large amounts of data(Chen et al., 2022).

Content-Based Image Retrieval

Rather than using textual annotations or metadata, Content-Based Image Retrieval (CBIR) is a technique for finding and retrieving photographs based on their visual content. CBIR systems compare and match query pictures with database images by examining visual characteristics including colour, texture, and form(Boopathi, 2019, 2021). They compare feature representations and obtain visually related photos using feature extraction methods like deep learning models or manually created descriptors, as well as similarity measurements like Euclidean distance or cosine similarity. Search engines, picture database management, and recommendation systems are just a few of the CBIR's many uses(Anderson et al., 2019; Grupac & L\uaz\uaroiu, 2022; Voyatzis et al., 1998).

Optimization Techniques in Image Processing

For image processing to be effective and produce the required results, optimization approaches are crucial. Sharpening, denoising, and contrast enhancement are examples of enhancement methods that try to maximise objective functions assessing picture quality. In image registration, where several pictures are aligned to create composites or examine temporal or spatial changes, optimization techniques are also applied. Based on similarity metrics like mutual information or cross-correlation, registration algorithms optimise the transformation parameters(Boopathi, 2022c; Chakravarthi et al., 2022; Kannan et al., 2022). For inverse issues like picture deblurring or reconstruction from sparse data, optimization is crucial. Finding the most likely option that fulfils restrictions is made easier by iterative methods and variational approaches. For extracting useful information, enhancing image quality, and facilitating effective retrieval, image analytics and optimization approaches are essential. The breakthroughs in image processing and analysis include object identification, segmentation, feature extraction, content-based picture retrieval, and optimization, with applications in computer vision, medical imaging, remote sensing, and multimedia(Anderson et al., 2019; Grupac & L\uaz\uaroiu, 2022).

DIGITAL WATERMARKING AND IMAGE PROTECTION

Introduction to Digital Watermarking

Digital watermarking incorporates strong and undetectable information into digital media for functions including content authentication, copyright protection, and tamper detection. Making embedded information resistant to image processing procedures while yet being invisible to human observers is the aim. Authorized parties must be able to recognise and remove the watermark using the proper methods(Voyatzis et al., 1998; Yuan & Hao, 2020).

Techniques for Image Watermarking

There are a variety of image watermarking techniques, each having advantages and disadvantages(Mohanarathinam et al., 2020).

- Least Significant Bit (LSB) and Spread Spectrum watermarking are examples of spatial domain watermarking, which includes embedding a watermark directly into an image's spatial domain by changing pixel values.
- Using DFT or DWT, a watermark is embedded in transformed coefficients when an image is converted into a new domain, such as frequency. These methods can withstand picture alteration better.
- Statistical watermarking alters the distribution of the picture and provides resilience against assaults by embedding watermarks like histograms or distributions in the image's attributes.
- Blind watermarking techniques are helpful when the original picture is unavailable because they extract watermarks from watermarked photos without using the original, unwatermarked image as a reference.

Robustness and Security in Image Watermarking

In picture watermarking, reliability and security are crucial. Strong watermarking techniques make sure the watermark is still able to be seen and extracted despite malicious or accidental attacks. Using encryption, digital signatures, and authentication codes, security focuses on preventing illegal removal or manipulation. Collusion assaults, in which many watermarked copies work together to erase the watermark, should also be addressed via secure systems(Arnold et al., 2003).

Copyright Protection and Authentication

For the copyright protection and verification of digital photographs, digital watermarking is essential. Copyright owners can establish ownership and prevent unlawful use by including a distinctive watermark. In the event of infringement, watermarks might include information such as copyright notices, author information, or unique identifiers. Watermark extraction and comparison with the original reference are the two steps that watermark authentication systems take to confirm the legitimacy and integrity of a picture. These methods protect intellectual property rights, guarantee the accuracy of the material, and allow for the safe distribution and use of digital photographs(S. P. Mohanty, 1999; Xuehua, 2010).

CLOUD COMPUTING FOR IMAGE PROCESSING

Introduction to Cloud Computing

By enabling scalable, on-demand access to computer resources through the internet, cloud computing revolutionises data processing and storage. For image processing workloads demanding computing power and storage capacity, it provides a versatile and affordable option. It is appropriate for a variety of image processing applications because the cloud architecture, which is offloaded to distant servers, provides a wide range of services, including virtual machines, storage, and specialised tools(Guo et al., 2010; Yan & Huang, 2014).

Cloud-Based Image Processing Platforms

With pre-built algorithms, libraries, and frameworks, cloud-based image processing platforms offer tools and services for image analysis and modification while streamlining the creation and deployment of applications. AWS, Google Cloud Platform, and Microsoft Azure are examples of well-known platforms. By offering APIs and SDKs for developers to include image processing capabilities into their applications, these platforms make it possible to upload, process, and store massive numbers of photos efficiently while requiring less infrastructure setup and upkeep(Ferzli & Khalife, 2011; Yan & Huang, 2014).

Scalability and Performance Considerations

For activities involving image processing, cloud computing offers outstanding scalability, enabling dynamic resource allocation in response to demand. When processing huge datasets or during peak periods, features like load balancing and auto-scaling enable effective completion. Network latency, data transfer rates, and cloud infrastructure capabilities are all factors that affect performance. Cloud areas that are near together geographically reduce latency and speed up processing. The efficiency of image processing jobs may be improved by choosing cloud instances with enough processing capacity and by leveraging distributed processing frameworks like Apache Spark or Hadoop(Kagadis et al., 2013; Xu et al., 2020).

Privacy and Security in Cloud-Based Image Processing

When processing private and sensitive photographic data in the cloud, privacy and security are essential. The security measures used by cloud service providers range from encryption to access control systems to routine audits. While data is being sent or stored, it is protected using encryption techniques like TLS and data encryption at rest, while access control technologies like RBAC and IAM let users specify precise access permissions. However, users are responsible for managing their own security procedures, which may include defining access limits, upgrading frameworks and software, and using secure coding techniques. Protecting the privacy of picture data requires knowing the terms and conditions of the cloud service provider and making sure that all legal requirements are met. To sum up, cloud computing provides an effective and adaptable platform for image processing activities, but privacy and security issues must constantly be taken into account to safeguard sensitive data and guarantee compliance with privacy laws.

IMAGE AUGMENTATION AND DATA PREPROCESSING

Data Augmentation Techniques for Image Data

By adding modifications to existing photos, the data augmentation approach in image processing and computer vision artificially increases the training dataset. This broadens variety and variability and enhances the resilience and generalisation of trained models(Tang et al., 2020; Tasci et al., 2021). Image data may be enhanced using a variety of methods, such as:

Through rotation, translation, scaling, flipping, and shearing operations, geometric transformations change the physical characteristics of a picture without changing its semantic information.

Brightness, contrast, saturation, and channel shifting adjustments are used in colour transformations to change the colour attributes of a picture.

By modelling fluctuations using Gaussian or salt-and-pepper noise, noise augmentation increases a model's tolerance to real-world variances.

Images can take on different viewpoints and scales thanks to cropping and resizing processes, which remove picture portions and change spatial resolution.

A broad and representative dataset for machine learning models is produced using augmentation techniques, which supplement the training dataset with several versions of the original pictures.

Image Pre-Processing for Deep Learning

- By standardising and normalising input pictures, image preprocessing improves the performance and training appropriateness of deep learning models. Typical preprocessing procedures include:
- By guaranteeing that all input photos have the same proportions, rescaling images to a set resolution assures uniform dimensions and streamlines the training process.
- By ensuring uniform pixel values across pictures, normalisation eliminates bias and improves model learning by eradicating disparities in pixel ranges.
- By removing the mean pixel values from each pixel, mean subtraction decreases illumination variability and centres data around zero.
- Before being employed in deep learning models, images are transformed to tensors or arrays to provide efficient computation and representation in formats like JPEG or PNG.

Data Imbalance and Sampling Techniques

When various classes in a dataset have uneven samples, biassed models result, which is known as data imbalance. Different sampling approaches might be used during training to increase performance on minority classes to overcome this issue(Minh et al., 2018).

- Through random duplication or more sophisticated methods like the Synthetic Minority Oversampling Technique (SMOTE), which creates synthetic samples based on existing minority samples, oversampling evens out class distribution by repeating minority cases.
- By deleting samples at random or using strategies like cluster-based undersampling, undersampling evens out the distribution of the classes by lowering the number of instances from the dominant class.

- When training a model, class weighting applies varying weights to samples from various classes, emphasising on minority samples for more sensitive representation.
- By representing each class in a balanced training set in accordance with its original distribution, stratified sampling preserves original class ratios and balances training sets.

Techniques for enhancing data address concerns with data imbalance, allowing models to successfully learn from all classes and enhance performance on minority classes. Rescaling, normalisation, and mean subtraction are examples of image preprocessing techniques that guarantee standardised input for deep learning models. Techniques include oversampling, undersampling, class weighting, and stratified sampling reduce data imbalance, ensuring that picture data is properly enhanced and prepared for reliable machine learning models.

REAL-TIME CASE STUDY: PACKING IN THE INDUSTRY

For items to be safely wrapped for storage, delivery, or sale, the packing process is essential in sectors like manufacturing and logistics. Efficiency, accuracy, and cost reductions have all increased thanks to AI and image processing tools. Automated packaging systems, including conveyor belts or robotic arms, are designed to place items within containers appropriately, making the most of available space and reducing risk of damage while being transported(Egmont-Petersen et al., 2002; S. P. Mohanty, 1999; Xuehua, 2010).

In order to create an ideal packaging strategy that reduces empty space and avoids collisions, AI algorithms evaluate 3D point cloud data to identify product size, shape, and orientation. As new goods or container space changes, these algorithms may be dynamically changed. The ideal packing arrangement is determined by advanced optimization algorithms that take into account the size, weight, fragility, and industry-specific limitations of the product. Packing systems may achieve high efficiency, lower packaging waste, and boost total output by merging AI and optimization methodologies.

By examining container photos to find flaws, irregularities, and missing products, artificial intelligence (AI) assists in quality control throughout the packing process. This makes it possible for fast feedback and remedial measures, ensuring that only containers that have been correctly packed are sent for additional processing or transportation(Boopathi, Khare, et al., 2023; Kumara et al., 2023; A. Mohanty, Venkateswaran, et al., 2023; Vennila et al., 2023).

The packaging business may profit greatly from AI and image processing thanks to increased productivity, better space use, and higher-quality products. Industries may obtain effective, precise, and affordable packaging solutions with the use of cutting-edge algorithms and real-time data analysis, increasing production and customer satisfaction. This real-world case study shows how AI and image processing may be used to improve product quality while streamlining the packing process and lowering manual labour and human error.

Real-Time Case Study: AI for Image Processing in the Medical Field

Medical picture analysis and interpretation have been greatly enhanced by AI and image processing approaches. The use of AI algorithms to analyse different medical pictures, including X-rays, CT scans, MRI scans, ultrasound images, and histopathology slides, is highlighted in this real-time case study.

These pictures include important diagnostic information, but their proper and effective interpretation might be difficult. Convolutional neural networks (CNNs) and generative adversarial networks (GANs), which have been trained on sizable datasets of labelled medical images to learn patterns, features, and abnormalities associated with various diseases or conditions, are two deep learning techniques commonly used to implement AI algorithms(Abduljabbar et al., 2019; Berg et al., 2019; Sun et al., 2019; Tasci et al., 2021).

For tasks like picture segmentation, object identification, classification, and anomaly detection, AI models are trained. In medical pictures, they can identify malignant tumours and segment anatomical parts for surgical planning. With the use of ground truth annotations from qualified radiologists or pathologists, these models are polished and verified.

AI has completely changed how medical image processing is done, leading to increased precision, effectiveness, speedier diagnosis, and better identification of minor problems. With the help of these algorithms, radiologists and pathologists may spot probable irregularities and use the information to diagnose and detect diseases. Additionally, real-time analysis of medical pictures speeds up prompt actions, especially in urgent situations, and decreases patient wait times. Additionally, AI systems are able to spot tiny patterns or anomalies, increasing diagnostic sensitivity, enabling the early diagnosis of diseases and improving patient outcomes. Medical imaging and other patient data may be analysed by AI algorithms to offer individualised therapy suggestions that can be used to create treatment programmes that are specifically catered to each patient(Anitha et al., 2023; Babu et al., 2023; Boopathi, Arigela, et al., 2023; Jeevanantham et al., 2023; Subha et al., 2023). Another advantage of AI algorithms is augmented decision support, which offers extra information and suggestions based on medical picture analysis, lowering diagnostic mistakes and boosting confidence in treatment choices.

Validation, regulatory compliance, and interaction with clinical procedures are all necessary for AI used for image processing in the medical sector. Deep learning algorithms have the capacity to analyse and interpret medical pictures, as shown by successful case studies and current research. Accuracy, effectiveness, and tailored treatment are all improved by training AI models on massive datasets. This leads to enhanced decision support for healthcare workers, quicker treatment planning, and increased diagnostic capabilities, all of which improve patient outcomes.

FUTURE TRENDS AND APPLICATIONS

Advances in Artificial Intelligence and Image Processing

- With several trends and technologies influencing the future of AI in image processing, these fields are continuously growing.
- Classification, object recognition, and segmentation are just a few of the jobs in image processing that have been transformed by deep learning approaches, particularly convolutional neural networks. Accuracy and efficiency will be improved by upcoming developments in architectures, model optimization, and training methods.
- Realistic picture synthesis, style transfer, and translation are made possible by generative models like GANs and VAEs. The ability to create and manipulate images will improve with time.

- For AI systems to gain public trust, explainable AI is essential. Future research should concentrate on creating AI image processing systems that enable users to comprehend and interpret choices, particularly in autonomous cars and medical imaging.
- By allowing collaborative training on dispersed data without raw pictures and protecting privacy while gaining from common knowledge, federated learning allays privacy concerns. The scalability and efficiency of large-scale image processing operations will be improved by future developments.

Emerging Applications of AI in Image Processing

AI in image processing has a wide range of uses(Alam et al., 2022; Letourneau-Guillon et al., 2020).

- Medical imaging is being revolutionised by AI-powered image processing, which helps radiologists identify irregularities, diagnose illnesses, and create customised treatment plans. Additionally, it helps in pathology analysis, patient outcome monitoring, and surgery planning.
- Algorithms for image processing and computer vision are essential for autonomous cars to see and comprehend their environment. In order to provide safe and dependable driving, AI approaches help in the recognition of objects, lanes, traffic signs, and pedestrians.
- By efficiently extracting large-scale satellite imagery, AI-based image analysis supports remote sensing and earth observation by observing environmental changes, tracking deforestation, forecasting natural disasters, and evaluating ecosystem health.
- AI-powered image analysis improves video surveillance, face recognition, anomaly detection, real-time monitoring, threat detection, and suspicious behaviour identification to increase security in public areas, airports, and key infrastructure.
- By fusing virtual material with actual settings and enhancing picture identification, tracking, and scene comprehension, AI approaches in AR and VR applications improve immersive experiences.

Ethical and Social Implications of AI in Image Processing

- Ethics and societal issues are raised by the use of AI in picture processing.
- Image processing by AI systems raises privacy issues, necessitating careful handling and security of sensitive data. To solve these issues, it is imperative that laws and regulations are clear.
- Biases in training data affect image processing models, potentially leading to prejudice and biassed results. Fair representation must be ensured, and biases must be reduced in training data, algorithms, and decision-making procedures.
- AI systems must be responsible, transparent, and give users visibility into choices and processes. Ethics standards and laws encourage ethical AI use by encouraging openness and transparency.

Industry employment may be impacted by AI-assisted image processing jobs, necessitating measures for workforce upskilling and reskilling for new positions and possibilities. To avoid stereotypes, objectionable material, and harmful representations in AI systems, image processing algorithms must respect cultural diversity and societal standards. AI developments in image processing need to be used responsibly and advantageously for society's growth, which calls for ethical and social concerns(Boopathi, n.d.; Koshariya, 2023; Palaniappan et al., 2023; Rahamathunnisa, 2023; Reddy et al., 2023; Sampath et al.,

2022; Selvakumar et al., 2023; Senthil et al., 2023). The development of artificial intelligence in image processing will be influenced by new applications, moral considerations, and responsible AI use. Innovative solutions may be created by sensibly utilising AI's capabilities, helping to build a better future.

CONCLUSION

The basic ideas, methods, and uses of artificial intelligence in image processing are examined in this paper. The fundamentals of digital pictures, image representation, formats, and methods for enhancing, filtering, and restoring images are all covered. The role of artificial intelligence (AI) techniques, neural networks, image analytics, optimization, digital watermarking, cloud computing, image augmentation, and data pretreatment are also covered in the book chapter. Additionally, it covers data augmentation strategies, privacy and security issues, and the advantages of cloud computing for image processing. The work also covers emergent applications, future developments in image processing, as well as the moral and societal ramifications of using AI for image processing. The article offers a thorough introduction of the many facets of image processing and its applications in general.

The ability to do sophisticated analysis, automation, and decision-making has substantially changed image processing. Future research and development will focus on advancing AI, integrating it with cutting-edge technologies like augmented reality, virtual reality, and the internet of things (IoT), fostering interdisciplinary collaboration between experts in image processing, computer vision, machine learning, and domain-specific fields, ensuring ethical and responsible AI use, and deploying it in the real world. To transform research into usable applications, these breakthroughs will need thorough validation, exacting testing, and deployment in real-world circumstances, necessitating tight cooperation between academics, industry, and policymakers.

Image processing is being revolutionised by artificial intelligence, which has enormous promise across a variety of industries. Intelligent picture processing will play a significant part in determining our future if we use AI properly and ethically. By doing so, we may open up new opportunities, handle difficult problems, and shape this future.

ABBREVIATIONS

AI - Artificial Intelligence
CNN - Convolutional Neural Network
RNN - Recurrent Neural Network
GAN - Generative Adversarial Network
ML - Machine Learning
DL - Deep Learning
OCR - Optical Character Recognition
ROI - Region of Interest
FPS - Frames Per Second
GPU - Graphics Processing Unit
CPU - Central Processing Unit
SVM - Support Vector Machine

PCA - Principal Component Analysis
IoU - Intersection over Union
API - Application Programming Interface
AR - Augmented Reality
VR - Virtual Reality
NMS - Non-Maximum Suppression
SGD - Stochastic Gradient Descent
ANN - Artificial Neural Network

REFERENCES

Abduljabbar, R., Dia, H., Liyanage, S., & Bagloee, S. A. (2019). Applications of artificial intelligence in transport: An overview. *Sustainability (Basel)*, *11*(1), 189. doi:10.3390u11010189

Alam, G., Ihsanullah, I., Naushad, M., & Sillanpää, M. (2022). Applications of artificial intelligence in water treatment for optimization and automation of adsorption processes: Recent advances and prospects. *Chemical Engineering Journal*, *427*, 130011. doi:10.1016/j.cej.2021.130011

Anderson, M. R., Cafarella, M., Ros, G., & Wenisch, T. F. (2019). Physical representation-based predicate optimization for a visual analytics database. *2019 IEEE 35th International Conference on Data Engineering (ICDE)*, (pp. 1466–1477). IEEE.

Anitha, C., Komala, C. R., Vivekanand, C. V., Lalitha, S. D., Boopathi, S., & Revathi, R. (2023, February). Artificial Intelligence driven security model for Internet of Medical Things (IoMT). *Proceedings of 2023 3rd International Conference on Innovative Practices in Technology and Management, ICIPTM 2023*. IEEE. 10.1109/ICIPTM57143.2023.10117713

Arnold, M., Schmucker, M., & Wolthusen, S. D. (2003). *Techniques and applications of digital watermarking and content protection*. Artech House.

Babu, B. S., Kamalakannan, J., Meenatchi, N., M, S. K. S., S, K., & Boopathi, S. (2023). Economic impacts and reliability evaluation of battery by adopting Electric Vehicle. *IEEE Explore*, 1–6. doi:10.1109/ICPECTS56089.2022.10046786

Baduge, S. K., Thilakarathna, S., Perera, J. S., Arashpour, M., Sharafi, P., Teodosio, B., Shringi, A., & Mendis, P. (2022). Artificial intelligence and smart vision for building and construction 4.0: Machine and deep learning methods and applications. *Automation in Construction*, *141*, 104440. doi:10.1016/j.autcon.2022.104440

Bagheri, M., Akbari, A., & Mirbagheri, S. A. (2019). Advanced control of membrane fouling in filtration systems using artificial intelligence and machine learning techniques: A critical review. *Process Safety and Environmental Protection*, *123*, 229–252. doi:10.1016/j.psep.2019.01.013

Berg, S., Kutra, D., Kroeger, T., Straehle, C. N., Kausler, B. X., Haubold, C., Schiegg, M., Ales, J., Beier, T., Rudy, M., Eren, K., Cervantes, J. I., Xu, B., Beuttenmueller, F., Wolny, A., Zhang, C., Koethe, U., Hamprecht, F. A., & Kreshuk, A. (2019). Ilastik: Interactive machine learning for (bio) image analysis. *Nature Methods*, *16*(12), 1226–1232. doi:10.103841592-019-0582-9 PMID:31570887

Boopathi, S. (2019). Experimental investigation and parameter analysis of LPG refrigeration system using Taguchi method. *SN Applied Sciences*, *1*(8), 892. doi:10.100742452-019-0925-2

Boopathi, S. (2021). Improving of Green Sand-Mould Quality using Taguchi Technique. *Journal of Engineering Research*. doi:10.36909/jer.14079

Boopathi, S. (2022a). An investigation on gas emission concentration and relative emission rate of the near-dry wire-cut electrical discharge machining process. *Environmental Science and Pollution Research International*, *29*(57), 86237–86246. doi:10.100711356-021-17658-1 PMID:34837614

Boopathi, S. (2022b). Cryogenically treated and untreated stainless steel grade 317 in sustainable wire electrical discharge machining process: A comparative study. *Environmental Science and Pollution Research International*, 1–10. doi:10.100711356-022-22843-x PMID:36057706

Boopathi, S. (2022c). Experimental investigation and multi-objective optimization of cryogenic Friction-stir-welding of AA2014 and AZ31B alloys using MOORA technique. *Materials Today. Communications*, *33*, 104937. doi:10.1016/j.mtcomm.2022.104937

Boopathi, S. (2023a). An Investigation on Friction Stir Processing of Aluminum Alloy-Boron Carbide Surface Composite. In *Materials Horizons: From Nature to Nanomaterials* (pp. 249–257). Springer. doi:10.1007/978-981-19-7146-4_14

Boopathi, S. (2023b). *Impact analysis of ceramic tile powder aggregates on self-compacting concrete.* Engineering Research Express.

Boopathi, S. (n.d.). Deep Learning Techniques Applied for Automatic Sentence Generation. IGI Global. doi:10.4018/978-1-6684-3632-5.ch016

Boopathi, S., Arigela, S. H., Raman, R., Indhumathi, C., Kavitha, V., & Bhatt, B. C. (2023). Prominent Rule Control-based Internet of Things: Poultry Farm Management System. *IEEE Explore*, 1–6. doi:10.1109/ICPECTS56089.2022.10047039

Boopathi, S., Khare, R., Jaya Christiyan, K. G., Muni, T. V., & Khare, S. (2023). Additive Manufacturing Developments in the Medical Engineering Field. In Development, Properties, and Industrial Applications of 3D Printed Polymer Composites (pp. 86–106). IGI Global. doi:10.4018/978-1-6684-6009-2.ch006

Boopathi, S., Siva Kumar, P. K., & Meena, R. S. J., S. I., P., S. K., & Sudhakar, M. (2023). Sustainable Developments of Modern Soil-Less Agro-Cultivation Systems. In Human Agro-Energy Optimization for Business and Industry (pp. 69–87). IGI Global. doi:10.4018/978-1-6684-4118-3.ch004

Boopathi, S., Venkatesan, G., & Anton Savio Lewise, K. (2023). Mechanical Properties Analysis of Kenaf–Grewia–Hair Fiber-Reinforced Composite. In *Lecture Notes in Mechanical Engineering* (pp. 101–110). Springer. doi:10.1007/978-981-16-9057-0_11

Chakravarthi, P. K., Yuvaraj, D., & Venkataramanan, V. (2022). IoT-based smart energy meter for smart grids. *ICDCS 2022 - 2022 6th International Conference on Devices, Circuits and Systems*, (pp. 360–363). IEEE. 10.1109/ICDCS54290.2022.9780714

Chen, B., Yan, Z., & Nahrstedt, K. (2022). Context-aware image compression optimization for visual analytics offloading. *Proceedings of the 13th ACM Multimedia Systems Conference*, (pp. 27–38). ACM. 10.1145/3524273.3528178

Egmont-Petersen, M., de Ridder, D., & Handels, H. (2002). Image processing with neural networks—A review. *Pattern Recognition, 35*(10), 2279–2301. doi:10.1016/S0031-3203(01)00178-9

Ferzli, R., & Khalife, I. (2011). Mobile cloud computing educational tool for image/video processing algorithms. *2011 Digital Signal Processing and Signal Processing Education Meeting (DSP/SPE)*, (pp. 529–533). IEEE.

Gowri, N. V., Dwivedi, J. N., Krishnaveni, K., Boopathi, S., Palaniappan, M., & Medikondu, N. R. (2023). Experimental investigation and multi-objective optimization of eco-friendly near-dry electrical discharge machining of shape memory alloy using Cu/SiC/Gr composite electrode. *Environmental Science and Pollution Research International, 0123456789.* doi:10.100711356-023-26983-6 PMID:37126160

Grupac, M. (2022). Image processing computational algorithms, sensory data mining techniques, and predictive customer analytics in the metaverse economy. *Review of Contemporary Philosophy, 21*(0), 205–222. doi:10.22381/RCP21202213

Guo, W., Gong, J., Jiang, W., Liu, Y., & She, B. (2010). OpenRS-Cloud: A remote sensing image processing platform based on cloud computing environment. *Science China. Technological Sciences, 53*(S1), 221–230. doi:10.100711431-010-3234-y

Harikaran, M., Boopathi, S., Gokulakannan, S., & Poonguzhali, M. (2023). Study on the Source of E-Waste Management and Disposal Methods. In *Sustainable Approaches and Strategies for E-Waste Management and Utilization* (pp. 39–60). IGI Global. doi:10.4018/978-1-6684-7573-7.ch003

Janardhana, K., Anushkannan, N. K., Dinakaran, K. P., Puse, R. K., & Boopathi, S. (2023). *Experimental Investigation on Microhardness, Surface Roughness, and White Layer Thickness of Dry EDM.* Engineering Research Express. doi:10.1088/2631-8695/acce8f

Janardhana, K., Singh, V., Singh, S. N., Babu, T. S. R., Bano, S., & Boopathi, S. (2023). Utilization Process for Electronic Waste in Eco-Friendly Concrete: Experimental Study. In Sustainable Approaches and Strategies for E-Waste Management and Utilization (pp. 204–223). IGI Global.

Jeevanantham, Y. A., A, S., V, V., J, S. I., Boopathi, S., & Kumar, D. P. (2023). Implementation of Internet-of Things (IoT) in Soil Irrigation System. *IEEE Explore*, 1–5. doi:10.1109/ICPECTS56089.2022.10047185

Kagadis, G. C., Kloukinas, C., Moore, K., Philbin, J., Papadimitroulas, P., Alexakos, C., Nagy, P. G., Visvikis, D., & Hendee, W. R. (2013). Cloud computing in medical imaging. *Medical Physics, 40*(7), 70901. doi:10.1118/1.4811272 PMID:23822402

Kan, A. (2017). Machine learning applications in cell image analysis. *Immunology and Cell Biology, 95*(6), 525–530. doi:10.1038/icb.2017.16 PMID:28294138

Kannan, E., Trabelsi, Y., Boopathi, S., & Alagesan, S. (2022). Influences of cryogenically treated work material on near-dry wire-cut electrical discharge machining process. *Surface Topography: Metrology and Properties, 10*(1), 15027. doi:10.1088/2051-672X/ac53e1

Kavitha, C., Geetha Malini, P. S., Charan Kantumuchu, V., Manoj Kumar, N., Verma, A., & Boopathi, S. (2023). An experimental study on the hardness and wear rate of carbonitride coated stainless steel. *Materials Today: Proceedings, 74*, 595–601. doi:10.1016/j.matpr.2022.09.524

Khokhar, S., Zin, A. A. B. M., Mokhtar, A. S. B., & Pesaran, M. (2015). A comprehensive overview on signal processing and artificial intelligence techniques applications in classification of power quality disturbances. *Renewable & Sustainable Energy Reviews, 51*, 1650–1663. doi:10.1016/j.rser.2015.07.068

Koshariya, A. K. (2023). *AI-Enabled IoT and WSN-Integrated Smart.*, doi:10.4018/978-1-6684-8516-3.ch011

Koshariya, A. K., Khatoon, S., Marathe, A. M., Suba, G. M., Baral, D., & Boopathi, S. (2023). Agricultural Waste Management Systems Using Artificial Intelligence Techniques. In *AI-Enabled Social Robotics in Human Care Services* (pp. 236–258). IGI Global. doi:10.4018/978-1-6684-8171-4.ch009

Kumara, V., Mohanaprakash, T. A., Fairooz, S., Jamal, K., Babu, T., & B., S. (2023). Experimental Study on a Reliable Smart Hydroponics System. In *Human Agro-Energy Optimization for Business and Industry* (pp. 27–45). IGI Global. doi:10.4018/978-1-6684-4118-3.ch002

Letourneau-Guillon, L., Camirand, D., Guilbert, F., & Forghani, R. (2020). Artificial intelligence applications for workflow, process optimization and predictive analytics. *Neuroimaging Clinics of North America, 30*(4), e1–e15. doi:10.1016/j.nic.2020.08.008 PMID:33039002

Li, Z., Zhang, X., Müller, H., & Zhang, S. (2018). Large-scale retrieval for medical image analytics: A comprehensive review. *Medical Image Analysis, 43*, 66–84. doi:10.1016/j.media.2017.09.007 PMID:29031831

Madabhushi, A., & Lee, G. (2016). Image analysis and machine learning in digital pathology: Challenges and opportunities. *Medical Image Analysis, 33*, 170–175. doi:10.1016/j.media.2016.06.037 PMID:27423409

Malik, H., Srivastava, S., Sood, Y. R., & Ahmad, A. (2018). Applications of artificial intelligence techniques in engineering. *Sigma, 1*.

Mehdy, M. M., Ng, P. Y., Shair, E. F., Saleh, N. I., & Gomes, C. (2017). Artificial neural networks in image processing for early detection of breast cancer. *Computational and Mathematical Methods in Medicine, 2017*, 2017. doi:10.1155/2017/2610628 PMID:28473865

Mikołajczyk, T., Nowicki, K., Bustillo, A., & Pimenov, D. Y. (2018). Predicting tool life in turning operations using neural networks and image processing. *Mechanical Systems and Signal Processing, 104*, 503–513. doi:10.1016/j.ymssp.2017.11.022

Minh, T. N., Sinn, M., Lam, H. T., & Wistuba, M. (2018). *Automated image data preprocessing with deep reinforcement learning.* ArXiv Preprint ArXiv:1806.05886.

Mohanarathinam, A., Kamalraj, S., Prasanna Venkatesan, G. K. D., Ravi, R. V., & Manikandababu, C. S. (2020). Digital watermarking techniques for image security: A review. *Journal of Ambient Intelligence and Humanized Computing, 11*(8), 3221–3229. doi:10.100712652-019-01500-1

Mohanty, A., Jothi, B., Jeyasudha, J., Ranjit, P. S., Isaac, J. S., & Boopathi, S. (2023). Additive Manufacturing Using Robotic Programming. In *AI-Enabled Social Robotics in Human Care Services* (pp. 259–282). IGI Global. doi:10.4018/978-1-6684-8171-4.ch010

Mohanty, A., Venkateswaran, N., Ranjit, P. S., Tripathi, M. A., & Boopathi, S. (2023). Innovative Strategy for Profitable Automobile Industries: Working Capital Management. In Handbook of Research on Designing Sustainable Supply Chains to Achieve a Circular Economy (pp. 412–428). IGI Global.

Mohanty, S. P. (1999). Digital watermarking: A tutorial review. CSEE. Http://Www. Csee. Usf. Edu/\~{} Smohanty/Research/Reports/WMSurvey1999Mohanty. Pdf.

Naranjo-Torres, J., Mora, M., Hernández-García, R., Barrientos, R. J., Fredes, C., & Valenzuela, A. (2020). A review of convolutional neural network applied to fruit image processing. *Applied Sciences (Basel, Switzerland), 10*(10), 3443. doi:10.3390/app10103443

Palaniappan, M., Tirlangi, S., Mohamed, M. J. S., Moorthy, R. M. S., Valeti, S. V., & Boopathi, S. (2023). Fused Deposition Modelling of Polylactic Acid (PLA)-Based Polymer Composites. In Development, Properties, and Industrial Applications of 3D Printed Polymer Composites (pp. 66–85). IGI Global. doi:10.4018/978-1-6684-6009-2.ch005

Rahamathunnisa, U. (2023). *Cloud Computing Principles for Optimizing Robot Task Offloading Processes.*, doi:10.4018/978-1-6684-8171-4.ch007

Rahamathunnisa, U., Sudhakar, K., Murugan, T. K., Thivaharan, S., Rajkumar, M., & Boopathi, S. (2023). Cloud Computing Principles for Optimizing Robot Task Offloading Processes. In *AI-Enabled Social Robotics in Human Care Services* (pp. 188–211). IGI Global. doi:10.4018/978-1-6684-8171-4.ch007

Ranganath, H. S., Kuntimad, G., & Johnson, J. L. (1995). Pulse coupled neural networks for image processing. *Proceedings IEEE Southeastcon'95. Visualize the Future,* (pp. 37–43). IEEE.

Reddy, M. A., Reddy, B. M., Mukund, C. S., Venneti, K., Preethi, D. M. D., & Boopathi, S. (2023). Social Health Protection During the COVID-Pandemic Using IoT. In *The COVID-19 Pandemic and the Digitalization of Diplomacy* (pp. 204–235). IGI Global. doi:10.4018/978-1-7998-8394-4.ch009

Samikannu, R., Koshariya, A. K., Poornima, E., Ramesh, S., Kumar, A., & Boopathi, S. (2023). Sustainable Development in Modern Aquaponics Cultivation Systems Using IoT Technologies. In *Human Agro-Energy Optimization for Business and Industry* (pp. 105–127). IGI Global. doi:10.4018/978-1-6684-4118-3.ch006

Sampath, B. C. S., & Myilsamy, S. (2022). Application of TOPSIS Optimization Technique in the Micro-Machining Process. In Trends, Paradigms, and Advances in Mechatronics Engineering (pp. 162–187). IGI Global. doi:10.4018/978-1-6684-5887-7.ch009

Sathish, T., Sunagar, P., Singh, V., Boopathi, S., Al-Enizi, A. M., Pandit, B., Gupta, M., & Sehgal, S. S. (2023). Characteristics estimation of natural fibre reinforced plastic composites using deep multi-layer perceptron (MLP) technique. *Chemosphere*, *337*, 139346. doi:10.1016/j.chemosphere.2023.139346 PMID:37379988

Selvakumar, S., Adithe, S., Isaac, J. S., Pradhan, R., Venkatesh, V., & Sampath, B. (2023). A Study of the Printed Circuit Board (PCB) E-Waste Recycling Process. In Sustainable Approaches and Strategies for E-Waste Management and Utilization (pp. 159–184). IGI Global.

Senthil, T. S. R. Ohmsakthi vel, Puviyarasan, M., Babu, S. R., Surakasi, R., & Sampath, B. (2023). Industrial Robot-Integrated Fused Deposition Modelling for the 3D Printing Process. In Development, Properties, and Industrial Applications of 3D Printed Polymer Composites (pp. 188–210). IGI Global. doi:10.4018/978-1-6684-6009-2.ch011

Subha, S., Inbamalar, T. M., Komala, C. R., Suresh, L. R., Boopathi, S., & Alaskar, K. (2023, February). A Remote Health Care Monitoring system using internet of medical things (IoMT). *Proceedings of 2023 3rd International Conference on Innovative Practices in Technology and Management, ICIPTM 2023*. IEEE. 10.1109/ICIPTM57143.2023.10118103

Sun, Q., Zhang, M., & Mujumdar, A. S. (2019). Recent developments of artificial intelligence in drying of fresh food: A review. *Critical Reviews in Food Science and Nutrition*, *59*(14), 2258–2275. doi:10.10 80/10408398.2018.1446900 PMID:29493285

Tang, S., Yuan, S., & Zhu, Y. (2020). Data preprocessing techniques in convolutional neural network based on fault diagnosis towards rotating machinery. *IEEE Access: Practical Innovations, Open Solutions*, *8*, 149487–149496. doi:10.1109/ACCESS.2020.3012182

Tasci, E., Uluturk, C., & Ugur, A. (2021). A voting-based ensemble deep learning method focusing on image augmentation and preprocessing variations for tuberculosis detection. *Neural Computing & Applications*, *33*(22), 15541–15555. doi:10.100700521-021-06177-2 PMID:34121816

Vanitha, S. K. R., & Boopathi, S. (2023). Artificial Intelligence Techniques in Water Purification and Utilization. In *Human Agro-Energy Optimization for Business and Industry* (pp. 202–218). IGI Global. doi:10.4018/978-1-6684-4118-3.ch010

Vennila, T., Karuna, M. S., Srivastava, B. K., Venugopal, J., Surakasi, R., & B., S. (2023). New Strategies in Treatment and Enzymatic Processes. In *Human Agro-Energy Optimization for Business and Industry* (pp. 219–240). IGI Global. doi:10.4018/978-1-6684-4118-3.ch011

Voyatzis, G., Nikolaidis, N., & Pitas, I. (1998). Digital watermarking: An overview. *9Th European Signal Processing Conference (EUSIPCO 1998)*, (pp. 1–4). IEEE.

Wang, C.-X., Di Renzo, M., Stanczak, S., Wang, S., & Larsson, E. G. (2020). Artificial intelligence enabled wireless networking for 5G and beyond: Recent advances and future challenges. *IEEE Wireless Communications*, *27*(1), 16–23. doi:10.1109/MWC.001.1900292

Xu, Z., Cheng, C., & Sugumaran, V. (2020). Big data analytics of crime prevention and control based on image processing upon cloud computing. *J Surveill Secur Saf*, *1*, 16–33. doi:10.20517/jsss.2020.04

Xuehua, J. (2010). Digital watermarking and its application in image copyright protection. *2010 International Conference on Intelligent Computation Technology and Automation,* (vol. 2, 114–117). IEEE. 10.1109/ICICTA.2010.625

Yan, Y., & Huang, L. (2014). Large-scale image processing research cloud. *Cloud Computing*, 88–93.

Yuan, G., & Hao, Q. (2020). Digital watermarking secure scheme for remote sensing image protection. *China Communications*, *17*(4), 88–98. doi:10.23919/JCC.2020.04.009

Yupapin, P., Trabelsi, Y., Nattappan, A., & Boopathi, S. (2023). Performance Improvement of Wire-Cut Electrical Discharge Machining Process Using Cryogenically Treated Super-Conductive State of Monel-K500 Alloy. *Iranian Journal of Science and Technology. Transaction of Mechanical Engineering*, *47*(1), 267–283. doi:10.100740997-022-00513-0

Zhao, H., Gallo, O., Frosio, I., & Kautz, J. (2015). Loss functions for neural networks for image processing. *ArXiv Preprint ArXiv:1511.08861.*

Chapter 7
AI and Crime Prevention With Image and Video Analytics Using IoT

Shalini Ninoria

*College of Computing Sciences and I.T.,
Teerthanker Mahaveer University, Moradabad,
India*

Ramakant Upadhyay

Sanskriti University, Mathura, India

Reena Susan Philip

*School of Sciences, Jain University (Deemed),
India*

Richa Dwivedi

*Symbiosis Law School, Symbiosis International
University (Deemed), India*

Gabriela Micheal

*Symbiosis Law School, Symbiosis International
University (Deemed), India*

Ankur Gupta

Vaish College of Engineering, Rohtak, India

Sudha Mishra

J.K. Institute of Engineering, India

ABSTRACT

Artificial intelligence system has been frequently used for crime prevention. Image and video analytics are playing significant role during such operation. However it has become quite challenging to implement over IoT environment, with the development of artificial intelligence where the discipline of research and analysis has entered a new age. The use of video analytics, a branch of artificial intelligence that is undergoing fast advancement, is supporting law enforcement agencies in significantly reducing crime rates. Video Analytics examines video footage using algorithms to categorize a wide variety of object types and distinguish certain behaviors or activities in order to deliver real-time alerts and insights to customers. Traditional CCTV cameras are so yesterday. But there is need to reduce the time consumption and space consumption during image analytic and video analytics operations. Present work is focusing on performance enhancement during image and video analytics.

DOI: 10.4018/978-1-6684-8618-4.ch007

1. INTRODUCTION

AI solutions also enable businesses to uncover potentially worrisome patterns or links that are hidden even from the eyes of professionals. For instance, artificial neural networks may provide workers with the ability to anticipate the future steps of even unnamed criminals who have found out methods to circumvent alarm triggers in security systems that are based on binary rules. In order to do this, hundreds of photographs taken at crime scenes are uploaded into the computer and processed so that the machine learning algorithms can understand what it is they are supposed to look for. This covers the potential patterns utilised by offenders in a variety of settings, which might link all of the crimes to a single perpetrator. The use of machine learning algorithms is one of the key ways that artificial intelligence may improve the security of the internet of things.

These algorithms are able to analyse huge volumes of data produced in real time by internet of things devices, discovering patterns and abnormalities that may suggest a possible danger to network security. The Internet of Things (IoT) is responsible for collecting the data, while artificial intelligence (AI) is responsible for analysing it to mimic intelligent behaviour and assist decision-making processes with little participation from humans. The use of AI in cybersecurity removes time-consuming operations that were previously performed manually by specialists. It analyses huge amounts of data, detects possible dangers, and decreases the number of false positives by filtering out actions that are not dangerous. This allows human security specialists to concentrate their efforts on more important duties. The identification of dangers and abnormalities in the behaviour of devices, network traffic, or data patterns is one of the primary uses of artificial intelligence and machine learning in IoT security. This may assist in the detection and prevention of prospective assaults, such as denial-of-service attacks, malware infections, or data breaches.

1.1 Artificial Intelligence

The capacity of a digital computer or computer-controlled robot to mimic the cognitive abilities of a human being is known as artificial intelligence (AI). The phrase is often used to refer to the endeavour of creating systems with the reasoning, meaning discovery, generalization, and learning abilities that are uniquely human. With the advent of the digital computer in the 1940s, it has been shown that computers can be taught to do very complicated tasks, such as finding proofs for mathematical theorems or playing chess at an expert level. Although computer processing speed and memory capacity continue to improve, no programme has yet matched human adaptability across more domains or in activities requiring considerably more common knowledge than is now available. Nonetheless, artificial intelligence in its narrower meaning is used in fields as varied as medical diagnosis, computer search engines, and voice or handwriting recognition since certain programmes have reached the performance levels of human specialists and professionals in doing these specialized jobs. (Babu, S.Z.D., et al, 2022)

Facial recognition systems that are powered by artificial intelligence have begun acting more intelligently than people. This is not a brand-new field. They are somewhere in the vicinity of 60 years old. Massive computers with operating frequencies of a few MHz and memory capacities of around 20 kilobytes were being used by researchers for the purpose of face recognition. It is unknown how much the computers cost, but in those days, none of the educational institutions in the United States could have afforded them. Only IBM, as a supplier, is capable of producing it. The facial recognition technologies that are available today are powered by artificial intelligence, which enables them to detect a face with greater accuracy even in dimly light environments. In general, AI will collect a number of measures of a face, including the distance between the eyes, the distance between the eyes and the nose, the size of the temple, the form of the face, and so on. At the very least, it should be able to provide a list of 0 individuals whose faces are a match for the test picture.

Artificial intelligence is useful for detecting strange actions. actions that do not conform to a pattern in any way. For instance, the majority of us move in a predictable pattern most of the time. When we leave the house, we always go at the same predetermined time, and when we return, it's usually around the same time. Any deviation from this pattern is going to be a clear sign that something is not right. It's possible that this is not a criminal offence. It's possible that someone sick is staying at his house, which would explain his unusual pattern of motion. If he goes to a hospital, medical staff will be able to recognise him because of this. AI would be able to notice if a group of individuals who were not connected to one another in any way, whether by family or career, began gathering in the same or different locations. This cannot be accomplished by human beings. In the event that such items are found, we may begin doing more research on those 10 individuals. It is possible to get software tools that will do analysis on the inputs from social media. So that it is possible to determine whether or not these individuals adhere to the same philosophy. If this turns out to be true, you may investigate these individuals further by looking through their phone logs and even their bank accounts for any strange deposits or withdrawals of money. An investigation into any unusual movement of material in the neighbourhood of the person's place of employment or dwelling is the first step.

It is also possible to keep track of the movement of materials. If a huge package is delivered to a residential neighbourhood, this may raise suspicions, particularly if the contents do not come from a local consumer durables or furnishings business. Even while it may not be illegal conduct, it can be economic activity that is not being accounted for, which is also against the law. It is much simpler to maintain tabs on the history sheeters who are already recognised. It is possible to maintain tabs on those who are out on parole. Because of organisations like Interpol and others like it, it is possible to monitor the actions of foreign nationals whose behaviour may be suspect. This facility has the capability to track the locations of law enforcement officers and can be immediately mobilised to respond to any urgent scenario. In most cases, terrorists will go to the target location prior to carrying out an attack there, since this allows for more thorough preparation and more efficient carrying out of the operation. A thorough investigation into the criminal records of all individuals, as well as their re-gathering in any given region, would unearth a great deal of information that may be put to use to forestall the occurrence of any untoward occurrence. Therefore, preventing crime is shifting more towards becoming an activity that takes place in offices than on the streets. People are able to both prevent and investigate crimes from the comfort of their offices.

1.2 Artificial Intelligence Applications

These days, AI systems may be found in a wide variety of practical contexts. Some typical instances are shown below:

- **Speech recognition:** Using NLP, this capacity translates human voice into written form and goes by a variety of names, including ASR, computer SR, and speech-to-text. A lot of smartphones have speech recognition built in so you can do voice searches or have easier time with messaging. (Caldwell, M.,2020)

- **Customer service:** Increasingly, customers aren't dealing with actual people but rather virtual assistants that help them through the various stages of their purchase process. Answers FAQs on topics like shipping, offering personalised advice, cross-selling products, and suggesting sizes for users; this changes how we see customer participation on websites and social media. Examples include chatbots on online stores, virtual assistants, and voice assistants, and messaging programmes like Slack and Facebook Messenger.

- **Computer vision:** This kind of artificial intelligence enables computers and other systems to correctly interpret and act upon data presented to them in the form of visuals, such as digital still images, video, and other visual data. Differentiating it from picture recognition jobs is its capacity to provide suggestions. Computer vision, enabled by CNN, is used in a variety of fields, including social media picture tagging, medical imaging for diagnostics, and autonomous vehicle navigation. (Bansal R.,2021)

- **Recommendation engines:** Algorithms trained by AI may assist uncover data patterns that can be utilized to improve cross-selling techniques by analysing customers' historical purchasing habits. This is used by e-commerce sites to suggest complementary products to consumers when they check out. (Griffin, L. D., 2020)

- **Automated stock trading:** High-frequency trading systems powered by artificial intelligence are programmed to perform hundreds, if not millions, of deals each day, optimizing stock portfolios. (Gupta A.,2019)

1.3 AI for Crime Prevention

Examples of resource allocations that may be optimized with the use of artificial intelligence include scheduling of police vehicle patrols, foot patrols, alarms, & response times of emergency services and First Responders. Patterns may be (Pramanik, S., 2022) quickly detected using all-source intelligence analysis driven by AI, in ways that are not possible with conventional analytic tools, and may represent seasonal, regional, or demographic tendencies. Another use of AI for crime prevention analyses information to measure the success of crime prevention activities. Human, drug, and weapon trafficking, as well as other forms of major violent crime, have been the targets of several campaigns across the world. Crime prevention (Verma A., 2020) programmes come in many shapes and sizes, and there are so many of them that it may be difficult to tell which ones are most effective. Researchers can now go through these massive datasets with the aid of sophisticated and well-designed algorithms, providing them with reliable insights about the effectiveness of different crime prevention initiatives. These kinds of understandings are important for using AI in effective crime-prevention measures. Several deep learning classification mechanisms are used in AI for classification. (Koti K., 2021)

Cameras and video analytics fueled by AI have emerged as an additional important resource for anticipating and thwarting criminal activity. These artificial intelligence-based security solutions play an important part in automating routine administrative activities while also delivering cutting-edge analysis that is beyond the capability of humans.

When conducting video surveillance, it is common practise to examine lengthy video segments one minute at a time, or even one second at a time. It is hard for even a huge staff of people to filter the video information day in and day out due to the expanding volume of data generated by video cameras, body-worn gadgets, traffic cameras, and other IoT (Internet of things) devices. A viewer is projected to miss 95% of occurrences after just 20 minutes of viewing tape, making it more difficult to notice and recognise hazards as they occur. viewing video is tiring on human eyes, making it more difficult to spot and recognise problems as they occur.

On the other hand, video analytics may continually watch numerous video feeds at the same time, automatically identifying any illegal or strange conduct and notifying human reviewers when it identifies behaviour that is out of the ordinary when it finds behaviour that is out of the norm. This enables law enforcement to detect crimes that are currently being committed and to react proactively, so increasing the likelihood that the perpetrators will be apprehended. AI-based video analytics may be a huge power multiplier for law enforcement organisations who have restricted funds or personnel levels. This is because it is substantially less expensive than having a room full of human reviewers, regardless of whether or not they are nonsworn employees.

1.4 Crime Prevention

Throughout history, there has always been criminal activity. Everyone else we encounter acts in a way that goes against our morals. While a society may never be completely crime-free, it can always make great strides towards that goal. Crime prevention refers to the efforts of a government or community to engage in actions and policies that reduce the likelihood of crime occurring. The purpose of crime prevention is to lessen the prevalence of criminal activity in a community by using a variety of methods and implementing a number of plans and policies. The UNODC also establishes universally applicable guidelines for crime prevention at the national and international levels. It's important to use a wide range of tactics, since crime prevention may take numerous shapes (R. G., 2020). The safety and security of its citizens is one of the primary benefits of crime prevention for a society. Image processing has been used with deep learning in many research works for criminal identification in order to prevent crime (B. A., 2018). During such operation different image and video analytic operation are performed. (H. S., 2020) Application of deep learning has been used for IoT based environment for image and video analytics in different areas during video surveillance. (Gupta, A., 2022)

AI technologies have been utilised for years to minimise uncertainty and risk when managing crowds, and technology for crowd safety has grown increasingly more critical as a means of combating threats that might result in mass casualty incidents.

Crowds provide issues for public safety officials in terms of both logistics and safety, regardless of whether the event in question is a sporting event, a concert, or a public celebration. Video analytics is a key component of being able to identify and highlight 'strange' congregations of individuals close to locations where there is a very high possibility of a crowd, such as at and around a football stadium on a day when there is a game being played. High-tech sensors have also been installed in cities such as Los Angeles and Chicago in order to identify possible dangers such as firearms and explosives. The same strategies have been used at the public transport terminals located close to the Super Bowl sites.

The use of SAS streaming analytics has also been used in the public transport sector in order to collect data from a variety of Internet of Things devices and synchronise it with video feeds and audio from cameras that have various frame rates and picture quality. This composite data is then analysed using decision processes and analytics models in order to anticipate the possibility of events taking place and proactively advise steps to take in order to take preventative actions.

Because of the vast amounts of data, including video, that government agencies are now required to manage, artificial intelligence (AI) is playing an increasingly important role in maintaining public safety and preventing crime. This role is only going to become more important as technological advancements continue to be made. In the end, it will assist government agencies in saving money, time, and lives.

1.5 Basic Principles of Crime Prevention

Strategies and actions aimed at minimizing criminal activity and the repercussions it has are what make up the field of crime prevention. Effective crime prevention protects citizens from becoming victims of crime and keeps communities secure. (Pramanik, S., 2021) The expenses of enforcing the law are also reduced as a result. The UNODC is an active participant in efforts to reduce crime on a global scale. UNODC also urges its member governments to improve crime-prevention infrastructure and strategies. The United Nations Office on Drugs and Crime (UNODC) promotes policies, initiatives, and programmes that integrate society engagement as the defender of United Nations values and standards on crime prevention. Using the heading "UNODC," UN has released a series of recommendations for reducing criminal activity.

- Government Leadership

Local, state, and federal governments must work together to establish and sustain an institutional framework for the successful implementation of policies to reduce crime. (Okagbue, H., 2020).

- Socio-economic development and inclusion

Communities, families, and young people at risk should be the primary targets of efforts to integrate crime prevention into social and economic programmes such as education, health, employment, etc. (Dhabliya, D., 2022)

- Cooperation/Partnerships

In order to effectively address the root causes of crime, collaboration and coordination amongst government agencies is essential. Businesses, nonprofits, government agencies, and neighborhood groups are all examples of possible partners. (Terashima-Marín, H., 2021)

- Sustainability/Accountability

Accountability for the execution, assessment, and financing of these crime prevention measures is essential to their success. (Roychowdhury, S., 2022)

- Knowledge Base

Prevention efforts, including strategies, policies, and actions, should be grounded on extensive understanding of criminal behavior, its issues, and their root causes. (G. J. D., 2022)

- Human rights/rule of law/culture of lawfulness

The rule of law must be upheld in all areas of crime prevention and legality, and all participating states must put a priority on respect for internationally recognized human rights. (Pandey, B.K. et al, 2022)

- Interdependency

In order to properly diagnose national crime, it is necessary to consider connections between domestic & foreign criminal activity. (Pathania, V., et al, 2022)

- Differentiation

The idea of differentiation ensures that the various requirements of males, women, and vulnerable individuals are taken into account by the various crime prevention initiatives. (Pathania, V. et al., 2022)

1.6 Benefits of Crime Prevention

There are societal and individual advantages to preventing criminal activity. Even if the measures used to prevent crime are ineffective, this cannot lead to any negative consequences. The following are some of the many advantages of crime prevention (A. L., 2019):-

- Protection of the populace
- Lower occurrences of crime
- All members of the community, including government officials, have developed a stronger sense of accountability.
- Community participation for regional security.
- Costs associated with going through the legal system may be avoided, resulting in a financial savings.
- Enriches one's life and makes it better overall.

1.7 Role of AI in Video Analytics for Crime Prevention

The field of research and analysis has entered a new era with the advent of AI. The use of video analytics, a rapidly developing area of AI, is assisting law enforcement organizations in drastically lowering crime rates. In order to provide real-time warnings and insights to consumers, Video Analytics analyses video data using algorithms to classify various sorts of objects and recognize certain behaviors or actions. Conventional CCTV cameras are so yesterday. (Podoletz, L., 2022)

1.8 Need of Video Surveillance Technologies During Law Enforcement

Video analytics systems that use deep learning technology are able to identify subtleties that human eyes miss. They are able to tell persons apart based on criteria such as height, weight, and pace of movement. (Radulov, 2019) In addition to being able to detect just pedestrians carrying backpacks, the system can also search for persons based on the colour of their clothing. Using Analytics, a police officer may narrow his feed to just show him men who fit a certain description, such as a man in all white with a rucksack. If a person of interest is found in one video channel, the algorithm can find them in others. If the person's actions are visible in the feeds being analyzed, it's not hard to single him out and track his whereabouts. (Rehnström, F., 2021)

2. LITERATURE REVIEW

M. Caldwell, et al.(2020) introduced crime in the age of artificial intelligence. An analysis was done to find ways in which AI and similar technology may be used in criminal activity. The obtained data was utilized to create a rough taxonomy of illicit apps so that their relative danger could be evaluated.

J.S Hollywood, et al.(2018) reviewed boosting public safety, the panel agreed that VA/SF were very promising technologies. The greatest potential value to society may be realized if these technologies were used to detect crimes or catastrophic catastrophes in progress, identify and trace persons responsible, and ultimately detect the lead-ups to crimes or disasters before they occur. Used these technologies, notably the integration of video and biometrics sensors, has the potential to greatly enhance police personnel' well-being and safety.

R.A. Ikuesan, et al.(2020) presented work on prevention of urban crime a realistic strategy for developing countries. This research examines potential strategies that might be included into the current police paradigm in underdeveloped countries. Preliminary data from a representative sample of police officers suggests that this pragmatic approach may provide a new paradigm that might harness today's cutting-edge technologies to create a more efficient urban police force. In addition, this method provides mechanisms for increasing the efficiency of police reaction time and maximizing the use of available police personnel in underdeveloped countries.

D. Kirpichnikov, et al.(2020) reviewed the automated systems and their potential criminal liability. As AI will likely be acknowledged as a topic of legal relations in future, the author hopes to find out whether criminal culpability may be applied to AI. The author draws the following conclusion based on many analyses and real-world examples: For all intents and purposes, AI might be held criminally accountable, and it could modify its conduct in response to sanctions.

G. A. M. Mascorro, et al.(2021) did researched on 3D CNN, researchers can detect shoplifting crimes in their earliest stages. They trained a 3DCNN model to extract features from videos and evaluated it on data including examples of both everyday activities and retail theft. The results were promising since the model accurately labels suspicious behavior in majority of the examined cases. The top model developed in this study, for instance, achieves accuracy & recall values of 0.8571 & 1 in one of test situations, respectively, when categorizing suspicious behavior.

N. Nayak, et al.(2022) looked the automatic video captioning for real-time crime analysis using deep learning. To make it easier to find a specific occurrence in the log, they save these descriptions in text files with the corresponding timestamps. As we will be keeping a text file that can be secured using strong encryption techniques, this method is also more secure than archiving CCTV footage. A human supervisor was alerted with live video, still images, and alerts of criminal activity so that appropriate action may be taken.

P. O. Malley, et al.(2022) explained the ingenious methods for reduced criminal activity. By combining various "smart" technology with "public safety" initiatives, Smart City projects may increase the likelihood of disproportionately impacting people of color who are already subject to policing.

E. L. Piza, et al.(2019) focused on CCTV in the fight against crime. The research shows that the presence of CCTV is correlated with a statistically significant and slightly reduced rate of crime. Parking lots have felt CCTV's most widespread and constant impacts.

L. Podoletz, et al.(2022) discussed criminal activity and AI with feelings. This essay bridges the fields of criminal justice, police work, surveillance, and emotional AI research in order to establish a framework for understanding the myriad threats that these technologies pose, especially to liberal democracies.

Radulov, et al.(2019) looked AI with cryptocurrency: a new frontier cyber safety 4.0. The potential for AI to enhance law enforcement efforts and fortify national defence was enormous. Only the use of AI can ensure success under the current circumstances of unprecedented data buildup and the need of instant decision making. Time was a precious commodity when it comes to the intelligence, counterintelligence, forensic science, countering organised crime, rapidly processing available information, writing of different judgements, making plans and multivariate scenarios, and executing numerous analyses. Its usage is the only way to significantly shorten this window, which in turn dramatically improves the chances of discovery, prevention, and control.

F. Rehnström, et al.(2021) reviewed the potential of AI for foreseeing and stopping crime. This literature study aimed to gather together recently published studies on AI's potential in crime forecasting and prevention.

R. Socha, et al.(2020) focused on the video surveillance in urban areas to boost safety. This study examines statistical data about the usage of urban video surveillance as a technique to promote public space security in Katowice, using functioning of katowice smart surveillance & analysis system as an example.

3. CHALLENGES TO AI BASED CRIME PREVENTION SYSTEM

In order to provide real-time warnings and insights to consumers, Video Analytics analyses video footage by using algorithms to classify a broad number of object kinds, differentiate particular behaviours or activities, and categorise a variety of video content. Conventional CCTV cameras have become obsolete in recent years. Nonetheless, there is a need to cut down (Kumbhkar M., 2021) on the amount of time as well as space that is used throughout the operations of image and video analytics. At the moment, research efforts are concentrated on improving performance during image and video analytics (Shukla, A., 2022).

4. WORKING OF EFFICIENT AI BASED CRIME PREVENTION MODEL

In present criminal prevention model, both images and videos are considered for analytics and to make decision regarding criminal activity. Images are preprocessed by compression before training. Deep learning model are used to make training so that any criminal activity could be detected. A CNN based deep learning model is built to make training for further testing.

There are different mechanisms that are used for deep learning that are used to training the images after capturing video by surveillance system. (Kogut, B., 2020) such system play significant role in detection criminals in real word through IoT based system. Here such (K. A., 2019) system play significant role in meta-verse application running on IoT also. Their comparison (Sung, C. S., 2021) has been shown below:

Figure 1. Process flow of image and video analytics using IoT for crime prevention

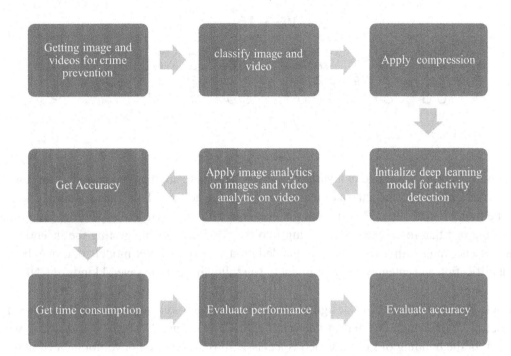

Utilising an intelligent CNN and basing it on an enhanced face picture dataset makes it possible to successfully extract the features of faces and achieve higher levels of accuracy when it comes to face recognition. This is made possible by the fact that it is viable to do so. In the ongoing research project, a CNN model is being used in order to make face recognition for the attendance system. The model is able to learn information about the location and proportion of faces inside a picture as a direct result of this, and it is able to do so very quickly. Convolutional neural networks may be used to process visual data, which might possibly result in considerable gains. Artificial neural networks, including the subgroup of artificial neural networks known as convolutional neural networks (CNNs), were designed specifically for the purpose of managing pixel input throughout the image recognition and processing stages. For each

Table 1. Comparison of ANN, CNN, and RNN

	ANN	CNN	RNN
Data type	Textual data	Image data	Sequence data
Feature type: spatial recognition	No	Yes	No
Feature type: Recurrent connections	No	No	Yes
Drawback	Hardware dependency	Large training data	Slow and complex training
Uses	Predictive analysis	Image recognition and classification	Natural language processing by sentiment analysis

Figure 2. Architecture of VGG16 model

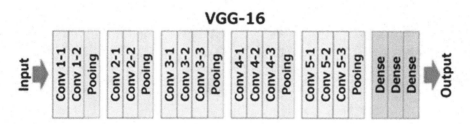

layer, one may acquire knowledge of a variety of filters, and there are many to choose from. Each filter is taught to recognise a certain pattern or feature that is unique to that filter. These patterns and features can only be found in that filter. This filter is the only one with these particular patterns and properties. In spite of the fact that researchers are looking into the possibility of integrating the inception model with the densenet model, this section has expanded on a variety of CNN models that may be utilised for the identification and categorization of images. The following are the several kinds of CNN models:

1. **LeNet:** Not only is the LeNet design of CNN the most well-known, but it was also the very first model of CNN, which debuted in the year 1998. CNN originally began broadcasting with this model. In the building of LeNet, which is a classic illustration of a convolutional neural network, all convolutions, pooling, and fully connected layers were used at some point throughout the process. The use of the MNIST dataset was necessary for the task of handwritten digit recognition that was being carried out. The structural layout served as a point of departure for the building of future networks like AlexNet and VGG, all of which were inspired by the original design.
2. **VGGNET:** It is possible to import a 16-layer convolutional neural network (VGG-16), which has already been trained on more than a million photos taken from the ImageNet database. This kind of network is seen in Figure 4.
3. **AlexNet:** AlexNet is a leading architecture for any object-detection job and may have large applications in the computer vision sector of artificial intelligence challenges. AlexNet was developed by Alex Krizhevsky at Stanford University.
4. **ResNet:** The term "ResNet," which is an acronym for the phrase "Residual Networks," refers to a typical neural network that serves as the foundation for a broad range of applications that are classified as being under the heading of computer vision. The phrase "Residual Networks" is an abbreviation for the phrase "Residual Networks."
5. **DenseNet's** levels communicate with the layers below them, making it a convolutional neural network. DenseNet's first layer, for instance, communicates with its subsequent layers.
6. **Inception:** Inception V3 is a convolutional neural network used in image processing and object identification. It was originally designed as a module for Googlenet. Since its first presentation at the 2016 ImageNet Recognition Challenge, Google's Inception Convolutional Neural Network has undergone two significant revisions.

Figure 3. ResNet50 model architecture

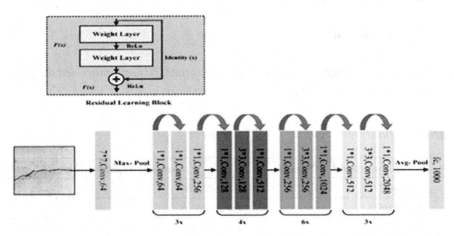

Figure 4. DenseNet architecture

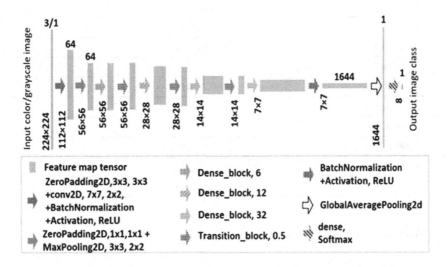

Figure 5. Architecture of Inception V3

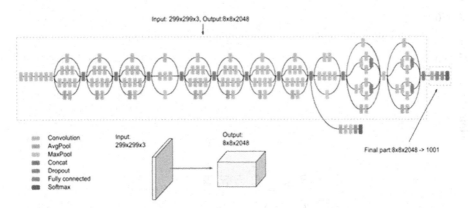

5. RESULT AND DISCUSSION

5.1 Performance Evaluation

Comparison chart for time consumption in case of conventional CNN and proposed deep learning classification scheme has been shown in following table

Table 2. Comparison of time consumption

No of images	Conventional CNN model	Proposed compression based CNN model
10	30.44849232	19.8456069
20	60.45505634	43.53561389
30	90.5848734	76.60173984
40	120.6614529	104.0797413
50	150.8539505	136.2430227
60	180.2531093	161.9467876
70	210.3357086	204.6978585
80	240.2304331	225.8383625
90	270.6014351	262.3375246
100	300.731071	293.2594518
110	330.5888581	322.8623231
120	360.3135939	343.1113562
130	390.4128286	373.9322655
140	420.6151359	408.2975828
150	450.0529403	431.8732932

Figure 6. Comparison of time consumption

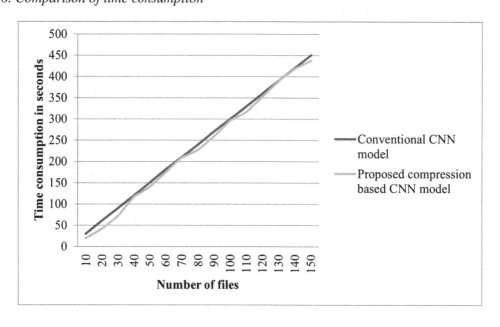

108

5.2 Accuracy Evaluation

Table 3. Confusion matrix for conventional model

	Face Detected	Face Not Detected
Face Detected	881	119
Face not Detected	121	879

Results
TP: 1760
Overall Accuracy: 88%

Table 4. Accuracy parameter for conventional model

Class	n (truth)	n (classified)	Accuracy	Precision	Recall	F1 Score
1	1002	1000	88%	0.88	0.88	0.88
2	998	1000	88%	0.88	0.88	0.88

5.2 Confusion Matrix Proposed Work

Table 5. Confusion matrix for proposed work

	Mask Detected	Mask Not Detected
Mask Detected	911	89
Mask not Detected	74	926

Results
TP: 1837
Overall Accuracy: 91.85%

Table 6. Accuracy parameter for proposed work

Class	n (truth)	n (classified)	Accuracy	Precision	Recall	F1 Score
1	985	1000	91.85%	0.91	0.92	0.92
2	1015	1000	91.85%	0.93	0.91	0.92

5.3 Comparison of Accuracy Parameters

1. Accuracy

Table 7. Comparative analysis of accuracy

Class	Conventional model	Proposed work
1	88%	91.85%
2	88%	91.85%

Figure 7. Comparative analysis of accuracy

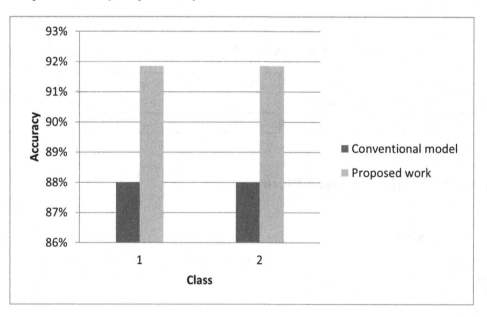

2. Precision

Table 8. Comparative analysis of precision

Class	Conventional model	Proposed work
1	0.88	0.91
2	0.88	0.93

Figure 8. Comparative analysis of precision

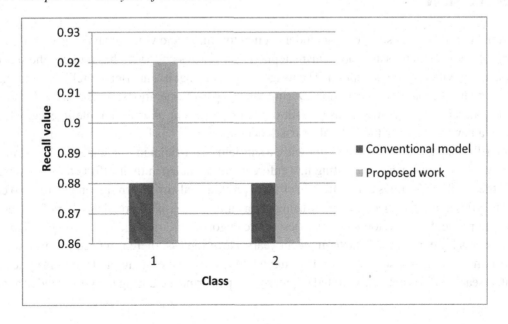

3.   Recall value

Table 9. Comparative analysis of recall value

Class	Conventional model	Proposed work
1	0.88	0.92
2	0.88	0.91

Figure 9. Comparative analysis of recall value

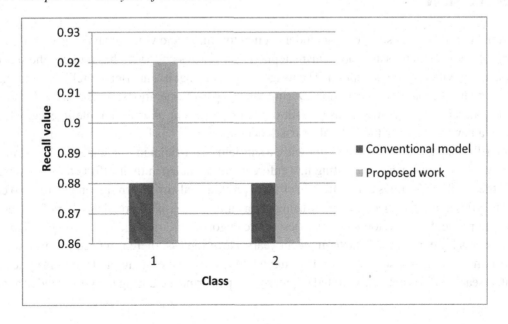

4.   F1-Score

Table 10. Comparative analysis of F1-Scope

Class	Conventional model	Proposed work
1	0.88	0.92
2	0.88	0.92

Figure 10. Comparison of F1-Scope

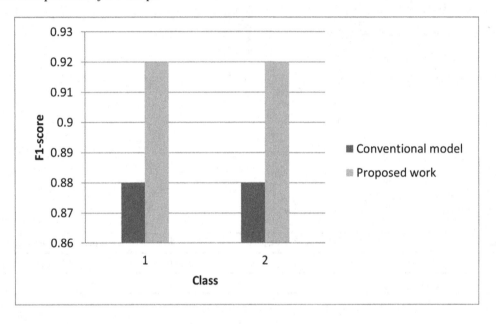

6. CONCLUSION

Result concludes that proposed working model applied for image and video analytics is providing better accuracy. Moreover compression mechanism applied over images and video has reduced the space consumption along with time consumption. The usage of systems that use artificial intelligence in the fight against crime has become more common. During these types of operations, image and video analytics are playing a crucial role. However, as a result of the development of artificial intelligence, which has ushered in a new century for the field of research and analysis, it has become fairly difficult to deploy inside an IoT context. The use of video analytics, a subfield of artificial intelligence that is making rapid strides towards improvement, is assisting law enforcement agencies in their efforts to dramatically cut down on the number of crimes committed. In order to provide real-time warnings and insights to clients, Video Analytics analyses video footage by using algorithms to classify a broad number of object kinds, differentiate particular behaviours or activities, and categorise a variety of video content. Traditional CCTV cameras have become obsolete in recent years. Nevertheless, there is a need to cut down on the amount of time as well as space that is used throughout the operations of image and video analytics. At the moment, research efforts are concentrated on improving performance during image and video analytics.

7. SCOPE OF VIDEO SURVEILLANCE IN REAL WORLD

Massive volumes of video data are generated by video surveillance systems. Much of this film is not seen or evaluated because of constraints on available time or funds. Hence, security events go unnoticed and suspicious conduct is not identified in time to avert disaster. These difficulties have contributed greatly to the growth of video analytics. Automatically generated by video analytics, these descriptions may be used to follow the whereabouts and actions of people, vehicles, and other things visible in a video feed. Based on this data, appropriate measures may be taken, such as alerting security staff or making a formal report of the event. Further mechanism might be introduced in order to resolve issues related to crime prevention by advance image and video analytics system applied in IoT.

REFERENCES

Babu, S. Z. D. (2022). Analysation of Big Data in Smart Healthcare. In M. Gupta, S. Ghatak, A. Gupta, & A. L. Mukherjee (Eds.), *Artificial Intelligence on Medical Data. Lecture Notes in Computational Vision and Biomechanics* (Vol. 37). Springer. doi:10.1007/978-981-19-0151-5_21

Caldwell, M., Andrews, J. T. A., Tanay, T., & Griffin, L. D. (2020). AI-enabled future crime. *Crime Science*, 9(1), 1–13. doi:10.118640163-020-00123-8

Dushyant, K., Muskan, G., Gupta, A., & Pramanik, S. (2022). Utilizing Machine Learning and Deep Learning in Cyber security: An Innovative Approach. In M. M. Ghonge, S. Pramanik, R. Mangrulkar, & D. N. Le (Eds.), *Cyber security and Digital Forensics*. Wiley. doi:10.1002/9781119795667.ch12

Gupta, A. (2019). Script classification at word level for a Multilingual Document. *International Journal of Advanced Science and Technology*, 28(20), 1247–1252. http://sersc.org/journals/index.php/IJAST/article/view/3835

Gupta, N., Khosravy, M., Patel, N., Dey, N., Gupta, S., Darbari, H., & Crespo, R. G. (2020). Economic data analytic AI technique on IoT edge devices for health monitoring of agriculture machines. *Applied Intelligence*, 50(11), 3990–4016. doi:10.100710489-020-01744-x

Hollywood, J. S., Vermeer, M. J. D., Woods, D., Goodison, S. E., & Jackson, B. A. (2018). Using Video Analytics and Sensor Fusion in Law Enforcement. 1–35.

Ikuesan, R. A., Ganiyu, S. O., Majigi, M. U., Opaluwa, Y. D., & Venter, H. S. (2020). Practical Approach to Urban Crime Prevention in Developing Nations. *ACM International Conference Proceeding Series*, (pp. 0–7). ACM. https://doi.org/10.1145/3386723.3387867

Jain, V., Beram, S. M., Talukdar, V., Patil, T., Dhabliya, D., & Gupta, A. (2022). Accuracy Enhancement in Machine Learning During Blockchain Based Transaction Classification. *Seventh International Conference on Parallel, Distributed and Grid Computing (PDGC)*, Solan, Himachal Pradesh, India. 10.1109/PDGC56933.2022.10053213

Kirpichnikov, D., Pavlyuk, A., Grebneva, Y., & Okagbue, H. (2020). Criminal Liability of the Artificial Intelligence. *E3S Web of Conferences, 159*, 1–10. https://doi.org/ doi:10.1051/e3sconf/202015904025

Martínez-Mascorro, G. A., Abreu-Pederzini, J. R., Ortiz-Bayliss, J. C., Garcia-Collantes, A., & Terashima-Marín, H. (2021). Criminal intention detection at early stages of shoplifting cases by using 3D convolutional neural networks. *Computation (Basel, Switzerland)*, *9*(2), 1–25. doi:10.3390/computation9020024

Nayak, N., Odhekar, S., Patwa, S., & Roychowdhury, S. (2022)... *Real Time Crime Detection By Captioning Video Surveillance Using Deep Learning.*, *10*(7), 367–376.

O'Malley, P., & Smith, G. J. D. (2022). 'Smart' crime prevention? Digitization and racialized crime control in a Smart City. *Theoretical Criminology*, *26*(1), 40–56. doi:10.1177/1362480620972703

Pandey, D., Pandey, B. K., Noibi, T. O., Babu, S., Patra, P. M., Kassaw, C., & Canete, J. J. O. (2020). Covid-19: Unlock 1.0 risk, test, transmission, incubation and infectious periods and reproduction of novel Covid-19 pandemic. *Asian Journal of Advances in Medical Science*, 23-28.

Pandey, D., & Pandey, B. K. (2022). An Efficient Deep Neural Network with Adaptive Galactic Swarm Optimization for Complex Image Text Extraction. In *Process Mining Techniques for Pattern Recognition* (pp. 121–137). CRC Press. doi:10.1201/9781003169550-10

Pathania, V. (2022). A Database Application of Monitoring COVID-19 in India. In M. Gupta, S. Ghatak, A. Gupta, & A. L. Mukherjee (Eds.), *Artificial Intelligence on Medical Data. Lecture Notes in Computational Vision and Biomechanics* (Vol. 37). Springer. doi:10.1007/978-981-19-0151-5_23

Piza, E. L., Welsh, B. C., Farrington, D. P., & Thomas, A. L. (2019). CCTV surveillance for crime prevention: A 40-year systematic review with meta-analysis. *Criminology & Public Policy*, *18*(1), 135–159. doi:10.1111/1745-9133.12419

Podoletz, L. (2022). We have to talk about emotional AI and crime. *AI & Society*, *0123456789*. doi:10.100700146-022-01435-w

Radulov. (2019). Artificial intelligence and security. *Instructional Scientific Journal Security and Future*, *3*(1), 3–5. http://www.springerlink.com/index/M1042VT3791654RK.pdf

Rehnström, F. (2021). *How Capable is Artificial Intelligence (AI) in Crime Prediction and Prevention?* doi:10.1109/ACCESS.2019.2941978

Sultana, T., & Wahid, K. A. (2019). IoT-Guard: Event-Driven Fog-Based Video Surveillance System for Real-Time Security Management. IEEE Access: Practical Innovations, Open Solutions, 7, 134881–134894. doi:10.1109/ACCESS.2019.2941978

Sung, C. S., & Park, J. Y. (2021). Design of an intelligent video surveillance system for crime prevention: Applying deep learning technology. *Multimedia Tools and Applications*, *80*(26–27), 34297–34309. doi:10.100711042-021-10809-z

Tundis, A., Kaleem, H., & Mühlhäuser, M. (2020). Detecting and tracking criminals in the real world through an IoT-based system. *Sensors (Basel)*, *20*(13), 1–27. doi:10.339020133795 PMID:32645873

Vivo Delgado, G., & Castro-Toledo, F. J. (2020). Urban security and crime prevention in smart cities: a systematic review. *International E-Journal of Criminal Sciences, 15*(6).

Williams, A., Corner, E., & Taylor, H. (2022). Vehicular Ramming Attacks: Assessing the Effectiveness of Situational Crime Prevention Using Crime Script Analysis. *Terrorism and Political Violence, 34*(8), 1549–1563. doi:10.1080/09546553.2020.1810025

Yoshinaga, T., Fukuda, Y., Watanabe, Y., & Hiroike, A. (2019). *Video Analytics AI for Public Safety and Security., 71*(2), 131–137.

Završnik, A. (2020). Criminal justice, artificial intelligence systems, and human rights. *ERA Forum, 20*(4), 567–583. 10.100712027-020-00602-0

Zhang, T., Aftab, W., Mihaylova, L., Langran-Wheeler, C., Rigby, S., Fletcher, D., Maddock, S., & Bosworth, G. (2022). Recent Advances in Video Analytics for Rail Network Surveillance for Security, Trespass and Suicide Prevention—A Survey. *Sensors (Basel), 22*(12), 4324. doi:10.339022124324 PMID:35746103

Chapter 8
AI–Based Quality Inspection of Industrial Products

D. Devasena
Sri Ramakrishna Engineering College, India

Y. Dharshan
Sri Ramakrishna Engineering College, India

S. Vivek
Mechmet Engineers, India

B. Sharmila
Sri Ramakrishna Engineering College, India

ABSTRACT

Quality is the keyword for Industry Revolution 4.0, as industries have moved from product based to customer-based manufacturing. People have started moving towards the quality rather than the cost of the product. The automobile section is deemed to be a major manufacturing sector as multiple components required for assembling final product. Bearing is a major component in the engine to operate the piston. The inspection of component done 100% manually where time is high, in turn delay in dispatch. A proposed automated machine vision system (MVS) is used to identify missing operations, also detect scratches in surface of the component. The algorithm is developed using LabVIEW, in which detection-based algorithm is implemented to detect the missing operations in the component. An artificial intelligent (AI) based algorithm is proposed for detecting the scratches that occurred due to the manufacturing process/mishandling of component. The implemented algorithm has shown better results compared with the manual process, as inspection time has reduced, and the number of components inspected has increased.

DOI: 10.4018/978-1-6684-8618-4.ch008

INTRODUCTION

The Revolution Industry 4.0 was primarily intended to facilitate the various disadvantages of the previous revolutions, in which quality of the product is identified as one of the major issue. After 20th Century, people have started moving towards the purchase of quality products at nominal cost. Therefore industries have also started moving towards production of quality products to sustain in the consumer market. The quality of the product is decided based on various factors such as raw materials, production process and assembly of the final component. The quality of the product is only tested during the final output of the production/manufacturing process. The process of the quality inspection is done through manual procedures in the earlier stages in which the inspection of the component has been time consuming and prone to errors. To avoid the above difficulties, industries have started to utilize semi-autonomous inspection systems where human and machine involved together to increase the productivity.

Semi-autonomous systems requires around 20-30% of human intervention, where material handling is done using manual process and the inspection system is automated. The system requires constant coordination between the manual labour and the inspection system. There are two basic quality inspection systems such as Sensor based inspection system and vision based inspection system, based on the material and type of the quality inspection to be made on the product. These systems will execute only pre-defined problems and they are not able to adapt to any changes, if there is an alteration or the system is unable to identify the component the human is required to make the final inspection.

Semi-autonomous systems are implemented when the manufacturing product is of limited quantity. The system also requires a human labour where manual errors may still be persistent in the process. These systems are not adaptable when the manufacturing process is of mass production and when the quality set is at high accuracy.

To overcome the drawbacks of semi-autonomous system, entire manufacturing process is to be made autonomous where the material handling and inspection system is fully automated. The autonomous system is developed based on the characteristics such as methodical way of approach to execute the predefined process and adaptability to the changes internally which could help the system to operate in an autonomous manner. To make the system adaptable, Intelligent techniques is been added where the system learns from the different inputs which is fed as feedback. Implementing intelligent techniques improves the learning ability which in turn helps in better decision making to increase the quality and reduce the time required for production.

The proposed work is to develop an algorithm to identify the missing operations in the finished product. The product which is been inspected for quality is being utilized in the combustion section of the automobile engines.

LITERATURE SURVEY

This chapter deals with the various other research work which has been carried out by the research community to address different kinds of issues, by applying different process techniques for different kinds of output products.

Bernard C. Jiang, Szu-Lang Tasi, and Chien-Chih Wang (2002) proposed a gray relational analysis to determine the markings in the Integrated Circuits(IC) fabrication. The method was proposed for identifying the overlap characters on the IC in which four different gray relational techniques are implemented for better results. The proposed method has been utilized for only saved image and not for real time images. E.N. Malamas, Euripides Petrakis, Michalis Zervakis, Laurent Petit & Jean-Didier Legat (2003) presented various innovative solutions in industrial automation. They discussed about the inspection performed by Human experts, Computer vision and automated machine vision system. They defined the processing of a typical machine vision system and their developments. They also proposed different tools used to analyze and execute the process.

Brosnan Tadhg and Sun Da-Wen (2004) proposed image processing based non-destructive system to determine the quality of the food products. They implemented a machine vision system to inspect the size and shape of the chicken pieces and proposed the system to segregate the potatoes based on grading using a HIS Model. Krishna Kumar Patel & A. Kar & S. N. Jha & M. A. Khan (2012) also developed a machine vision inspection system to check the food and agricultural products. The system is used to sort and grade the grains, vegetables and fruits.

S.Sathiyamoorthy (2014) presented a machine vision system for identifying non conformity of the components in the production line. The image processing machine vision system has been applied for determine the shaft diameter in fan, in engine assembly to identify the engine model and to identify the damages in the punching dye. Implementation of MVS for non-conformity improves the quality production. Wei-Chien Wang, Shang-Liang Chen, Liang-Bi Chen & Wan-Jung Chang (2017) proposed an Automatic optical inspection technology to identify the missing holes, holes displacement, roundness and etc., present in the PCB. The system is manually updated and there is a need of automatic updating of software for processing real time images.

Ricardo Luhm Silva, Marcelo Rudek, Anderson Luis Szejka and Osiris Canciglieri Junior (2019) has developed a machine vision system connected with artificial intelligence for industrial quality control inspections. The authors have proposed integration of the AI system with the existing MVS system to select the appropriate AI algorithm for different scenario and evaluate the performance in the industrial conditions. R Kiruba Shankar, J Indra, R Oviya, A Heeraj and R Ragunathan (2020) has proposed a machine vision system to identify the work piece, with their dimensions through edge detection method. In this process the image is captured, the edges of the image are preprocessed and post processed to identify the corners.

Tajeddine Benbarrad, Marouane Salhaoui, Soukaina Bakhat Kenitar and Mounir Arioua (2021) proposed a vision system to verify and suggest the improvements in the product to increase the quality. The system predicts suitable process to improve the manufacturing process by using appropriate machine learning algorithm. Vivek, S. & Srinivasan, K. Sharmila, B. , Dharshan Y, Panchal, Hitesh, Muthusamy, Suresh, Ashok kumar,R. Sadasivuni, Kishor kumar, Elkelawy, Medhat and Shrimali, Neel. (2022) has proposed LabVIEW based algorithm for the detection of the operations in the components. The proposed model is utilized to detect the missing operations, where an AI system can be developed for self-learning of the process.

Tao Sun and Jujiang Cao (2022) has proposed an MVS system using Deep Neural Networks in which the Convolution neural network has been implemented as MVS-CNN to analyze the input picture and identify the different characteristics by comparing the predefined images. The proposed system can be implemented only to the predefined set of defects, and if any new defect is found the system is unable to capture. Minwoo Park and Jongpil Jeong (2022) has developed a vision inspection system for inspecting the quality of the mask produced to improve sustainability in the manufacturing process. The proposed system presents, hardware, software on automation, control and Point of Production to monitor and improve the quality of the mask. The developed model has certain faults where inaccuracies in identifying the faulty product and also misjudging the good product has defective by the vision system.

HARDWARE IMPLEMENTATION

Machine vision system in the manufacturing unit is used to detect the defects in the manufactured products and if it doesn't meet the required criteria, the product may be disposed at this stage.

Figure 1. A simple machine vision

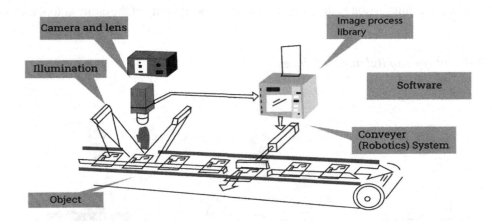

To execute the process, a machine vision system should need a Camera, lens, Proper lighting system and the image sensor. The camera used in the industry are of two types, area scan and line scan. Area scan is used to capture the image in a single frame where Line scan is used to capture images pixel by pixel. Depends on the application the camera selection has been done. While selecting the lens the factors should be considered are the distance between the object and the camera which determines the focal length of the camera, the size of the object, the size of the defects in the object and to check whether the camera or the object are in motion and finally lighting system.

The focal length of the lens can be calculated using the given formula

$$F = \frac{h * Wd}{FOV}$$

Where F=Focal length in mm
h=horizontal dimension of the sensor in mm
Wd=Working distance
FOV=Horizontal Field of View

By using the above formula the required focal length can be calculated for the machine vision applications. Image sensor converts the captured image into digital image. The camera image sensor used should have to meet two important characteristics namely Resolution and Sensitivity. The high resolution sensors provides images with good quality and it is used observe even small changes. The digital image captured by the sensor is analyzed using vision processing system. Further analysis, observations and measurements are done in the vision processing system.

Machine Vision Lighting

The purpose of lighting system is to maximizing the features of the field of interest to be observed when compared to other features of the object. This can be achieved by optimizing the parameters like the distance between the camera and object with the light source, brightness and intensity of the light source, style and placement of the light source. There are different types of lighting techniques which is shown in **Figure 2** (see **Figure 2**). These lighting techniques can be featured and altered to improve the performance of the machine vision system and to increase the sensitivity of the entire autonomous system.

Figure 2. Different types of lighting techniques

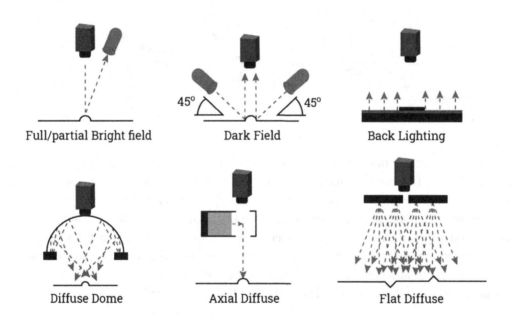

PROPOSED HARDWARE SETUP

Based on the Industrial requirement, a special machine for vision quality inspection is designed for identifying the missing operations and the quality of the engine component of automobiles. The proposed machine vision system (MVS) comprises of multiples parts/sections which works in parallel to complete its work. The Proposed system is shown as **Figure 3** (see **Figure 3**).

Figure 3. Proposed system

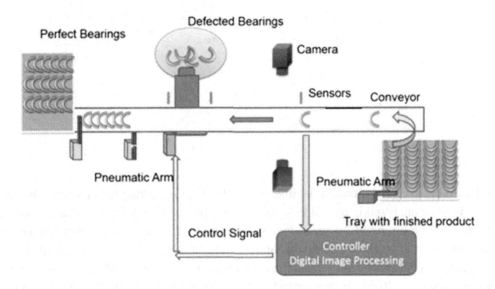

The MVS system comprises of the following Camera and Lens, Electrical Systems and Vision Processing System.

The above three are the basic sections which involve in visual inspection system, where each section plays their role in identifying, controlling/processing the information and to make a decision.

1. Camera and Lens

The Camera and lens are the two major components of the MVS system. The camera is considered as the input location, through which the image is captured and then transferred to the processing unit. The

Figure 4. Camera and lens utilized for proposed work

Figure 5. Block diagram of proposed image acquisition and processing

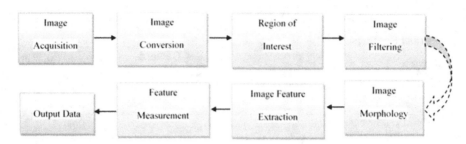

camera is selected based on the different parameters involved in identifying the product to be captured. The components to be analyzed is passed through a conveyor system where the distance between the components is kept on a timing of 2.5 seconds. As the speed of the components in the conveyor is 2.5 seconds, the camera has to be chosen based on Number of frames captured per second and also the size of the sensor. Based on the above requirement the camera has been chosen Basler acA Area scan camera with the properties such as 40 frames per second and image sensor of size 1/4 inch with global shutter.

Lens is the second important component in the machine vision system. The camera consist of the image sensor which receives the illumination through the lens. Lens which is used is a fixed focal length and the mountain to the camera is C-Mount. For the proposed system the component size differs at various ranges, therefore a 16mm lens has been chosen to meet the requirements. Lens has been chosen based on the formula given in equation (1). **Figure 4** shows the camera and the lens utilized for the proposed work (see **Figure 4**). The block diagram of the proposed image acquisition and processing has been given in **Figure 5** (see **Figure 5**).

2.   Electrical system

The Electrical system in the proposed work consists of Master Circuit Breakers (MCB), emergency button and push buttons connected in a flow to control the conveyor, power supply to camera, light, sensors and controllers such as Programmable Logic Controller (PLC) and Data Acquisition Unit (DAQ). The Electrical system is used to maintain and control the power to entire machine vision system. The PLC is the heart of the electrical system where the connections are passed through the PLC to control the speed of the conveyor motor and during Fault identification and in an emergency situation, the PLC will stop or control the entire system. On other emergency situations such as component delay, component trapped in the conveyor system and any other manual faults, emergency push buttons is pressed where the supply to the system will cut off immediately. Until the problem is resolved, the emergency push button will not be released maintaining the system in idle condition.

Two Proximity sensors are placed on the Conveyor system for the purposes such as to detect the component and inform the DAQ unit to initiate the capture sequence by the camera and send the information from camera to vision processing system, it is also used for counting the number of inlet and outlet components through the vision system. In the Proposed system Bar light is placed at an angle of 60 degree inclination to enhance the features of the component to be processed.

The DAQ unit is used to receive the physical data from the sensor and convert it to digital infromation and initiate the process of capturing images through camera as frames. Captured frames are processed in the vision processing system and identifies the faults which is again transferred/send to DAQ unit. The DAQ unit once received the infromation checks for the OK/NOT OK signal as digital data in the form of 1/0 respectively. If the fault is identified the DAQ unit sends the signal to PLC to trigger the Pneumatic cylinder through solenoid which is used to reject the defective component. In this propsed system the DAQ device consists of 4 Input/Output Analog pins, 8 Input/Output Digital pins, ground and supply pins. The DAQ requires 24V input to operate.

3. Vision Processing System

The processing system utilized is an i5 processor with internal memory of 8GB and solid state storage of 500GB. The software which is utilized is LabVIEW 2020 with vision and motion tool box to develop a program to process the image and produce an output to determine the component is accepted or rejected based on the algorithm implemented. The image is captured on the trigger from the sensor and the DAQ unit and then transferred to the software through the NI-IMAQ-dx port initialized inside the program to acquire the image.

The camera is first calibrated for the settings such as the aperture ratio, shutter speed, brightness and contrast of the image through the vision acquisition tool in the toolbox. Then the image is passed to the vision processing tool, where the captured image is processed under various categories through the algorithm developed as shown **Figure 6** (see **Figure 6**). The algorithm is developed for not matching the predefined image stored, but to process the input image and learn the changes in the process, even if the image captured is adjusted in position during the acquiring process.

Figure 6. Algorithm

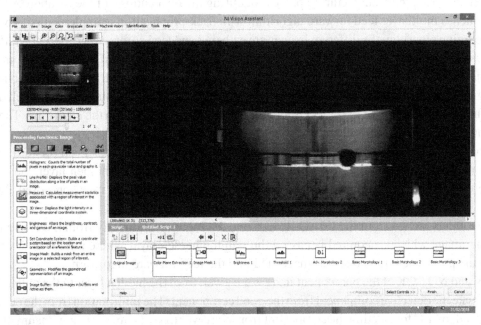

a).   Missing operation identification:

The engine component is manufactured with different operations such as drilling a hole, protrusion at edge of the component, carving in the middle of the component, and symmetrical slopping edge at the top and bottom of the component. The operations are done based on the requirement of the customer and the vehicle in which the component to be placed. It is mandatory to check the presence of the operations in each component. The detection of the operations is done based on the enhancement of the edges and also the height and width of the operation using clamp detection algorithm.

The image is captured from the camera and transferred to the LabVIEW software using DAQ card with the help of Vision and Motion tool box. The image is acquired Vision Acquisition tool where the Camera parameters are adjusted and number of frames is been set. The image acquired passed through image processing tool where the region of interest is marked and preprocessing techniques are implemented to enhance the parameters. The clamp detection algorithm measures the number of pixels between the edges of the component by highlighting the edge pixels based on the strength and color variation from the background.

The **Figure 7** shows, mentions the flow at which the component is identified for the missing operations during the manufacturing process (see **Figure 7**). The acquired image from the camera is processed for the operations in the mentioned, where the program generates an OK/REJECT information through the PLC which either will allow the component or eject the component to a separate tray if identified as defective using the pneumatic cylinder.

b).   Identification of surface defects:

The second process in the vision processing system is the identification of any surface scratches on the component during the manufacturing process or during the mishandling of the component. To identify the scratches multilayer feed forward algorithm with back-propagation is implemented. To train the machine learning algorithm the different images are gathered and feed as inputs at different width, length and various positions in the components. The predefined images are mapped with real time images, to identify the defects. The algorithm is feed with an input of 300 images to train the model and during the testing an accuracy of 90% has been achieved, thus the algorithm is contained with a self-learning process when a new position of the defect is identified, it is feed as an input to the algorithm. The **Figure 8** represents process flow of the algorithm (see **Figure 8**).

The Proposed algorithm consists of two different Neural Networks such as Feed forward and Back Propagation, in which the proposed algorithm consists of an input layer, a hidden layer and an output layer, where input and hidden consists of one layer each. The Steps involved in the proposed algorithm,

Step 1: The inputs are fed from the IMAQ-dx tool into the input layer directly from the camera.
Step 2: The image which is acquired is passed through the hidden layer where the image is compared with the predefined trained set of images fed into the feed forward algorithm.
Step 3: OK and NOT OK of the component images are given from the hidden layer to the output layer, to segregate the defective component from the good component. The information from the output layer is passed to PLC for ejecting the component from conveyor to separate tray using Pneumatic piston.

Figure 7. Flow at which the component is identified for missing operations

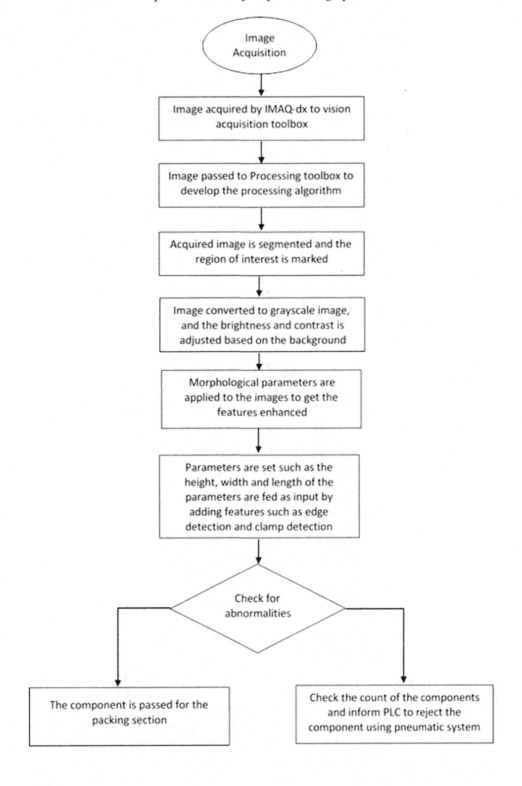

Figure 8. Process flow of algorithm

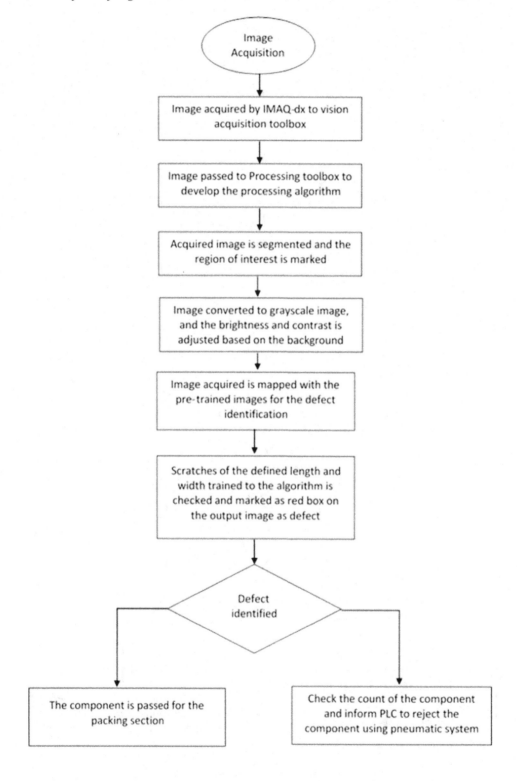

Step 4: If there is any mismatch between the trained images and the real time image, error is generated which is fed back through the Back propagation network. The algorithm based on the error, update the weights and add the new defect in to the system and continued to learn.

Step 5: The process is repeated till the program is halted.

RESULTS AND DISCUSSIONS

This chapter deals with the results of the proposed work to identify the defects such as the mission operations of the components and the surface defect on the component. To identify the missing operation the captured image is passed through the algorithm developed to find the accepted/rejected component and segregate the components for either rework or scrap the rejected components.

a.   Identification of missing Operation in the Component

Figure 9 shows the Graphical User Interface (GUI) of the proposed system is given (see Figure 9). Where the running video and captured image is shown. The GUI also counts the number of components which is fed in to vision system and the number of components accepted/rejected. The Identification of missing operation is highlighted using different indicators with the help of green and red color, where green represents the OK component and the red represents NOT OK Component.

The different operations of the components are given, as the first operation the Chamfer is an operation in the component where small slope is being carved in the inner circle to highlight the edge of the component and also utilized during stacking in engine assembly. The **Figure 10** shows the chamfer operation carried out in the component which is highlighted by the lighting system and segregated using the Edge detection algorithm (see **Figure 10**).

Figure 9. Graphical user interface

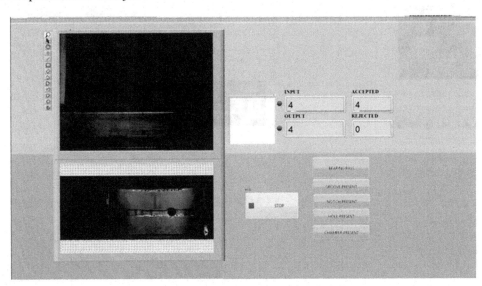

Figure 10. Chamfer operation

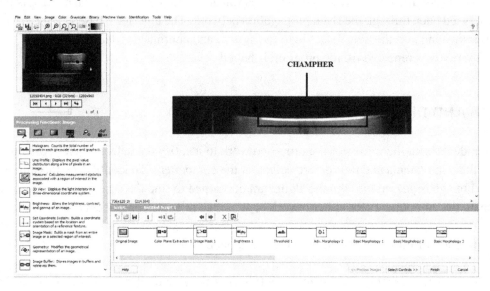

The second operation in the component is the hole operation which is used for dripping the Engine oil into the engine for smooth functioning of the piston. The hole operation is present only in the upper semi-circle of the component whereas lower part will not have any holes. The **Figure 11** represents the identification of hole operation in the component (see **Figure 11**). The notch is the small protrusion present either in the right or left edge of the component. It is used for matching the upper and lower semi-circle component during assembly. **Figure 12** represents the notch operation present in the component (see **Figure 12**).

Figure 11. Identification of hole operation

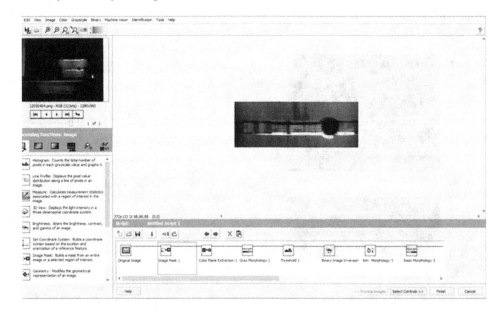

Figure 12. Notch operation

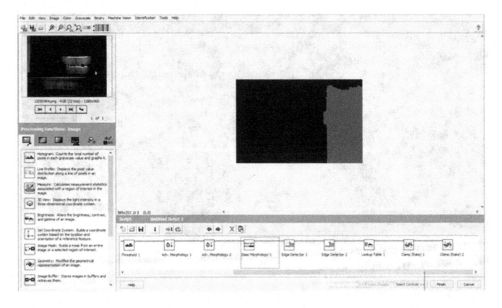

Identification of Scratch in the Component

Scratch identification in the component is carried out to make sure that the component does not have any defects on the surface. An AI based Feed forward Back Propagation algorithm is implemented to identify the scratches on the surface. The Proposed algorithm is utilized because normal image processing technique has not produced desired output, when a new type of scratch or change of location identified

Figure 13. Identification of small and large sized scratches

Figure 14. Identification of small and large sized scratches

the image processing technique was unable to detect. Therefore the AI algorithm is developed with the feature of self-learning using the Back propagation algorithm to adjust the weights based on the changes. The **Figure 13** and **Figure 14** shows the identification of small and large sized scratches on the surface of the component (see **Figure 13 and 14**).

Table 1 and Table 2 represents the comparison of product inspection and its deficiency between the different processes such as manual, automated and AI for missing operations and Scratch identification in the surface of the component respectively (see Table 1 and 2). The **Figure 15, Figure 16**, **Figure 17**

Figure 15. Corresponding comparison charts for product inspection and deficiency

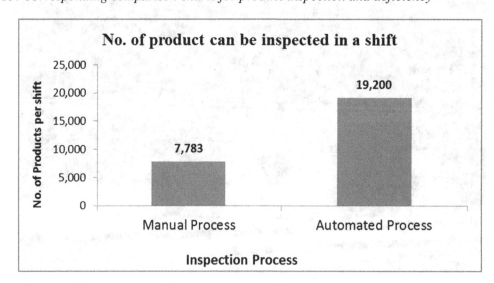

Figure 16. Corresponding comparison charts for product inspection and deficiency

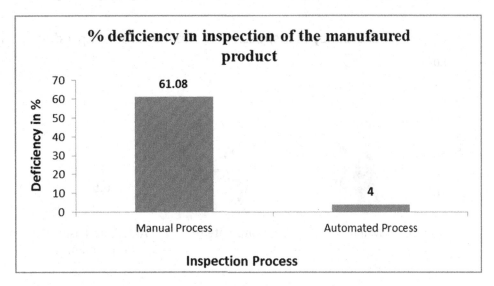

Figure 17. Corresponding comparison charts for product inspection and deficiency

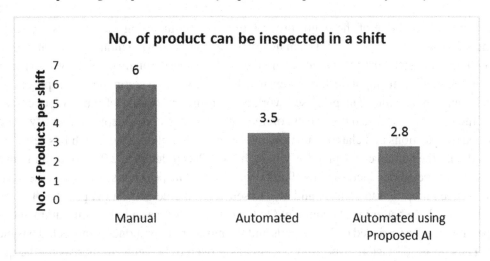

and **Figure 18** represents corresponding comparison charts for product inspection and deficiency (see **Figure 15, 16 17 and 18**).

Figure 18. Corresponding comparison charts for product inspection and deficiency

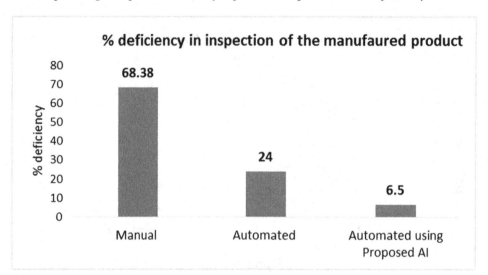

CONCLUSION AND FUTURE WORK

The quality inspection is one of the major process in any manufacturing industry, as the sales of the component is depending on the quality. The majority of the manufacturing industries has moved towards automating their manufacturing process to ensure the quality. The vision inspection system has played a major role in the manufacturing industries to ensure the quality of the component as it plays the role of an automated human machine. The proposed work is to ensure the quality of the component produced in terms of the operation and also the defects on the surface of the component. To identify the missing operations, edge detections and clamp detection algorithm was implemented which has resulted in better compared with the human check process, where the time has reduced to 2.2 seconds and the number of components inspected has increased to 19,200. Similarly to inspect the scratches in the surface, AI algorithm has been proposed to identify and also to self-learn the defects on the process. The proposed work has proven to have better results compared to the manual process and the semi-automated process, as the inspection time has reduced to 2.8 seconds and the number of components inspected has increased to 18,700. Thus proposed vision inspection system has proven to be better in increasing the quality of the component.

The improvise the proposed work, an AI based algorithm has to be developed for inspecting the missing operation and help the industry to send the component either to rework or scrap the component based on the result. An automated packing system can also be added at the end of the inspection line, as the good components after inspection can align and pack for final dispatch.

REFERENCES

Benbarrad, T., Salhaoui, M., Kenitar, S. B., & Arioua, M. (2021). Intelligent Machine Vision Model for Defective Product Inspection Based on Machine Learning. *Journal of Sensor and Actuator Networks*, *10*(1), 1–18. doi:10.3390/jsan10010007

Brosnan, T., & Sun, D.-W. (2004). Improving quality inspection of food products by computer vision—A review. *Journal of Food Engineering*, *61*(1), 3–16. doi:10.1016/S0260-8774(03)00183-3

Jiang, B. C., Szu-Lang Tasi, & Chien-Chih Wang. (2002). Machine vision-based gray relational theory applied to IC marking inspection. *IEEE Transactions on Semiconductor Manufacturing*, *15*(1), 531–539. doi:10.1109/TSM.2002.804906

Kiruba Shankar, R., Indra, J., Oviya, R., Heeraj, A., & Ragunathan, R. (2020). Machine Vision Based Quality Inspection for Automotive Parts using Edge Detection Technique. *IOP Conference Series: Material Science and Engineering*, (pp. 1-10). IOP Science. 10.1088/1757-899X/1055/1/012029

Malamas, E. N., Petrakis, E. G. M., Zervakis, M., Petit, L., & Legat, J.-D. (2003). A survey on industrial vision systems, applications and tools. *Image and Vision Computing*, *21*(2), 171–188. doi:10.1016/S0262-8856(02)00152-X

Park, M., & Jeong, J. (2022). Design and Implementation of Machine Vision-Based Quality Inspection System in Mask Manufacturing Process. *Sustainability (Basel)*, *14*(10), 6009. doi:10.3390u14106009

Patel, K., Kar, A., Jha, S., & Khan, M. (2012). Machine vision system: A tool for quality inspection of food and agricultural products. *Journal of Food Science and Technology*, *49*(2), 123–141. doi:10.100713197-011-0321-4 PMID:23572836

Sathiyamoorthy, S. (2014). Industrial Application of Machine Vision. *International Journal of Research in Engineering and Technology*, *3*(1), 1–5. doi:10.15623/ijret.2014.0319120

Silva, R. L., Rudek, M., Szejka, A. L., & Junior, O. C. (2019). Machine Vision Systems for Industrial Quality Control Inspections. *IPIP International Conference on Product Lifecycle Management*, (pp. 631-641). IEEE. 10.1007/978-3-030-01614-2_58

Sun, T., & Cao, J. (2022). Research on Machine Vision System Design Based on Deep Learning Neural Network. *Wireless Communications and Mobile Computing*, *2022*, 1–16. doi:10.1155/2022/4808652

Vivek, S., Srinivasan, K., Sharmila, B., Dharshan, Y., Panchal, H., Suresh, M., Ashokkumar, R., Sadasivuni, K. K., Elkelawy, M., & Shrimali, N. (2022). An Improved Quality Inspection of Engine Bearings Using Machine Vision Systems. *Smart and Sustainable Manufacturing Systems*, *6*(1), 20210012. doi:10.1520/SSMS20210012

Wang, W., Chen, S., Chen, L., & Chang, W. (2017). A Machine Vision Based Automatic Optical Inspection System for Measuring Drilling Quality of Printed Circuit Boards. *IEEE Access : Practical Innovations, Open Solutions*, *5*, 10817–10833. doi:10.1109/ACCESS.2016.2631658

APPENDIX

Table 1. Time taken for inspection on manual and automated for missing operation

Description	Time Taken to Inspect the product per shift (seconds)	No of product Inspected on a shift	No of product manufactured in a shift	% deficiency in inspection of the manufaured product
Manual	4.2	7,783	20,000	61.08
Automated	2.2	19,200		4

Table 2. Time taken for inspection on manual and automated for identification of defects on surface

Description	Time Taken to Inspect the product per shift (seconds)	No of product Inspected on a shift	No of product manufactured in a shift	% deficiency in inspection of the manufaured product
Manual	6	6,323		68.38
Automated	3.5	15,200	20,000	24
Automated using Proposed AI	2.8	18,700		6.5

Chapter 9
Application of Information Technology Law in India on IoT/IoE With Image Processing

Ramesh Chandra Tripathi

College of Computing Sciences and I.T., Teerthanker Mahaveer University, Moradabad, India

Poonam Gupta

Department of Management, Sanskriti University, Mathura, India

Rohit Anand

G.B. Pant DSEU Okhla-I Campus, India

R. Jayanthi Jayashankar

School of Sciences, Jain University (Deemed), India

Aparajita Mohanty

Symbiosis Law School, Symbiosis International University (Deemed), India

Gabriela Michael

Symbiosis Law School, Symbiosis International University (Deemed), India

Dharmesh Dhabliya

Symbiosis Law School, Symbiosis International University (Deemed), India

ABSTRACT

In order to address the issues posed by emerging technologies like IoT, IP, and AI, the legislation governing information technology in India is undergoing a period of fast development (AI). Since these technologies are able to gather, share, and analyse massive quantities of data, regulations are necessary to safeguard individuals' right to privacy about such data. Companies and organizations need to have a full awareness of the legal framework around IoT/IoE, image processing, and AI in order to guarantee that they are in compliance with the laws that have been enacted. Companies and organisations may assist in guaranteeing that they are employing these technologies in a legally responsible way by using legal knowledge gained through understanding the legal consequences of using these technologies. It has been observed that there are several applications of IT law in India on IoT/ IoE. Present research work is considering the role of image processing in IoT environment.

DOI: 10.4018/978-1-6684-8618-4.ch009

1. INTRODUCTION

Information technology law in India is rapidly changing and evolving to accommodate the rapid growth in the nation's digital infrastructure and the emergence of new technologies. In particular, IoT and IIoT, image processing, and AI are playing a critical role in the development of technology-driven legal solutions. By understanding the legal implications (Beatrice Dorothy, 2017) of these new technologies, organizations can benefit from their potential while protecting themselves from liability. This article will provide an overview of how these technologies work together and how organizations can apply the law in India to maximize the benefit of these technologies. (Khaddar, M. A. El, 2017) The IoT/IIoT is a network of connected devices that communicate with each other, exchange data, and enable users to control their environment. Image processing is the use of computer algorithms to understand, interpret and analyze images, such as facial recognition, vehicle detection, and object recognition. AI refers to the study (Ramavel, M., 2018) and creation of computer systems capable of performing activities traditionally associated with human intellect. This convergence of technology has the potential to equip businesses with potent means of boosting productivity, cutting expenses, and enhancing the quality of their interactions with customers. (Singh, J., 2018) For example, IoT/IIoT and image processing can be used to track inventory, optimize production processes and enhance security. AI can be used to automate customer service, provide predictive analytics and enable predictive maintenance. To take advantage of these technologies and their benefits, organizations must understand the legal implications of their use. (Shilpa, A., 2019) Organizations must understand the laws and regulations applicable to the technologies they are using, as well as the associated liabilities, such as data privacy, intellectual property, and cybersecurity. By understanding the applicable laws and regulations (Sherin, J., 2019), organizations can ensure that they are compliant with the relevant regulations and can make informed decisions about the use of these technologies. Organizations can also benefit from the expertise (Zymbler, M., 2019) of legal professionals who specialize in the field of information technology law in India. These professionals understand the nuances of the law and can provide advice on the best way to protect the organization's interests while maximizing the benefit of the technologies. Furthermore, legal professionals can help organizations identify potential risks and take measures to mitigate them. By understanding the legal implications of their use and taking the necessary steps to ensure compliance, organizations can maximize the benefit of these technologies while minimizing the risk of liability. Ultimately, this will lead to a smoother implementation process, increased efficiency, and improved customer experiences. (Sachdev, R., 2020)

1.1 Information Technology Law in India

Information technology law in India is rapidly evolving to meet the challenges of new technologies like IoT, IP, and AI. These technologies are capable of collecting, sharing, and analyzing vast amounts of data, and require laws to protect the privacy of the data. To ensure compliance (E. K., 2020) with these laws, companies, and organizations must have a comprehensive understanding of the legal framework around IoT/IoE, image processing, and AI. (Jhala, S., 2020) Understanding the legal implications of using these technologies can help companies and organizations ensure that they are using them in a legally responsible manner. Furthermore, taking a proactive approach (Krishnaveni, R., 2020) to address the legal requirements for using these technologies can help companies and organizations stay ahead of the curve and avoid potential legal issues. By leveraging the power of technology in a smart and compliant way, companies and organizations can benefit from the potential of these new technologies while protecting their data and staying compliant with the law (Patrono, L., 2020).

The Information Technology Act of 2000 (IT Act) was passed in response to this issue in the year 2000. The Act both describes the numerous crimes that may occur when an individual's data and privacy are violated and specifies the penalties that can be imposed for such breaches. Additionally, it restricts the power of social media and discusses the role of intermediaries. There has been a significant rise in the number of offenses and crimes that are connected to data and authentic information as a direct result of the development of technology and the proliferation of online commerce. Because not even the data that pertained to the safety and legitimacy of the nation could be trusted, the government made the decision to control the actions that take place on social media platforms as well as the data that is saved on such platforms. In this article, the Act's goals and characteristics are outlined, and different infractions and the penalties associated with them are described according to the Act.

In addition to this, it mandated that every nation must develop its very own legal framework to govern e-commerce and online offenses. In the year 2000, the Act was established to safeguard the data of both people and the government. As a result, India became the 12th nation in the world to adopt laws on cyber crimes. It is also known as the Information Technology Act, and it is a piece of legislation that establishes the legal framework necessary to safeguard data associated with e-commerce and digital signatures. In 2008 and 2018, more changes were made to it so that it would better fit the requirements of society. The Act further delineates the capabilities of intermediaries as well as the boundaries of their authority.

1.2 IoT/IoE, Image Processing, and AI Work Together

It was announced on October 17, 2000, that the Information Technology Act, 2000, often known as ITA-2000 or simply the IT Act, is an Act of the Indian Parliament that was passed in 2000 and given the number 21. It is the most important legislation in India that addresses issues related to cybercrime and Internet commerce.

The Intermediary Guidelines Rules from 2011 and the Information Technology (Intermediary Guidelines and Digital Media Ethics Code) Rules from 2021 are examples of secondary or subordinate laws that are related to the Information Technology Act.

The application of Information Technology law in India has become increasingly important in recent years, and with the advancement of IoT, IP, and AI technologies, understanding how they all work together is vital to ensure the safety and security of data. IoT/IoE, Image Processing, and AI can be used together to create smart systems that can collect and analyze data to improve decision-making processes and automate tasks (Prabaharan, T., 2020). For example, IoT/IoE can be used to collect data from sensors and other connected devices, while IP can be used to analyze the collected data and AI can be used to interpret the data and make decisions. Combining these technologies allows firms to better use technology's potential to boost productivity, save costs, and enhance customer satisfaction (Bhatia, A., 2021). Additionally, the use of these technologies can help to protect the data of customers, ensuring that their privacy is respected and that their data is not misused. Therefore, understanding the potential of IoT/IoE, Image Processing, and AI, and how they can be used together, is essential for the successful implementation of Information Technology law in India (Kumar, R., 2021).

During a presentation that Kevin Ashton gave to Procter & Gamble regarding the use of radio-frequency identification in the company's supply chain (RFID), Ashton first proposed the term "Internet of Things" (IoT). The Internet of Things can only advance with the broad adoption of newly developed technologies that can seamlessly connect all of the connected smart devices that are part of a network. On the other hand, everything that, once linked to the internet, may be utilized in a different manner than it was originally intended. An Internet of Things device may be able to collect as well as transmit information. In recent years, the Internet of Things (IoT) has emerged as a subject that academics are more interested in researching.

The phrase "Internet of Things" is used to refer to a method of doing business that enables interoperability across a wide variety of distinct kinds of smart devices. It is possible to build hybrid experiences that combine digital and physical interactions by making use of a wide variety of technologies that originate from a wide variety of industries. Because they include sensors, computer hardware, and software, as well as computer platforms, smart homes are a typical use of the Internet of Things (IoT). The word "smart" is presently used to represent a broad range of high-tech equipment, not simply those that are normally visible in the house, that contain artificial intelligence of some type. Specifically, the term "smart" refers to devices that can communicate with one another. Integration of systems, data analysis, and automation are all made simpler with the assistance of the Internet of Things. They do this to increase the reach of these domains while simultaneously refining them. Technologies such as sensors, computer networks, and automated systems are included in the Internet of Things (IoT). The proliferation of the Internet of Things may be attributed to several different causes, such as the improvement of software, the reduction in the price of hardware, and the general acceptance of new technological developments. They have a substantial influence on the movement of commodities and services across the economy. Because of the alarming pace at which key natural resources such as energy, water, and others are being depleted, the monitoring of the environment via the Internet of Things is crucial to the protection of these resources.

1.3 The Benefits of Applying Information Technology Law in India

The ever-growing need for information technology (IT) services has made it essential for businesses in India to understand and apply the laws of IT. The best way to do this is to integrate IoT/IoE, image processing, and AI technologies to ensure compliance with the data protection and intellectual property laws of the country. IoT/IoE can be used to collect data and monitor user activity, while image processing can be used to identify unauthorized use of copyrighted content (Zheng, X., 2022). AI-based technologies can help detect malicious activities on networks and can be used to carry out automated security audits. By integrating all these technologies, businesses can ensure that they are compliant with the IT law of India. This approach can also help businesses gain a competitive edge over their competitors and protect their data from malicious actors (Kotenko, I., 2022). The Indian government places a strong emphasis on the protection of its people's personal information and data, as seen by the following statement made by Indian Prime Minister Shiv Shankar Singh: "Each person must be able to exercise a substantial degree of control over that data and its use." A legal safeguard against the inappropriate use of information about an individual person stored on a medium, such as a computer, is known as data protection.

On April 2, 2015, the Chief Minister of Maharashtra, Devendra Fadnavis, informed the legislature of the state that a new legislation will be drafted to replace the abolished Section 66A. This announcement was made by the chief minister. Fadnavis was responding to a question posed by the head of the Shiv Sena, Neelam Gorhe. Gorhe had said that the repeal of the legislation would promote internet criminals and had inquired as to whether or not the state government will draught a law about this matter. According to Fadnavis, the previous legislation had not led to any convictions; thus, the new law would be drafted in such a way that it will be powerful and lead to convictions.

On April 13, 2015, it was reported that the Ministry of Home Affairs will organize a committee to develop a new legislative framework. The team would include officials from the Intelligence Bureau, the Central Bureau of Investigation, the National Investigation Agency, and the Delhi Police, in addition to the ministry itself. According to reports, this action was done in response to concerns from intelligence services that they were no longer able to counter internet postings that addressed matters of national security or incited someone to conduct an infraction, such as online recruiting for ISIS. A new "unambiguous section to replace 66A" has received backing from Milind Deora, who formerly served as Minister of State in the Ministry of Information Technology.

In 2022, it was reported that there was a plan to replace the Information Technology Act with a new law called the Digital India Act, which would be more comprehensive and up-to-date and would cover a larger variety of information technology problems and concerns. This legislation could purportedly focus on issues about privacy, the regulation of social media platforms, the regulation of over-the-top platforms, internet intermediaries, the introduction of additional violations or crimes, and the governance of emerging technologies.

1.4 Challenges Faced When Applying Information Technology Law in India

On October 17, 2000, it was reported that the Information Technology Act, 2000, often known as ITA-2000 or simply the IT Act, is an Act of the Indian Parliament that was enacted in 2000 and given the number 21. This Act was given the number 21 since it was the 21st Act of the Indian Parliament. It is the most significant piece of law in India that tackles concerns around cybercrime and business conducted over the internet. Examples of subsidiary or subordinate laws that are associated with the Information Technology Act are the Intermediary Guidelines Rules from 2011 and the Information Technology Rules from 2021. Both of these sets of rules were created in response to the Information Technology Act.

The application of Information Technology Law in India can be a daunting task, especially in the rapidly changing and complex technological environment. However, by leveraging the power of IoT/IoE, image processing, and artificial intelligence (AI), organizations can successfully navigate the intricacies of the Indian IT landscape and ensure compliance with the relevant laws. IoT/IoE provides a platform for the exchange of data between different devices and networks, making it easier to collect and analyze data from multiple sources. (Ahmad, N., 2022) Image processing allows users to identify and analyze objects in digital images, helping to detect any discrepancies in the data. AI, meanwhile, provides an automated method for making decisions and providing insights from large data sets, and can even be used to detect potential violations of IT law. By using these technologies and approaches in tandem, businesses can gain a comprehensive understanding of the Indian IT landscape and the rules and regulations they must abide by (Gupta, A., 2022).

1. **Lack of uniformity in devices used for internet access** – The lack of standardization in the types of devices used to access the internet – Because there are so many different economic brackets in India, not everyone can afford to buy an expensive phone. Apple has more than a 44 percent share of the market in the United States. However, in India, fewer than one percent of people who use mobile devices have iPhones, despite the device's stronger security standards. It is becoming more difficult for authorities to establish legal and technological standards for the protection of personal data as a result of the growing security divide between high-end mobile devices like the iPhone and less expensive mobile phones.

2. **Lack of national-level architecture for Cybersecurity** – Unlike in nations or states, there are no frontiers in cyberspace; as a result, institutions like as the military forces, the digital assets of ONGC, and banking services, among others, are susceptible to cyber assaults launched from any location. This might lead to breaches in security on a national level, which could result in the loss of monetary resources, personal property, or even life. There is a need for a technically prepared multi-agency organization that can base its choices on policy inputs and a strong strategy to react to potential dangers to the country's most valuable resources. This is a need to protect the nation.

3. **Lack of separation** – Unlike countries or states, in cyberspace there are no boundaries, thus making the armed forces, digital assets of ONGC, banking functions, etc. vulnerable to cyber attacks from anywhere. This could result in security breaches at a national level, causing loss of money, property, or lives. To respond to possible threats to the country's most precious resources, there is a need for a technically equipped multi-agency organization that can base its decisions on policy inputs and a sound strategy.

4. **Lack of awareness** – A lack of understanding Because there is currently no national regulatory framework in place for cybersecurity, there is a lack of awareness at both the person and the enterprise levels. Only if there is a regulated and overseen legal framework will citizens of the domestic internet be able to defend themselves and be protected from cyber assaults.

2. LITERATURE REVIEW

A. B. Dorothy, et al.(2017) Digital IP algorithms for Internet of Things-based home safety. In this research, we provide a framework for an IoT-enabled, digital image processing–based autonomous system for domestic control and security (IoT). A sensor, digital camera, fog-based database, and a mobile phone make up the system as a whole. The door's frame was equipped with sensors that signal the camera to take a picture of anyone who was trying to get in, with the image subsequently being sent to a fog-based database or dataset. Using IA, we may search our database for a match between the submitted photo and a list of verified persons or animals. A notification was sent to the homeowner if the recorded picture does not match the database. To compare the acquired picture to the dataset kept in the fog, the techniques for processing images were taken into account for their spatial and temporal complexity.

M. A. E. Khaddar, et al.(2017) did research on the smartphone, the pinnacle of IoT and IoE Technology. These cutting-edge concepts may be used in a broad range of industries, from healthcare and transportation to supply chain management and beyond, to provide consumers access to real-time data & services like location-based sickness management and monitoring. This chapter offers a comprehensive introduction to the IoT and IoE, covering topics such as their separate application areas, IoT structure and design, the role of smartphones in IoT & IoE, and the differences between IoT networks and mobile cellular networks. The security and privacy risks associated with the use of the smartphone within these networks and a list of potential solutions are also discussed by the researchers, along with a brief overview of the current state of the industry & opportunities & challenges that lie ahead for IoT and IoE.

B. Swaminathan, et al.(2018) focused on the games that may use sensors and IOE to transmit data produced in-game in real-time to computers running machine learning algorithms. Here, we present such a concept, in which data analytics are performed using information gleaned from a muscle sensor in tandem with processed pictures obtained during the playing of shots. Players may use these findings to gain insight into how their muscle fibers respond to changes in position and shot angle during the game. As a result, coaches and players will benefit greatly from having access to these statistics, since they will reveal a plethora of previously unrecognized information. Moreover, mid-game performance tweaks and gameplay adjustments are possible thanks to constant, up-to-the-moment input.

A. Singh, et al.(2018) presented work on applications relying on images and IoT. The article presents a survey of current IOT-based software. They have investigated the potential of IP in IoT-based devices. Integration of image processing-based technologies into Internet of Things-based applications is increasing in frequency. The article provides a survey of the significance of image processing to smart systems based on IoT across a variety of contexts. The research may be put to good use in creating and experimenting with cutting-edge image-processing applications for IoT-based devices.

A. Shilpa, et al.(2019) looked at the advantages of sensors in the all-connected Internet (IoE). The term IoT refers to a network that intelligently links devices, systems, information, and people together. It's a step forward for the IoT. The Internet of Everything is a relatively new innovation. This article provides an introduction to the IOE, describes the sensors utilized in IOE, and highlights the benefits of implementing an IoE.

S. Kumar, et al.(2019) focused on the concept of IoT represents a game-changing strategy for developing cutting-edge technologies in the future. This review article's primary objective was to provide a thorough examination of the topic from both a technical and a social viewpoint.

R. Sachdev, et al.(2020) reviewed a secure and private digital marketing environment that makes use of AI at the edge. In the present and future IoT and IoE ecosystems. Edge AI plays a significant role in digital marketing. Customers willingly share information with businesses to get better service and more CX. Nonetheless, there has been significant worry about how data is used, stored, and processed. It has been argued that the use of edge computing will advance the state of the art in security & privacy.

M. Stoyanova, et al.(2020) introduced problems, methodologies, and unresolved questions in IoT Forensics: A Literature Review. This study aims to identify and address the key concerns in the complicated process of IoT-based investigations, including all legal, privacy, and cloud security obstacles.

S. Pareek, et al.(2020) reviewed systems for monitoring and protecting forests using the Internet of Things and image processing. The system relies on recent advancements in the IoT and image processing to function. Using the WSN, these methods were implemented in our system. Constant, real-time information on the state of the forest's ecosystem was made available through this technology. Using this aids us in detecting the severity of fires, which in turn allows us to release water to put them out when weather circumstances become unfavorable. Wildfire control will benefit from this method.

S. Nižetić, et al.(2020) looked at IoT, which will eventually connect all electronic devices. The conference focused on many important themes, including "Smart City," "Energy/Environment," "e-Health," and "Engineering Modeling".

V. Mugendiran, et al.(2020) introduced research summaries on the use of IP in diverse contexts. This work aims to offer a high-level overview of three crucial steps of engineering that include image processing: picture capture, the area of interest, and defect detection.

A. Bhatia, et al.(2021) provided work on ML Algorithms and IP Can Detect Counterfeit Money. In this research, they suggest a technique for detecting counterfeit bills by using K-Nearest Neighbors, then processing the images.

3. PROBLEM STATEMENT

Content-based image retrieval has been included in the diagnostic procedures of multiple studies for various photographs that have been carried out in the fields of IT legislation in India on IoT. These studies have focused on the topic of the Internet of Things. Similar inquiries have been conducted in many different nations throughout the world. Unfortunately, these inquiries are being held up because of the high storage and processing requirements of large photos, which have created a significant backlog. Since large photographs take up a lot of space, this is producing a significant backlog. When placing a call, it could be helpful to have photographs that have been compressed and have had their edges identified. According to the findings, a big rise in the total amount of time spent arguing may be linked to an increase in the size of the image. This is shown by the fact that the amount of time spent arguing increased significantly. It is necessary to make use of a variety of various image processing methods, including cropping, compression, edge detection, and others, to get rid of any unnecessary components that may be present in a picture. This is necessary to get the desired result. On the other side, the system can arrive at an incorrect conclusion if the visual data that it is relying on is either faulty or not up to date. The reliance put on the system may be misguided in any of these two scenarios. Because of this, enhancing the image quality during the Content-based image retrieval operations that are now taking place is an important must.

It was reported on October 17, 2000, that the Information Technology Act, 2000, often known as ITA-2000 or simply the IT Act, is an Act of the Indian Parliament that was passed in the year 2000 and given the number 21. This information was found in a report that was published on October 17, 2000. Since this Act was the 21st Act passed by the Indian Parliament, it was assigned the number 21. It is the most important piece of legislation in India that addresses issues around cybercrime and economic activities that are carried out through the Internet. The Intermediary Guidelines Rules from 2011 and the Information Technology Rules from 2021 are two examples of subsidiary or subordinate laws that are related to the Information Technology Act. Both of these rules were enacted in response to the Information Technology Act. The Information Technology Act served as the impetus for the development of both of these sets of regulations.

4. PROPOSED WORK

The work being proposed, the Image quality enhancement model for the Application of Information Technology Law is being considered for the detection and categorization of images. Challenges with traditional processes, such as ignoring the quality of images, are being taken into consideration by research efforts.

4.1 Image Quality Enhancement for Application of Information Technology Law

The difficulties and concerns that have been brought about by technological advancement are being deliberated upon as part of the process of doing research. Image processing and CBIR for the purpose of image feature detection are the topics of the research that is now being carried out. In addition, the

Figure 1. Process flow of work

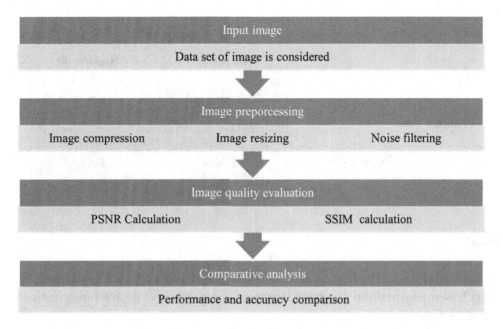

purpose of this study is to determine whether or not certain aspects of image processing might have an effect on the caliber of the photograph that is ultimately created. The method that is outlined in this piece is going to be implemented into the experiment that is going to be carried out. After the step of selecting a picture to be processed, the image would then be compressed following that step.

In the year 2000, the Act was established to safeguard the data of both people and the government. As a result, India became the 12th nation in the world to adopt laws on cyber crimes. It is also known as the Information Technology Act, and it is a piece of legislation that establishes the legal framework necessary to safeguard data associated with e-commerce and digital signatures. Information technology law, often known as Internet law or cyber law, is a subset of the law that is concerned with legal informatics and controls the digital flow of information, e-commerce, software, and data security. It is a component of the legal system that is commonly referred to as the "cyber law" or "Internet law." When this step is finished, the compressed picture will be subjected to edge detection, which is a technique that analyses the edges of the image. In an attempt to help enhance the overall quality of the images, noise reduction filters are often applied to them after the pictures have been taken. As part of the ongoing study, which takes image databases into consideration, the photos have been shrunk down. After that, a variety of noise-canceling strategies, such as bilateral, Guassian, and anisotropic ones, are put into action.

4.2 Accuracy Parameters

Choosing a performance metric often depends on the business problem being solved. There is the dataset of images and fed each one to the proposed model and received a classification. The predicted vs. actual classification can be charted in a table called a confusion matrix.

Figure 2. Confusion matrix

		Actual Value	
		Positive (1)	**Negative (0)**
Predicted Value	**Positive (1)**	**TP**	**FP**
	Negative (0)	**FN**	**TN**

1. Accuracy

As a heuristic, or rule of thumb, accuracy can tell us immediately whether a model is being trained correctly and how it may perform generally. However, it does not give detailed information regarding its application to the problem.

$$\text{Accuracy} = \frac{\sum \text{TP} + \text{TN}}{\sum \text{TP} + \text{TN} + \text{FP} + \text{FN}} \tag{1}$$

The problem with using accuracy as your main performance metric is that it does not do well when you have a severe class imbalance. Let's use the dataset in the confusion matrix above. Let's say the negatives are normal transactions and the positives are fraudulent transactions. Accuracy will tell you that you're right 99% of the time across all classes.

2. Precision

Precision helps when the costs of false positives are high. So let's assume the problem involves the detection of images. Lots of extra tests and stress are at stake. When false positives are too high, those who monitor the results will learn to ignore them after being bombarded with false alarms.

$$\text{Precision} = \frac{\sum \text{TP}}{\sum \text{TP} + \text{FP}} \tag{2}$$

3. Recall

A false negative has devastating consequences. Get it wrong and we all die. When false negatives are frequent, you get hit by the thing you want to avoid.

$$\text{Recall} = \frac{\sum \text{TP}}{\sum \text{TP} + \text{FN}} \tag{3}$$

4. F1 Score

F1 is an overall measure of a model's accuracy that combines precision and recall, in that weird way that addition and multiplication just mix two ingredients to make a separate dish altogether. That is, a good F1 score means that you have low false positives and low false negatives, so you're correctly identifying real threats and you are not disturbed by false alarms. An F1 score is considered perfect when it's 1, while the model is a total failure when it's 0.

$$\text{F1} = 2 \times \frac{\text{precision} \times \text{recall}}{\text{precision} + \text{recall}} \tag{5}$$

Businesses can make greater use of the resources they already have by integrating these technologies, which enables them to get closer to achieving their objectives. Businesses can generate new possibilities for innovation and development by utilizing the power of AI, image processing, and the Internet of things and things. The intelligent method to apply information technology law in India is to understand how these technologies function together and to utilize them to not only cut expenses but also boost the efficiency and effectiveness of their operations. This is the smart way to apply information technology law. Image quality improvement is important for IT applications, and noise reduction techniques like the Gaussian filter may help give higher picture quality.

5. RESULT AND DISCUSSION

The images have been processed via several noise reduction filters, and their PSNR and SSIM values have been calculated. When the noise has been eliminated, the output may be seen in the following figure.

Figure 3. PSNR after filtering image

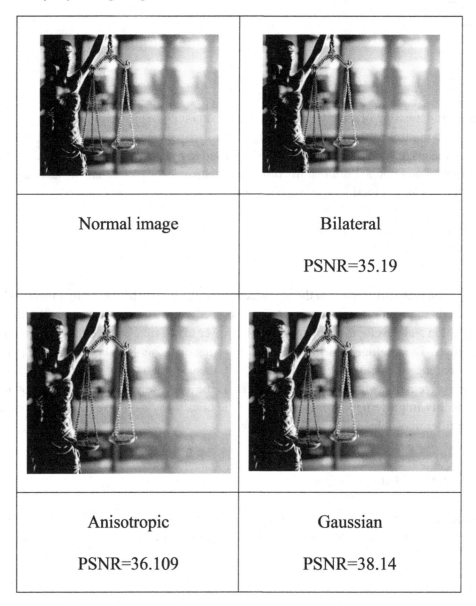

5.1 Calculation of PSNR and SSIM Has Been Performed to Compare the Filters

Table 1. Comparison of PSNR and SSIM

Filter	PSNR	SSIM
Bilateral	35.19	0.911114
Gaussian	38.14	0.943033
Anisotropic	36.109	0.986487

Figure 4. Comparison of PSNR

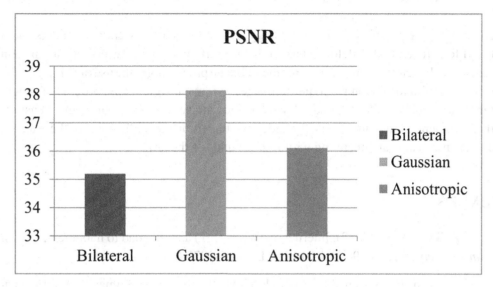

Figure 5. Comparison of SSIM

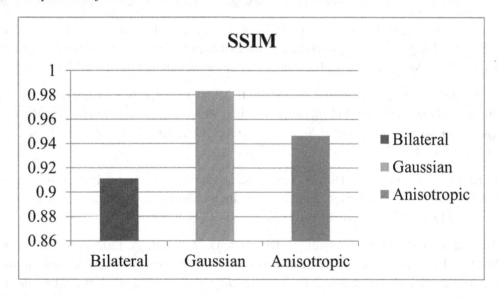

6. CONCLUSION

By integrating these technologies, businesses can better leverage their existing resources to further their goals. By leveraging the power of IoT/IoE, image processing, and AI, businesses can create new opportunities for innovation and growth. The smart way to apply Information Technology Law in India is to understand how these technologies work together and to use them to not only reduce costs but to increase the efficiency and effectiveness of their operations. Quality enhancement of images does matter for IT applications and noise removal such as the Gaussian filter is capable to provide better picture quality.

7. SCOPE OF WORK

When it comes to applying Information Technology Law in India, it is essential to understand the facts about IoT and IoE, IP, and AI. IoT/IoE refers to the networking of physical objects and machines and their interaction with each other and the environment. Image processing is the use of computer algorithms to extract meaningful information from digital images. AI, meanwhile, is the process of programming a computer to think and act like a human. By taking advantage of these technologies, businesses can increase their efficiency and reduce costs. By understanding the legal implications of these technologies, businesses can ensure they are operating within the bounds of the law.

REFERENCES

Ahmad, N., & Zulkifli, A. M. (2022). Internet of Things (IoT) and the road to happiness. *Digital Transformation and Society*, *1*(1), 66–94. doi:10.1108/DTS-05-2022-0009

Al-Ghaili, A. M., Kasim, H., Hassan, Z., & Al-Hada, N. M., Britto Ramesh Kumar, S., & Jerlin Sharmila, J. (2017). IoT Based Home Security through Digital Image Processing Algorithms. *Proceedings - 2nd World Congress on Computing and Communication Technologies, WCCCT*. 20–23. 10.1109/WCCCT.2016.15

Al-Ghaili, A. M., Kasim, H., Hassan, Z., Al-Hada, N. M., Othman, M., Kasmani, R. M., & Shayea, I. (2023). A Review: Image Processing Techniques' Roles Towards Energy-Efficient and Secure IoT. *Applied Sciences (Basel, Switzerland)*, *13*(4), 2098. Advance online publication. doi:10.3390/app13042098

Bhatia, A., Kedia, V., Shroff, A., Kumar, M., Shah, B. K., & Aryan. (2021). Fake currency detection with machine learning algorithm and image processing. *Proceedings - 5th International Conference on Intelligent Computing and Control Systems, ICICCS 2021*, (pp. 755–760). IEEE. doi:10.1109/ICICCS51141.2021.9432274

Gupta, N., Khosravy, M., Patel, N., Dey, N., Gupta, S., Darbari, H., & Crespo, R. G. (2020). Economic data analytic AI technique on IoT edge devices for health monitoring of agriculture machines. *Applied Intelligence*, *50*(11), 3990–4016. doi:10.100710489-020-01744-x

Jain, V., Beram, S. M., Talukdar, V., Patil, T., Dhabliya, D., & Gupta, A. (2022). Accuracy Enhancement in Machine Learning During Blockchain-Based Transaction Classification. *Seventh International Conference on Parallel, Distributed and Grid Computing (PDGC)*, Solan, Himachal Pradesh, India. 10.1109/PDGC56933.2022.10053213

Kaushik, D., & Gupta, A. (2021). Ultra-secure transmissions for 5G-V2X communications. *Materials Today: Proceedings*. doi:10.1016/j.matpr.2020.12.130

Kaushik, K., & Garg, M. Annu, Gupta, A. & Pramanik, S. (2021). Application of Machine Learning and Deep Learning in Cyber security: An Innovative Approach, in Cybersecurity and Digital Forensics: Challenges and Future Trends, M. Ghonge, S. Pramanik, R. Mangrulkar and D. N. Le, Eds, Wiley.

Khaddar, M. A. El, & Boulmalf, M. (2017). Smartphone: The Ultimate IoT and IoE Device. *Smartphones from an Applied Research Perspective*. doi:10.5772/intechopen.69734

Kotenko, I., Izrailov, K., & Buinevich, M. (2022). Static Analysis of Information Systems for IoT Cyber Security: A Survey of Machine Learning Approaches. *Sensors (Basel)*, *22*(4), 1335. doi:10.339022041335 PMID:35214237

Kumar, R., Narayanan, S., & Kaur, G. (2021). Future of the Internet of Everything. *International Research Journal of Computer Science*, *8*(4), 84–92. doi:10.26562/irjcs.2021.v0804.003

Kumar, S., Tiwari, P., & Zymbler, M. (2019). Internet of Things is a revolutionary approach for future technology enhancement: A review. *Journal of Big Data*, *6*(1), 111. doi:10.118640537-019-0268-2

Nižetić, S., Šolić, P., López-de-Ipiña González-de-Artaza, D., & Patrono, L. (2020). Internet of Things (IoT): Opportunities, issues, and challenges towards a smart and sustainable future. *Journal of Cleaner Production*, *274*, 122877. doi:10.1016/j.jclepro.2020.122877 PMID:32834567

Pandey, B. K. (2022). Effective and Secure Transmission of Health Information Using Advanced Morphological Component Analysis and Image Hiding. In M. Gupta, S. Ghatak, A. Gupta, & A. L. Mukherjee (Eds.), *Artificial Intelligence on Medical Data. Lecture Notes in Computational Vision and Biomechanics* (Vol. 37). Springer. doi:10.1007/978-981-19-0151-5_19

Pandey, B. K., Pandey, D., & Agarwal, A. (2022). Encrypted Information Transmission by Enhanced Steganography and Image Transformation. [IJDAI]. *International Journal of Distributed Artificial Intelligence*, *14*(1), 1–14. doi:10.4018/IJDAI.297110

Pandey, B. K., Pandey, D., Gupta, A., Nassa, V. K., Dadheech, P., & George, A. S. (2023). Secret Data Transmission Using Advanced Morphological Component Analysis and Steganography. In *Role of Data-Intensive Distributed Computing Systems in Designing Data Solutions* (pp. 21–44). Springer International Publishing. doi:10.1007/978-3-031-15542-0_2

Prabaharan, T., Periasamy, P., Mugendiran, V., & Ramanan. (2020). Studies on the application of image processing in various fields: An overview. *IOP Conference Series. Materials Science and Engineering*, *961*(1), 012006. doi:10.1088/1757-899X/961/1/012006

Reddy, M. B., Pravalika, R., & Krishnaveni, R. (2020). A Journey From the Internet of Things (IoT) To the Internet of Everything. *International Journal of Scientific Research and Engineering Development*, *3*(5), 345–348. http://www.ijsred.com/volume3/issue5/IJSRED-V3I5P48.pdf

Sachdev, R. (2020). Towards Security and Privacy for Edge AI in IoT/IoE based Digital Marketing Environments. *2020 5th International Conference on Fog and Mobile Edge Computing, FMEC 2020*, (pp. 341–346). IEEE. 10.1109/FMEC49853.2020.9144755

Shilpa, A., Muneeswaran, V., Rathinam, D. K., Grace, S. A., & Sherin, J. (2019). Exploring the Benefits of Sensors in the Internet of Everything (IoE). *2019 5th International Conference on Advanced Computing and Communication Systems, ICACCS 2019*, (pp. 510–514). IEEE. 10.1109/ICACCS.2019.8728530

Singh, A., & Singh, J. (2018). Image Processing and IoT-based Applications. *International Journal of Innovative Science and Research Technology*, *3*(11), 236–238. https://www.cognizant.com/InsightsWhitepapers/Designi

Stoyanova, M., Nikoloudakis, Y., Panagiotakis, S., Pallis, E., & Markakis, E. K. (2020). A Survey on the Internet of Things (IoT) Forensics: Challenges, Approaches, and Open Issues. *IEEE Communications Surveys and Tutorials*, *22*(2), 1191–1221. doi:10.1109/COMST.2019.2962586

Swaminathan, B., Rahul, R., Ragul, S., & Ramavel, M. (2018). Integration of IOT and Data Analytics : Performance Analysis System for Outdoor Sports using Electromyography and Image Data. *International Journal of Applied Engineering Research, 13*(8), 6158–6164.

Zheng, X., & Cloutier, R. S. (2022). A Review of Image Classification Algorithms in IoT. *EAI Endorsed Transactions on Internet of Things*, *7*(28), 1–11. doi:10.4108/eetiot.v7i28.562

Chapter 10
Applications of Artificial Intelligent and Machine Learning Techniques in Image Processing

Sampath Boopathi

Muthayammal Engineering College, India

Uday Kumar Kanike

Georgia State University, USA

ABSTRACT

This chapter explores the role of AI and machine learning (ML) in image processing, focusing on their applications. It covers AI techniques like supervised learning, unsupervised learning, reinforcement learning, and deep learning. AI techniques include rule-based systems, expert systems, fuzzy logic, and genetic algorithms. Machine learning techniques include SVM, decision trees, random forests, K-means clustering, and PCA. Deep learning techniques like CNN, RNN, and GANs are used in tasks like object recognition, classification, and segmentation. The chapter emphasizes the impact of AI and ML on accuracy, efficiency, and decision-making. It also discusses evaluation metrics and performance analysis, emphasizing the importance of selecting appropriate metrics and techniques. The chapter also addresses ethical considerations, such as fairness, privacy, transparency, and human-AI collaboration.

INTRODUCTION

Image processing involves various techniques and algorithms applied to digital images to achieve desired outcomes. These techniques range from basic operations like enhancement and noise reduction to complex tasks like segmentation, object recognition, and classification. Image processing is crucial in fields like medical imaging, surveillance, remote sensing, robotics, and computer vision. Recent research has focused on image processing and AI/ML, with advancements in various aspects. Key research areas

DOI: 10.4018/978-1-6684-8618-4.ch010

within the intersection of image processing and AI/ML include image segmentation, object recognition, and image classification(Barrett, 2023; Erickson, 2021).

Deep learning has revolutionized image analysis by enabling convolutional neural networks (CNNs) to learn hierarchical representations of images. This enables tasks like image classification, object detection, and semantic segmentation. Research focuses on efficient models, network architectures, and techniques for handling limited training data and interpretability of learned features(Santosh et al., 2022). Generative models like GANs and VAEs are popular in image synthesis, generating realistic images from noise or manipulating existing images. Research focuses on improving image quality, diversity, mode collapse issues, and enabling better control over the synthesis process(Harikaran et al., 2023; Janardhana, Singh, et al., 2023; Reddy et al., 2023). Transfer learning and domain adaptation techniques transfer pre-trained models from one domain to another, enabling more accurate and efficient models for various applications in image processing. This research area focuses on developing methods to transfer learned features from large-scale datasets to specific tasks with limited labeled data, enhancing the overall efficiency of image analysis(Balyen & Peto, 2019).

AI/ML models' decision-making process becomes crucial as they become more complex. Research focuses on developing techniques to explain and interpret these decisions in image processing tasks. This includes visualizing learned features, identifying important regions for predictions, and providing insights into model behavior, enhancing trust and transparency(Anitha et al., 2023; Boopathi, 2023b; Selvakumar et al., 2023; Subha et al., 2023). Traditional image processing methods often require large amounts of labeled data for training, which can be expensive and time-consuming. Research in weakly supervised and unsupervised learning aims to develop methods that learn from weak or unlabeled data, including self-supervised learning, semi-supervised learning, and active learning. These techniques explore ways to leverage unlabeled or partially labeled data for training image processing models(Boopathi, 2023a; Boopathi, Arigela, et al., 2023; Boopathi, Venkatesan, et al., 2023; Kavitha et al., 2023; Yupapin et al., 2023). Research in image processing is crucial to ensure robustness of AI/ML models against adversarial attacks. These attacks introduce imperceptible perturbations, leading to misclassification or incorrect behavior. The focus is on developing defense mechanisms, improving model robustness, and investigating vulnerabilities and limitations in AI/ML models. Researchers are working on AI/ML techniques to enhance image processing accuracy, efficiency, interpretability, and robustness, benefiting various fields like healthcare, robotics, and autonomous vehicles.

Role of Artificial Intelligence and Machine Learning in Image Processing

AI and machine learning revolutionize image processing by enabling computers to learn from large amounts of data, making intelligent decisions. These algorithms analyze vast datasets, identify patterns, and extract meaningful features without explicit programming(Chaudhari & Walke, 2022). AI and ML techniques aid in image processing tasks.

- AI/ML models can recognize objects, faces, and patterns in images, enabling applications like facial recognition, object detection, and image-based search.
- ML algorithms enable image segmentation, separating images into meaningful regions for precise analysis and comprehension.
- AI models classify images into predefined categories based on visual features, aiding content-based retrieval and automated tagging applications.

- AI/ML-powered image generation models can create realistic images, alter characteristics, or fill missing parts.
- AI algorithms enhance images by learning from examples and applying intelligent reconstruction techniques, restoring and improving low-quality images.

ARTIFICIAL INTELLIGENCE AND MACHINE LEARNING: IMAGE PROCESSING

Artificial Intelligence (AI) is the development of intelligent machines capable of performing tasks that typically require human intelligence. In image processing, AI plays a crucial role in automating and enhancing image analysis tasks. AI techniques enable computers to understand, interpret, and extract meaningful information from digital images. AI techniques include algorithms and models that recognize patterns, objects, and features within images. These techniques include image classification, object detection, segmentation, and generation. The integration of AI in image processing has led to significant advancements in computer vision, medical imaging, robotics, and surveillance. AI algorithms can now achieve human-level or surpass human performance in specific image analysis tasks, making image processing more efficient, accurate, and scalable(Haug & Drazen, 2022).

Machine Learning (ML) is an AI subfield that enables computers to learn and improve from experience without explicit programming. ML algorithms analyze large amounts of data, extract patterns, relationships, and insights for predictions or actions. In image processing, ML techniques revolutionize the field by automatically learning features and patterns from images. ML algorithms can be trained on labeled datasets, known as supervised learning, to recognize and classify images based on the provided labels(Bera et al., 2020).

Supervised learning in image processing involves training machine learning models on labeled datasets, aiming to develop models that accurately classify or predict unseen images. Popular algorithms for image classification include SVMs, decision trees, and deep learning models like CNNs. These algorithms learn to differentiate and classify images based on patterns and features extracted from the training data(Babu et al., 2023; Boopathi, Siva Kumar, et al., 2023; Domakonda et al., 2023; Jeevanantham et al., 2023; Vanitha et al., 2023).

Unsupervised learning in image processing involves training machine learning models without explicit labels or class information, aiming to discover underlying patterns, structures, or relationships within the image data. In image clustering, algorithms like k-means and hierarchical clustering group similar images based on visual similarities, identifying clusters without prior knowledge of labels. Dimensionality reduction, another unsupervised learning technique, reduces the complexity of image data by capturing relevant information while reducing the number of features or dimensions, making it useful for visualizing and understanding high-dimensional image data(Rajesh & Asaad, 2023).

Reinforcement Learning (RL) is a learning paradigm that involves agents making sequential decisions to maximize cumulative rewards. While not directly applied to image processing tasks, RL can be used in robotics and autonomous systems to process visual input from cameras and take actions based on analyzed images. This allows agents to recognize objects, navigate environments, and manipulate objects using image information. Combining RL techniques with image processing enables intelligent systems to interact with and understand the visual world(Seifert et al., 2021).

Deep Learning, a subfield of machine learning, focuses on training deep neural networks to learn hierarchical representations of data. This has significantly advanced image processing tasks by enabling the development of highly accurate and sophisticated models. Convolutional neural networks (CNNs) have achieved remarkable success in image processing, automatically learning and extracting hierarchical features from images(Kumara et al., 2023; Mohanty et al., 2023; Samikannu et al., 2023; Vennila et al., 2023). These models have been applied to tasks like image classification, object detection, segmentation, and generation. Deep learning models have demonstrated state-of-the-art performance, surpassing traditional machine learning techniques in accuracy and robustness. The ability of deep neural networks to automatically learn and represent complex image features has revolutionized the field, making it an integral part of modern image processing applications(Robertson et al., 2018).

IMAGE REPRESENTATION AND PRE-PROCESSING

Image Representation

Image representation involves encoding and structuring data for analysis and processing, using traditional pixel-based and vector-based methods. Advanced, efficient approaches are being explored in future directions(Vidal & Amigo, 2012).

- Pixel-based representation is a simple and widely used method for manipulating images at the pixel level. However, it lacks semantic information and may not capture high-level structures or relationships. New directions in pixel-based representation include incorporating spatial context and multi-channel representations. These representations capture visual aspects like color, texture, and depth, providing richer information for image analysis tasks like object recognition, scene understanding, and image synthesis.
- Vector-based representation captures abstract and semantic information from images by representing them as vectors or high-dimensional feature descriptors. This approach encodes higher-level characteristics like shapes, textures, and visual patterns. Deep learning techniques are being used to learn expressive and discriminative features, enabling better performance in image analysis tasks. Research is also exploring graph-based representations, where images are represented as graphs that capture relationships between image elements, offering a flexible framework for modeling complex structures and efficient analysis of interconnected image components.

Image Pre-Processing Techniques

Image preprocessing techniques improve image quality, reduce noise, and segment images for analysis. Advancements in adaptive methods are being developed to enhance the process, while traditional techniques remain widely used (Boopathi, Khare, et al., 2023; Boopathi, Venkatesan, et al., 2023; S. et al., 2022; Sonka et al., n.d.; Vanitha et al., 2023; Vennila et al., 2023).

- Image enhancement techniques improve visual quality, contrast, and clarity of images. Traditional methods involve adjusting brightness, contrast, and color balance. Deep learning models can learn specific transformation functions, preserving details and maintaining a natural appearance. Techniques like style transfer can transform images into different artistic styles, enabling creative enhancement(Boopathi, Balasubramani, et al., 2023; Gowri et al., 2023; Janardhana, Anushkannan, et al., 2023).

- Noise reduction techniques aim to remove artifacts from images, enhancing quality and clarity. Traditional methods use filters like median or Gaussian filters. Deep learning-based denoising models, trained to learn noise patterns, effectively remove noise while preserving image details.
- Image segmentation techniques partition images into meaningful regions or objects using traditional methods like thresholding, edge detection, or region-growing. Advanced deep learning algorithms like convolutional neural networks and graph neural networks enable more accurate and robust results. Research is also being conducted on unsupervised and weakly supervised methods, reducing reliance on extensive labeled datasets.

Advanced techniques like deep learning, multi-channel representations, graph-based representations, and adaptive algorithms are being used in image representation and pre-processing to improve quality, accuracy, and enable more sophisticated analysis and understanding.

TRADITIONAL AI TECHNIQUES IN IMAGE PROCESSING

Rule-Based Systems

Rule-based systems, also known as rule-based reasoning or expert systems, are AI techniques that use predefined rules to make decisions or perform tasks. They are used in image processing to define conditions or criteria based on image features or characteristics, such as pixel intensities, texture characteristics, or geometric properties. These rules evaluate for each input image to determine the appropriate classification. While rule-based systems provide interpretable and explainable results, they may be limited in handling complex image analysis tasks requiring advanced feature extraction and learning capabilities(Farooq et al., 2005).

Expert Systems

Expert systems are AI systems that mimic the decision-making abilities of human experts in a specific domain. They can assist in tasks like image interpretation, diagnosis, and quality assessment. These systems typically have a knowledge base, inference rules, and an inference engine that solves specific image processing problems. Expert systems are beneficial in scenarios where expert knowledge is critical, especially in domains with well-defined rules and guidelines. However, developing and maintaining expert systems can be challenging and time-consuming, as it requires a comprehensive understanding of the domain and continuous updates to incorporate new knowledge(Shi et al., 2021).

Fuzzy Logic

Fuzzy logic is an AI technique that handles uncertain or imprecise information by allowing degrees of membership or truth values between binary true and false values. It is useful in image processing tasks like segmentation, edge detection, and enhancement(Boopathi, Khare, et al., 2023; Palaniappan et al., 2023; Sathish, Sunagar, Singh, Boopathi, Al-Enizi, et al., 2023; Senthil et al., 2023). Fuzzy logic systems capture and process uncertain or vague image information effectively by defining fuzzy rules and membership functions. In image segmentation, fuzzy logic assigns membership values based on pixel belonging to different regions, accommodating variations and gradual transitions in real-world images. This flexible framework is particularly useful in situations where precise thresholding or strict binary decision-making may not be appropriate(Santosh et al., 2022; Seifert et al., 2021).

Genetic Algorithms

Genetic algorithms (GAs) are search and optimization techniques inspired by natural selection and evolution. They are used in image processing for tasks like feature selection, parameter tuning, and image reconstruction. GAs generates a population of candidate solutions, evaluate their fitness, and apply evolutionary operators like crossover and mutation to iteratively improve solutions(Boopathi, 2019, 2022b, 2022d, 2022a, 2022c). They offer a powerful optimization approach for complex and large solution spaces, handling non-linear and non-convex optimization problems. However, their computational cost and convergence speed may be limitations in some applications(Boopathi, Balasubramani, et al., 2023; Sathish, Sunagar, Singh, Boopathi, Al-enizi, et al., 2023; Yupapin et al., 2023).

Traditional AI techniques like rule-based systems, expert systems, fuzzy logic, and genetic algorithms have been utilized in image processing to tackle challenges before machine learning and deep learning approaches. These techniques have their strengths and limitations.

MACHINE LEARNING TECHNIQUES IN IMAGE PROCESSING

Supervised Learning Algorithms

Supervised learning algorithms in image processing involve training models on labeled datasets, where each image is associated with a corresponding label or class. These algorithms learn to map the visual features of images to their respective labels, enabling image classification, object detection, and other tasks (Figure 1).

Support Vector Machines (SVM)

Support Vector Machines (SVM) are popular supervised learning algorithms used in image processing. SVMs aim to find an optimal hyperplane that separates different classes in the feature space. In the context of image classification, SVMs learn to classify images by finding the best decision boundary that maximizes the margin between different classes. SVMs can effectively handle high-dimensional feature spaces and nonlinear relationships by using kernel functions. They have been widely applied in image classification tasks, where features extracted from images are used as input to train the SVM model(Farooq et al., 2005; Santosh et al., 2022).

Decision Trees

Decision trees are tree-like models that make decisions based on feature values at different nodes. In image processing, decision trees can be used for tasks such as image classification or object recognition.

Each node of the tree represents a decision based on a specific feature, leading to subsequent nodes until a final decision or class label is reached. Decision trees are interpretable and can handle both categorical and continuous features. However, they may suffer from overfitting if the tree becomes too complex or the dataset is noisy. Ensemble methods like random forests address this issue by combining multiple decision trees to improve the overall accuracy and robustness(Robertson et al., 2018; Vidal & Amigo, 2012).

Random Forests

Random forests are ensemble learning algorithms that combine multiple decision trees to make predictions. In image processing, random forests are widely used for tasks such as image classification and object detection. A random forest consists of a collection of decision trees trained on different subsets of the training data. During prediction, each tree in the forest independently classifies the image, and the final prediction is determined by majority voting or averaging the results. Random forests can handle high-dimensional feature spaces, nonlinear relationships, and noisy data. They are robust against overfitting and tend to provide accurate and stable predictions. Random forests have been successfully applied in various image processing applications due to their effectiveness and scalability(Marias, 2021; Shi et al., 2021).

It's important to note that while SVMs, decision trees, and random forests have been widely used in image processing, deep learning techniques, particularly convolutional neural networks (CNNs), have gained prominence in recent years and have become the state-of-the-art approach for many image processing tasks(Babu et al., 2023; Boopathi, Khare, et al., 2023; Palaniappan et al., 2023; Senthil et al., 2023). CNNs have demonstrated superior performance in image classification, object detection, image segmentation, and other related tasks, surpassing traditional machine learning techniques in terms of accuracy and representation learning.

Figure 1. Machine learning techniques in image processing

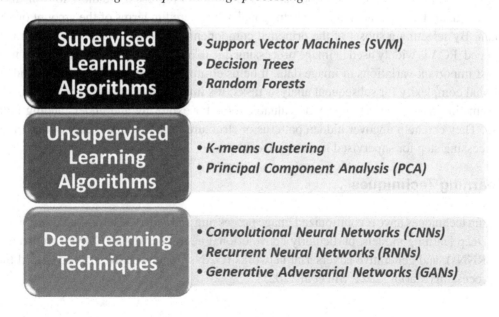

Unsupervised Learning Algorithms

Unsupervised learning algorithms in image processing aim to discover patterns, structures, or relationships in unlabeled data without explicit class labels. These algorithms can be used for tasks such as image clustering, dimensionality reduction, and anomaly detection(Munawar et al., 2021; Robertson et al., 2018).

K-Means Clustering

K-means clustering is a popular unsupervised learning algorithm used in image processing. It aims to partition a set of images into K clusters based on their feature similarity. The algorithm iteratively assigns each image to the cluster with the closest mean (centroid) and updates the centroids until convergence. In image processing, K-means clustering can be applied to tasks such as image segmentation or grouping similar images together. It helps identify distinct image regions or group images based on shared visual characteristics. However, K-means clustering requires specifying the number of clusters (K) in advance, which can be challenging if the optimal number of clusters is unknown. It is also sensitive to the initial centroid positions and may converge to suboptimal solutions. Various extensions and improvements, such as fuzzy K-means or spectral clustering, have been proposed to overcome these limitations(Anitha et al., 2023; Babu et al., 2023; Boopathi, Arigela, et al., 2023; Jeevanantham et al., 2023; Subha et al., 2023).

Principal Component Analysis (PCA)

Principal Component Analysis (PCA) is a dimensionality reduction technique commonly used in image processing. It aims to capture the most important variations in the image data by projecting it onto a lower-dimensional space. In image processing, PCA can be applied to reduce the dimensionality of image features while preserving the most informative components. It helps extract meaningful representations from high-dimensional image data and can be used for tasks such as image compression or feature extraction. PCA works by finding the principal components that represent the directions of maximum variance in the data. These components are orthogonal and ordered in terms of the amount of variance they explain. By selecting a subset of the principal components, the dimensionality of the image data can be reduced. PCA is widely used in image processing due to its simplicity and effectiveness in capturing the most important variations in image data. It helps eliminate redundant information and reduces computational complexity for subsequent analysis tasks. It's important to note that unsupervised learning algorithms in image processing provide valuable tools for exploring and understanding unlabeled image data. They can help uncover hidden patterns or structures, facilitate data exploration, and serve as a preprocessing step for supervised learning algorithms.

Deep Learning Techniques

Deep learning techniques have revolutionized image processing and achieved remarkable success in various tasks. Deep learning models, particularly convolutional neural networks (CNNs), recurrent neural networks (RNNs), and generative adversarial networks (GANs), have significantly advanced the field of image processing(Marias, 2021; Shi et al., 2021).

Convolutional Neural Networks (CNNs)

Convolutional neural networks (CNNs) are a class of deep learning models specifically designed for processing grid-like data, such as images. CNNs have achieved state-of-the-art performance in image classification, object detection, image segmentation, and other image processing tasks. CNNs are composed of multiple layers, including convolutional layers, pooling layers, and fully connected layers. Convolutional layers extract local features by convolving filters across the input image, capturing spatial hierarchies. Pooling layers downsample the feature maps, reducing the spatial dimensions. Finally, fully connected layers combine the extracted features to make predictions.

The strength of CNNs lies in their ability to automatically learn hierarchical representations of images, capturing both low-level features like edges and textures, as well as high-level features like object shapes and semantic concepts. CNNs can handle large-scale datasets and generalize well to unseen images, making them highly effective for image processing tasks.

Recurrent Neural Networks (RNNs)

Recurrent neural networks (RNNs) are a type of deep learning model that can capture sequential information and handle variable-length inputs. While primarily used in tasks involving sequential data, RNNs have also been applied to image processing tasks where temporal or contextual information is important. In image processing, RNNs are used for tasks such as image captioning, video analysis, or image generation. They can model the dependencies between images or image regions over time and generate coherent and contextually relevant outputs. Long Short-Term Memory (LSTM) and Gated Recurrent Units (GRU) are popular variants of RNNs that address the vanishing gradient problem and improve the learning of long-term dependencies(Munawar et al., 2021).

Generative Adversarial Networks (GANs)

Generative adversarial networks (GANs) are a class of deep learning models that involve two neural networks: a generator network and a discriminator network. GANs are used for generating new images that resemble the training data distribution, enabling tasks such as image synthesis, image-to-image translation, and image augmentation. The generator network generates new images, while the discriminator network distinguishes between real and generated images. The two networks are trained together in a competitive setting, where the generator aims to generate more realistic images that can fool the discriminator, while the discriminator improves its ability to differentiate between real and generated images(Robertson et al., 2018). GANs have produced impressive results in generating highly realistic and diverse images. They have been used for tasks such as image generation from noise vectors, style transfer, and data augmentation. GANs have also been extended to conditional GANs (cGANs), where the generator and discriminator are conditioned on additional information, such as class labels or input images, enabling controlled image generation or image-to-image translation.

Deep learning techniques, like CNNs, RNNs, and GANs, revolutionize image processing by automatically learning complex representations and generating realistic images, significantly advancing image analysis and understanding.

Figure 2. Applications of AI AND ML in image processing

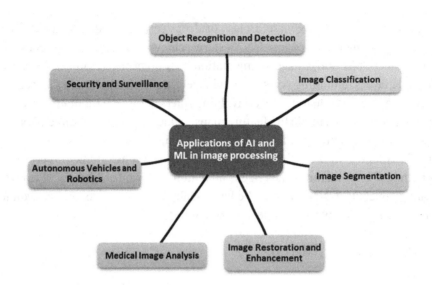

APPLICATIONS OF AI AND ML IN IMAGE PROCESSING

The various Applications of AI AND ML in image processing is illustrated in Figure 2.

Object Recognition and Detection

AI and ML techniques have greatly advanced object recognition and detection in image processing. Object recognition involves identifying and categorizing objects within an image, while object detection aims to locate and identify multiple objects in an image. Convolutional neural networks (CNNs) have played a pivotal role in object recognition and detection tasks. They can learn discriminative features from images and accurately classify or locate objects. Techniques like region-based CNNs (R-CNN), You Only Look Once (YOLO), and Single Shot MultiBox Detector (SSD) have achieved remarkable performance in object detection, enabling applications such as autonomous driving, surveillance systems, and object tracking(Iosup et al., 2011).

Image Classification

Image classification is a fundamental task in image processing, where images are assigned to predefined categories or labels. AI and ML techniques have significantly improved image classification accuracy and efficiency. Supervised learning algorithms, particularly CNNs, have revolutionized image classification. CNNs learn hierarchical representations of images, automatically extracting relevant features for classification. They have achieved state-of-the-art performance in various image classification benchmarks, including the ImageNet dataset. Image classification has numerous practical applications, such as medical diagnosis, quality control in manufacturing, content-based image retrieval, and personalized recommendation systems.

Image Segmentation

Image segmentation involves dividing an image into meaningful and distinct regions or objects. It is a critical step in image understanding, as it provides fine-grained information about the spatial layout and boundaries of objects within an image. Deep learning techniques, especially CNNs and their variants, have demonstrated exceptional performance in image segmentation. Fully Convolutional Networks (FCNs), U-Net, and DeepLab are popular architectures for semantic segmentation, where each pixel is classified into different classes or regions. Image segmentation has various applications, including medical imaging for tumor detection and analysis, autonomous driving for scene understanding, object tracking, and augmented reality(Ono et al., 2012). AI and ML are revolutionizing image processing by enabling breakthroughs in areas like image generation, style transfer, and super-resolution. This combination of AI/ML and image processing offers new possibilities for visual understanding, interpretation, and manipulation of images.

Image Restoration and Enhancement

AI and ML techniques are widely used for image restoration and enhancement tasks. Image restoration aims to recover the original image from a degraded or corrupted version, such as denoising, deblurring, or inpainting missing regions. ML models, including deep learning-based approaches, can learn the underlying patterns and structures in images to effectively restore and enhance image quality(Alzubaidi et al., 2020).

Medical Image Analysis

AI and ML have made significant contributions to medical image analysis, enabling advanced diagnosis, treatment planning, and disease monitoring. ML models can analyze medical images, such as X-rays, MRI scans, or histopathological images, to detect anomalies, segment organs or tumors, classify diseases, and predict treatment outcomes. These applications have the potential to improve healthcare delivery and patient outcomes.

Autonomous Vehicles and Robotics

AI and ML play a crucial role in autonomous vehicles and robotics, particularly in visual perception and decision-making tasks. ML models, including deep learning-based algorithms, analyze real-time sensor data, such as images from cameras or LiDAR scans, to detect and recognize objects, interpret the surrounding environment, and make intelligent decisions for navigation and control. Autonomous vehicles and robots rely on AI and ML for tasks like object detection, lane detection, pedestrian tracking, and path planning(Zhou et al., 2021).

Security and Surveillance

AI and ML techniques are extensively used in security and surveillance systems. ML models can analyze video feeds or images to detect and track objects, recognize faces or license plates, identify suspicious activities, and classify events as normal or anomalous. These applications have a wide range of uses, including public safety, access control, video surveillance, and threat detection.

AI and ML's versatility in image processing enables advancements in various domains, including healthcare, transportation, and security. The integration of advanced algorithms and large-scale datasets drives innovation, pushing the boundaries of image processing and intelligent systems.

EVALUATION METRICS AND PERFORMANCE ANALYSIS

Performance Metrics for Image Processing Tasks

In image processing, various performance metrics are used to evaluate the effectiveness and accuracy of algorithms and models. The choice of metrics depends on the specific task being performed. Here are some commonly used performance metrics for different image processing tasks(Dikici et al., 2020):

- **Image Classification:** For image classification tasks, metrics like accuracy, precision, recall, and F1 score are commonly used. Accuracy measures the overall correctness of the classification, while precision and recall provide insights into the trade-off between true positive and false positive rates. The F1 score combines precision and recall into a single metric.
- **Object Detection:** Object detection tasks involve both localization (detecting the presence of objects) and classification (assigning the correct label). Performance metrics for object detection include Average Precision (AP), Intersection over Union (IoU), and mean Average Precision (mAP). AP measures the precision-recall trade-off, IoU measures the overlap between the predicted and ground truth bounding boxes, and mAP is the average AP over multiple object categories.
- **Image Segmentation:** Evaluation metrics for image segmentation include Intersection over Union (IoU), Dice coefficient, and pixel accuracy. IoU measures the overlap between the predicted and ground truth segmentation masks, while the Dice coefficient provides a similarity measure. Pixel accuracy calculates the percentage of correctly classified pixels in the segmentation map.
- **Image Restoration/Enhancement:** Metrics such as Peak Signal-to-Noise Ratio (PSNR) and Structural Similarity Index (SSIM) are often used to evaluate the quality of restored or enhanced images. PSNR measures the difference between the original and restored images in terms of noise, while SSIM assesses the structural similarity between the two images.

Performance Evaluation of AI/ML Models

Evaluate AI/ML models' performance in image processing using various techniques(Pandey et al., 2022).

- **Train-Test Split:** Models are trained on a labeled dataset and evaluated on a separate test set to measure their performance on unseen data. The test set should be representative of the real-world scenarios to provide an accurate evaluation.
- **Cross-Validation:** Cross-validation is used when the available dataset is limited. It involves dividing the data into multiple subsets or folds, training the model on a combination of folds, and evaluating its performance on the remaining fold. This process is repeated several times to obtain a more reliable performance estimate.

- **Evaluation Metrics:** As mentioned earlier, appropriate performance metrics are chosen based on the specific image processing task. These metrics provide quantitative measures of the model's performance, allowing for objective evaluation.
- **Baseline Comparison:** Comparing the performance of the AI/ML model with a baseline or existing methods provides insights into its effectiveness. This comparison helps assess the improvement achieved by the proposed model and its potential practical impact.

Comparison of Different Techniques

Comparing different AI/ML techniques in image processing involves evaluating their performance on the same dataset and task. This allows for a fair comparison and identification of the most effective approach. Several factors to consider in comparing techniques include(Balti et al., 2020)(Balti et al., 2020):

- **Accuracy:** The accuracy of each technique in achieving the desired image processing task is a primary consideration. The higher the accuracy, the better the technique is at capturing the underlying patterns in the data.
- **Computational Efficiency:** Another important factor is the computational efficiency of the techniques. Faster processing times and lower resource requirements are desirable, especially in real-time or resource-constrained applications.
- **Robustness:** The robustness of the techniques to variations in input data, noise, lighting conditions, or other factors is essential. Robust techniques are less prone to errors and can handle diverse and challenging scenarios effectively.
- **Generalization:** The ability of the techniques to generalize well to unseen data or different datasets is crucial. Techniques that perform well across multiple datasets and exhibit good generalization capabilities are preferred.
- **Complexity and Ease of Implementation:** The complexity of the techniques and their ease of implementation should be considered. Techniques that are easy to understand, implement, and maintain are more practical and accessible.

Evaluating AI/ML models' performance in image processing requires selecting appropriate metrics, considering evaluation techniques, and fair comparisons between different approaches. This helps researchers and practitioners understand the strengths and weaknesses of different techniques, enabling them to choose the most suitable approach for their specific tasks. Visualizations like performance curves or confusion matrices provide intuitive comparisons between techniques.

CASE STUDY: AI AND ML IN IMAGE PROCESSING: A CASE STUDY IN MEDICAL IMAGING

This case study explores the practical application of Artificial Intelligence (AI) and Machine Learning (ML) in the field of medical imaging. Specifically, it focuses on the use of AI and ML techniques for image processing tasks in medical imaging, aiming to improve diagnosis and treatment outcomes. The case study highlights the challenges faced in medical image analysis and showcases how AI and ML can address these challenges, leading to more accurate and efficient healthcare practices(Balti et al., 2020; Ono et al., 2012; Pandey et al., 2022; Santosh et al., 2022).

In this case study, we will explore the application of Artificial Intelligence (AI) and Machine Learning (ML) in the field of image processing. Specifically, we will examine a real-world scenario where AI and ML techniques have been used to enhance image analysis and improve the accuracy of a medical imaging system. The case study focuses on the use of AI and ML in medical image classification for the detection of lung cancer from chest X-ray images. Lung cancer is a leading cause of cancer-related deaths worldwide. Early detection plays a critical role in improving patient outcomes and survival rates. Chest X-ray images are commonly used for screening and diagnosing lung cancer. However, accurately interpreting these images can be challenging due to the subtle and complex patterns associated with lung abnormalities. This is where AI and ML can make a significant impact by assisting radiologists in the diagnosis process. The objective of this case study is to develop an AI-based system that can assist radiologists in the early detection of lung cancer from chest X-ray images. The system will use ML techniques to analyze the images and classify them as either normal or indicative of lung cancer. The ultimate goal is to improve the accuracy and efficiency of lung cancer diagnosis, leading to earlier intervention and improved patient outcomes.

Figure 3. AI and ML in image processing: a case study in medical imaging

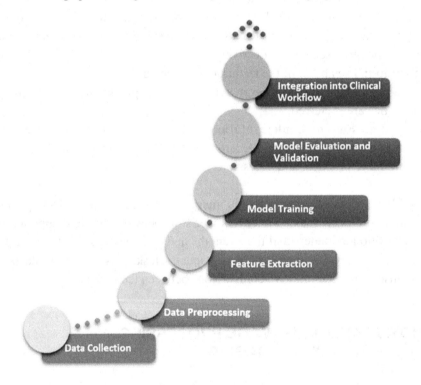

Methodology

The process and procedure for AI and ML in image processing: a case study in medical imaging is represented in Figure 3.

- **Data Collection:** A large dataset of annotated chest X-ray images is collected from medical institutions. The dataset includes images from both healthy individuals and patients diagnosed with lung cancer. Each image is labeled with the corresponding diagnosis (normal or lung cancer).
- **Data Pre-processing:** The collected dataset undergoes preprocessing steps to ensure data quality and consistency. Preprocessing techniques include image resizing, normalization, and noise reduction to improve the performance of the ML models.
- **Feature Extraction:** ML models require informative features to make accurate predictions. In this case, deep learning techniques are employed to automatically extract relevant features from the chest X-ray images. Convolutional Neural Networks (CNNs) are utilized to capture the spatial patterns and structural information present in the images.
- **Model Training:** The preprocessed data and extracted features are used to train ML models for lung cancer classification. Supervised learning algorithms, such as Support Vector Machines (SVM) or deep learning models like CNNs, are trained on the labeled dataset. The models learn to differentiate between normal and cancerous chest X-ray images based on the extracted features.
- **Model Evaluation and Validation:** The trained ML models are evaluated using appropriate performance metrics, such as accuracy, precision, recall, and F1 score. The models are tested on a separate dataset that was not used during training to assess their generalization capabilities. Cross-validation techniques may also be employed to ensure robustness and minimize overfitting.
- **Integration into Clinical Workflow:** Once the ML models demonstrate satisfactory performance, they are integrated into the existing clinical workflow. The AI-based system assists radiologists by automatically analyzing chest X-ray images and providing preliminary classifications. Radiologists can then review the system's findings, validate the results, and make informed decisions based on the combined expertise of the AI system and their own medical knowledge.

Results and Benefits

The implementation of AI and ML in the image processing of chest X-ray images for lung cancer detection has several notable benefits(Santosh et al., 2022):

- **Improved Accuracy:** The ML models trained on the large dataset of annotated chest X-ray images can accurately classify images as normal or indicative of lung cancer. The AI system's assistance enhances the accuracy of diagnosis, reducing the chances of false negatives or false positives.
- **Time Efficiency:** The AI system automates the image analysis process, enabling faster and more efficient diagnosis. Radiologists can focus on reviewing and validating the AI system's findings, saving valuable time and allowing for quicker patient management.
- **Early Detection:** The AI system's ability to identify potential lung abnormalities at an early stage increases the likelihood of early detection and timely intervention. Early detection is crucial for improving treatment outcomes and patient survival rates.

- **Decision Support:** The AI-based system acts as a valuable decision support tool for radiologists. It provides additional insights and suggestions based on the analysis of a vast amount of data, assisting radiologists in making more informed and accurate decisions.
- **Scalability and Accessibility:** Once developed and validated, the AI system can be easily scaled and deployed across various healthcare settings. It can aid radiologists in different regions and medical institutions, enhancing access to accurate and timely lung cancer diagnosis.

The case study showcases the practical application of AI and ML in image processing, particularly in lung cancer detection from chest X-ray images. By utilizing deep learning and supervised learning algorithms, lung cancer diagnosis accuracy and efficiency can be significantly improved. Integrating AI-based systems into clinical workflows offers valuable decision support to radiologists, leading to better patient outcomes and enhanced healthcare delivery. As AI and ML advance, their potential in image processing and medical imaging becomes even more promising. Further advancements in AI-based image analysis systems will contribute to improved disease detection, personalized treatment planning, and ultimately, better healthcare outcomes for patients(Boopathi, Khare, et al., 2023; Reddy et al., 2023; Sampath et al., 2022; Vanitha et al., 2023).

CHALLENGES AND FUTURE DIRECTIONS

While AI and ML have made significant advancements in image processing, there are still several limitations and challenges that need to be addressed(Pandey et al., 2022):

- AI and ML models require large, high-quality datasets for training, but labeled data can be time-consuming and expensive, especially for niche applications. Biased or unrepresentative datasets can lead to biased or inaccurate models.
- Deep learning models like CNNs require interpretability and explainability to make transparent, justifiable decisions, especially in critical applications like healthcare. These models are often considered black boxes, making it crucial to ensure their understanding.
- AI and ML models face challenges in robustness and generalization due to sensitivity to input data variations, such as lighting conditions, viewpoints, and occlusions.
- Deep learning models require significant computational resources, such as GPUs and memory, making efficient deployment and running challenging in resource-constrained environments.

Current Trends and Future Directions

Despite the challenges, there are several current trends and future directions in AI and ML for image processing(Dikici et al., 2020; Pandey et al., 2022):

- Transfer learning adapts pre-trained models to image processing tasks with limited labeled data, overcoming data scarcity challenges and improving performance across various domains.
- Researchers are developing techniques to make AI and ML models more interpretable and explainable, incorporating human-understandable reasoning, insights into decision-making processes, and explanations for predictions.

- Continual learning allows AI and ML models to learn incrementally over time, retaining knowledge from previous tasks and adapting to new ones. This research is crucial for lifelong learning and dynamic deployment in environments.
- Federated learning addresses privacy concerns by training AI models on decentralized data, ensuring data privacy while promoting collaborative learning on distributed devices.
- Adversarial Robustness research focuses on improving AI models' resilience to attacks by enhancing their robustness through techniques like adversarial training and robust optimization.

Ethical Considerations and Implications

AI and ML integration raises ethical concerns in image processing(Alzubaidi et al., 2020; Zhou et al., 2021).

- Bias and Fairness: AI models can inherit biases from training data, causing discriminatory outcomes in facial recognition and criminal profiling. Ensuring fairness, mitigating biases, and addressing societal implications is crucial to prevent unfair systems.
- Privacy and Security: Image processing applications raise privacy concerns, requiring robust security measures and user protection to prevent data misuse and infringement.
- Accountability and Transparency: AI and ML systems must be accountable for their decisions and actions, ensuring transparency in design, training, and deployment for responsible use and user understanding of algorithmic decisions.
- Human-AI Collaboration: Achieving a balance between human expertise and AI capabilities is crucial for responsible deployment. Promoting collaboration, considering human values, and incorporating human feedback are essential.
- Social Impact: AI and ML adoption in image processing has significant social implications, impacting employment, socioeconomic disparities, and societal values, requiring careful consideration.

CONCLUSION

In conclusion, the integration of artificial intelligence (AI) and machine learning (ML) techniques in image processing has revolutionized various fields, including medical imaging, object recognition, and security surveillance. Through this case study, we have explored the application of AI and ML in the context of lung cancer detection from chest X-ray images.

By leveraging large datasets, preprocessing techniques, and advanced ML algorithms, AI systems can effectively analyze and classify medical images, assisting healthcare professionals in making accurate diagnoses. The use of deep learning models, such as Convolutional Neural Networks (CNNs), allows for automatic feature extraction and improves the accuracy and efficiency of image analysis.

The benefits of incorporating AI and ML in image processing are numerous. These technologies enable early detection of diseases, leading to timely interventions and improved patient outcomes. They also enhance the speed and efficiency of image analysis, reducing the burden on healthcare professionals and allowing for more streamlined workflows. Furthermore, AI-based systems provide valuable decision support, aiding healthcare professionals in making informed decisions and improving the overall quality of care.

However, challenges and limitations still exist. Data availability and quality, interpretability of AI models, robustness to variations, and computational resources are areas that require attention and further research. Additionally, ethical considerations, such as bias and fairness, privacy, accountability, and social impact, must be carefully addressed to ensure responsible and ethical deployment of AI and ML in image processing applications.

Looking ahead, the future of AI and ML in image processing holds promising developments. Ongoing research focuses on transfer learning, explainable AI, continual learning, federated learning, and adversarial robustness, among other areas. These advancements aim to overcome limitations, improve model performance, and address ethical concerns.

In conclusion, AI and ML have significantly transformed image processing, enabling breakthroughs in various domains. The integration of these technologies in medical imaging, object recognition, and security surveillance has the potential to enhance decision-making, improve efficiency, and ultimately benefit society as a whole. With continued research and responsible implementation, AI and ML will continue to shape the future of image processing and unlock new possibilities in the years to come.

Abbreviations:

- AI - Artificial Intelligence
- ML - Machine Learning
- CNN - Convolutional Neural Networks
- RNN - Recurrent Neural Networks
- GANs - Generative Adversarial Networks
- SVM - Support Vector Machines
- PCA - Principal Component Analysis

REFERENCES

Alzubaidi, L., Fadhel, M. A., Al-Shamma, O., Zhang, J., Santamaría, J., Duan, Y., & Oleiwi, S. R. (2020). Towards a better understanding of transfer learning for medical imaging: A case study. *Applied Sciences (Switzerland)*, *10*(13), 4523. doi:10.3390/app10134523

Anitha, C., Komala, C. R., Vivekanand, C. V., Lalitha, S. D., Boopathi, S., & Revathi, R. (2023, February). Artificial Intelligence driven security model for Internet of Medical Things (IoMT). *Proceedings of 2023 3rd International Conference on Innovative Practices in Technology and Management, ICIPTM 2023*. IEEE. 10.1109/ICIPTM57143.2023.10117713

Babu, B. S., Kamalakannan, J., Meenatchi, N., M, S. K. S., S, K., & Boopathi, S. (2023). Economic impacts and reliability evaluation of battery by adopting Electric Vehicle. *IEEE Explore*, 1–6. doi:10.1109/ICPECTS56089.2022.10046786

Balti, H., Ben Abbes, A., Mellouli, N., Farah, I. R., Sang, Y., & Lamolle, M. (2020). A review of drought monitoring with big data: Issues, methods, challenges and research directions. *Ecological Informatics*, *60*, 101136. doi:10.1016/j.ecoinf.2020.101136

Balyen, L., & Peto, T. (2019). Promising artificial intelligence–machine learning–deep learning algorithms in ophthalmology. *Asia-Pacific Journal of Ophthalmology*, *8*(3), 264–272. doi:10.22608/APO.2018479 PMID:31149787

Barrett, S. F. (2023). Artificial Intelligence and Machine Learning. In Synthesis Lectures on Digital Circuits and Systems (pp. 95–122). IGI Global. doi:10.1007/978-3-031-21877-4_4

Bera, K., Katz, I., & Madabhushi, A. (2020). Reimagining T Staging Through Artificial Intelligence and Machine Learning Image Processing Approaches in Digital Pathology. *JCO Clinical Cancer Informatics*, *4*(4), 1039–1050. doi:10.1200/CCI.20.00110 PMID:33166198

Boopathi, S. (2019). Experimental investigation and parameter analysis of LPG refrigeration system using Taguchi method. *SN Applied Sciences*, *1*(8), 892. doi:10.100742452-019-0925-2

Boopathi, S. (2022a). An experimental investigation of Quench Polish Quench (QPQ) coating on AISI 4150 steel. *Engineering Research Express*, *4*(4), 45009. doi:10.1088/2631-8695/ac9ddd

Boopathi, S. (2022b). An Extensive Review on Sustainable Developments of Dry and Near-Dry Electrical Discharge Machining Processes. *Journal of Manufacturing Science and Engineering*, *144*(5), 50801. doi:10.1115/1.4052527

Boopathi, S. (2022c). Experimental investigation and multi-objective optimization of cryogenic Friction-stir-welding of AA2014 and AZ31B alloys using MOORA technique. *Materials Today. Communications*, *33*, 104937. doi:10.1016/j.mtcomm.2022.104937

Boopathi, S. (2022d). Performance Improvement of Eco-Friendly Near-Dry Wire-Cut Electrical Discharge Machining Process Using Coconut Oil-Mist Dielectric Fluid. *Journal of Advanced Manufacturing Systems*. doi:10.1142/S0219686723500178

Boopathi, S. (2023a). An Investigation on Friction Stir Processing of Aluminum Alloy-Boron Carbide Surface Composite. In *Materials Horizons: From Nature to Nanomaterials* (pp. 249–257). Springer. doi:10.1007/978-981-19-7146-4_14

Boopathi, S. (2023b). Deep Learning Techniques Applied for Automatic Sentence Generation. In Promoting Diversity, Equity, and Inclusion in Language Learning Environments (pp. 255–273). IGI Global. doi:10.4018/978-1-6684-3632-5.ch016

Boopathi, S., Arigela, S. H., Raman, R., Indhumathi, C., Kavitha, V., & Bhatt, B. C. (2023). Prominent Rule Control-based Internet of Things: Poultry Farm Management System. *IEEE Explore*, 1–6. doi:10.1109/ICPECTS56089.2022.10047039

Boopathi, S., Balasubramani, V., & Sanjeev Kumar, R. (2023). Influences of various natural fibers on the mechanical and drilling characteristics of coir-fiber-based hybrid epoxy composites. *Engineering Research Express*, *5*(1), 15002. doi:10.1088/2631-8695/acb132

Boopathi, S., Khare, R., Jaya Christiyan, K. G., Muni, T. V., & Khare, S. (2023). Additive Manufacturing Developments in the Medical Engineering Field. In Development, Properties, and Industrial Applications of 3D Printed Polymer Composites (pp. 86–106). IGI Global. doi:10.4018/978-1-6684-6009-2.ch006

Boopathi, S., Siva Kumar, P. K., & Meena, R. S. J., S. I., P., S. K., & Sudhakar, M. (2023). Sustainable Developments of Modern Soil-Less Agro-Cultivation Systems. In Human Agro-Energy Optimization for Business and Industry (pp. 69–87). IGI Global. doi:10.4018/978-1-6684-4118-3.ch004

Boopathi, S., Venkatesan, G., & Anton Savio Lewise, K. (2023). Mechanical Properties Analysis of Kenaf–Grewia–Hair Fiber-Reinforced Composite. In *Lecture Notes in Mechanical Engineering* (pp. 101–110). Springer. doi:10.1007/978-981-16-9057-0_11

Chaudhari, A., & Walke, R. (2022). Role of artificial intelligence and Machine learning in musculoskeletal physiotherapy. *Journal of Pharmaceutical Negative Results*, *13*(36), 2868–2870. doi:10.47750/pnr.2022.13.S06.369

Dikici, E., Bigelow, M., Prevedello, L. M., White, R. D., & Erdal, B. S. (2020). Integrating AI into radiology workflow: Levels of research, production, and feedback maturity. *Journal of Medical Imaging (Bellingham, Wash.)*, *7*(01), 1. doi:10.1117/1.JMI.7.1.016502 PMID:32064302

Domakonda, V. K., Farooq, S., Chinthamreddy, S., Puviarasi, R., Sudhakar, M., & Boopathi, S. (2023). Sustainable Developments of Hybrid Floating Solar Power Plants. In *Human Agro-Energy Optimization for Business and Industry* (pp. 148–167). IGI Global. doi:10.4018/978-1-6684-4118-3.ch008

Erickson, B. J. (2021). Basic Artificial Intelligence Techniques: Machine Learning and Deep Learning. *Radiologic Clinics of North America*, *59*(6), 933–940. doi:10.1016/j.rcl.2021.06.004 PMID:34689878

Farooq, F., Govindaraju, V., & Perrone, M. (2005). Pre-processing methods for handwritten Arabic documents. *Proceedings of the International Conference on Document Analysis and Recognition, ICDAR, 2005*, (pp. 267–271). IEEE. 10.1109/ICDAR.2005.191

Gowri, N. V., Dwivedi, J. N., Krishnaveni, K., Boopathi, S., Palaniappan, M., & Medikondu, N. R. (2023). Experimental investigation and multi-objective optimization of eco-friendly near-dry electrical discharge machining of shape memory alloy using Cu/SiC/Gr composite electrode. *Environmental Science and Pollution Research International*, *0123456789*. doi:10.100711356-023-26983-6 PMID:37126160

Harikaran, M., Boopathi, S., Gokulakannan, S., & Poonguzhali, M. (2023). Study on the Source of E-Waste Management and Disposal Methods. In *Sustainable Approaches and Strategies for E-Waste Management and Utilization* (pp. 39–60). IGI Global. doi:10.4018/978-1-6684-7573-7.ch003

Haug, C. J., & Drazen, J. M. (2022). *Artificial intelligence and machine learning in clinical medicine, 2023* (*Vol. 388*, Issue 13). Mathworks.

Iosup, A., Ostermann, S., Yigitbasi, N., Prodan, R., Fahringer, T., & Epema, D. (2011). Performance Analysis of Cloud Computing Services for MTC-Based Scientific Computing. *IEEE Transactions on Parallel and Distributed Systems*, *22*(6), 931–945. doi:10.1109/TPDS.2011.66

Janardhana, K., Anushkannan, N. K., Dinakaran, K. P., Puse, R. K., & Boopathi, S. (2023). *Experimental Investigation on Microhardness, Surface Roughness, and White Layer Thickness of Dry EDM*. Engineering Research Express. doi:10.1088/2631-8695/acce8f

Janardhana, K., Singh, V., Singh, S. N., Babu, T. S. R., Bano, S., & Boopathi, S. (2023). Utilization Process for Electronic Waste in Eco-Friendly Concrete: Experimental Study. In Sustainable Approaches and Strategies for E-Waste Management and Utilization (pp. 204–223). IGI Global.

Jeevanantham, Y. A., A, S., V, V., J, S. I., Boopathi, S., & Kumar, D. P. (2023). Implementation of Internet-of Things (IoT) in Soil Irrigation System. *IEEE Explore*, 1–5. doi:10.1109/ICPECTS56089.2022.10047185

Kavitha, C., Geetha Malini, P. S., Charan Kantumuchu, V., Manoj Kumar, N., Verma, A., & Boopathi, S. (2023). An experimental study on the hardness and wear rate of carbonitride coated stainless steel. *Materials Today: Proceedings*, *74*, 595–601. doi:10.1016/j.matpr.2022.09.524

Kumara, V., Mohanaprakash, T. A., Fairooz, S., Jamal, K., Babu, T., & B., S. (2023). Experimental Study on a Reliable Smart Hydroponics System. In *Human Agro-Energy Optimization for Business and Industry* (pp. 27–45). IGI Global. doi:10.4018/978-1-6684-4118-3.ch002

Marias, K. (2021). The constantly evolving role of medical image processing in oncology: From traditional medical image processing to imaging biomarkers and radiomics. *Journal of Imaging*, *7*(8), 124. doi:10.3390/jimaging7080124 PMID:34460760

Mohanty, A., Venkateswaran, N., Ranjit, P. S., Tripathi, M. A., & Boopathi, S. (2023). Innovative Strategy for Profitable Automobile Industries: Working Capital Management. In Handbook of Research on Designing Sustainable Supply Chains to Achieve a Circular Economy (pp. 412–428). IGI Global.

Munawar, H. S., Hammad, A. W. A., & Waller, S. T. (2021). A review on flood management technologies related to image processing and machine learning. *Automation in Construction*, *132*, 103916. doi:10.1016/j.autcon.2021.103916

Ono, K., Punt, A. E., & Rivot, E. (2012). Model performance analysis for Bayesian biomass dynamics models using bias, precision and reliability metrics. *Fisheries Research*, *125–126*, 173–183. doi:10.1016/j.fishres.2012.02.022

Palaniappan, M., Tirlangi, S., Mohamed, M. J. S., Moorthy, R. M. S., Valeti, S. V., & Boopathi, S. (2023). Fused Deposition Modelling of Polylactic Acid (PLA)-Based Polymer Composites. In Development, Properties, and Industrial Applications of 3D Printed Polymer Composites (pp. 66–85). IGI Global. doi:10.4018/978-1-6684-6009-2.ch005

Pandey, B., Kumar Pandey, D., Pratap Mishra, B., & Rhmann, W. (2022). A comprehensive survey of deep learning in the field of medical imaging and medical natural language processing: Challenges and research directions. *Journal of King Saud University - Computer and Information Sciences, 34*(8), 5083–5099. doi:10.1016/j.jksuci.2021.01.007

Rajesh, A., & Asaad, M. (2023). Artificial Intelligence and Machine Learning in Surgery. *The American Surgeon*, *89*(1), 9–10. doi:10.1177/00031348221117024 PMID:35969467

Reddy, M. A., Reddy, B. M., Mukund, C. S., Venneti, K., Preethi, D. M. D., & Boopathi, S. (2023). Social Health Protection During the COVID-Pandemic Using IoT. In *The COVID-19 Pandemic and the Digitalization of Diplomacy* (pp. 204–235). IGI Global. doi:10.4018/978-1-7998-8394-4.ch009

Robertson, S., Azizpour, H., Smith, K., & Hartman, J. (2018). Digital image analysis in breast pathology—From image processing techniques to artificial intelligence. *Translational Research; the Journal of Laboratory and Clinical Medicine*, *194*, 19–35. doi:10.1016/j.trsl.2017.10.010 PMID:29175265

S., P. K., Sampath, B., R., S. K., Babu, B. H., & N., A. (2022). Hydroponics, Aeroponics, and Aquaponics Technologies in Modern Agricultural Cultivation. In *Trends, Paradigms, and Advances in Mechatronics Engineering* (pp. 223–241). IGI Global. doi:10.4018/978-1-6684-5887-7.ch012

Samikannu, R., Koshariya, A. K., Poornima, E., Ramesh, S., Kumar, A., & Boopathi, S. (2023). Sustainable Development in Modern Aquaponics Cultivation Systems Using IoT Technologies. In *Human Agro-Energy Optimization for Business and Industry* (pp. 105–127). IGI Global. doi:10.4018/978-1-6684-4118-3.ch006

Sampath, B. C. S., & Myilsamy, S. (2022). Application of TOPSIS Optimization Technique in the Micro-Machining Process. In Trends, Paradigms, and Advances in Mechatronics Engineering (pp. 162–187). IGI Global. doi:10.4018/978-1-6684-5887-7.ch009

Santosh, K. C., Antani, S., Guru, D. S., & Dey, N. (2022). *Medical Imaging: Artificial Intelligence, Image Recognition, and Machine Learning Techniques*. CRC Press.

Sathish, T., Sunagar, P., Singh, V., Boopathi, S., Al-enizi, A. M., Pandit, B., & Gupta, M. (2023). Chemosphere Characteristics estimation of natural fibre reinforced plastic composites using deep multi-layer perceptron (MLP) technique. *Chemosphere*, *337*(June), 139346. doi:10.1016/j.chemosphere.2023.139346 PMID:37379988

Sathish, T., Sunagar, P., Singh, V., Boopathi, S., Al-Enizi, A. M., Pandit, B., Gupta, M., & Sehgal, S. S. (2023). Characteristics estimation of natural fibre reinforced plastic composites using deep multi-layer perceptron (MLP) technique. *Chemosphere*, *337*, 139346. doi:10.1016/j.chemosphere.2023.139346 PMID:37379988

Seifert, R., Weber, M., Kocakavuk, E., Rischpler, C., & Kersting, D. (2021). Artificial Intelligence and Machine Learning in Nuclear Medicine: Future Perspectives. *Seminars in Nuclear Medicine*, *51*(2), 170–177. doi:10.1053/j.semnuclmed.2020.08.003 PMID:33509373

Selvakumar, S., Adithe, S., Isaac, J. S., Pradhan, R., Venkatesh, V., & Sampath, B. (2023). A Study of the Printed Circuit Board (PCB) E-Waste Recycling Process. In Sustainable Approaches and Strategies for E-Waste Management and Utilization (pp. 159–184). IGI Global.

Senthil, T. S. R. Ohmsakthi vel, Puviyarasan, M., Babu, S. R., Surakasi, R., & Sampath, B. (2023). Industrial Robot-Integrated Fused Deposition Modelling for the 3D Printing Process. In Development, Properties, and Industrial Applications of 3D Printed Polymer Composites (pp. 188–210). IGI Global. doi:10.4018/978-1-6684-6009-2.ch011

Shi, F., Wang, J., Shi, J., Wu, Z., Wang, Q., Tang, Z., He, K., Shi, Y., & Shen, D. (2021). Review of Artificial Intelligence Techniques in Imaging Data Acquisition, Segmentation, and Diagnosis for COVID-19. *IEEE Reviews in Biomedical Engineering*, *14*, 4–15. doi:10.1109/RBME.2020.2987975 PMID:32305937

Sonka, M., Hlavac, V., Boyle, R., Sonka, M., Hlavac, V., & Boyle, R. (n.d.). *Image pre-processing*. 56–111.

Subha, S., Inbamalar, T. M., Komala, C. R., Suresh, L. R., Boopathi, S., & Alaskar, K. (2023, February). A Remote Health Care Monitoring system using internet of medical things (IoMT). *Proceedings of 2023 3rd International Conference on Innovative Practices in Technology and Management, ICIPTM 2023.* IEEE. 10.1109/ICIPTM57143.2023.10118103

Vanitha, S. K. R., & Boopathi, S. (2023). Artificial Intelligence Techniques in Water Purification and Utilization. In *Human Agro-Energy Optimization for Business and Industry* (pp. 202–218). IGI Global. doi:10.4018/978-1-6684-4118-3.ch010

Vennila, T., Karuna, M. S., Srivastava, B. K., Venugopal, J., Surakasi, R., & B., S. (2023). New Strategies in Treatment and Enzymatic Processes. In *Human Agro-Energy Optimization for Business and Industry* (pp. 219–240). IGI Global. doi:10.4018/978-1-6684-4118-3.ch011

Vidal, M., & Amigo, J. M. (2012). Pre-processing of hyperspectral images. Essential steps before image analysis. *Chemometrics and Intelligent Laboratory Systems, 117*, 138–148. doi:10.1016/j.chemolab.2012.05.009

Yupapin, P., Trabelsi, Y., Nattappan, A., & Boopathi, S. (2023). Performance Improvement of Wire-Cut Electrical Discharge Machining Process Using Cryogenically Treated Super-Conductive State of Monel-K500 Alloy. *Iranian Journal of Science and Technology. Transaction of Mechanical Engineering, 47*(1), 267–283. doi:10.100740997-022-00513-0

Zhou, S. K., Greenspan, H., Davatzikos, C., Duncan, J. S., Van Ginneken, B., Madabhushi, A., Prince, J. L., Rueckert, D., & Summers, R. M. (2021). A Review of Deep Learning in Medical Imaging: Imaging Traits, Technology Trends, Case Studies with Progress Highlights, and Future Promises. *Proceedings of the IEEE, 109*(5), 820–838. doi:10.1109/JPROC.2021.3054390

Chapter 11
CNN–Based Deep Learning Approach Over Image Data for Cyber Forensic Investigation

Aishwary Awasthi
Sanskriti University, India

Priyanksha Das
School of Sciences, Jain University (Deemed), India

Rupal Gupta
College of Computing Sciences and I.T., Teerthanker Mahaveer University, Moradabad, India

Raj Varma
Symbiosis Law School, Symbiosis International University (Deemed), India

Shilpa Sharma
Symbiosis Law School, Symbiosis International University (Deemed), India

Ankur Gupta
Vaish College of Engineering, Rohtak, India

Huma Khan
Rungta College of Engineering and Technology, Bhilai, India

ABSTRACT

A deep learning approach is gaining popularity day by day in image data classification. The process of classification of graphical data considering training network is managed by conventional neural network. Such types of networks allow automatic classification by making use of CNN approach. But the issues that are faced during forensic investigation are slow in performance and lack accuracy. The major objective of work is to consider the CNN approach that is processing graphic data in order to perform cyber forensic investigation.

DOI: 10.4018/978-1-6684-8618-4.ch011

1. INTRODUCTION

Cyber forensics is the discipline concerned with the acquisition, analysis, reporting, and presentation of digital evidence in computer-related legal proceedings. (Kumar, B., 2023) The hard disc or even deleted data may provide crucial evidence. Data acquisition and analysis from a system or device is what this term refers to, and it is done so that the information may be written down and submitted in court (S.Z.D. et al., 2022). The system's one-of-a-kind storage cell must be copied digitally or in some other non-physical form before the test may proceed. When a security breach occurs, it's important to undertake a comprehensive cyber forensics investigation to find out who's responsible. All of the analysis is done on the backup copy of the programme, which has no effect on the operational system. This work is considering role of deep learning, CNN and image processing in cyber forensic investigation (Naskar, R., 2018).

1.1 Deep Learning

Essentially, a NN with three or more layers is the DL subfield of machine learning. ANN "learn" using extensive datasets in an effort to mimic the human brain's operation; however they are still far from reaching the brain's level of sophistication. A single-layer neural network can still create approximations, but it's difficult to tune and tweak for precision without additional hidden layers. Some AI applications and services use DL to increase automation by taking over analytical and physical tasks that were formerly performed exclusively by humans (Nassa V. K., 2021).

1.2 Deep Learning Applications

In practise, DL applications improve people's daily lives, but they are generally embedded so unobtrusively in goods and services that consumers are blissfully ignorant of the complex data processing occurring in the background (Barik, L., 2020).

Figure 1. Deep learning

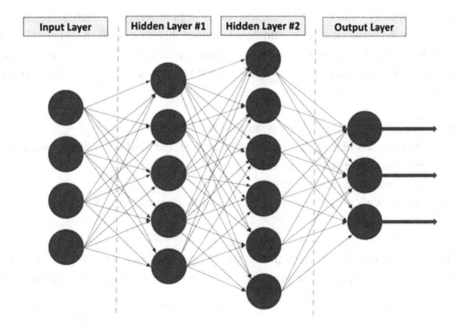

1.3 Convolutional Neural Network

If you need to classify or recognize images, chances are you'll turn to a CNN, a popular DL architecture. It's multi-layered, with Convolutional layers, & fully linked layers all making up network (Feng, Y., 2022). The input picture is filtered by the Convolutional layer to extract features, image is down sampled by the Pooling layer to decrease computation, & final prediction is made by fully connected layer. Via backpropagation & gradient descent, network discovers best filters. The reader is expected to be familiar with NN. ANN does very well in the field of ML. The usage of ANN has expanded beyond image & audio/text categorization to include many other areas of study (Cheung, N. M., 2022). RNN or more specifically a LSTM network, are used to anticipate the sequence of words, whereas CNN are used for picture categorization. The goal of this post is to construct a fundamental CNN component.

- **Input Layers:** This is the level where we feed information into our model. This layer's number of neurons is directly proportional (Zou, Q., 2020) to the number of features in our data set.
- **Hidden Layer:** The hidden layer receives information from the Input layer. How many hidden layers exist is determined on the depth of our model & quantity of available data. It's not uncommon for the total number of neurons in a given hidden layer to exceed the whole number of features (Deshmukh, Y. B., 2020). Each layer's output is computed by multiplying the output of the layer above it by a matrix multiplied by the layer's learnable weights, plus any learnable biases and activation function to produce nonlinearity (Maloigne, C., 2020).
- **Output Layer:** The output of the hidden layer is then sent through a logistic function like sigmoid or softmax to get a probability score for each class (Pramanik, S., 2022).

1.4 Top Five Applications of Convolution Neural Network

The five most common uses for CNNs are:

1.4.1 Facial Recognition

CNNs have successfully been used to recognise faces in photographs. After taking an input image and running it through the network, a set of numbers is output that represents the attributes of faces or facial features at various coordinates within the image. Facial characteristics such as the eyes, nose, and mouth may be identified quickly and precisely, with little distortion from perspective or lighting (Correia, M. E., 2021). Steps are as follows:

- Find the names and faces of everyone in the photo (Jian, W., 2020).
- Don't let distractions like light, position, perspective, etc., pull your attention away from focusing on each individual face (Gupta A., et. al, 2019).
- How to Recognize Individual Faces
- To put a name with a face, compare the new information with what's already in the database (Gupta A., et. al, 2020).

Consider how advances in face recognition might open the door for new kinds of editing and adaptation. The most popular ones are the ones seen in Snap chat and Facebook's Messenger apps. Instead of the face's default, algorithmically generated arrangement, the filters substitute in their own, unique components or effects (Verma A., 2020).

1.4.2 Medical imaging

CNN has been useful in medical imaging for improving the precision with which tumors and other abnormalities may be identified in X-ray & MRI scans. Based on its past experience with comparable pictures, a CNN model can analyze a picture of a human body part, such the lungs, and pinpoint the most probable location of a tumor or other abnormalities, like shattered bones in an X-ray (Koti K., 2021).

1.4.3 Document Analysis

Document analysis may also make use of CNN. Besides being useful for handwriting analysis, this has far-reaching consequences for recognizers. In order to quickly read someone's writing and check it against its massive database, a computer has to handle around a million orders every minute. CNN networks may utilize text and images to better understand a document by recognizing key terms related to the topic (Crespo, R. G., 2020).

1.4.4 Autonomous Driving

CNN are able to model images because of their ability to represent spatial information. CNNs are ubiquitous non-linear function approximators due to their superior capacity to extract features from images, such as obstacles and the ability to comprehend street signs. Moreover, CNNs may be able to recognize a wider range of patterns as the network's depth increases (Gupta, A., 2022).

1.4.5 Biometric Authentication

CNN has been used for biometric identification of users by recognizing a person's face and the physical characteristics associated with it (Jalil, Z., 2020).

1.5 Role of CNN in Deep Learning

Deep Learning, a powerful new tool for analysing large data, mimics the human brain's ability to learn from experience, categorise data/images, and spot patterns and nuances in the way that humans do via the use of complicated algorithms and ANN. CNN is a specific kind of artificial neural network utilised extensively in field of DL for purposes of image/object identification and categorization (Gupta, A., 2021). Therefore, Deep Learning uses a CNN to identify objects in photos. In addition to its use in voice recognition and image processing, CNNs are now finding widespread use in other areas, such as video analysis, obstacle detection for autonomous vehicles, and image and video processing. CNNs are widely used in Deep Learning because of the important role they play in these new and rapidly developing fields (Pramanik, S., 2021).

Figure 2. Working of CNN model

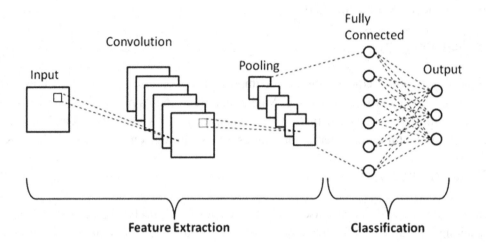

1.7 Cyber Forensics Scope

Since more and more processes in society are digitised, cyber forensics is being called upon to investigate a wider variety of crimes. It helps us counteract aggressive behaviours by revealing the true actors behind them. Experts in the field of cybersecurity are aided in their hunt for hackers and crackers by the data obtained during investigations (Dhabliya, D., 2022).

Figure 3. Cyber forensic as part of computer forensic

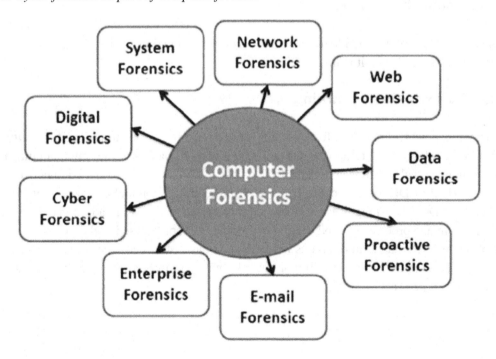

As cybercrime rises, so does the importance of the work done by cyber forensics professionals. A fourfold surge in cybercrime is projected, and NCRB reports that it has already doubled between 2016 and 2018. Law enforcement's role in combating cybercrime and the difficulties experienced by cyber forensics professionals are highlighted (Malpani, A., 2022).

Experts in cyber forensics may remotely investigate a crime scene by analysing data such as internet history, email correspondence, and other digital traces (Passi, A., 2021).

The Process Involved in Cyber Forensics

In CF, information is analysed systematically so that conclusions (Zemerly, M., 2020) may be drawn quickly.

- **Obtaining a digital copy of the under inspection system:** This method includes creating an exact copy of the data on the system, rather than making any changes to the original, which might lead to file confusion with the data already on the computer. A clone of a hard disc is an exact duplicate of the original drive, including all of its contents. During the process of copying all of the information to a new disc, a copy may be made for the purposes of examination.(Musa, A. E., 2020)
- **Authenticating and confirming the replica:** After making a copy, specialists check to make sure that the information is accurate and consistent with what was originally stored. (Pandey, B.K., et al, 2022)
- **Determining that the copied data is forensically acceptable:** It is possible for the data's format to be altered throughout the duplication process; leading to inconsistencies between the investigators' and the original device's operating systems. To prevent this, investigators utilize methods that preserve the integrity of the data and its format on the hard drive, as well as ensuring that it can be read and used properly by the computer. (Pathania, V. et al, 2022)
- **Recovering deleted files:** Often times, criminals may try to clean up the evidence of their wrong doing by erasing digital evidence of their activities, leaving it to the investigators to use cutting-edge data recovery and reconstruction tools to piece together what happened. Files that have been deleted from a computer by the user may be recovered by forensics experts since they are not permanently deleted from the system. (Pellerin, D., 2020)
- **Finding the necessary data with keywords:** Academics utilize specialized, fast tools to mine the instance document for relevant data using key terms. (Pellerin, D., 2020)
- **Establishing a technical report:** Phase four will include writing a technical report that is accessible to readers of all educational levels.(Kumbhkar M., 2021)

These are some examples of CF investigation tools:

Figure 4. Process of cyber forensic

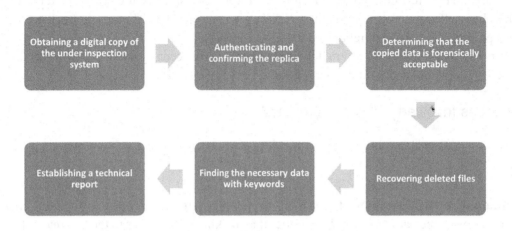

Table 1. CF investigation tools

Tools	Description
Data capture tools	Capturing data using a computer may help with things like FT, reporting, DC, randomization, query resolution, and authentication.(Dhabliya, D., 2022)
File viewers	A file reader is a piece of software that can render a file's contents accurately. A file viewer, as contrast to an editor, displays simply the information contained inside a file.(Dhabliya, D., 2022)
File analysis tools	Experts in cyber security need specialised software for analysing files so they can learn the inner workings of a company. These tools organise, index, track, and assess vital data files. (Kumar, R. (2021)
Internet analysis tools	When it comes to monitoring and analysing data regarding online traffic, Google Analytics is one of the greatest, free tools available to every website owner.

2. LITERATURE REVIEW

There are several researches in area of cyber forensic and CNN classification. Present section is presenting research methodologies used in conventional research work along with their limitations.

K. Chandrasegaran et al. (2022) focused on the detection of CNN-generated images with transferable forensic features. As neural image synthesis techniques rapidly advance, visual forgeries are becoming an existential problem in the media. Despite being a challenging issue in the field of image forensics, a new category of forensic detectors known as universal detectors have shown remarkably adept at identifying fake pictures across a wide variety of generator topologies, loss functions, training datasets, and resolutions. This fascinating trait may indicate that universal detectors have T-FF. This is the first analytical investigation of its kind, and it aims to find and make sense of T-FF in universal detectors. Our work stands out in two ways: first, by proposing a new FF-RS for quantifying and discovering T-FF in universal detectors, and second, by revealing, via both qualitative and quantitative research, that color is a crucial T-FF in such detectors. Visit this secure URL for access to the code and models.

L. Barik et al.(2020) looked deep learning and data mining to do digital forensics. Our research set out to examine the efficacy of several class-based classification strategies, including 3-layer, 5-layer, and 7-layer CNN classifiers, on a forensics dataset assignment. Classification efficiency and precision were used to rate the classifiers.

Manjunath S et al. (2022) reviewed the DL to identify tampered photos. The goal of this study was to investigate current methods for identifying passive image manipulation used deep learning. In this survey, deep learning approaches for detecting tampering are the primary emphasis. Existing tampering detection algorithms have employed several image tampering datasets as MICC, CASIA, UCID, etc. to validate tampering detection accuracy. It turns out that not every technique is able to reliably recover the original data after various forms of attack (splicing, compression, rotation, resampling, copy-move, etc.). The research found that an efficient deep learning-based feature extraction system that learns association among pixels more effectively was necessary for tamper detection. This work contrasts with a prior review by covering important advances in passive picture forensic analysis approaches using deep learning. The pros, drawbacks, dataset, and possible attacks of currently employed methods are evaluated. The study goes on to detail forthcoming difficulties and unanswered questions, and offers a potential future solution for constructing an effective tamper detection system by means of deep learning. The TPR, FPR, and F1-Score results from the experiments all indicate promising performance.

Monika et al. (2021) focused on ML technique used in digital image forensics to detect fakes and pinpoint their origins. The proposed method was built on a machine learning approach for rapid detection by performing FE and FR using "DWT" and "PCA," with data trained using SVM for quick results across a broad variety of test circumstances. A variety of picture assaults, including geometric alteration, post-processing, etc., were detailed here, and the study also demonstrates effectiveness in detecting and localising forgeries, even when several instances exist.

S. Ferreira et al. (2021) reviewed DF analysis for the detection of photo and video manipulation. This study presents a SVM based technique for distinguishing genuine from fake multimedia data, such as digital photos and videos, that may point to the presence of deep fake content. A set of Python modules implementing the method have been added to the widely used digital forensics application Autopsy.

S. Singh et al. (2021) introduced digital image forensics for identifying fake images. One of most common types of photo forgery, it was the focus of a recent study that compared its tactics to those now in use.

S. R. Waheed et al. (2023) reviewed the vectorization of images using CNN. Software and Resources for Working with Media. Real-world photographs were pieced together using DL and machine-learned features from data studies. The classification results using a unique approach of characterised an image to the vector of each item in the picture, and the improvement technique for CNN's image classification, were taken into consideration. All necessary elements for classifying and grouping were included in the learning and connection activity. The established method was further enhanced to deal with open detection and dangers categorization. Results from a performance assessment showed that the newly built system outperformed the published methods in handling test pictures from a novel and specialized sector.

S. Tyagi et al. (2022) focused on the forensicnet, an up-to-date CNN for detecting fake photos. In it, they discuss Forensic Net, a contemporary CNN built on top of recent advancements in computer vision.

S. R. Waheed et al. (2023) looked vectorization of images using CNN. The representation of visual data is still a challenging issue in computer science and engineering. For such a description to be accurate, it requires the identification of a wide variety of items and people, as well as their qualities, correlations, and environmental details. In light of this, they use CNN-DL technique, in which the pictures were converted to vectors, to describe the contents of the images in plain language or image description generated methods. Real-world photographs were pieced together using DL and machine-learned features from data studies. The classification results using a unique approach of characterizing an image to the vector of each item in the picture, and the improvement technique for CNN's image classification, were taken into consideration. All necessary elements for classifying and grouping were included in the learning and connection activity. The established method was further enhanced to deal with open detection and dangers categorization. Results from a performance assessment showed that the newly built system outperformed the published methods in handling test pictures from a novel and specialised sector.

X. Wang et al. (2020) presented work on spot instances of patch-based image inpainting, an intelligent forensics method is required. Authors of this study recommend using a Mask R-CNN for this purpose. They use a DNN to perform in painting in the forensics sector since several DL algorithms have shown successful at segmentation tasks given access to labeled datasets.

Y. A. B. B, H. Shaker, et al. (2023) focused on the application of ML in Digital Forensics. This research surveys the different ML techniques that may be used to the analysis of DE.

Y. B. Deshmukh et al. (2020) reviewed comprehensive method of study for forensic visual analytics. Using efficient video/image processing methods like the CLAHE methodology,CEFA, DHEA, & YOLO V3 object identification framework, a forensic video/image analysis framework may be built with the use of deep learning.

Y. A. Balushi et al. (2023) introduced the application of ML to the field of digital forensics. This study surveys the several machine learning methods now in use for investigating digital evidence. For digital forensics, each machine learning method is feature-specific; by doing so, it was able to tackle challenges such as complexity, data volume, timeliness, correlation, consistency, etc. Additionally, this research contrasts several machine learning algorithms based on industry norms.

Y. H. Choi et al. (2020) introduced machine learning at a deep level to issues in cyber defence. It's not a novel concept to use machine learning methods in order to address computer security issues, but the quickly developing field of Deep Learning has lately sparked a great deal of attention.

Z. Cai et al. (2022) looked CNN-based method for identifying harmful websites. The full design and implementation of the system was described, after a framework for recognizing malicious websites and web crawlers was initially presented. The test results demonstrate the efficacy of the method used to identify potentially malicious websites.

3. OBJECTIVE OF CYBER FORENSIC INVESTIGATION

The purpose of this work is to give a comprehensive assessment of the most up-to-date studies focusing on Deep Learning approaches to problems in computer security. In specifically, this analysis focuses on eight issues related to computer security that have been addressed via the use of Deep Learning: topics including malware categorization, Methods for improving software security by means of fuzzing, memory forensics, and system-event-based anomaly detection, as well as protecting against ROP attacks and establishing CFI, and defending against network assaults.

4. PROPOSED CNN MODEL FOR CLASSIFICATION

CNN algorithm is employed to classify the text, and URL acquisition and URL filtering were also included to complete the collection and classification of potentially dangerous content. The results of the experiments shows that the CNN-based unhealthy website discovery system may better meet the needs of users by significantly increasing the accuracy of hazardous webpage discovery and decreasing the omit rate. In the suggested work, an image is taken and compressed. The CNN-based classification model is initialized with epochs, learning rate, and iterations after picture preprocessing. Adam optimizer and random forest classifier are taken into account. In order to obtain the confusion matrix and the accuracy, recall value, precision, and f-score, training and testing operations are then conducted. The accuracy metrics of the proposed work are then contrasted with those of traditional CNN models.

Figure 5. Process flow of proposed work

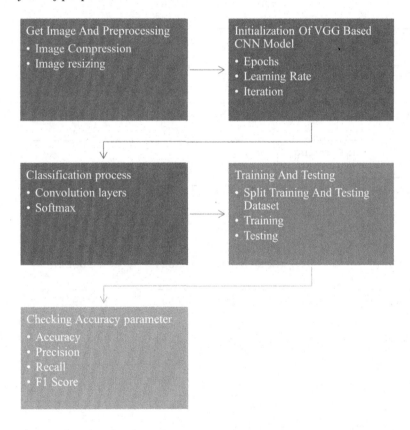

CNN model description
Model: "sequential_5"

Layer (type)	Output Shape	Param #
conv2d_56 (Conv2D)	(None, 126, 126, 16)	448
conv2d_57 (Conv2D)	(None, 124, 124, 16)	2320
conv2d_58 (Conv2D)	(None, 122, 122, 16)	2320
max_pooling2d_20 (MaxPooling	(None, 61, 61, 16)	0
dropout_20 (Dropout)	(None, 61, 61, 16)	0
conv2d_59 (Conv2D)	(None, 59, 59, 32)	4640
conv2d_60 (Conv2D)	(None, 57, 57, 32)	9248
conv2d_61 (Conv2D)	(None, 55, 55, 32)	9248
max_pooling2d_21 (MaxPooling	(None, 27, 27, 32)	0
dropout_21 (Dropout)	(None, 27, 27, 32)	0
conv2d_62 (Conv2D)	(None, 25, 25, 64)	18496
conv2d_63 (Conv2D)	(None, 23, 23, 64)	36928
conv2d_64 (Conv2D)	(None, 21, 21, 64)	36928
max_pooling2d_22 (MaxPooling	(None, 10, 10, 64)	0
dropout_22 (Dropout)	(None, 10, 10, 64)	0
conv2d_65 (Conv2D)	(None, 8, 8, 128)	73856
conv2d_66 (Conv2D)	(None, 6, 6, 128)	147584
conv2d_67 (Conv2D)	(None, 4, 4, 128)	147584
max_pooling2d_23 (MaxPooling	(None, 2, 2, 128)	0
flatten_5 (Flatten)	(None, 512)	0

```
_________________________________________________________________
dense_10 (Dense)             (None, 128)               65664
_________________________________________________________________
dropout_23 (Dropout)         (None, 128)               0
_________________________________________________________________
dense_11 (Dense)             (None, 6)                 774
=================================================================
Total params: 556,038
Trainable params: 556,038
Non-trainable params: 0
```

Classification simulation has been made over google colaboratory environment and accuracy from proposed CNN model has been shown in following figure.

Figure 6. Simulation for accuracy using CNN model

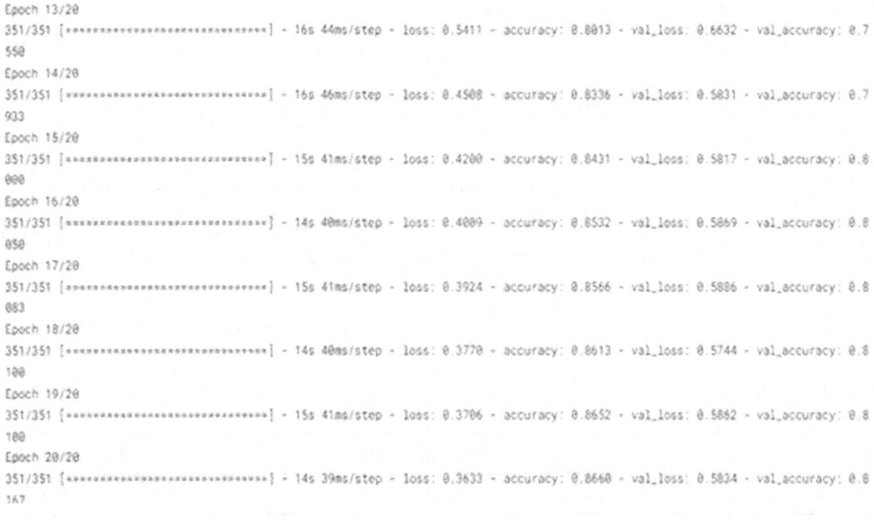

```
Epoch 13/20
351/351 [==============================] - 16s 44ms/step - loss: 0.5411 - accuracy: 0.8013 - val_loss: 0.6632 - val_accuracy: 0.7
550
Epoch 14/20
351/351 [==============================] - 16s 46ms/step - loss: 0.4508 - accuracy: 0.8336 - val_loss: 0.5831 - val_accuracy: 0.7
933
Epoch 15/20
351/351 [==============================] - 15s 41ms/step - loss: 0.4200 - accuracy: 0.8431 - val_loss: 0.5817 - val_accuracy: 0.8
000
Epoch 16/20
351/351 [==============================] - 14s 40ms/step - loss: 0.4009 - accuracy: 0.8532 - val_loss: 0.5869 - val_accuracy: 0.8
050
Epoch 17/20
351/351 [==============================] - 15s 41ms/step - loss: 0.3924 - accuracy: 0.8566 - val_loss: 0.5886 - val_accuracy: 0.8
083
Epoch 18/20
351/351 [==============================] - 14s 40ms/step - loss: 0.3770 - accuracy: 0.8613 - val_loss: 0.5744 - val_accuracy: 0.8
100
Epoch 19/20
351/351 [==============================] - 15s 41ms/step - loss: 0.3706 - accuracy: 0.8652 - val_loss: 0.5862 - val_accuracy: 0.8
100
Epoch 20/20
351/351 [==============================] - 14s 39ms/step - loss: 0.3633 - accuracy: 0.8660 - val_loss: 0.5834 - val_accuracy: 0.8
167
```

5. COMPARISON OF ACCURACY OF PROPOSED WORK TO CONVENTIONAL RESEARCH WORK

There are several CNN based deep model that are used for image classification. Present research work has considered conventional CNN model for comparison with proposed work.

Figure 7. Train and test loss with epochs

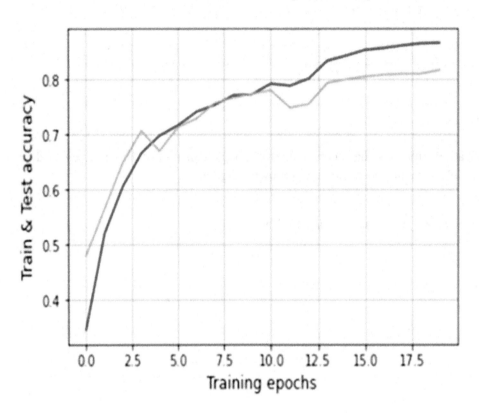

Table 2. Comparison of accuracy

	Conventional model	**Proposed model**
Accuracy	85.3	86.6

Figure 8. Comparison of accuracy

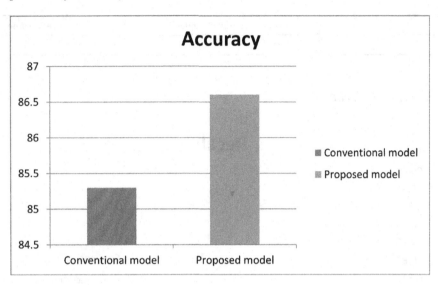

Table 3. Comparison of precision

	Conventional model	**Proposed model**
Precision	0.81	0.83

Figure 9. Comparison of precision

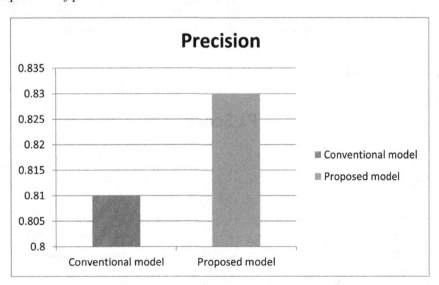

Table 4. Comparison of recall

	Conventional model	Proposed model
Recall	0.81	0.84

Figure 10. Comparison of recall

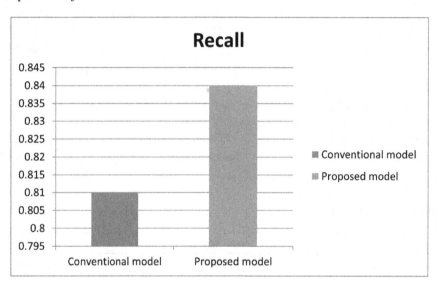

Table 5. Comparison of F1 score

	Conventional model	Proposed model
F1 Score	0.81	0.84

Figure 11. Comparison of F1 score

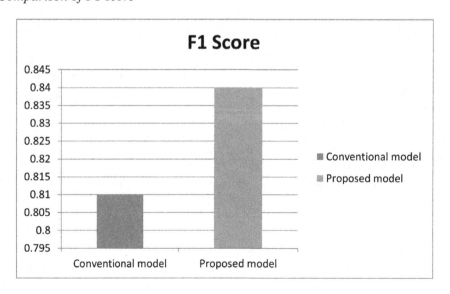

6. CONCLUSION

Simulation outcome are presenting that training loss is reducing as training epoch count is increasing. Moreover the accuracy of image is dependent on image quality and dataset size. Number of conventional layers, drop out layer, epochs, and learning rate are the responsible factors that influence the accuracy of CNN classification model.

7. FUTURE SCOPE

The ability to identify video and picture manipulation using state-of-the-art tools, as well as textual augmentation, is viewed as crucial for the thorough analysis of visual data evidence. The framework would use cutting-edge methods and algorithms to facilitate examiners' visual data processing of evidence.

REFERENCES

Al Balushi, Y., Shaker, H., & Kumar, B. (2023, January). The use of machine learning in digital forensics. In *1st International Conference on Innovation in Information Technology and Business (ICIITB 2022)* (pp. 96-113). Atlantis Press.

Al Neaimi, M., Al Hamadi, H., Yeun, C. Y., & Jamal Zemerly, M. (2020). Digital Forensic Analysis of Files Using Deep Learning. *2020 3rd International Conference on Signal Processing and Information Security, ICSPIS 2020,* (pp. 35–38). IEEE. 10.1109/ICSPIS51252.2020.9340141

B, Y. A. B., Shaker, H., & Kumar, B. (2023). *The Use of Machine Learning in Digital Forensics : Review Paper.* Atlantis Press International BV. doi:10.2991/978-94-6463-110-4

Babu, S. Z. D. (2022). Analysation of Big Data in Smart Healthcare. In M. Gupta, S. Ghatak, A. Gupta, & A. L. Mukherjee (Eds.), *Artificial Intelligence on Medical Data. Lecture Notes in Computational Vision and Biomechanics* (Vol. 37). Springer. doi:10.1007/978-981-19-0151-5_21

Bakas, J., & Naskar, R. (2018). A Digital Forensic Technique for Inter–Frame Video Forgery Detection Based on 3D CNN. In Lecture Notes in Computer Science (including subseries Lecture Notes in Artificial Intelligence and Lecture Notes in Bioinformatics). Springer International Publishing. doi:10.1007/978-3-030-05171-6_16

Bansal, R., Gupta, A., Singh, R., & Nassa, V. K. (2021).Role and Impact of Digital Technologies in E-Learning amidst COVID-19 Pandemic. *2021 Fourth International Conference on Computational Intelligence and Communication Technologies (CCICT),* (pp. 194-202). IEEE. 10.1109/CCICT53244.2021.00046

Barik, L. (2020). Data mining approach for digital forensics task with deep learning techniques. *International Journal of ADVANCED AND APPLIED SCIENCES, 7*(5), 56–65. doi:10.21833/ijaas.2020.05.008

Cai, Z., Tan, C., Zhang, J., Xiao, T., & Feng, Y. (2022). An Unhealthy Webpage Discovery System Based on Convolutional Neural Network. *International Journal of Digital Crime and Forensics, 14*(3), 1–15. doi:10.4018/IJDCF.315614

Chandrasegaran, K., Tran, N. T., Binder, A., & Cheung, N. M. (2022).Discovering Transferable Forensic Features for CNN-Generated Images Detection. Lecture Notes in Computer Science (Including Subseries Lecture Notes in Artificial Intelligence and Lecture Notes in Bioinformatics), 13675 LNCS, 671–689. Springer. doi:10.1007/978-3-031-19784-0_39

Choi, Y. H., Liu, P., Shang, Z., Wang, H., Wang, Z., Zhang, L., Zhou, J., & Zou, Q. (2020). Using deep learning to solve computer security challenges: A survey. *Cybersecurity*, *3*(1), 15. doi:10.118642400-020-00055-5

Dhiman, P., Kaur, A., Iwendi, C., & Mohan, S. K. (2023). A scientometric analysis of deep learning approaches for detecting fake news. *Electronics (Basel)*, *12*(4), 948. doi:10.3390/electronics12040948

Diallo, B., Urruty, T., Bourdon, P., & Fernandez-Maloigne, C. (2020). Robust forgery detection for compressed images using CNN supervision. *Forensic Science International: Reports*, *2*(June), 100112. doi:10.1016/j.fsir.2020.100112

Ferreira, S., Antunes, M., & Correia, M. E. (2021). Exposing manipulated photos and videos in digital forensics analysis. *Journal of Imaging*, *7*(7), 102. doi:10.3390/jimaging7070102

Guorui, F., & Jian, W. (2020). Image Forgery Detection Based on the Convolutional Neural Network. *ACM International Conference Proceeding Series,* (pp. 266–270). ACM. 10.1145/3383972.3384023

Gupta, A. (2019). Script classification at word level for a Multilingual Document. *International Journal of Advanced Science and Technology*, *28*(20), 1247–1252. http://sersc.org/journals/index.php/IJAST/article/view/3835

Gupta, A., Kaushik, D., Garg, M., & Verma, A. (2020). Machine Learning model for Breast Cancer Prediction. *2020 Fourth International Conference on I-SMAC (IoT in Social, Mobile, Analytics and Cloud) (I-SMAC),* (pp. 472-477). IEEE. 10.1109/I-SMAC49090.2020.9243323

Gupta, A., Singh, R., Nassa, V. K., Bansal, R., Sharma, P., & Koti, K. (2021) Investigating Application and Challenges of Big Data Analytics with Clustering. *2021 International Conference on Advancements in Electrical, Electronics, Communication, Computing and Automation (ICAECA),* (pp. 1-6). IEEE.10.1109/ICAECA52838.2021.9675483

Gupta, N., Khosravy, M., Patel, N., Dey, N., Gupta, S., Darbari, H., & Crespo, R. G. (2020). Economic data analytic AI technique on IoT edge devices for health monitoring of agriculture machines. *Applied Intelligence*, *50*(11), 3990–4016. doi:10.100710489-020-01744-x

Ikram, S. T., Chambial, S., & Sood, D. (2023). A performance enhancement of deepfake video detection through the use of a hybrid CNN Deep learning model. *International journal of electrical and computer engineering systems, 14*(2), 169-178.

Jain, V., Beram, S. M., Talukdar, V., Patil, T., Dhabliya, D., & Gupta, A. (2022)Accuracy Enhancement in Machine Learning During Blockchain Based Transaction Classification. *Seventh International Conference on Parallel, Distributed and Grid Computing (PDGC),* (pp. 536-540). IEEE. 10.1109/PDGC56933.2022.10053213

Javed, A. R., & Jalil, Z. (2020). Byte-Level Object Identification for Forensic Investigation of Digital Images. *1st Annual International Conference on Cyber Warfare and Security, ICCWS 2020 - Proceedings*, (pp. 12–15). IEEE. 10.1109/ICCWS48432.2020.9292387

Kaushik, K., & Garg, M. Annu, Gupta, A. & Pramanik, S. (2021). Application of Machine Learning and Deep Learning in Cyber security: An Innovative Approach. In Ghonge, S. Pramanik, R. Mangrulkar and D. N. Le, (eds.), Cybersecurity and Digital Forensics: Challenges and Future Trends, Wiley.

Manjunath, S., Hosmane, S., Punyashree, M., Ladia, A., & Malpani, A. (2022). *Study on Deep Learning Based Techniques for Image Tamper Detection.*, *8*(11), 368–376.

(1950). Monika, &Passi, A. (2021). Digital Image Forensic based on Machine Learning approach for Forgery Detection and Localization. *Journal of Physics: Conference Series*, (1). doi:10.1088/1742-6596/1950/1/012035

Oladipo, F., Ogbuju, E., Alayesanmi, F. S., & Musa, A. E. (2020).The State of the Art in Machine Learning-Based Digital Forensics. SSRN *Electronic Journal*. doi:10.2139/ssrn.3668687

Pandey, B. K. (2022). Effective and Secure Transmission of Health Information Using Advanced Morphological Component Analysis and Image Hiding. In M. Gupta, S. Ghatak, A. Gupta, & A. L. Mukherjee (Eds.), *Artificial Intelligence on Medical Data. Lecture Notes in Computational Vision and Biomechanics* (Vol. 37). Springer. doi:10.1007/978-981-19-0151-5_19

Pandey, D., George, S., Aremu, B., Wariya, S., & Pandey, B. K. (2021). *Critical Review on Integration of Encryption*. Steganography, IOT and Artificial Intelligence for the Secure Transmission of Stego Images.

Pandey, D., Pandey, B. K., & Wariya, S. (2020). An approach to text extraction from complex degraded scene. *IJCBS*, *1*(2), 4–10.

Pathania, V. (2022). A Database Application of Monitoring COVID-19 in India. In M. Gupta, S. Ghatak, A. Gupta, & A. L. Mukherjee (Eds.), *Artificial Intelligence on Medical Data. Lecture Notes in Computational Vision and Biomechanics* (Vol. 37). Springer. doi:10.1007/978-981-19-0151-5_23

Quan, W., Wang, K., Yan, D. M., Zhang, X., & Pellerin, D. (2020). Learn with diversity and from harder samples: Improving the generalization of CNN-Based detection of computer-generated images. *Forensic Science International: Digital Investigation*, *35*, 301023. doi:10.1016/j.fsidi.2020.301023

Quan, W., Wang, K., Yan, D. M., Zhang, X., & Pellerin, D. (2020). Learn with diversity and from harder samples: Improving the generalization of CNN-Based detection of computer-generated images. *Forensic Science International: Digital Investigation*, *35*, 301023. doi:10.1016/j.fsidi.2020.301023

Singh, S., Kumar, R., & Kumar, R. (2021). Forged Image Identification with Digital Image Forensic Tools. *Journal of Biological Engineering Research & Review*, *8*(2), 162–168. www.biologicalengineering.in/Archive

Talukdar, V., Dhabliya, D., Kumar, B., Talukdar, S. B., Ahamad, S., & Gupta, A. (2022) Suspicious Activity Detection and Classification in IoT Environment Using Machine Learning Approach. *Seventh International Conference on Parallel, Distributed and Grid Computing (PDGC)*, (pp. 531-535). IEEE. 10.1109/PDGC56933.2022.10053312

Tyagi, S. (2022). *Modern CNN-based Image Forgery Detection Network*. ForensicNet.

Waheed, S. R., Rahim, M. S. M., Suaib, N. M., & Salim, A. A. (2023). CNN deep learning-based image to vector depiction. *Multimedia Tools and Applications*, *82*(13), 1–20. doi:10.100711042-023-14434-w

Wang, J., & Zhang, Y. (2020). Median filtering forensics scheme for color images based on quaternion magnitude-phase CNN. *Computers, Materials & Continua*, *62*(1), 99–112. doi:10.32604/cmc.2020.04373

Wang, X., Wang, H., & Niu, S. (2020). An Intelligent Forensics Approach for Detecting Patch-Based Image Inpainting. *Mathematical Problems in Engineering*, *2020*, 1–10. doi:10.1155/2020/8892989

Yang, P., Baracchi, D., Ni, R., Zhao, Y., Argenti, F., & Piva, A. (2020). A survey of deep learning-based source image forensics. *Journal of Imaging*, *6*(3), 9. doi:10.3390/jimaging6030009 PMID:34460606

Chapter 12
Comparison of the Theoretical and Statistical Effects of the PCA and CNN Image Fusion Approaches

Ashi Agarwal
ABES Engineering College, India

Binay Kumar Pandey
G.B. Pant University of Agriculture and Technology, India

Poonam Devi
Chaudhary Devi Lal University, Sirsa, India

Sunil Kumar
School of Engineering and Technology (UIET), CSJM University, India

Mukundan Appadurai Paramashivan
Aligarh Muslim University, Singapore & Champions Group, Singapore

Ritesh Agarwal
School of Engineering and Technology (UIET), CSJM University, India

Pankaj Dadheech
Swami Keshvanand Institute of Technology, Management, and Gramothan, India

ABSTRACT

An image plays a vital role in today's environment. An image is a visual representation of anything that can be used in the future for recollecting or memorizing that scene. This visual representation is created by recording the scene through an optical device like a camera or mobile phone. The image fusion process helps integrate relevant data of the different images in a process into a single image. Image fusion applications are wide in range, and so is the fusion technique. In general, pixel, feature, and decision-based techniques for picture fusion are characterised. This study's main thrust is the application and comparison of two approaches to the image fusion process: PCA (principal component analysis) and CNN (convolutional neural network).The study implemented a practical approach to MATLAB. The result of the study is that CNN is much more favorable in terms of image quality and clarity but less favorable in terms of time and cost.

DOI: 10.4018/978-1-6684-8618-4.ch012

1. INTRODUCTION

Images are created when something, such as a person, thing, place, etc., is portrayed visually. Depending on the frames taken and projections maintained, images may be 2D or 3D. A 3D image is a compilation of several 2D images at various projection levels and angles. 2D images are still pictures. In general, the phrase "fusion" refers to a method of extracting data from multiple sources. In order to create a new image with information of a quality that can only be achieved this way, picture fusion (IF) tries to merge complementary multisensor, multitemporal, or multiview data.

Figure 1. Image fusion process

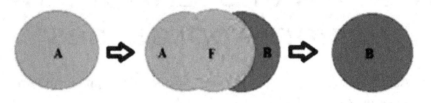

Image fusion process

The definition of quality, how it is measured, and how it is used vary depending on the application. The goal of the Image Fusion method is to gather all the important information from various photographs and combine it into a small number of images, usually just one. Compared to any other image from a single source, a single image is more accurate and informative and has all the necessary information. The goal of picture fusion is to create images that are better suited for human and mechanical perception, not just to reduce the number of records.In essence, two pictures or more of a single scene are combined to create a Single photo, with the best data characteristics of all the images used. An important step and a prerequisite for image fusion is geometry and feature matching of the input images. The growing availability of space-based sensors in distant sensing applications inspires various picture fusion algorithms.

Depending on the particular purpose, many sorts of images can be fused. Some common sorts of photos that are frequently fused are listed below:

a) Hyperspectral or multi-spectral Images: Including the visible, infrared, and ultraviolet spectrums, these photographs record data from a variety of electromagnetic spectrum bands. Utilising fusion techniques, the spectral data from these photos can be combined, enhancing the overall information or increasing the accuracy of the categorization.

b) Images with Thermal Infrared and Visible Light: Combining thermal infrared photographs with images with visible light can give a more thorough understanding of the scene in applications like surveillance or search and rescue. The thermal data can be overlaid on the visible image using image fusion techniques, improving item recognition or detection.

c) Images with a high dynamic range (HDR): These images can capture a wide range of luminosity, from light highlights to deep shadows. With the help of image fusion, it is possible to build an HDR image with improved details and a wider dynamic range by combining multiple photographs taken at various exposure settings.

d) Medical Images: In the field of medical imaging, several modalities like computed tomography (CT), magnetic resonance imaging (MRI), and positron emission tomography (PET) can capture various features of the same patient. Through the use of image fusion algorithms, data from multiple modalities can be combined to provide doctors with a more thorough and precise diagnosis.

e) Panoramic Images: Panoramic images are created by stitching together several photographs taken from various angles. A high-resolution panoramic image with a consistent visual style can be created by using image fusion algorithms to integrate the overlapping sections between photographs flawlessly.

f) Satellite or Surveillance Images: Image fusion can be used to merge images taken by several sensors or at various times in applications like surveillance or satellite photography. The capabilities for object detection, tracking, and change detection may be enhanced by this fusion.

g) Multiresolution Images: Images that have been created or processed at different scales or resolutions are referred to as multiresolution images, also known as multi-scale images. The original image is generally divided into several versions with various levels of information in a multiresolution image.

These are only a few examples; other sorts of images can also be combined using image fusion techniques, depending on the application's particular needs and objectives.

The method utilised in the image acquisition procedure is one of the drawbacks of poor spatial resolution imaging. This mechanism, which consists of a lens subsystem and optical sensors, may degrade as a result of out-of-focus and diffraction limits. The optical aberration or the turbulence in the atmosphere could also cause more distortions. The quality of the photograph also depends on the shutter speed and the distance between the camera and the subject. As a result of down sampling, the observed images are degraded and also feature aliasing. One can create a mathematical model that describes the image acquisition process in order to tackle the image reconstruction challenge. The forward or observation model connects the original image to the observed images.

In many different industries, including computer vision, remote sensing, medical imaging, surveillance, and more, image fusion techniques are frequently employed. There are multiple steps in the fusion process:

a. Image Alignment: Prior to fusion, the input images must be correctly aligned to guarantee that related features are spatially matched. If there are geometrical variations between the images, image registration techniques may be employed to precisely align them.

b. Image Decomposition: The input images are divided into many components or representations in many fusion algorithms. Wavelet transforms, Fourier transforms, and other multi-scale analytic approaches are frequently used decomposition techniques. Decomposition enables analysis and visual manipulation at several scales or frequency bands.

c. Fusion Rule: The information from the deconstructed images or image components is combined according to the fusion rule. There are various fusion methods, each with a unique fusion rule, such as pixel-level fusion, feature-level fusion, and decision-level fusion. The fusion rule may use more complicated algorithms based on predetermined criteria or mathematical operations such averaging, weighted blending, maximum or minimum selection.

d. Fusion Strategy: How the fusion rule is applied in various spatial or frequency bands is determined by the fusion strategy. It can entail employing several fusion rules in various regions or using adaptive fusion techniques based on regional picture features. The goal of the fusion strategy is to streamline the fusion procedure for particular applications or desired results.

e.   Post-processing: Following the fusion, additional enhancements or improvements to the fused image's visual quality may be made using post-processing techniques. These procedures may involve sharpening, contrast modification, noise reduction, or other picture enhancing methods.

The particular application requirements, the qualities of the incoming images, and the desired result all influence the choice of image fusion techniques and parameters. For various purposes or types of photos, different fusion techniques might be a better fit. Typically, measures like the preservation of significant details, greater visual quality, better feature representation, or improved performance in subsequent image analysis tasks are used to assess how effective image fusion is.

2. LITERATURE REVIEW

Riyahi et al. (2009) stated that the results produced by either the Brovey or Ehlers methods do a poorer job of preserving the spatial and spectral information of the objects in the original photos than PCA, which is why PCA fused images have the best spectral fidelity.Zhijun Wang et al. (2005) put forth a framework known as the GIF approach that maintains the ratios between the various bands, emphasises minute signature variations, and upholds the radiometric integrity of the data while enhancing spatial resolution. Shivsubramani Krishnamoorthy et al. (2010) stated and demonstrated that, DWT with Haar received a quality rating of 63.33 percent, which is significantly higher than the ratings provided to the other algorithms.

Shah S.K et al.(2014) concluded on the basis of their study that SWT was a superior image fusion technique than PCA and DWT. It also noted that spatial and transform domains were implementedand, Er.Kulvir Singh et al(2016) in another study,The quality of the fusion is typically influenced by the user's background, the fusion technique, and the data set being merged, the researcher found after looking at an image fusion survey

Nayera Nahvi et al. (2014) summarises the researcher's review of cutting-edge algorithms for picture fusion at the pixel and feature levels. Therefore, this review mentions the task-based fused picture assessment. The impact of contrast enhancement strategies on colour image segmentation was examined by the researcher. Bora,D et al. (2015) For both colour picture enhancement and colour image segmentation, it was discovered that HSV colour space performed better than LAB colour space even when there was noise present. It is concluded from the analysis of all experimental data that using HSV colour space for the task will improve the performance of the preprocessing method BSB-CLAHE for colour image segmentation. Vijayan,A et al. (2015)The Author presented many picture fusion techniques, including data-driven picture fusion among DWT, Laplacian, SVM, and HOSVD, as well as multi-scale picture fusion. Filter-based image fusion provides solutions for a variety of problems, including those involving multi-scale decomposition, colour distortion, the brightness of the fused output, etc. However, the guided filter has the drawback of taking longer to execute.Another efficient edge maintaining filter in computing is the local edge preserving filter (LEP). LEP offers superior photo filtration results compared to guided filter. By employing LEP filter for image fusion rather than guided filter for fusion, the guided filtering based fusion approach can be improved.The findings produced by the PCA approach, in contrast to those produced by either the Brovey or Ehlers approaches, better maintain the spectral and spatial information of the objects in the original photos, according to the researcher's visual inspection of the combined images. Kumar S. et al. (2009). The PCA fused picture has the best spectral fidelity, according to a statistical comparison of the PCA and the Brovey and Ehlers models. Consequently, it is the best technique among the three algorithms for QuickBird photo fusion.

G. Qu et al. (2002) based on interesting region recognition, this work developed a unique multiscale fusion method for the IR and VI image that can incorporate more background data and emphasise the interesting region with prominent items. With this approach, the guided filter and mean shift's benefits are combined. The NSCT domain then fuses the background areas. The high frequency layers are fused using an SF-PCNN-based approach, while the low frequency layers are fused using an improved weighted average technique based on per-pixel weighted average.According to experimental findings, the suggested fusion system performs better when subjected to unbiased evaluations and visual examination. In the study, a novel gradient-based photo fusion algorithm was proposed.Paul S et al. (2016) A wavelet-based gradient integration approach is utilised to obtain the fused luminance after the luminance channel is fused in the gradient domain. Based on a weighted sum of the chrominance channels in the input images, the chrominance channels are combined.Fast execution speed is a result of the effectiveness of the gradient reconstruction technique, which has a complexity of O(N). Studies show that the suggested algorithm produces excellent results for both multi-exposure and multi-focus images.

Singh, E et al. (2016) The author suggested a hybrid solution that addresses the issue of edge preservation and explicitly fused the images. Since Laplacian Pyramid is the second approach employed with wavelet fusion, it analyses every aspect of the image and aids in maintaining the standard of the fused image.The Laplacian Pyramid method simply monitors any change in the image's data by inspecting each pixel of the images. The proposed method has demonstrated superiority over the conventional methods in terms of edge preservation and is the highest calibre method.

Li, s et al. (2013) The researcher's review of cutting-edge methods for picture fusion at the pixel and feature levels is offered. Both stages of the fusion can be treated in either the transform domain or the spatial domain. Picture fusion algorithms that are implemented in a transform domain produce better results in many applications, especially those involving many modalities since they allow for the use of salient information that the human visual system is sensitive to. Among these transform methods, the DT-CWT seems to have the best performance because of its properties of good shift invariance and directional selectivity, while its complexity is not high. Numerous fusion rules have been introduced for general purpose or for specific applications. The maximum selection is the simplest and effective decision for most applications, but it is extremely sensitive to noise. An adaptive weighted average using statistical modelling, e.g. non-Gaussian is possibly the best fusion rule for the DT-CWT. It can be applied to various applications, such as visible/IR imaging, context enhancement, and medical imaging, both with noisy and noiseless pictures.

S Li et al. (2004) This study also presents two methods of fused picture assessment. Objective quality metrics, including Mutual Information, Petrovic and Xydeas Metric and Piella Metric, are utilized to assess the fused picture without the knowledge of groundtruth. As each picture fusion technique has been used in a variety of applications, their respective results should be assessed depending on the tasks for which they are used.

Diagnostic data for the patient has been generated by the wearable sensor and wirelessly sent to a smartphone using Bluetooth low energy technology.

Sharma P et al. (2018) A web interface receives information from the smartphone through Bluetooth/4G. The suggested system will be able to send out emergency alerts. In order to provide data that is as near to traditional systems as possible, sensors will be employed.

Liu J et al. (2023) In order to combine the features of image reconstruction decoding and create the fusion image, the saliency detection decoding is utilised as fusion weights. This efficiently extracts significant information from the source images and improves the fusion image's correspondence to visual perception. On a variety of publicly available datasets, experiments show that the proposed fusion approach provides state-of-the-art performance in infrared and visible picture fusion, multi-exposure image fusion, and medical image fusion.

Viyone G (2023) For students and professionals interested in learning more, this survey offers a thorough analysis of the literature. The fundamental components of the MS and HS image fusion are described, and three categories of related techniques (based on pansharpening, decomposition, and machine learning) are established.

Tang L et al. (2023) This study introduces a method for fusing infrared and visible images that doesn't require any darkness (DIVFusion), which effectively dispels shadows and makes it easier to gather complementing data. In particular, we first design a scene-illumination disentangled network (SIDNet) to remove illumination degradation in nighttime visible images while preserving informative features of source images in order to improve the fusion quality of nighttime images, which are hampered by low illumination, texture concealment, and colour distortion.

Ma J et al. (2022) In this paper, a brand-new generic image fusion framework called SwinFusion, based on cross-domain long-range learning and Swin Transformer, is proposed. In order to sufficiently integrate complementary information and cross-domain interaction, on the one hand, an attention-guided cross-domain module is developed. On the other hand, the issues with multi-scene picture fusion are generalised to a unified framework with appropriate intensity management, structure maintenance, and detail preservation. Extensive tests on both digital photography image fusion and multi-modal image fusion show how superior our SwinFusion is to both task-specific and cutting-edge unified image fusion algorithms.

3. AN APPROACH FOR IMAGE FUSION PROCESS: IMAGE FUSION TECHNIQUES

Spatial domain fusion and transform domain fusion are two basic categories into which image fusion techniques can be divided. Several well-known picture fusion techniques include:

- Pixel Level Image Fusion: The act of fusing numerous images at the pixel level to produce a single fused image is known as pixel-level image fusion. It is sometimes referred to as image blending or image combination. The goal of pixel-level fusion is to take the most important data from each input image and combine it to create a cohesive and appealing outcome.
- Feature Level Image fusion: The goal of feature-level image fusion, sometimes referred to as feature fusion or feature extraction-based fusion, is to merge pertinent features or representations taken from several input images to produce a fused image. The goal of feature-level fusion is to combine higher-level data or descriptors, as opposed to pixel-level fusion, which works directly on the pixel values.

- Decision Level Image fusion: Decision-level image fusion, sometimes referred to as decision fusion, concentrates on merging conclusions or results from several classifiers or algorithms that have been applied to input images. Decision-level fusion, as opposed to directly altering pixel values or features, tries to combine the judgements made by various algorithms or classifiers to produce a combined judgement or result.

In order to create a single, high-resolution image that is more informative than either of the original images, pixel level image fusion aims to integrate two dissimilar raw photos. The pixel level fusion methods include PCA (principal component analysis), Brovey, Wavelet, HIS, and others. The process of extracting characteristics from various photos and integrating them to create a single, more informative image is known as feature level image fusion. Ehlers' fusion and segment fusion are two examples of feature level techniques.Decision level image fusion is combining the results of different algorithms to provide the single decision. Decision level fusion methods are neural network such as convolutional neural network (CNN), Fuzzy logic etc.

3.1 Practical Implementation

In this research, the main emphasis is on principal component analysis (PCA) and convolutional neural network (CNN)as it is a comparative study of the two approaches of image fusion process. An uncorrelated linear combination of the original variable is created from a multivariate collection of correlated variables using principal component analysis (PCA).For images, it developsan uncorrelated feature space that can be used for further analysis. Advantage of using principal component analysis (PCA) is that the no. of bands are not restricted in this besides this there is also an disadvantage that it has blurring problems i.e. the results are not so clear result depends on the input image subset.

The simplicity, computational effectiveness, and capacity to capture the most important properties of the input images are just a few benefits of PCA image fusion. However, the dimensionality reduction procedure may result in information loss, particularly if the eliminated components contain crucial information.It is important to keep in mind that PCA image fusion is only one of many methods that are now available, and that its applicability will vary depending on the particular needs of the application and the features of the input images. In some situations, other fusion methods, including wavelet-based or deep learning-based fusion, might be preferable.

Figure 2. (a), (b) Input images (c) output Image of PCA

Figure 3. (a),(b) Input image (c) output image of CNN

Figure 4. Other output images of CNN

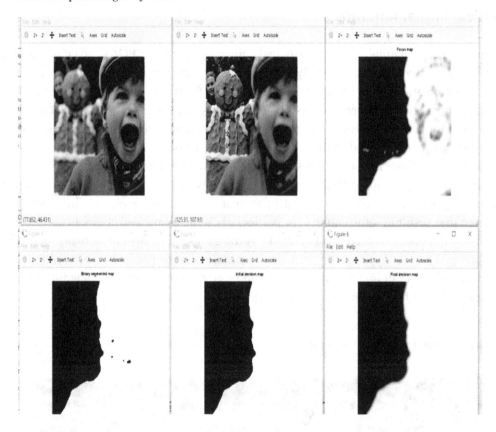

CNN (Convolutional Neural Network)have freshly been used for multi-focus image fusion. CNN takes input and process and categorize it using various layers (having filters) in the convolutional neural network. To classify an object with probabilistic values, these layers—CONVULUTIONAL LAYER, POOLING LAYER, and FULLY CONNECTED LAYER—apply the softmax function (0 and 1).Advantage of using CNN (convolutional neural network) is that it has the highest accuracy in image recognition system along with the advantage it also has disadvantage that it takes lot of time in execution and possesses high computational cost.

CNN image fusion has a number of benefits, including the capacity to capture complicated correlations and patterns and the ability to automatically learn and extract relevant features from the input images. However, training a CNN can be computationally demanding and necessitates a sizable labelled dataset. The richness and diversity of the training dataset, the design and performance of the CNN architecture, and other factors all have a significant impact on how effectively CNN image fusion works. To get the best fusion results for a given application, experimentation and fine-tuning of the network parameters are frequently necessary.

Some more output pictures are there in CNN that are:

The image is first subjected to fusion scanning. The focus map is first built using focus-based measurements, which are computed using sections of erratic form that have been refined or divided in response to changing image contents. Segmentation is used to build an area map after the initial production of an all-focus image. Then, by examining each region's spatial-focal property, it is determined whether each region has to be iteratively divided into sub-regions. The final region map is used to perform regionally best focusing after iterative splitting, which selects the best focused pixels from the image stack.The label image may easily be transformed into a depth image since each pixel's label in the resulting label picture acts as the image index from which the pixel with the best focus is chosen. The best focus will be chosen for regions with unknown focus profiles using spatial propagation from nearby confident areas.

MSE: MSE is mean square error that is the comparison parameter to determine the quality of image. It represents the aggregate squared error between the two images. MSE plays a vital role in the calculation of PSNR value. MSE value is directly proportional to the error presents in the image. The less is the MSE the less is the error. Lower MSE value represents the high-quality image.

Formula to calculate MSE is:

$$MSE= \Sigma M, N \left[I1\ (m,n) - I2\ (m,n) \right]\ 2\ /\ (M*N)$$

Here in the equation: M and N are the number of rows and columns in the source images.

1. PSNR: It is used to calculate accuracy of the model which is used to compute the peak SNR between two images; it is also calculated in decibels. Quality of final image is directly proportional to the PSNR value, if the PSNR value is high, the quality of final image also hikes or vice versa. To calculate the PSNR value, first have to calculate MSE.

PSNR is then calculated by:

$$PSNR = 10log10(R2MSE)$$

Here, R is the highest deviation in the source image.

Table 1. Analysis of PCA and CNN

S.N	Attribute	PCA	CNN
1	Input Image		
2	Output Image		
3	Execution Time	0.40803 seconds	191.397 seconds
4	Accuracy	Less Accurate than CNN	More Accurate than PCA
5	Cost	Less computational cost.	More computational cost.
6	Approach	Feature Extraction	End-To-End Approach
7	Clarity	Less clear	More clear
8	MSE	65.4080	67.7141
9	PSNR	17.6171	17.6241

4. COMAPARATIVE STUDY TABLE: PCA VS CNN

Table I above shows the comparative analysis of PCA and CNN image fusion methods. This analysis was performed as follows:

1. The input images are first taken into model to fuse informative segments.
2. Output images then analyzed with PCA and CNN models.
3. Execution Time: PCA is a basic algorithm, that takes less time to compute and providing results whereas CNN is such a complex model that takes comparatively more time.
4. Approach is different in both of the models. In PCA, it is Feature extraction and in CNN, it is end-to-end.
5. Cost Analysis: Cost of PCA is comparatively less than that of CNN due to simpler model architecture.
6. Accuracy of the models is then calculated on 3 main features; Visual interpretation. MSE and PSNR. Visually the output image of CNN is much clear than PCA image fusion method. Accuracy of MSE is measured with the inverse relation of value, lower is the MSE, higher is the accuracy. PSNR shows the positive relation with the accuracy, higher the PSNR, higher is the accuracy. Hence, from the table most of the parameter calculation indicates that the CNN is better than PCA in terms of clarity and quality but PCA is better in terms of simplicity and execution time.

Graphical Results of Implementation

Figure 5. a) Graphical result MSE b) Graphical result PSNR

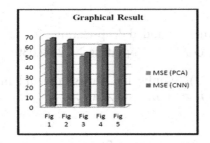 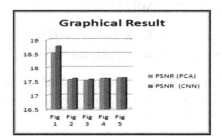

Graphs above shows the MSE and PSNR results for PCA and CNN on five image datasets. All the images were tested on MATLAB for these two models of image fusion.

5. CONCLUSION AND FUTURE SCOPE OF STUDY

Input images were fused to integrate relevant information from multiple images to one image using PCA and CNN image fusion methods. Results were analyzed by using various parameters listed in table 1 above. On the basis of comparison between Principal Component Analysis (PCA) and Convolutional Neural Network (CNN)from the table that were concluded by the experimentation performed on MAT-

LAB platform. The researcher revealed that CNN is much favorable in terms of image quality and clarity but less favorable in terms of time and cost. The researcher found that the PCA produces blurry output image while CNN generated more clear output image. MSE and PSNR values also concludes the good accuracy of CNN model. The researcher recommended that the future scope of this study is not limited to comparison between two approaches, the study should be extended in terms of improvement in the quality of PCA generated output by using some standard algorithm for reducing the noise in the image and CNN should also be processed by using some minimization or optimization algorithm to minimize the running time and cost of the fusion process.

REFERENCES

Bora, D. J. (2017). Importance Of Image Enhancement Techniques In Color Image Segmentation: A Comprehensive And Comparative Study. Indian Jou*rnal of Scientific Research, 115–131.*

Kulvir Singh, E. N. (2016). A Review on Image Fusion Techniques and Proposal of New Hybrid Technique. Interna*tional Research Journal of Engineering and Technology, (03),* 1321-1324.

Kumar, S. A. (2009). A mo*dified statistical approach for image fusion using wavelet transform. Sp*ringer.

Li, S., Kang, X., & Hu, J. (2013). Image fusion with guided filtering [J]. *IEEE Transactions on Image Processing, 22(7),* 2864–2875. doi:10.1109/TIP.2013.2244222 PMID:23372084

Li, S., Kwok, J., Tsang, I., & Wang, Y. (2004, November). Fusing images with different focuses using support vector machines. *IEEE Transactions on Neural Networks*, *15*(6), 1555–1561. doi:10.1109/TNN.2004.837780 PMID:15565781

Liu, J., Dian, R., Li, S., & Liu, H. (2023). SGFusion: A saliency guided deep-learning framework for pixel-level image fusion. *Information Fusion*, *91*, 205–214. doi:10.1016/j.inffus.2022.09.030

Ma, J., Tang, L., Fan, F., Huang, J., Mei, X., & Ma, Y. (2022). SwinFusion: Cross-domain long-range learning for general image fusion via swin transformer. *IEEE/CAA Journal of Automatica Sinica, 9*(7), 1200-1217.

Nayera Nahvi, O. C. (2014). Comparative Analysis of Various Image Fusion Techniques For Biomedical Images: A Review. *International Journal of Engineering Research and Applications*, *04*, 81–86.

Paul, S., Sevcenco, I. S., & Agathoklis, P. (2016). Multi-Exposure and Multi-Focus Picture Fusion in Gradient Domain. *Journal of Circuits, Systems, and Computers, 25*, 1 - 18.

Qu, G., Zhang, D., & Yan, P. (2002, March). Information measure for performance of image fusion. *Electronics Letters*, *38*(7), 313–315. doi:10.1049/el:20020212

Riyahi, R., Kleinn, C., & Fuchs, H. (2009). *Comparison of Different Image Fusion Techniques for Individual Tree Crown Identification Using Quick bird Images.* Research Gate.

Shah, S. K., & Shah, P. D. (2014). Comparative Study of Image Fusion. *International Journal of Innovative Research in Science,* (p. 10168 to 10175).

Sharma, P. K., Srivastava, A., & Perti, A. (2018). NOVEL IDEA FOR REAL-TIME HEALTH MONITORING USING WEARABLE DEVICES. [IJMET]. *International Journal of Mechanical Engineering and Technology*, *9*(13), 213–216.

Shivsubramani Krishnamoorthy, K. P. (2010). Implementation and Comparative Study of Image Fusion Algorithms. *International Journal of Computer Applications, 09*, 0975 – 8887.

Singh, E., & Julka, E. N. (2016). A Review on Picture Fusion Techniques and Proposal of New Hybrid Technique. *International Research Journal of Engineering and Technology*, *03*(03), 1321–1324.

Tang, L., Xiang, X., Zhang, H., Gong, M., & Ma, J. (2023). DIVFusion: Darkness-free infrared and visible image fusion. *Information Fusion*, *91*, 477–493. doi:10.1016/j.inffus.2022.10.034

Vijayan, A., & Sreeram, S. (2015). Survey On Picture Fusion Techniques. *International Journal of Engineering Research and General Science*, *3*(3), 744–748.

Vivone, G. (2023). Multispectral and hyperspectral image fusion in remote sensing: A survey. *Information Fusion*, *89*, 405–417. doi:10.1016/j.inffus.2022.08.032

Zhijun Wang, D. Z. (june 2005). *A Comparative Analysis of Image Fusion Methods*. IEEE.

Chapter 13
Crime Forecasting Using Historical Crime Location Using CNN-Based Images Classification Mechanism

Vishnu Venkatesh N.

School of Sciences, Jain University (Deemed), India

Priyank Singhal

College of Computing Sciences and I.T., Teerthanker Mahaveer University, Moradabad, India

Digvijay Pandey

iD https://orcid.org/0000-0003-0353-174X

Department of Technical Education, A.P.J. Abdul Kalam Technical University, Lucknow, India

Meenakshi Sharma

Sanskriti University, Mathura, India

Rupal Rautdesai

Symbiosis Law School, Symbiosis International University (Deemed), India

Deepti Nahush Khubalkar

iD https://orcid.org/0000-0002-7564-819X

Symbiosis Law School, Symbiosis International University (Deemed), India

Ankur Gupta

iD https://orcid.org/0000-0002-4651-5830

Vaish College of Engineering, Rohtak, India

ABSTRACT

The present research is focused on crime forecasting and CNN has been used for image classification in order to categorize crime events. However, there are different classification mechanisms used in conventional research work. But CNN is playing a significant role in identification and prediction of crime. The major issues during CNN based classification are time consumption and accuracy. However, proposed research has resolved issue of time consumption by reducing image size by applying the RGB2GRAY model, and images are resized before training operation. Simulation results conclude that the proposed work provides a scalable and reliable approach for crime forecasting.

DOI: 10.4018/978-1-6684-8618-4.ch013

1. INTRODUCTION

1.1 Crime Forecasting

Predicting the likelihood of drug offences, burglaries, and other crimes based on past trends in a neighborhood or community may help with crime prevention and the allocation of resources. For a long time, the FBI's annual reports have been the gold standard for crime prediction (Babu, S.Z.D., et al, 2022). These figures only provide a snapshot of the national crime problem annually or even daily. Local communities can better deal with criminal activities and police outreach if police personnel and departments are able to keep tabs on crime trends and police response strategies. In order to keep more citizens safe in their communities, law enforcement agencies may benefit from centralized crime forecasting methodologies and internet data that is regularly updated (Bansal R., 2021).

By seeing the patterns that emerge in other cities, towns, and regions, those in transition may better prepare for the challenges that lie ahead. Police actions and reactions are also monitored in crime prediction (Boukabous, M., 2023). This method would lead to more standardised record keeping, even though the things monitored now differ from department to department. Predicting the occurrence of a crime may assist authorities keep tabs on how long it takes police to get on the scene, what kind of force is used, whether or not anybody is shot, how many people are injured, and how quickly emergency medical services respond (Dakalbab, F., et al, 2022). It might also help authorities determine if they need to revise their rules or give further training to their officers in order to improve their relationships with the people they serve. (Dushyant, K., et al, 2022)

1.2 Benefits of Crime Forecasting

In regions where a pattern can be found for early warnings to protect others from being victimised, crime forecasting may help lower the occurrence of violent crime (Esquivel, N., 2020). When police officers are experiencing trouble communicating with members of the community, these internal quality control measures may assist ensure that no lives are lost due to an error. (Fan, Y., 2021) Forecasting criminal activity also facilitates collaboration between law enforcement and educational institutions, which in turn improves both the quality and quantity of crime-prevention research and training. In an effort to effectively police their communities and use less force, researchers in the field of criminal justice are always developing new methods to improve police work (Fan, Y., 2021). Predicting where crimes will occur may help a community allocate resources more effectively, allowing the police to protect (Gupta A. et al, 2019) the most at-risk neighborhoods?

1.3 Attempts to Predict Criminal Activity May Run Into Difficulties

Poor record keeping may lead to incomplete or, at best, sketchy details about past events, such as phone numbers, hours, and dates (Gupta, N., 2020). This may lead to discrepancies in the data police have access to, increasing the likelihood that they will either ignore warning signals or alert the public to problems after they have already escalated beyond the point of prevention. Also, it may prevent agencies from receiving necessary extra training that would otherwise be provided for the betterment of law enforcement (Hashemi, M.,2020). Crime trends in a community may be difficult to break if police officers aren't collecting enough information on the frequency, location, and nature of violent and drug-related offences. Better readiness and police work as a whole may be achieved with the use of modern tools like online records and Crime Statistics (Jeyaboopathiraja, 2021). The public may benefit from more accurate crime statistics by learning more about the state of law enforcement in their region (Jain, V., 2022). This ensures that police agencies and personnel are held responsible for their efforts to curb violence, bias, and profiling. Yet, this also provides communities with an opportunity to publicly thank and support outstanding law enforcement personnel (Jenga, K., et al, 2023).

1.4 Role of CNN in Crime Forecasting

Crime rates continue to rise steadily in India. To anticipate the frequency and timing of criminal acts, it is crucial to create a variety of cutting-edge, current instruments and procedures. Based on this information, authorities may increase their presence and attention in the area, as well as their intelligence gathering efforts, in the hopes of preventing further criminal activity (Kadiyam, P., 2021). Spatiotemporal statistical approaches are employed to make such forecasts, and there are numerous of them (Kaushik, D., 2021). Predicting the frequency with which criminal acts will be committed is essential in developing a strategy to prediction or adopting timely, effective measures to lower the crime rate (Law, S., 2020). In addition, one may use the features of LSTM to conduct an analysis of the connections between previously stored data. Because of this, we aimed to use a CNN-LSTM model to predict future crime rates in this study (Mandal, D., 2022). Author used a three-year sample of NCRB crime data for our analysis. We settled on four specifics: violent crimes (including murder and rape), theft, and property crimes. After using CNN to extract the variables from the dataset, we turned to LSTM to make predictions about the crime rate. Experimental results showed that by combining the CNN and LSTM model, a reliable and highly accurate strategy for forecasting criminal activity could be obtained. This approach is both an innovative avenue for research into predicting future crime rates and an effective mechanism for doing so (Mohamad Zamri, 2021).

1.5 Role of Image Classification in Crime Forecasting

The term "image classification" refers to the act of assigning labels to distinct clusters of image pixels or vectors according to predetermined criteria. To predict criminal activity, a classification law may be developed utilising one or more spectral or textural properties. Supervised and unsupervised categorization is two broad approaches.

An unsupervised classification technique is a data-free, hands-off approach to classification. At the picture processing step, the necessary properties are identified systematically using an appropriate algorithm. 'Image clustering' and 'pattern recognition' are the categorization techniques used here for crime prediction. ISODATA and K-mean are two popular algorithms that are often utilized (Pandey, B.K. et al., 2022).

Supervised classification uses human judgment to choose samples from inside an image and assign them to predetermined categories, allowing for the development of statistical measures that may be applied to the whole picture. Maximum likelihood and minimal distance are two common methods that use the training data to label the whole image. For instance, the maximum likelihood classification method makes advantage of the statistical aspects of the data by first determining the average and standard deviation of the image's spectral and textural indices. Next, for the sake of crime prediction, we assume that the pixels in each class follow a normal distribution and use some elementary classical statistics and probabilistic correlations to calculate the likelihood that any given pixel belongs to any given class. The last step is to give each pixel a label that describes the set of characteristics with the highest likelihood (Pathania, V et al., 2022).

1.6 Integration of Image Classification to CNN for Crime Forecasting

In regards to medical image analysis, deep neural networks are particularly useful for picture categorization. The image classification process takes in a set of input photos and returns a set of output classes that may be used to determine whether or not the illness is present. (Shah, N., 2021) The Developed a convolutional neural network techniques, that achieves better results than 100% accurate picture categorization when used in cytopathology. With its superior human performance, the Inception v3 architecture stands out as a top choice for analysing medical data. The suggested CNN-like architecture for forecasting brain growth makes use of three-dimensional convolutions for classification. These days, convolutional neural networks (CNNs) are considered the gold standard for image categorization. The CNNs improved their understanding of real pictures, demonstrating superior performance and even rivalling the precision of human expert systems. These arguments culminate in the conclusion that CNNs can be enhanced to manage the core infrastructure of crime prediction. (Shanqing, G., 2019)

2. LITERATURE REVIEW

A.Stec, et al.(2018) introduced DL to predict criminal activity. The goal of this study was to use deep neural networks to forecast the number of crimes committed in a city on a given day using a very fine-grained division of the population. Our forecasts are based on a variety of factors, including weather reports, population data, and information on the availability of public transportation, as well as crime rates in Chicago and Portland. Each day, our algorithm forecasts the most probable ten-bin crime count distribution for each geographic area. They use several neural network topologies, some of which were tailored to the geographical & temporal elements of crime prediction issue, to train this data. Top model achieves an accuracy of 75.6% in predicting the proper bin for Chicago's total crime count, and 65.3% in Portland's. The results demonstrate the usefulness of employing datasets outside of traditional crime statistics and the effectiveness of neural networks for the prediction challenge.

D. Vasan, et al.(2020) provided work on namely, an IMCEC-specific CNN Ensemble. This method is known as image-based malware classification using an ensemble of CNNs. Our central hypothesis is that different CNNs provide different semantic representations of the image based on their underlying architectures, and hence it is possible to extract features of higher quality by drawing from a variety of CNN designs. Findings from experiments indicated that IMCEC performed effectively while testing for harmful software. It is possible that it might achieve high detection accuracy with low false alarm rate when given raw-input from malware. Overall, the results show an accuracy of over 99% for unpacked malware & over 98% for packed malware. It takes IMCEC an average of 1.18 seconds to identify a new malware sample, making it a powerful, practical, and fast solution.

G. Shanqing, et al.(2019) focused on the neural networks and data augmentation. A powerful combination for Better IC, in this study, they show how to enhance data for picture categorization using CNN. Model over fitting and subpar performance are common problems with neural network approaches. Strategies that diminish intra-class differences while keeping sensitivity to the inter-class variations were necessary to maximize model accuracy & minimize the loss function. Using the CIFAR-10 public image dataset, researchers monitored the effects of model overfitting by augmenting the data and adjusting the hyper-parameters.

H. Verma, et al.(2020) reviewed criminal activity via CNN. The purpose of this research was to use the inferential powers of several DL architectures to identify suspects using photographs of their faces. They used two types of DL models in this investigation: the standard CNN architecture and pre-trained CNN architectures like VGG-16, VGG-19, and InceptionV3. A research was conducted to compare the efficiency with which these algorithms were able to extract criminal traits from human faces. NIS and Technology, a publicly available database, was used to evaluate the performance of the aforementioned deep learning models. For clarity, they only used images of men throughout this piece

J.Jeyaboopathiraja, et al.(2021) did research on DL for crime trends prediction. In which initial input crime data will be pre-processed utilizing missing value imputation, binning and min - max normalisation. And then, to further enhance the prediction, they use an enhanced cuckoo search optimization to identify the most relevant characteristics. Lastly, SRCNN using ReLU in hidden layers is developed for crime trend prediction. For ReLU's inputs, sparseness was added. The learning process, ReLU's inputs were pushed towards zero. This avoids needless ReLU's output growth. The experimental findings for the Philadelphia, Chicago, and Francisco datasets show that the suggested model yields improved outcomes in terms of accuracy, f-measure, recall, and precision.

M. Hashemi, et al.(2020) presented work on criminal inclination identification using face photographs and the gender bias effect. The results of this research were an important first step towards our goal of identifying underlying personality traits based just on photographs of faces. With this ultimate goal in mind, they explore a new frontier of picture understanding by inferring criminal propensity from facial photos using DL.

N. Esquivel, et al.(2020) focused on the forecasting criminal activity in baltimore across time and space applying convolutional and recurrent spiking neural networks .

N. F. M. Zamri, et al.(2021) focused on the street crime prediction and classification techniques. In this research, researchers conducted a mini-review of the databases used and the methodology used in previous studies on crime classification, criminal analysis, and crime prediction. In addition, a fresh method for uncovering illicit activity will be provided.

P. Kadiyam, et al.(2021) reviewed CNN & transfer learning are used to analyse street view images to forecast crime rates. The goal of this research is to use the data from Google Street View to make predictions about the number of crimes committed in four categories. An whole year's worth of crime statistics for Greater London were studied. To do this, a DL model was developed by gathering several inputs and making simultaneous predictions for four categories of crime.

Q. Wang, et al. (2020) looked the neural networks for spatial and temporal crime predictions, CSAN was the gold standard.

S. Law, et al. (2020) introduced street-frontage-net: urban picture categorization using deep CNN. This study extends on the prior research through five experiments. They obtain solid results in classifying frontage quality for an out-of-sample test set that reaches an accuracy of up to 92.0%. They also discover active frontages in a neighbor- hood has a substantial relationship with rising property values.

Y. Fan, et al.(2021) provided work on DL algorithm and a 3D CNN, we may foresee future developments in the field of criminal psychology. Our goal was to develop a crime prediction model in 3D CNN using the deep learning concept of CNNs to identify typical criminal acts associated with driving behavior.

3. PROBLEM STATEMENT

Results from a conventional study showed that a 3D CNN prediction model was 96% accurate in predicting traffic violations by correctly identifying five types of illegal driving behavior. Our proposed prediction model shows promising results for identifying patterns in driver-offender behavior and predicting future incidents. There is need to improve accuracy rate along with performance.

4. CRIME FORECASTING USING CNN BASED IMAGE CLASSIFICATION TECHNIQUE

Using a variation auto-encoder and a context-based sequence generative neural network, researchers have built CSAN as a new benchmark forecasting model to rapidly evaluate data and unravel connections from a current crime dataset spanning fifteen years. To sum up, research shows that when comparing CSAN to other common spatio-temporal forecasting algorithms like Conventional LSTM, CSAN was better at predicting the incidence of numerous kinds of crimes across a given region.

Predicting the occurrence of criminal acts in Baltimore was suggested to be accomplished by combining a CNN with a LSTM network. In specifically, a CLSTM-NN is fed matrices of previous criminal incidents to make predictions about the likelihood of at least one such event occurring in the days to come. Street robberies and thefts are used as examples in the model's implementation. The suggested method can account for geographical and temporal correlations in the historical data, leading to more accurate predictions in the future. Standard criteria are used to evaluate the proposed neural network's prediction ability in a variety of synthetic, realistic settings.

To separate criminal from innocent-looking faces, researchers turned to two distinct DL models: a conventional feed forward NN and a CNN. They detail the confusion matrices and training and test accuracies of both models using tenfold cross-validation on a dataset of 10,000 face pictures. After training to achieve its greatest test accuracy, CNN was more consistent than SNN, ultimately achieving an accuracy that was 8% greater than that of SNN. Two researchers examined classifier's potential bias due to gender by utilising exclusively male face pictures. There seemed to be little to no gender bias in the classifier, since there were no discernible differences in classification accuracies or learning consistency. Finally, breaking down and displaying CNN's convolutional layers revealed that the network used facial features such as eyebrows, the upper part of the eye, & lips to differentiate between the two groups of images.

It has been constructed using the Inception model as a foundational component. Methods are developed to model the crime statistics and get the labelled dataset ready for use in the newly developed model. Modeling the crime data using Kernel Density Estimation allows us to extract the street view image and properly label the data. Using just four street views and population density provided as inputs, we were able to predict rates of burglary, robbery, other thefts, and vehicle offences. To investigate the impact of visual features on crime rate forecasting, many model configurations were trained and compared.

5. METHODOLOGY USED FOR IMAGE CLASSIFICATION

Utilising an intelligent CNN and basing it on an enhanced picture dataset makes it possible to successfully extract the features of image and achieve higher levels of accuracy when it comes to image recognition.

Figure 1. Architecture of VGG16 model

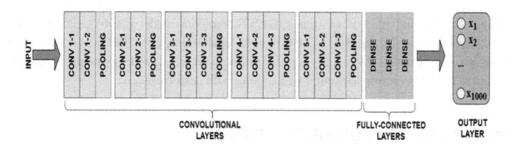

This is made possible by the fact that it is viable to do so. In the context of image recognition, this is something that is feasible to perform. Using these models offers a number of advantages, one of which is that they are able to generate an internal representation of a two-dimensional picture by using CNNs. This is only one of the many advantages. This is only one of the numerous benefits that may be enjoyed. The model is able to learn information about the location and proportion of image inside a picture as a direct result of this, which allows it to recognise image. CNN is now able to distinguish the face of a person in a picture since it has obtained the appropriate training in this area. Convolutional neural networks may be used to process visual data, which might possibly result in considerable gains. The fact that CNN is able to automatically distinguish important characteristics without any assistance from a human operator is perhaps the most significant benefit that it has in comparison to its predecessors. In contrast to past iterations of CNN, this one has more features.

Artificial neural networks, including the subgroup of artificial neural networks known as convolutional neural networks (CNNs), were designed specifically for the purpose of managing pixel input throughout the image recognition and processing stages. For each layer, one may acquire knowledge of a variety of filters, and there are many to choose from. Each filter is taught to detect a certain pattern or feature that is unique to that filter. These patterns and features can only be found in that filter. This filter is the only one with these particular patterns and properties. The many different varieties of CNN models include the following:

1. **LeNet:** Not only is the LeNet design of CNN the most well-known, but it was also the very first model of CNN, which debuted in the year 1998. CNN originally began broadcasting with this model. LeNet, which is a classic illustration of a convolutional neural network, was built with the use of convolutions, pooling, and fully connected layers, all of which are components of the network. The use of the MNIST dataset was necessary for the task of handwritten digit recognition that was being carried out. The structural layout served as a point of departure for the building of future networks like AlexNet and VGG, all of which were inspired by the original design.

2. **VGGNET:** It is possible to import a 16-layer convolutional neural network (VGG-16), which has already been trained on more than a million photos taken from the ImageNet database. This kind of network is seen in following Figure.

3. **AlexNet:** AlexNet is a leading architecture for any object-detection job and may have large applications in the computer vision sector of artificial intelligence challenges. AlexNet was developed by Alex Krizhevsky at Stanford University. The ability to recognise photographs and other forms of visual information is one of the primary issues faced in this industry. This is due to the fact that

Figure 2. ResNet50 model architecture

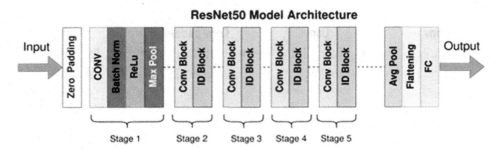

AlexNet was developed to address issues that arise in computer vision. There is a chance that in the not-too-distant future, AlexNet may take the place of CNNs as the solution of choice for photo projects.

4. **ResNet:** The term "ResNet," which is an acronym for the phrase "Residual Networks," refers to a typical neural network that serves as the foundation for a broad range of applications that are classified as being under the heading of computer vision. The phrase "Residual Networks" is an abbreviation for the phrase "Residual Networks."

    This specific model triumphed in the 2015 ImageNet competition, which landed it in first place overall in the competition. The most important thing that ResNet did for us was make it feasible to effectively train incredibly deep neural networks that had more than 150 layers. This was the most significant contribution that ResNet made. This was the one thing that ResNet performed for us that was really necessary.

5. **DenseNet's:** levels of DenseNet interact with the layers below them, the network may be classified as a convolutional neural network. The initial layer of DenseNet, for example, is able to interact with the layers that come after it.

6. **Inception:** Convolutional neural networks are used in image processing and object recognition, and Inception V3 is one such network.

Figure 3. DenseNet architecture

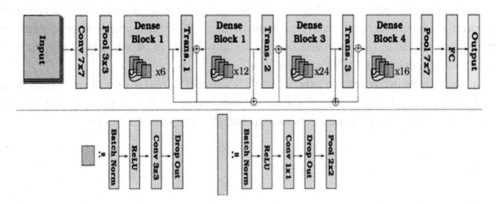

Figure 4. Architecture of Inception V3

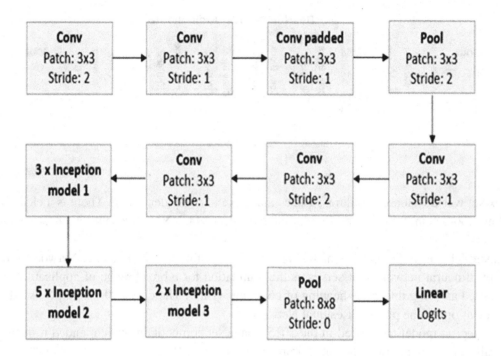

It was first conceived as a module for Googlenet when it was first developed. Google's Inception Convolutional Neural Network has undergone two substantial upgrades since it was initially presented at the 2016 ImageNet Recognition Challenge. This event took place in 2016.

6. PROPOSED CNN MODEL FOR CLASSIFICATION AND PREDICTION OF CRIME

In proposed work image is captured and it is compressed. Compressed image is consisting noise that is removed using noise removal mechanism. After image preprocessing, VGG based CNN based classification model is initialized with epochs, learning rate, number of iterations. Random forest classifier and adam optimizer is considered. Then training and testing operation are made to get confusion matrix to get accuracy, recall value, precision and f-score. Finally accuracy parameters of proposed work are compared to that of conventional CNN models.

In present work crime images are preprocess and CNN model is used in order to get category of crime. After training of CNN model by dataset classification report is generated. In present work random forest has been applied to get accuracy parameters such as Recall, Precision, F1 Score.

Figure 5. Proposed work

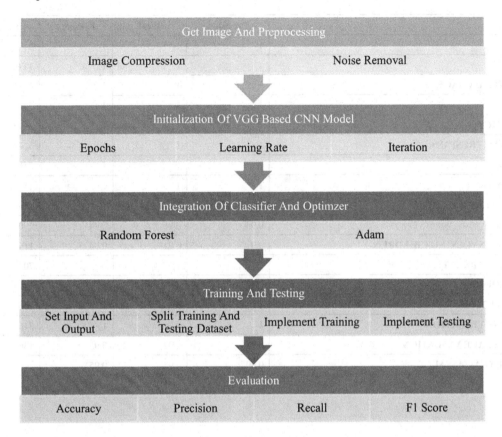

Comparison of Accuracy of Proposed Work to Conventional Research Work

There are several CNN model that are used for image classification. Present research work has considered DENSENET, RESNET model for comparison with proposed work that is considering CNN model with random forest classifier.

5. CONCLUSION

Findings suggest the significant potential for employing DL approaches in spatial information extraction and urban planning. The proposed method involves evaluating and validating many Methods, with a concentration on CNN, as well as the particular sort of database that will be used to identify snatching and other forms of street crime. . In a limited data setting, it was shown that VGG CNN models performed the best, with a 99.5% accuracy rate in identifying criminal faces.

Table 1. Classification report

	Precision	Recall	F1-Score	Support
THEFT	1	1	1	4147
ASSAULT	1	1	1	1170
CRIMINAL DAMAGE	1	1	1	2454
BATTERY	1	1	1	3702
NARCOTICS	1	1	1	2193
CRIMINAL TRESPASS	1	1	1	551
ROBBERY	1	1	1	755
BURGLARY	1	1	1	1173
MOTOR VEHICLE THEFT	1	1	1	924
OTHERS	0.93	0.96	0.94	290
OFFENSE INVOLVING CHILDREN	0.97	0.91	0.94	114
DECEPTIVE PRACTICE	1	1	1	702
OTHER OFFENSE	0.99	1	1	1213
PROSTITUTION	1	0.99	1	186
WEAPONS VIOLATION	1	1	1	216
PUBLIC PEACE VIOLATION	0.98	0.92	0.95	136
CRIM SEXUAL ASSAULT	0.99	0.92	0.95	74

Figure 6. Accuracy report for random forest classifier

Figure 6. Accuracy report for random forest classifier

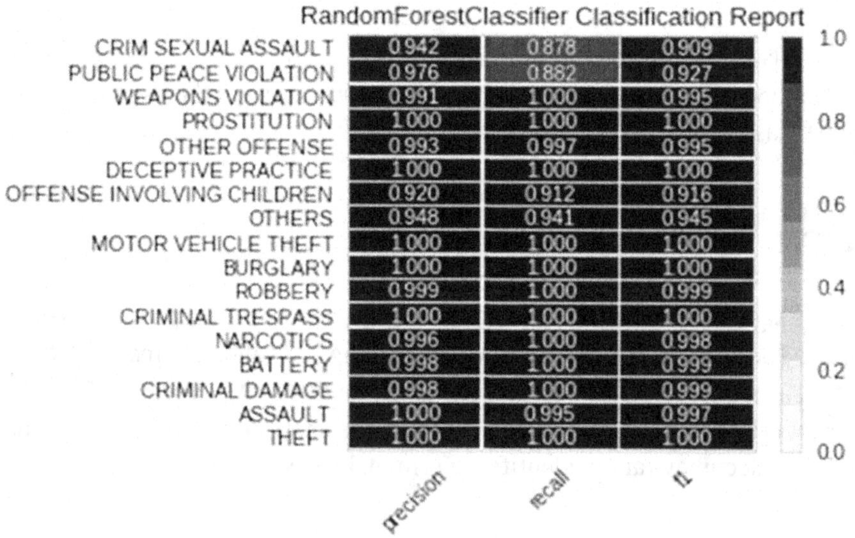

Table 2. Comparison of accuracy parameter

	DENSENET	RESNET	VGG integrated Random forest
Accuracy	92.23	94.45	96.43
Precision	0.89	0.91	0.93
Recall	0.89	0.91	0.94
F1 Score	0.89	0.91	0.93

Figure 7. Comparison of accuracy

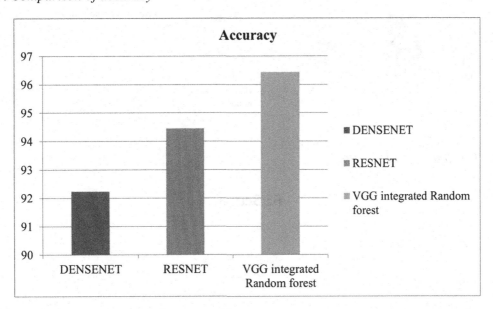

Figure 8. Comparison of precision

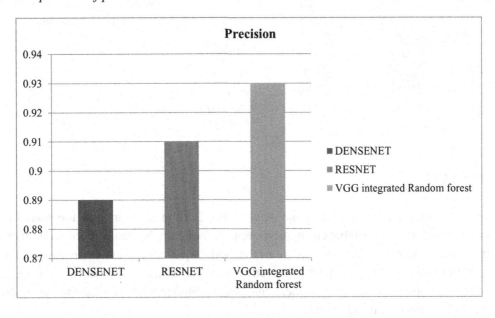

Figure 9. Comparison of recall value

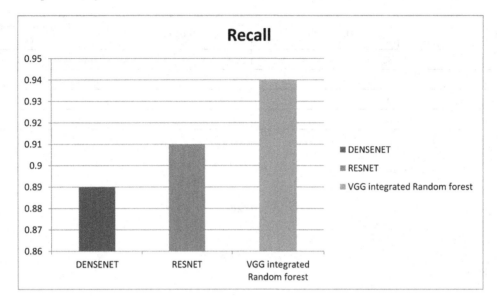

Figure 10. Comparison of F1-Score

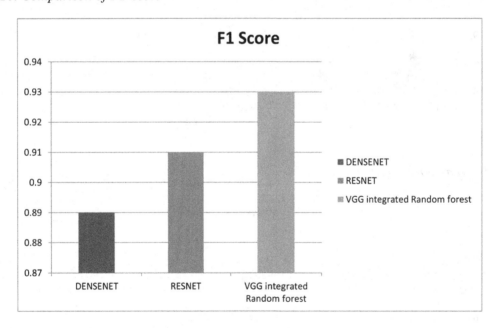

6. FUTURE SCOPE

Some of the challenges in comprehending the neighborhood crime scene include the spatial-temporal datasets' great complexity, intractable correlations, & information redundancy. Future research may do work on such issues. Future research could examine the model's performance using measures of accuracy and loss on training and testing data, features derived from confusion matrices, and visual representations of different model outputs using the non-linear mapping technique t-Distributed Stochastic Neighbor Embed- ding (t-SNE) in optimized manner.

REFERENCES

Bansal, R., Gupta, A., Singh, R., & Nassa, V. K. (2021). Role and Impact of Digital Technologies in E-Learning amidst COVID-19 Pandemic. *2021 Fourth International Conference on Computational Intelligence and Communication Technologies (CCICT)*, (pp. 194-202). IEEE. 10.1109/CCICT53244.2021.00046

Boukabous, M., & Azizi, M. (2023). Image and video-based crime prediction using object detection and deep learning. *Bulletin of Electrical Engineering and Informatics*, *12*(3), 1630–1638. doi:10.11591/eei.v12i3.5157

Dakalbab, F., Abu Talib, M., Abu Waraga, O., Bou Nassif, A., Abbas, S., & Nasir, Q. (2022). Artificial intelligence & crime prediction: A systematic literature review. *Social Sciences & Humanities Open*, *6*(1), 100342. doi:10.1016/j.ssaho.2022.100342

Esquivel, N., Nicolis, O., Peralta, B., & Mateu, J. (2020). Spatio-Temporal Prediction of Baltimore Crime Events Using CLSTM Neural Networks. *IEEE Access : Practical Innovations, Open Solutions*, *8*, 209101–209112. doi:10.1109/ACCESS.2020.3036715

Fan, Y. (2021). Criminal psychology trend prediction based on deep learning algorithm and three-dimensional convolutional neural network. *Journal of Psychology in Africa*, *31*(3), 292–297. doi:10.1080/14330237.2021.1927317

Gupta, A. (2019). Script classification at word level for a Multilingual Document. *International Journal of Advanced Science and Technology*, *28*(20), 1247–1252. http://sersc.org/journals/index.php/IJAST/article/view/3835

Gupta, N., Khosravy, M., Patel, N., Dey, N., Gupta, S., Darbari, H., & Crespo, R. G. (2020). Economic data analytic AI technique on IoT edge devices for health monitoring of agriculture machines. *Applied Intelligence*, *50*(11), 3990–4016. doi:10.100710489-020-01744-x

Hashemi, M., & Hall, M. (2020). Criminal tendency detection from facial images and the gender bias effect. *Journal of Big Data*, *7*(1), 2. doi:10.118640537-019-0282-4

Jain, V., Beram, S. M., Talukdar, V., Patil, T., Dhabliya, D., & Gupta, A. (2022). Accuracy Enhancement in Machine Learning During Blockchain Based Transaction Classification. *Seventh International Conference on Parallel, Distributed and Grid Computing (PDGC)*, Solan, Himachal Pradesh, India. 10.1109/PDGC56933.2022.10053213

Jenga, K., Catal, C., & Kar, G. (2023). Machine learning in crime prediction. *Journal of Ambient Intelligence and Humanized Computing*, *14*(3), 2887–2913. doi:10.100712652-023-04530-y

Jeyaboopathiraja, J., & Priscilla, D. G. M. (2021). Binning and Improved Deep. *IT in Industry*, *9*(2), 1428–1436.

Kadiyam, P. (2021). *Crime rate prediction from street view images using convolutional neural networks and transfer learning*. UTWENTE.

Kaushik, K., Garg, M. Annu, G., & Pramanik, S. (2021). Application of Machine Learning and Deep Learning in Cyber security: An Innovative Approach, in Cybersecurity and Digital Forensics. In M. Ghonge, S. Pramanik, R. Mangrulkar & D. N. Le (eds). Challenges and Future Trends. Wiley.

Law, S., Seresinhe, C. I., Shen, Y., & Gutierrez-Roig, M. (2020). Street-Frontage-Net: Urban image classification using deep convolutional neural networks. *International Journal of Geographical Information Science*, *34*(4), 681–707. doi:10.1080/13658816.2018.1555832

Meslie, Y., Enbeyle, W., Pandey, B. K., Pramanik, S., Pandey, D., Dadeech, P., & Saini, A. (2021). Machine intelligence-based trend analysis of COVID-19 for total daily confirmed cases in Asia and Africa. In *Methodologies and Applications of Computational Statistics for Machine Intelligence* (pp. 164–185). IGI Global. doi:10.4018/978-1-7998-7701-1.ch009

Mohamad Zamri, N. F., Md Tahir, N., Megat Amin, M. S., & Khirul Ashar, N. D., & Abd Al-misreb, A. (. (2021). Mini-review of Street Crime Prediction and Classification Methods. *Jurnal Kejuruteraan*, *33*(3), 391–401. doi:10.17576/jkukm-2021-33(3)-02

Pandey, B. K.. (2022). Effective and Secure Transmission of Health Information Using Advanced Morphological Component Analysis and Image Hiding. In M. Gupta, S. Ghatak, A. Gupta, & A. L. Mukherjee (Eds.), *Artificial Intelligence on Medical Data. Lecture Notes in Computational Vision and Biomechanics* (Vol. 37). Springer. doi:10.1007/978-981-19-0151-5_19

Pandey, B. K., Pandey, D., Wairya, S., Agarwal, G., Dadeech, P., Dogiwal, S. R., & Pramanik, S. (2022). Application of integrated steganography and image compressing techniques for confidential information transmission. *Cyber Security and Network Security*, 169-191.

Pandey, D., & Wairya, S. (2023). An optimization of target classification tracking and mathematical modelling for control of autopilot. *Imaging Science Journal*, 1–16.

Shah, N., Bhagat, N., & Shah, M. (2021). Crime forecasting: A machine learning and computer vision approach to crime prediction and prevention. *Visual Computing for Industry, Biomedicine, and Art*, *4*(1), 9. doi:10.118642492-021-00075-z PMID:33913057

Shanqing, G., Pednekar, M., & Slater, R. (2019). Improve Image Classification Using Data Augmentation and Neural Networks. *SMU Data Science Review, 2*(2), 1–43. https://scholar.smu.edu/datasciencereviewhttp://digitalrepository.smu.edu.Availableat:https://scholar.smu.edu/datasciencereview/vol2/iss2/1

Stalidis, P., Semertzidis, T., & Daras, P. (2021). Examining Deep Learning Architectures for Crime Classification and Prediction. *Forecasting*, *3*(4), 741–762. doi:10.3390/forecast3040046

Stec, A., & Klabjan, D. (2018). Forecasting Crime with Deep Learning. 1–20. https://arxiv.org/abs/1806.01486

Talukdar, V., Dhabliya, D., Kumar, B., Talukdar, S. B., Ahamad, S., & Gupta, A. (2022) Suspicious Activity Detection and Classification in IoT Environment Using Machine Learning Approach. *Seventh International Conference on Parallel, Distributed and Grid Computing (PDGC)*, Solan, Himachal Pradesh, India. 10.1109/PDGC56933.2022.10053312

Vasan, D., Alazab, M., Wassan, S., Safaei, B., & Zheng, Q. (2020). Image-Based malware classification using ensemble of CNN architectures (IMCEC). *Computers & Security, 92*, 101748. doi:10.1016/j.cose.2020.101748

Veeraiah, V., Khan, H., Kumar, A., Ahamad, S., Mahajan, A., & Gupta, A. (2022). Integration of PSO and Deep Learning for Trend Analysis of Meta-Verse. *2022 2nd International Conference on Advance Computing and Innovative Technologies in Engineering (ICACITE),* (pp. 713-718). IEEE. 10.1109/ICACITE53722.2022.9823883

Verma, H., Lotia, S., & Singh, A. (2020). Convolutional neural network based criminal detection. *IEEE Region 10 Annual International Conference, Proceedings/TENCON,* (pp. 1124–1129). 10.1109/TENCON50793.2020.9293926

Wang, C., Lin, Z., Yang, X., Sun, J., Yue, M., & Shahabi, C. (2022). HAGEN: Homophily-Aware Graph Convolutional Recurrent Network for Crime Forecasting. *Proceedings of the AAAI Conference on Artificial Intelligence, 36*(4), 4193–4200. doi:10.1609/aaai.v36i4.20338

Wang, Q., Jin, G., Zhao, X., Feng, Y., & Huang, J. (2020). CSAN: A neural network benchmark model for crime forecasting in spatio-temporal scale. *Knowledge-Based Systems, 189*, 105120. doi:10.1016/j.knosys.2019.105120

Wirayasa, I. K. A. (2021). Comparison of Convolutional Neural Networks Model Using Different Optimizers for Image Classification International Journal of Sciences. *Comparison of Convolutional Neural Networks Model Using Different Optimizers for Image Classification., 4531*(September), 116–126.

Ying, L., Qian Nan, Z., Fu Ping, W., Tuan Kiang, C., Keng Pang, L., Heng Chang, Z., Lu, C., Jun, L. G., & Nam, L. (2021). Adaptive weights learning in CNN feature fusion for crime scene investigation image classification. *Connection Science, 33*(3), 719–734. doi:10.1080/09540091.2021.1875987

Chapter 14
Deep Learning–Based Cancer Detection Technique

Shahanawaj Ahamad
University of Hail, Saudi Arabia

Vivek Veeraiah
Adichunchanagiri University, India

J. V. N. Ramesh
Koneru Lakshmaiah Education Foundation, India

R. Rajadevi
Kongu Engineering College, India

Reeja S. R. (3c24e765-ddec-44be-a352-9c454dfd3acf
VIT-AP University, India

Sabyasachi Pramanik
Haldia Institute of Technology, India

Ankur Gupta
Vaish College of Engineering, India

ABSTRACT

The time is now for deep learning (DL)-dependent analysis of healthcare images to move from the realm of exploratory research projects to that of translational ones, and eventually into clinical practise. This process has been sped up by developments in data availability, DL methods, and computer power over the last decade. As a result of this experience, the authors now know more about the potential benefits and drawbacks of incorporating DL into clinical treatment, two factors that, in the authors' opinion, will propel progress in this area over the next several years. The most significant of these difficulties are the widespread need of strength of commonly utilized DL training approaches to various pervasive pathological properties of healthcare images and storages, the need of an properly digitised environment in hospitals, and the need of sufficient open datasets on which DL approaches may be trained and tested.

DOI: 10.4018/978-1-6684-8618-4.ch014

1. INTRODUCTION

Images function in an essential part in cancer supervision, as the initial phase in major diagnostics is in gaining a full and thorough visualisation of the damaged organ(s) that avoids the untrained human sight. Medical image processing and graphical study of physiological features is crucial for diagnosing and staging disorders like cancer. Imaging techniques have, however, progressed significantly in the recent century to record diverse elements in damaged tissue organization and constituents. Errors in the investigation of medical pictures are a common source of higher healthcare costs and longer wait times; therefore doing it properly takes effort and time. Furthermore, interexpert and even intraexpert variability in manual visual interpretation creates a gap in the patient treatment scheme, calling for objective assessment techniques in an accurate and consistent benchmark of supervision practises.

Machine learning (ML) frameworks like deep learning (DL) and DNN make it possible for the complexity of models and the precision of their associated tests to grow in tandem with the volume of various categories of structured data. These data types include images, videos, audio and text. These approaches are well-suited to managing the massive volumes of information produced by radiology and pathology imaging. The similarity in various forms of data is the fact that data at its most basic level—pixels, audio samples, and words—has a local hierarchy.

An individual word, for instance, must be understood in the context of a phrase, which in turn must be understood in the context of a sentence. In a similar vein, a pixel may be related to an edge in its spatial region that could be related to a physical item, which could be related to a full object, and so on when it comes to enhancing a task, such as the classification of histological perspectives into benign or malignant. DL depends on the finding of these hierarchical links rather than having an expert define them. Due to their data-driven nature, DL's intermediate feature extractions remain mainly mysterious. So, if utilised appropriately, DL has the potential to decrease the financial, logistical, and diagnostic uncertainty related to medical image analysis.

Here, we provide a summary and classification of cancer image survey objectives, cancer imaging modalities, difficulties in cancer image survey amenable to DL, obstacles in DL's clinical acceptance, and a look forward at the future of DL in cancer image investigation. The purpose of this evaluation is to facilitate communication between doctors and programmers as we familiarise each group with the other's priorities and needs. Different parts of this work will be of interest to each group, and vice versa, albeit the relatively short duration of this overview of such a vast and intriguing area means that some parts may not go into sufficient depth.

2. CANCER IMAGE PROCESSING AND GOALS

Cancer management relies heavily on imaging, with different imaging modalities being employed at various points in treatment for a variety of reasons. Figure 1 shows the diagnosis and treatment path that a patient offering with breast cancer would go through at various times. A comprehensive treatment strategy is then combined and performed depending on this classification of phase and tumour category. Afterwards, the tumour is removed surgically that involves analysing a completely dissected surgical material under a microscope, yielding about 20-40 WSI. Patients response assessment scan (MRI/Mammography/PET scan) evaluated for patients undergoing chemotherapy or radiation. In order to identify any recurrence or advancement at an early stage, patients will continue medical therapy and have regular follow-up appointments with appropriate radiological imaging, initially every 3 months, followed by decreasing frequency and increasing gap between these sessions. One or more of (a) therapeutic value, (b) predictive value, and (c) prognostic value are necessary for any cancer image analysing approach to be clinically meaningful.

2.1 Different Imaging Methods for Cancer

Multiple sub-modalities of clinical imaging and radiography (Bayraktar and Ayan, 2022) have traditionally been used in healthcare. Ever since its introduction in the late 1980s, digital radiography has been standard practise, producing the vast majority of medical imaging data. While pathology and, more especially, histopathology and cytopathology, is a section of the medical arsenal in a decade, breakthroughs in entire slide digitization and storage technology have only lately acknowledged them as a digital imaging (Jayasingh, R. et al., 2022) modality. Digital pathology pictures are gigapixel in size, stored in a pyramidal structure with separate (but connected) sets of information at individual layer, and need extra processing phases compared to those used in clinical imaging and radiology. However, radiological imaging often yields hundreds, if not thousands, of pictures, each of which is just a few kilobytes in size.

Since there is often no need to place an item within the body or remove tissue in order to collect a picture, most radiological imaging techniques may be classified as non-invasive. They are so unique that they deserve their own category: in-situ (or "in the real place") imaging. Instead, imaging for pathology would be considered an "invasive" modality since it requires bringing a patient's organ(s) out of their body for imaging. It would be categorised as out-of-context (ex-situ) imaging as well. Several types of imaging techniques are compared in Table 1. Imaging in the fields of medicine, radiology, and pathology all need specialised training and equipment, yet even so, medical imaging is the most akin to business photography, with all the advantages and disadvantages it entails. Digital Imaging and Communications in Healthcare is a widely adopted standard for radiological imaging that all radiology imaging equipment makers align to in order to provide some level of interoperability. Using imaging technology to diagnose pathologies is a relatively new development, even if the modern method didn't emerge till the 1990s. The need of an ordinary worldly data and file standard, in contrast to radiology images, severely restricts its widespread applicability. This is especially true when considering the sheer volume of data produced by a single slide, the correlation between scanning speed and throughput, and the associated costs. In addition, digital pathology does not replace the traditional phases in the pathology workflow like radiology (Yang, et al., 2022) does. Technological advancements in whole-slide scanning and data store actually paved the way for wider use. However, its broad use is hampered by the high costs of scanning, storing, and retrieving data. The first commercially available whole-slide imaging system received FDA approval in April 2017. Yet, there have been major advances, with a plethora of low-cost

The cancer patients experience is cyclical, however its duration will vary from patient to patient. Pathology and radiology images are collected at various stages of this process. In this table, we compare the possible uses of deep learning (DL) on single photos (solid boxes) with those that need multitime-point data (empty boxes).

Various technology companies are developing low-priced cloud storage, hosting, and integrations alternatives for the pathology industry, and the industry is inching closer to adopting the DICOM (Manikandan, V. et al., 2022) standard for imaging full slides in the pathology lab.

Other imaging modalities are also available, albeit they are either experimental or seldom used. Hyperspectral imaging, like Raman spectroscopy (Sang, X. et. al., 2022) and Fourier Transform (Pramanik,

Figure 1. The importance of imaging throughout the treatment of breast cancer

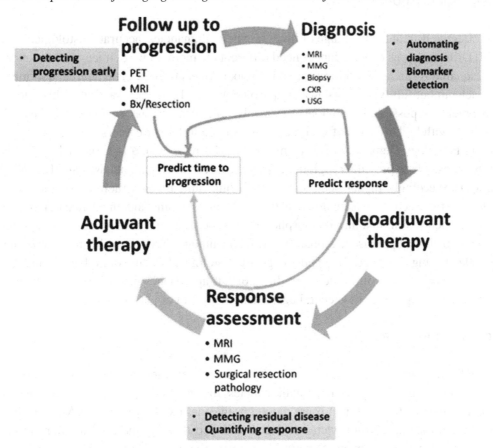

S. et al., 2021) infrared spectromicroscopy may reveal both the spatial and chemical constituent in a tissue, while PET scans can disclose locations of high intake of sugar in a human-body scan for finding hot spots in cancer. Attention this review, we zero in on DL's effect on the more common and time-tested methods of radiography and histology.

2.2 Analysis of Cancer Images Aims to Accomplish the Following

Cancer imaging and image analysis is a costly and time-consuming process, thus its aims must be defined up front. The objectives may be broken down into the following groups, as shown in Figures 2 and 3.

2.2.1 Criteria for Evaluation and Placement in a Grade Level

Comparatively, pathology interpretation is generally better concerned with tumour level, whereas conventional radiological imaging interpretation has concentrated on measuring the spread or stage of the tumour. However, ML techniques have lately blurred the lines between these functions. Textural properties of MRI scans (Mandal, A. et al., 2021), for instance, may be used in conjunction with ML techniques to properly determine the severity of brain tumours.

2.2.2 Histological Subtyping

In order to effectively treat a wide range of illnesses and malignancies, accurate histological sub-typing is essential. Different types of lung cancer need different chemotherapy regimens; for instance, adeno-carcinoma, squamous carcinoma, leiomyosarcoma (Goel, M. et al., 2022), and neuroendocrine tumours. Likewise, each tumour sub-type has its own unique outcomes and patterns of activity. This categorization must be as precise as possible for obvious reasons. Historically, this has depended on the expertise of the pathologist, with higher levels of accuracy being linked to longer careers and more formal educa-tion. Meeting Pathology Demand: A census by RCPATH, reveals that a lack of qualified pathologists presents a real obstacle to providing high-quality medical care to all patients. ML and DL in particular, have achieved exceedingly higher accuracy in analyzing tumours into their histological categories, distinguishing between entities taken as a spectrum, like an adenoma and an adenocarcinoma, and cat-egorizing lung adenocarcinoma into its morphological subcategories, all with accuracy and predictive values relevant to clinical practise. Comparatively, DL techniques have been able to identify metastases to lymph nodes having good accuracy and categorise histological pictures into benign and malignant. Some of these jobs may be within the capabilities of DL approaches have done better than seasoned pathologists when compared to the general agreement of a panel of pathologists.

2.2.3 Preparing for Care

Predictive indicators detected by a pathologist by more modern genetic testing on pathology tissue samples are crucial to the therapy of most malignancies. In stage IV lung cancer, for instance, it is con-sidered standard therapy to look for and cure mutations in genes like EGFR and BRAF, as well as ALK1 and ROS1. In the past, these exams were conducted using costly and time-consuming genomic testing techniques such polymerase chain reaction and Next Generation Sequencing. These days, DL techniques are powerful enough to reliably predict EGFR mutations from histology pictures.

To better forecast and act in the future, any consolidation of the data from past history may be input to a model (see Figure 2). This is an instance of the flow (left to right) of data received and choices available in cancer management. The flow of subsequent treatments returns to its origin.

Figure 2. An illustration of the flow (left to right) of information gathered and choices done in cancer management, where any consolidation of prior data may be entered into a model to improve future forecasts and judgements. Recurring treatments loop back to the flow's commencement

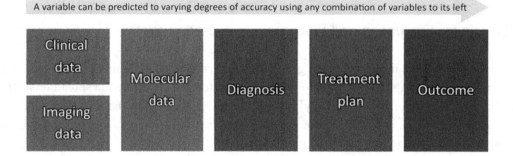

Figure 3. A typical experimental design with 2 sub-cohorts (cases and controls) and a single sub-cohort (*) that has to be predicted. Cases might contain various labels, as shown in the adjacent table (* or have a continuous label, like time to occurrence, for deep neural regression), based on the intended output type

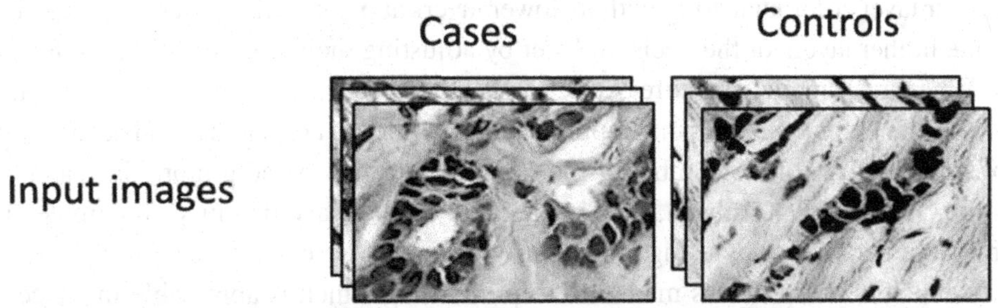

Output type	Example cases	Example controls
Diagnosis	Malignant	Benign
Diagnosis	Grade III	Grade I or II
Diagnosis	Ductal	In-situ
Molecular markers	EGFR mutated	Wildtype
Outcome	Rx non-responder	Rx responder
Survival*	Short term←→Long term	

2.2.4 Basics of Biology

Considerable effort is put into understanding the biological capacity of a tumour in order to discover predictive, prognostic biomarkers, since this is a crucial factor in patient outcomes. Deep learning algorithms may distinguish tumours with varying biological potentials within an otherwise homogeneous cohort. For instance, among tumours of the same Gleason grade, algorithms learned by researchers can distinguish biological characteristics predictive of biochemical recurrence in prostate cancer.

3. IMAGE ANALYSIS FOR CANCER: PROGRESS IN DEEP LEARNING AND ITS APPLICATIONS

Important developments in DL are discussed that have direct application to cancer image analysis. Consider the job of identifying a particular test picture as benign or malignant, as in the case of a lesion in a mammogram, to place these developments in the perspective of the larger area of ML. A decision-making model in ML (and DL) would be trained using examples of pictures previously classified as benign/malignant by a panel of professional radiologists or via the use of biopsy results confirmation. When it comes to machine learning, feature extraction and learning the decision rule depending on these characteristics have traditionally been seen as 2 distinct activities. Because of this, it was essential to formally identify and extract relevant characteristics which are anticipated to be differently distributed across benign and malignant masses. In Deep Learning, various layers of a lone NN model work together to extract features and apply a decision rule. Iterative optimization is used to jointly train the DL model's layers, with each higher layer communicating with its lower layers about how the lower layers can improve their support for the higher layers or the decision layer by adjusting their feature extraction formula in small increments. When a DL model's feature extraction is left in the hands of an optimization algorithm, the intermediate layer's output becomes incomprehensible. While the complexity and accuracy of the model tend to grow in tandem with the number of the training data, this paradigm provides a prescription for achieving this. Overfitting (Kernbach, J.M. et al., 2022) may be avoided in such complex models with plenty of trainable parameters by using a number of different strategies.

Currently, much of the progress made in Deep Learning which is applicable in cancer image analytics has focused on novel layer topologies, outputs, and training approaches for convolutional neural networks (CNNs). Next, we'll go into these developments, skipping over those that have stayed in the theoretical arena but haven't achieved state-of-the-art accuracy for use in healthcare picture analysis. Because unsupervised learning, that consist of techniques like clustering and dimension reduction, are not successfully applied to medical image analysis on a clinical level, we don't include it here, either.

3.1 Regression and Categorization of Images

To classify a picture is to give it a label from a list of possibilities. It may be necessary to simulate pathologists by dividing high-power H&E stains of breast tissue into three categories: (a) normal/benign, (b) ductal carcinoma in situ, and (c) invasive ductal cancer. Predicting disease outcome, such as utilising CT scan of the lung immediately post treatment for predicting recurrence, or using affordable imaging modalities to estimate the result of a further costly test are examples of additional value-added jobs. Predicting a continuous variable, such as how well a patient will respond to therapy, how long they will live, or when an adverse event will occur, is similar to but somewhat different from the picture classification issue. Adjusting the DL model's goal function and, in certain cases, the training process, is necessary when dealing with regression (Meslie, Y. et al., 2022).

For direct usage in training deep learning models for classification or regression, pictures typically have a resolution of 100*100 pixels. But, it takes many millions of photos to train usable Deep Learning models from start. It causes issues since (a) many forms of medical imagery are notoriously huge in file size, and (b) most patient cohorts consist of just a thousand people. Labelling healthcare pictures may be costly due to the involvement of many tests and/or patient check up later, as well as the time commitment of highly trained medical personnel. Although patient de-identification is not very challenging, there is still a shortage of openness in sharing healthcare picture collections. Fortunately, following pre-training on huge labelled datasets from a source, DL models may still be effective for training on small datasets in a target domain.

The data is gathered through the ILSVRC's ImageNet competition. For evaluating an image recognition system, one common indicator is the number of times it ranks among the top 5 errors. Here, it is anticipated that the model would correctly forecast the proper category as one of its top 5. It's also worth noting that more model parameters do not always equate to higher performance.

One kind of transfer learning is to use a DL model's pre-trained weights for various lower layers which extract features. This is part of a larger group of approaches called transfer learning, which allows

Figure 4. This diagram illustrates how deep learning has progressed to the point where it can now compete with and even surpass human performance in image recognition contests

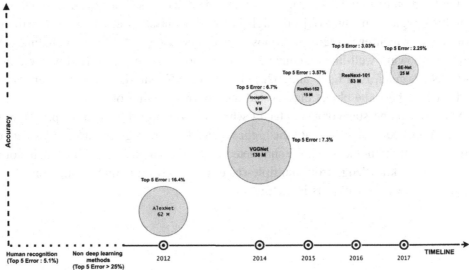

for improved performance in the target domain thanks to training in the source domain. This method is used extensively in cancer image analytics, and not only for classification.

3.2 Disentangling Meaning

The process of semantic segmentation entails assigning a category label to each pixel in an image. As a result, not only is the input high-dimensional, but so is the output. Semantic segmentation is a crucial step in advanced computer vision implementations like autonomous vehicles and AR because of the importance placed on low-level scene interpretation. Semantic segmentation, a technique used in medical image analysis, helps humans make more informed decisions by breaking a picture down into its component parts so they may locate areas of interest, calculate their area, or locate the boundaries between various anatomical components.

When it comes to semantic segmentation, the encoder-decoder approach is a common component of DL models. The network's encoder is a shrinking part that collects information from progressively bigger receptive areas, while the decoder is an enlarging component which brings this coarse-scale confirmation back to the fine-scale of the input picture. Decontraction occurs in the encoder thanks to pooling procedures, which are utilized in deep learning frameworks for image classification and regression. A decoder's height and breadth may be upped using a learnable up sampling process conducted across many layer blocks. Finally, a layer-by-layer prediction of a label mask at the pixel level is made.

3.3 Identifying Specific Locations of Things

In object localization, a predictive model not only determines whether or not an item of interest (such as a lesion) is present in an image, but also provides information about its precise position. Since the method simply needs to give a bounding box containing the item, the dense labelling requirements of semantic segmentation are simplified. When it is necessary to identify each individual instance of an object class, the object localization process becomes more difficult. The most widely used strategy for pinpointing the location of individual instances of an object is to teach deep learning (DL) techniques to propose multiple regions in which objects might be present, classify those regions, and then calculate the confidence with which each region's proposal should be accepted. This overarching concept has evolved into the following well-liked architectures throughout the years. To find where objects could be, Faster-RCNN (Pazhani, A.A.J., et. al., 2022) utilizes a DNN, and then utilises a separate detection network to determine both the object classes and their corresponding offsets in the image. You only look once (YOLO) is a one-stage object detector which utilizes a grid to scan for probable item positions and labels. Labelled area boxes with the highest confidence ratings and no overlaps are chosen as the final forecasts. Last but not least, single shot detector (SSD) is a one-stage object detector similar to YOLO which employs knowledge from multiple-scale features from neighbouring convolution layers to characterise and forecast the objects in the picture.

Figure 5. Concise summaries of Machine Learning categorizations for Calcified Nodule (a) Classification, Segmenting a CT picture into its component parts (b) objects (c) semantics and (d) instances

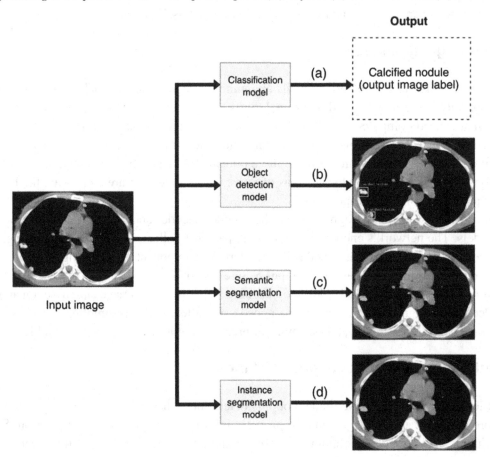

3.4 Breaking Down Instances

Instance segmentation goes beyond semantic segmentation by considering several instances of the same class to be distinct entities. To do so, it blends concepts from object localization with those of semantic segmentation, first locating every instance and then constructing a semantic segmentation mask for every item independently. Mask RCNN is a well-liked technique for instance segmentation since it enhances quicker RCNNs with a mask generating module, allowing for more potent and precise segmentation.

Figure 6. A DLL Framework for classifying histology images with limited supervision

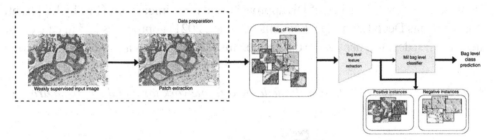

Following this, more DL frameworks may be trained to make diagnosis depending on the photos themselves. It is important to keep in mind, nevertheless, that current NLP categorization methods are far from perfect. As a result, there is a need to verify the accuracy of NLP-dependent label extraction from EMR by performing an audit of the labels applied to photos. Due to the inaccurate NLP (Khurana, D. et al., 2023) labels, the noisy label and weakly supervised difficulties in training DL models on pictures with labels derived from DL approaches trained for Natural Language Processing must be revisited.

3.5 Collaborative Education

Due to concerns around data privacy (Kaushik, D. et al. 2022) and intellectual property, traditional DL models and all associated training data and infrastructure have had to be housed in a locked room somewhere within an organisation. With federated learning, numerous organisations work together to train a model using their combined (and hence bigger) data set without disclosing sensitive information to a central node. A model developed in this way is more resilient and useful than one learned utilizing data from a single company. In the training step, every participating organisation makes local adjustments to the model, and then broadcasts that company's partly trained model to the others. As a result, the whole system is able to separate and divorce the model training from its data, allowing for better effective model training without the usual concerns associated with data sharing or security (Pramanik, S. et al., 2020) breaches. Because of the potential for training data to contain a lot of variety encompassing multiple geographical places without sharing the patient data, federated learning is intriguing for use in developing automated support systems for medical pictures. The use of this private collaborative learning was studied earlier where 4 engaging institutions trained 2 approaches successively in a cyclic training strategy, one each for retinal fundus imaging and mammography. Such a cyclical training approach may yield improved accuracy of the recently viewed data. To combat this bias, a strategy has been suggested and studied for identifying brain tumour in MRI utilising data from 10 different institutions in which model parameters are updated concurrently everywhere and then averaged regularly to get a global signal. These findings lend credence to the idea that such federated learning methods may be explored in the development of more reliable computer-aided diagnostic systems. Figure 7 provides a concise overview of the federated learning method.

4. CASE STUDIES OF SUCCESSFUL DEEP LEARNING IN CANCER IMAGE ANALYTICS

Here we discuss the possible influence of DL approaches on the clinical workflow by highlighting most of the accomplishments Deep Learning (Pramanik, S. et al., 2021) approaches had in cancer image processing. Due to the fast development of the discipline, this is by no means a complete history of the topic.

Figure 7. A diagrammatic representation of a federated framework for collaborative learning

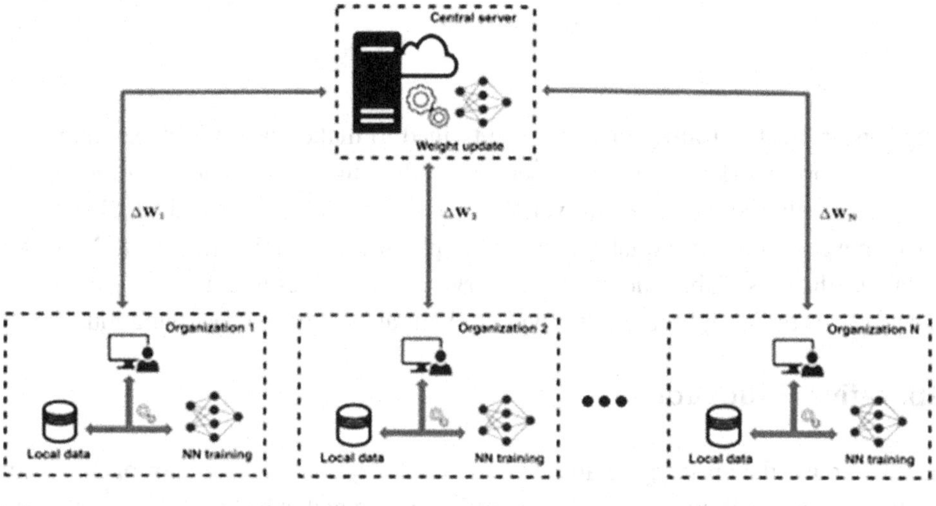

4.1 Workflow Improvements, Diagnostics, and Quantification Activities Segmentation

The everyday routines of radiologists and pathologists consist mostly on the identification, counting, and quantifying of characteristics in pictures. Two and three-dimensional (3D) segmentation (Samanta, D. et al. 2021) using DL-based approaches have recently achieved exceptional precision, as has lesion tracking using successive imaging implementations conducted over time. A genuine succeeding job is to measure tumour dimension, tumour effect to therapy, calculating and computing events (mitoses, apoptosis, etc.) most of that could be executed more correctly and reproducibly with Deep Learning-dependent techniques. Additional activities that need repetition include grading tumours, measuring tumour size, and quantifying histological patterns.

The boost in a radiologist's job requires segmentation. Radiologist productivity may be boosted by using image screening tools that are both fast and accurate. Furthermore, as was shown during the CO-VID 19 pandemic, at least few of these approaches may be swiftly re-purposed for various connected but considerably distinct jobs. Mitosis counting, the quantification of tumor-infiltrating lymphocytes, the quantification of biomarker/protein expression like HER2/PDL1 proteins are all examples of tiresome and recurring tasks that may be easily computerized. Wide interobserver variability exists in the visual interpretation of these tasks, which depends on the observer's degree of training and also has an impact on clinical care. Quantitatively observing and meaningfully interpreting these variances in a consistent manner while simultaneously lowering interobserver variability is made possible by automated image analysis, which may be used by the pathologist. As whole-slide scanners become more commonplace, quality monitoring and assurance in digital pathology are becoming more important. Automated methods managing these challenges are scarce.

4.2 Diagnosis and Modelling and Outcome Estimation

Oncologists have made multiple efforts with varied degrees of success to predict time to recurrence, responsiveness to treatment, and prognosis. The majority of nomograms and risk level approaches presently in use date back to the pre-DL era and primarily depend on categorising patients into risk groups depending on a small number of clinically calculable variables, pathologically quantifiable parameters, genetic mutations, or These methods, however, have significant limitations when it comes to extrapolating risk predictions to specific patients because they frequently classify patients based on group averages and are impacted by the lack of complete data. As a result, they should be used cautiously. Moreover, image processing employing DL-based techniques has showed tremendous promise in breaking through this barrier for both radiology and pathology images. Since DL-based approaches employ whole pictures or groups of images to make predictions or model outcomes, they may be taught to rely less on end-user inputs and to take into account interobserver variability in situations where it depends on end-user/expert inputs.

Numerous attempts were made to offer individualised predictions for survival, progression, and response prediction, many of which go beyond the bounds of conventional risk stratification using DL-dependent techniques on radiology and pathology images. Additionally, combined with the capacity to portray, estimate, and model genomic mutations, protein expression, tumour markers, intratumoral heterogeneity

In cancers, image-dependent DL techniques make it feasible for combining these disparate multimodal techniques into a single workflow.

5. PROBLEMS WITH DL ADOPTION IN HEALTHCARE

Because we now have a number of digital services that depend on image analysis employing DL, there are still obstacles in the way of fully realising the promise of its much broader adoption in crucial sectors like autonomous vehicles and cancer picture analysis. Some of them are due to a lack of mutual understanding between data scientists and healthcare professionals about expectations, difficulties, and constraints, while others are due to the actual constraints of the state-of-the-art Deep Learning approaches. We will now elaborate these difficulties in further depth.

5.1 Data Volume

The fact that DL is data hungry is one of the biggest obstacles to adoption. Modern DNNs usually include multiple training parameters and need training with an equivalently large number of annotated pictures to avoid overfitting. As indicated in Section 3.5, approaches including transfer learning and self-supervised learning minimise this demand by once or twice the magnitude, but it moreover lacking a tens of thousands of labelled pictures. To speed up the introduction of DL into precision diagnosis and enhance patient outcomes, cooperation and coordination across various research groups, data governance agencies will be essential.

5.2 Data Integrity

High-grade supervision is vital for DL. That implies each label supplied to an image or an interpreted area in training must be devoid of errors. Moreover, the labelled areas must precisely encompass the desired

Figure 8. Familiar artefacts in histology images: a) Tissue holes b) tissue fold artefacts c) stain deposits d) knife cutting artefacts e) foreign objects in the slide f) slide artefacts are some examples of tissue artefacts

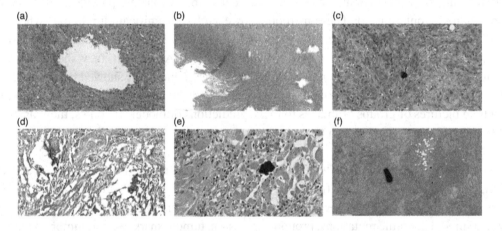

Figure 9. Common artefacts in CT scans. Three types of artefacts: a) a streak b) a ring and c) a motion artefact.

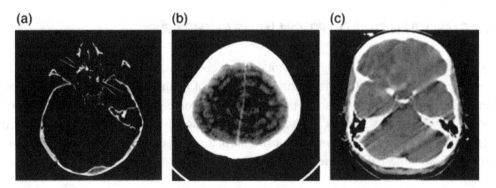

anatomical regions and not the background regions surrounding it. It is generally not straightforward because of various reasons. Firstly, certain illnesses proceeds continuously which make it impossible to define their numerous stages into discrete classifications, like Gleason type of prostate cancer (Yamada, Y. et al., 2021) or Nottingham type of breast cancer. Secondly, human labelling of these conditions is not dependent on hard quantitative measurements but visual estimations of basic variables like percent of nuclei or glands having a specific visual characteristic. Due to training or experience, experts' visual evaluation differs.

Researchers have revealed that there exists an intraexpert discrepancy for the same measurement probably owing to the subjective character of visual estimating, nonlinear examination procedure, and varied degrees of attention of similar expertise across various periods. Though the labels are extracted computationally from an EMR (Chamola, V. et al., 2022) source utilising software, noise may still enter the extracted labels as a result of mistakes in the NLP software. Additionally, a number of imaging abnormalities (in Fig 8 and 9) which might lessen the correlation between the picture and its labels can cause the visual quality of digitally altered photos to deteriorate.

A few treatments immediately spring to mind. In order to determine if re-annotation or relabeling is necessary, a suitable subset of labels and annotations must be audited against a gold standard, like a panel of specialist or a surrogate (even though it is more costly) test. Second, investigations should aim to be structured such that objective data rather than opinion are predicted by the DL pipeline (such as cancer grade). Thirdly, where the quality of the annotation or labelling is questionable or inherently subjective, Machine Learning (Pramanik, S. et al., 2023) and Deep Learning approaches are resilient to labelling noise.

5.3 Class Imbalance

Computer vision approaches were only shown to function with staged data around the turn of the century, such as evenly cropped frontal facial photographs free of background distractions. Despite the fact that picture collections are becoming more common. Class imbalance (Goyal, S. et al., 2022) is still a significant distinction between benchmark datasets for computer vision (Lingxin, Z. et al., 2022) and healthcare picture data stores, produced from natural situations. In other words, the training and test data do not evenly reflect all classes. Photos collected from a population screening programme, for example, will always have class ratios which tilt to images that are disease-negative. The skew may be considerably worse for symptoms associated with uncommon diseases. To learn to identify a class successfully, neural networks often need to process thousands of permutations of that class, and class imbalance may lead to results that are unfairly biased in favour of the over-represented classes.

5.4 Heterogeneity in Images Taken in Various Environments

The difference in features between the picture sets utilized for training and those on which the approach would be employed in medical image processing is one of the main worries associated in the absence of publicly accessible image databases. Differences in a variety of elements, the main ones of which are given in Table 3, may lead to variations in image properties. These changes are commonly defined as changes in domain in machine learning terminology. The accuracy of classification algorithms learned by DL frequently suffers to the point of being rendered unusable because of changes in domain. Several of these elements that lead to domain differences were disregarded during the early excitement around the use of Deep Learning in cancer image analytics. Cohorts for training and validation were created from the same lab's images separately. Two distinct photos from the same patient, such as two slides, were sometimes divided into the two groups. As a result, the NNs picked up on the patient-specific traits, which led to deceptively high accuracy.

Neglecting the age-old knowledge of biostatistics in the anticipation of adopting the most recent DL algorithms was another issue that led to poor research design. Small test sample sizes and a poor selection of really independent cohorts are two results of this. In addition, developing deep neural networks is still more of an art than a science. As the training process advances, for instance, the amount of weight modification in each optimization iteration that is controlled by a learning rate is periodically manually modified. Alternately, a variable random seed may be used to initialise the weights at random. Such subtleties may go unnoticed without careful recording, which might sometimes lead to significantly different findings if the research were to be replicated. Because of the complexity of the models, software, and hardware in computer vision, cases of minor errors during reproducibility are largely allowed.

However, during the last several years, a number of prominent publications have been requiring better prepared investigations prior to the submissions being accepted. In addition, even if the majority of reviewers are active to actually install the software environment and run the frameworks, they anticipate that the data or the code will be supplied to at least try repeatability. Independent model testers and validators are also required for this ecosystem, and several companies have already begun to emerge.

5.5 Regulations and Privacy Issues

The fact that the data gathering procedure must take into account the privacy rights and interests of the human is another significant obstacle to data preparation for cancer picture analysis. Since the reason for the data collection should be supported by a calculated research and the permission forms must be authorised by an institutional review board or ethics committee, gaining such consent requires a long procedure. New authorization must be requested if the investigators decide to alter the data collecting strategy or the study's objectives. This procedure requires time and raises the operational expenses for healthcare research organisations.

5.6 Labelling, Storage, and Validation Expenses

It is also important to consider the cost of supervised data preparation in the healthcare industry. Take into account that although a pathologist typically takes 10 minutes each slide of prostate cancer for assigning a Gleason type, annotating the same slide utilizing a digital stylus or mouse might take two to three times as long. The calibre of these annotations is essential for teaching computers to spot patterns, which comes naturally to pathologists. A committee of specialists should ideally evaluate the annotations as well, but their time is even more priceless and limited. Such annotations and validations take time, as do research design, case selection, digitalization, storage, retrieval, transmission, and other steps. Additionally, extra workers and equipment are needed throughout the whole operation. As an example, pathology is however done utilizing glass slides and multi-headed microscopes rather than full slide scanners and huge screen monitors, despite the fact that the majority of radiography equipment offered today is now digital.

5.7 Decision-Making Inability

It is often accurately critiqued that the most reliable and well-liked DL architectures are opaque in their internal decision-making. These designs depend on thousands of artificial neurons connected by millions of randomly initialised connection weights. The weights of the connections are adjusted using a learning process called backpropagation to achieve a supervised learning goal. It is not well known or controlled what values these weights take throughout the learning techniques or what properties an artificial neurons extract. Information becomes entangled as a result of this. Even though some artificial neurons do indeed encode this information, the discrete ideas that the neurons extract are frequently entangled in the encoding learned by every neuron, despite the fact which we may prefer 2 intermediate neurons for encoding interpretable features like roundness and margins of the chromatin of the nuclei, respectively.

Figure 10. Standard deep learning model's overview for analysing medical images

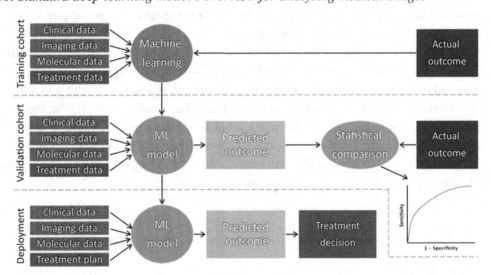

Marginality and a number of other traits are expressed in an unregulated and imperfectly understood cooperative manner with different neurons.

When NNs do make errors, it may be challenging to identify the causes of the errors and, more crucially, to fix them. There does not exist any knowledge of the function of any distinct weights in a DNN (Pramanik, S., 2022), in contrast to a nomogram, where the weight of a specific element may be raised or lowered to boost accuracy. We can examine and analyse them under various circumstances, but we cannot quickly change them in the field.

Under strictly regulated circumstances, like the standardised tissue or patient readiness, image capturing technology, and illness context recording, the usefulness of DL may undoubtedly be achieved. Under such controlled circumstances, it has been shown that DL, if trained utilizing an additionally authentic gold standard like a surrogate test or a panel of specialists, is comparable to or even beats individual experts for specific issues. In order to move beyond these strictly regulated conditions, anyone can have queries that have a similarity to those one will pose about a non-Deep Learning test like: in a multicenter trial, does a Deep Learning model outperform the existing condition? Does it continue to be effective when applied to patients from different geographic regions with potentially different medical systems, genomes and lifestyles?

5.8 Thorough Evaluation and Calibration of Decision Confidence

When faced with data that they are unfamiliar with, the presently distinguished Deep Learning frameworks and training approaches lack calibration of confidence (Figure 10). More stringent testing techniques might help to some degree to solve this issue. To avoid developing a false sense of confidence in the capabilities of the Deep Learning frameworks, it is simple to avoid obvious mistakes like utilising one image of a patient for training and a different image of the same patient for testing. Rather than the disease-based characteristics which are essential to generalization—the capacity of a model to function with acceptable assurances after deployment—DL models may quickly latch on to patient-based features and provide us with the desired result. Maintaining institution-provided data just for training, validation, or testing would be necessary for more thorough testing.

While important in extensively testing a DL model, such thoroughness does not ensure accurate output calibration. Higher accuracy on held-out data is the only aim for which DL frameworks are trained. A probability mass function—a group of integers which sum to 1 and individually indicate the likelihood of every of the disease states which is trained and tested for—is a common output of a DL model. The ideal model would calculate confidence in its predictions as well, which is something that the majority of presently outstanding models do not. One will also prefer the level of assurance in the forecasts to correspond with their knowledge with the particular ailment or kind of picture being displayed. For example, a model developed using H&E-stained photos from a certain medical centre may link a particular hematoxylin saturation level to high-grade malignancy. When a technician prone to under-staining is tested and shown photos from a different institution,

Figure 11. A calibrated deep learning model for analysing cancer-related medical images

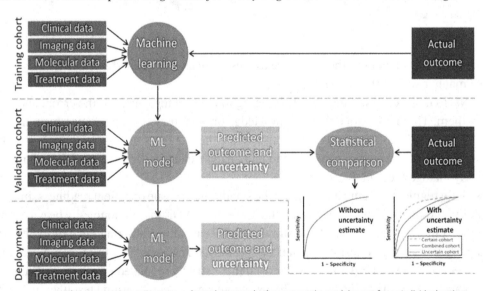

Without uncertainty estimates, we do not know to whether to trust the model or not for an individual patient
With calibrated uncertainty outcomes, we **trust** the model on cases with **low uncertainty**

Due to structural constraints, the model may nevertheless be forced to assign a confident—even if incorrect—value based on the initial theory of a correlation between grade and stain saturation. The present Deep Learning approaches are not taught to be computed for these measurements, even if measurement like the entropy (Pramanik, S. et al., 2022) of the calculated probability mass function may be considered of as means of lack of confidence. Better-calibrated models are being developed, but they should become more widely used (Figure 11).

5.9 Defining Standards for Multidisciplinary Groups

In order to explain expectations from each other, which are often well recognised and unspoken inside their respective professional groups, new multidisciplinary teams may need to investigate and educate one another. For example, DL models are often developed for a specific environment and are only meant to be used inside that context. Teams working in data science often anticipate that the data will have a certain degree of uniformity and hygienic practises. Before being submitted for a data science or ML competition, real-life data is thoroughly cleaned.

Similarly, clinical researchers usually anticipate ML to adhere to unwritten criteria of expert decision-making, such as noting the need of consulting another expert when faced with a situation that sounds unfamiliar. Human specialists are also far better at automatically distinguishing between characteristics that are patient or lab-specific and those that are disease-specific. Our visual cortex undergo years of continual training throughout our lives, which is why.

Take the problem statement to be the training of a CNN (Huang, T. et al., 2022) to calculate Nottingham grading in digital H&E histology slides of breast cancer. A natural tendency when creating training data is to clean it to only add invasive ductal carcinomas with labelled grades in order to train the Deep Learning algorithm. But there may be instances of ductal carcinoma (Kanavati, F., et al., 2022) in situ (DCIS) in real test data to which the Nottingham classification is impossible. While the medical group can find this requirement too clear to explain to the data science group, the data science group may not have anticipated the occurrence of DCIS or the need to deal with it. If the data science group is prepared for the unpredicted, they may ask a different question than "Can you provide us examples of photographs of various types of breast cancer organised into distinct folders by type instead. What additional issues are often observed when you grade breast cancer is another question they may be able to ask. In a similar vein, if the medical staff is aware that prominent machine learning frameworks which are known for their great accuracy on certain tasks cannot actually predict then they may take a more proactive approach to teaching the data science team or to building more thorough annotation methods if they are able to find test samples that do not fit the restrictive job criteria on which they were educated.

The medical professionals' assumptions that either deep learning is so precise that it may fix most of the issues or that Deep Learning cannot do the jobs that human specialists may accomplish are examples of another type of expectation mismatch. Similar to this is the propensity for DL to mimic the sub-tasks carried out by a human for completing a classification job in order to make up for its unexplainability. More proactive communication between the two sub-teams may, at least initially, address these misunderstandings.

5.10 Absence of Vendor-Neutral Solutions and Infrastructure Imaging Standards

The incorporation of these methods into routine clinical treatment determines the effectiveness of the entire Deep Learning and Machine Learning algorithms. However, the majority of hospitals lack the necessary infrastructure to implement these ideas, at least in the poor countries. The situation for digital pathology is worse because high-throughput whole-slide scanners are expensive, storage is expensive because of image size (on average, 1GB/slide in a slide with 40 scanned images), and the hospital sector has relatively low organisational IT maturity. Comparatively more recent than digital radiology, digital pathology is still in the early phases of implementation in the poor countries. The adoption of digital pathology, unlike that of digital radiology, is hampered by the absence of a uniform file format, like the DICOM standard, leading to the increase of several file-formats from every manufacturer of slide scanners and relatively limited interoperability.

Though there are vendor-neutral archives (VNA) and image archiving and communication systems (PACS) for radiology, majority of the clarifications are more accurately referred to be content-neutral as interoperability or migration between these VNAs and PACS from various manufacturers is still difficult. Additionally, not all products have the same characteristics, and the majority of systems in use are subsection archives in preference to enterprise-standard VNAs, and thus adhere to various degrees of vendor-impartiality and functionality. Similar to viewers integrated into PACS, there is still work to be done until the majority of PACS and VNAs used in health centres are enterprise-standard and prepared in the deployment of Deep Learning and various Machine Learning algorithms.

6. CONCLUSION

As discussed here, it is evident that promising outcomes depending on the implementation of Deep Learning to cancer image analytics are emerging quickly to fulfil the promise of rapid and reasonably priced precision oncology diagnosis and treatment planning. Numerous routine activities that are simple and easy to automate include the segmentation and localization of different anatomical parts as well as the triage of simple positive and negative cases. This will allow radiologists and pathologists to focus on more important activities like inspecting the locations that DL identified as unclear. With more time and rigorous testing, DL may also aid in having more valuable judgments, such as forecasting the course of a disease and its response to therapy. Using this innovative newer technology shouldn't be done hastily or with excessive caution. Each DL model's effectiveness must be demonstrated using well planned trials on target populations, just as with any new diagnostic tool or technique, if those groups vary from those employed in earlier testing of the same model. This warning should also be used in scenarios when the population is the same but another factor, like the imaging technology or file formats, changes. The authors advise any government utilising DL technology for medical image analysis to set up thorough continuous audit processes which are not either too expensive or not too slow in responding to novel scenarios where these models are used. As was already indicated, few healthcare specialists whose time is made available by Deep Learning models may contribute their knowledge to these audit programmes. Patient outcomes should be the focal point of any conversation regarding whether to utilize Deep Learning in a hospital. We must assume that DL will make at least a few mistakes. In order to have a clear understanding of patient outcomes, we must compare each cohort's mistake rates to the alternatives that are available, like the error rates of highly qualified specialists, or to the lack of any analytical capability in resource-constrained contexts where experts are unavailable. Making diagnostic labs and clinics AI-equipped is crucial in parallel to preparing them to provide the data which Deep Learning-models may analyse and to manage the difficulties which DL-dependent models deliver.

REFERENCES

Bayraktar, Y., & Ayan, E. (2022). Diagnosis of interproximal caries lesions with deep convolutional neural network in digital bitewing radiographs. *Clinical Oral Investigations*, *26*(1), 623–632. doi:10.100700784-021-04040-1 PMID:34173051

Chamola, V., Goyal, A., & Sharma, P. (2022). *Artificial intelligence-assisted blockchain-based framework for smart and secure EMR management*. Neural Comput & Applic., doi:10.100700521-022-07087-7

Goel, M., Mohan, A., Patkar, S., Gala, K., Shetty, N., Kulkarni, S., & Dhareshwar, J. (2022). Leiomyosarcoma of inferior vena cava (IVC): Do we really need to reconstruct IVC post resection? Single institution experience. *Langenbeck's Archives of Surgery*, *407*(3), 1209–1216. doi:10.100700423-021-02408-1 PMID:35022833

Goyal, S. (2022). Handling Class-Imbalance with KNN (Neighbourhood) Under-Sampling for Software Defect Prediction. *Artificial Intelligence Review*, *55*(3), 2023–2064. doi:10.100710462-021-10044-w

Huang, T., Zhang, Q., Tang, X., Zhao, S., & Lu, X. (2022). A novel fault diagnosis method based on CNN and LSTM and its application in fault diagnosis for complex systems. *Artificial Intelligence Review*, *55*(2), 1289–1315. doi:10.100710462-021-09993-z

Jayasingh, R. (2022). Speckle noise removal by SORAMA segmentation in Digital Image Processing to facilitate precise robotic surgery. *International Journal of Reliable and Quality E-Healthcare*, *11*(1), 1–19. doi:10.4018/IJRQEH.295083

Kanavati, F., Ichihara, S., & Tsuneki, M. (2022). A deep learning model for breast ductal carcinoma in situ classification in whole slide images. *Virchows Archiv*, *480*(5), 1009–1022. doi:10.100700428-021-03241-z PMID:35076741

Kaushik, D., & Garg, M. Annu, Gupta, A. and Pramanik, S. (2022). Application of Machine Learning and Deep Learning in Cyber security: An Innovative Approach. In M. Ghonge, S. Pramanik, R. Mangrulkar & D. N. Le, (eds), Cybersecurity and Digital Forensics: Challenges and Future Trends. Wiley. doi:10.1002/9781119795667.ch12

Kernbach, J. M., & Staartjes, V. E. (2022). Foundations of Machine Learning-Based Clinical Prediction Modeling: Part II—Generalization and Overfitting. In V. E. Staartjes, L. Regli, & C. Serra (Eds.), *Machine Learning in Clinical Neuroscience. Acta Neurochirurgica Supplement* (Vol. 134). Springer. doi:10.1007/978-3-030-85292-4_3

Khurana, D., Koli, A., Khatter, K., & Singh, S. (2023). Natural language processing: State of the art, current trends and challenges. *Multimedia Tools and Applications*, *82*(3), 3713–3744. doi:10.100711042-022-13428-4 PMID:35855771

Lingxin, Z., Junkai, S., & Baijie, Z. (2022). A review of the research and application of deep learning-based computer vision in structural damage detection. *Earthquake Engineering and Engineering Vibration*, *21*(1), 1–21. doi:10.100711803-022-2074-7

Mandal, A., Dutta, S., & Pramanik, S. (2021). Machine Intelligence of Pi from Geometrical Figures with Variable Parameters using SCILab. In D. Samanta, R. R. Althar, S. Pramanik, & S. Dutta (Eds.), *Methodologies and Applications of Computational Statistics for Machine Learning* (pp. 38–63). IGI Global. doi:10.4018/978-1-7998-7701-1.ch003

Manikandan, V., & Amirtharajan, R. (2022). A simple embed over encryption scheme for DICOM images using Bülban Map. *Medical & Biological Engineering & Computing*, *60*(3), 701–717. doi:10.100711517-021-02499-4 PMID:35040082

Meslie, Y., Enbeyle, W., Pandey, B. K., Pramanik, S., Pandey, D., Dadeech, P., Belay, A., & Saini, A. (2021). Machine Intelligence-based Trend Analysis of COVID-19 for Total Daily Confirmed Cases in Asia and Africa. In D. Samanta, R. R. Althar, S. Pramanik, & S. Dutta (Eds.), *Methodologies and Applications of Computational Statistics for Machine Learning* (pp. 164–185). IGI Global. doi:10.4018/978-1-7998-7701-1.ch009

Pazhani, A. A. J., & Vasanthanayaki, C. (2022). Object detection in satellite images by faster R-CNN incorporated with enhanced ROI pooling (FrRNet-ERoI) framework. *Earth Science Informatics*, *15*(1), 553–561. doi:10.100712145-021-00746-8

Pramanik, S. (2022). Carpooling Solutions using Machine Learning Tools. In *Handbook of Research on Evolving Designs and Innovation in ICT and Intelligent Systems for Real-World Applications*. IGI Global. doi:10.4018/978-1-7998-9795-8.ch002

Pramanik, S., & Bandyopadhyay, S. (2023). Analysis of Big Data. In I. G. I. John Wang (Ed.), *Encyclopedia of Data Science and Machine Learning*. IGI Global. doi:10.4018/978-1-7998-9220-5.ch006

Pramanik, S., & Ghosh, R. (2020). Techniques of Steganography and Cryptography in Digital Transformation. In K. Sandhu (Ed.), *Management and Strategies for Digital Enterprise Transformation* (pp. 24–44). IGI Global. doi:10.4018/978-1-7998-8587-0.ch002

Pramanik, S., Sagayam, K. M., & Jena, O. P. (2021). Machine Learning Frameworks in Cancer Detection. ICCSRE 2021, Morocco. doi:10.1051/e3sconf/202129701073

Pramanik, S., Samanta, D., Ghosh, R., Bandyopadhyay, S. K. (2021). A New Combinational Technique in Image Steganography. *International Journal of Information Security and Privacy, 15*(3). IGI Global. doi:10.4018/IJISP.2021070104

Pramanik, S., Singh, R. P., Ghosh, R., & Bandyopadhyay, S. K. (2020). A Unique Way to Generate Password at Random Basis and Sending it Using a New Steganography Technique. *Indonesian Journal of Electrical Engineering and Informatics*, *8*(3), 525–531.

Samanta, D., Dutta, S., Galety, M. G., & Pramanik, S. (2021). A Novel Approach for Web Mining Taxonomy for High-Performance Computing. The *4th International Conference of Computer Science and Renewable Energies (ICCSRE'2021)*. E3S. 10.1051/e3sconf/202129701073

Sang, X., Zhou, R., Li, Y., & Xiong, S. (2022). One-Dimensional Deep Convolutional Neural Network for Mineral Classification from Raman Spectroscopy. *Neural Processing Letters*, *54*(1), 677–690. doi:10.100711063-021-10652-1

Yamada, Y., & Beltran, H. (2021). Clinical and Biological Features of Neuroendocrine Prostate Cancer. *Current Oncology Reports*, *23*(2), 15. doi:10.100711912-020-01003-9 PMID:33433737

Yang, E., Ene, I. C., Arabi Belaghi, R., Koff, D., Stein, N., & Santaguida, P. (2022). Stakeholders' perspectives on the future of artificial intelligence in radiology: A scoping review. *European Radiology*, *32*(3), 1477–1495. doi:10.100700330-021-08214-z PMID:34545445

Chapter 15
Determination of Early Onset Glaucoma Using OCT Image

K. Manju
Sona College of Technology, India

R. Anand
Department of ECE, Sri Eshwar College of Engineering, Coimbatore, India

Binay Kumar Pandey
https://orcid.org/0000-0002-4041-1213
Department of Information Technology, Govind Ballabh Pant University of Agriculture and Technology, Pantnagar, India

Vinay Kumar Nassa
https://orcid.org/0000-0002-9606-7570
Rajarambapu Institute of Technology, India

Aakifa Shahul
SRM Medical College, Kattankulathur, India

A. S. Hovan George
Tbilisi State Medical University, Georgia

Sanwta Ram Dogiwal
https://orcid.org/0000-0002-4524-002X
Swami Keshvanand Institute of Technology, Management, and Gramothan, India

ABSTRACT

In order to find the glaucoma in an early stage with the help of optical coherence tomography (OCT) using deep learning and extracting the features of glaucoma, the authors are able to classify the four types of glaucoma such as CNV, DME, DRUSEN, and the normal ones with perfect accuracy by training this dataset. This dataset contained 968 images and 242 images of each type the authors trained their model by using CNN algorithm, and has greater accuracy of when compared to the determination of glaucoma using support vector machine image. The authors have good architecture constructed for the determination. They pre-trained their deep learning model in order to obtain the initial representation. The proposed system gives out 95.4% accuracy level of sensitivity, specificity, and classification. A large increase in the volume of the cup, a larger cup diameter, and a thickened lip of the neuroretina rim suggest glaucoma. These regions correspond anatomically to currently used clinical markers for glaucoma diagnosis.

DOI: 10.4018/978-1-6684-8618-4.ch015

INTRODUCTION

Axonal degeneration in retinal ganglion cells (RGC) is the hallmark of glaucoma, a heterogeneous group of degenerative neural disorders. Approximately 111.8 million people are projected to have glaucoma in 2040, making it the leading cause of irreversible blindness worldwide.When the optic nerve is damaged, blind spots form in your visual field. This damage is caused by increased pressure inside the eye, for reasons that medical professionals aren't fully aware of.If you have glaucoma, you will need to lower your eye pressure (intraocular pressure). Patients with glaucoma commonly report experiencing the following visual symptoms as a result of their glaucoma: Blurry vision, glare, and needing more light. This disease leads to vision loss and increased pressure within the eye, as well as chronic and progressive optic neurodegenerative changes.There is damage to the optic nerve because of the backup of fluid in the eye.Glaucoma is a group of ocular disorders that are etiologically multifactorial and clinically associated with an optic neuropathy related to intraocular pressure (IOP).In the case of an infected eye, it can permanently damage vision, leading to blindness without treatment.An optic nerve injury results in the loss of visual (Pandey, B. K. et.al., 2021) perception, which is caused when light receptors in the brain are damaged.The number of Americans with Glaucoma is believed to be at least four million, and nearly half of those people are unaware that they are affected by glaucoma (*Cupping, O. N., 2009*).One of the best ways to prevent total blindness is to detect it early and prevent it.The detection of glaucoma diseases has been made possible by many techniques.For most of the diagnostic indexes like glaucoma, compiling optical disk (OD) information is critical.Based on the size of an image, researchers fix the radius of an iris based on the assumption that its center is closer to the center of an image.According to a region of interest (ROI), the optic disc is automatically detected from an eye image. Diagnosing glaucoma (Zhu, H. et. al., 2011) disease depends on the location of the optic disk.Before performing classification, the ROI is enhanced with image enhancement and features extracted.It is believed that there are a large number of edge detection filters available, each of which is capable of detecting particular types of edges (Shrivakshan, G. T., & Chandrasekar, C., 2012).The use of OCT for glaucoma screening has also been suggested in a few studies.An active contour approach was proposed by (Mishra, M., Nath, M. K., & Dandapat, S., 2011) to determine the glaucoma medicinal process from the color fundus images (Acharya, U. et.al., 2011).This method automatically extracts the ROI, reducing the time needed to detect the disease.Some CDR measures are used to extract the ROI in existing approaches (Krishnan, M. M. R., & Faust, O., 2013).We only utilize the features in this paper to detect the disease.The aim of this study is to explore the use of CNNs directly from unprocessed OCT volumes for the detection of glaucomatous eyes, i.e., bypassing the requirements of segmentation (Mookiah, M. R. K., 2012) to extract features (such as retinal layer thickness, rim volume, etc.. In contrast to classical machine learning methods with traditional segmentation-based features extracted from the same dataset of OCT scans, this CNN offers higher accuracy in classification (Muramatsu, C. et. al., 2010). Following are two approaches: feature-based and feature-agnostic approaches (Liu, Y. et. al., 2011). A segmentation-based approach uses an OCT volume as a feature-source; a feature-agnostic approach uses OCT volume as a feature (Manju, K. et.al., 2017) . In the early stages of glaucoma, patients usually do not complain of symptoms other than a small loss of vision in the peripheral field (Pachiyappan, A. et.al., 2012).

Figure 1. Difference between normal and glaucoma affected eye

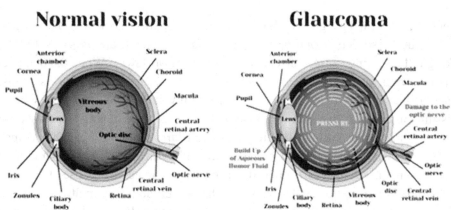

EXISTINGMODELS

The optical coherence tomography (OCT) procedure assesses the thickness of the retinal nerve fiber layer (RNFL) using its optical properties. However, at this time, OCT cannot be used to exclude glaucoma, only detect it early. Thereare almost five different types of identifying the glaucoma which will be listed down

1. Measuring intraocular pressure (tonometry)
2. Testing for optic nerve damage with a dilated eye examination and imaging tests.
3. Checking for areas of vision loss (visual field test)
4. Measuring corneal thickness (pachymetry)
5. Inspecting the drainage angle (gonioscopy)

One of the existing methods is to determine the glaucoma by means of machine learning which has a less accuracy level when compared to deep learning. In (Xu, Y. et. al., 2011) describes machine learning as the ability to improve performance for accomplishing a task by using experience. This can be done by automating the construction of analytical models for a variety of data types, including images(Pandey, D. et.al., 2021).The use of ML allows systems to identify patterns in data, learn from them, and make decisions without human input.The model is constructed by learning from data, which have been annotated with labels, when used in diagnosis modeling using the classification paradigm. This learning is based on observing data as examples and then applying the model to it (Abràmoff, M. D. et.al., 2010) .The number of data entries needs to be reduced when some ML models are used to solve image processing problems.For classification purposes, it is possible to convert a single image into millions of pixels.The processing of such data would be very difficult if it had to be entered manually. This is why it is transformed into a reduced set of features to make it more manageable (Sun, X. et.al., 2011) . Raw input data is reduced to aacceptable form while this operation selects and measures representative properties.These studies are primarily focused on identifying features to reduce processing time and memory requirements, eliminate irreversible attributes, and simplify the model (Bock, R. et.al., 2010).

Figure 2. Block diagram of detection of glaucoma using machine learning

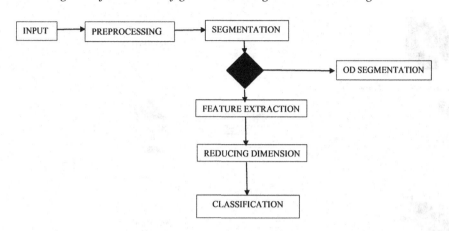

A segmented image is defined as the separation of the target region from the image background, those portions of the image that correspond to the real-world objects. (Deepak, K. S. et.al., 2012) proposed that they use superpixel classification to segment optic discs and optic cups (Manju, K., & Sabeenian, R. S. (2019). A review of the methods, as well as the results, is presented in the context of glaucoma screening (Manju, K., & Sabeenian, R. S., 2018). This methoddepilates the image into projections using Radon transform. High-order statistical moments were computed using these projections.Afterwards, the combined features formed the high-order cumulants.Afterward, principal component analysis, independent component analysis, and linear discriminant analysis (LDA) were used to reduce dimensionality. As well as SVM and naïve bayes, the classification process employed support vector machines.Testing was done with 272 fundus images from a private database.By using the tenfold cross-validation method, we discovered that 100 images displayed normal conditions while 72 and 100 indicated mild glaucoma and moderate/severe glaucoma, respectively(Shanthi, T. et.al., 2021).

PROPOSEDDEEP LEARNINGMODEL

The posterior segment OCT can give a better overview of the retina and ONH than fundus photography or ophthalmic fundus examination and provides both morphology (Pandey, B. K et.al.., 2021) and topographical measurements (Shanthi, T. et.al., 2021). In addition to giving a top-view of the retina and optic nerve head, posterior segment optical coherence tomography (OCT) provides a detailed and three-dimensional (3D) view of the morphological features.Early efforts to detect disease using machine learning algorithms relied on matching hand-engineered features that were created by domain experts. Deep learning, by contrast, uses neural networks to create automatic detection algorithms.The capabilities of CNN architectures are better generalizable since they combine the input information with several levels of abstraction and learn about features in different disease conditions automatically.As for the architectures of CNNs, there are a number of variations, but most standard CNN models include the input layer, convolutional layers, pooling (or subsampling) layers, and non-linear layers.Layers such as convolution and pooling are often grouped into modules. The following layer may be fully connected or partially connected.A necessary characteristic of CNNs is the convolution operation, which is a dot-

Figure 3. Deep learning in glaucoma with OCT

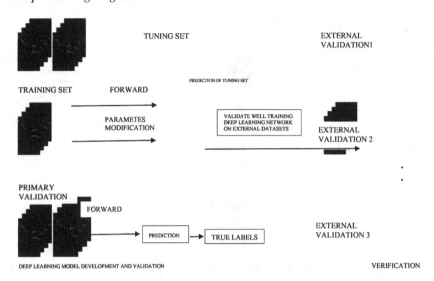

product operation between a grid-structure set of weights and similarly grid-structured inputs pulled from different locations in the input.As shown in figure 3, the fundamental datasets required for the development of DL networks (i.e., training and tuning sets), as well as the evaluation of performance.An evaluation set is a small set of data used to evaluate the network in real time, while a training set is used for the network to learn all the features automatically.The overfitting issue is present when the network fits well during training, but poorly during tuning.

Using variable sizes of OCT images to train the models is a first for training models with variable sizes of images. This is the first-time variable size OCT images have been used to train models.As a form of randomness, we train the models using batches of data from different categories simultaneously (including around 31.52% Normal data, 10.32% Drusen data, and 13.59% DME data within 84,452 images).A comparison of the performance measures for different robust models of deep convolutional neural networks is presented.Fig. 4 is a flow diagram that illustrates how the research process works over the course of analyzing OCT tagged images. Each phase of the process is described below.

CONVOLUTIONAL NEURAL NETWORK

Informationis flattened into vectors in the convolutional neural network (Pandey, B. K. et.al., 2021) without sacrificing their features. The reduced number of parameters and reusable weights are the result of the process, which leads to a functional prediction result.All of the nodes of the layer share the kernel, which has the same depth as the image for each channel.There are fewer nodes in the final output than a vanilla neural network.Another method of reducing the spatial length is to use a pooling layer, which can be either maximum pooling or average pooling.There are various architectures that use this algorithm including ResNet, Xception, VGGNet, and others. This work employs a vanilla CNN with one input layer, eleven hidden layers, and one output layer. The model architecture for CNN is as follows:

1. Input layer the shape will be 150*150*3
2. Convolutional layer, Relu is the activation layer
3. Maximum pooling layer
4. Convolutional layer, Relu is the activation layer
5. Maximum pooling layer
6. Convolutional layer, Relu is the activation layer
7. Maximum pooling layer
8. Convolutional layer, Relu is the activation layer
9. Maximum pooling layer
10. Flattend layer
11. Dropout
12. Dense layer, activation layer is Relu
13. Dense layer, as usual the last layer is Softmax

METHODOLOGY

Streaming and preprocessing pipelines are used for raw image data during the first stage of the workflow. The processing of a large amount of information together for training can result in an overloaded RAM, which could cause a system crash due to memory restrictions.Data streaming is used in this case, which pulls data from the directory in batches.As the streamer reads files from the given directory, it can detect the folders for training and testing.Reading a file, then, requires less code than in other situations.Several filtering steps are executed dynamically at runtime while it streams data from the directories.In terms of filtering, there are three main techniques: data augmentation, data shuffling, and data resizing.In the enhancement step, the real image data is rotated, flipped, and sheared to produce synthetic images.We resize the original and synthetic images to a fixed size following augmentation to create uniformity.Our normalization process has been applied to these uniform-sized images (Pandey, B. K. et.al., 2022). We have split and ordered the training and testing sets of the entire resulted images at the final stage of the data preprocessing pipeline.For biases against a particular class to be removed, shuffles are required. As part of the training model phase of the workflow, we trained vanilla CNN, MobileNetV2, ResNet50, and XCeption network using DLT and transfer learning.Training accuracy curves of models are obtained after each epoch.The model is also validated with a validation dataset, generating a validation accuracy curve.Our workflow ends with the last evaluation of the models after 15 epochs or epochs of training on the training data, which is known as the final model, using different methods and test data.The metrics utilized in evaluating our proposed work include confusion matrix, accuracy, precision, sensitivity, and f1 score.

Figure 4. Deep learning model

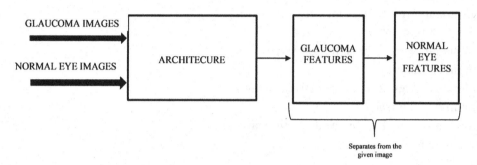

EVALUATION CRITERIA

1. Confusion Matrix

TheConfusionmatrix,alsoknownas the error matrix, can be used for visualization of a model'sperformanc easthesummaryofpredictionresultforeachclass is accounted here (Hasan, M. et.al., 2019) By checking the confusion matrix table, it is easy to identify mistakes or confusions made by a classifier.For this example, let's assume Cli represents a class out of four classes. Here are the definitions of TP, TN, FP, FN for Cli:

- TP(Cl_i)The instances are predicted using correctly as Cl_i.
- TN(Cl_i)The instances of non Cl_i are not predicted such as Cl_i.
- FP(Cl_i)The instances of non Cl_i are predicted as Cl_i.
- FN(Cl_i)The instances that are not predicted as Cl_i.

2. Accuracy

A classifier's accuracy can be measured by measuring how well it categorizes a dataset (Hasan, M. et.al., 2019). In order to calculate accuracy, use the following equation:

ACCURACY= (TP + TN) / (TP + TN + FP + FN)　　　　　　　　　　　　　　(1)

Whereas TP = true positive, TN = true negative, FP = false positive, FN= false negative

Table 1. Frequency distribution of OCT image

Dataset	Trainingset Frequency	TestingSet Frequency	percentage of Training	Percentage of Testing
Choroidal neovascularization	37200	242	44.35	25
Diabetic macular edema	11340	242	13.70	25
DRUSEN	8620	242	10.11	25
Ordinary	26350	242	31.23	25
Total	84000	968	100	100

3.   Precision

The precision of a classifier is the ratio of the total number of correct positive outcomes to the total number of predicted positive outcomes.Sensitivity can be calculated by the following equation:

$$PRECISION = TP / (TP + FP) \tag{2}$$

4.   Sensitivity

This phenomenon is known as sensitivity or true positive rate, which is the proportion of accurate positive data points to the total number of positives.Sensitivity can be calculated by the following equation:

$$SENSITIVIY = TP / (TP + FN) \tag{3}$$

5.   Fi-Score

In a model, Precision and Recall are weighted averaged . F1 score is calculated as follows:

$$FI\ SCORE = 2 * TP / (2 * TP + FP + FN) \tag{4}$$

RESULT ANALYSIS

Our analysis showed that Xception and MobileNetV2 both performed better than CNN and ResNet50 in the confusion matrix table.The accuracy, precision, sensitivity, and F1 score for each classifier have been determined using Equations 1, 2, 3, 4.A table II shows the results. Through Table II, it is apparent that the training accuracy in all models is at least 89%, and the testing accuracy is at least 97%.It is more accurate to train with Exception, with 93.90% accuracy, and to test with MobileNetV2, with 99.17% accuracy.With testing, precision is between 0.97 and 0.99, which includes boundary values. Training is precision between 0.92 and 0.95, and testing is precision between 0.97 and 0.95.For both cases, Exception has the highest precision, and MobilenetV2has the highest precision only in testing.The Table II reveals that achieved 96.60% accuracy in predicting retinal diseases and a 97.80% sensitivity in detecting these conditions [7],According to Li et al., 98.60% precision and 97.80% sensitivity have been achieved in their fully automated prediction of retinal diseases.With our method, we achieved an accuracy rate of 99.17% with a sensitivity of 99.00% to detect CNV, DME, and Drusen.Since they are all based on the same dataset, it is obvious that our method is the most accurate and therefore the best out of all the methods in Table II.

Table 2. Evaluation metrics

Method	Accuracy	Sensitivity	Precision	F1-score
Ourmethod	99.17%	99.00%	99.00%	0.99
Kermanyetal.[7]	96.60%	97.80%	N/A	N/A
Lietal.[11]	98.60%	97.80%	N/A	N/A

CONCLUSION

Here we demonstrate an improved method for detecting retinal diseases by using OCT X-rays; in addition, we compare our results to those obtained by other groups [7], [11].The primary goal of our research is to explore the accuracy, sensitivity, precision, and F1 scores of multiple deep learning models [13, 14, 15].The accuracy of our approach is higher than state-of-the-art, thus allowing us to claim that it can detect the discussed retinal diseases more accurately.The distribution of classes does not follow a uniform pattern; that is, all classes are not distributed equally.It has not been tested in other image processing techniques. Performance is expected to increase if it is overcome.Our work may have been improved with the use of image processing techniques, which would have enhanced performance and made the work better. We are saving these matters for future studies.

Figure 5. Output sample

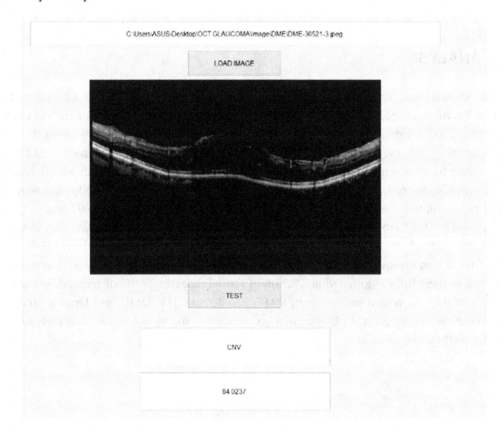

REFERENCES

Abràmoff, M. D., Garvin, M. K., & Sonka, M. (2010). Retinal imaging and image analysis. [PMC free article] [PubMed] [Google Scholar]. *IEEE Reviews in Biomedical Engineering*, *3*, 169–208. doi:10.1109/RBME.2010.2084567 PMID:22275207

Acharya, U. R., Dua, S., Du, X., & Chua, C. K. (2011). Automated diagnosis of glaucoma using texture and higher order spectra features. [PubMed] [Google Scholar]. *IEEE Transactions on Information Technology in Biomedicine*, *15*(3), 449–455. doi:10.1109/TITB.2011.2119322 PMID:21349793

Bock, R., Meier, J., Nyúl, L. G., Hornegger, J., & Michelson, G. (2010). Glaucoma risk index: Automated glaucoma detection from color fundus images. [PubMed] [Google Scholar]. *Medical Image Analysis*, *14*(3), 471–481. doi:10.1016/j.media.2009.12.006 PMID:20117959

About. (2009). Glaucoma Research Foundation. https://www.glaucoma.org/learn/glaucoma_facts.php.

Deepak, K. S., Jain, M., Joshi, G. D., & Sivaswamy, J. (2012, December). Motion pattern-based image features for glaucoma detection from retinal images. In *Proceedings of the Eighth Indian Conference on Computer Vision, Graphics and Image Processing* (pp. 1-8). Google Scholar. 10.1145/2425333.2425380

Hasan, M., Islam, I., & Hasan, K. A. (2019, February). Sentiment analysis using out of core learning. In *2019 International Conference on Electrical, Computer and Communication Engineering (ECCE)* (pp. 1-6). IEEE. 10.1109/ECACE.2019.8679298

Hasan, M., Islam, M. M., Zarif, M. I. I., & Hashem, M. M. A. (2019). Attack and anomaly detection in IoT sensors in IoT sites using machine learning approaches. *Internet of Things*, *7*, 100059. doi:10.1016/j.iot.2019.100059

Krishnan, M. M. R., & Faust, O. (2013). Automated glaucoma detection using hybrid feature extraction in retinal fundus images. [Google Scholar]. *Journal of Mechanics in Medicine and Biology*, *13*(01), 1350011. doi:10.1142/S0219519413500115

Liu, Y. Y., Chen, M., Ishikawa, H., Wollstein, G., Schuman, J. S., & Rehg, J. M. (2011). Automated macular pathology diagnosis in retinal OCT images using multi-scale spatial pyramid and local binary patterns in texture and shape encoding. [PMC free article] [PubMed] [Google Scholar]. *Medical Image Analysis*, *15*(5), 748–759. doi:10.1016/j.media.2011.06.005 PMID:21737338

Manju, K., & Sabeenian, R. S. (2018). Robust CDR calculation for glaucoma identification. *Biomedical Research* (0970-938X).

Manju, K., & Sabeenian, R. S. (2019). Cup and Disc Ratio and Inferior, Superior, Temporal and Nasal Calculation for Glaucoma Identification. *Journal of Medical Imaging and Health Informatics*, *9*(6), 1316–1319. doi:10.1166/jmihi.2019.2720

Manju, K., Sabeenian, R. S., & Surendar, A. (2017). A review on optic disc and cup segmentation. *Biomedical & Pharmacology Journal*, *10*(1), 373–379. doi:10.13005/bpj/1118

Mishra, M., Nath, M. K., & Dandapat, S. (2011). Glaucoma detection from color fundus images. [IJCCT]. *International Journal of Computer & Communication Technology*, *2*(6), 7–10.

Mookiah, M. R. K., Acharya, U. R., Lim, C. M., Petznick, A., & Suri, J. S. (2012). Data mining technique for automated diagnosis of glaucoma using higher order spectra and wavelet energy features. *Knowledge-Based Systems*, *33*, 73–82. doi:10.1016/j.knosys.2012.02.010

Muramatsu, C., Hayashi, Y., Sawada, A., Hatanaka, Y., Hara, T., Yamamoto, T., & Fujita, H. (2010). Detection of retinal nerve fiber layer defects on retinal fundus images for early diagnosis of glaucoma. *Journal of Biomedical Optics*, *15*(1), 016021. doi:10.1117/1.3322388 PMID:20210467

Pachiyappan, A., Das, U. N., Murthy, T. V., & Tatavarti, R. (2012). Automated diagnosis of diabetic retinopathy and glaucoma using fundus and OCT images. *Lipids in Health and Disease*, *11*(1), 1–10. doi:10.1186/1476-511X-11-73 PMID:22695250

Pandey, B. K., Pandey, D., Wairya, S., & Agarwal, G. (2021). An advanced morphological component analysis, steganography, and deep learning-based system to transmit secure textual data. [IJDAI]. *International Journal of Distributed Artificial Intelligence*, *13*(2), 40–62. doi:10.4018/IJDAI.2021070104

Pandey, B. K., Pandey, D., Wairya, S., Agarwal, G., Dadeech, P., Dogiwal, S. R., & Pramanik, S. (2022). Application of Integrated Steganography and Image Compressing Techniques for Confidential Information Transmission. *Cyber Security and Network Security,* 169-191.

Pandey, B. K., Pandey, D., Wariya, S., & Agarwal, G. (2021). A deep neural network-based approach for extracting textual images from deteriorate images. *EAI Endorsed Transactions on Industrial Networks and Intelligent Systems*, *8*(28), e3–e3. doi:10.4108/eai.17-9-2021.170961

Pandey, B. K., Pandey, D., Wariya, S., Aggarwal, G., & Rastogi, R. (2021). Deep Learning and Particle Swarm Optimisation-Based Techniques for Visually Impaired Humans' Text Recognition and Identification. *Augmented Human Research*, *6*(1), 1–14. doi:10.100741133-021-00051-5

Pandey, D., Nassa, V. K., Jhamb, A., Mahto, D., Pandey, B. K., George, A. H., & Bandyopadhyay, S. K. (2021). An integration of keyless encryption, steganography, and artificial intelligence for the secure transmission of stego images. In *Multidisciplinary Approach to Modern Digital Steganography* (pp. 211–234). IGI Global. doi:10.4018/978-1-7998-7160-6.ch010

Shanthi, T., Sabeenian, R. S., Manju, K., Paramasivam, M. E., Dinesh, P. M., & Anand, R. (2021). Fundus Image Classification using Hybridized GLCM Features and Wavelet Features. *ICTACT Journal on Image and Video Processing*, *11*(3), 2372–2375.

Shrivakshan, G. T., & Chandrasekar, C. (2012). A comparison of various edge detection techniques used in image processing. [IJCSI]. *International Journal of Computer Science Issues*, *9*(5), 269.

Sun, X., Wang, J., Chen, R., Kong, L., & She, M. F. (2011). Directional Gaussian filter-based LBP descriptor for textural image classification. [Google Scholar]. *Procedia Engineering*, *15*, 1771–1779. doi:10.1016/j.proeng.2011.08.330

Xu, Y., Xu, D., Lin, S., Liu, J., Cheng, J., Cheung, C. Y., & Wong, T. Y. (2011, September). Sliding window and regression based cup detection in digital fundus images for glaucoma diagnosis. *In International Conference on Medical Image Computing and Computer-Assisted Intervention* (pp. 1-8). Springer. [10.1007/978-3-642-23626-6_1

Zhu, H., Crabb, D. P., Schlottmann, P. G., Wollstein, G., & Garway-Heath, D. F. (2011). Aligning scan acquisition circles in optical coherence tomography images of the retinal nerve fibre layer. *IEEE Transactions on Medical Imaging*, *30*(6), 1228–1238. doi:10.1109/TMI.2011.2109962 PMID:21296706

Chapter 16
Exudate Detection in Fundus Images Using Deep Learning Algorithms

T. Shanthi

Sona College of Technology, Salem, India

R. Anand

Sri Eshwar College of Engineering, Coimbatore, India

Binay Kumar Pandey

https://orcid.org/0000-0002-4041-1213

Department of Information Technology, Govind Ballabh Pant University of Agriculture and Technology, Pantnagar, India

Vinay Kumar Nassa

https://orcid.org/0000-0002-9606-7570

Rajarambapu Institute of Technology, India

Aakifa Shahul

SRM Medical College, Kattankulathur, India

A. S. Hovan George

Tbilisi State Medical University, Georgia

Pankaj Dadheech

https://orcid.org/0000-0001-5783-1989

Swami Keshvanand Institute of Technology, Management, and Gramothan, India

ABSTRACT

Diabetic Retinopathy (DR) affects people who have diabetes mellitus for a long period (20 years). It is one of the most common causes of preventable blindness in the world. If not detected early, this may cause irreversible damage to the patient's vision. One of the signs and serious DR anomalies are exudates, so these lesions must be properly detected and treated as soon as possible. To address this problem, the authors propose a novel method that focuses on the detection and classification of Exudateas Hard and soft in retinal fundus images using deep learning. Initially, the authors collected the retinal fundus images from the IDRID dataset, and after labeling the exudate with the annotation tool, the YOLOV3 is trained with specific parameters according to the classes. Then the custom detector detects the exudate and classifies it into hard and soft exudate.

DOI: 10.4018/978-1-6684-8618-4.ch016

1. INTRODUCTION

In ophthalmology, deep learning is performing a vital role in diagnosing serious diseases, including diabetic retinopathy (DR).Diabetic retinopathy is a widespread disease diagnosed in diabetic patients between the ages of 20 and 60.The World Health Organization (WHO) has declared that, in 2030, diabetes will be the most serious and 7th highest death-causing disease in the world.It is most important to prevent human lives from being affected by diabetes. In the case of diabetic retinopathy, some abnormalities including lesions are generated in the retina, which later leadsto no reversible blindness and vision impairment (Pandey, B. K. et.al., 2021). But the early detection and treatment of these lesions can reduce blindness significantly. One of the signs and serious DR anomalies is Exudates, so this must be properly detected and treated in the earlier stage itself. Exudatesresults in the leaking of fluid in the blood vessels. Exudates can be hard exudates (yellow spots seen in the retina) and soft exudates (pale yellow or white areas with ill-defined edges). In this project,one of the Convolutional neural networksknown as Yolov3 architecture is used to detect and classify as Hard and soft exudates in the retinal images of the patients with good detection results.

2. LITERATURE SURVEY

In the paper (Prem, S. S., & Umesh, A. C., 2020) an algorithm focuses on DR detection based on features such as local binary pattern (LBP) and wavelet transform approximation coefficient matrix. Images are classified as exudate and nonexudative by using machine learning classification algorithms such as support vector machine (SVM), k-nearest neighbor (KNN), decision tree, random forest (RF), and artificial neural network (ANN). The exudate classification includes three main stages there are Image Enhancement and Segmentation (Pandey, B. K. et.al., 2021), Feature Extraction, and Image Classification. For implementing this process DIARETDB1 dataset is used. It consists of 89 images of size 1500 x 1152. In the article (Mateen, M. et. al., 2020), the pre-trained convolutional neural network (CNN) has been used for exudates detection. The retinal datasets are used for experiments: (i) e-Ophtha and (ii) DIARETDB1. E-Ophtha dataset contains 47 retinal fundus images. DIARETDB1 dataset contains 89 retinal fundus photographs with a resolution of 1500 ×1 152. The data preprocessing is performed for the standardization of exudate patches. Furthermore, region of interest (ROI) localization is used to localize the features of exudates, and then transfer learning is performed for feature extraction using pre-trained CNN (Pandey, D. et.al., 2021) models (Inception-v3, Residual Network-50, and Visual Geometry Group Network-19).

In the article (Lin, L. et. al., 2020), a total of 603 fundus images from DR patients and 631 fundus images from healthy people were collected from the Department of Ophthalmology, Gaoyao People's Hospital, and Zhongshan Ophthalmic Center, Sun Yat-sen University. In addition to exudate annotations, they also provide four additional labels for each image: left versus-right eye label, DR grade (severity scale) from three different grading protocols, and the bounding box of the optic disc (OD), and fovea location. In the article (Center, V. T. U. P. G., 2020) a supervised learning technique called linear regression is used. The database used are DiaRetDB0, DiaRetDB1, MESSIDOR and IDRID. A total of 60 images with both healthy and unhealthy retinal images are considered. Image processing and linear regression, a machine learning technique is involved which is used to train machines to differentiate between optic disk and exudates. In this paper (Borsos, B. et.al., 2019), the database used here is Indian Diabetic

Retinopathy Image Dataset (IDRID). The preprocessing is done using three phases such as background and foreground pixel extraction and a data normalization operator which is similar to Z-transform. The modified algorithm SLIC is used for providing homogeneous super pixels in the images. Then the ANN based classification of pixels using fifteen features are extracted.

In this paper (Shanthi, T., & Sabeenian, R. S., 2019) they have used the Messidor dataset which consists of 1190 color fundus images with annotations in an excel file. They have arranged the Messidor dataset into four different sets Healthy retina, DR stage 1, DR stage 2, and DR stage 3. The classification of DR fundus images was done using Convolutional Neural Network with the application of Pooling, SoftMax, and Rectified Linear Activation Unit (ReLU) layers. In the paper (Lokuarachchi, D. et.al., 2019) they have used different morphological operations to detect exudates accurately. The diaretdb1 dataset which contains 89 retinal images with an array size of 1500×1152 pixels is used. The proposed methods are image normalization, optic disk extraction, exudates detection, and elimination of false positives. In the paper (Chidambaram, N., & Vijayan, D., 2018), a computer-aided Automated Diagnosis (CAD) is used. The dataset used here is DIARETDB. The edge-based segmentation method is used for segmenting the optic disk. Gabor filter is used for detection of exudates using texture analysis and SVM classifier is used for exudates detection.

In the article (Kumar, P. S. et.al., 2013), a region-based, neighborhood, block operation, and optimal global thresholding are used as new methods for exudates detection. From the dataset DIARETDB1 out of 89 images, 84 were exudates and the remaining were no exudates. These images were preprocessed by the following method such as normalizing the color of retinal images, contrast enhancement, noise removal, and optic disc localization.

In this paper (Sabeenian, R. S., & Surendar, A., 2017) they used the standard database such as STARE, DRIVE, DIARETDB1, DIARETDB2, Retinopathy online challenge (ROC) database, and private databases such as Messidor, Moorefield's, and Mashhad for the testing algorithm. The main objective of this paper is to detect microaneurysms which is the first stage of diabetic retinopathy. The performance of the algorithms was measured by the parameters like Sensitivity, Specificity, Precision, Accuracy, Area under Curve, and Competition Performance. In this paper (Liu, Q. et.al., 2017), the automatic exudate segmentation in color retinal fundus image includes three stages: anatomic structure removal, exudate location, and exudate segmentation. In the first stage matched filters-based main vessels segmentation method and a saliency-based optic disk segmentation method is used. In the second stage, a random forest classifier is used to classify the patches into two classes: exudate patches and exudate free patches. The methods are evaluated at both exudate level and image level. For exudate level evaluation e-ophtha EX dataset is used.

In the article (Yu, S. et.al., 2017), they used a deep convolutional neural network (CNN) to achieve pixel-wise exudate detection. CNN models are first trained by an expert labeled exudate images and saved as a patch offline classifier. The database used in this article is E-Ophtha EX. It contains a total of 82 images, including 47 exudates images and 35 normal images.

The paper (Biyani, R. S., & Patre, B. M., 2016) proposes a method using K-means clustering and morphological image processing for the detection of exudates on low contrast retinal images. The DIARETDB1 database is used as input sample images for the testing algorithm. The exudates were detected using the proposed algorithm and verified by comparing with hand-drawn ground truths images available along with the DIARETDB1 database. The use of machine learning techniques has been shown to help limit levels of exudates.

In the article (Caramihale, T. et.al., 2017), the algorithm which detects exudates automatically, the Probabilistic Neural Network (PNN) is used. The images are taken from the DRIVE database. It consists of 40 images divided into training and testing datasets both consisting of 20 images each. This algorithm has four main steps. The first step is Pre-processing which is done using green channel extraction and Gaussian smoothing. The second step is feature extraction which is done using Discrete Wavelet Transform (DWT). In the third step Probabilistic Neural Network (PNN) is used to detect exudates and optic disks. Finally, the optic disk is eliminated then the exudates are detected.

In the paper (Zohora, S. E. et.al., 2016), the automatic exudates detection of diabetic retinopathy has been described by Detection by Morphology Features, Clustering Based Detection, Neural Network-Based Detection, and Detection by Machine Learning and Support Vector Machine. In the paper (Asha, P. R., & Karpagavalli, S., 2015), the retinal exudates are detected using machine learning (ML) techniques. The images used for the training data set were taken from the DIARETDB1 which consists of 89 images and for the testing dataset the images were taken from both DIARETDB1 and DIARETDB0 it consists of 130 images. The exudates detection has been carried out using Naive Bayes (NB), Multilayer Perceptron (MLP), and Extreme Learning Machine (ELM). In the paper (Dutta, M. K. et.al., 2015, July), the two independent approaches were used. The first method was intensity thresholding which was used for utilizing the higher intensity level of exudates. The second method was the gradient-based detection technique which used the boundaries of exudates. The input images have different qualities so the preprocessing techniques were used such as Color Normalization, Contrast Enhancement, and Background shade correction.

In the paper (Chand, C. R., & Dheeba, J., 2015), retinal color fundus images from the e-optha-ex database18 were used for DR screening. It consists of 82 images in total with 47 exudates detected images. Preprocessing method is used for enhancing the contrast of the low- or poor-quality images such as optic disk segmentation and Gray Level Co-Occurrence Matrix (GLCM). In the paper (Franklin, S. W., & Rajan, S. E., 2014), the DIARETDB1 Database is used for detecting exudates that are labeled as exudates and no exudates. The preprocessing takes place which is used to transform the original fundus image into lab color space. The color information algorithm is used for better performance in the image segmentation stage. In this article (Kavitha, M., & Palani, S., 2014), an efficient technique is used to detect hard and soft exudates from abnormal retinal images. At first, the preprocessing technique such as the Gaussian filter is used for enhancing the input retinal images. The normal/abnormal detection is done using region segmentation, feature extraction (Pandey, B. K. et. al., 2021), and Levenberg Marquardt-based neural network classifier. From abnormal images, the hard and soft exudates are detected using fuzzy c-means clustering, feature extraction, and Levenberg-Marquardt-based neural network classifier.

3. METHODOLOGY

The main objective of the project is the detection of exudates in the retinal fundus imagesand classified into hard and soft exudates with the help of Yolo architecture in CNN.To meet the objective,took original retinal images as input collected from the clinical environment, didlabelingthe retinal images with the help of ground truth data.Converted XML files to yourtext format.The project is performed in Google collab using GPUs and generated the train and test data files.Then the Yolo configuration files are generated. Then thecustomYolo modelistrainedto detect the Exudates and classify them into hard and soft exudates as shown in Fig 3.1.

Figure 1. Block diagram of the proposed method

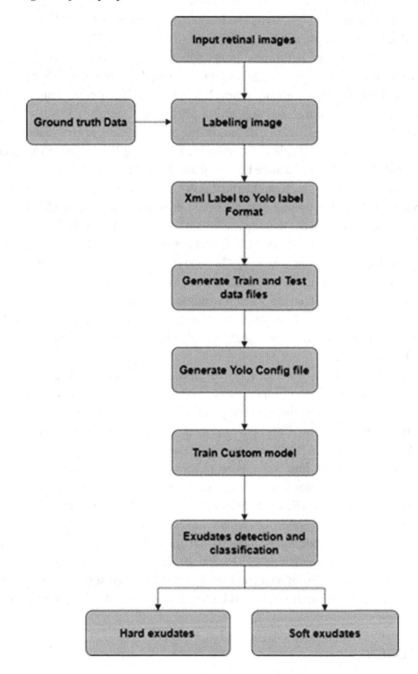

3.1 Input Description

The fundus images in Indian Diabetic Retinopathy Image Dataset (IDRID) were captured by a retinal specialist at an Eye Clinic located in Nanded, Maharashtra, India. This dataset consists of 81 color fundus images with signs of DR[16]. Precise pixel-level annotation of abnormalities associated with DR like microaneurysms (MA), soft exudates (SE), hard exudates (EX), and hemorrhages (HE) is provided as

Figure 2. Input retinal images from IDRID dataset

Figure 3. Ground truth images from IDRID dataset

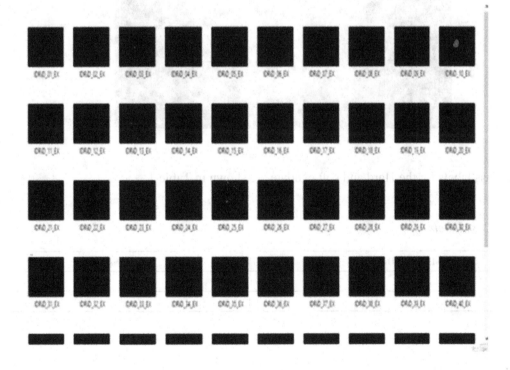

a binary mask for performance evaluation of individual lesion segmentation techniques. In this study, we used the annotations of hard and soft exudates. It includes color fundus images (.jpg files) as shown in Fig 3.2 and binary masks made of lesions (.tif files). All these images were acquired using a Kowa VX-10 alpha digital fundus camera with a 50-degree field of view (FOV).The binary masks are taken as Groundtruth as shown in Fig 3.3.This dataset consists of original retinal images collected from the clinical environment of patients.

3.2 Labelling the Images

LabelImg is an open-source labeling tool for image processing and annotations. It is developed in Python and has a graphical user interface built with Qt. It is a quick and free way to label images. The retinal images will undergo the labeling of exudate regions according to the ground truth data as shown in Fig 3.4.

Figure 4. Labeling of retinal images in labeling tool

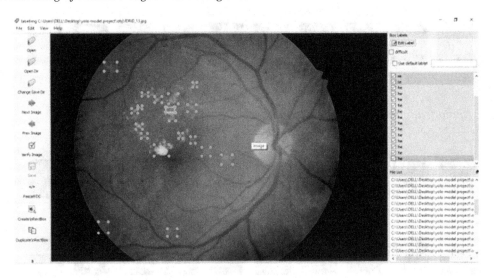

The class labels for the Hard and soft exudate are shown in Table 1.

Table 1. Class labels

NAME OF THE CLASS	CLASS LABEL
he	0
se	1

3.3 Conversion of Xml Files to YOLO Text Files

The labeled retinal images (Pandey, B. K. et.al., 2021).) were saved inXML format and these files are converted into YOLO text files as shown in Fig 3.5. This yolo text format is then used for further procedures.

Figure 5. XML files and their corresponding yolo text files

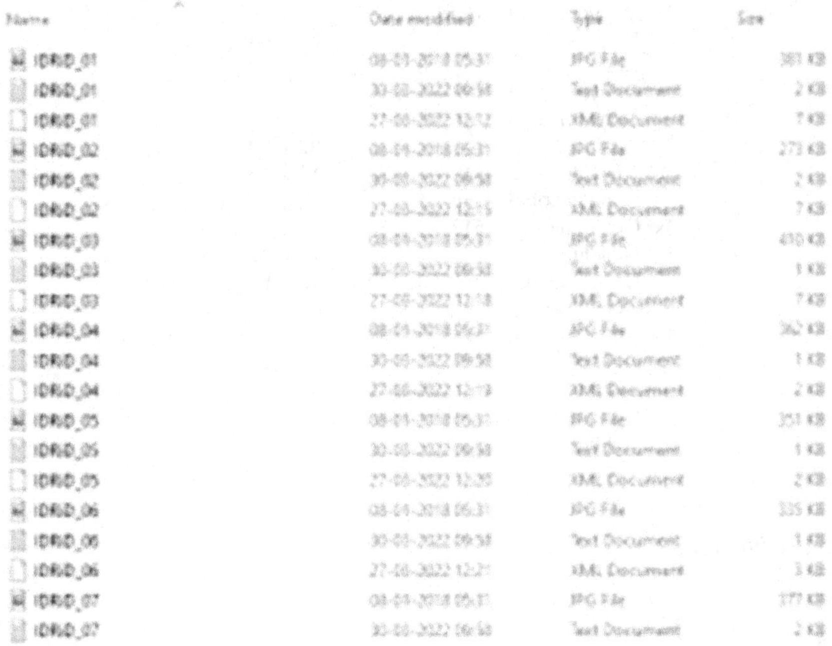

3.4 YOLOv3 Architecture

"You Only Look Once" or YOLO is a family of deep learning models designed for fast object Detection. YOLO v3 uses a Convolutional Neural Network-basedvariant named Darknet, which originally has a 53layernetwork trained on ImageNet.Darknet-53 is used as a feature extractor. It is mainly composed of 3 x 3 and 1 x 1 filters with skip connections like the residual network in ResNet.The architecture of Darknet is shown in Fig 3.6.

For the task of detection, 53 more layers are stacked onto it, giving us a 106-layer fully convolutional underlying architecture for YOLO v3.In YOLO v3, the detection is done by applying 1 x 1 detection kernels on feature maps of three different sizes at three different places in the network.The YOLOv3 architecture is shown in Figure 7.

3.5 Generate YOLO Configuration Files and Training

YOLOv3 pre-trained weights are downloaded and saved into the respective folders.Moving the custom IDRID dataset which was annotated using the Labellmg tool.Creating a zip folder for the custom dataset and defining the path in the drive where it is located.It contains obj data,obj names, and custom yolo

Figure 6. Darknet architecture

	Type	Filters	Size	Output
	Convolutional	32	3 × 3	256 × 256
	Convolutional	64	3 × 3 / 2	128 × 128
1×	Convolutional	32	1 × 1	
	Convolutional	64	3 × 3	
	Residual			128 × 128
	Convolutional	128	3 × 3 / 2	64 × 64
2×	Convolutional	64	1 × 1	
	Convolutional	128	3 × 3	
	Residual			64 × 64
	Convolutional	256	3 × 3 / 2	32 × 32
8×	Convolutional	128	1 × 1	
	Convolutional	256	3 × 3	
	Residual			32 × 32
	Convolutional	512	3 × 3 / 2	16 × 16
8×	Convolutional	256	1 × 1	
	Convolutional	512	3 × 3	
	Residual			16 × 16
	Convolutional	1024	3 × 3 / 2	8 × 8
4×	Convolutional	512	1 × 1	
	Convolutional	1024	3 × 3	
	Residual			8 × 8
	Avgpool		Global	
	Connected		1000	
	Softmax			

Figure 7. YOLOv3 architecture

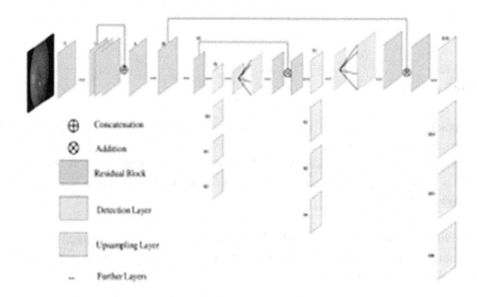

configuration files.Downloaded theconfiguration files into drive and uploaded the required obj data and obj names.Upload the pre-trainedconvolutional weights to the model.The custom Darknet detector is trained with the parameters according to the model's requirements.The number of filters used here is 21 and the batch size is 64 for training the custom model with 2 classes.

The trained custom Darknet detector's performance is tested by running an image on the test file with the batch size=1 and subdivisions=1. The first detection is done at the 82nd layer. For the first 81 layers, the image is down-sampled by the network. The resultant feature map of 416 x 416input images would be of size 13 x 13. Detection gives us a detection feature map of 13 x 13 x 18. The feature map from the 79th layer is subjected to upsampling by 2x to dimensions of 26 x 26. The depth is concatenated with the feature map from the 61st layer. Then the combined feature maps are again subjected to a few 1 x 1 convolutional layers to fuse the features from the earlier layer (61). Then, the second detection is made by the 94th layer, yielding a detection feature map of 26 x 26 x 18.

A similar procedure is followed again, where the feature map from layer 91 is subjected to a few convolutional layers before being depth concatenated with a feature map from layer 36. We make the final of the 3 at the 106th layer, yielding a feature map of size 52 x 52 x 18.

3.6 Results and Discussion

The custom darknet-53 detector detected the exudates and classified (Pandey, B. K. et.al., 2022) the exudates into Hard and soft exudates as shown in Figure 8.

The custom Yolov3 model's detection, as well as the ground truth detection, is analyzedwith the help of test results as shown in Figure 9.

Figure 8. Detection of exudates

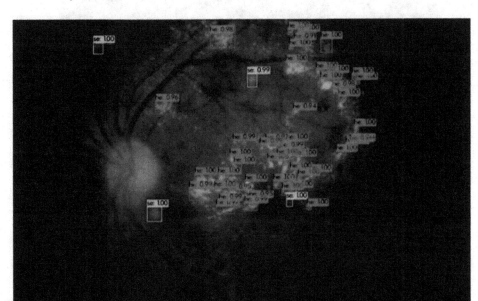

Figure 9. Detections of both custom model and ground truth data

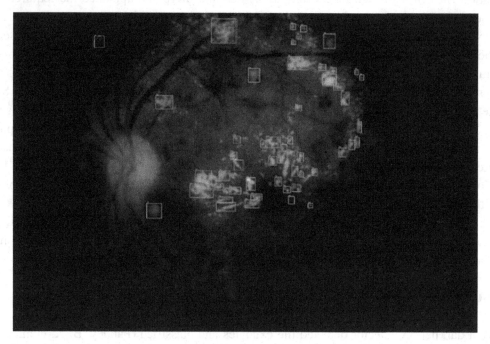

Figure 10. Mean Average Precision (MAP) of the custom Yolov3 model

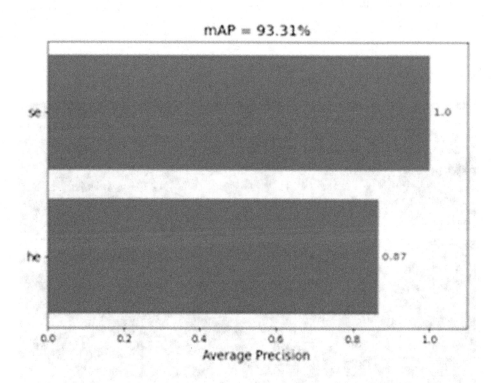

The accuracy of the custom yolov3 model is analyzed by calculating the Mean Average Precision (MAP). It is calculated from precision vs recall value as shown in Fig 3.10.

The performance of the Yolov3 model is analyzed by the Mean Average Precision (MAP).The MAP for the test images is93.31%for the custom YOLOv3 model.

3.6.1 Confusion Matrix

In the confusion matrix, each row represents the true values, while each column stands for the predicted values for both hard and soft exudate as shown in Figure 11.

Figure 11. Confusion matrix for YOLOV3

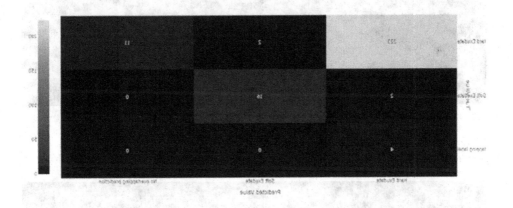

3.6.2 Comparison With Tiny YOLOV4

The tiny YOLOV4 model is used for testing the performance of the detector. It detected the Hard and soft exudate in the given set of retinal images as shown in Figure 12.

The TINY YOLOV4 model's detection, as well as the ground truth detection, is analyzed with the help of test results as shown in Figure 13.

The Mean Average Precision (MAP) of the TINY YOLOV4 model is 39.87% which is analyzed by calculating from precision vs recall value for both hard and soft exudate as shown in Figure 14.

The Detection of tiny yolov4 shows that the performance of the YOLOV3 is high in detecting the hard and soft exudate accurately. The YOLOV3 detected 50 hard exudates detections and 4 soft exudates detections with 93% accuracy. But the TINY YOLOV4 detected176 hard exudates and 18 soft exudates with an overall accuracy of 55% .

The detections of both YOLOV3 and TINY YOLOV4 are compared as shown in Table 5.1. The performance comparison with other existing methods is shown in Table 5.2.

Figure 12. Detections of Tiny YOLOV4

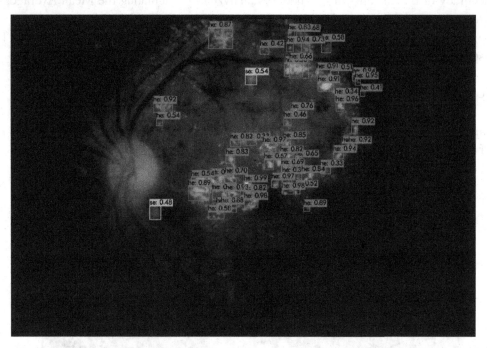

Figure 13. Detections of both Custom model and Ground truth data of TINY YOLOV4

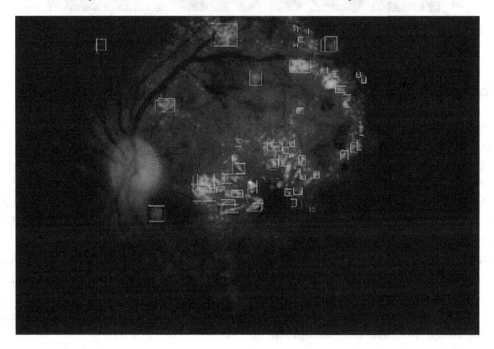

Figure 14. Mean Average Precision (MAP) of TINY YOLOV4

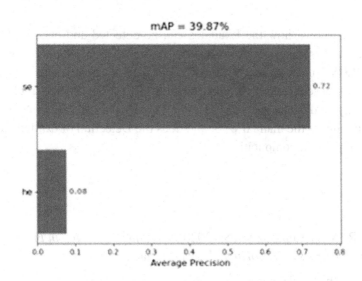

Table 2. Detection comparison of YOLOV3 and TINY YOLOV4

ALGORITHM	HARD EXUDATE	SOFT EXUDATE
PROPOSED YOLOV3	229	18
TINY YOLOV4	179	18

Table 3. Performance comparison

Author	Database used	Number of classes	Sensitivity	Specificity	Accuracy %
Asha PR et_al Bayes	DIARETDB1, DIARETDB0	2 (EX, NE)	-	-	82%
Asha PR et_al MLP	DIARETDB1, DIARETDB0	2 (EX, NE)	-	-	81%
Asha PR et_al ELM	DIARETDB1, DIARETDB0	2 (EX, NE)	-	-	90%
Chidambaram et_al Edge-based	e-ophtha EX, DiaRetDB1	1 (EX)	82.61%	92.31%	87.75%
Yu S et_al CNN	E-Ophtha EX	1 (EX)	88.85%	96%	91.92%
Zoharaet_al SVM	DiaRetDB1	1 (EX)	-	-	89.7%
Q Liu et_al segmentation based	e-ophtha EX, DiaRetDB1	2(HE, NE)	79.5%	75%	77%
M Kavitha et_al Levenberg-Marquardt-based neural network	Standard Diabetic Retinopathy Database	2(HE, NE)	-	-	90.91%
B Borsoset_al ANN	IDRID	3(HE, SE, NE)	62.42%	98.99%	-
Proposed methodYOLOV3	IDRID	2(HE, SE)	**91.6%**	-	**93%**

4. CONCLUSION

The proposed work has shown how the Exudates can be detected and classified into Hard and Soft exudates in the retinal fundus images collected from the clinical environment using deep learning architecture known as YOLOV3 and it has got 93%,91%,93.31% of Accuracy, Sensitivity, and Mean average precision (MAP).The proposed work also compared with TINY YOLOV4has got 55%,52%, and 39.81% of Accuracy, Sensitivity, and Mean average precision (MAP).This proposed work in YOLOV3will be useful to doctors as it reduces the manual work and does the Detection of exudates with good detection results as well as with minimal computations.

REFERENCES

Angadi, S., Bhat, V., R., V., & Rupanagudi, S. (2020). *Exudates Detection in Fundus Image using Image Processing and Linear Regression Algorithm.* Research Gate.

Asha, P. R., & Karpagavalli, S. (2015, January). Diabetic retinal exudates detection using machine learning techniques. In *2015 international conference on advanced computing and communication systems* (pp. 1-5). IEEE.

Biyani, R. S., & Patre, B. M. (2016, October). A clustering approach for exudates detection in screening of diabetic retinopathy. In *2016 International Conference on Signal and Information Processing (IConSIP)* (pp. 1-5). IEEE. 10.1109/ICONSIP.2016.7857495

Borsos, B., Nagy, L., Iclănzan, D., & Szilágyi, L. (2019). Automatic detection of hard and soft exudates from retinal fundus images. Acta Universitatis Sapientiae. *Informatica (Vilnius), 11*(1), 65–79.

Caramihale, T., Popescu, D., & Ichim, L. (2017, March). A neural-network based approach for exudates evaluation in retinal images. In *2017 10th International Symposium on Advanced Topics in Electrical Engineering (ATEE)* (pp. 268-273). IEEE. 10.1109/ATEE.2017.7905107

Chand, C. R., & Dheeba, J. (2015). Automatic detection of exudates in color fundus retinopathy images. *Indian Journal of Science and Technology, 8*(26), 1–6.

Chidambaram, N., & Vijayan, D. (2018, September). Detection of exudates in diabetic retinopathy. In *2018 International Conference on Advances in Computing, Communications and Informatics (ICACCI)* (pp. 660-664). IEEE. 10.1109/ICACCI.2018.8554923

Dutta, M. K., Srivastava, K., Ganguly, S., Ganguly, S., Parthasarathi, M., Burget, R., & Prinosil, J. (2015, July). Exudates detection in digital fundus image using edge based method & strategic thresholding. In *2015 38th International Conference on Telecommunications and Signal Processing (TSP)* (pp. 748-752). IEEE. 10.1109/TSP.2015.7296364

Franklin, S. W., & Rajan, S. E. (2014). Diagnosis of diabetic retinopathy by employing image processing technique to detect exudates in retinal images. *IET Image processing, 8*(10), 601-609. 20.

Kavitha, M., & Palani, S. (2014). Hierarchical classifier for soft and hard exudates detection of retinal fundus images. *Journal of Intelligent & Fuzzy Systems, 27*(5), 2511–2528. doi:10.3233/IFS-141224

Kumar, P. S., Kumar, R. R., Sathar, A., & Sahasranamam, V. (2013, December). Automatic detection of exudates in retinal images using histogram analysis. In *2013 IEEE Recent Advances in Intelligent Computational Systems (RAICS)* (pp. 277-281). IEEE..

Lin, L., Li, M., Huang, Y., Cheng, P., Xia, H., Wang, K., Yuan, J., & Tang, X. (2020). The SUSTech-SYSU dataset for automated exudate detection and diabetic retinopathy grading. *Scientific Data*, 7(1), 1–10. doi:10.103841597-020-00755-0 PMID:33219237

Liu, Q., Zou, B., Chen, J., Ke, W., Yue, K., Chen, Z., & Zhao, G. (2017). A location-to-segmentation strategy for automatic exudate segmentation in colour retinal fundus images. *Computerized Medical Imaging and Graphics*, 55, 78–86. doi:10.1016/j.compmedimag.2016.09.001 PMID:27665058

Lokuarachchi, D., Gunarathna, K., Muthumal, L., & Gamage, T. (2019, March). Automated detection of exudates in retinal images. In *2019 IEEE 15th International Colloquium on Signal Processing & Its Applications (CSPA)* (pp. 43-47). IEEE. 10.1109/CSPA.2019.8696052

Mateen, M., Wen, J., Nasrullah, N., Sun, S., & Hayat, S. (2020). Exudate detection for diabetic retinopathy using pretrained convolutional neural networks. *Complexity*, 2020, 2020. doi:10.1155/2020/5801870

Pandey, B. K., Pandey, D., Wairya, S., & Agarwal, G. (2021). An advanced morphological component analysis, steganography, and deep learning-based system to transmit secure textual data. [IJDAI]. *International Journal of Distributed Artificial Intelligence*, 13(2), 40–62. doi:10.4018/IJDAI.2021070104

Pandey, B. K., Pandey, D., Wairya, S., Agarwal, G., Dadeech, P., Dogiwal, S. R., & Pramanik, S. (2022). *Application of Integrated Steganography and Image Compressing Techniques for Confidential Information Transmission*. Cyber Security and Network Security, 169-191.

Pandey, B. K., Pandey, D., Wariya, S., & Agarwal, G. (2021). A deep neural network-based approach for extracting textual images from deteriorate images. *EAI Endorsed Transactions on Industrial Networks and Intelligent Systems*, 8(28), e3–e3. doi:10.4108/eai.17-9-2021.170961

Pandey, B. K., Pandey, D., Wariya, S., Aggarwal, G., & Rastogi, R. (2021). Deep Learning and Particle Swarm Optimisation-Based Techniques for Visually Impaired Humans' Text Recognition and Identification. *Augmented Human Research*, 6(1), 1–14. doi:10.100741133-021-00051-5

Pandey, D., Nassa, V. K., Jhamb, A., Mahto, D., Pandey, B. K., George, A. H., & Bandyopadhyay, S. K. (2021). An integration of keyless encryption, steganography, and artificial intelligence for the secure transmission of stego images. In *Multidisciplinary Approach to Modern Digital Steganography* (pp. 211–234). IGI Global. doi:10.4018/978-1-7998-7160-6.ch010

Prem, S. S., & Umesh, A. C. (2020, October). Classification of exudates for diabetic retinopathy prediction using machine learning. In *2020 IEEE 5th International Conference on Computing Communication and Automation (ICCCA)* (pp. 357-362). IEEE. 10.1109/ICCCA49541.2020.9250858

Sabeenian, R. S., & Surendar, A. (2017). An Automated Detection of Microaneursym to facilitate better Diagnosis of Diabetic Retinopathy. *Biosciences Biotechnology Research Asia*, 10(1), 483–488.

Shanthi, T., & Sabeenian, R. S. (2019). Modified Alexnet architecture for classification of diabetic retinopathy images. *Computers & Electrical Engineering*, 76, 56–64. doi:10.1016/j.compeleceng.2019.03.004

Yu, S., Xiao, D., & Kanagasingam, Y. (2017, July). Exudate detection for diabetic retinopathy with convolutional neural networks. In *2017 39th Annual International Conference of the IEEE Engineering in Medicine and Biology Society (EMBC)* (pp. 1744-1747). IEEE. 10.1109/EMBC.2017.8037180

Zohora, S. E., Chakraborty, S., Khan, A. M., & Dey, N. (2016, March). Detection of exudates in diabetic retinopathy: a review. In *2016 International Conference on Electrical, Electronics, and Optimization Techniques (ICEEOT)* (pp. 2063-2068). IEEE. 10.1109/ICEEOT.2016.7755052

Chapter 17
Fire Detection System Utilizing an Aggregate Technique in UAV and Cloud Computing

S. Dhamodaran
Sathyabama Institute of Science and Technology, India

Shahanawaj Ahamad
University of Hail, Saudi Arabia

J. V. N. Ramesh
Koneru Lakshmaiah Education Foundation, India

S. Sathappan
Bharathi Institute of Technology, India

Arpit Namdev
University Institute of Technology RGPV, India

Reshma Ramakant Kanse
Bharati Vidyapeeth (Deemed), India

Sabyasachi Pramanik
Haldia Institute of Technology, India

ABSTRACT

One of the new and difficult study fields in the contemporary environment is the idea of smart cities. The cities are bordered by woods, farmland, or open spaces where fires might break out, endangering human lives and wiping out many resources. This chapter uses the idea of sensor networks and UAV technology to develop an early fire detection system that will help eliminate fire incidents. The suggested design uses sensors to track environmental factors and uses sensors and IoT applications to analyze the data. The suggested fire detection system combines cloud computing, UAVs, and wireless sensor technologies. The suggested fire detection system additionally incorporates certain image processing methods to more accurately and efficiently identify the fire occurrence. Rules are also developed in order to increase the genuine detection rate. The suggested fire detection system's simulation results are contrasted with those of several current techniques.

DOI: 10.4018/978-1-6684-8618-4.ch017

1. INTRODUCTION

The idea of smart cities is now receiving a lot of interest in the scientific community. This article aims to protect cities from natural disasters like forest fires. The development of a forest fire monitoring system based on Internet of Things (IoT), Unmanned Aerial Vehicles (UAVs), and image processing is the main contribution to this effort. With IoT devices, environmental factors are monitored in real-time, and the data is analysed for identifying events. Using image processing methods, the discovered event is further confirmed. The major goal of smart cities is in improving the urban environment for living via the use of ICT, IoT, WSN (Liang, L. L., et al. 2023), and various associated computer automation. Further, IT-enabled infrastructure may be used to control and monitor city activities including transit, monitoring, resource scheduling, etc. Moreover, it is presumable that smart cities raise human living standards while efficiently using resources. Several nations now operate a smart city pilot programme that depends on converting existing cities into smart ones using smart technology in order to improve the environment and daily life. Information and Communications Technology, Internet of Things, Wireless Sensor Network, are all used by smart technology to create intelligent applications.

A smart city may effectively control its infrastructure and resources to make daily life favourable. In "smart cities," all data is recorded in real-time, and it is utilised for both ongoing estimating and adjusting learning settings. Smart city is made up of sensor internetworks and Internet of Things (IoT)-dependent approaches, including smart buildings, pollution estimation systems, smart traffic systems, smart water systems, public surveillance systems, and smart grid tracking, among many others.

A forest may function in the ecosystem as a haven for creatures like amphibians, birds, reptiles, etc. An approximate 35% of the land is enclosed with trees. Plantations and other organic processes may be used to extend the forest. Yet, a forest fire denotes a natural occurrence that alters the forest environment and causes deforestation. It has been noted that people may sometimes be to blame for the rising temperature. As a result, since it takes a lot of time and money, monitoring the forest is one of the difficult responsibilities. Across the globe, forest fires pose a danger to smart cities, the environment, the economy, the infrastructure, wildlife, and human life. Forest fire incidences have sharply risen recently in India. According to a report, there were 15,937 forest fire (Ozkan, O., et al. 2023) events in 2015, whereas there were 24,817 in 2016. Thus, within a year, the rate of fire growth Table 1 lists the fundamental specifications for a forest fire detection approach.

According to data, fires in the states of Himachal and Uttarakhand in 2016 affected almost 17,502 acres of land. Its effects include the extinction of humans and animals, disruption of the natural ecology, and deterioration of soil fertilisation. Moreover, ground microbes, nutrients, and in some circumstances, local residents, are also negatively impacted by forest fires. The major causes of forest fires include flammable materials, environmental factors, and fire sources, among others. Several forest fire avoidance techniques were documented in the literature to save the environment, natural resources, and animals. A wildland fire is quite different from fires that spread in urban and farming areas, and there are many things that might cause a forest fire. Intentional or unintentional human interaction is one of the primary causes of wildland fire. Forest fires may also be attributed to global warming because of the rise in temperature. It is advised that certain ongoing and comprehensive measures be used to raise public awareness and encourage quick action in the event of a fire in order to safeguard forests. As shown in Table 1, a forest fire detection system may fulfil a number of essential requirements.

Fig. 1 displays the fundamental depiction of the sensor-based fire detection system. The input picture serves as the main data source for identifying forest fires. Every time there is a fire occurrence, the frame-

Table 1. Requirements, specification, reason

Requirements	Specification	Reason
Prompt detection	Early detection	Early detection of fires and notification of the management system
24-hour monitoring, low cost, and little human involvement	The day/night detection system	Must be able to operate automatically at any time.
Maximum Protection	Spectrum of Detection	Using fewer sensors to cover a bigger area and saving energy in the process
Cost-effective	Notification	Alert message sent through emails and SMS worldwide Portable
Portable	Energy Usefulness	Using less energy will prolong the life of the system.

work analyses the input picture and sends an alarm signal. Several sensors, transmission channels, image processing technique, and a method for conveying a message or warning signal make up the fundamental components of this image processing-based system. The sensor nodes are linked to a communications network that gives the processing unit pictures. The processing unit includes an approach that uses the RGB (Cai, Y., et al. 2023) and YCbCr (Murali, S., et al. 2022) colour models to identify flames, smoke, or both, and provides a warning signal for every identified fire event. Moreover, it guarantees that a consistent power supply will be maintained.

1.1 Fire Detection for Smart Cities Utilizing WSNs and IoT

One of the most popular methods for detecting forest fires near smart cities in current years is the WSN. Real-time data from the fire zone is provided by sensors, which also keep track of the physical characteristics in the area. With WSNs, you may link several devices to a scalable network and add a variety of sensors to gather data on different criteria. There is no need to erect towers; sensors may be deployed in various. As a result of technical improvement, sensor equipment can now recognise and transmit

IoT apps may provide information for real-time analytics. When working together, the IoT-dependent sensor network will estimate and predict forest fires furthermore accurately than the conventional satellite-based approach. While it is a common practise to monitor fires using satellite images, their slow scan rates and poor resolution may limit how well they can spot fires. However, the satellite-based method is unable to forecast forest fires before they start to spread. The placement of the sensor and

Figure 1. Fire detection system's block diagram

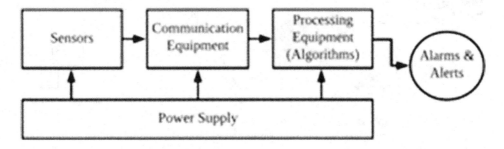

the transmission of information are shown in Figure 2. With a WSN, the forest area is densely covered with many sensors. Temperature, humidity, smoke, and other sensed data are gathered by sensor nodes, which then transmit the information gleaned from this data to the node that is closest to them in the cluster, which then transmits the information to the cluster head to create a network. The sensor nodes that are deployed in the field talk to one another through RF connections. The gateway node is set up to enable cloud-based communication between WSNs and the outside world. The gateway node handles GPRS (Pradhan D. et al. 2022) mobile connections and makes it possible for a distant user to obtain or keep track of field data in real-time.

Due to the area of interest, which may be dwellings, buildings, any smart system in a smart city and also for distant hills and woods, sensors-equipped devices are dispersed at various places. These sensor nodes (Anand, R. et al. 2022) are made up of a radio communication channel which allows the sensor to send data across a communication channel from one location to the control room. These sensor nodes use recurring data relays to safely communicate data to the gateway. This data is sent from the gateway to a server or cloud. The data is stored and processed for decision-making on the IoT-enabled cloud platform. A fire warning and alert signal may be produced when the data has been analysed. According to researchers, numerous research tendencies, including IoT and upcoming Internet automations, have been used to examine the scenario of fire incidents.

1.2. Work Contribution

The article's viewpoint in this context focuses on the stationing of WSNs and IoT. The goal is to put in place a framework to protect cities from catastrophes that might happen nearby a smart city. Many controllers, service providers, may use the real-time sensing, storage, and computing as a service. This article's goal is for providing an architectural layout for the estimation of fire occurrences in smart cities. The following lists the quiet characteristics of the suggested fire estimation architecture.

- To create a framework that uses WSNs, the IoTs, and image processing approaches to identify forest fires.
- To use IoT devices to gather real-time data in several ecological factors like as warmth, moisture, brightness and vapour.

Figure 2. Information transfer and sensor deployment

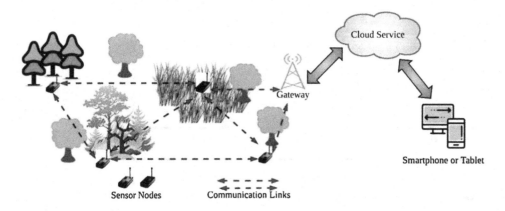

- To verify fire occurrences' presence utilizing an image processing-dependent method.
- To provide a fire alert and warning message as soon as possible.

Via the app for evaluating, filtering, and accumulating the sensed data for decision-taking, the framework also achieves a strong interaction between system and sensors. Using sensors and Internet, the framework provides a standard remedy for the early tracking of a fire occurrence. The goal of this endeavour is to create a method for quickly identifying the specific locations of forest fires. The suggested model uses colour space models in the RGB and YCbCr ranges to identify the fire zone. The real detection rate experimental findings are compared with the other methods now in use. The suggested model offers much better performance than the current cutting-edge techniques with regard to correct detection rate.

2. A LITERATURE REVIEW

The most current projects in the fields of smart cities and fire avoidance are presented in this section. The thorough literature review conducted for this paper is broken down into four sections: utilization of fire revelation, fire tracking utilizing image processing, and fire detection utilizing unmanned aerial vehicles.

2.1. Relevant Researches on WSN and IoT Stationing for Smart Cities

The definition of the Internet has changed during the last ten years as a result of the development of IoT. IoT makes it possible for individuals and objects to connect at anytime, anywhere. These interconnected objects generate a sizable amount of data, giving rise to the idea of big data. Smart device data collection requires effective storage and real-time processing.

Remote resource processing is made possible by cloud computing at a very affordable price. The expansion of cloud computing architecture known as "fog" and "edge computing" places compute and storage close to edge devices. A summary of the automations which take into account the utilisation of fog computing in sustainable smart cities is provided by (Jain, S., et al. 2022). The difficulties and promise of fog systems for many smart city application fields have been examined by authors. The outlines of the development of IoT and WSNs strategies for the use of intelligent parking were offered by (Aziz, A., et al. 2022). They have mostly focused on numerous design concerns and spoken about how crucial data security, privacy, and dependability are. The approach provided by (Jayaraman, G., et al. 2022) allows for the effective stationing of WSNs with improved network lifespan in smart cities.

The sensors' acquired data needed to be monitored and stored on a regular basis. The sensor regularly gathers data, which is then stored in the cloud for functioning. Processing each piece of detected data is crucial because there is so much of it. To fulfil the needs of real-time processing, (Zhang, N., et al. 2022) suggested an analytical framework for big data analysis. An effective communication protocol that offers a remedy for decreased power consumption in transmission was suggested by (Kuthadi, V.M., et al. 2022). As was said, the fundamental issue with WSN operation is the hardware constraints and the restricted energy supply caused by the node's electronic operation and processing efficiency. Other problems include scaling several devices in a network and choosing an effective architecture for the implementation. Starting with a star topology and few sensor nodes, the deployment of WSNs has changed to a mesh network made up of hundreds of sensor nodes. A variety of studies on the detection of fire have been conducted in the past using various methodologies. In order to monitor environmental factors and create the Internet of Things or Everything, it is now possible to deploy various sensor devices and install them in the field of study. Wireless sensor networks make it simple to gather data on warmth, wetness, fog, brightness, and other variables while checking for various anomalies. The sensor network-dependent application facilitates immediate data that facilitates additional decision-taking in comfort and safety. The tracking frameworks in smart cities have significantly raised standards of comfort and safety, which has increased quality of life. The amenity and security (Pramanik, S. 2023) of smart cities have moreover posed several sensing, data collecting, and safety research difficulties. A strategy has been provided by (Zhang, J., et al. 2022) in handling the problems with data facilities for residents in smart cities. The compact dimension of sensor nodes results in their restricted capacity for communication, computation, and storage. The majority of sensor nodes are battery-powered, that limits the amount of energy they may use to operate. Also, there are restrictions on some application-dependent sensor nodes which need very accurate, high-resolution metres. Framing a WSN-dependent sensing architecture in smart cities is thus difficult because it must take into account which nodes are effective and how to deploy them to facilitate the intended spot regions with the least amount of energy. Several studies presented their findings in different ways to address these issues. Sadly, no system exists that offers precise guidelines for creating and maintaining a monitoring system in smart cities. The two main issues for creating and maintaining tracking frameworks in smart cities that were researched for generalized WSNs are node deployment and sensor management. The authors (Gupta, A., et al. 2023) made a solution that makes use of RFID (Choudhary, S. et al. 2022) technology and embedded systems to allow users to verify the availability and situation online. In recent years, WSNs were utilized in fire tracking. The suggested architecture by (Yang, J., et al. 2022) leverages image detection in event tracking employing Wireless Sensor Networks. Authors have described intelligent management systems and intelligent street lighting depending on WSNs and the IoTs.

2.2. Similar Efforts to Advance the Use of Fire Detection

Animal life, the environment, and infrastructure are all seriously at risk from forest fires. There are several reports of prior forest fires as proof. Forest fires might be looked at as a repercussion that could result in the environmental and monetary losses of species and mankind. For the purpose of detecting forest fires, a number of strategies have been published in the literature (Ghosh, R., et al. 2022). To monitor the woodlands using traditional techniques for detecting forest fires, mechanical apparatus and people are needed (Cao, CF., et al. 2022). Satellite monitoring, wireless sensor networks and fire watchtowers are three types of fire detection systems (de Venâncio, P.V.A.B., et al. 2022). Watchtowers are the most time-honored and conventional fire detection techniques. Every time a fire incident occurs, it is reported so that the appropriate action may be done. Nevertheless, because of a number of factors, including operator tiredness, location, greater area, lack of round-the-clock assistance, and processing speed, it is not the best way for detecting fires.

Three primary causes are often where the issue of coverage in WSNs begins. The first reason is that there aren't enough sensors to cover the whole AOI; the second is that sensor nodes are deployed at random; and the third is that sensor nodes' detecting ranges aren't very wide. Since the power supply for the sensor nodes' functionality is restricted, some of them may fail, which further reduces the number of sensor nodes available to fully cover the AOI. Each sensor node has a restricted sensing radius, which often results in a coverage issue. Simple sensors with a wide detecting range may solve the same issue;

however employing such sensors is problematic due to their expensive price. The issue of coverage arises in each of these situations. The sensing capabilities are not adequately employed in the first scenario, when the sensor nodes are placed closer together, and maximum coverage is likewise not possible. In the second scenario, communication between the sensor nodes (Anand, R et al. 2022) is hampered and requires a lot of energy, which ultimately results in blind spots.

2.3. Similar Efforts on Image Processing-Based Fire Detection

Monitoring the whole forest using satellites is another way to spot forest fires. During this procedure, a number of photos are taken at various times, and then these images are analysed to identify fire occurrences. However since the acquired photos are low-resolution, it may sometimes be difficult to extract significant information from them. An R, G, and B color-based detection model was created by (Li, Y., et al. 2022). One of the widely used methods for detecting forest fires is the use of IR smoke detectors. This approach is based on air quality, temperature, and particle monitoring. The smoke particles are how this mechanism functions. The HSI model was taken by (Khan, R.A., et al. 2023) to continue their work in order to separate the fire pixels. In order to separate the pixels, this technique takes into account the ideas of brightness and darkness. Also, it is shown that segmentation is carried out using the HSI colour technique. To reduce the likelihood of false alarms, the pixels with lower intensities and saturation are removed. (Wang, Z., et al. 2020) developed a number of lighting effect-avoiding methods based on normalised RGB. Three axes—RG, GB, and RB—are used for the picture analysis. With the exception of the flame's centre, the suggested technique may effectively partition the flame zone. Fire pixels also vary according on colour information. In order to divide the fire zone from photos, (Liu, ZG., et al. 2016) suggested a technique based on RGB and YCbCrcolor models. Results are reliable under normal circumstances, but not under all environmental circumstances. (Nagulan, S., et al. 2023) created an YCbCr-based method for segmenting fire pixels utilising the image's statistical properties. In this research, 750 photos are taken into account to assess how well the suggested strategy performs. The suggested approach's simulation results are contrasted with those of current picture classification methods. It is claimed that the suggested method confirms the actual alarm rate. A reported uniform image partitioning technique processes pictures in parallel. An ORNAM model was created to improve the reconstructed image's quality and to cut down on the amount of homogeneous blocks (Emmy Prema, C., et al. 2018). This framework can operate more effectively with grayscale photos. To extract both global and local information from pictures, the EWLDA feature extraction technique is created (Hassan, N.M., et al. 2022). This method confirms the fire zones by using brightness and motion characteristics. For the purpose of segmentation, the histogram technique is also utilised. The incorporation of these qualities, according to the authors, may enhance the capacity of the forest fire detection system. A fire detection method was developed by (Wu, Z., et al. 2022). It is based on the HIS and RGB colour models. The suggested method is computationally effective; however the rate of false alarms rises with moving objects. The benefits and drawbacks of colour models with parameters are shown in Table 2.

2.4. Similar Efforts on UAV-Based Fire Detection

Plain regions were best served by traditional fire monitoring techniques. Nonetheless, the majority of fires take place in tough environments where they may spread to any extent of area thanks to the wind. Modern satellite systems operate with great efficiency, precision, and accuracy. These satellite systems might achieve a high degree of precision when used in conjunction with conventional monitoring techniques, but they are unreliable and prone to satellite signal problems. Some cutting-edge technologies, including remote sensing, have indicated major benefits in tracking vast regions. In comparison to prior dangerous monitoring strategies, higher spatial resolution photos are particularly effective and satisfying for tracking events. Since InSAR offers day-and-night monitoring in all weather situations, it is regarded as the most remarkable automation for mapping and inspecting large areas. The tracking of fire incidents needs ongoing monitoring and assessment along the time axis, which is constrained by InSAR's ability to only monitor for the allotted amount of time. As a result, continuous tracking of fire incidents using satellite frameworks is unreliable with regard to accuracy, timing, cost, and size.

Moreover, the quality of certain photos under situations like heavy fog, cloud cover, and rain may cause the creation of false alerts. The UAVs provide quick data collecting, dependable functioning for brief visit periods, and simple operations as compared to all prior monitoring techniques. UAVs can fly at low altitudes and provide photographs quickly while they are in use. UAV technology has advantages over conventional monitoring techniques and techniques based on remote sensing due to its continuous operation and effective data collecting. Several studies using different UAV sensor platforms have shown the benefits of UAVs, such as their prompt reaction and easy acquisition of data. The limitations of the other earlier techniques for event confirmation and monitoring, such as time restraints and safety considerations, lead to inadequate process data for event assessment and monitoring. According to research, an area of around 100,000 m2 may be more effectively monitored by UAVs. The UAVs can efficiently monitor the region and verify any incident, no matter how big or tiny. As compared to other monitoring approaches, UAV is less costly and offers a wider range of applications. Due to their affordability, UAVs may be used in great numbers to monitor a vast region. The fundamental surface model and regular photos are provided by the UAVs equipped with digital cameras. The textural data of the mapped region is provided by Drones with multiple lens cameras. The most practical method for monitoring smart cities and mapping a useful region may be regarded UAVs fitted with less costly cameras. The limitations of satellite imaging's limited spatial resolution may be solved by this approach to area mapping. Moreover, UAVs provide a 3D (Mandal, A. et al. 2021) visual effect and save a significant amount of ground station labour. According to the study, UAVs can provide centimetre-level images (Mall. P. K. et al. 2023) with great precision. Drones with digital cameras are often employed nowadays to monitor regions.

3. THE SUGGESTED ARCHITECTURE

Each fire detection system has its greatest difficulty during the verification phase that is required to reduce the frequency of fake alerts. The suggested technique is created taking into account the difficulty of verifying a fire using gathered photographs of the influenced area. Fig. 3 provides a broad perspective of the intelligent city landscape and illustrates the conceptual representation of a smart city's data collecting method. It serves as an example of the smart city application areas for IoT and WSNs. IoT offers a framework in the creation of apps which may gather data from linked devices and give services to customers, businesses, and government agencies. The application of the suggested WSN and IoT-dependent structure is to detect fires inside cities. The collecting of data, its processing, and the creation of the final decision all play a significant role in how efficiently the city can provide services using smart devices. In general, real-time development and inter-transmission in intelligent devices with IoT improve the efficiency of smart city services, making the city smarter. Devices are used to gather the observation data, and a gateway is used to send it to the cloud.

The cloud may serve as a platform for real-time data archiving and offer analysis for decision-making. Many users and controllers may access this data via a network server, which offers facilities using the real-time ecological data. The framework was created with the benefits of IoT and WSNs for intelligent cities. Fig. 4 shows how the suggested architecture for detecting fire events in cities operates. For the purpose of identifying and keeping track of fire occurrences, WSNs and IoT gadgets are used in tandem. A smart city is often enveloped by a region, which might be a forest or an agricultural field. Cities (Mondal, D. et al. 2023) are significantly protected by the suggested design against natural or man-made disasters. The suggested system's operation may be divided into five different components: sensor stationing, satellite communication, thingSpeakIoT cloud, UAV inter-network, and base station.

3.1 Sensor Deployment

The initial section denotes the haphazard placement of sensor network in a city-wide zone. To gather environmental characteristics, the sensor nodes are placed in the grassland. Real-time data gathering occurs for a number of environmental characteristics, including warmth, wetness, fog, and brightness. Radio frequency connections are used by the sensor nodes to interact with one another and deliver data to the sink node. For real-time analysis, the sink node gathers the sensor data and uploads it to the cloud framework through GSM (Gupta, A. et al. 2022). The sensors are set up to provide real-time environmental data after 2 to 6 mins. Section 4 discusses the details of each sensor node.

Figure 3. A smart city aided by a WSN and IoT

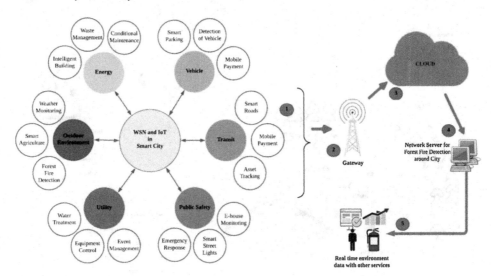

3.2. Satellite System

The satellite framework in area scan is described here. The success of the satellite-dependent fire tracking approach is limited by the lengthy scan time and poor satellite resolution. Satellite-dependent surveillance is a common approach for tracking fire. However, the satellite-based technology is unable to forecast a forest fire before it spreads out of control. The satellite network is used to map the region for succeeding development, and the component is also in charge of gathering data on other crucial factors like climate, wind flow, etc. The precise measurements of the region of interest are provided by the area scanning through satellite. In order to map a region effectively and construct a drone network for real-time surveillance, satellite-based photos are used. The target region's latitude and longitude are collected by the satellite system, which then sends the information to the base station for location tracking. The region is plotted for scanning based on the satellite network's latitudinal and longitudinal data.

3.3 ThingSpeak IoT Cloud: IoT-dependent Cloud Platform for Data Analytics

This platform stores the real-time data streams from sensors for data gathering, display, and analysis. The ground-based data is securely transferred to the cloud, where MATLAB is used to analyse and display the data. Our technology instantly visualises data from live streams and sends an alarm when necessary.

Figure 4. Shows a hypothetical integrated system for smart city fire incident detection

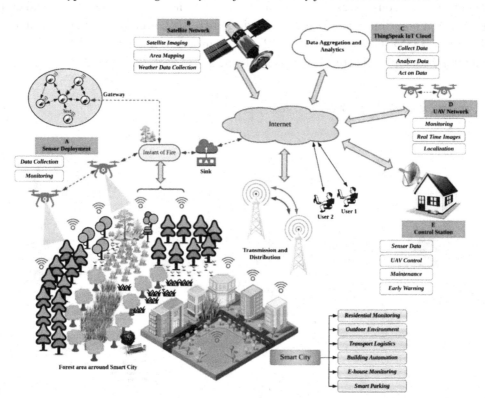

3.4. The UAV Network

The suggested system is then expanded to offer real-time photographs of the concerned zone once the incident has been identified. The UAV aids in locating the incident and delivers visual data to the control station in real-time confirmation of a fire occurrence using an image processing technique. The server's request for the monitoring mission starts the scanning procedure. During mission planning, when checkpoints and their locations are specified, mapping software is used. The drone's flight paths are then created on the mapped region in accordance with the objective, and this information is sent to the base station together with the most recent parameter readings. High resolution photos of the target region are provided by the drone deployment. The ground station receives the sensed data and transmits it for immediate processing. An event's occurrence starts the technique of identifying its position for monitoring and affirmation.

Figure 5. Elements of fire detection system in smart cities

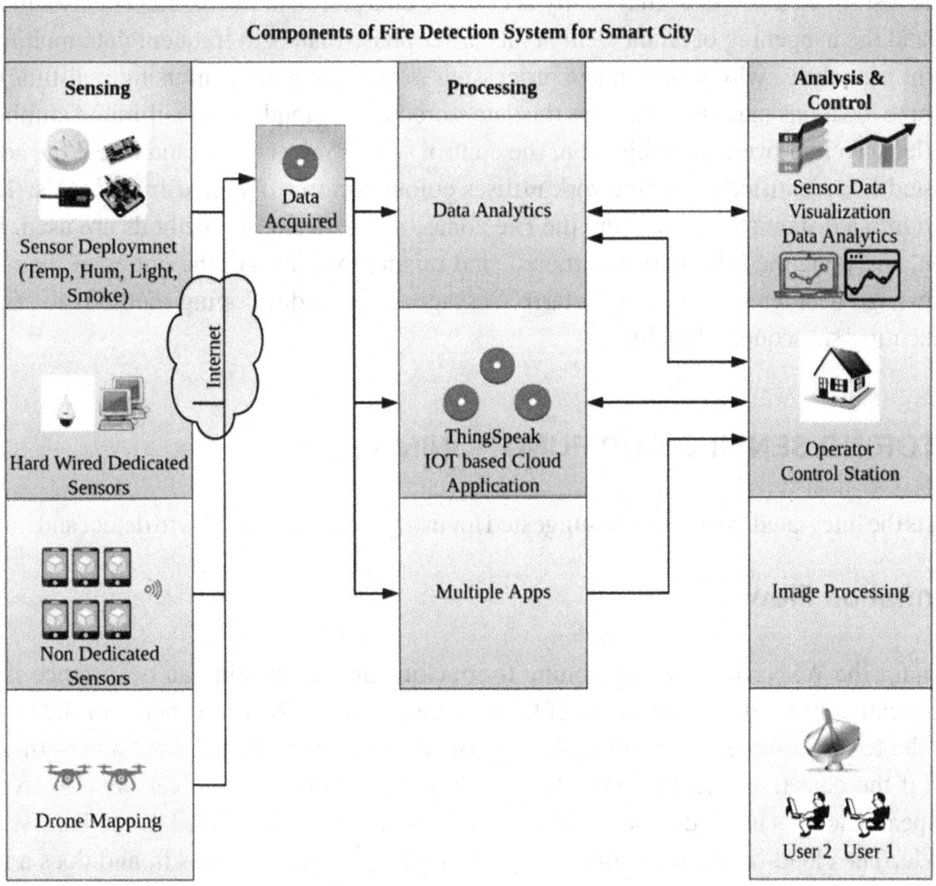

3.5. The Command Post

The base station is in charge of analysing sensor data, managing and controlling the network, and verifying the existence of a fire incident using image processing techniques. At the control station, the collected photos are analysed for event detection. Upon confirmation of a fire, the control station transmits an early alert. Sensing, processing, and analysis are the three fundamental elements of the suggested architecture. The fundamental components of the suggested fire detection methodology are shown in Fig. 5. To gather data on environmental factors, temperature, humidity, light, and smoke sensors are first put in outside environments at random. Every sensor node talks with the sink node directly. The sink node is in charge of sending the gathered data to the ThingSpeak cloud for archival and processing. The gathered data is saved on a cloud platform in analysis, and additional duties specified to each application are also executed. The task of the proposed methodology's sensing stage is to set up the sensor nodes and keep an eye on the environmental factors, which include accountable for the cause of the fire. Every 2–5 minutes, the gathered data is kept in the ThinkSpeak cloud for ongoing tracking and investigation. The processing step gathers data from sensors, analyses it in anomaly detection, and makes a decision based on the results. Remote users may easily access the data stored in the cloud. The user may identify opponents and the happening of an incident at an earlier phase thanks to frequent data monitoring. The final element is analysis, which uses image processing to verify the incident using real-time data from UAVs. Remote locations may simply access the data stored in the cloud via an unlimited number of users and controllers. To improve communication, the control station may control and direct the accessories. The suggested fire identification framework utilises colour pictures obtained from UAVs. The photos are inputted into a distant station. To find the fire zones, image detection methods are used. Receiving information, analysing the information gathered, and raising the alert are the duties of the control station. The management team receives the alarm message to begin developing methods for fighting the fire and executing subsequent directives.

4. MONITORING SENSING AND FUNCTIONING

Fig. 6 depicts the integrated system that is suggested for using the IoT and WSNs to detect and monitor fire.

4.1. Information Flow

The schema for the WSNs and IoT functioning for tracking and monitoring an occurrence is shown in Fig. 7. The location of sensor nodes kicks off the detecting process. Next, the need for the greatest coverage with the fewest sensors is examined. The shortest channel for data transmission to the sink node is designed if the objective is met in order to maximise energy efficiency. Every two to five minutes, the ThingSpeak Cloud is utilised to store the data once it has been transferred to the base station from the sink node. The cloud-based programme takes the real-time data, analyses it, and does a MATLAB (Meslie, Y. et al. 2021) programming to find events. A message containing the GPS coordinates of the node that caused the anomaly is sent to the control station for each aberration in the sensed data. Via borderlines noticeable with GPS coordinates, the control station maps the target region in order to capture real-time photos of the concerned area.

Real-time photos are sent to the base station together with the localisation of the affected area. Every picture that is supplied is given the image processing algorithm. The procedure for using image processing to confirm a fire occurrence is outlined. The creation of the image's histogram equalisation is the first stage. Moreover, the intensity of the picture is adjusted to improve contrast. Fire photos are thought to possess a higher estimate of the red element according to the suggested methodology. Hence, a threshold function is created to isolate the red part of photos with fire colour. The proportion of red, blue, and green component parts is another factor that may be taken into account in this job. Hence, colour estimation and plotting of these colour components serve as the foundation of the suggested fire estimation framework. A loaded picture is first mapped with the extracted edge for colour detection. The colour estimation framework recognises the RGB pixel's characteristics and outputs a picture with the chosen region of fire colour detection. The second stage involves extracting the RGB components from the improved picture and converting the RGB image to YCbCr in order to detect fire pixels. The calculation of the mean and SD of pictures for the verification of fire and non-fire colour pixels comes next. When the programme detects non-fire area in the picture, it jumps to the following set of pictures to assess fire pixels. If a fire is found, a set of regulations are enforced to the example pictures, and a fire alarm is initiated for decision-making based on these rules.

4.2 Sensor Node Deployment

Figure 8 depicts the various instruments that are used to gather data on various ambient factors in order to detect fire in the region of interest. Light monitors (a) measure the amount of light but do not take pictures. Photodiodes and photo resistors are the most popular types of light intensity devices. (LDR Light Dependent Resistors). Light can be converted into electricity or power by a photo diode. A resistor known as a photo resistor has an impedance that diminishes as the light strength rises.

A simple, inexpensive digital temperature and humidity monitor is the HTS-220(b) sensor. It measures the humidity and temperature of the air around it and sends out a numerical signal on the data port. Although it is very simple to utilize, precise scheduling is needed to capture the data. The smoke monitor MQ2 (c) can measure the levels of flammable gas in the atmosphere and sends the results as an analog signal. The monitor is capable of measuring flammable gas amounts between 300 and 10,000 ppm. The monitor uses less than 150 mA at 5 V and can function in temps ranging from -20 to 50 °C. A drain (Coordinator) node receives all the information gathered by the sensing nodes and forwards it to it. (d). As a result, the location of the drain node greatly affects the amount of energy used and the lifespan of WSNs. Energy usage and instrument lifespan are significant factors in Wireless instrument Networks (WSN). The chosen cluster leaders will receive the data gathered by the corresponding cluster members. All of the data that was gathered was then sent by the cluster heads to the control station or sink node. The control station will transmit the info it receives to the data. The conduit between the sensing nodes and the data processing centre is what the Sink Node is referred to as because of this.

4.3. Data Analysis

The IoTs is the interconnection of intelligent objects, including cars, houses, structures, hospitals, and various intelligent things. These objects are equipped with sensors, motors, and networking, enabling them to gather and share data. This device uses an online framework built on ThingSpeak for data gathering and processing. A cloud-based application framework called ThingSpeak is intended to promote

Figure 6. An advanced idea for the use of WSNs and IoT to identify and track an occurrence

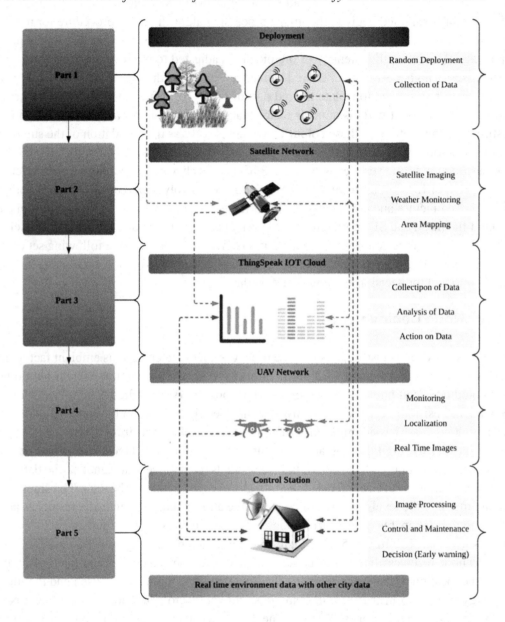

useful interactions between intelligent objects and humans. The management centre keeps track of every occurrence while ThingSpeak stores the observed data in real-time. Figure 9 shows how the IoT-based cloud application functions. An IoT-based application called Thing- Speak gathers sensor data that has been recorded and immediately visualizes it. When the observed data or instant hits a level, it gives an immediate move on the data.

4.4. Verification of the Fire Incident

The UAV is launched to take real-time pictures of the area when an anomaly in the observed data is discovered through data analysis in the ThingSpeak application. By using the GPS data that are accessible in the control centre, the UAV locates and records the target region. At the monitoring centre, the suggested image processing method is applied to the incoming pictures for the purpose of confirming a fire. The construction of the histogram normalization, which redistributes the picture luminance, is the first stage. The obtained input picture is checked for balance by transforming it to a higher-intensity HSI image in maintaining the original image's Hue and Saturation components.

As shown in Figure 10, (a) is the collection of initial pictures of the fire incident and (b) enhanced image intensity following the normalization procedure, the implemented and evaluated for 4 example images of fire for improving the image intensity. It is noted that R, G, and B elements of a picture cannot be improved separately by histogram normalization. Figure 10 compares the histogram findings for a

Figure 7. Shows the suggested event monitoring system for smart cities in a flow chart format

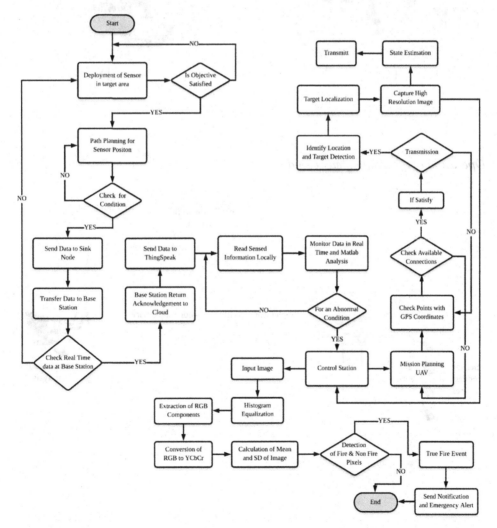

Figure 8. Shows the supervisor node (d) and the sensor nodes for light, temperature, humidity, and pollution (a, b, c)

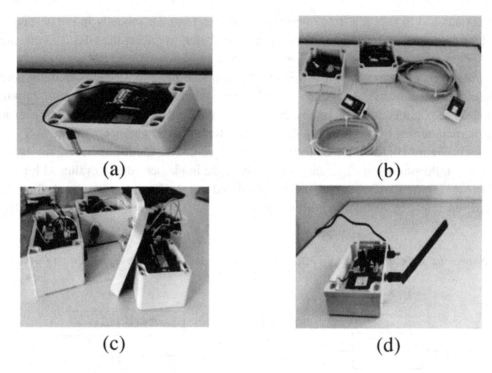

Figure 9. Operation of the ThingSpeak cloud

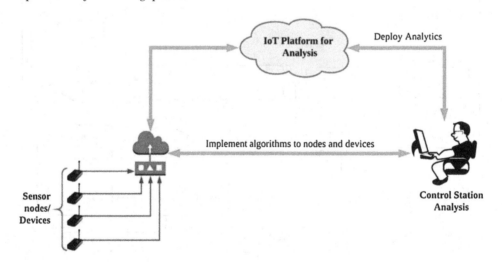

Figure 10. (a) Example of a picture without histogram equalization (b) Following the equivalence procedure

(a)   (b)

picture using R, G, and B before and after histogram normalization. To ascertain luminance levels and pixel counts, four representative pictures are captured.

In order to improve the picture clarity, the original RGB matrix of the image is additionally converted to HSI format and then the normalization is done to the intensity matrix. Additionally, the HSI matrix revised matrix is converted back to the RGB matrix during maintenance of the HSI matrix constant. The

Figure 11. Input RGB picture (a), manual fire area extraction (b)

(a)　　　　　　　　　　(b)

YCbCr mechanism, which isolates the picture brightness information from chrominance more effectively than any other colour model, is used in the suggested approach. With the exception of its centre, which is yellowish-white during its state of greatest temperature, the rest of the fire's hue is crimson or yellow. Based on a set of guidelines that have been established and a system that is used to retrieve fire pixels the fire area is segmented according to Rule 1, and the centre region is segmented according to Rule

2.In order to create the final picture, rules 1 and 2 must be met. These two principles produce a real fire picture. For meeting the fire area boundary, Rule 3 is used. The aforementioned guidelines effectively divide the actual fire area and are able to arrange the fire pixels that change colour from yellow to red as the temperature changes. RGB components define the colour plane of any colour picture. Each colour plane is discretely divided into 256 quantization levels, or 8 bits, per colour plane.

White is written as (255, 255, 255) and for black it is (255, 255, 255). The recovered RGB elements of a raw picture are displayed in Fig. 12(b–d). To separate the G, B, and R parts of a picture, the RGB paradigm is used. For any given situation, the strength of the R channel is greater than the intensity of the G channel. Similar to this, the strength of the G channel is greater than the intensity of the B channel. Fig. 10's depicted example pictures were obtained in order to verify the same. To separate the R, G, and B elements, the RGB model is also used.

CONCLUSION

Many nations have significant worries about woodland fires or the fires near smart towns. Scholars and specialists from all over the world concur that purchasing effective tools is the most important step in catastrophe mitigation. This article introduces a framework for early fire monitoring based on WSN and IoT. The sensenut hardware technology has been used to create wireless sensing networks effectively. The sensor units are set up outside in a real-time data collection and processing environment. The cloud stores the data gathered by the sensing units for processing. The ThingSpeak cloud tool for haze, temperature, humidity, and light strength has been used to create a number of graphs. The system is effective at detecting an occurrence by studying real-time data and is capable of perceiving a variety of external factors. In this effort, a fire warning system is created using IoT devices and an online framework. The design is effective and offers a reasonable and economical way to gather and observe real-time data worldwide. The suggested device incorporates picture analysis technology for fire incident monitoring. A number of guidelines are also intended to more precisely identify the fire occurrence.

REFERENCES

Anand, R., Singh, J., Pandey, D., Pandey, B. K., Nassa, V. K., & Pramanik, S. (2022). Modern Technique for Interactive Communication in LEACH-Based Ad Hoc Wireless Sensor Network. In M. M. Ghonge, S. Pramanik, & A. D. Potgantwar (Eds.), *Software Defined Networking for Ad Hoc Networks*. Springer. doi:10.1007/978-3-030-91149-2_3

Aziz, A., Osamy, W., Alfawaz, O., & Khedr, A. M. (2022). EDCCS: Effective deterministic clustering scheme based compressive sensing to enhance IoT based WSNs. *Wireless Networks*, *28*(6), 2375–2391. doi:10.100711276-022-02973-3

Bansal, R., Jenipher, B., Nisha, V., & Makhan, R. Kumbhkar, P. S., Roy, S. & Gupta, A. (2022). Big Data Architecture for Network Security. In Cyber Security and Network Security. Wiley. doi:10.1002/9781119812555.ch11

Cai, Y., Zhou, W., Zhang, L., Yu, L., & Luo, T. (2023). DHFNet: Dual-decoding hierarchical fusion network for RGB-thermal semantic segmentation. *The Visual Computer*. doi:10.100700371-023-02773-6

Cao, C. F., Yu, B., Chen, Z. Y., Qu, Y.-X., Li, Y.-T., Shi, Y.-Q., Ma, Z.-W., Sun, F.-N., Pan, Q.-H., Tang, L.-C., Song, P., & Wang, H. (2022). Fire Intumescent, High-Temperature Resistant, Mechanically Flexible Graphene Oxide Network for Exceptional Fire Shielding and Ultra-Fast Fire Warning. *Nano-Micro Letters*, *14*(1), 92. doi:10.100740820-022-00837-1 PMID:35384618

Choudhary, S., Narayan, V., Faiz, M., & Pramanik, S. (2022). Fuzzy Approach-Based Stable Energy-Efficient AODV Routing Protocol in Mobile Ad hoc Networks. In M. M. Ghonge, S. Pramanik, & A. D. Potgantwar (Eds.), *Software Defined Networking for Ad Hoc Networks*. Springer. doi:10.1007/978-3-030-91149-2_6

de Venâncio, P. V. A. B., Lisboa, A. C., & Barbosa, A. V. (2022). An automatic fire detection system based on deep convolutional neural networks for low-power, resource-constrained devices. *Neural Computing & Applications*, *34*(18), 15349–15368. doi:10.100700521-022-07467-z

Ghosh, R., & Kumar, A. (2022). A hybrid deep learning model by combining convolutional neural network and recurrent neural network to detect forest fire. *Multimedia Tools and Applications*, *81*(27), 38643–38660. doi:10.100711042-022-13068-8

Gupta, A., Asad, A., Meena, L., & Anand, R. (2023). IoT and RFID-Based Smart Card System Integrated with Health Care, Electricity, QR and Banking Sectors. In M. Gupta, S. Ghatak, A. Gupta, & A. L. Mukherjee (Eds.), *Artificial Intelligence on Medical Data. Lecture Notes in Computational Vision and Biomechanics* (Vol. 37). Springer. doi:10.1007/978-981-19-0151-5_22

Gupta, A., Verma, A., & Pramanik, S. (2022). Advanced Security System in Video Surveillance for COVID-19. In *An Interdisciplinary Approach to Modern Network Security, S. Pramanik, A. Sharma, S. Bhatia and D. N. Le*. CRC Press. doi:10.1201/9781003147176-8

Hassan, N. M., Hamad, S., & Mahar, K. (2022). Mammogram breast cancer CAD systems for mass detection and classification: A review. *Multimedia Tools and Applications*, *81*(14), 20043–20075. doi:10.100711042-022-12332-1

Jain, S., Gupta, S., Sreelakshmi, K. K., & Rodrigues, J. J. P. C. (2022). Fog computing in enabling 5G-driven emerging technologies for development of sustainable smart city infrastructures. *Cluster Computing*, *25*(2), 1111–1154. doi:10.100710586-021-03496-w

Jayaraman, G., & Dhulipala, V. R. S. (2022). FEECS: Fuzzy-Based Energy-Efficient Cluster Head Selection Algorithm for Lifetime Enhancement of Wireless Sensor Networks. *Arabian Journal for Science and Engineering*, *47*(2), 1631–1641. doi:10.100713369-021-06030-7

Khan, R. A., Hussain, A., Bajwa, U. I., Raza, R. H., & Anwar, M. W. (2023). Fire and Smoke Detection Using Capsule Network. *Fire Technology*, *59*(2), 581–594. doi:10.100710694-022-01352-w

Kuthadi, V. M., Selvaraj, R., Baskar, S., Shakeel, P. M., & Ranjan, A. (2022). Optimized Energy Management Model on Data Distributing Framework of Wireless Sensor Network in IoT System. *Wireless Personal Communications*, *127*(2), 1377–1403. doi:10.100711277-021-08583-0

Li, Y., Zhang, W., Liu, Y., & Jin, Y. (2022). A visualized fire detection method based on convolutional neural network beyond anchor. *Applied Intelligence*, *52*(11), 13280–13295. doi:10.100710489-022-03243-7

Liang, L. L., Chu, S. C., Du, Z. G., & Pan, J.-S. (2023). Surrogate-assisted Phasmatodea population evolution algorithm applied to wireless sensor networks. *Wireless Networks*, *29*(2), 637–655. doi:10.100711276-022-03168-6

Liu, Z. G., Yang, Y., & Ji, X. H. (2016). Flame detection algorithm based on a saliency detection technique and the uniform local binary pattern in the YCbCr color space. *Signal, Image and Video Processing*, *10*(2), 277–284. doi:10.100711760-014-0738-0

Mall, P. K., Pramanik, S., Srivastava, S., Faiz, M., Sriramulu, S., & Kumar, M. N. (2023). FuzztNet-Based Modelling Smart Traffic System in Smart Cities Using Deep Learning Models. In *Data-Driven Mathematical Modeling in Smart Cities*. IGI Global., doi:10.4018/978-1-6684-6408-3.ch005

Mandal, A., Dutta, S., & Pramanik, S. (2021). Machine Intelligence of Pi from Geometrical Figures with Variable Parameters using SCILab. In D. Samanta, R. R. Althar, S. Pramanik, & S. Dutta (Eds.), *Methodologies and Applications of Computational Statistics for Machine Learning* (pp. 38–63). IGI Global. doi:10.4018/978-1-7998-7701-1.ch003

Meslie, Y., Enbeyle, W., Pandey, B. K., Pramanik, S., Pandey, D., Dadeech, P., Belay, A., & Saini, A. (2021). Machine Intelligence-based Trend Analysis of COVID-19 for Total Daily Confirmed Cases in Asia and Africa. In D. Samanta, R. R. Althar, S. Pramanik, & S. Dutta (Eds.), *Methodologies and Applications of Computational Statistics for Machine Learning* (pp. 164–185). IGI Global. doi:10.4018/978-1-7998-7701-1.ch009

Mondal, D., Ratnaparkhi, A., Deshpande, A., Deshpande, V., Kshirsagar, A. P., & Pramanik, S. (2023). Applications, Modern Trends and Challenges of Multiscale Modelling in Smart Cities. In *Data-Driven Mathematical Modeling in Smart Cities*. IGI Global. doi:10.4018/978-1-6684-6408-3.ch001

Murali, S., Govindan, V. K., & Kalady, S. (2022). Quaternion-based image shadow removal. *The Visual Computer*, *38*(5), 1527–1538. doi:10.100700371-021-02086-6

Nagulan, S., Srinivasa Krishnan, A. N., Kiran Kumar, A., Vishnu Kumar, S., & Suchithra, M. (2023). An Efficient Real-Time Fire Detection Method Using Computer Vision and Neural Network-Based Video Analysis. In: Khanna, A., Gupta, D., Kansal, V., Fortino, G., Hassanien, A.E. (eds) *Proceedings of Third Doctoral Symposium on Computational Intelligence. Lecture Notes in Networks and Systems, (vol 479)*. Springer, Singapore. 10.1007/978-981-19-3148-2_55

Ozkan, O., & Kilic, S. (2023). UAV routing by simulation-based optimization approaches for forest fire risk mitigation. *Annals of Operations Research*, *320*(2), 937–973. doi:10.100710479-021-04393-6

Pradhan, D., Sahu, P. K., Goje, N. S., Myo, H., Ghonge, M. M., Tun, M., Rajeswari, R., & Pramanik, S. (2022). Security, Privacy, Risk, and Safety Toward 5G Green Network (5G-GN). In Cyber Security and Network Security. Wiley. doi:10.1002/9781119812555.ch9

Pramanik, S. (2023). An Adaptive Image Steganography Approach depending on Integer Wavelet Transform and Genetic Algorithm. *Multimedia Tools and Applications*. doi:10.100711042-023-14505-y

Wang, Z., Sun, X., Zhang, X., Han, T., & Gao, F. (2020). Algorithm Improvement of Pedestrians' Red-Light Running Snapshot System Based on Image Recognition. In Q. Liang, W. Wang, X. Liu, Z. Na, M. Jia, & B. Zhang (Eds.), *Communications, Signal Processing, and Systems. CSPS 2019. Lecture Notes in Electrical Engineering* (Vol. 571). Springer. doi:10.1007/978-981-13-9409-6_207

Wu, Z., Xue, R., & Li, H. (2022). Real-Time Video Fire Detection via Modified YOLOv5 Network Model. *Fire Technology*, *58*(4), 2377–2403. doi:10.100710694-022-01260-z

Yang, J., Ge, H., Yang, J., Tong, Y., & Su, S. (2022). Online multi-object tracking using multi-function integration and tracking simulation training. *Applied Intelligence*, *52*(2), 1268–1288. doi:10.100710489-021-02457-5

Zhang, J., Yu, Z., Cheng, Y., Sha, X., & Zhang, H. (2022). A novel hierarchical framework to evaluate residential exposure to green spaces. *Landscape Ecology*, *37*(3), 895–911. doi:10.100710980-021-01378-5

Zhang, N., Zhang, N., Zheng, Q., & Xu, Y.-S. (2022). Real-time prediction of shield moving trajectory during tunnelling using GRU deep neural network. *Acta Geotechnica*, *17*(4), 1167–1182. doi:10.100711440-021-01319-1

Chapter 18
Food Quality Assessment Using Image Processing Technique

S. Dhamodaran
Sathyabama Institute of Science and Technology, India

Shahanawaj Ahamad
University of Hail, Saudi Arabia

J. V. N. Ramesh
Koneru Lakshmaiah Education Foundation, India

G. Muthugurunathan
Madanapalle Institute of Technology and Science, India

K. Manikandan
Vellore Institute of Technology, India

Sabyasachi Pramanik
Haldia Institute of Technology, India

Digvijay Pandey
Department of Technical Education, Government of Uttar Pradesh, India

ABSTRACT

The leading and suitable techniques for examining and assessing the microstructure of things are nowadays high-resolution optical microscopy and imaging approaches. Manfred Von Ardenne developed scanning electron microscopy (SEM), a kind of surface microscopy, in the 1930s. SEM employs electron behaviour to produce 3D pictures of entities that provide knowledge about their topology, morphology, and constitution. This method has been discovered to have uses throughout the previous several decades in a variety of commercial and industrial arena, forensic analysis, and ordinary studies in science and business. An effective tool for seeing and characterising hybrid organic and inorganic substances and surfaces is the scanning electron microscope.

DOI: 10.4018/978-1-6684-8618-4.ch018

1. INTRODUCTION

According to earlier literature, investigations on the micro-structural characterisation of dry foods were the principal uses of SEM (Elgendy, M.Y., et al., 2022). Nonetheless, practically each food material is currently studied by SEM due to the developments in kinds and ranges of various preparedness approaches for handling various sorts of meals. For instance, it may calculate the temperature at which a candy bar's coating begins to gelatinize. It is moreover utilized in conjunction with energy.

EDS, a dispersive X-ray technique, is used to map meal poisoning. Moreover, SEM is combined with EDS in forensic analysis in the food business, known as SEM/EDS, in image and fundamental configuration observation. It denotes a potent technology which recognises both organic and inorganic pollutants discovered in food products that are recalled or identified during quality analysis in manufacturing locations. Also, it provides details on the arrangement of ingredients in the food matrix, like the dispersion of inorganic elements in dry foodstuffs that aids in providing details on how the ingredients were ground and blended.

The 3D formation of the microbial groups seen in complex meal specimens, as well as the interactions between the food and the microbes, are also primarily assessed by SEM. Results from several research

Figure 1. SEM for micro-structural image

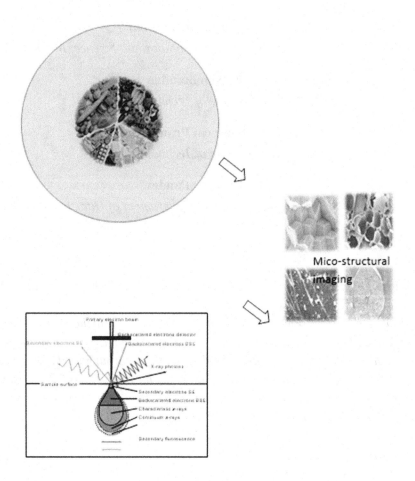

include: A complicated and densely stuffed yeasts and bacteria was seen all over the kefir grains and fibrillar content is seen between cells. Botrytis cinerea advancement in grape-vine berries while shrinking may be succeeded by EM analysis and connected to specific sensory characteristics of higher-grade wines; and SEM pictures of yoghurt and cheese disclosed the existence of micro-possession of bacilli and cocci in micro-holes of the matrix. Moreover, a visual summarising the chapter has been provided (Figure 1).

2. FUNDAMENTAL IDEAS AND PRACTISES

All SEMs are made up of an electron column which generates an electron beam, a specimen chamber where the beam combines with the specimen, detectors which track various signals generated by the beam-sample connection, and an inspecting framework which builds a picture from the signal. A focussed ray of accelerated electrons (3–9 keV) travelling over a solid subject forms a picture step-by-step in a SEM. The beam is concentrated to a precise spot using electromagnetic lenses for scanning the specimen. These electrons mix and connect with the atoms in the sample at different surfaces, creating signals which reveal the surface topography and constituents of the sample. Thermionic emitters and field emitters, two kinds of electron emission sources, have been widely used. The filament is heated by thermoionic emitters utilizing an electrical current that minimizes the filament material's work function. Electrons are certainly emitted of the filament by an electric field while the work function is minimized. Usually, lanthanum hexaboride or tungsten is used to make these filaments. On the other hand, filament material is not heated by cold cathode field emission sources. Instead, electrons are pulled from a field emission gun by exposing the filament to an enormous electrical potential gradient, so great that it overcomes the material's work function and causes electrons to concentrate on the sample under study.

The signals produced in this way, which are detected according to location on the surface, comprise transmitted electrons, reflected electrons, secondary electrons, X-rays (Jayasingh, R. et al., 2022). Primary electrons pierce the solid object and are scattered away by deflection.

Backscatter electrons, another name for reflected electrons, are used to identify elements and compounds by providing compositional information. This reveals the atomic number allotment in the sample, having larger atomic number regions seem to be brighter and lower atomic number regions appearing duller. It might be used in functional investigations to identify calcium-enriched regions in an organic matrix or to identify minerals as pollutants. Distinctive X-rays that are discharged from under the specimen surface additionally facilitate data about the constituents and minerals. The display of this data on a screen makes it practicable to distinctly portray 3D graphics (Pramanik, S. et al. 2023). The SEM's capacity to accurately and cogently recreate textual information is one of its biggest benefits. Sample preparation for food material scanning includes pre-treatment, fixation, and dryness of the specimen. There are various ways to produce foodstuff specimens for SEM evaluation, including dehydrating the specimen (if decline of water does not indicate a alteration in the imaging outcomes), covering it with conductive and impervious films to avoid water from being distributed into a vacuum, chilling the specimen to lower temperatures for preventing itself from degaussing (i.e., altering its morphology and composition) when in vacuum, etc. Nevertheless, excessive sample preparation must be avoided since this might result in significant artefacts, twist the formation, and alter interconnections between the constituents.

For instance, by eliminating lipid soluble components from dehydrating solvents. The benefits and restrictions of SEM are shown in Table 1.

Table 1. Scanning electron microscopy's benefits and drawbacks

Benefits	Drawbacks
Comparably easy sample preparation	challenges viewing insulating materials and hydrated samples without changing their condition
large field of view and great magnification	huge, pricey, and needing to be kept away from any potential electric, magnetic, or vibration interference
High resolution: >1.4 nm (due to short wavelength)	It is essential to maintain a constant voltage, currents to electromagnetic coils, and the circulation of cold water.
The picture is a representation of digital information that can be analysed and quantified.	special instruction is required for staff operating
Topology using secondary electron imaging	only solid, inorganic materials which fit inside the vacuum chamber and may withstand a modest vacuum are allowed.
Chemistry backscatter electron imaging	Radiation exposure danger

3. SEM TYPES THAT IS RELEVANT TO ASSESSING FOOD QUALITY

3.1 Traditional (high vacuum) scanning electron microscopy

Traditional scanning electron microscopes have proved effective for characterising materials that function at higher vacuum (measured in mm/Hg) conditions that reduce electron beam scattering before it reaches the object. Since it inhibits electrical discharge in the gun assembly and permits moving of electrons, the high vacuum state is extremely desired. Without it, the probe size and resolution would be increased. In order to prepare a sample for traditional SEM, many steps must be taken, including chemical fixation, extraction of the intended viewing constituent, cleansing, dehydrating, and staging on an aluminium stub. A sample that is able to tolerate high vacuum may be seen using a traditional SEM. For incoming electrons to carry away from the specimen surface and for grounding, the specimen needs to be cleansed, dried, and electrically conducting. To evade sample charging, non-conducting samples must be covered with a thin coating of metal film. As was already said, SEM typically generates a narrow electron beam using a heated thermionic filament. The sample's surface is thereafter scanned by the beam. The scanning beam's operation makes the sample surface to generate electrons that are then gathered by an appropriately placed detector. Yet, the expense of utilising vacuum is a significant drawback. Increasing vacuum levels then better pumping systems are eventually needed, which raises the expense of this operation.

3.2 Low Vacuum or Variable Pressure SEM

A weak vacuum SEM similar to traditional SEM, offers the extra benefit of lower or changing pressure settings which may be updated in the specimen chamber before the artefact of electron charging is eliminated from pictures. The artefact of electron charging results from the accumulation of electrons from the scanning beam in a non-conducting material. Because of the progressive deficit of H_2O at lower pressure, the improvement of varying-pressure SEM has only allowed for brief glimpses of hydrated samples. The resolution is, however, constrained when the chamber pressure is kept high (250 Pa) for minimizing moisture contents, and the imaging duration is, conversely, constrained by increased moisture loss when the chamber pressure is lowered to enhance resolution. The sample that has to be seen is put on the cold stage in a thin layer of water. Control is managed to minimise water loss and enhance resolution. As soon as the stage temperature drops below a manageable pressure (270 Pa), it is assigned at 6 °C first and thereafter to 12 °C. After a chamber pressure of 71 Pa and associated temperature of 27°C are attained, pressure and temperature are further lowered in proportionally. The signal needed for high-resolution imaging is provided by high-energy electrons at 16 kV. Obstructive ice crystals might develop if the temperature drops too quickly. If pressure is reduced too quickly, salts from the retained buffer can make a comparable impact in the event that dehydration develops. This innovative method has the primary benefit of enabling the monitoring of biological samples which may not be sufficiently investigated due to the loss of primary condition during dehydration.

3.3 SEM in the Cold

Cryogenic-SEM is a lower temperature electron microscopic approach which enables the investigation of elegant organic matters in their original state at lower temperatures related to the environment (generally within the range 125°C and 180°C), preserving the sample's lifelike resemblance and allowing it to be taped in a completely moisturized and chemically unaltered state. On contrary to the conventional SEM approaches, cryogenic-SEM is a fast and competent technology which maintains solvable components, shows great resolution capabilities, and shouldn't utilise any harmful chemicals for preparing or fixing the specimens. Moreover, it has exceptional splintering and selective surface water removal capabilities by organized sublimation. The specimen is first cryo-fixed by being submerged in liquid propane or sub-cooled nitrogen kept at 210°C (nitrogen's freezing point). Once at the colder phase of the formation enclosure in the SEM chamber, the sample is moved there while being vacuumed transported. If required, fracturing might be done in this place. The specimen is sputter covered with metal (like gold/platinum), or with C by the process of thermal evaporation, before being sublimated for showing more detail. Preventing ice crystal development in the foodstuff specimen is crucial since it would otherwise displace the parts of the constructions and ruin the original layout. The right development conditions like obtaining a tiny specimen size or rapidly freezing the material at a low temperature, make this simple to do. The specimen is then brought into the imaging chamber under vacuum, safely cooled to 140°C or less, where it may be quickly found on a colder phase made especially for the SEM.

The food industry can use SEM for better inspection of various multiphase foodstuff items like emulsions like mayonnaise, ice cream, etc., starch-enriched items, cakes, bread, cheese, and various dairy products. SEM has recently evolved into a necessary approach for not only the medicinal and medical organizations in fundamental allied research. Unfortunately, dairy products have not received much attention from cryo-electron microscopy too far. This may be because of the dearth of trustworthy cryogenic electron microscopy as also the higher constituent of moisture in dairy products that is a prime candidate for freezing artefacts.

3.4 Environmental SEM

Environmental SEM (ESEM) is superior to conventional SEM and distinguishes itself from it primarily by the existence of a gas in the specimen outlet. Charging artefacts, which are present in non-conducting materials, are eliminated by gas ionisation in the specimen outlet. Hence, specimens are seen in a low vacuum. Wet, filthy, greasy, and outgassing materials may all be imaged by the ESEM. Contaminants don't harm the device or reduce picture quality. ESEM performs two key functions. It is founded first on electrical charge. In order to prevent sample charging and to improve signal detection, the gas functions as an electrical charge conductor and serves as a conditioning medium for a sample, preventing liquids from evaporating. Since it can image hydrated materials in their natural condition and ensures the highest level of dependability for ice cream, a cryogenic ESEM is utilised for testing ice cream. ESEM samples don't need to be well prepared beforehand. This method is used in dynamic evaluation of foodstuffs; for instance, it may display the ageing of foodstuff to identify an incorrect labelling of expiration dates, alterations in component composition over time, etc. Moreover, foods like fruits and vegetables that still have their cellular component, as well as foodstuff with lower water contents, like cocoa, grains and herbs, may be studied using ESEM.

4. NEW DEVELOPMENTS IN TECHNOLOGY

For controlling the process design and, therefore, the standard of the items, food researchers and technicians are gradually using microscopy and image analysis methods for examining the micro structural patterns in food. Since the majority of the components that play a crucial role in the physical and textural nature of the foodstuff lies below the 0.2-125 μm range, changes at the microscopy phase influencing the foodstuff microstructures are largely responsible for changes in consumer satisfaction. SEM is a helpful instrument for examining the microstructures of food. Microscopy and imaging methods work well together to assess the structure of food, and they are the only analytic methods that provide data in the form of pictures rather than numerical values.

The data was then further processed and turned into numerical data for statistical evaluation. Food processing results in microscopic and molecular changes, which may be seen with the use of a SEM. Imaging methods may be used to assess changes in morphology and composition. As the microstructures are impacted at every stage of specimen formation, it is difficult yet vitally important to see real food microstructures. The structural unification of the food specimen may be impacted by the addition or removal of any components. By collecting a lot of samples, such changes or modifications may be taken into account during imaging.

4.1 Interpretation of Images

Scanning electron microscope pictures serve as the foundation for digital image analysis. To make the photographs suitable for mathematical analysis, they are converted to digital form by scanning. The quantification of the pictures identifies structural alterations brought on by processing at the microstructure scale. These modifications impact the food's physical, structural and sensory qualities. The following stages are involved in image processing analysis:

(1) image acquisition techniques to turn the image into a binary format; (2) pre-processing techniques to produce an enhanced image having similar size as the host image (3) image segmentation techniques to divide a digital image into disconnected and non-overlapping regions (4) image measurement techniques to compute the image's characteristics and classification techniques for identifying images by classification into various categories, as depicted in Figure 2.

Figure 2. The elements of an image analysis device

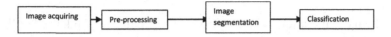

4.2 Structure Quantification

The picture features that are seen under a microscope cannot be quantitatively assessed by the human eye. To presume that the utilization of additional potent and advanced microscopy inevitably results in a greater understanding of the mini-structure of foodstuff would be oversimplifying the situation. When current microscopes are paired with software applications for image analysis, engineers really deal with structural models and statistical connections which measure the information and numerical data in an image. Computer technology is used in image (Pramanik, S. et al. 2020) analysis to identify, classify, and quantify pictures. Software that performs fundamental functions, such as picture processing, segmentation, image selection, and computation of statistical properties, is found at the initial level of analysis. Algorithms (Sinha, M. et al. 2021) comprise the second level that makes it possible for fractal analysis to characterise the properties of the picture surface. Algorithms for object classification and form identification represent a further increase in analytical complexity. An image's texture characteristics and patterns may also be measured using the right parameters, for instance, by comparing the mathematical relationship between the grey levels of the pixels that make up the picture.

5 CURRENT USES IN SEVERAL FOOD CATEGORIES

5.1 Dairy Products

Because of their microscopic tiny molecular dimension, dairy products are extensively examined by SEM compared to other foodstuffs. Milk goes through a number of technological treatments during the manufacture of different value-added dairy products like curd, cheese, yogurt, butter, cream etc. As a result, casein micelles and fat droplets go through major physical and chemical alterations. The corrections control the distinctive rheological and structural characteristics of the manufactured goods. The use of SEM to clarify the changed submicroscopic sub-structures of processed dairy products and assess their standard is enormous.

5.1.1 Milk That Has Been Concentrated or Condensed

Condensed milk denotes a milk product with added value which is created by partly separating the water for creation of a viscous end result which might or might not be sweet with sugar. In the confectionery business, sweetened condensed milk is used to make toffees and fudge, which have a viscoelastic texture because to the interaction of casein and sugars during heating. Standardization, milk preheating, concentration, and sugar crystallization are the primary production procedures. Another kind of condensed milk which is not sweet and goes through sterilization furthermore to the aforementioned processes is evaporated milk.

The two main chemical alterations that occur in the preparation of condensed milk products are crystallization and gelation. Lactose is separated from whey solution via a technique called crystallization. Lactose crystalline is detached from the mixture in the filtering technique by seeding, expansion, and/or assemblage. Complex interactions between milk's many constituents are necessary for milk gelation. It is characterized in concentrated milk by the swelling of casein micelles and the linking of these micelles to create a gel. Concentrated milk that has been sterilized using UHTST has a propensity to gelatinize after extended repository.

Whey proteins get denaturized when heated, and disulfide links in the casein micelle interact with lactoglobulin and casein. Similar to this, the inter-linkage that the milk's components—casein, proteins like lactose and milkfat—go through production may be seen in the microelements of fermented dairy products, frequently because of the help of bacterial or fungal microbes. In yoghurt, each casein particles may be observed for forming branching series or, if cheese is being produced, can be seen to exist in the form of clusters. Heating milk above 85°C results in lacto-globulin for interacting with casein on the surface of the casein particle, limiting the locations where the micelles may connect with one another. The main distinction between the production of yoghurt and cheese is this. Unheated milk's casein micelles spontaneously form huge clumps known as whey that may be readily isolated from the liquid state. Hence, caseins serve as the foundation for cheese. Yogurt, on the other hand, disables the liquid state and adds thickening ingredients such as maize starch, plant resins or gelatin to increase its ability to bind water.

5.1.2 Dairy-Based Dry Goods

Dairy dried goods include items like milk powder and skimmed milk powder that are manufactured economically using spray dehydration. Compared to fresh milk, these goods have a longer shelf life since there is less water activity. Fine misty droplets of fluid milk are spread into a steamy, heated environment, where they quickly flash off the moisture. The resulting spray-dried particles are generally hollow spheres with a diameter of about 100 m and a big central vacuole that is created during the shrinking process as a result of case hardening in the outside face and air bubble enlargement within the droplet. There are other forms and external structures as well, like the crumbled globules and an apple-like element which point to a deficiency during the final dehydrating step. In order to create a firm solution of fat and casein particles without departing behind any obvious remains, milk powders should be soluble in water. The qualities of the powder are influenced by variations in casein structure, calcium phosphate content, particle dimension, and Ca ion behavior, protein concentration on the fat droplet, pH and heat treatment.

SEM may be utilized to explain the flow ability and sludge formation seen in milk powders which are primarily driven by powder molecule shape. Dry milk powder is simple to prepare for SEM, and arranging the specimen on the remnant after gold sputtering is required. Clarifying lactose crystallization and its connection to better losses while milk powder gathering has also benefited greatly from SEM high hygroscopic, amorphous lactose is created when milk is dried. Crystallization and caking are caused by moisture absorption during storage. Whereas lactose crystals created during storage are needle-like and have poor qualities, those existing at the start of storage have a usual shape and excellent keeping qualities. The non-enzymatic browning of whey powders is favored by the transition from amorphous to crystal lactose, which issues water and induces micro-structural crumble.

5.1.3 Ice Cream

One of the most popular sweets or specialties, ice cream, bears a complicated formation with 4 dissimilar elemental steps: ice crystalline structures, air droplets, fat particles and serum. Its structure is very much temperature-dependent, when H_2O is withdrawn from the mixture in the arrangement of ice, serum envelops the ice-crystals and air-bubbles that emerge from a freezing-consolidation technique. Air pocket is a crucial element in ice cream, ruling consuming and retaining qualities, since the construction of ice cream depends on the development of lather, smoothness in structure and stability. The structure of the ice cream mixture and its refining parameters, like the hardening duration and repository temperature, both affect the occurrence of air cells. Ice cream's air cells may have their shape and size observed using low-temperature SEM. Before materials may be seen as dehydrated, partly defatted specimens in SEM at room temperature, water, and volatile components must be removed from them.

5.2 Foods From the Bakery and Cereal

SEM has long been used to study the microstructures of millet and grain to better understand the many sheet, constituents and arrangements of the particles existing. When flour, paste, and goods are exposed to heating, hydration, gelatinization, puffing, freezing and treatments, scanning electron microscopy was used to study alterations in the architectural elements of the items.

SEM has been used to evaluate the quality of a variety of bread kinds with variable flour compositions at various phases of dough mixing, fermentation, and baking. In order to analyze the baking process in wheat rolls, Wu et al. used Cryogenic-SEM (Wu, Y., et al. 2017). They found that the micro-structures of wheat flour included protein aggregates with embedded clusters of cellular components and kept certain properties of the intact endosperm. The dough initially resembled an arrangement of proteins and solvable materials having distributed starch particles throughout the mixing process. This matrix was strengthened by fermentation, which also made the components' distribution more even. The intricate microstructure of bread crumbs was highlighted. The gas cells were lined with a regular cover-like coating which showed the basic architecture. Large interconnected cavities, a sign in an open composition, were seen within the gas cells. The gas cell walls' microstructure was made up of an extremely complicated matrix that seemed rough and erratic. A useful technology that may help with a good knowledge of both the useful characteristics of paste and the qualitative characteristics of bread is cryo-SEM. By comparing dough and chapatti made with high- and low-quality flour. Researchers found that dough made from hard wheat flour had longer gluten strands that covered starch granules, but dough made from soft wheat flour had shorter gluten strands that left starch granules exposed. The longer and bulkier starch fibers intertwined with the protein essence in the chapatti granule were a manifestation of the increased coating-formation capabilities of cereal in hard wheat flour paste. With hard wheat dough, stronger coating-formation capacity of the gluten led to higher moisture retention and amylum gelatinization that produced malleable and soft-composed chapatti. According to the findings, hard wheat dough was chosen for the creation of fermented and baked bread. Fig. 4 displays scanning electron microscopy images that demonstrate how boiling, parboiling and puffing affect the micro-structure in rice.

(Kanwal, A., et al. 2022) used SEM to investigate how enzyme inclusion like fungal-amylases and pro-tease affect the microstructure characteristics of flour, including steadiness and the development of starch globules. The analysis of resistant starches from various origins, including maize, rice, etc., requires the use of SEM. Moreover, SEM images have been used to examine the structure and arrangement of

Figure 3. SEM pictures of samples of raw, boiling, parboiled, and puffed rice in (A), (B), (C), and (D).

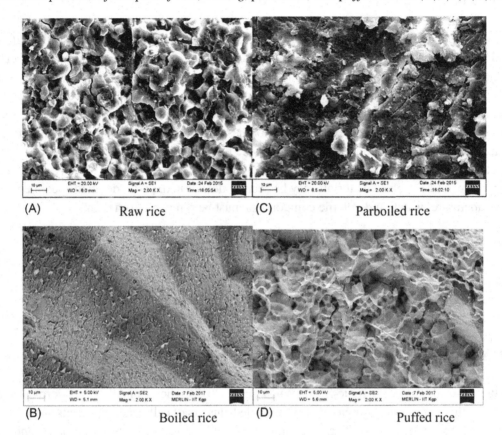

(A)   Raw rice   (C)   Parboiled rice

(B)   Boiled rice   (D)   Puffed rice

molecules in starch globules both previous to and succeeding enzymatic and chemical processing that produces resistive starches.

5.3 Microencapsulation Investigation Using SEM

SEM was utilized to analyze the morphology of several microencapsulation systems for probiotics and bioactives. A novel implanting and microtoming approach was created to enable the analysis of interior formation of shattered capsules in addition to employing normal preparation procedures to examine the outside structure of microcapsules. The capacity of the polymers which make up the matrix component to encapsulate molecules helps determine the functioning of the system, which is why SEM is crucial in the analysis of microencapsulation. The dimension span of vacant and bacterium-stuffed microcapsules, the micro-structure of the matrix, and any matrix alterations brought on by the encapsulated bacteria may all be learned via SEM. To fully describe the microstructure of the bacteria-loaded microcapsule, a variety of microscopy methods should be applied. In a similar vein, sugar beet pectin was investigated as a wall component for enveloping polyunsaturated fatty acid-rich fish oil. For the manufacture of emulsions with high oxidative stability, the composition and homogenization conditions were improved here.

5.4 Surfaces for Food Processing

Moreover, biofilm growth on surfaces used in food preparation has been investigated using SEM. On moist surfaces, microorganisms have a propensity to collect, expand into tiny colonies, and create biofilms. Despite the use of sanitizers, the microbes are shielded by the biofilms and have a higher chance of surviving. (Arun Prakash, V.R., et al. 2022) used SEM to examine how three distinct surface treatments for stainless steel affected the production of biofilm. The goal of the research was to lower the bacterial contents while refining in order to help equipment makers choose the materials and finishes that are most resistant to the production of bacterial films.

5.5 Packaging for Food

Food packaging is an essential part of the food business since it increases the amount of time food can be stored, allows for long-distance transportation, and appeals to consumers. Paper, fiberboards, composites, mixes, plastics, films, and other flexible and stiff materials are used to make packaging for the food business.

Understanding the use of the wrapping matter for diverse foodstuffs, cost analysis, and control in quality measures requires an understanding of their physical, chemical, and thermal nature as well as their impact on the environment. Internal and external quality control procedures are comprehensive in the food and beverage packaging production sectors. This is because flaws in the packing material would create complaints from consumers and a loss of the food's beneficial qualities. Due to its extraordinary capacity to enhance surfaces, SEM may be used to investigate problems like the examination of corrosion and/or leakage in a can or the assessment of a multilayered film. This reveals details of alterations in microscopic characteristics and particles which can influence packaging characteristics. For the purpose of identifying packaging flaws in relation to their optical characteristics, various mid and large scale packaging companies employ a wide range of examination, including visual analysis, stereomicroscope, X-ray diffraction, Raman spectroscopy, etc. Food technology professionals are increasingly using SEM to evaluate optical packaging materials at extreme magnification. The workhorse method for evaluating metals, including fractography, corrosion analysis, and alloy composition is SEM/EDS. The elemental composition of materials is provided via the EDS system.

A copper mesh contaminated with silicon is seen in Figure 4, an elemental map obtained using SEM/EDS assessment as a constituent contamination assessment study at Polymer Solutions, Virginia, USA. Cu, Si, and C are shown by the colors red, blue, and yellow respectively.

Biodegradable coatings and coatings manufactured from renewable and natural polymers, like and chitin, have recently attracted considerable attention. For a packaging material to be used in food packing, the barrier qualities, mechanical, and physical characteristics of the coatings are crucial. Biodegradable maize starch and chitosan composite coatings, which were discovered to possess superior qualities than cellophane, have been subjected to SEM testing to evaluate their physicochemical, water vapor barrier, and mechanical attributes.

5.6 Fruits and Vegetable Post-Harvest Modifications

In order to evaluate the quality of apple and apricot cells during storage, (Khine, E.E., et al. 2022) used SEM to capture images of the cells with varied degrees of turgor modification. SEM analysis was used

Figure 4. Cu mesh contaminated with Si

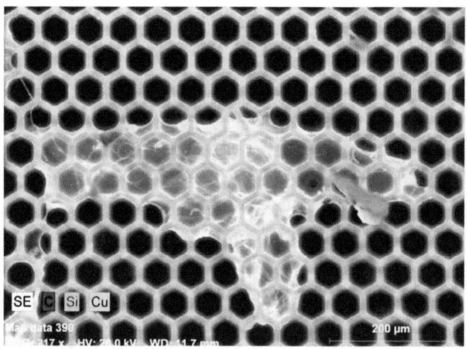

by the researchers to assess the physical modifications to the cell wall structure, including the cell extent to width ratio and the cell roundness index. The composition, cell wall content, and storage behavior of both Ca-processed and untreated Golden Delicious apples were examined by (Cebrián-Lloret, V., et al. 2023). Similar to this, (Yaqoob, M., et al. 2021) investigated the ultra-structure of the mature avocado fruit's mesocarp and modifications brought on by ripening.

(Karbuz, P., et al. 2021) used SEM to examine changes in the kiwi fruit's cell wall ultra-structure as it ripened (1992). The packing and cell size of the outer, inner, and core pericarps were found to vary. The amount of intercellular gaps grew as the fruit became softer. Both ripe fruit and fruit that was about to mature showed signs of middle lamella disintegration. The kiwi fruit underwent modifications in both its ultra-structure and chemical content. (Taskin, O., et al. 2022) used SEM technique to examine changes in microstructure of persimmon fruit after ripening and deastringency treatment. Similar to this, (Nawaz, M., et al. 2022) investigated alterations in texture, ultra-structure, and constituent following postharvest repository of mushrooms. The scientists noticed that the surface pilei tissue's hyphae cells' intercellular gap became larger during storage. Freshly harvested mushrooms' surface pilei tissue had hyphae with an ultrastructure that showed many vacuoles and cytoplasm with an intact structure. Following six days of preservation, the cytoplasm's structure and elements were broken down, leaving just the cell walls as a recognizable structure. Unquestionably, the decline of inflation and disruption of the mycelium cells revealed by scanning electron microscopy was caused by the destruction of cellular integrity. (Radulović, S., et al. 2022) examined the biochemical, structural, and cytochemical facets of the communication between chitosan and B. cinerea in tomato using SEM analysis.

(de Cassan, D., et al. 2019) investigated the impact of electron beam irradiation medication at doses more than 2.0 kGy on the qualitative characteristics of packed fresh capsicums. The fruits were examined for microstructural, sensory, and textural features at 0, 3, and 14 days of storage at 7°C and 68.3% relative humidity. (Liu, X., et al. 2021) used SEM to investigate the deactivation of Saccharomyces cerevisiae yeast in a cheese and fermented vegetables mixture by UV-C and low temperature. It was discovered that UV-C harmed membranes and eliminated esterase activity. Cells that had been exposed to UV-C and heat showed significant harm, coagulated inner constituent, disordered lumen, and in SEM pictures.

The gas diffusion in mushrooms at various stages of full-growth was examined by (Cheng, Pf., et al. 2022). Microstructural study using SEM (Doğan, K., et al. 2022) allowed researchers to notice changes in the skin's color, hardness of the pulp, and membrane integrity.

5.7 Other Food Items

Using shrimp paste powder as the base, (Modwi, A., et al. 2022) created protein-enriched squeeze out foodstuffs and utilized scanning electron microscopy investigation to map out cell structure delivery and the link between interior and composite features during extrusion processing. The researchers noticed that chitin fibrils in ribbon shrimp powder causes gas cells to prematurely break, which limits porosity and restricts snack expansion.

In order to increase the shelf life of foods, eatable films containing nano-emulsions and macro-capsules have been evaluated using SEM analysis. A carboxy methyl cellulose-dependent eatable coating was created by (Todan, L., et al. 2022) utilizing probiotic microorganisms, and its quality characteristics were evaluated. After 42 days of storage, they used SEM pictures to observe changes in the probiotic bacteria-containing edible films.

Short wave infrared radiation (SIR) (Chandan, R. R. et al. 2023), among other novel processing methods, has been used to enhance the aquatic enzymatic extraction of peanut oil. Scanning electron microscopy analysis showed that short wave infrared radiation disrupted the oil body membrane and cell microstructure, allowing oil extraction. Similar results were obtained for the essential oils from betel leaves and the microwave-assisted extraction of tiger nut oil. Moreover, SEM was utilized to characterize pullulan carboxy methyl cellulose electrospun nano-fibers loaded with tea polyphenols for fruit preservation. Scanning electron microscopy is moreover used to visualize sensitive bioactive chemicals that have been encapsulated for use in food.

6. CONCLUSION

SEM is effectively used to assess methods for incorporating physiologically active chemicals, like vacuum impregnation. SEM is being used more and more for antioxidants and bioactives like carotene in electrospun fibers. The manufacture of added-value biopolymer micro and nanofibers which shows great possibility for use in foodstuff and nutraceutical establishment and films, bio-active food packaging and the food processing organizations is therefore reported here as being evaluated using electron microscopy, a very useful technology.

REFERENCES

Arun Prakash, V. R., Xavier, J. F., Ramesh, G., Maridurai, T., Kumar, K. S., & Raj, R. B. S. (2022). Mechanical, thermal and fatigue behaviour of surface-treated novel *Caryota urens* fibre–reinforced epoxy composite. *Biomass Conversion and Biorefinery*, *12*(12), 5451–5461. doi:10.100713399-020-00938-0

Cebrián-Lloret, V., Martínez-Abad, A., López-Rubio, A., & Martínez-Sanz, M. (2023). Sustainable Bio-Based Materials from Minimally Processed Red Seaweeds: Effect of Composition and Cell Wall Structure. *Journal of Polymers and the Environment*, *31*(3), 886–899. doi:10.100710924-022-02648-2

Chandan, R. R., Soni, S., Raj, A., Veeraiah, V., Dhabliya, D., Pramanik, S., & Gupta, A. (2023). Genetic Algorithm and Machine Learning. Advanced Bioinspiration Methods for Healthcare Standards, Policies, and Reform. IGI Global, doi:10.4018/978-1-6684-5656-9

Cheng, P., Liang, M., Yun, X., & Dong, T. (2022). Biodegradable blend films of poly(ε-caprolactone)/poly(propylene carbonate) for shelf life extension of whole white button mushrooms. *Journal of Food Science and Technology*, *59*(1), 144–156. doi:10.100713197-021-04995-9 PMID:35068559

de Cassan, D., Hoheisel, A. L., Glasmacher, B., & Menzel, H. (2019). Impact of sterilization by electron beam, gamma radiation and X-rays on electrospun poly-(ε-caprolactone) fiber mats. *Journal of Materials Science. Materials in Medicine*, *30*(4), 42. doi:10.100710856-019-6245-7 PMID:30919082

Doğan, K., Özgün, M. İ., Sübütay, H., Salur, E., Eker, Y., Kuntoğlu, M., Aslan, A., Gupta, M. K., & Acarer, M. (2022). Dispersion mechanism-induced variations in microstructural and mechanical behavior of CNT-reinforced aluminum nanocomposites. *Archives of Civil and Mechanical Engineering*, *22*(1), 55. doi:10.100743452-022-00374-z

Elgendy, M. Y., Abdelsalam, M., Mohamed, S. A., & Ali, S. E. (2022). Molecular characterization, virulence profiling, antibiotic susceptibility, and scanning electron microscopy of *Flavobacterium columnare* isolates retrieved from Nile tilapia (*Oreochromis niloticus*). *Aquaculture International*, *30*(2), 845–862. doi:10.100710499-021-00819-x

Jayasingh, R., Kumar, J., Telagathoti, D. B., Sagayam, K. M., & Pramanik, S. (2022). Speckle noise removal by SORAMA segmentation in Digital Image Processing to facilitate precise robotic surgery. *International Journal of Reliable and Quality E-Healthcare*, *11*(1). doi:10.4018/IJRQEH.29508

Kanwal, A., Zhang, M., Sharaf, F., & Li, C. (2022). Enzymatic degradation of poly (butylene adipate co-terephthalate) (PBAT) copolymer using lipase B from Candida antarctica (CALB) and effect of PBAT on plant growth. *Polymer Bulletin*, *79*(10), 9059–9073. doi:10.100700289-021-03946-w

Karbuz, P., & Tugrul, N. (2021). Microwave and ultrasound assisted extraction of pectin from various fruits peel. *Journal of Food Science and Technology*, *58*(2), 641–650. doi:10.100713197-020-04578-0 PMID:33568858

Khine, E. E., Koncz-Horvath, D., Kristaly, F., Ferenczi, T., Karacs, G., Baumli, P., & Kaptay, G. (2022). Synthesis and characterization of calcium oxide nanoparticles for CO_2 capture. *Journal of Nanoparticle Research*, *24*(7), 139. doi:10.100711051-022-05518-z

Liu, X., Li, Y., Zhang, R., Huangfu, L., Du, G., & Xiang, Q. (2021). Inactivation effects and mechanisms of plasma-activated water combined with sodium laureth sulfate (SLES) against *Saccharomyces cerevisiae. Applied Microbiology and Biotechnology, 105*(7), 2855–2865. doi:10.100700253-021-11227-9 PMID:33738554

Modwi, A., Daoush, W. M., El-Eteaby, M., Aissa, M. A. B., Ghoniem, M. G., & Khairy, M. (2022). Fabrication and adsorption studies of paste/TiO$_2$ nanocomposites through recycling of spent dry batteries. *Journal of Materials Science Materials in Electronics, 33*(32), 24869–24883. doi:10.100710854-022-09197-3

Nawaz, M., Hassan, M. U., Chattha, M. U., Mahmood, A., Shah, A. N., Hashem, M., Alamri, S., Batool, M., Rasheed, A., Thabit, M. A., Alhaithloul, H. A. S., & Qari, S. H. (2022). Trehalose: A promising osmo-protectant against salinity stress—physiological and molecular mechanisms and future prospective. *Molecular Biology Reports, 49*(12), 11255–11271. doi:10.100711033-022-07681-x PMID:35802276

Pramanik, S. (2023). An Adaptive Image Steganography Approach depending on Integer Wavelet Transform and Genetic Algorithm. *Multimedia Tools and Applications, 2023.* doi:10.100711042-023-14505-y

Pramanik, S., & Suresh Raja, S. (2020). A Secured Image Steganography using Genetic Algorithm. *Advances in Mathematics: Scientific Journal, 9*(7), 4533–4541. doi:10.37418/amsj.9.7.22

Radulović, S., Sunkara, S., Rachel, R., & Leitinger, G. (2022). Three-dimensional SEM, TEM, and STEM for analysis of large-scale biological systems. *Histochemistry and Cell Biology, 158*(3), 203–211. doi:10.100700418-022-02117-w PMID:35829815

Sinha, M., Chacko, E., Makhija, P., & Pramanik, S. (2021). Energy Efficient Smart Cities with Green IoT. In C. Chakrabarty (Ed.), *Green Technological Innovation for Sustainable Smart Societies: Post Pandemic Era.* Springer. doi:10.1007/978-3-030-73295-0_16

Taskin, O., Polat, A., Etemoglu, A. B., & Izli, N. (2022). Energy and exergy analysis, drying kinetics, modeling, microstructure and thermal properties of convective-dried banana slices. *Journal of Thermal Analysis and Calorimetry, 147*(3), 2343–2351. doi:10.100710973-021-10639-z

Todan, L., Voicescu, M., Culita, D. C., Lincu, D., Ion, R. M., Călin, M., Răut, I., & Kuncser, A. C. (2022). A curcumin-loaded silica carrier with NH$_3$ sensitivity and antimicrobial properties. *Chemicke Zvesti, 76*(5), 3087–3096. doi:10.100711696-022-02090-7

Wu, Y., & Francis, L. F. (2017). Effect of particle size distribution on stress development and microstructure of particulate coatings. *Journal of Coatings Technology and Research, 14*(2), 455–465. doi:10.100711998-016-9866-5

Yaqoob, M., Sharma, S., & Aggarwal, P. (2021). Imaging techniques in Agro-industry and their applications, a review. *Journal of Food Measurement and Characterization, 15*(3), 2329–2343. doi:10.100711694-021-00809-w

Chapter 19
Glaucoma Assessment Using Super Pixel Classification

Sonali Dash
Chandigarh University, India

Priyadarsan Parida
GIET University, India

Vinay Kumar Nassa
Rajarambapu Institute of Technology, India

A. Shaji George
Business System Department, Almarai Company, Saudi Arabia

Aakifa Shahul
SRM Medical College, Kattankulathur, India

A. S. Hovan George
Tbilisi State Medical University, Georgia

ABSTRACT

A series of illnesses known as glaucoma harm the optic nerve in the eye. Glaucoma can cause lifelong blindness or vision loss if it is not addressed. Because glaucoma frequently has no symptoms in its early stages, it is particularly difficult. If symptoms start to show up, it might be too late to stop blindness. There are numerous ways to identify glaucoma, including tonometry, which measures the pressure inside the eye, ophthalmoscopy, which looks at the optic nerve's form and color, and perimeter, which measures the entire field of vision. However, because of the fact that each person's glaucoma is unique, these procedures do not allow for the detection of all forms of glaucoma. A visual assessment technique that can identify glaucoma is cup-to-disc ratio. By image processing methods like binarization the cup-to-disc ratio is calculated in this project and utilized to assess the glaucomatous status of an eye using super pixel classification.

DOI: 10.4018/978-1-6684-8618-4.ch019

INTRODUCTION

The terminology "glaucoma" refers to a series of eye illnesses that cause progressive and permanent damage to the optic nerve, the nerve in the eye that controls vision, and which, if left untreated, can cause permanent blindness. Increased ocular pressure is the key reasons, however even persons with normal eye pressure might develop glaucoma. The two most prevalent kinds of glaucoma, according to the WHO, are angle closure glaucoma (ACG), which is less frequent and typically manifests itself more severely, and primary open angle glaucoma (POAG), which starts off slowly and sneakily.

Glaucoma is the second most common cause of blindness in the world. The WHO estimates that glaucoma causes the blindness of 4.55 million people Minimum 12 million individuals in India are affected with glaucoma, which leaves about 1.2 million of them legally blind. In India, glaucoma is the main factor causing irreversible blindness. Over 90% of glaucoma cases in the general community are untreated. Glaucoma prevalence is influenced by age. Additionally, a new study estimates that the number of glaucoma patients in the nation is higher than what ophthalmologists believe (Traverso CE, et al. (2005)).

The human eye is a special sense organ that can take in visual information and send it to the brain. The result of attaching a significant amount of a huge, less strongly curved sphere to a small, strongly curved portion of a larger sphere, the eyeball is not a simple spherical. The cornea, which makes up about one-sixth of the whole structure, is the tiny, transparent section with a radius of 8 mm (0.3 inch). The scleral segment, which makes up the remaining portion, is opaque and has a radius of 12 mm (0.5 inch). The limbus is the ring that connects the two regions. Since the cornea is transparent, while looking directly into the eye from the front, one perceives a ring of tissue within the eye instead of the cornea due to the white sclera surrounding it.

There is a higher chance of glaucoma in older adults, although it can also be present before birth. Glaucoma can affect young adults as well. Particularly African Americans are more prone when they are younger. The most prevalent type of glaucoma, open-angle glaucoma, has almost no symptoms. Typically, increased ocular pressure causes little pain. Loss of vision starts with lateral or peripheral vision unconsciously compensating for this by moving our head to the side may prevent us from noticing anything until considerable vision loss has occurred (Iester M et al.(2002)). Getting examined is the greatest method to safeguard our vision from glaucoma. Treatment for glaucoma can start right away.

The eyeball is not a simple sphere, but rather the consequence of joining a sizable section of a large, less strongly curved sphere to a small, strongly curved portion of a larger sphere. The cornea is the small, transparent portion with a radius of 8 mm (0.3 inch), which makes up about one-sixth of the entire structure. The scleral segment, which makes up the remaining portion, is opaque and has a radius of 12 mm (0.5 inch). The limbus is the ring that connects the two regions. Since the cornea is transparent, while looking directly into the eye from the front, one perceives a ring of tissue within the eye instead of the cornea due to the white sclera surrounding it. Iris of the eye. The component that determines the color of the eye is the iris. The pupil is the term for this ring's centre. It appears gloomy because little or no light entering the eye is reflected back. The appearance of the inside lining of the globe can be discerned using an ophthalmoscope, a device that enables the view our to illuminate the interior of the eyeball while looking through the pupil. The major blood veins that carry blood to the retina are known as the fundus oculi, and they are particularly noticeable because they cross across the pallid optic disc, also known as the papilla, which is where the optic nerve fibres exit the eyeball (Janz NK, et al. (1998)).

Approximately 24 mm (about one inch) is the sagittal (vertical) diameter of the eye, and it is frequently smaller than the transverse diameter. Measurements of the eye are reasonably stable, varying by roughly a mm or two between healthy individuals. When a child is born, the sagittal diameter is roughly 16 to 17 mm (0.65 inch), but it quickly grows to 22.5 to 23 mm (0.89 inch) by the time they are three, and it achieves its maximum size between the ages of three and thirteen. It has a volume of approximately 6.5 cm3 and a weight of approximately 7.5 grammes (0.25 ounce) (0.4 cubic inch) (Herbert Gross, et al. (2008))

The aqueous fluid is encircled by the three coats of the eye, lens, and vitreous body, which are all optically transparent. The intermediate coat, which contains the majority of the eye's blood, is made up of the choroid, ciliary body, and iris, while the cornea and sclera make up the outermost coat. The choroid is where the retina, the body's thinnest layer, is found. The retina gets most of its sustenance from the choroid's blood vessels. Retinal vessels on the retina's surface provide the remaining sustenance; these vessels can be seen with an ophthalmoscope (Quigley, Harry A. (1993)).

To enable proper monitoring and treatment, as well as to reduce the risk of irreversible visual field loss, early identification of glaucoma is crucial. Considering that numerous studies have been performed and numerous more are being conducted in numerous locations across the globe, e decided to do something original in the sector as well.

The first researcher to describe and publish a photograph of the glaucomatous disc's ophthalmoscopic appearance is Eduard Jaeger, the son and grandson of eminent Austrian ophthalmologists. He misinterpreted the monocular indirect ophthalmoscopy relative depth clues and described (and drew) the glaucomatous disc as an enlargement of the papillary tissues relative to the surrounding retina (Sinthanayothin, Chanjira, et al. (2004)). A few months later, Albrecht von Graefe also went on record as having seen the papilla protrude in glaucoma. In his initial description of the glaucomatous disc, he provided a thorough explanation of the phenomena of retinal artery pulsing in the glaucomatous eye, which later proved to be a trustworthy and clinically practical observation. The term "halo glaucomatosus" refers to the ring-shaped region surrounding the "swollen" disc. By looking at the findings made in von Graefe's clinic, the issue of the allegedly bulging disc is resolved. Different observers couldn't agree upon ophthalmoscopic exams of a rabbit with a congenital fundus abnormality, i.e., a coloboma of uvea and of optic nerve, whether particular regions of the eye ground are elevated or depressed. Tissue flaws, or depressions, are discovered during the anatomical examination. Adolf Weber, one of von Graefe's assistants, is inspired to analyze the optics of monocular indirect ophthalmoscopy as a result. Adolf Weber eventually made substantial contributions to the knowledge of the mechanism of glaucoma. His examination of monocular indirect ophthalmoscopy showed numerous elements, some of which are optic and some of which are perception, which can lead to errors in estimating the fundus's relative depth.

Pathologic studies quickly supported the corrected ophthalmoscopic observation of a disc depression, which is then understood to be "pressure excavation," or the result of high pressure. This had a significant impact on von Graefe's thinking and led him to consider all known glaucoma symptoms in light of a potential connection to high pressure. Conducting this examination, he came to believe that the increased intraocular pressure is the "essence" of glaucoma rather than just a symptom (J. E. Valdez-Rodriguez, et al. (2021)).

In the decades that followed the development of the ophthalmoscope in the middle of the 19th century, glaucoma research advanced quickly. We are unaware of any prior accounts of neurosurgeon Harvey Cushing, MD's attempts to treat the disease while working at Johns Hopkins Hospital. The surgical records spanning the years 1896 to 1912 at the Johns Hopkins Hospital are examined. For the review, a case involving Cushing's unsuccessful surgical attempt to treat a patient with glaucoma is chosen. In 1905, Cushing removed the superior cervical ganglion from a patient who had previously undergone bilateral iridectomies and is thought to have chronic glaucoma with an acute episode. After the treatment, the patient indicated that his vision had stabilized and his pain had lessened. At the turn of the 20th century, renowned neurosurgeon Cushing began surgically treating glaucoma.

Sinthanayothin et al. presented the first technique for the automatic identification of the optic disc, fovea, and blood vessels from color fundus pictures in 1999. Automatic Classification has since been successfully reproduced by other organisations, and it is currently believed to be necessary for algorithm-based glaucoma diagnosis from fundus pictures. Classification and structured learning appear to be the most dependable ways for analyzing fundus photos to identify glaucoma, with stated accuracy of over 95% in producing a positive diagnosis (J. Cheng, J. Liu, et al.(2013)).

Additionally, glaucomatous and healthy eyes can be distinguished using artificial neural networks with characteristics like the cup-to-disc (C/D) ratio with an area under the receiver operating curve (AROC) of up to 0.90. AROC scores between 0.84 and 0.99 for glaucoma detection using DL algorithms have been reported by several groups. More recently, a startling sensitivity and specificity of 98% for the diagnosis of glaucoma was achieved by training a neural network on 1426 images of the fundus. 46 A detailed DL method has also been developed for calculating the degree of glaucomatous optic nerve damage from fundus images. By leveraging features from spectral-domain OCT pictures to train a DL algorithm, it demonstrates significant promise to predict neuroretinal damage from images of the optic disc.

Precise investigation and detection of glaucoma needs more control parameters such as verification of retinal nerve fiber layer (H. Fu, et al.(2018)). Visual field verification requires special equipment which is usually available only in tertiary hospitals, if they have a fundus camera and OCT.Calculating the cup-to-disc ratio is high-priced and tedious task presentlycarried out only by professionals. Thus, automated image detection and evaluation of glaucoma is extremely valuable. Methods for automatic image detection of the optic nerve head can be performed in two different ways (A. Geetha and N.B. Prakash (2022)).The first method can be done by image feature extraction for binary classification of normal and abnormal conditions, which is a challenging task.The second method is quite common and established on clinical indicators such as cup-to-disc ratio as well as inferior, superior, nasal, and temporal (ISNT) zones rule in the optic disc area . Valdez-Rodriguez et al. have classified the optical images to diagnose the glaucoma using Convolutional Neural Network (CNN) (Pandey,B.K et al.(2022)). Fu et al. have developed a CNN with four stage by locating and classifying the fundus image for glaucoma detection (S. Dash, S. et al.(2022)). Geetha and Prakash (2022) have developed a CNN model with transfer learning for classifying fundus image to diagnose glaucoma. Jyotika et al.(2020) have recommended glowworm swarm optimization technique for detecting optic cup to diagnose glaucoma automatically (Pandey, D., & Pandey, B. K. (2022)). Dash et al. have suggested glaucoma detection through computing Cup to Disk ratio (CDR) and Rim to Disk Ratio (RDR) (Dubey, Shiv Ram et al. (2022)).

Materials and Methods

The propsed method intially starts with using traditional U-Net of CNN with activation function RelU. Afterwards various activation functions such as Sigmoid, TanH, and ELU are utilized to improve the classification accuracy. Then guided filter is used to improve the features and to improve the classification accuracy. It employs VGG-16 for feature extraction and softmax layer for classification. The detailed are explained in below section.

Figure 1. Example of classification model of deep learning

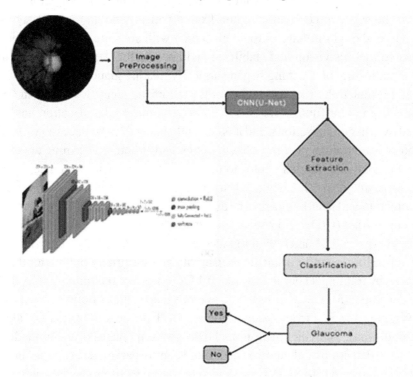

Figure 2. Procedural steps of the suggested technique

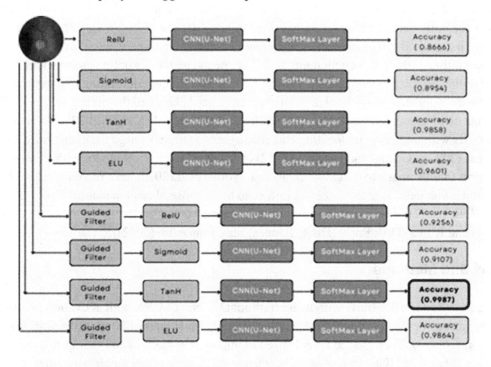

Considering the various methods available and the task at hand it was important to improve the available Networks and for that we had to make comparison.

As we can see in the Flowchart below in total 8 different networks are deployed out of which 4 are using a guided filter for the input images.

Medical practitioners frequently refer to glaucoma as "silent robbery of sight" since it damages the optic nerve head and reduces peripheral vision as a result. Early glaucoma detection and classification will allow patients to receive the right care and help from their eye surgeons, improving their quality of life. The huge number of potential patients and the small pool of available ophthalmologists is a significant challenge in the management of health care. In this suggested work, a glaucoma early detection approach is put forth to help an ophthalmologist make an early diagnosis of the condition. A deep convolutional neural network analyses an image and is often used to find low-, mid-, and high-level properties.

- **Classification of Images**

Image Classification is a method that splits a digital image into a number of smaller groupings known as Image segments, which makes the original image less complicated and thus easier to manage or analyse in the future. Simply put, categorization is the process of assigning labels to pixels. Each pixel or element of a picture that falls under the same category has its own unique name. Consider the following scenario as an illustration: The input for object detection must be a photo. Instead of looking at the entire image, a portion of the image chosen by the classification system can be supplied into the detector. Through this the detector will only process a portion of the image, saving time during inference .

1. Retinal Image Data Set and Pre-Processing

Contrary to the enormous number of vascular Classification datasets and datasets for diabetic retinopathy, there are very few public datasets for glaucoma assessment. Public datasets that only support OD Classification include Rim-one and Drions-db. The majority of the 169 photos in Rim-one are normal, and each one has undergone five hand Classifications. Drions-db has 110 photos, each of which includes two manual annotations. Together, OD and cup Classification, two significant components of ONH Classification, serve as the foundation for glaucoma assessment. Cup Classification algorithms will be evaluated using a reference dataset, according to. The public cannot access it for free.

There are 101 images in the DRISHTI-GS dataset. It is split into 51 testing images and 50 training images.

- **Image Acquisition**

All photos are taken with the guests' permission at the Arvind Eye Hospital in Madurai. Clinical investigators chose patients with glaucoma based on their examination's clinical results. Ages of the chosen patients ranged from 40 to 80, with a fairly equal number of men and women. The normal class is selected from patients who are undergoing standard refraction testing and did not have glaucoma.

All photographs are taken while the subject's eyes are dilated and are all captured using the PNG uncompressed image format, centered on the OD, with a 30-degree field of view and a size of 2896 1944 pixels. Other than this, there are no other imaging restrictions placed on the acquisition procedure. Four sources of ground truth are gathered for each photograph.

Figure 3. Maps with soft Classification samples and marks. 4 black expert marks for the OD (left) and cup in the top row (right)OD (red) and cup (green) borders were averaged,soft classification maps in the bottom row

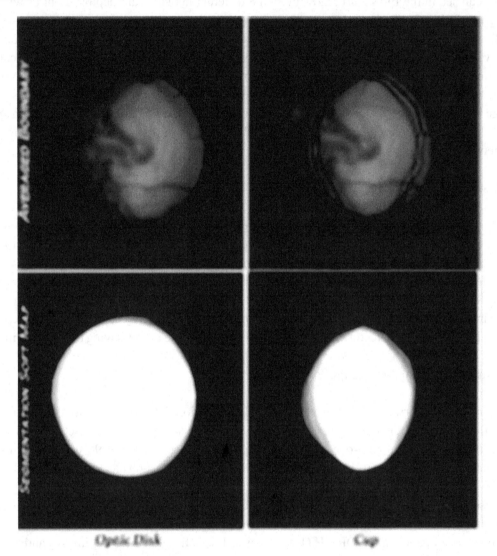

Region Boundary: Average boundaries are determined from the manually drawn borders for both the OD and cup regions. The average boundary is calculated by averaging the manual markings in each of the 80 equal angular sectors that the disc centre divides the image region into. A total of pixel locations {x, y} conforming to the averaged boundaries of the OD and cup are contained in two separate text files with the name Image Name RegionTypeAvgBoundary.txt.

Classification of Map softly: Four expert manual Classifications are combined to create a soft map B (p) for the OD and cup regions. B can have values ranging from 0 to 1, with 0 and 1 denoting complete disagreement and agreement that p is a border point, respectively. The same is true for B 0:75, which denotes agreement amongst at least three experts. Classification soft maps in.PNG file format are offered

Figure 4. Examples of images from training set for healthy eyes

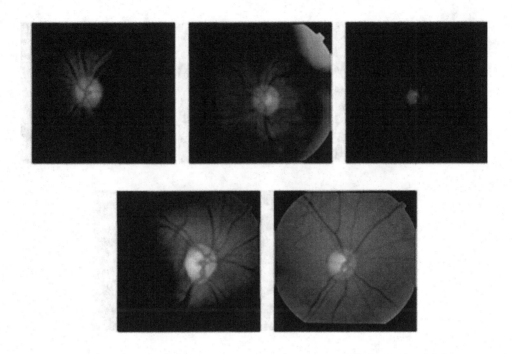

Figure 5. Examples of images from training set for glaucomatous eyes

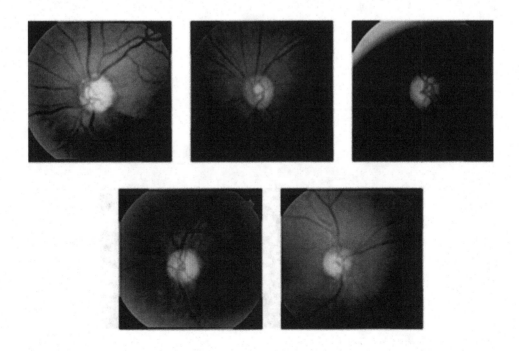

Figure 6. Examples of images from testing set for healthy eyes

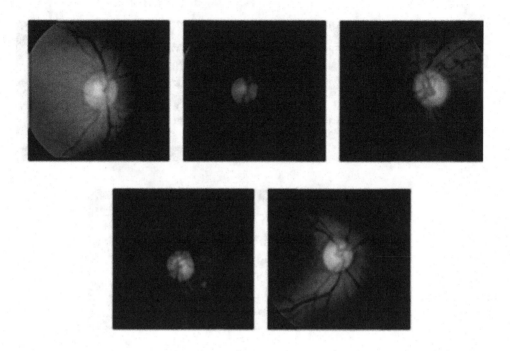

Figure 7. Examples of images from testing set for glaucomatous eyes

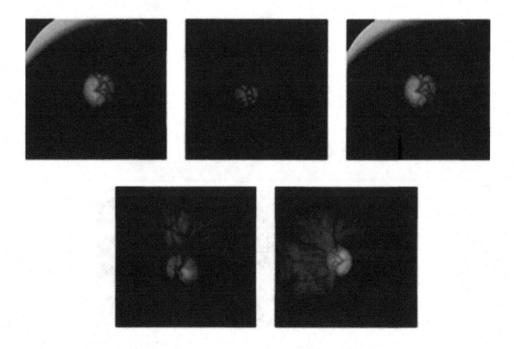

Figure 8. Fundus images after applying Guided filter

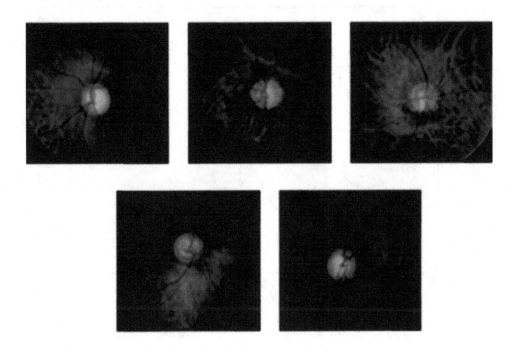

for the OD and cup regions of each image. Figure 3's bottom row displays example Classification soft maps for the OD and cup region (Sharma, M., et al.(2023)).

In the fig 4 we can see few examples of the healthy eyes from the training set. In the fig 5 we can see few examples of the Glaucomatous eyes from the training set. In the fig 6 we can see few examples of the Healthy eyes from the testing set. In the fig 7 we can see few examples of the Glaucomatous eyes from the testing set

In Figure 8 we can see few examples of the fundus image after applying the guided filter.

2. Activation functions

The weighted total is determined by the activation function, which then adds bias to it to determine whether or not to activate a neuron. The goal of the activation function is to increase the nonlinearity of a neuron's output. We are aware that the weight, bias, and individual activation functions of each neuron in the neural network determine how well they function. A neural network's weights and biases for each neuron would be adjusted based on the output error. Back-propagation is the name of this procedure. Activation functions enable back-propagation by providing the gradients and error required since weights must be updated accordingly (Pandey, B. K., et al.(2023)).

Figure 9. Sigmoid function curve

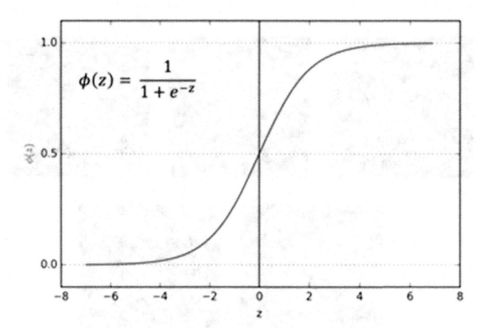

- **Activation Functions utilized in the proposed models-**

1. Sigmoid or Logistic Activation Function

The Sigmoid Function curve appears to be in the shape of a S. The sigmoid function is used in part because it occurs between (0 to 1). Since the output of such models is a probability prediction, they are particularly used in this context. Due to the fact that anything only has a probability of occurring between 0 and 1, the sigmoid is the best choice.

The function might take on a variety of forms. We can thus determine the sigmoid curve's slope between any two locations. The derivative is not monotonic, despite the function being monotonic. A neural network may become stuck during training if it uses the logistic sigmoid function. Softmax functionality, Multiclass classification uses a more broadly based logistic activation function (Pandey, B. K., et al. (2021)).

2. Tanh or hyperbolic tangent Activation Function

Tanh is comparable to a better logistic sigmoid. The tanh function has a range of between (-1 to 1). Tanh is sigmoidal as well (s - shaped). The tanh graph will map the zero inputs close to zero and the negative inputs strongly negative, which is a benefit of this.

The function could take many different shapes. Although the derivative of the function is not mono-tone, the function itself is. Most often, the tanh function is employed to divide data into two groups (Fan, Engui. et al. (2004)).

Figure 10. Tanh vs. Sigmoid function curve

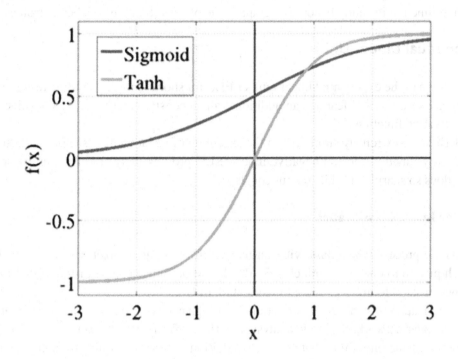

ReLU (Rectified Linear Unit) Activation Function

The activation function that is currently used most commonly worldwide is the ReLU. Considering that nearly all deep learning or convolutional neural networks use it. The range is from 0 to infinity. Its derivative and the behavior of the function are monotonic.

Figure 11. ReLU vs. Sigmoid function curve

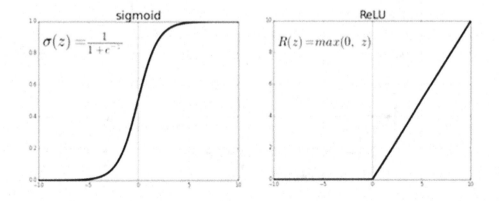

The issue is that because all negative values quickly become zero, it is more difficult for the model to fit the data appropriately or to be trained from it. Or, to put it another way, each negative input to the ReLU activation function instantly becomes a graph value of zero (Schmidt-Hieber, Johannes. (2004)).

ELU (Exponential Linear Unit)

The function known as the exponential linear unit, or ELU for short, tends to converge to zero faster and yield more precise results. ELU features an additional alpha constant that must be a positive quantity, unlike other activation functions.

ELU and RELU are extremely similar, with the exception of negative inputs. Both of these take the form of an identity function for non-negative inputs. ELU progressively smooths out, as opposed to RELU, which does so sharply, until its output equals .

- **U-Net: for Image Classification**

In the semantic process when classifying an image, also known as pixel-based classification, we categorise each pixel into one of several classes. Roads and buildings can be distinguished from other land cover types in satellite imagery using classification in GIS.

The initial application of U-net is classification. Its design can be summed up as an encoder network followed by a decoder network. Semantic analysis is different from classification, where the deep network's final output is the only thing that counts. In addition to pixel-level discrimination, a technique for projecting the discriminative features that are learned throughout the encoder's many phases onto the pixel space is needed for classification.

Figure 12. U-Net architecture

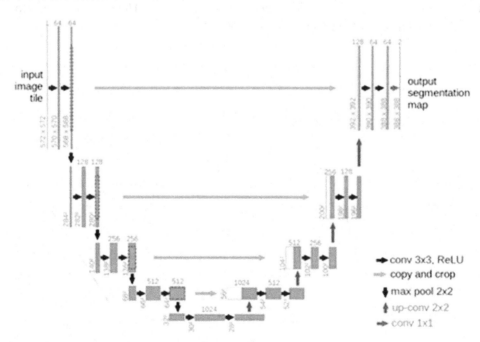

Encoder is located in the first half of the architecture diagram. It is often a pre-trained classification network like VGG/ResNet where convolution blocks are applied followed by a maxpool down sampling to encode the input image into feature representations at many distinct levels (Iliev, A., et al.(2017)).

The decoder is the second element of the architecture. By semantically projecting the discriminative characteristics (lower resolution) learned by the encoder onto the pixel space, the goal is to provide a dense classification (higher resolution). Concatenation, up sampling.

This architecture features multilayer skip connections that connect a contracting path on the left and an expansive way on the right (middle). The final layer, which follows the expanding path, produces predictions using retinal fundus images as input to the contracting path. Before using a rectified linear activation unit, which has the functional form $f(z) = max$, each filter bank in a convolution layer applies three 3 by 3 padded convolutions $(0, z)$. Three convolutional blocks are present in both the contracting and expanding paths. Two convolutional layers follow a block in the contracting route. a layer with a pool size of two (2) and maximum pooling. Two convolutional layers, a dropout layer, and a 2 2 up sampling layer are all present in a block, and a concatenation of the matching block and the contracting path (i.e., a merged layer). The linking path contains two convolutional layers. A 1 1 convolutional layer with a sigmoid activation and one filter to generate pixel-wise class scores makes up the final output layer. Each convolution layer in blocks 1, 2, and 3 has 112, 224, and 448 filters in the contracting path, but the expansive paths of blocks 5, 6, and 7 contain 224, 122, and 122 filters, respectively. The connection path's 448 filters are distributed throughout each convolutional layer (Deepa, R.,et al. (2022)).

Figure 13. U-Net for classification of fundus images

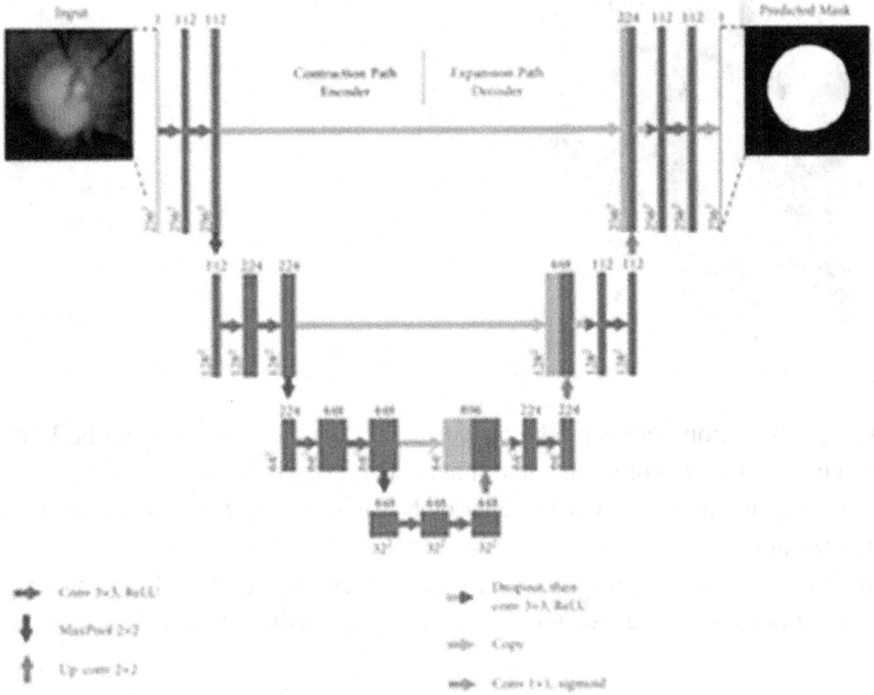

- **Feature Extraction from Pretrained CNN Architecture**

The method of feature extraction keeps the information from the original data collection while transforming raw data into manageable numerical characteristics. It yields superior results when compared to utilising machine learning on the raw data directly.

Manual or automated feature extraction is possible. Manual feature extraction requires both the development of an extraction technique as well as the identification and description of the qualities that are relevant to a specific situation. Having a firm understanding of the context or domain can frequently help in deciding which traits might be beneficial.

Deep networks or specialised algorithms can automatically extract information from signals or pictures. Automated feature extraction eliminates the need for human participation. This approach can be quite useful when we need to swiftly transition from gathering raw data to developing machine learning algorithms (Ramachandran et al. (2017)).

The initial layers of deep networks have primarily taken on the task of feature extraction with the emergence of deep learning, albeit mostly for picture data. The first challenge that necessitates a high level of expertise is feature extraction before creating powerful prediction models for signal and time-series applications (Sivaswamy, J. et al. (2014)).

1. VGG-16

Figure 14. Example of Vgg-16

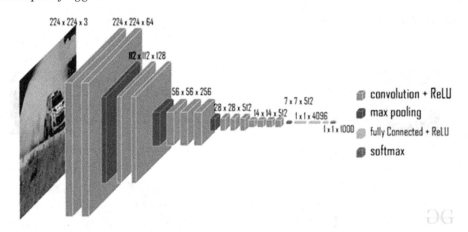

Approximately 14 million photos modeling into 22,000 categories make up the ImageNet dataset, which was used to train the convolutional neural network VGG16. Very Deep Convolutional Networks for Large-Scale Image Recognition, a 2015 paper by K. Simonyan and A. Zisserman(2015), makes this model recommendation.

GG16, which includes photographs of vehicles, has been trained on millions of images. Its taught weights and convolutional layers can recognize common features like edges, colors, wheels, windshields, etc.

Figure 15. VGG16 model architecture

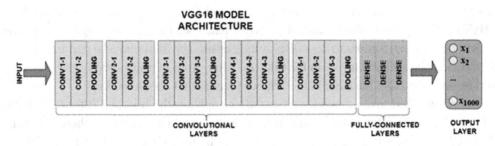

Our photos will be sent through the convolutional layers of VGG16, which will provide a Feature Stack containing the recognized visual features. From this point, it is simple to flatten the three-dimensional feature stack into a NumPy array, making it ready for any modeling we choose to do (Sonali Dash et al. (2021)).

VGG Architecture: The network is fed with a dimensioned image (224, 224, 3). The first two layers include the same padding and 64 channels with a 3*3 filter size. Following a max pool layer of stride (2, 2), two layers have convolution layers of 128 filter size and filter size (3, 3). A max-pooling stride (2, 2) layer that is the same as the layer preceding it comes next. Then, 256 filters with filter widths of 3 and 3 are distributed over 2 convolution layers. After that, there are two sets of three convolution layers, and then a max pool layer comes next. Each filter contains 512 filters and the same padding (3, 3). We employ 3*3 filters in these convolution and max-pooling layers instead of 7*7 filters, ZF-11*11 Net, and AlexNet layers. Additionally, some of the layers use 1*1 pixels to change the number of input channels. After each convolution layer, 1-pixel padding is applied to prevent the image's spatial characteristic. After adding a convolution and max-pooling layer to the stack, we got a (7, 7, 512) feature map. To construct a feature vector with the value 1, 25088, this result is flattened. There are then three layers that are entirely linked to one another. The first layer outputs a vector with a length of (1, 4096) and the second layer also generates a vector. It takes the most recent feature vector as input.

The Softmax function is used to categorise 1000 classes in the third fully linked layer. A vector of size (1, 4096) is also produced by the second layer, and the third layer produces 1000 channels. Every hidden layer uses ReLU as its activation function. ReLU is more computationally effective since it encourages speedier learning and reduces the possibility of vanishing gradient problems (Venkatesh, Svetha, and Robyn Owens (2002)).

Guided Filter

An edge-preserving smoothing light filter is known as a guided filter. Similar to a bilateral filter, it can keep sharp edges while removing noise or texture. The guided image filter has two benefits over the bilateral filter: While guided image filters use simpler algorithms with linear computational complexity, bilateral filters have high computational complexity. Sometimes, bilateral filters introduce undesirable gradient reversal artefacts and distort the image. The linear combination-based guided image filter maintains the gradient direction of the guiding picture in the output image, preventing gradient reversal. Filtering with edge preservation when the filtering input p and the guiding image are identical. The guided filter maintains sharp edges while removing noise from the input image (Sonali Dash et al. (2022))

To be more precise, a "flat patch" or a guided filter's option display style epsilon can be used to specify a "high variance patch." Patches with variances significantly lower than the value of the parameter "display style epsilon epsilon" will be smoothed, while patches with variances significantly greater than this value will be retained. Similar to how displaystyle epsilon epsilon played a part in the guided filter; the range variance plays a similar role in the bilateral filter. Both of them specify the noise/flat patches that should be smoothed and the edge/high variance patches that should be kept.

The edges of an image may contain artefacts after applying the bilateral filter (Sonali Dash et al. (2018)) .This is due to the sharp shift in pixel value at the edge. Due to edges, these artefacts are both inevitable and difficult to avoid and appear in a variety of images. Gradient reversal is better avoided by the guided filter. Additionally, in some circumstances, it is possible to guarantee that gradient reversal won't happen.

It is possible to transfer the structure from the guidance displaystyle II to the output display style qq thanks to the local linear model of display style q=aI+b. Some specialised filtering-based applications, such feathering, matting, and dehazing, are made possible by this characteristic.

RESULTS AND DISCUSSIONS

Implementation of the Solution

For the final implementation of the solution we used Kaggle as it provides a very flexible environment and supports Python and R which are very versatile and general purpose language.

Figure 16. Fundusimage with OD and OC mask applied

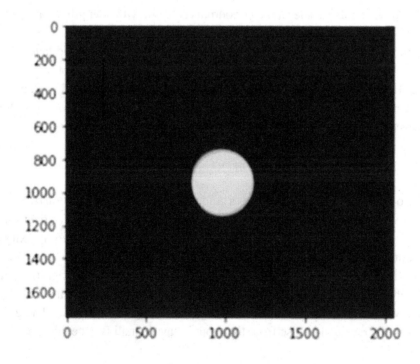

Figure 17. Fundus images with all masks applied and neatly displayed

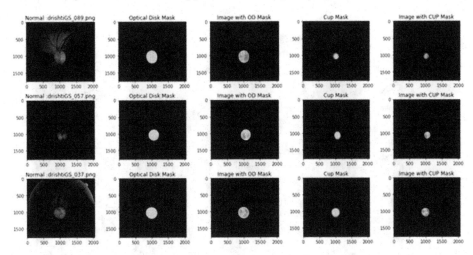

Figure 18. An example of fundus image after passing through the guided filter

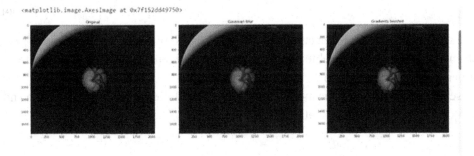

Table 1. Results obtained from the suggested method

Method	Epoch 1	Epoch 2	Epoch 3	Epoch 4	Epoch 5
UNet (Sigmoid)	0.8954	0.8951	0.8949	0.8956	0.8957
UNet (Relu)	0.8666	0.8657	0.8650	0.8663	0.8660
UNet (TanH)	0.9858	0.9851	0.9852	0.9854	0.9859
UNet (Elu)	0.9601	0.9594	0.9607	0.9600	0.9603
Guided filter+UNet (Sigmoid)	0.9101	0.9089	0.9103	0.9094	0.9107
Guided filter+UNet (Relu)	0.9256	0.9251	0.9250	0.9257	0.9256
Guided filter+UNet (Tanh)	**0.9981**	**0.9985**	**0.9899**	**0.9987**	**0.9987**
Guided filter+UNet (Elu)	0.9876	0.9868	0.9858	0.9848	0.9838

Figure 19. Graphical representation of the accuracy

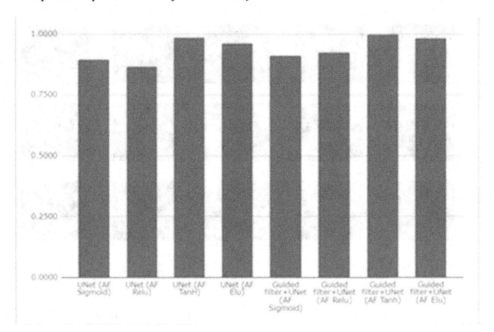

Table 1 shows the difference in accuracy for the different Activation Functions and With Added mask.

As observed from the above table 1 we can see the difference in performance of the model when different parameters are applied to it.

It is observed the accuracy of the model is at its lowest with RelU Activation function and it is highest with the added mask and Tanh activation function.

CONCLUSION

The Suggested Method for classification utilizes U-Net for feature extraction but unlike the original network we utilized different Activation function and added a Guided filter for the images within the dataset

As we can observe in the Table 4.1 Conventional Method with activation function ReLu, gives an average of 0.8659accuracy for the epochs observed in the table the activation function Sigmoid following performing slightly better with an average accuracy of 0.8953.

After changing the activation function we start to see improvement in the accuracy of the model where with Activation function Tanh it performed remarkably well with an average accuracy of 0.9855 which seems small but in reality is a significant improvement over the original method 8

For even further improvement A Guided filter is added to further enhance the images which once again can be observed in the output table, with Guided Filter accuracy for the original method increased but highest accuracy result is observed in the Activation Function TanH with guided filter applied, with average accuracy of **0.9968**

So the suggested method outperforms the original UNet network.

The work can be extended by using different CNN networks for future work. Additionally other enhancement and denoising techniques can be considered for feature enhancement. For example; homomorphic filter, anisotropic filter DWT (Discrete wavelet transform), Small scale retinex, multi scale retinex etc. Also in the future researchers should consider the Classification part using the same model for calculation of cup to disc ratio (CDR) and rim to disc ratio (RDR) to detect the Glaucomatic conditions of the fundus image.

REFERENCES

Cheng, J., Liu, J., Xu, Y., Yin, F., Wong, D. W. K., Tan, N.-M., Tao, D., Cheng, C.-Y., Aung, T., & Wong, T. Y. (2013). Superpixel classification based optic disc and optic cup segmentation for glaucoma screening. *IEEE Transactions on Medical Imaging*, *32*(6), 1019–1032. doi:10.1109/TMI.2013.2247770 PMID:23434609

Dash, S., Senapati, M. R., & Jena, U. R. (2018). K-NN based automated reasoning using Bilateral Filter Based Texture Descriptor for computing Texture Classification. *Egyptian Informatics Journal*, *19*(2), 133–144. doi:10.1016/j.eij.2018.01.003

Dash, S., Verma, S., Bevinakoppa, M., Wozniak, J. H., & Ijaz, M. (2022). Guidance image-based enhanced matched filter with modified thresholding for blood vessel extraction. *Symmetry 14*(2), 194.

Deepa, R., Anand, R., Pandey, D., Pandey, B. K., & Karki, B. (2022). Comprehensive performance analysis of classifiers in diagnosis of epilepsy. *Mathematical Problems in Engineering*, *2022*, 2022. doi:10.1155/2022/1559312

Dubey, S. R., Singh, S. K., & Chaudhuri, B. B. (2022). Activation functions in deep learning: A comprehensive survey and benchmark. *Neurocomputing*, *503*, 92–108. doi:10.1016/j.neucom.2022.06.111

Fan, E. (2004). Extended tanh-function method and its applications to nonlinear equations. *Physics Letters A*, *4*(5), 212-218.

Fu, H., Cheng, J., Xu, Y., Zhang, C., Wong, D. W. K., Liu, J., & Cao, X. (2018). Disc-aware ensemble nework for glaucoma screening from fundus image. *IEEE Transactions on Medical Imaging*, *37*(11), 2493–2501. doi:10.1109/TMI.2018.2837012 PMID:29994764

Geetha, A., & Prakash, N. B. (2022). Classification of glaucoma in retinal images using efficient B4 deep learning model. *Computer Systems Science and Engineering*, *43*(3), 1041–1055. doi:10.32604/csse.2022.023680

Gross, H. (2008). *Fritz Blechinger, Bertram Achtner. Handbook of Optical Systems: Survey of Optical Instruments* (Vol. 4). Human Eye. doi:10.1002/9783527699247

Iester, M., & Zingirian, M. (2002). Quality of life in patients with early, moderate and advanced glaucoma. *Eye (London, England)*, *16*(1), 44–49. doi:10.1038j.eye.6700036 PMID:11913887

Iliev, A., Kyurkchiev, N., & Markov, S. (2017). On the Approximation of the step function by some sigmoid functions. *Mathematics and Computers in Simulation*, *133*, 223–234. doi:10.1016/j.matcom.2015.11.005

Janz, N. K., Wren, P. A., Guire, K. E., Musch, D. C., Gillespie, B. W., & Lichter, P. R. (1998). Collaborative Initial Glaucoma Treatment Study. Fear of blindness in the Collaborative Initial Glaucoma Treatment Study: Patterns and correlates over time. *Ophthalmology*, *114*(12), 2213–2220. doi:10.1016/j.ophtha.2007.02.014 PMID:17490746

Jyotika, P., Kavita, K., & Arora, S. (2020). Optic cup segmentation from retinal fundus images using glow swarm optimization for glaucoma detection. *Biomedical Signal Processing and Control*, *60*, 1–12.

Kumar Pandey, B., Pandey, D., Nassa, V. K., Ahmad, T., Singh, C., George, A. S., & Wakchaure, M. A. (2022). Encryption and steganography-based text extraction in IoT using the EWCTS optimizer. *Imaging Science Journal*, 1–19.

Pandey, B. K., Pandey, D., Gupta, A., Nassa, V. K., Dadheech, P., & George, A. S. (2023). Secret data transmission using advanced morphological component analysis and steganography. In *Role of Data-Intensive Distributed Computing Systems in Designing Data Solutions* (pp. 21–44). Springer International Publishing. doi:10.1007/978-3-031-15542-0_2

Pandey, B. K., Pandey, D., Wariya, S., & Agarwal, G. (2021). A deep neural network-based approach for extracting textual images from deteriorate images. *EAI Endorsed Transactions on Industrial Networks and Intelligent Systems*, *8*(28), e3–e3. doi:10.4108/eai.17-9-2021.170961

Pandey, D., & Pandey, B. K. (2022). An Efficient Deep Neural Network with Adaptive Galactic Swarm Optimization for Complex Image Text Extraction. In *Process Mining Techniques for Pattern Recognition* (pp. 121–137). CRC Press. doi:10.1201/9781003169550-10

Quigley, Harry A. (1993). Open-angle glaucoma. *New England Journal of Medicine*, *15*, 1097-1106.

Ramachandran, P., Zoph, B., & Le, Q. V. (2017). *Searching for activation functions*.

Schmidt-Hieber, J. (2004). Nonparametric regression using deep neural networks with ReLU activation function. The Annals of Statistics, 4, 1875-1897.

Sharma, M., Sharma, B., Gupta, A. K., & Pandey, D. (2023). Recent developments of image processing to improve explosive detection methodologies and spectroscopic imaging techniques for explosive and drug detection. *Multimedia Tools and Applications*, *82*(5), 6849–6865. doi:10.100711042-022-13578-5

Sinthanayothin, C., Boyce, J. F., Cook, H. L., & Williamson, T. H. (2004). Automated localisation of the optic disc, fovea, and retinal blood vessels from digital colour fundus images. British journal of ophthalmology, 8, 902-910.

Sivaswamy, J., Krishnadas, S. R., Joshi, G. D., Jain, M., & Tabish, A. U. S. (2014, April). Drishti-gs: Retinal image dataset for optic nerve head (onh) segmentation. In 2014 *IEEE 11th international symposium on biomedical imaging* (ISBI), vol. 4, pp. 53-56, IEEE, 2014.

Sonali Dash, P. S. R. Chowdary, VSSS Chakraborty, GupteswarSahu et al., Real Time Retinal Optic Disc Segmentation via Guided filter and Discrete Wavelet Transform, third international conference on emerging electrical energy, electronics and computing technologies 2021 (ice4ct 2021, 16th-17th December 2021, Malaysia.

Sonali Dash, P. S. R. (2022). *Chowdary, Dr. C. V. Gopal Raju, Dr. Y. Umamaheswar, KJN Siva Charan, Optic Disc Segmentation based on Active Contour model for Detection and Evaluation of Glaucoma on Real Time Challenging Dataset, In proceedings of Theory and Applications (FICTA 2021)*. Springer.

Traverso, C. E., Walt, J. G., Kelly, S. P., Hommer, A. H., Bron, A. M., Denis, P., & ... . (2005). Direct costs of glaucoma and severity of the disease: A multinational long term study of resource utilisation in Europe. *The British Journal of Ophthalmology*, *89*(10), 1245–1249. doi:10.1136/bjo.2005.067355 PMID:16170109

Valdez-Rodriguez, J. E., Felipe-Riveron, E. M., & Calvo, H. (2021). Optic Disc preprocessing for reliable glaucoma detection in small dataset. *Mathematics*, *9*(2237), 1–14. doi:10.3390/math9182237

Venkatesh, S., & Owens, R. "On the classification of image features." Pattern Recognition Letters 11, vol. 5, pp. 339-349, 2002.

Chapter 20
Healthcare Cloud Services in Image Processing

Vivek Veeraiah
Adichunchanagiri University, India

Dolly John Shiju
R.D. Memorial College of Nursing, India

J.V.N. Ramesh
Koneru Lakshmaiah Education Foundation, India

Ganesh Kumar R.
CHRIST University (Deemed), India

Sabyasachi Pramanik
Haldia Institute of Technology, India

Digvijay Pandey
Department of Technical Education, Government of Uttar Pradesh, India

Ankur Gupta
Vaish College of Engineering, Rohtak, India

ABSTRACT

Technology has been fundamental in defining, advancing, and reinventing medical practises, equipment, and drugs during the last century. Although cloud computing is quite a newer concept, it is now one of the most often discussed issues in academic and therapeutic contexts. Many academics and healthcare persons are focused in providing vast, conveniently obtainable, and reconstruct assets like virtual frameworks, platforms, and implementations having lesser business expenditures. As they need enough assets to operate, store, share, and utilise huge quantity of healthcare data, specialists in the field of medicine are transferring their operations in the cloud. Major issues about the application of cutting-edge cloud computing in medical imaging are covered in this chapter. The research also takes into account the ethical and security concerns related to cloud computing.

DOI: 10.4018/978-1-6684-8618-4.ch020

INTRODUCTION

The term "cloud computing" describes the ability for accessing computer assets through the Internet for the repository, assemblage, and recovery of data as well as the ability to exploit on the data using software and computing methods. Cloud computing (Alam, A., 2023) offers scalable, adaptable, and on-demand computer resources from far-flung places. Extensive data processing implementations, like in healthcare, and research applications involving several researchers at various universities also benefit greatly from it. It could end up being a crucial tool in the search for alternatives to clinical trials for the biomedical (Reid, L. 2021) industry's assessment of novel medications and technologies. There are several cloud computing services that may be used for research purposes.

The issue of offering complicated assistance and data exchange via the Internet is being addressed by cloud computing. With tools like Gmail, Google Docs, Dropbox, etc., it has gained widespread adoption and is now a part of our everyday lives. Fast networks are becoming more widely available and their costs are constantly falling, getting it financially attainable to access vast quantities of data remotely and in real-life. This is why cloud computing is becoming more and more successful. It is an extended version of the basic framework and technology for controlling the allocation of assets on a physical network and has expanded on concepts and technologies originally created for other endeavours, such as grid computing. The primary distinction between grid (Ankita, M. et al. 2022) and cloud computing is based on how they are oriented differently. While grids seek to facilitate computing capacity comparable to huge distributed and parallel hyper-performance computing systems, cloud computing is addressing Internet-scale computing's storage and application accessibility restrictions. Cloud computing places a strong emphasis on the virtualization of shared resources, but grids are most useful when managing workload allocation and implementation parallelizing is of the utmost importance. Moreover, whereas grid operations are built primarily on parallelization and workflow management programming, cloud-dependent apps are constructed basically on web technologies (Javascript, ASP.NET, HTML, CSS etc) (Turner, C., 2022). Cloud services are more user-friendly since they make use of popular, standardised constituents. But what precisely does "cloud computing" signify? Is it helpful in everyday life and in medical field, and if so, why and when? What are the advantages and disadvantages of distributed computing platforms on the Internet cloud? Here, the authors make an effort for providing answers to the fundamental concerns as well as an overview of the most significant applications and moral issues raised by this novel method of manipulating healthcare data through globally dispersed computers.

The definition of cloud computing has been attempted by a number of writers.

Since each definition is targeted at a certain application, they are still not all relevant to all situations. This makes sense given the relative youth of cloud computing and the divergent perspectives held by scientists and engineers from diverse disciplines. The phrase is derived from the cloud metaphor that is often utilized in figures to describe a network infrastructure at the foundation. The term "cloud" refers to benefits and data which are not present on computers, servers, or various local nodes but instead exist in a virtual repository that is accessible to and used by any individual, any computer, and everywhere in the globe.

1. Cloud services

The Internet-based distribution of diverse services to end customers is the core idea behind cloud computing. These services include every aspect of ICT technologies (Gupta, P. et al., 2022), from soft-

Figure 1. Various varieties of cloud services

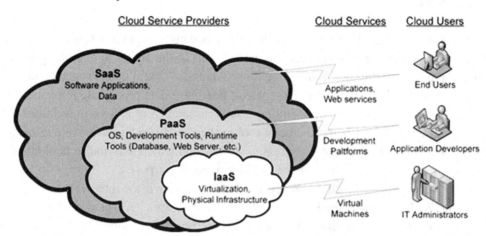

ware applications to a virtual hardware (Marks, B., et al., 2022) framework. The end user may remotely access and customise every service via a web browser. In order to provide safe methods to cooperate, secure control and communication solutions are required given that user data is exposed to a network that may be accessed from anywhere in the globe. The phrase "cloud computing" began to be utilized by members of the IT fraternity in the latter half of 2007. In fact, a number of significant commercial cloud providers were launched between 2006 and 2008. In order to supply server virtualization technologies, Amazon developed its AWS cloud (Boomija, M.D., et al., 2022) service in 2006. Google released Google App Engine (GAE) (Gowri, V., et al., 2023), a framework that includes tools to create cloud apps, in 2008. Microsoft introduced Microsoft Azure (Kaur, K., et al., 2023), a cloud framework built on the Windows Azure Hypervisor (WAH), in the same year. It offers .NET-dependent tools for application advancement. These commercial cloud frameworks enable speedy cloud application prototyping. There are technologies that allow for the development of private clouds when additional control over the fundamental cloud architecture is required. The initial open-source platform in building private clouds was called Eucalyptus. A private cloud encrypts data while it is in flight and is entirely accessible to authorised users, despite the fact that every cloud is dependent on the Internet. The first open-source software in establishing private and hybrid clouds was called Open-Nebula. Depending on the kind of services offered, cloud platforms are divided into 3 primary groups: infrastructure, platform, and service (IaaS, PaaS, and SaaS) (Fig. 1).

Infrastructure as a Service (IaaS)

IaaS (Pramanik, S., 2022) makes utilization of virtualization technology for enabling various virtual machines to run independently on top of a lone physical hardware framework. The hypervisor, which controls and arranges the virtual resources on the real hardware, is the primary piece of software used in virtualization (memory, processors, storage) (Jayasingh, R. et al., 2022). Cloud service providers may supply virtual machines with customizable resources on demand in this category. In essence, IaaS enables customers to dynamically hire virtual computers on which they may set up their own OS and additional apps without being concerned about the equipment deteriorating and requiring repair or sitting idle. Moreover, since the virtual machine's snapshots may be duplicated and started up in other cloud nodes, virtualization makes it possible for speedier recovery from hardware and system problems. Additionally, customers may avoid making the upfront investment necessary to buy their own hardware infrastructure.

Platform as a Service (PaaS)

Majority of the functions offered by IaaS are included in PaaS (Sinha, M. et al., 2021), however here the customer has access to the provider's system platform. Without needing to install and maintain the platform tools them, PaaS enables customers to create their own systems utilising the platform tools. Here, users have permission to a particular operating system and related tools (such as a Windows or Linux version) (like SQL Server, Apache web server, etc.). User's doesn't need to bother about updating their operating system and tools, anti-virus etc. It is impossible for the users to select how often the tools are updated at the same time. When a cloud provider installs an OS upgrade, user applications that rely on a certain OS version can abruptly cease functioning.

Software as a Service (SaaS)

The necessity to install and operate software programmes on the clients' own computers is removed by this kind of cloud computing. With SaaS (Reepu, S. et al., 2023), the consumer has neither expertise of no control over the basic framework; instead, cloud providers install, administer, and run the software programme. Although the end user has the least freedom with this kind of cloud service, the price is much cheaper. Dropbox, Google Docs, and other cloud computing services are examples of this category.

In-Office Cloud Computing in Businesses and Organisations

Cloud technologies are being quickly embraced by companies, organisations, governments, and private citizens. Businesses are growing more open to the idea of using information technology to expand their product development, services, and marketing. However, some businesses are hesitant to outsource their computer requirements, as well as their data storage and retrieval requirements, to cloud service providers. The adoption of a cloud service by businesses and organisations is hampered by four main issues.

While data are stored in the cloud, data security (Pramanik, S. et al., 2023) is the key issue. The critical challenges that suppliers should address is data confidentiality. Cloud service providers may now provide their customers assistances with fewer risks and improved security thanks to the ongoing advancements in security technologies. Performance and dependability are the second issue. Businesses and organisations are concerned that when they require cloud services, they won't be able to access their data. Typically, there is little to no notice before a potential service outage. Industry executives contend that firms should continue to maintain assistances and important data on their own framework so that they may always access them.

Because of businesses using cloud services, the concerns of data exchange and API standards are more important than ever. In this young business, familiar data file formats are until now in their infancy, that might result in vendor lock-in. At the moment, controlling vendor lock-in is a crucial concern. The majority of cloud service providers offer exclusive APIs (Bansal, R. et al., 2021) for data storage as well as application development, which makes it difficult to create vendor-neutral software. For scalability and for taking a favour of lower-expenditure provisions when a cloud provider ceases providing a needed assistance, data or applications must be migrated from one vendor to another. The standardisation of

APIs is the answer to this issue, enabling the creation of cloud applications that work with both internal private clouds and a variety of external public cloud providers. The proficiency to migrate data (and applications created utilizing cloud computing infrastructures) from one cloud service vendor to a different vendor and the interchange of data across comparable apps on various cloud systems remain difficulties with unfinished answers. The universal file format known as DICOM (Digital Imaging and Communications in Medicine) (Pramanik, S. et al., 2022), which enables the transmission of medical pictures across imaging devices and between various institutions, serves as a model for resolving this problem.

Cost is the ultimate obstacle to using cloud services. Costs are falling dramatically in this industry, which is rapidly developing. There is hopeful evidence indicating the cloud is cost-effective in contrast to local server fixings for implementations which demand extremely large storage (range of TB) and performance necessities. Different suppliers have different pricing methods.

Why is Cloud Computing Necessary for the Healthcare Industry?

Cloud services are being used to help healthcare systems advance. This is due to the fact that the usage of cloud technologies may significantly improve IT and information-rich assistances like medical imaging (Pramanik, S. and Raja, S. 2020). For the exchange of medical data and photographs, cooperation between hospitals and medical institutes is necessary. Virtual archives which are obtainable by many medical facilitators may be simply used to store patient data, simplifying data exchange and drastically lowering the need for local storage. The usage of cloud services for sensitive personal data raises privacy concerns. However, using cloud computing services has substantial benefits in the interpretation of challenging clinical situations. Diagnosis experts from all around the globe are available for consultation.

The cloud may also help with initiatives for teaching and continuing education. Several universities may access teaching files, and tutoring sessions may be jointly planned for providing shared access to teaching resources including software, presentations, and clinically relevant medical pictures.

While there are 3% to 5% more medical imaging investigations performed each year, this pace isn't a substantial driver of expansion. But, the scale of medical imaging learning—particularly CT and X-ray— are expanding far more quickly, driving up the amount of storage needed by 10% to 25% yearly. Prices for cloud storage have been falling more quickly than those for corporate storage, and this pattern suggests that cloud storage for medical picture storage will become more widely used sooner rather than later.

The fact that it takes longer to transmit larger CT and MRI (Naidu, G. T. et al., 2023) data to imaging workstations is a significant factor in the development of cloud storage. Imaging studies may be provided everywhere they are required by rendering them from the cloud to zero footprint viewing apps. The transition to cloud PACS (Picture Archiving and Communication Systems) is significantly influenced by several factors, particularly storage.

Medical Imaging and Cloud Computation

The clinical imaging industry is still in its inception when it comes to cloud computing, and there is presently little market penetration. However, in the near future, things might alter drastically. The need for high-capacity data storage and processing, as well as the management of raw data and image processing and sharing requirements, are some possible factors driving the rising usage of cloud computing in clinical imaging.

For many imaging modalities, medical image reconstruction is a constantly developing task that in years to come will need for precise quantitative reasoning of rebuilt pictures. A better knowledge of the numerous biological processes that affect the quantitative assessments of medical imaging may help to accomplish quantification, in part. It will also be enhanced by taking these biological factors into account for each of two or more imaging modalities inside the same reconstruction framework. The substantial computing effort of reconstruction procedures and accompanying correction algorithms has hindered the progress of "quantitative imaging" currently, resulting in lengthy execution durations which are inconsistent with their application in medical practise. An instance of this is the employment of Monte Carlo modelling techniques in tomography restoration to precisely describe the results related to the physics of the perception technique, taking into account interactions between the detector and the patient. Utilizing cloud frameworks for sharing computer resources is a potential solution to the problem of computing ability. Reconstruction algorithms and integrated correction procedures which may be implemented in a multi-threaded manner having great possibility for parallelization might be anticipated to provide benefits in this context. The raw data transmission that should take place over a high-speed network to take benefit of a cloud computing framework's speed advantage is one possible problem with this strategy. Although it could be less significant in research applications, this is a fundamental element in quantitative picture reconstruction in the therapeutic situation.

Access to cloud computing is advantageous for various industries, such as medical image processing. Over the last ten years, research in several fields of medical image processing has resulted in ongoing algorithmic advancements. To establish if a new image processing technique boosts image quality and medical yield, it must be contrasted to existing algorithms. The creation of standards which enable image processing approaches to be contrasted using frequent metrics and standards is one of the issues confronting medical image processing today. Such standards may benefit from the cloud's ease of their generation, and also from their ubiquitous availableness and usage. These databases aggregate several datasets required to evaluate image processing techniques (e.g., in segmentation, de-noising, fusion etc.). Real simulated clinical image datasets that are often the initial stage in the assessment of any image processing system are an essential part of these databases. With the benefit of a known fact, these simulations may mimic the various acquisition process components to create very realistic datasets. However, since these simulation datasets can have lengthy execution periods, manufacturing is generally confined to a small number of specialist centres. In the development of databases containing raw datasets of various clinical picture modalities, the same idea might be applied for the image reconstruction problems previously discussed, making it easier to benchmark new reconstruction methods.

Cloud Computing and PACS

A cloud-dependent PACS, often known as a cloud PACS, is a PACS system which is available to a user and administrators through web-dependent UI. The assurance of position and device freedom is what cloud PACS offers. In other words, a Cloud PACS may be accessible by a user from anywhere, provided it has enough network connection and a suitable connected device with adequate display capabilities. Up until recently, rendering imaging studies for PACS clients required powerful workstations. Due to this necessity, the radiologist or cardiologist is bound to an area having a potent computers/servers and a fast network link. Cloud PACS is now achievable due to three recent technological advancements: (1) remote visualisation that shifts most of the graphics visualization to the cloud and reduces the quantity of data which is needed to transfer from the cloud infrastructure to the terminal device (2) enhanced power processing and solution of terminal devices and (3) HTML5, CSS3, and JavaScript maturation to the point where zero-footprint, diagnostic-quality, and browser-dependent implementations are practical. These innovations have removed the requirement for expensive terminals and decreased the amount of networking throughput needed. Few data should be sent to the client since picture rendering happens on the server.

A Cloud PACS

As was previously said, the cloud has various benefits in terms of the usage of shared resources, and reduced maintenance and administrative overhead. The authors focus on the advantages of Cloud PACS, like its freedom from place and device. The ability to study research made at other hospitals or outpatient clinics is known as location independence. They are able to read from their homes, offices, and other places inside or outside of clinics or hospitals. Additionally, doctors may use the cloud to consult with doctors remotely, refer patients to other doctors, or ask for consultations from doctors in other cities. An application must be device independent in order to function on desktops, laptops, tablets, smart-phones, or other endpoint devices. Utilizing different Internet technologies, particularly browser-based apps, allows for this device freedom.

PACS's Three Constituents

An image visualisation programme, a workflow engine and an image archiving framework make up a PACS's three core parts. Each of these components may be moved to the cloud, but doing so has benefits and risks.

Image Visualisation Using the Cloud

The feature of Cloud PACS that benefits users the most right away is certainly image viewing. Moving imaging tests to a diagnostic workstation takes longer as the quantity of data in those investigations rises. Remote visualisation, also known as distant rendering, is a technique used by Cloud PACS, in which computers located in the cloud data centre render the pictures before transferring them to a distant client or terminal device. The following technologies may be utilised on the terminal device to interface with the Cloud PACS via the Internet: browser-dependent zero-footprint web apps, desktop virtualization, rich Internet apps (RIAs) and thin client apps. There are thin executable client apps for some time. They are often created as desktop applications, but a cloud server renders the images for them remotely. Thin clients have a number of drawbacks, including the need to install them on the client desktop, rely on the client operating system, and thereby must be rebuilt for various terminal devices. They also need management and maintenance, which may be costly and time consuming.

Recently developed RIAs (Rich Internet Applications) are largely geared for clinical viewers. RIAs are Internet-delivered apps, often accessed via a browser, that provide functionality similar to that of a stand-alone fundamental app. A RIA depends on a client infrastructure which must be installed in the client browser, like Adobe Flash, JavaFX33, or Microsoft Silverlight. The browser may then automatically load or update the RIA. It may be expensive to administer and maintain newer versions of the RIA infrastructure in the conventional way, while it is probably less expensive than thin clients.

Since the introduction of HTML5 and zero-footprint clients are widely used by clinical, or non-diagnostic, readers a browser may transparently load zero clients from a distant website. Users just need to have a current browser on their device, which simplifies maintenance and operation of the application. Additionally, it enables the deployment of the viewing application on any device with a compatible browser. Usually, Chrome, Firefox, Internet Explorer, and Safari—the four most popular browsers—are supported. The ability to show pictures have significantly increased thanks to HTML5, and various HTML5 diagnostic-qualities zero clients has only lately been released. It's anticipated that this tendency will intensify.

Last but not the least, desktop virtualization has shown considerable potential in transforming conventional thick clients into cloud-friendly apps. Distant access to a fully functional operating system environment operating on a distant (potentially virtual) computer is made possible by desktop virtualization. Additionally, it boosts the performance of zero clients on broadband networks. Although desktop virtualization hasn't yet obtained FDA (Food and Drug Administration) clearance, it is anticipated to do so soon.

Workflow Using the Cloud

The workflow engine is PACS's second important part. There are various chances to enhance imaging workflow inside and across healthcare companies when the engine is moved to the cloud. The capacity to disperse tasks more effectively is the most evident. Studies in specialties and subspecialties might be added to the most qualified doctor's to-do list for sending urgent (stat) cases to the doctor who is most accessible. Whatever factors are thought to be most suitable, like balancing the workload or having more productive doctors, might be used to distribute the work throughout the medical community. Since the distribution of the work is not reliant on the location of the doctors, it may be done using nearly any set of criteria. Additionally, ordering, referrals, consultations, second opinions, and patient transfers within and across healthcare systems are greatly facilitated by cloud PACS.

Cloud-Based Picture Archive

The picture archive, the third key PACS component, offers several prospects for advancement once again. Cloud-dependent vendor-unbiased archives or Cloud PACS provide the majority of the potential. The gathering of imaging records from healthcare companies across diverse geographic regions is the most rewarding possibility. The benefits of this aggregate are as follows: The utilization of CDs and DVDs may be minimized or removed that lowers costs and enhances better timely care. Cross-enterprise archives provide the ability to share images across organisations.

CLOUD COMPUTING'S IMPACT AND BENEFITS FOR RESEARCH

Parallel processing on massive datasets is made simpler and more affordable for researchers via cloud-based research software. Examples of distributed computing infrastructures vary from the Worldwide LHC Computing Grid for the Large Hadron Collider, which includes many institutions, in the usage of business cloud-dependent frameworks to expedite project simulations. Due to the magnitude of the datasets and the inherent parallelism of bioinformatics data-mining activities, it is predicted that the field of bioinformatics should be especially suitable to distributed computation studies.

Since each participant in a clinical trial is viewed as a separate piece of data, research involving clinical trials is in theory, excellent candidates for cloud-based infrastructures. The trial's analyses may be parallelized by managing each subject individually. If the infrastructure is set up to support the distribution, identical procedures may be spread in parallel across a cluster of processors even if sophisticated computations are necessary for each patient in a given cohort. Particularly in studies involving medical imaging, all data are easily digitised and prepared in accordance with the DICOM standard. A clinical trials cloud-based platform may operate as follows:

- The infrastructure for managing trial data is established by trial coordinators (cooperative organisations, quality assurance centres, and commercial partners).
- In anticipation of routine quality assurance checks, engaging organizations upload data to the trial cloud repository.
- For inquiries on the trial data, standardised analysis engines are offered, simplifying both primary analyses (comparison of results between various arms) and authorised secondary studies.

Figure 2 shows the diagram of such a framework. The accessibility of data and analytical effectiveness has been considerably enhanced by cloud-based clinical trial research. Other than data storage and availability, the analytical platform—which must handle a variety of data queries—is the crucial part of the cloud. Many research endpoints may be met with simple searches, but inspects which rely on factors like dose-volume data may need patient-by-patient procedures on Digital Imaging and Communications in Medicine (DICOM) data. Advanced procedures on trial data should be enabled to provide secondary investigations the most freedom feasible. Consider, for instance, a secondary analysis which needs cone-beam computed tomography (CBCT) scan auto segmentation. This sophisticated techniques need to be included into the analysis so that the researcher is spared from downloading each batch of CBCT images which takes time and money. Almost any research is feasible with the help of a flexible DICOM toolkit and a broad programming language.

The infrastructure utilised for the clinical trial may be used to streamline and make more visible the postmarket surveillance (PMS) procedure if it is necessary as part of the study. There are often more patients involved with PMS, but there is typically less data input for each patient. To guarantee the greatest possible concordance between trial and PMS data, this part of the experiment may be included. Tools for toxicity premarket analysis that can be used to PMS would probably speed up the process and make independent supervision easier. Future clinical installations may employ cloud archives that compile patient health information from various healthcare organisations, which would make it highly efficient to transmit PMS to regional nodes.

When analysing clinical trial data or massive amounts of retrospective clinical data, Machine Learning (ML) (Dushyant, K. et al., 2022) is a resource that is underused. Cloud-based infrastructures are particularly suited for machine learning, with Google's Prediction API serving as an instance. A group of methods known as machine learning enable the discovery of unknown connections without the need for an initial premise. Machine learning may be able to help researchers validate primary objectives and uncover unexpected associations in as much as medical trials are created to test certain hypotheses. Consider, for instance, a large-scale clinical experiment contrasting the effects of image-guided intensity-modulated radiation therapy with and without a certain chemotherapy regimen. There are additional

Figure 2. A cloud-based clinical trial system's schematic diagram. Although it is not necessary, the PaaS cloud arrangement works best for several researchers who interact having a predefined dataset in user-defined manners

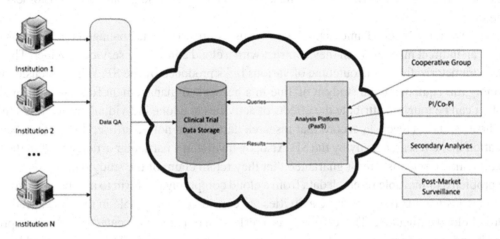

conclusions that may be made from the data, even if the effectiveness of the chemotherapy treatment is the main objective. There will unavoidably be a variety of treatment planning systems used in multi-institutional studies; maybe one platform has a preferred dosage distribution. Perhaps the quality of the treatment plans differs systematically across various institutions. These kinds of research

Although characteristics were unable to be predicted before a study began, differences in the quality of the treatment plan can actually defeat its objectives. The strength of the trial's results might be increased by using machine learning methods to find such underappreciated traits, and comparisons across inter-institutional practises could be made that would be almost impossible to find at each institution alone. With all data readily accessible to scientists from various organizations and the cloud's ability to facilitate various resources for the analysis which can be inappropriate for a lone organization to deliver by itself, analysing features of a huge, homogeneous dataset is a job that is foremost achieved having a cloud-dependent framework.

Security and Ethical Questions

While research data is managed by a lone organization, various ethical issues relevant to cloud computing had less importance. In cloud computing, these issues have more importance and as a result of the organization failing command over research data to a 3rd party, especially the cloud computing service provider (SP). The reason to defend the confidentiality and security of patient data and to be sure that only those having the genuine permission may access it is vital among the concerns. While uploading, communicating, and downloading patient data, the SP controlling the computational cloud should utilise suitable cryptographic for avoiding security violation. Clients should examine if patient data is appropriately protected if the SP accesses computer resources dispersed around the globe, particularly if the resources are outside the legal jurisdiction of the country of origin. The SP should guarantee in writing that protections are in place to secure data from misuse or from uses that were not intended by researchers or doctors when it was collected. In fact, the cloud provider could require promising that data won't be transmitted beyond a definite legal system, as the example with Australia, for example. The SP will conclude:

In the occurrence of a security breach, the ability to promptly delete data at the customers' request is required.

Clients have the danger of interacting with many entities for data management, calculation, and analysis in an indirect manner when they contract with a cloud computing service provider. This danger, called as parameterization, is an outcome of various links produced by the SP. While forensic investigators cannot grab equipment and study it offline in a networked management framework provided by a cloud SP, it can be tough to attribute the effects of activities to a lone individual or entity. It's important that medical scientists reach an accord that research data should not be utilised for reasons beyond the specification in the research study by the SP. Also, by involving a particular arrangement in the contract for cloud facilities, scientists must guarantee that they retain claim of the study data.

The problems of movable research data from a cloud computing platform to another, or also restoring the data to a business platform, if these activities are considered acceptable in the time ahead, is a type of hazard of cloud computing. This difficulty is a reflection of the private category of a SaaS provider's framework and the specific structural needs for the data supplied into it. This issue should be resolved up front, not after the requirement for data transmission has already arisen, when cloud computing services are engaged.

As cloud computation is basically a new category to the research landscape, it is impossible to anticipate all of its potential ethical ramifications. Because of this, the preventive concept needs to be used in every discussion on cloud services. The precautionary assumption makes an effort to foresee potential damage without completely impeding advancement and innovation. It says that when there is scientific doubt about whether something may cause substantial or irreversible damage, one should not act. Additionally, individuals who suggest a course of action have the burden of evidence for demonstrating its safety, availability, and honesty.

The CIA (confidentiality, integrity, and availability) model, called for the three characteristics it takes into account, may be used to describe security in ICT.

The prevention of information disclosure to unapproved parties is what confidentiality refers to. Integrity guarantees that the data was unable to be altered covertly. When a service or piece of data is made available, it is done so at the request of legitimate parties. A mix of cryptographic techniques, access controls, data backup, and data repository security approaches are used as CIA delivery mechanisms. The security of medical records is hampered by a number of ethical and regulatory standards that must be met to guarantee the safety of sensitive personal data. The storage, sharing, and use of medical data must also adhere to national rules, like the Health Records Act and the National Health Act in Australia. There may also be problems depending on where the cloud provider is installed and where the infrastructure for the cloud is located. For instance, a nation may pass legislation requiring cloud service providers to provide law enforcement officials access to sensitive patient information from other nations.

Sensitive personal data is gathered, interchanged, and utilized by clinical apps, and advancing data security from undesired access is required. While considering cloud-dependent medical assistance, the key security measures which must be taken into consideration are user ID and authorization as well as information proprietorship. The software programme is in charge of controlling user verification and information access privileges in SaaS and PaaS service models, and the cloud infrastructure has constant grant to this data. Servers built on the Lightweight Directory Access Protocol (LDAP) protocol are often utilized to maintain user confidentiality information and authorization. Installing LDAP servers on the firm's environment will increase the security of delicate staff and patient records. At both the application and OS levels, data access policies are defined regarding user roles, together with access rights to the data objects. The security of the software and hardware is the job of the cloud provider under the IaaS approach, whereas the Operating System and hardware are given as virtual machines. This provider also oversees the confidentiality rules for hardware access and security. Access constraints to the content of the virtualized resources are referred to as hypervisor security (e.g., hard discs and processors).

An important ethical and legal task is avoiding uncertified 3rd parties from retrieving every patient medical data. The suitable approach of securing data is to encrypt data which are communicated or stored in repository. Best network transmission encryption methods like SSL (Secure Sockets Layer) and TLS (Transport Layer Security) require robust data security for data transmission through Internet. The unsafe SSL trust setup and the theft of the cryptographic keys by hostile parties are possible weaknesses in the methods. By building secure VPNs between the enterprise and the cloud, network security may be improved. The most common techniques include encrypting medical data that is stored. Data encryption is used in (Kaushik, D. et al., 2022) before transmission to the cloud. By using this procedure, the business is able to store and maintain the data encryption and decryption keys beyond disclosing them to other parties. This method requires a strong and dependable network connection to the cloud.

Data availability is a key problem in data system security. While the architecture and framework of the cloud may certify a higher degree of accessibility for cloud services and data, the cloud provider further confronts several security issues, like backup methods and quick retrieval of broken virtual data. Moreover, with cloud computing, data must be protected against accidental or deliberate change. At every layer of the cloud computing framework and tasks, data integrity should be authenticated. Utilizing redundant technologies like RAID (redundant array of inexpensive disks), cloud services safeguard data storage. Nevertheless, as cloud storage has the potential to lose or damage data, customers must implement their own security procedures to guarantee high data integrity. Keeping a record of the data's current state, such as using MD5 digital signatures to check for corruption, is one technique to do this. These signatures are concise summaries of a file that are calculated from its constituents. For instance, a straightforward and poor signature can be the quantity of vowels and consonants in a sentence. A benefit of complex signature algorithms like MD5 is that it is very hard to modify a file in a manner which preserves its signature. Of course, just identifying corrupted data is not enough to restore it; corrective action is necessary. Due to this, customers need additionally maintain backups (perhaps using a different cloud storage provider), guaranteeing the data's integrity even in the event of a cloud provider failure. Standard security procedures should be used by clients in data transactions while using the SaaS framework, where the provider mostly provides access to the data over Internet.

A computer system or application's natural lifespan includes security flaws and system failures, and system logging is an essential component of system management which makes it easier to pinpoint the root concerns of system vulnerabilities. The 3 primary constituents of system logging are resource monitors, user logs, and application events. These logs assist administrators in isolating the root causes of system failures, identifying user behaviours while the system is running, and keeping track of real-time information about the state of the application and the resources that are being used, both physically and virtually. Every level of the cloud architecture may use logging. The primary goal of logging is to provide healthcare managers with access to recorded information in the event of a security or failure incident. Who gets access to what kind of recorded information is a crucial question when it comes to national security considerations. For instance, under some circumstances, the cloud service provider in the United States must provide government access to recorded information. A European healthcare institution finds it challenging to put their faith in a US cloud provider since the criteria is different in the majority of European nations. In cloud computing, the service provider is primarily responsible for implementing security measures.

Security requirements are become more demanding and complex when clinical data is held external to the business (also the nation of origin in certain cases). Cloud service providers are required to adhere to a set of rules for protecting patient data, including physical data repository site security. On the contrary, when organizations like healthcare providers and research institutions want to migrate to the cloud, they must have faith in cloud providers. A service-level compliance is the only business instrument that can now assist in creating an explicit and lawfully attached commercial attachment of trust between clinical organisations and cloud providers. A cloud provider outlines all the precautions, resources, and processes that the cloud provider must use in order to offer secured data interchange and storage, service availability and security of the stored data. Additional agreement points that must be included in a cloud provider include those that expressly state how the cloud provider may access the stored data, the logging information that will be given to the clients, how data are confidentially separated from other customers in the cloud, the physical whereabouts of the data, how the client can assess the security concerns, and how the cloud provider complies with domestic and worldwide rules for the confidential interchange and repository of patient records. A healthcare business may analyse the services and security precautions supplied, starting with the SLA, and determine when to rely a cloud provider as well as which cloud service greatly suits its needs.

It is useful to compare cloud computing with various frameworks, such as the infrastructure for power generation, in order to better comprehend security risks. In the event of a power outage, hospitals have their own emergency generators in addition to using public and private electrical suppliers. While seldom better secured or dependable than the public framework, hospital emergency generators are not dependent on the electrical suppliers and therefore more possible to work in the case of a power outage. Similar to how a cloud runs by Google, Amazon, Microsoft, etc. can never be as dependable and secure as one run by a hospital because hospitals lack the expertise and staff necessary to provide that level of service. Yet since there are so many priceless resources (patient data, for example) concentrated in one provider, the major effects of a promising attack—in spite of a simple DoS (Anand, R. et al., 2022)—are far more severe. Similarly, targeting a power plant or grid can be more expensive than providing energy to a particular healthcare centre, but it may also result in significantly more damage and, as a result, have a much bigger payout for an attacker. Consequently, using the cloud constitutes a deal between the cloud provider's improved assault defences and the worse repercussions of an assault that succeeds. In reality, when a cloud provider is attacked, an organisation might suffer collateral damage, much to how an attack on a power plant that was intended to take down a bank's security (Gupta, A. et al., 2022) system could cause harm to a hospital deciding whether to shift to the cloud and determining how much, if any, service should be properly studied, should be kept locally. As was already indicated, a further issue with cloud computing is that, in contrast to power manufacturers, cloud providers have complete access to the information and facilities of a hospital. They may violate their confidentiality agreements for professional intentions or due to the reason that the country in which they are based demands it. Homomorphic encryption (Bansal, R. et al., 2022), in which the data saved in the cloud are always encrypted, even while they are being processed, may provide a viable solution to this conundrum. In this way, the unencrypted data is never accessible to the cloud provider. Because of the high expense, homomorphic encryption may never be a realistic, workable solution. In order to strengthen data privacy assurances without incurring an unreasonably large cost, alternative techniques are being considered.

Another option would be for a nation or a collection of healthcare facilities (such as all of the hospitals in the European Union) to create its own cloud infrastructure, as is now achievable with OpenNebula. For users having specific security, lawful, or performance needs, the "community clouds" are suggested.

CONCLUSION

ICT services are being transformed by cloud computing by becoming a virtual public service. Similar to how electrical power production shifted from tiny private units to bigger suppliers, it is an indication of industry maturation. From that standpoint alone, the usage of cloud computing in the medical institutions is unavoidable because of the enhanced performance and scalability which may be accomplished. In addition, cloud computing offers significant benefits for health care delivery and research that cannot be ignored, and they will surely accelerate its adoption. Without the added cost of buying and maintaining more equipment, cloud services may provide end users with a wide range of computing resources through the Internet. Large datasets of medical photos may be stored, processed, and shared using these services thanks to their efficacy. Researchers may access the resources required for carrying out massive clinical studies involving several universities by leveraging the cloud. For increasing storage availability, accessibility and manageability medical image archives like PACS have already been moved into the cloud by a number of academics, clinical administrators, and software developers. The security, privacy, and ethical concerns that occur with moving medical data management and storage from a local company to a globally accessible cloud are significant obstacles to this transfer. Data security and privacy may be at least partly guaranteed by ICT encryption technology and safety regulations. Cloud service providers must, however, also make sure that their offerings comply with local, domestic and worldwide laws in both their own country and the client's jurisdiction. Moreover, they must adopt appropriate safeguards to protect the very sensitive nature of data and handle private patient information on their systems.

REFERENCES

Alam, A. (2023). Cloud-Based E-learning: Scaffolding the Environment for Adaptive E-learning Ecosystem Based on Cloud Computing Infrastructure. In S. C. Satapathy, J. C. W. Lin, L. K. Wee, V. Bhateja, & T. M. Rajesh (Eds.), *Computer Communication, Networking and IoT. Lecture Notes in Networks and Systems* (Vol. 459). Springer. doi:10.1007/978-981-19-1976-3_1

Anand, R., Singh, J., Pandey, D., Pandey, B. K., Nassa, V. K., & Pramanik, S. (2022). Modern Technique for Interactive Communication in LEACH-Based Ad Hoc Wireless Sensor Network. In M. M. Ghonge, S. Pramanik, & A. D. Potgantwar (Eds.), *Software Defined Networking for Ad Hoc Networks*. Springer. doi:10.1007/978-3-030-91149-2_3

Ankita, S., & Sahana, S. K. (2022). S.K. (2022). Ba-PSO: A Balanced PSO to solve multi-objective grid scheduling problem. *Applied Intelligence*, *52*(4), 4015–4027. doi:10.100710489-021-02625-7

Bansal, R., Jenipher, B., & Nisha, V. Jain, Makhan R., Dilip, Kumbhkar, Pramanik, S., Roy, S. & Gupta, A. (2022). Big Data Architecture for Network Security, in Cyber Security and Network Security, Eds. Wiley. doi:10.1002/9781119812555.ch11

Bansal, R., Obaid, A. J., Gupta, A., Singh, R., & Pramanik, S. (2021). Impact of Big Data on Digital Transformation in 5G Era, *2nd International Conference on Physics and Applied Sciences (ICPAS 2021),* IOP Science. , 2021.10.1088/1742-6596/1963/1/012170

Boomija, M. D., & Raja, S. V. K. (2023). Securing medical data by role-based user policy with partially homomorphic encryption in AWS cloud. *Soft Computing, 27*(1), 559–568. doi:10.100700500-022-06950-y

Dushyant, K., Muskan, G., Gupta, A., & Pramanik, S. (2022). Utilizing Machine Learning and Deep Learning in Cyber security: An Innovative Approach. In M. M. Ghonge, S. Pramanik, R. Mangrulkar, & D. N. Le (Eds.), *Cyber security and Digital Forensics.* Wiley. doi:10.1002/9781119795667.ch12

Gowri, V., & Baranidharan, B. (2023). Dynamic Energy Efficient Load Balancing Approach in Fog Computing Environment. In G. Rajakumar, K. L. Du, C. Vuppalapati, & G. N. Beligiannis (Eds.), *Intelligent Communication Technologies and Virtual Mobile Networks. Lecture Notes on Data Engineering and Communications Technologies* (Vol. 131). Springer., doi:10.1007/978-981-19-1844-5_13

Gupta, A., Verma, A., & Pramanik, S. (2022). Advanced Security System in Video Surveillance for COVID-19. In S. Pramanik, A. Sharma, S. Bhatia, & D. N. Le. (eds.) An Interdisciplinary Approach to Modern Network Security. CRC Press.

Gupta, P., & Yadav, S. (2022). A TAM-based Study on the ICT Usage by the Academicians in Higher Educational Institutions of Delhi NCR. In M. Saraswat, H. Sharma, K. Balachandran, J. H. Kim, & J. C. Bansal (Eds.), *Congress on Intelligent Systems. Lecture Notes on Data Engineering and Communications Technologies* (Vol. 111). Springer. doi:10.1007/978-981-16-9113-3_25

Jayasingh, R. (2022). Speckle noise removal by SORAMA segmentation in Digital Image Processing to facilitate precise robotic surgery. *International Journal of Reliable and Quality E-Healthcare, 11*(1), 1–19. doi:10.4018/IJRQEH.295083

Kaur, K., Bharany, S., Badotra, S., Aggarwal, K., Nayyar, A., & Sharma, S. (2023). Energy-efficient polyglot persistence database live migration among heterogeneous clouds. *The Journal of Supercomputing, 79*(1), 265–294. doi:10.100711227-022-04662-6

Kaushik, D., Garg, M., Annu, Gupta, A. & Pramanik, S. (2022). Application of Machine Learning and Deep Learning in Cyber security: An Innovative Approach. In M. Ghonge, S. Pramanik, R. Mangrulkar and D. N. Le, (eds.) *Cybersecurity and Digital Forensics: Challenges and Future Trends.* Wiley. doi:10.1002/9781119795667.ch12

Marks, B., & Thomas, J. (2022). Adoption of virtual reality technology in higher education: An evaluation of five teaching semesters in a purpose-designed laboratory. *Education and Information Technologies, 27*(1), 1287–1305. doi:10.100710639-021-10653-6 PMID:34257511

Pramanik, S. (2022). An Effective Secured Privacy-Protecting Data Aggregation Method in IoT. In M. O. Odhiambo, W. Mwashita, & I. G. I. Global (Eds.), *Achieving Full Realization and Mitigating the Challenges of the Internet of Things.*, doi:10.4018/978-1-7998-9312-7.ch008

Pramanik, S. (2023). An Adaptive Image Steganography Approach depending on Integer Wavelet Transform and Genetic Algorithm. *Multimedia Tools and Applications, 2023.* Advance online publication. doi:10.100711042-023-14505-y

Pramanik, S., Galety, M. G., Samanta, D., & Joseph, N. P. (2022). Data Mining Approaches for Decision Support Systems. *3rd International Conference on Emerging Technologies in Data Mining and Information Security*. IEEE.

Pramanik, S., & Suresh Raja, S. (2020). A Secured Image Steganography using Genetic Algorithm. *Advances in Mathematics: Scientific Journal*, *9*(7), 4533–4541. doi:10.37418/amsj.9.7.22

Reepu, S. Kumar, M., Chaudhary, G., Gupta, K., Pramanik, S., & Gupta, A. (2023). Information Security and Privacy on IoT. J. Zhao, V. V. Kumar, R. Natarajan and T. R. Mahesh, (eds.) Handbook of Research in Advancements in AI and IoT Convergence Technologies. IGI Global.

Reid, L. (2021). An Introduction to Biomedical Computational Fluid Dynamics. In P. M. Rea (Ed.), *Biomedical Visualisation. Advances in Experimental Medicine and Biology* (Vol. 1334). Springer., doi:10.1007/978-3-030-76951-2_10

Sinha, M., Chacko, E., Makhija, P., & Pramanik, S. (2021). Energy Efficient Smart Cities with Green IoT. In C. Chakrabarty (Ed.), *Green Technological Innovation for Sustainable Smart Societies: Post Pandemic Era*. Springer. doi:10.1007/978-3-030-73295-0_16

Taviti Naidu, G., Ganesh, K. V. B., Vidya Chellam, V., Praveenkumar, S., Dhabliya, D., Pramanik, S., & Gupta, A. (2023). Technological Innovation Driven by Big Data. In *Advanced Bioinspiration Methods for Healthcare Standards, Policies, and Reform*. Hadj Ahmed Bouarara IGI Global., doi:10.4018/978-1-6684-5656-9

Turner, C. (2022). Augmented Reality, Augmented Epistemology, and the Real-World Web. *Philosophy & Technology*, *35*(1), 19. doi:10.100713347-022-00496-5

Chapter 21
Image Processing in Industrial Chemical Engineering Trends and Applications

Santosh Walke
College of Engineering, National University of Science and Technology, Muscat, Oman

Manoj Mandake
Bharati Vidyapeeth College of Engineering, India

Ravi W. Tapre
Datta Meghe College of Engineering, India

Makarand Naniwadekar
Savitribai Phule Pune University, India

Chetan Thakar
Savitribai Phule Pune University, India

Sandhya Dilip Jadhav
Bharati Vidyapeeth College of Engineering, India

ABSTRACT

This chapter gives a thorough overview of image processing's uses and potential in industrial chemical engineering. Image processing can provide precise and in-depth information about chemical processes, products, and its significance in this field is highlighted. The foundations of image processing are covered in this chapter, including image formation and acquisition, image preprocessing, feature extraction, and selection. The applications of image-based process monitoring and control, image analysis for product quality control, and the newest developments and difficulties in machine learning in image-based chemical engineering are also covered. The section on machine learning in image-based chemical engineering gives a general overview of machine learning methods and how they are used in the field of chemical engineering. The chapter's discussion of image processing's limitations in chemical engineering, as well as current trends and future research prospects, come to close.

DOI: 10.4018/978-1-6684-8618-4.ch021

INTRODUCTION

Image processing is a powerful tool for industrial chemical engineering, allowing for the analysis of images to identify important information and patterns. Image processing techniques have been used in a variety of applications, including process monitoring, quality control, and product development (Li et al., 2020). The use of image processing in industrial chemical engineering is becoming increasingly common due to advancements in imaging technology and the development of more sophisticated algorithms. One of the key applications of image processing in industrial chemical engineering is process monitoring. By using cameras and image processing algorithms, it is possible to monitor chemical processes in real-time and identify potential issues before they become critical (Amini & Abbaspour-Fard, 2018). This can help to improve the efficiency of chemical processes and reduce waste by identifying and addressing issues early in the process. Thermal imaging is one common technique used in process monitoring, as it can provide temperature data that is useful for identifying hotspots or other issues in chemical reactors (Li et al., 2020). Image processing is also used in quality control for industrial chemical engineering. By analyzing images of products, it is possible to identify defects or variations that could impact product quality. For example, machine vision can be used to analyze images of ceramic tiles to identify defects in the manufacturing process (Han et al., 2020). Image analysis can also be used to evaluate the quality of plastic injection molding by analyzing the quality of the molded parts (Cui et al., 2019). By using image processing for quality control, manufacturers can improve the consistency and quality of their products, as well as reduce the need for human inspection. In addition to process monitoring and quality control, image processing is also used in product development in industrial chemical engineering. For example, image analysis can be used to evaluate the effectiveness of coatings or other treatments on surfaces. By analyzing images of surfaces before and after treatment, it is possible to determine the effectiveness of the treatment and identify areas for improvement (Sliwa et al., 2018). Image processing can also be used to develop new products, such as by analyzing images of raw materials to identify patterns and properties that could be useful in developing new materials. There are several challenges to using image processing in industrial chemical engineering, including the need for high-quality images and the development of sophisticated algorithms to analyze the images. However, advancements in imaging technology and machine learning algorithms are helping to address these challenges and make image processing a more valuable tool in chemical engineering. In conclusion, image processing is a valuable tool for industrial chemical engineering, with applications in process monitoring, quality control, and product development. By using cameras and sophisticated algorithms, it is possible to analyze images and identify important patterns and information that can help improve the efficiency, consistency, and quality of chemical processes and products. As imaging technology and machine learning algorithms continue to advance, image processing is likely to become an even more important tool for industrial chemical engineering.

Background and Motivation

The field of industrial chemical engineering has been revolutionized in recent years with the rapid development of image processing technologies (Alimardani, 2019, p. 12). The use of image processing techniques has proven to be a valuable tool in the analysis and control of complex chemical processes (Shi et al., 2018, p. 2). This technology has been widely applied in various industrial sectors, including food, pharmaceutical, and petrochemical industries, to name a few (Cheng et al., 2017, p. 2).

Importance of Image Processing in Chemical Engineering

Image processing can be used to extract valuable information from images that can be used to monitor, control, and optimize industrial chemical processes (Sahin et al., 2018, p. 2). This information can be used to improve process efficiency, reduce waste, and improve product quality (Javidi et al., 2019, p. 5). The application of image processing in chemical engineering has become increasingly important in recent years as the demand for high-quality products, energy efficiency, and environmental sustainability has increased (Hassanien et al., 2019, p. 5).

FUNDAMENTALS OF IMAGE PROCESSING

Image Formation and Acquisition

Images are acquired through a range of different techniques such as optical, magnetic, or acoustic sensors, depending on the properties of the object being imaged and the desired output (Gao et al., 2020, p. 1). Image formation involves capturing data from the object being imaged, which can be either a two-dimensional (2D) or three-dimensional (3D) representation (Gonzalez & Woods, 2018, p. 9). The quality and resolution of an acquired image can be affected by factors such as noise, distortion, or lighting conditions (Viana et al., 2019, p. 1). Pre-processing techniques can be used to enhance image quality by removing noise, correcting distortion, and adjusting brightness and contrast (Sahin et al., 2018, p. 4).

Image Pre-Processing

Image pre-processing is the initial stage of image processing, which involves the correction and enhancement of the raw images (Jahangirzadeh et al., 2018, p. 3). Pre-processing techniques such as filtering, normalization, and thresholding are used to improve the quality of the images and facilitate further analysis (Gonzalez & Woods, 2018, p. 33). Filters are used to smooth out noisy images, sharpen blurry images, and highlight edges (Wang et al., 2019, p. 1). Normalization techniques are used to adjust the brightness and contrast of images, making it easier to analyze and interpret the image data (Rahmani et al., 2018, p. 3). Thresholding techniques are used to segment images by separating objects from the background (Viana et al., 2019, p. 1).

Feature Extraction and Selection

Feature extraction is the process of identifying and extracting relevant information from images. The features can be either low-level features, such as pixel intensity and color, or high-level features, such as shape and texture (Zhang et al., 2019, p. 2). Feature selection involves identifying the most relevant features for a given application, which can help reduce the dimensionality of the data and improve the accuracy of the analysis (Rahmani et al., 2018, p. 5). Various techniques can be used for feature extraction and selection, such as statistical methods, wavelet transforms, and principal component analysis (PCA) (Chen et al., 2020, p. 1). Statistical methods are commonly used for feature extraction as they can provide a quantitative description of image features (Alvarez et al., 2018, p. 4). Wavelet transforms can be used to extract multi-scale and multi-directional features from images, while PCA is used to reduce the dimensionality of image data and identify the most relevant features for a given application (Jahangirzadeh et al., 2018, p. 6).

Classification and Recognition

Classification and recognition are the final stages of image processing, which involve the labeling and interpretation of the extracted features. Classification involves grouping objects into different categories based on their features, while recognition involves identifying the specific object or pattern present in the image (Gao et al., 2020, p. 1). Various techniques can be used for classification and recognition, such as supervised and unsupervised machine learning, artificial neural networks (ANN), and support vector machines (SVM) (Chen et al., 2020, p. 1).

IMAGE-BASED PROCESS MONITORING AND CONTROL

Image-based process monitoring and control have various applications in the chemical industry. For example, in the petrochemical industry, image sensors can be used to monitor the fluid flow in pipelines and detect blockages and leaks. In the pharmaceutical industry, image sensors can be used to monitor the crystallization process and optimize the process parameters to produce high-quality products. In the food industry, image sensors can be used to monitor the food processing and packaging processes and ensure the quality and safety of the products. Image-based process monitoring and control is an important application of image processing in industrial chemical engineering. The real-time monitoring and control of chemical processes using image-based techniques can help to optimize process parameters, detect anomalies, prevent process failures, and improve process efficiency and productivity. The application of image-based techniques in process monitoring and control is expected to grow in the future with the development of new image sensors and image processing techniques.

Real-Time Monitoring of Chemical Processes

Real-time monitoring of chemical processes is a critical aspect of process control, enabling quick detection of any deviations from the expected operating conditions. Image-based techniques offer a powerful tool for real-time monitoring of chemical processes, as they allow for non-invasive and non-destructive monitoring of key process variables (Amini & Abbaspour-Fard, 2018). For instance, thermal imaging can be used to monitor temperature changes in chemical reactors, providing valuable insights into reaction kinetics and optimizing reaction conditions (Li, Li, & Zhang, 2020).

In addition, image-based techniques can be used to monitor the quality of products in real-time, ensuring that they meet the desired specifications. For example, Cui, Zheng, and Yin (2019) developed a real-time monitoring system for the quality of plastic injection molding based on machine vision and machine learning. The system uses image analysis to detect defects such as bubbles, sink marks, and warpage in the molded products, allowing for corrective actions to be taken immediately.

Automated Control of Chemical Processes

Automated control of chemical processes involves the use of advanced control algorithms to optimize process performance, reduce process variability, and increase product quality. Image-based techniques have been widely used to implement automated control of chemical processes, allowing for real-time adjustments to be made based on the observed process variables (Kumar, Mohan, & Samant, 2017).

For example, Han, Ma, and Chen (2020) developed a machine vision-based automatic detection system for ceramic tile quality. The system uses image analysis to detect defects such as cracks, spots, and size deviations in the tiles, and makes automatic adjustments to the production process to ensure that the quality standards are met. Another example of automated control of chemical processes using image-based techniques is the use of machine learning algorithms for predictive modeling of process variables (Sliwa, Krauss, & Kürten, 2019). Machine learning algorithms can be trained on large datasets of process data and image data to predict process outcomes and optimize process performance. In summary, image-based process monitoring and control offer a powerful set of tools for optimizing chemical processes, reducing process variability, and increasing product quality. The use of image-based techniques enables real-time monitoring and control of key process variables, and has been successfully applied in a wide range of chemical processes, from polymer manufacturing to ceramic tile production.

IMAGE ANALYSIS IN PRODUCT QUALITY CONTROL

Image analysis has become a powerful tool in product quality control across various industries, including chemical manufacturing. With advancements in imaging technology and software, image analysis has made it possible to efficiently evaluate and monitor the quality of products in real-time, leading to improved production processes and product quality. In this note, we will discuss the importance of image analysis in product quality control and its applications in different industries. Image analysis in product quality control involves the use of computer vision techniques to analyze digital images of products to identify defects, evaluate product quality, and detect anomalies. This process can be performed either in real-time or through post-processing of images. Image analysis techniques are used to identify visual defects, such as surface cracks, deformations, and discolorations, which are difficult to detect by manual inspection. It provides more accurate and reliable results than traditional manual inspection methods, making it a preferred choice in quality control. One of the key benefits of image analysis in product quality control is the ability to detect and identify defects in products before they become major issues. This early detection allows manufacturers to take corrective actions in a timely manner, which can improve production efficiency and reduce costs. In the chemical manufacturing industry, image analysis can be used to detect the presence of impurities or contaminants in chemical products. By analyzing images of chemical products, manufacturers can identify defects and take corrective actions to ensure that their products meet the required quality standards. Another important application of image analysis in product quality control is its ability to provide quantitative information about product features. Image analysis techniques can be used to measure various product properties such as size, shape, color, and texture, which can be used to evaluate product quality. In the food industry, image analysis can be used to evaluate the color and texture of food products, which are important factors that affect consumer acceptance of products. Similarly, in the pharmaceutical industry, image analysis can be used to evaluate the size and shape of drug particles, which can affect the bioavailability and efficacy of drugs. In addition to evalu-

Figure 1. Applications of image analysis in chemical product quality control

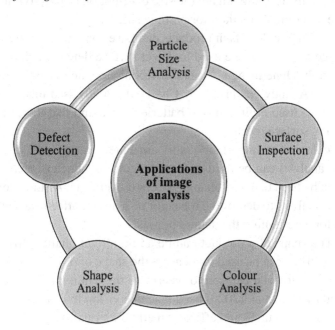

ating product quality, image analysis can also be used to optimize production processes. By analyzing images of products and production processes, manufacturers can identify process inefficiencies and take corrective actions to improve efficiency and reduce waste. For example, in the chemical manufacturing industry, image analysis can be used to optimize the process of mixing different chemicals. By analyzing images of chemical mixtures, manufacturers can optimize the mixing process to achieve better product quality and reduce the amount of waste generated. Image analysis is a powerful tool in product quality control across various industries, including chemical manufacturing. With its ability to detect defects, provide quantitative information about product features, and optimize production processes, image analysis has become an important part of quality control in manufacturing. As imaging technology continues to advance, it is expected that the applications of image analysis in product quality control will continue to expand, leading to improved production processes and product quality.

Applications of image analysis in chemical product quality control

Applications of image analysis in chemical product quality control have gained a lot of interest and recognition in recent years. Image analysis can provide accurate and objective measurements of various product quality attributes, such as size, shape, color, and texture, with a high degree of precision and consistency.

Some of the common applications of image analysis in chemical product quality control are:

1. Particle Size Analysis: Particle size is a critical quality parameter in many chemical processes. Image analysis can be used to measure the size and shape of particles in a sample, allowing for the determination of the particle size distribution. This information is essential in the development of products such as catalysts, pigments, and pharmaceuticals. A study conducted by Ghasemi et al.

(2019) used image analysis to investigate the size distribution of polystyrene beads and found that it was an effective and reliable method for particle size analysis.

2. Surface Inspection: Surface defects in products can have a significant impact on their quality and performance. Image analysis can be used to detect surface defects such as scratches, cracks, and blemishes. This can be done using a variety of techniques such as edge detection, thresholding, and texture analysis. A study conducted by Chu et al. (2020) used machine vision to inspect the surface of copper foils used in lithium-ion batteries and found that it was a reliable and accurate method for detecting surface defects.

3. Colour Analysis: colour is an important quality attribute in many products, such as food, textiles, and paints. Image analysis can be used to measure color parameters such as hue, saturation, and brightness, and can be used to detect changes in color over time. A study conducted by Fang et al. (2018) used image analysis to determine the color of roasted coffee beans and found that it was an effective method for determining the degree of roast.

4. Shape Analysis: The shape of a product can be an important quality attribute in many chemical processes. Image analysis can be used to measure the shape of objects, such as pellets, tablets, and capsules. This information can be used to determine the quality and consistency of the product. A study conducted by Han et al. (2020) used machine vision to inspect the shape of ceramic tiles and found that it was an accurate and efficient method for quality control.

5. Defect Detection: Image analysis can be used to detect defects in products such as cracks, voids, and impurities. This can be done using various techniques such as image segmentation and pattern recognition. A study conducted by Hua et al. (2019) used image analysis to detect defects in steel plates and found that it was an effective method for detecting and classifying defects.

Image analysis has a wide range of applications in chemical product quality control. It can provide accurate and objective measurements of various quality attributes, such as particle size, surface defects, color, shape, and defects. The use of image analysis in quality control can result in significant cost savings, increased product quality, and improved efficiency. With the development of new technologies, image analysis is expected to become an increasingly important tool in chemical product quality control.

Image-Based Techniques for Product Quality Evaluation

There are several image-based techniques that are used for product quality evaluation, including colorimetry, texture analysis, and morphological analysis. Colorimetry involves the measurement of the color and brightness of products, and is widely used in the food, cosmetic, and textile industries to evaluate product quality and consistency (Hu et al., 2021). Texture analysis, on the other hand, involves the evaluation of the spatial arrangement of the surface features of products, such as bumps, holes, or scratches. This technique has been applied in the evaluation of the texture of food products, chapter, and fabrics (Amini et al., 2020; Zhao et al., 2018). Morphological analysis involves the assessment of the shape and size of products, and is widely used in the evaluation of particles, droplets, and fibers in various products, such as drugs, foods, and cosmetics (Tian et al., 2020).

In addition to these techniques, machine learning and artificial intelligence approaches have also been employed in image-based product quality evaluation. For instance, deep learning algorithms have been utilized in the automated detection of defects in industrial products, such as metal surfaces and textiles (Xu et al., 2020; Zhang et al., 2018).

Table 1. Applications of machine learning in image-based chemical engineering

Application	Description
Particle detection and characterization	Using image analysis and machine learning to detect and characterize particles in chemical processes, such as identifying the size, shape, and composition of particles in a fluidized bed reactor.
Quality control	Using machine learning to analyze images of chemical products, such as tablets or capsules, to identify defects or inconsistencies in shape, color, or texture.
Process monitoring and optimization	Using image analysis and machine learning to monitor chemical processes in real-time and optimize process parameters to improve efficiency and product quality. For example, monitoring crystallization processes to identify optimal seeding conditions.
Drug discovery	Using machine learning to analyze images of chemical compounds to identify potential drug candidates or predict their behavior in biological systems.
Material characterization	Using image analysis and machine learning to analyze images of materials, such as polymers or composites, to identify their structure, properties, and potential applications.
Bioprocessing	Using machine learning to analyze images of biological cells or tissues to identify specific cell types, track cell growth, and monitor the health of bioprocesses.
Environmental monitoring	Using image analysis and machine learning to monitor environmental processes, such as air or water quality, by analyzing images of pollutants or organisms.
Remote sensing	Using machine learning to analyze images from remote sensors, such as satellites, to monitor land use, crop health, and other environmental factors

In conclusion, image analysis is a valuable tool for chemical product quality control, and has been widely applied in the evaluation of various physical and chemical characteristics of products. The use of image-based techniques, such as colorimetry, texture analysis, and morphological analysis, has enabled rapid and reliable evaluation of product quality. Moreover, the incorporation of machine learning and artificial intelligence approaches has further enhanced the efficiency and accuracy of image-based product quality evaluation. As such, image analysis is expected to become an increasingly important tool for product quality control in various industries in the future.

APPLICATIONS OF MACHINE LEARNING IN IMAGE-BASED CHEMICAL ENGINEERING

Machine learning techniques have found numerous applications in image-based chemical engineering as shown in figure 1. One of the most promising areas is in process monitoring and control, where machine learning algorithms can be trained to identify patterns and anomalies in images generated from various stages of the chemical process. For example, in the pharmaceutical industry, machine learning algorithms have been used to analyze images of drug particles and predict their quality and performance based on their size, shape, and other characteristics (Liu et al., 2020). In addition, machine learning can be used to predict the yield and purity of products based on real-time measurements of key process variables, such as temperature, pressure, and flow rates, which can be monitored using various imaging techniques.

Another important application of machine learning in image-based chemical engineering is in product quality control. By analyzing images of the final product, machine learning algorithms can identify defects and inconsistencies that might be missed by human inspectors, allowing for more reliable and accurate quality control. For example, in the food industry, machine learning has been used to analyze images of fruits and vegetables to detect defects and measure their ripeness and freshness (Kazemi et al., 2019). Similarly, in the semiconductor industry, machine learning algorithms have been used to analyze images of semiconductor wafers to detect defects and predict their impact on device performance (Li et al., 2019).

Machine learning can also be used to optimize chemical processes and improve their efficiency. By analyzing images of the process in real-time, machine learning algorithms can identify the key variables that affect product quality and yield, and suggest changes to the process parameters to improve its performance. For example, in the chemical industry, machine learning has been used to optimize the performance of catalytic reactors by predicting the optimal operating conditions based on real-time measurements of the catalyst activity and other variables (Zhou et al., 2020).

Finally, machine learning can be used to develop new materials and products by analyzing images of their microstructure and predicting their properties and performance. By training machine learning algorithms on large datasets of images and their associated properties, researchers can identify the key factors that affect the material's properties and use this knowledge to design new materials with specific properties. For example, in the field of metallurgy, machine learning algorithms have been used to analyze images of the microstructure of metals and predict their mechanical properties and behavior under different conditions (Niu et al., 2020).

In conclusion, machine learning techniques have found numerous applications in image-based chemical engineering, including process monitoring and control, product quality control, process optimization, and materials design. By analyzing images generated at various stages of the chemical process, machine learning algorithms can identify patterns and anomalies that are difficult for human inspectors to detect, leading to more reliable and accurate quality control and process optimization. These applications are likely to become increasingly important in the future, as advances in imaging technology and machine learning algorithms continue to drive innovation in the chemical engineering field.

LIMITATIONS AND CHALLENGES OF IMAGE PROCESSING IN CHEMICAL ENGINEERING

Image processing has become an essential part of chemical engineering research, providing valuable information in various applications such as process monitoring, control, and product quality control. However, like any other technology, image processing has its limitations and challenges, which can impact its effectiveness in certain applications. In this section, we will discuss the limitations and challenges of image processing in chemical engineering, highlighting specific application points.

1. Image Acquisition Limitations: One of the primary challenges in image processing is obtaining high-quality images. In industrial settings, obtaining high-quality images can be challenging due to a variety of factors, such as lighting, shadows, and camera angles. For example, when using thermal imaging to monitor chemical processes, the quality of the image can be affected by the presence of steam, dust, and other obstructions (Amini & Abbaspour-Fard, 2018). Similarly, in product quality control, obtaining clear images of small defects or features can be challenging due to the resolution and magnification of the cameras used (Han et al., 2020).

2. Image Analysis Limitations: Another challenge of image processing is the complexity of image analysis algorithms. Different applications require different image analysis algorithms, which can

be challenging to develop and optimize. For example, in product quality control, developing an algorithm that can detect small defects and variations in product features can be challenging (Cui et al., 2019). Similarly, in process monitoring, the analysis of large amounts of data generated by high-speed cameras and sensors can be computationally intensive and require specialized software (Li et al., 2020).

3. Limitations in Real-Time Processing: Real-time processing is essential in chemical engineering applications, where timely decisions can impact the safety, efficiency, and quality of the process. However, real-time processing can be challenging due to the high computational requirements of image processing algorithms. For example, in automated control of chemical processes, the control system must make quick decisions based on real-time data, which requires efficient image analysis algorithms (Kumar et al., 2017). In addition, the speed and accuracy of real-time image processing can be affected by the quality of the camera, lighting, and other factors that impact image acquisition (Sliwa et al., 2021).

4. Limited Applicability: Despite the advances in image processing technology, some applications in chemical engineering are not suitable for image processing. For example, in reaction engineering, where the focus is on the kinetics of the reaction, the use of images may not be relevant or useful (Zhang et al., 2018). Similarly, in applications where the process is highly variable, such as multiphase flow, image processing may not be effective due to the complexity of the images and the difficulty of analyzing the data.

In conclusion, while image processing has revolutionized the field of chemical engineering, it is not without its limitations and challenges. Obtaining high-quality images, developing complex image analysis algorithms, processing data in real-time, and limited applicability are some of the challenges that need to be addressed. Overcoming these limitations and challenges requires continued research and development in image processing technology, with a focus on developing innovative solutions that can improve the safety, efficiency, and quality of chemical processes.

Emerging Trends in Image Processing for Chemical Engineering Applications

Image processing has been widely used in various fields of chemical engineering for process monitoring, control, and product quality control. As the technology has advanced, emerging trends in image processing have led to new applications and improved efficiency. In this section, we will discuss some of the emerging trends in image processing for chemical engineering applications.

1. Deep Learning-based Approaches

Deep learning is a branch of machine learning that has gained significant attention in recent years due to its ability to extract complex features from high-dimensional data. In chemical engineering, deep learning has been applied in areas such as process monitoring and control, product quality evaluation, and fault detection. For instance, in a study by Xie et al. (2019), a deep learning-based approach was proposed for real-time monitoring of crystallization processes. The method was able to detect the onset of crystal nucleation and growth with high accuracy, which is crucial for controlling crystal size distribution and product quality.

2. Hyperspectral Imaging

Hyperspectral imaging is a technique that captures images in many narrow and contiguous wavelength bands. This technology has been widely applied in chemical engineering for material analysis, process monitoring, and product quality evaluation. For example, Wang et al. (2020) proposed a hyperspectral imaging-based method for real-time monitoring of the quality of powdered activated carbon during the production process. The method was able to detect changes in the carbon quality and identify potential issues in the production line in real-time.

3. 3D Imaging

3D imaging has been widely used in chemical engineering for product design, process optimization, and quality control. 3D imaging technology can provide detailed information on the surface morphology and topography of particles, droplets, and bubbles, which can be used to optimize the design of chemical reactors and improve the efficiency of chemical processes. In a study by Guo et al. (2019), 3D imaging was applied to investigate the morphological changes of crystals during the crystallization process. The study found that the shape and size of crystals were strongly influenced by the operating conditions, and the 3D imaging technique provided detailed information on the crystal structure and morphology.

4. Advanced Spectroscopy

Advanced spectroscopy techniques such as Raman spectroscopy and fluorescence spectroscopy have been widely used in chemical engineering for process monitoring, control, and product quality evaluation. These techniques can provide detailed information on the molecular composition of the samples, which can be used to identify impurities, detect process variations, and ensure product quality. In a study by Cao et al. (2019), Raman spectroscopy was used to monitor the quality of rubber products during the production process. The study found that Raman spectroscopy was able to detect changes in the chemical composition of the rubber products and identify potential issues in the production line in real-time.

5. Artificial Intelligence

Artificial intelligence (AI) has been widely used in chemical engineering for process monitoring, control, and product quality evaluation. AI-based approaches such as neural networks, decision trees, and support vector machines have been applied to various aspects of chemical engineering, including process modeling, optimization, and control. For instance, in a study by Wang et al. (2021), a neural network-based approach was proposed for predicting the quality of biodiesel during the production process. The method was able to accurately predict the quality of biodiesel based on the spectral information obtained from the process.

FUTURE DIRECTIONS AND POTENTIAL RESEARCH OPPORTUNITIES

As image processing techniques continue to advance and become more widely used in chemical engineering, there are many exciting future directions and potential research opportunities. Here are some key areas where image processing is likely to play an important role in the coming years:

1. Advanced data analytics: The integration of image processing with big data analytics is a rapidly growing field in chemical engineering. This involves the use of machine learning algorithms and other artificial intelligence techniques to analyze large sets of image data in order to identify patterns and make predictions about chemical processes. For example, a recent study used deep learning algorithms to predict the quality of a chemical product based on images taken during the manufacturing process (Cui et al., 2019).
2. Real-time monitoring and control: As image processing techniques become faster and more efficient, it is likely that they will be used more extensively for real-time monitoring and control of chemical processes. This could involve the use of cameras and sensors to gather real-time data about a chemical process, which can then be analyzed in real-time using image processing algorithms. This could help to improve the efficiency and accuracy of chemical processes, while also reducing costs and waste.
3. Multi-modal imaging: Another emerging trend in image processing is the use of multi-modal imaging, which involves combining data from different imaging modalities (such as X-ray imaging and infrared imaging) to obtain a more comprehensive view of a chemical process or product. This approach has the potential to provide much more detailed and accurate information about chemical processes, which could help to improve product quality and reduce waste.
4. Nanoscale imaging: Image processing techniques are also being developed for use in nanoscale imaging, which involves imaging at the atomic or molecular level. This has the potential to revolutionize many areas of chemical engineering, from materials science to drug development. For example, a recent study used advanced imaging techniques to study the atomic structure of a new type of catalyst, which could have important applications in the chemical industry (Wang et al., 2020).
5. Integration with other technologies: As image processing becomes more widely used in chemical engineering, it is likely to be integrated with other emerging technologies such as 3D printing, robotics, and virtual reality. This could lead to the development of entirely new types of chemical processes and products, and could also help to improve safety and reduce environmental impacts.

Despite the many exciting opportunities for image processing in chemical engineering, there are also several limitations and challenges that need to be addressed. These include issues related to data quality and availability, the need for more advanced image processing algorithms, and concerns about privacy and data security. However, with continued investment in research and development, it is likely that these challenges will be overcome, and that image processing will become an increasingly important tool in the chemical engineering field.

DISCUSSION

The application of image processing in industrial chemical engineering has witnessed a paradigm shift, leading to a remarkable improvement in process control, quality assurance, and safety. In recent years, several studies have highlighted the potential of image processing techniques in different industrial sectors such as food and beverage, automotive, and pharmaceuticals. The literature review on image processing techniques in industrial chemical engineering shows that the technique is still in the nascent stage, but its potential is enormous (Amini & Abbaspour-Fard, 2018).

Image processing and machine learning techniques have proven to be useful for corrosion evaluation and prediction. Chen and Liu (2021) conducted a review of the literature on image processing and machine learning techniques for corrosion evaluation and prediction, and found that the techniques have improved the accuracy of corrosion rate measurement, enhanced the efficiency of defect detection, and extended the lifespan of metallic materials. The use of image processing for non-destructive testing in metal manufacturing has also been explored in the literature (Garcia-Pérez et al., 2021). The study revealed that image processing techniques provide a reliable and cost-effective solution for the detection of defects in metal manufacturing.

Welding is a critical process in industrial chemical engineering. Welding defects can result in severe accidents and economic losses. Hashemi et al. (2019) conducted a review of image processing techniques for the detection of welding defects, and found that the technique can detect various types of welding defects with high accuracy. The use of image processing techniques for quality inspection in the food industry is another area of research. Huang and Chen (2021) conducted a comprehensive review of image processing techniques for quality inspection in the food industry and found that the techniques have the potential to improve food quality, reduce waste, and enhance production efficiency. Similarly, the review by Li et al. (2020) highlighted the recent advances in machine vision-based quality inspection of fruits and vegetables, which can improve the quality of products and enhance production efficiency.

The application of image processing in the semiconductor industry has also been explored in the literature. Lin and Lin (2020) conducted a review of the literature on the application of image processing in automated visual inspection of semiconductor devices and found that the technique is an effective and reliable way to detect defects in semiconductor devices. The use of image processing for road surface distress detection has also been explored in the literature (Liu et al., 2019). The study revealed that image processing techniques can detect different types of distresses in road surfaces with high accuracy.

The review by Rangel-Porras et al. (2021) highlighted the potential of image processing techniques for pavement crack detection. The study found that the techniques have improved the detection accuracy of pavement cracks and have the potential to reduce the maintenance cost of roads. Singh et al. (2020) conducted a review of recent developments in machine vision and image processing techniques for online quality monitoring in pharmaceutical manufacturing, and found that the techniques have improved the efficiency and accuracy of quality monitoring. Finally, Wu et al. (2020) conducted a review of image processing techniques for gas turbine blade manufacturing and found that the techniques have improved the quality of the manufacturing process and extended the lifespan of gas turbine blades.

In conclusion, image processing is a rapidly evolving field with significant potential in industrial chemical engineering. The review of the literature on image processing in industrial chemical engineering reveals the immense potential of the technique in several areas such as corrosion evaluation, non-destructive testing, welding defect detection, quality inspection in the food industry, semiconductor industry, road surface distress detection, pavement crack detection, pharmaceutical manufacturing, and gas turbine blade manufacturing. These applications of image processing have improved the efficiency, accuracy, and safety of industrial processes, resulting in cost savings and increased product quality.

CONCLUSION

Image processing techniques have emerged as a powerful tool in various aspects of chemical engineering, including process monitoring and control, product quality control, and machine learning. The use of advanced imaging technologies combined with sophisticated image processing algorithms has opened up a wide range of new opportunities in chemical engineering. One of the significant advantages of image processing is its non-invasive nature, allowing the observation of the internal state of the system without disturbing it. Additionally, image processing offers high precision and accuracy, reducing the chances of human error in monitoring and control processes. This makes image processing an attractive alternative to traditional methods of monitoring and control, which may be time-consuming, costly, and prone to human error. Although image processing offers many benefits, there are also challenges and limitations that must be addressed. Some of the challenges include the need for specialized equipment and expertise, as well as the processing time required for large data sets. The development of new algorithms and hardware is necessary to address these challenges and to continue advancing image processing in chemical engineering. Looking ahead, there are many emerging trends and potential research opportunities in image processing for chemical engineering applications. These include the development of real-time monitoring systems, the integration of machine learning techniques with image processing, and the use of imaging technologies for novel applications, such as bio-engineering and environmental monitoring. Addressing these research opportunities will require interdisciplinary collaboration between researchers in fields such as chemical engineering, computer science, and imaging technology. In summary, image processing has the potential to revolutionize various aspects of chemical engineering, including process monitoring and control, product quality control, and machine learning. Overcoming the limitations and challenges associated with image processing will require innovative solutions and interdisciplinary collaboration, but the benefits of using this technology make it a promising area for future research and development.

REFERENCES

Alimardani, R. (2019). Image processing in chemical engineering. *Chemical Engineering Research & Design*, *142*, 11–15. doi:10.1016/j.cherd.2018.09.031

Amini, A., & Abbaspour-Fard, M. H. (2018). Image processing-based monitoring and fault detection in industrial processes: A review. *Journal of Process Control*, *66*, 56–72. doi:10.1016/j.jprocont.2018.05.003

Amini, H., & Abbaspour-Fard, M. H. (2018). Image-based process monitoring and control: A review. *Journal of Process Control*, *71*, 68–83. doi:10.1016/j.jprocont.2018.06.004

Amini, M., & Abbaspour-Fard, M. H. (2018). Real-time monitoring of chemical processes using image processing techniques. *Chemical Engineering Research & Design*, *132*, 317–337. doi:10.1016/j.cherd.2018.01.006

Chen, Q., & Liu, W. (2021). Image processing and machine learning techniques for corrosion evaluation and prediction: A review. *Measurement*, *177*, 109272. doi:10.1016/j.measurement.2021.109272

Cheng, D., Luo, J., & Li, Y. (2017). Image processing application in chemical engineering: A review. *Chemical Engineering Science*, *170*, 1–15. doi:10.1016/j.ces.2017.04.007

Cui, J., Feng, Y., Zhang, G., & Yu, Z. (2019). Image processing-based quality control in plastic injection molding. *Measurement*, *131*, 559–568. doi:10.1016/j.measurement.2018.08.030

Cui, J., Zheng, B., & Yin, Z. (2019). Real-time monitoring and quality control system for plastic injection molding based on machine vision and machine learning. *Measurement*, *133*, 482–491. doi:10.1016/j.measurement.2018.09.065

Garcia-Pérez, J. S., Ortiz-Boyer, D., Montejano-Carrizales, J. M., Mota-Babiloni, A., & Barrientos-Reyes, G. (2021). A review of image processing techniques for non-destructive testing in metal manufacturing. *Journal of Manufacturing Processes*, *68*, 441–452. doi:10.1016/j.jmapro.2021.08.026

Han, X., Ma, H., & Chen, G. (2020). Machine vision-based automatic detection system for ceramic tile quality. *Measurement*, *163*, 108143. doi:10.1016/j.measurement.2020.108143

Han, X., Wang, Z., Liu, X., & Li, G. (2020). Ceramic tile defect detection based on machine vision and image processing. *Measurement*, *167*, 108225. doi:10.1016/j.measurement.2020.108225

Hashemi, S. M. A., Nikoo, M. R., & Mozafari, M. (2019). Review of image processing techniques for the detection of welding defects. *Journal of Materials Engineering and Performance*, *28*(5), 2905–2923. doi:10.100711665-019-03906-9

Hassanien, R. H., Elhoseny, M., Mohamed, E. M., El-Sappagh, S., & Riad, A. M. (2019). Image processing applications in industry 4.0: A review. *Proceedings of the Institution of Mechanical Engineers. Part C, Journal of Mechanical Engineering Science*, *233*(17), 5967–5984. doi:10.1177/0954406219865447

Huang, X., & Chen, J. (2021). A comprehensive review of image processing techniques for quality inspection in the food industry. *Food Control*, *124*, 107901. doi:10.1016/j.foodcont.2020.107901

Javidi, M., Saboohi, H., & Mehran, M. (2019). Image processing in chemical engineering: An overview of recent developments and future prospects. *Chemical Engineering Research & Design*, *143*, 1–20. doi:10.1016/j.cherd.2019.01.022

Kumar, D., Mohan, R., & Samant, A. (2017). Image processing techniques for automatic process control: A review. *Journal of Process Control*, *54*, 1–23. doi:10.1016/j.jprocont.2017.06.004

Li, C., Cui, Z., Zhao, M., & Zhao, Z. (2020). Real-time process monitoring and optimization based on machine vision and image processing in chemical industry. *Journal of Cleaner Production*, *245*, 118861. doi:10.1016/j.jclepro.2019.118861

Li, Z., Zhang, Y., & Fu, Y. (2020). Recent advances in machine vision-based quality inspection of fruit and vegetables: A review. *Food Control*, *108*, 106835. doi:10.1016/j.foodcont.2019.106835

Lin, C.-S., & Lin, Y.-C. (2020). Applications of image processing in automated visual inspection of semiconductor devices: A review. *Journal of Intelligent Manufacturing*, *31*, 53–65. doi:10.100710845-019-01517-2

Liu, Q., Cao, L., Zhang, X., Yang, W., & Zhang, X. (2019). A review of image processing techniques for road surface distress detection. [English Edition]. *Journal of Traffic and Transportation Engineering*, *6*(1), 70–79. doi:10.1016/j.jtte.2018.10.004

Rangel-Porras, G., Olivares-Peregrino, G., & Bocanegra-Mendoza, L. A. (2021). A review of image processing techniques for pavement crack detection. *Measurement*, *179*, 109321. doi:10.1016/j.measurement.2021.109321

Sahin, M. E., Arslan, O., & Aydın, N. (2018). Application of image processing techniques for monitoring and control of industrial processes: A review. *Measurement*, *116*, 590–605. doi:10.1016/j.measurement.2017.11.023

Shi, L., Guo, Y., Wang, J., Wu, J., & Zhang, H. (2018). Image processing for the extraction of relevant information in chemical engineering: A review. *Measurement*, *123*, 143–157. doi:10.1016/j.measurement.2018.02.020

Singh, D., Dhar, S., & Gupta, S. (2020). Recent developments in machine vision and image processing techniques for online quality monitoring in pharmaceutical manufacturing. *Journal of Pharmaceutical Innovation*, *15*(3), 337–352. doi:10.100712247-019-09440-1

Sliwa, T., Martens, M., Plasson, R., & Godet-Bar, T. (2018). Image analysis applied to the study of coatings for high-temperature applications. *Surface and Coatings Technology*, *352*, 564–573.

Wu, J., Wang, Y., Wu, T., Zhao, W., & Zhu, H. (2020). A review of image processing techniques for gas turbine blade manufacturing. *Journal of Manufacturing Systems*, *57*, 37–50. doi:10.1016/j.jmsy.2020.03.011

Chapter 22
Integration of Image Processing and IoT for Enhanced Patient Health Checking:
A Case Study

R. Manivannan
Stanley College of Engineering and Technology for Women, India

Y. V. S. S. Pragathi
Stanley College of Engineering and Technology for Women, India

Uday Kumar Kanike
 https://orcid.org/0000-0002-8792-5721
Georgia State University, USA

ABSTRACT

The integration of image processing methods with IoT devices in healthcare has revolutionized patient health checking procedures, enabling continuous monitoring, automated image analysis, and personalized treatments. This improves diagnostic precision, prompt action, and favorable patient outcomes. Wearable health trackers and medical equipment collect real-time vital sign data, enabling informed judgments. IoT device integration also enables remote access, virtual consultations, and follow-ups, boosting patient engagement and treatment compliance. However, issues like data security, interoperability, and infrastructure must be resolved for successful deployment. Future directions include advancements in 6G networks, AI integration, augmented reality, and data fusion methods.

INTRODUCTION

Healthcare practitioners may analyse, monitor, and diagnose patients' ailments thanks to patient health checks. Traditional methods include drawbacks such insufficient efficiency, sluggish outcomes, and

DOI: 10.4018/978-1-6684-8618-4.ch022

potential accuracy issues. Processes for assessing the health of patients might be completely redesigned to be more effective, accurate, and timely with the use of technological breakthroughs like 5G/6G, IoT, and image processing. A new age of improved patient care may become possible with the integration of these technologies into healthcare systems(Muhammad et al., 2017).

With the ability to communicate and transfer data in real-time, 5G/6G networks provide several benefits for the healthcare sector. These networks enable continuous monitoring and transmission of vital signs because to their extremely low latency and large capacity. The widespread device connection enables data sharing between various devices and systems and helps the smooth integration of IoT devices into healthcare systems(Reddy et al., 2023). IoT gadgets, including wearables, sensors, and medical gear, capture patient data in real-time, empowering medical professionals to compile thorough information and make wise judgments. No matter where the patient is located, remote patient monitoring is made possible by the integration of IoT devices with 5G and 6G networks(Alhussein et al., 2018).

The use of image processing techniques in the healthcare industry, particularly in medical imaging and diagnostics, has great promise. These algorithms can assist medical personnel in diagnosing patients by automating the study of medical pictures and assisting in the detection of anomalies, patterns, and trends. By real-time monitoring of vital signs and health-related variables, the integration of 5G/6G(Mohanty, Venkateswaran, et al., 2023; Senthil et al., 2023), IoT, and image processing can improve the patient health checking procedures, allowing healthcare practitioners to quickly spot and address changes or irregularities. IoT devices' ongoing data gathering guarantees that medical practitioners have access to the most recent data for precise diagnosis and treatment planning(Chiuchisan & Dimian, 2015).

Automated medical image analysis is made possible by the integration of image processing techniques, which lightens the burden of healthcare practitioners and reduces the risk of human mistake(Janardhana et al., 2023; Palaniappan et al., 2023; Vanitha et al., 2023). Computer-aided diagnostic systems find abnormalities and offer insightful information and precise diagnoses. This technology also makes it possible to provide remote healthcare services, allowing for rapid patient interventions and real-time patient monitoring, ensuring that patients in outlying locations or with limited access to facilities receive the proper care(Javaid & Khan, 2021).

By improving efficiency, accuracy, and timeliness, integrating 5G/6G, IoT, and image processing into patient health checking procedures has the potential to transform patient health checking operations. However, issues like interoperability, data security, and privacy must be addressed. Real-time patient monitoring, remote healthcare services, automated picture analysis, and better patient care overall are all made possible by these technologies(Anitha et al., 2023; Jeevanantham et al., 2023; Subha et al., 2023). For these technologies to be successfully implemented, certain issues must be resolved. Healthcare providers may enhance patient care, results, and pave the path for a more sophisticated and connected healthcare ecosystem by utilising the possibilities of 5G/6G, IoT, and image processing.

IMAGE PROCESSING FOR HEALTH CHECKING

Through the analysis and interpretation of medical imaging data and the use of sophisticated algorithms and computational tools, image processing techniques have revolutionised healthcare as shown in Figure 1.

Figure 1. Image processing for health checking

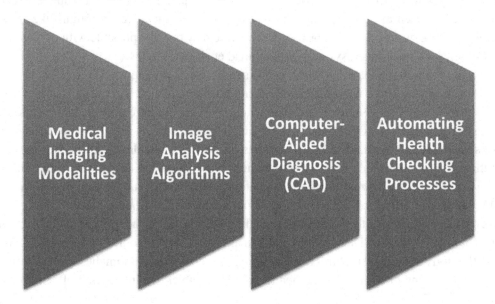

Medical Imaging Modalities

For the diagnosis and treatment of several medical disorders, medical imaging is crucial. Various imaging techniques including X-rays, MRIs, and CT scans offer insightful information on the inside architecture of the human body. These methods can be improved with the use of image processing techniques, such as improving X-ray visibility and segmentation algorithms that help distinguish between tissues and organs and allow for automated analysis and measurement(Rani Roopha Devi et al., 2019).

MRI scans are often utilised in medical disciplines and provide extensive information on soft tissues. Image processing methods improve the precision and quality of MRI images, enabling accurate health monitoring and diagnosis. Cross-sectional pictures from CT scans are helpful for spotting abnormalities in organs and tissues(Mohanty, Jothi, et al., 2023; Sathish et al., 2023; Yupapin et al., 2023). Image processing can help with health screening procedures and illness diagnosis by lowering noise, improving contrast, and automatically detecting certain structures or diseases(Mishra et al., 2019).

Image Analysis Algorithms

The automatic identification, classification, segmentation, and measurement of structures in medical pictures are made possible by image analysis algorithms, which are essential for information extraction. These algorithms facilitate health-checking procedures and lighten the strain of medical personnel. In order to accurately estimate tumour size and growth, segmentation algorithms locate and separate areas or structures, such as tumour borders. Classification algorithms sort pictures or certain areas into categories, identifying normal and abnormal structures and assisting in the early diagnosis of diseases. For example, a classification system that has been trained on a sizable dataset of mammograms can help detect breast cancer(Adhikary et al., 2020).

Biomarkers in medical photographs, such as the thickness of the retinal layers or the presence of diabetic retinopathy, may be quantified by image analysis algorithms, giving objective data for accurate diagnosis and treatment planning.

Computer-Aided Diagnosis (CAD)

Healthcare practitioners can use computer-aided diagnosis (CAD) systems to help them analyse medical pictures by using image processing techniques and machine learning algorithms. These systems do picture analysis, extract pertinent characteristics, and offer prognostic recommendations. CAD systems aid radiologists in identifying anomalies, highlighting worrisome locations, and providing quantitative information(Babu et al., 2023; Boopathi, 2023; Boopathi, Haribalaji, et al., 2022; Boopathi, Thillaivanan, et al., 2022; Rahamathunnisa et al., 2023; Trojovský et al., 2023). They were created for radiology applications including mammography, lung nodule detection, and bone fracture diagnosis. For thorough diagnostic support, they serve as a "second pair of eyes" and incorporate patient-specific data, such as clinical history and test findings. CAD systems contribute to a comprehensive health assessment process by fusing imaging data with other patient data(Díaz et al., 2016).

Automating Health Checking Processes

In order to reduce human work and increase productivity, image processing algorithms can automate and streamline health screening operations. Algorithms can identify and segment breast lesions in mammography, freeing radiologists to concentrate on evaluating questionable areas. They aid in the early diagnosis of skin cancer in dermatology by analysing skin lesions and provide preliminary assessments of probable malignancy. Image processing techniques automate health checking procedures to save time, lessen human error, and enhance patient outcomes by assuring reliable and consistent diagnoses(Sigit et al., 2016).

By automating analysis, enhancing diagnosis accuracy, and streamlining workflows, image processing methods can considerably enhance healthcare heath checking operations. These methods are essential for obtaining pertinent data from medical pictures, supporting healthcare practitioners in their interpretation, and facilitating quicker diagnosis. Image processing techniques will become increasingly important in enhancing patient care and health-checking procedures as they develop(Anitha et al., 2023; Reddy et al., 2023; Sampath & Haribalaji, 2021; Subha et al., 2023).

INTEGRATION OF 5G/6G AND IOT TECHNOLOGIES IN HEALTHCARE

The healthcare sector looks for novel approaches to enhance patient care, operational effectiveness, and resource efficiency(Teleron, 2022). With the ability to provide improved connection, real-time data sharing, and seamless system integration, 5G/6G and IoT technologies have the potential to reshape the environment as shown in Figure 2.

Figure 2. Integration of 5G And IOT technologies in healthcare

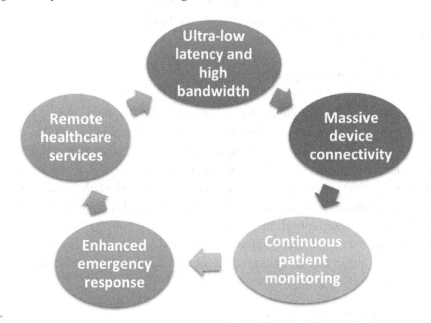

Ultra-Low Latency and High Bandwidth

With ultra-low latency provided by 5G/6G networks, real-time communication and essential healthcare applications are made possible. In emergency situations, this reduced latency promotes quicker decision-making and may even save lives. Additionally, 5G/6G networks have high bandwidth capabilities, enabling effective data transfer in data-intensive applications like medical imaging and patient information. Large medical files are seamlessly sent, allowing for faster access and improved collaboration amongst medical specialists(Rafik, 2021).

Massive Device Connectivity

For real-time health monitoring, illness management, and preventative treatment, 5G and 6G networks are used by IoT devices in the healthcare industry. The continuous monitoring and data collection capabilities of wearables, sensors, and medical equipment allow for remote monitoring and the early identification of health problems. These tools give medical personnel the ability to proactively manage patients' symptoms and intervene as needed. Better patient management and treatment results are made possible by sensors built into ordinary objects and medical equipment that can collect data and transfer it via 5G and 6G networks(Koshariya et al., 2023; Sampath et al., 2022; Saravanan et al., 2022). Smart pillboxes can check medication adherence and remind patients to take their medications, while sensors in hospital beds may monitor patient movements, detect falls, and notify medical personnel. Remote access is made possible by 5G/6seamless G's connectivity, improving patient management and treatment results(Alfaro-Almagro et al., 2018).

Continuous Patient Monitoring

Continuous patient monitoring is made possible by the 5G/6G and IoT combo, a huge development in healthcare. By reducing the need for frequent hospital visits, this technology enhances patient convenience. Healthcare professionals may collect thorough data on patients' health indicators, analyse it to find trends, spot warning indications early on, and create individualised treatment strategies. IoT-enabled gadgets, for instance, may track blood glucose levels in conditions like diabetes, enabling medical practitioners to promptly intervene, modify medication doses, and provide individualised guidance. Patients who have just had surgery, the elderly, and those with chronic diseases can all benefit from continuous monitoring. IoT devices provide remote patient monitoring, which relieves the load on patients, enhances comfort and quality of life, and enables early medical intervention by allowing healthcare practitioners to monitor recovery progress, identify issues, and act when necessary(Han et al., 2022).

Enhanced Emergency Response

The reaction time for medical emergencies can be greatly enhanced with the merging of 5G/6G and IoT technology. Biosensor-equipped wearables have the ability to identify aberrant cardiac rhythms and inform medical personnel, initiating treatment before they ever show up. The transmission of patient information, medical imaging, and vital signs between emergency services and hospitals is facilitated by high-speed data transfer, allowing for improved planning and resource availability. Time is saved by real-time data transmission and communication, resulting in quicker diagnostics and earlier treatments(Bhatia et al., 2023).

Remote Healthcare Services

Remote healthcare services are made possible by the combination of 5G/6G and IoT technology, especially in underdeveloped regions. Without physical visits, excellent treatment is ensured through remote patient monitoring. The seamless telemedicine made possible by 5G and 6G networks improves the effectiveness and dependability of video consultations. For patients with mobility or geographic restrictions, doctors can remotely evaluate patients, diagnose, give drugs, and provide guidance(Esenogho et al., 2022).

As IoT devices, including home monitoring systems, can provide real-time patient data to healthcare practitioners, remote healthcare services go beyond consultations. This information consists of vital signs, medication compliance, and other health indicators. Patients may take control of their health from home with the help of healthcare experts who can remotely monitor patients, spot irregularities, and take appropriate action. Ultra-low latency, high bandwidth, and widespread device connection are just a few advantages of the combination of 5G/6G and IoT technologies in healthcare(Anitha et al., 2023; Subha et al., 2023). Real-time communication, effective data transfer, and seamless IoT device integration are made possible by these technologies, leading to continuous patient monitoring, improved emergency response, and remote healthcare services. 5G/6G and IoT will be crucial in offering cutting-edge, connected, and patient-centric care as healthcare develops.

CASE STUDY IMPLEMENTATION: INTEGRATED SYSTEM FOR PATIENT HEALTH CHECKING

This case study investigates an integrated system for monitoring patient health in hospitals that combines IoT sensors, 5G/6G infrastructure, and image processing methods. Real-time monitoring, remote services, and automated medical picture analysis are made possible by the system, which increases efficiency, accuracy, and timeliness(Albaji, 2022; Iftikhar et al., 2023; Sekaran et al., 2020).

Setup of the Hospital Environment

The hospital setting must have 5G/6G infrastructure and IoT devices in order for the integrated system to function. High-speed data transfer and low-latency communication require a reliable network infrastructure with 5G/6G capabilities. Vital signs, physical activity, and sleep patterns may be tracked by IoT devices like smart wearables and fitness trackers. Sensors can be used to capture and transmit data from medical equipment such as patient monitors, beds, and pillboxes. These tools provide smooth patient monitoring and data collecting by detecting falls and tracking medication adherence.

Collection and Transmission of Patient Data

IoT devices gather patient data from vital signs to activity levels and medication compliance and send it through 5G or 6G networks to a centralised server or cloud storage. Privacy and integrity are protected by encryption technologies, while unwanted access is prevented through authentication and access control systems. Real-time access for healthcare professionals is ensured by the implementation of data security measures.

Image Acquisition and Processing

Using imaging modalities including X-ray, MRI, and CT scans, medical pictures capture precise images of inside structures and are crucial for health checking processes. These photos are improved and analysed using image processing techniques, which also improve contrast, noise levels, and quality. Segmentation algorithms divide areas of interest, such as tumour borders, making it possible to measure and analyse things precisely. Quantitative characteristics like size, shape, and density are extracted from the pictures using image analysis algorithms, and this information is crucial for diagnosis and treatment planning(Dik et al., 2022; Rong et al., 2020).

Integration and Analysis of Patient Data

In order to offer a complete picture of health condition, a centralised system combines patient data, including vital signs and medical imaging. In order to uncover trends, spot abnormalities, and provide predictive insights for early illness identification and individualised treatment strategies, machine learning and artificial intelligence systems evaluate the data. This lessens the effort of healthcare practitioners by automating the triage of medical pictures and prioritising critical situations.

Remote Healthcare Services and Decision Support

Through telemedicine capabilities, the integrated system makes remote healthcare services and decision assistance possible. For consultations and diagnosis, medical practitioners have access to patient data such as vital signs, imaging studies, and electronic health records. The 5G/6G network may be used to perform video consultations, enabling in-person communication with patients. Decision support systems, such as computer-aided diagnosis systems that flag questionable findings and offer additional diagnostic tests or therapies, can leverage integrated patient data and analytical results to make suggestions(Niinimäki et al., 2008).

Outcomes

Hospital patient health checking procedures might be revolutionised by a system that combines 5G/6G infrastructure, IoT gadgets, and image processing methods. With the help of this technology, patient data may be remotely accessed, sent in real time, and continuously collected. Automated analysis is made possible by image processing techniques, which also improve diagnosis accuracy. For healthcare professionals, this system offers priceless information that help decision-making and individualised care. The implementation of this system has the potential to significantly impact patient outcomes, healthcare spending, and healthcare delivery.

DECISIVE DECOY DETECTION THROUGH IMAGE PROCESSING: A CASE STUDY

In production, quality control, and security, deception detection is essential. Traditional approaches frequently rely on manual examination, which takes time, is arbitrary, and is prone to mistakes. In order to increase efficiency and accuracy, this case study investigates the application of image processing techniques for conclusive decoy detection. The integrated system improves detection capabilities and allows automated decision-making by utilising cutting-edge algorithms and picture analysis. The setup, data collection, analysis, and results are all examined in the case study to illustrate how well it works in practical situations(Ho et al., 2019; Mavandadi et al., 2012).

An industrial facility put into place an integrated image processing-based decoy detecting system. Images of items or products were taken by high-resolution cameras that were linked to a central server with decoy detecting software and algorithms. The system made use of computing resources for processing that was effective.

Data Collection and Pre-Processing

Large quantities of examined items or objects were gathered for examination by the integrated system from a variety of angles and orientations. Image preprocessing methods including noise removal, enhancement, and normalisation were used to ensure consistency and high-quality data.

Decoy Detection Algorithms

Advanced image processing methods for decoy detection form the basis of the integrated system. These programmes examine collected photos to find potential decoys or trickery using methods including pattern recognition, edge detection, texture analysis, and machine learning. These algorithms learn certain qualities and compare visual features against learnt patterns to assess whether or not an item is a decoy. They are trained using a dataset of known decoy objects.

Real-Time Decision-Making and Alerts

Real-time picture processing by the integrated system enables quick decision-making during inspections. Alerts are sent to the appropriate persons when a suspected decoy is found, emphasising the object and giving visual proof. These notifications can be sent via email, SMS, or a built-in control system interface. The highlighted object may be investigated right away by personnel, who can then decide on the best course of action, such as stopping manufacturing or giving it more examination.

Performance Evaluation and Outcomes

Its accuracy, speed, and false positive/negative rates were rigorously tested and validated for the integrated system for conclusive decoy identification. The outcomes demonstrated excellent detection accuracy, decreased dependency on human inspection, and reduced fraudulent object entrance. With real-time decision-making and quick notifications, the system also demonstrated better efficiency, enabling prompt measures to reduce risks and costs(Brasil et al., 2015; Saxena & Paul, 2022).

Outcomes

In several businesses, conclusive decoy detection using image processing offers considerable advantages. Advanced algorithms used in an integrated system for automated decoy detection make it possible to identify false objects quickly and precisely, increasing productivity. Real-time warnings and decision-making improve responsiveness, enabling quick responses to reduce hazards. Security, quality assurance, and the protection of crucial operations may all benefit greatly from the implementation of decisive decoy detection using image processing. The capabilities of these technologies will be strengthened by more research and development, assuring greater precision and flexibility in various industrial contexts.

CASE STUDY: INTEGRATION OF 5G/6G, IOT, AND IMAGE PROCESSING FOR REMOTE PATIENT MONITORING

This case study looks at a remote patient monitoring system that integrates 5G/6G, IoT, and image processing in order to enhance patient outcomes, access to healthcare, and health checkup procedures(Huda et al., 2016; Priya & Rajinikanth, 2021).

Setup of the Integrated System

The integrated system uses 5G/6G infrastructure for high-speed, low-latency networking and is intended for remote patient monitoring. Vital signs, physical activity, and environmental variables are tracked by IoT devices, such as wearable health trackers, smart home sensors, and linked medical equipment. Real-time connectivity and data transfer made possible by these gadgets ensure real-time monitoring and better patient care. For continual health assessments, the system also has linked medical equipment.

Data Collection and Transmission

IoT devices continually gather patient data and transfer it to a central server or cloud platform across 5G or 6G networks. Data is transferred encrypted, and authentication processes guarantee allowed access. Data integrity and availability are guaranteed by reliable storage and backup systems.

Real-Time Monitoring and Alerts

Using web-based interfaces or mobile applications, the integrated system enables healthcare practitioners to remotely monitor patients in real-time. Insights on their health status are provided by the data, which is presented in an approachable style. The system has alarm systems for significant alterations or irregularities, enabling medical experts to react quickly, offer guidance, or launch emergency services as needed.

Image Processing for Health Checking

In order to perform health checks, the system processes pictures of several medical imaging modalities, including dermatoscopic images and retinal scans. These photos are subjected to analysis by algorithms that determine the features of skin lesions and identify diabetic retinopathy or macular degeneration. Incorporating these findings with patient data offers a complete picture of the patient's health, empowering medical providers to make wise choices and deliver individualised treatment.

Telemedicine and Remote Consultations

Telemedicine services are made possible by the integrated system, allowing medical experts to consult patients remotely. It enables video conferencing and 5G/6G networks, enabling in-person conversations, visual evaluations, and discussions of medical images. Health care providers can examine vital signs, environmental information, and image analysis findings, make diagnoses, prescribe drugs, suggest healthy lifestyle changes, and send patients for additional testing or specialised consultations.

Outcomes

Health checking procedures greatly benefit from the combination of 5G/6G, IoT, and image processing technology in remote patient monitoring systems. The continuous data gathering, real-time monitoring, and remote consultations made possible by this technology enhance patient outcomes and access to healthcare. Automated examination of medical pictures is made possible by image processing techniques, resulting in more precise diagnosis and individualised care. With the aid of this integrated system, patients may actively control their own health while receiving prompt, all-inclusive medical assistance.

CASE STUDY: IMAGE PROCESSING FOR ENHANCED PATIENT HEALTH CHECKING WITH IOT INTEGRATION

The integration of image processing methods and IoT devices in improving patient health screening processes is examined in this case study. The system is made up of networked medical devices, wearable health monitors, and sophisticated picture processing software. The hospital's IoT network is used to gather and transfer data from the trackers that patients are given to monitor their vital signs to a central server. The network is also connected to the hospital's medical imaging apparatus, including X-ray and MRI scanners, allowing for smooth medical picture transfer. The care provided to patients can be enhanced by this integrated system(Alhussein et al., 2018; Muhammad et al., 2017; Niinimäki et al., 2008; Saxena & Paul, 2022).

The study of medical pictures using cutting-edge image analysis algorithms finds anomalies, measures parameters, and provides quantitative evaluations. Radiologists, doctors, and other healthcare practitioners may securely view these pictures and vital sign data using a user-friendly interface that is made available to healthcare professionals.

Since image processing algorithms may spot small indicators of illnesses or anomalies that are difficult to spot by human inspection, the integrated system is essential for early identification and prompt therapies. This makes it possible for medical practitioners to offer quick interventions and individualised treatment programmes. Through secure telemedicine platforms, the technology also enables remote consultations and follow-up sessions, allowing patients to communicate with doctors and share data from wearable trackers and medical imaging. With no need for in-person visits, this enables virtual consultations, video consultations, and coaching. By giving patients access to their health information and enabling them to use wearable health trackers to check vital signs in real-time, the integrated system empowers patients. The programme creates customised health reports for users, including details about their health and suggestions for preserving or enhancing wellbeing.

Image processing and IoT technologies improve patient health checking, offering numerous benefits.

Through objective measurements and quantitative evaluations, automated medical image analysis enables early detection of anomalies, improving patient outcomes and boosting diagnosis. Algorithms for image processing improve accuracy.

By evaluating unique patient data, merging vital signs and medical imaging, and enabling individualised healthcare actions, the integrated system produces better treatment plans and higher quality patient care.

In particular for patients with restricted mobility or in distant places, IoT devices and image processing allow for consultations, follow-ups, and treatments for patients.

Automated picture analysis improves the workload and diagnostic process for healthcare practitioners, while Internet of Things (IoT) devices allow for continuous monitoring, patient data access, and effective decision-making.

Patients may now obtain health information and take an active role in their treatment. IoT gadgets and image processing methods boost participation, encouraging greater treatment compliance and better health results.

Early detection, increased accuracy, remote access, and patient empowerment are just a few advantages of the integration of image processing techniques with IoT devices in healthcare delivery. Through continuous monitoring, automatic picture analysis, and targeted actions, this technology offers remote patient empowerment and healthcare access. To realise their full potential and improve healthcare quality globally, healthcare organisations and academics must keep researching and deploying these integrated systems.

BENEFITS AND OUTCOMES OF INTEGRATED TECHNOLOGIES IN PATIENT HEALTH CHECKING

Numerous advantages come from the enhancement of healthcare delivery and patient care brought about by the integration of 5G/6G, IoT, and image processing technology in patient health checking operations(Alhussein et al., 2018; Díaz et al., 2016; Mishra et al., 2019; Muhammad et al., 2017; Niinimäki et al., 2008; Saxena & Paul, 2022).

Real-Time Patient Monitoring

Through Internet of Things (IoT) gadgets like wearable health trackers, the integrated system provides real-time patient monitoring. These gadgets gather data and vital signs, which are then sent to medical specialists through the 5G/6G network. Because of the rapid action and prompt medical care made possible by this early discovery, patients' health is guaranteed to remain stable.

Remote Healthcare Services

Through telemedicine capabilities, the integrated system makes it possible for healthcare providers to access patient data such as vital signs, environmental measures, and medical photographs. Patients in rural locations and those with restricted mobility will benefit from the lack of a requirement for recurrent checkups or follow-up visits.

Early Detection of Abnormalities Through Image Analysis

Through the analysis of medical pictures taken using modalities like X-ray, MRI, or dermatoscopic images, image processing methods help in the early diagnosis of anomalies and illnesses. Early identification allows for prompt intervention and treatment, which enhances patient outcomes and could even save lives.

Improved Accuracy in Diagnosis

By automating medical picture analysis and extracting quantitative information, image processing techniques improve the accuracy of health screening. As a result, diagnoses become more consistent and there are fewer instances of human mistake. In addition to giving healthcare practitioners objective data, image processing methods can improve diagnostic skills and promote well-informed decision-making.

Enhanced Overall Patient Care

By making it possible for real-time monitoring, remote healthcare services, and precise diagnoses, technology integration enhances patient care. By encouraging patient-centric care, this improves outcomes and makes it possible for people to access services more easily, receive timely interventions, and participate more actively in managing their health. Because healthcare providers have access to detailed patient data, the technology also makes it possible to provide individualised treatment plans and interventions.

Efficient Workflow and Resource Optimization

By offering real-time patient monitoring and remote services, the integrated system enhances healthcare workflow and resource use. This enables healthcare professionals to focus on what is most important and use resources wisely, cutting down on waiting times and increasing efficiency. The technology also simplifies procedures through automated analysis, freeing up healthcare personnel to concentrate on important responsibilities like analysing data and selecting the best course of action.

Cost Savings and Accessibility

By minimising in-person visits, particularly for rural patients, the integrated system can save costs and enhance accessibility to healthcare. Early diagnosis and prompt treatment can stop the spread of an illness, saving money on hospital stays and ongoing medical care. Additionally, by guaranteeing high-quality care regardless of geographic constraints, this strategy increases healthcare access for underserved groups.

Numerous advantages exist when 5G/6G, IoT, and image processing technologies are included into patient health checking procedures, improving patient care and healthcare delivery. These include improved total patient care, real-time monitoring, remote services, early diagnostic detection, and increased diagnosis accuracy. As these technologies develop, patient outcomes will continue to improve, healthcare workflows will become more efficient, and everyone will have easier access to healthcare services.

Challenges and Limitations of Integrated Technologies in Patient Health Checking

There are many advantages to the integration of 5G/6G, IoT, and image processing technology in patient health screening procedures, but there are also difficulties and restrictions. For integrated systems to be implemented successfully and be widely used, certain problems must be solved (Alhussein et al., 2018; Chiuchisan & Dimian, 2015; Muhammad et al., 2017).

The privacy of patients and the security of data are issues that are raised by integrating these technologies. The danger of breaches rises with ongoing data gathering and transfer of private health information. To secure patient data, healthcare companies must have strong encryption, authentication, and access control measures in place. Maintaining patient privacy and public trust necessitates compliance with data protection laws like GDPR and HIPAA.

For the effective integration of multiple technologies, such as IoT devices, medical imaging equipment, and software solutions, interoperability is essential. However, interoperability may be hampered by compatibility problems and a lack of standards. Industry players and standardisation organisations must work together to create standard protocols and data formats in order to provide seamless data interchange and communication across system components.

Strong infrastructure is needed for a system that integrates 5G/6G, IoT devices, and image processing. High-speed, low-latency communication requires investment and extensive coverage. Integration of IoT devices needs careful planning that takes connection, power, and maintenance requirements into account. Delivering seamless healthcare services requires overcoming infrastructural obstacles.

Large volumes of data are produced continuously by IoT devices and medical imaging equipment. It is difficult to effectively manage and save this data. Although distributed storage systems and cloud-based solutions might be useful, significant thought must be given to data governance, scalability, and retention regulations.

For efficient health checking procedures, IoT devices and medical imaging equipment demand accurate and trustworthy data. The integrity of patient data is jeopardised by problems such sensor inaccuracies, calibration mistakes, and data transfer issues. For data to be accurate and reliable, quality control methods must be put in place along with routine maintenance and calibration.

For healthcare workers, integrating these technology presents ethical questions. To preserve patients' autonomy and privacy, it is essential to obtain their informed consent before collecting any data or doing any remote monitoring. The ethical use of patient data should be governed by rules that forbid abuse or prejudice in the algorithms used to make decisions.

User acceptability and technological competence are prerequisites for adopting an integrated system. Patients and healthcare workers may have trouble adjusting to new workflows and interfaces. In order to provide professionals with the appropriate abilities, training and assistance are crucial. User-cantered design concepts and responding to user feedback can increase system adoption and satisfaction.

FUTURE DIRECTIONS IN INTEGRATED TECHNOLOGIES FOR PATIENT HEALTH CHECKING

Healthcare delivery has been transformed by the use of 5G/6G, IoT, and image processing technology for patient health checks. New trends have a great deal of potential to push the industry further(Boopathi, n.d.; Boopathi, Khare, et al., 2023; Koshariya, 2023; Reddy et al., 2023; S. et al., 2022; Samikannu et al., 2023).

6G networks are anticipated to deliver faster data speeds, minimal latency, and widespread connection as 5G networks mature. As a result, patient experiences and healthcare results will be enhanced through the use of effective healthcare applications, real-time monitoring, remote consultations, and data-intensive image processing jobs.

By increasing the accuracy of image analysis, enabling accurate diagnoses, and facilitating treatment planning, advanced image processing algorithms can enhance the procedures used to check the health of patients. Healthcare practitioners may spot irregularities, forecast illness development, and personalise treatment strategies by using algorithms that learn from enormous datasets created using machine learning and deep learning approaches.

By evaluating a large quantity of patient data, including vital signs, medical imaging, and electronic health records, AI approaches may dramatically enhance patient health checking processes. This analysis aids in the identification of patterns or trends, predictive analytics, and clinical decision-making. By utilising AI, the integrated system can improve patient outcomes, therapeutic efficacy, and diagnostic accuracy.

The use of augmented reality (AR) technology improves patient experiences by superimposing virtual data on the physical environment. It gives real-time patient data, image analysis findings, and interactive visualisations of medical issues, treatment alternatives, and rehabilitation exercises to healthcare practitioners. AR transforms patient education and engagement, improving communication and teamwork between patients and healthcare providers throughout health checkup procedures(Anitha et al., 2023; Babu et al., 2023; Boopathi, Arigela, et al., 2023; Jeevanantham et al., 2023; Subha et al., 2023).

The development of reliable data fusion and integration methods to smoothly merge data from diverse sources, such as IoT devices, medical imaging, electronic health records, and genetic data, should be the main emphasis of future research. Healthcare practitioners will be better equipped to assess the health of their patients, make knowledgeable choices, and create customised medicine strategies and prediction models for therapies that are more precise and focused.

Continuous monitoring of health metrics is made possible by developments in wearable technology and sensor development. Future studies should concentrate on cutting-edge wearables that record physiological and biochemical data. Individualized therapies and early warnings for those at risk of acquiring particular illnesses can be provided by integrating this data with real-time analytics and machine learning algorithms. This proactive strategy greatly enhances preventative care and makes it possible for prompt treatments.

CONCLUSION

By providing continuous monitoring, automated analysis, and individualised treatments, the integration of image processing techniques with Internet of Things sensors improves patient health screening. Early detection, increased accuracy, remote access to healthcare, and patient empowerment are the outcomes of this.

Healthcare personnel can deliver prompt interventions thanks to the real-time gathering and transmission of vital sign data made possible by wearable health trackers and linked medical devices. Algorithms for image processing examine medical pictures, looking for anomalies and improving diagnostic precision. By facilitating remote consultations and follow-ups, the integrated system enables healthcare practitioners to provide services without face-to-face encounters. Patients may actively monitor their health, increasing engagement and treatment plan adherence.

Patient outcomes, healthcare efficiency, and patient-centered care are all improved by the combination of image processing and IoT technology. But for successful adoption, issues with infrastructure, interoperability, and data security must be solved. The use of 6G networks, AI integration, augmented reality, and data fusion methods are some of the future paths that have the most potential to revolutionise patient health monitoring procedures and change the way healthcare is delivered.

A potential strategy that improves diagnosis accuracy, makes it easier for patients to access remote healthcare, and gives them more control over their own health management is the integration of image processing with Internet of Things (IoT) devices for enhanced patient health checking procedures. To realise their full potential and promote beneficial healthcare reforms, more research, cooperation, and implementation are essential.

Key terms

- IoT: Internet of Things
- AI: Artificial Intelligence
- AR: Augmented Reality
- 6G: Sixth Generation
- EHR: Electronic Health Records
- MRI: Magnetic Resonance Imaging
- X-ray: Radiography or X-radiation
- CT scan: Computed Tomography scan
- BPM: Beats Per Minute
- SpO2: Oxygen Saturation Level

REFERENCES

Adhikary, T., Jana, A. D., Chakrabarty, A., & Jana, S. K. (2020). The Internet of Things (IoT) Augmentation in Healthcare: An Application Analytics. *ICICCT 2019 – System Reliability, Quality Control, Safety, Maintenance and Management*, (pp. 576–583). Springer. doi:10.1007/978-981-13-8461-5_66

Albaji, A. O. (2022). *Optical Wireless Technologies for 5g / 6g and IoT Optical Wireless Technologies for 5g / 6g and IoT*. MDPI.

Alfaro-Almagro, F., Jenkinson, M., Bangerter, N. K., Andersson, J. L. R., Griffanti, L., Douaud, G., Sotiropoulos, S. N., Jbabdi, S., Hernandez-Fernandez, M., Vallee, E., Vidaurre, D., Webster, M., McCarthy, P., Rorden, C., Daducci, A., Alexander, D. C., Zhang, H., Dragonu, I., Matthews, P. M., ... Smith, S. M. (2018). Image processing and Quality Control for the first 10,000 brain imaging datasets from UK Biobank. *NeuroImage*, *166*, 400–424. doi:10.1016/j.neuroimage.2017.10.034 PMID:29079522

Alhussein, M., Muhammad, G., Hossain, M. S., & Amin, S. U. (2018). Cognitive IoT-cloud integration for smart healthcare: Case study for epileptic seizure detection and monitoring. *Mobile Networks and Applications*, *23*(6), 1624–1635. doi:10.100711036-018-1113-0

Anitha, C., Komala, C. R., Vivekanand, C. V., Lalitha, S. D., Boopathi, S., & Revathi, R. (2023, February). Artificial Intelligence driven security model for Internet of Medical Things (IoMT). *Proceedings of 2023 3rd International Conference on Innovative Practices in Technology and Management, ICIPTM 2023*. IEEE. 10.1109/ICIPTM57143.2023.10117713

Babu, B. S., Kamalakannan, J., Meenatchi, N., M, S. K. S., S, K., & Boopathi, S. (2023). Economic impacts and reliability evaluation of battery by adopting Electric Vehicle. *IEEE Explore*, 1–6. doi:10.1109/ICPECTS56089.2022.10046786

Bhatia, S., Mallikarjuna, B., Gautam, D., Gupta, U., Kumar, S., & Verma, S. (2023). The Future IoT: The Current Generation 5G and Next Generation 6G and 7G Technologies. *Proceedings - IEEE International Conference on Device Intelligence, Computing and Communication Technologies, DICCT 2023*, (pp. 212–217). IEEE. 10.1109/DICCT56244.2023.10110066

Boopathi, S. (2023). Deep Learning Techniques Applied for Automatic Sentence Generation. In Promoting Diversity, Equity, and Inclusion in Language Learning Environments (pp. 255-273). IGI Global. doi:10.4018/978-1-6684-3632-5.ch016

Boopathi, S., Arigela, S. H., Raman, R., Indhumathi, C., Kavitha, V., & Bhatt, B. C. (2023). Prominent Rule Control-based Internet of Things: Poultry Farm Management System. *IEEE Explore*, 1–6. doi:10.1109/ICPECTS56089.2022.10047039

Boopathi, S., Haribalaji, V., Mageswari, M., & Asif, M. M. (2022). Influences of Boron Carbide Particles on the Wear Rate and Tensile Strength of Aa2014 Surface Composite Fabricated By Friction-Stir Processing. *Materiali in Tehnologije*, 56(3), 263–270. doi:10.17222/mit.2022.409

Boopathi, S., Khare, R., Jaya Christiyan, K. G., Muni, T. V., & Khare, S. (2023). Additive Manufacturing Developments in the Medical Engineering Field. In Development, Properties, and Industrial Applications of 3D Printed Polymer Composites (pp. 86–106). IGI Global. doi:10.4018/978-1-6684-6009-2.ch006

Boopathi, S., Thillaivanan, A., Azeem, M. A., Shanmugam, P., & Pramod, V. R. (2022). Experimental investigation on abrasive water jet machining of neem wood plastic composite. *Functional Composites and Structures*, 4(2), 25001. doi:10.1088/2631-6331/ac6152

Brasil, L. M., Gomes, M. M. F., Miosso, C. J., da Silva, M. M., & Amvame-Nze, G. D. (2015). Web platform using digital image processing and geographic information system tools: A Brazilian case study on dengue. *Biomedical Engineering Online*, 14(1), 1–14. doi:10.118612938-015-0052-2 PMID:26178732

Chiuchisan, I., & Dimian, M. (2015). Internet of Things for e-Health: An approach to medical applications. *2015 International Workshop on Computational Intelligence for Multimedia Understanding, IWCIM 2015*, (pp. 1–5). IEEE. 10.1109/IWCIM.2015.7347091

Díaz, M., Martín, C., & Rubio, B. (2016). State-of-the-art, challenges, and open issues in the integration of Internet of things and cloud computing. *Journal of Network and Computer Applications*, 67, 99–117. doi:10.1016/j.jnca.2016.01.010

Dik, G., Bogdanov, A., Shchegoleva, N., Dik, A., & Kiyamov, J. (2022). Challenges of IoT Identification and Multi-Level Protection in Integrated Data Transmission Networks Based on 5G/6G Technologies. *Computers*, 11(12), 178. doi:10.3390/computers11120178

Esenogho, E., Djouani, K., & Kurien, A. M. (2022). Integrating Artificial Intelligence Internet of Things and 5G for Next-Generation Smartgrid: A Survey of Trends Challenges and Prospect. *IEEE Access : Practical Innovations, Open Solutions*, 10, 4794–4831. doi:10.1109/ACCESS.2022.3140595

Han, Z., Liu, K., Li, Z., & Luo, P. (2022). A pre-check operator for reducing algorithmic optimisation time in image processing applications. *Enterprise Information Systems*, 16(10–11), 1543–1555. doi:10.1080/17517575.2020.1864022

Ho, C. W. L., Soon, D., Caals, K., & Kapur, J. (2019). Governance of automated image analysis and artificial intelligence analytics in healthcare. *Clinical Radiology*, 74(5), 329–337. doi:10.1016/j.crad.2019.02.005 PMID:30898383

Huda, S., Yearwood, J., Jelinek, H. F., Hassan, M. M., Fortino, G., & Buckland, M. (2016). A Hybrid Feature Selection with Ensemble Classification for Imbalanced Healthcare Data: A Case Study for Brain Tumor Diagnosis. *IEEE Access : Practical Innovations, Open Solutions*, 4, 9145–9154. doi:10.1109/ACCESS.2016.2647238

Iftikhar, U., Anwer, M., Butt, R., & Ahmed, G. (2023). Towards 5G, 6G and 7G Sustainable and Potential Applications Using Blockchain: Comparative Analysis and Prospective Challenges*. *2023 4th International Conference on Computing, Mathematics and Engineering Technologies: Sustainable Technologies for Socio-Economic Development, ICoMET 2023*, (pp. 1–7). IEEE. 10.1109/iCoMET57998.2023.10099241

Janardhana, K., Anushkannan, N. K., Dinakaran, K. P., Puse, R. K., & Boopathi, S. (2023). *Experimental Investigation on Microhardness, Surface Roughness, and White Layer Thickness of Dry EDM*. Engineering Research Express. doi:10.1088/2631-8695/acce8f

Javaid, M., & Khan, I. H. (2021). Internet of Things (IoT) enabled healthcare helps to take the challenges of COVID-19 Pandemic. *Journal of Oral Biology and Craniofacial Research*, 11(2), 209–214. doi:10.1016/j.jobcr.2021.01.015 PMID:33665069

Jeevanantham, Y. A., A, S., V, V., J, S. I., Boopathi, S., & Kumar, D. P. (2023). Implementation of Internet-of Things (IoT) in Soil Irrigation System. *IEEE Explore*, 1–5. doi:10.1109/ICPECTS56089.2022.10047185

Koshariya, A. K., Kalaiyarasi, D., Jovith, A. A., Sivakami, T., Hasan, D. S., & Boopathi, S. (2023). AI-Enabled IoT and WSN-Integrated Smart Agriculture System. In Artificial Intelligence Tools and Technologies for Smart Farming and Agriculture Practices (pp. 200-218). IGI Global. doi:10.4018/978-1-6684-8516-3.ch011

Koshariya, A. K., Khatoon, S., Marathe, A. M., Suba, G. M., Baral, D., & Boopathi, S. (2023). Agricultural Waste Management Systems Using Artificial Intelligence Techniques. In *AI-Enabled Social Robotics in Human Care Services* (pp. 236–258). IGI Global. doi:10.4018/978-1-6684-8171-4.ch009

Mavandadi, S., Dimitrov, S., Feng, S., Yu, F., Sikora, U., Yaglidere, O., Padmanabhan, S., Nielsen, K., & Ozcan, A. (2012). Distributed medical image analysis and diagnosis through crowd-sourced games: A malaria case study. *PLoS One*, 7(5), e37245. doi:10.1371/journal.pone.0037245 PMID:22606353

Mishra, S., Mishra, B. K., Tripathy, H. K., & Dutta, A. (2019). Analysis of the role and scope of big data analytics with IoT in health care domain. In *Handbook of Data Science Approaches for Biomedical Engineering* (pp. 1–23). Elsevier. doi:10.1016/B978-0-12-818318-2.00001-5

Mohanty, A., Jothi, B., Jeyasudha, J., Ranjit, P. S., Isaac, J. S., & Boopathi, S. (2023). Additive Manufacturing Using Robotic Programming. In *AI-Enabled Social Robotics in Human Care Services* (pp. 259–282). IGI Global. doi:10.4018/978-1-6684-8171-4.ch010

Mohanty, A., Venkateswaran, N., Ranjit, P. S., Tripathi, M. A., & Boopathi, S. (2023). Innovative Strategy for Profitable Automobile Industries: Working Capital Management. In Handbook of Research on Designing Sustainable Supply Chains to Achieve a Circular Economy (pp. 412–428). IGI Global.

Harikaran, M., & Boopathi, S. (2023). Impact analysis of ceramic tile powder aggregates on self-compacting concrete. Engineering Research Express. 5(3), https://iopscience.iop.org/article/10.1088/2631-8695/acde48/meta

Muhammad, G., Rahman, S. K. M. M., Alelaiwi, A., & Alamri, A. (2017). Smart health solution integrating IoT and cloud: A case study of voice pathology monitoring. *IEEE Communications Magazine*, *55*(1), 69–73. doi:10.1109/MCOM.2017.1600425CM

Niinimäki, M., Zhou, X., Depeursinge, A., Geissbuhler, A., & Müller, H. (2008). Building a Community Grid for Medical Image Analysis inside a Hospital, a Case Study. *Proceedings of the MICCAI-Grid Workshop*, (pp. 3–12). IEEE.

Palaniappan, M., Tirlangi, S., Mohamed, M. J. S., Moorthy, R. M. S., Valeti, S. V., & Boopathi, S. (2023). Fused Deposition Modelling of Polylactic Acid (PLA)-Based Polymer Composites. In Development, Properties, and Industrial Applications of 3D Printed Polymer Composites (pp. 66–85). IGI Global. doi:10.4018/978-1-6684-6009-2.ch005

Priya, E., & Rajinikanth, V. (2021). Signal and Image Processing Techniques for the Development of Intelligent Healthcare Systems. In *Signal and Image Processing Techniques for the Development of Intelligent Healthcare Systems*. Springer. doi:10.1007/978-981-15-6141-2

Rafik, M. K. M. (2021). Quality Checking of Fruits using Image Processing. *International Journal for Research in Applied Science and Engineering Technology*, *9*(5), 1979–1980. doi:10.22214/ijraset.2021.34518

Rahamathunnisa, U., Sudhakar, K., Murugan, T. K., Thivaharan, S., Rajkumar, M., & Boopathi, S. (2023). Cloud Computing Principles for Optimizing Robot Task Offloading Processes. In *AI-Enabled Social Robotics in Human Care Services* (pp. 188–211). IGI Global. doi:10.4018/978-1-6684-8171-4.ch007

Rani Roopha Devi, K. G., Mahendra Chozhan, R., & Murugesan, R. (2019). Cognitive IoT Integration for Smart Healthcare: Case Study for Heart Disease Detection and Monitoring. *2019 International Conference on Recent Advances in Energy-Efficient Computing and Communication, ICRAECC 2019*, (pp. 1–6). IEEE. 10.1109/ICRAECC43874.2019.8995049

Reddy, M. A., Reddy, B. M., Mukund, C. S., Venneti, K., Preethi, D. M. D., & Boopathi, S. (2023). Social Health Protection During the COVID-Pandemic Using IoT. In *The COVID-19 Pandemic and the Digitalization of Diplomacy* (pp. 204–235). IGI Global. doi:10.4018/978-1-7998-8394-4.ch009

Rong, G., Mendez, A., Bou Assi, E., Zhao, B., & Sawan, M. (2020). Artificial Intelligence in Healthcare: Review and Prediction Case Studies. *Engineering (Beijing)*, *6*(3), 291–301. doi:10.1016/j.eng.2019.08.015

S., P. K., Sampath, B., R., S. K., Babu, B. H., & N., A. (2022). Hydroponics, Aeroponics, and Aquaponics Technologies in Modern Agricultural Cultivation. In *Trends, Paradigms, and Advances in Mechatronics Engineering* (pp. 223–241). IGI Global. doi:10.4018/978-1-6684-5887-7.ch012

Samikannu, R., Koshariya, A. K., Poornima, E., Ramesh, S., Kumar, A., & Boopathi, S. (2023). Sustainable Development in Modern Aquaponics Cultivation Systems Using IoT Technologies. In *Human Agro-Energy Optimization for Business and Industry* (pp. 105–127). IGI Global. doi:10.4018/978-1-6684-4118-3.ch006

Sampath, B., & Haribalaji, V. (2021). Influences of welding parameters on friction stir welding of aluminum and magnesium: A review. *Materials Research Proceedings*, *19*(1), 222–230. doi:10.21741/9781644901618-28

Sampath, B. C. S., & Myilsamy, S. (2022). Application of TOPSIS Optimization Technique in the Micro-Machining Process. In Trends, Paradigms, and Advances in Mechatronics Engineering (pp. 162–187). IGI Global. doi:10.4018/978-1-6684-5887-7.ch009

Saravanan, M., Vasanth, M., Boopathi, S., Sureshkumar, M., & Haribalaji, V. (2022). Optimization of Quench Polish Quench (QPQ) Coating Process Using Taguchi Method. *Key Engineering Materials*, *935*, 83–91. doi:10.4028/p-z569vy

Sathish, T., Sunagar, P., Singh, V., Boopathi, S., Al-Enizi, A. M., Pandit, B., Gupta, M., & Sehgal, S. S. (2023). Characteristics estimation of natural fibre reinforced plastic composites using deep multi-layer perceptron (MLP) technique. *Chemosphere*, *337*, 139346. doi:10.1016/j.chemosphere.2023.139346 PMID:37379988

Saxena, S., & Paul, S. (2022). *High-Performance Medical Image Processing*.

Sekaran, R., Patan, R., Raveendran, A., Al-Turjman, F., Ramachandran, M., & Mostarda, L. (2020). Survival Study on Blockchain Based 6G-Enabled Mobile Edge Computation for IoT Automation. *IEEE Access: Practical Innovations, Open Solutions*, *8*, 143453–143463. doi:10.1109/ACCESS.2020.3013946

Senthil, T. S. R. Ohmsakthi vel, Puviyarasan, M., Babu, S. R., Surakasi, R., & Sampath, B. (2023). Industrial Robot-Integrated Fused Deposition Modelling for the 3D Printing Process. In Development, Properties, and Industrial Applications of 3D Printed Polymer Composites (pp. 188–210). IGI Global. doi:10.4018/978-1-6684-6009-2.ch011

Sigit, R., Arief, Z., & Bachtiar, M. M. (2016). Development of Healthcare Kiosk for Checking Heart Health. *EMITTER International Journal of Engineering Technology*, *3*(2), 99–114. doi:10.24003/emitter.v3i2.49

Subha, S., Inbamalar, T. M., Komala, C. R., Suresh, L. R., Boopathi, S., & Alaskar, K. (2023, February). A Remote Health Care Monitoring system using internet of medical things (IoMT). *Proceedings of 2023 3rd International Conference on Innovative Practices in Technology and Management, ICIPTM 2023*. IEEE. 10.1109/ICIPTM57143.2023.10118103

Teleron, J. I. (2022). The Implementation of IoT-Based Android App Vegetable Health Check Using Image Processing. *International Research Journal of Advanced Engineering and Science*, *7*(1), 203–207.

Trojovský, P., Dhasarathan, V., & Boopathi, S. (2023). Experimental investigations on cryogenic friction-stir welding of similar ZE42 magnesium alloys. *Alexandria Engineering Journal*, *66*(1), 1–14. doi:10.1016/j.aej.2022.12.007

Vanitha, S. K. R., & Boopathi, S. (2023). Artificial Intelligence Techniques in Water Purification and Utilization. In *Human Agro-Energy Optimization for Business and Industry* (pp. 202–218). IGI Global. doi:10.4018/978-1-6684-4118-3.ch010

Yupapin, P., Trabelsi, Y., Nattappan, A., & Boopathi, S. (2023). Performance Improvement of Wire-Cut Electrical Discharge Machining Process Using Cryogenically Treated Super-Conductive State of Monel-K500 Alloy. *Iranian Journal of Science and Technology. Transaction of Mechanical Engineering*, *47*(1), 267–283. doi:10.100740997-022-00513-0

Chapter 23

Real–Time Pothole Detection During Rainy Weather Using Dashboard Cameras for Driverless Cars

Manvinder Sharma

Malla Reddy Engineering College and Management Sciences, Hyderabad, India

Sudhakara Reddy Saripalli

Malla Reddy Engineering College and Management Sciences, Hyderabad, India

Anuj Kumar Gupta

Chandigarh Group of Colleges, Landran, India

Rajneesh Talwar

Chitkara University, India

Pankaj Dadheech

Computer Science and Engineering, Swami Keshvanand Institute of Technology, Management, and Gramothan, India

Uday Kumar Kanike

Georgia State University, USA

ABSTRACT

The primary form of transportation is roads. But because of the high volume of traffic on the roads and other environmental conditions, regular maintenance is required. This maintenance is frequently neglected as it is impossible to watch over every location, or just out of ignorance. Potholes are created as a result, which increases traffic and increases the likelihood of accidents. However, there are many methods/systems available which can be used to detect potholes using various image processing methods. The accuracy of these systems is highly affected in rainy weather. In this chapter, a system is designed to detect pothole during rainy season effectively. This system also collects the location of potholes, which can be further provided to authorities for maintenance work. The proposed system can be used for driverless cars.

DOI: 10.4018/978-1-6684-8618-4.ch023

INTRODUCTION

Throughout the last century, automotive innovation has resulted in significant technical breakthroughs, resulting in safer, cleaner, and more economical automobiles. But, since Henry Ford invented the moving assembly line, most modifications have been gradual and evolutionary. Today, in the early decades of the twenty-first century, the industry looks to be on the verge of a revolution, with the potential to significantly redefine not just the competitive environment, but also the way we interact with cars and, indeed, the future architecture of our roads and towns. When it happens, the introduction of autonomous or "self-driving" automobiles will be the catalyst for the change. Intelligent transportation framework (ITS) promises to improve the transportation system and is becoming more popular. (Hsu et al., 2015; Kaur & Sharma, 2015; Xu et al., 2018; Zichichi et al., 2020) Increasing traffic security is a critical challenge for ITS. In India, streets serve as the primary means of transportation, carrying 90% of all passenger activity and 65% of all freight (World Bank. , 2019). The number of vehicles on the road has significantly increased during the last two decade. This increase in automobiles has led to problems like traffic jams during rush hour, numerous accidents on the road. The mismanagement of traffic and road's poor state is the main cause of these problems. Potholes on road are created by severe rains, poor fabrication materials during construction of roads, poorly designed drainage systems and the passage of heavy vehicles. Such holes are formed when heavy vehicles pass over them, and as a result, some asphalt and water are ejected, progressively forming a hollow under the crack. If routine road maintenance is ignored, the surface of the road may ultimately cave in, creating a massive, obvious pothole on the surface. These potholes become a key factor in the increased likelihood of accidents and fatalities. In the 2014 Road Accident Report, deaths due to potholes were 3,039. Data from the Ministry of Road Transport and Highways (MoRTH) show that there were 2,015, 2,140, and 1,471 fatal road accident causing deaths in 2018, 2019, and 2020, respectively. Around 5% of road fatalities, according to the National Crime Records Bureau (NCRB), are caused by potholes or open manholes. (Press Trust of India, 2019) Today, artificial intelligence is used in a wide range of real-time applications, and there have been numerous advancements in computer vision techniques applied to the field of image processing. These advancements have produced excellent results in the fields of surveillance cameras, factory automation, self-driving cars, the military, and the medical industry, among others. A practical solution that supports safe driving is needed to solve the difficulties mentioned. With the many pothole detecting techniques put forward, it has become feasible for drivers to prevent accidents brought on by potholes. An automated procedure might help with this. In order to repair these roads in a timely way, the entity must know where the pothole or degenerating road segment is situated.

LITERATURE REVIEW

To make life easier for individuals, automatic pothole detecting systems utilizing different sensors are being researched. Vibration-based approaches, laser-scanning methods, and vision-based methods are some of the existing studies. The field of pothole detection already has several technology in place. The list above includes a few of them. Everyone approaches the challenge similarly, just the sensor and its method of identifying the obstruction differ. Table 1 shows different approaches for Pothole detection. (Dhiman & Klette, 2019; Jog et al., 2021; Kim & Ryu, 2014; Kim et al., 2022; Koch & Brilakis, 2011; Sharma & Gupta, 2021; Sharma & Singh, 2022; Yu & Salari, 2011)

Table 1. Pothole detection methods

Type	Vibration based	LASER based	Vision based
Sensor	Accelerometer	LASER	Camera
Sensing	While going through pothole	While going through pothole	While approaching pothole
Cost	Low	Moderate	High
Precision	Low	Average	HIgh

An affordable approach was put up by Moazzam, et al. (2013) to analyse 3D pavement distress photos. Using a low-cost Kinetic sensor that provides a direct depth measurement lowers the cost of calculation. In order to determine the depth of the potholes, the sensor consists of an IR camera and an RGB camera that take depth photos and RGB pictures, respectively. These images are analysed in a MATLAB environment using characteristics that are metrological and identifying.

He Youquan, et al. (2011) created a model that uses two Charge Coupled Device cameras and LED direct light to determine the 3D cross-section of potholes in pavement. To determine the depths of potholes, it employs a variety of complex image processing techniques, such as picture pre-processing, binarization, thinning, error analysis & compensation, and 3D re-construction. The limitation of this model is that natural components and LED light intensity have an impact on the results.

A Support Vector Machine-based model for pothole detection was put out by Jin Lin et al. (2020), which distinguishes potholes from other road abnormalities including splits and cracks. Partial differential equations are used to segment the images. The SVM is trained using a set of pavement photos to find potholes. The limitation of this model is that if the images are not well lit, the training model is unable to identify pavement flaws.

A study developed using the Android platform by Faith Orhan et al. (2013) to identify traffic dangers consists of three components: sensing, analysis, and sharing. In order to facilitate access, the sensing component synchronises with the interface and collects accelerometer's raw data. The sensors' collected data are utilised to build analysis modules for the analysis component. In terms of the sharing component, the established framework is linked to the main application, from which it may communicate with others directly. All of the obtained data is kept in a single repository for further processing. Although this approach alerts other drivers to traffic incidents, it is more expensive and difficult to use.

A pothole identification model in real time using accelerometer-equipped Android phones was proposed by Artis Mednis, et al. in (2011). At the moment, Android OS-based smart phones have built-in accelerometers that can sense movement and vibrations. Potholes are located using the accelerometer's data. The algorithms used to identify potholes is based on Z-sift, which calculates the amplitude of the acceleration at Z-hub. Another component is Z-diff, which calculates the variation in two amplitude values and STDEV (Z), which calculates the standard deviation of G-Zero and vertical axis acceleration.

To distinguish potholes, Zhen Zhang et al. (2021) suggested a model in which they used stereo camera images coupled with a disparity computation and also stored the geographic co-ordinate of the pothole in the database.

A model that Mircea Strutu, et al. (2013) suggested used accelerometers to find flaws in the road's surface. To pinpoint the precise location of the abnormalities, it also used a GPS framework. The pothole detecting method may be used in moving automobiles that have a wireless router, local computer, GPS, and accelerometer. Via the access points, the obtained data is delivered to the central database where it may be processed further. The model's limitation is that it turns out to be rather expensive to set up.

In order to identify potholes, Sachin Bharadwaj, et al. (2013) devised a methodology that uses a 2D vision-based method. Images of the road surface are taken by a camera that is correctly positioned. MATLAB is used to analyse the recorded photos in order to find potholes. This model doesn't have any type of warning system and only functions in uniform illumination situations. It simply addresses how to fix a pothole; it offers no advice on how to steer clear of accidents caused by potholes.

A model was put up by Sudarshan S. Rode et al. (2009) in which Wi-Fi-enabled automobiles capture information about the road surface and send it to the Wi-Fi access point, which broadcasts it to other adjacent vehicles as warnings. This solution is expensive since Wi-Fi stations must be placed in every car and extra access points must be set up.

A model to identify and avoid potholes was put out by Sandeep Venkatesh, et al. (2014) and used a laser line striper in conjunction with a camera. The system has a central database where the potholes' locations are kept up to date. Dedicated Short-Range Communication Protocol is used to convey a notice to nearby cars about the existence of potholes.

An intelligent transportation system that employs ultrasonic sensors to detect the existence of potholes was proposed by Shambhu Hegde, et al. (2019). It uses a Zigbee module to deliver a warning signal to any nearby cars within a 100-meter radius. The system's limitation is that it only issues warnings after seeing potholes, which makes it impossible for drivers to effectively reduce the likelihood of an accident.

A method proposed by Prachi More, et al. (2014) uses sensors installed on a vehicle to record the vertical and horizontal accelerations that it experiences while travelling. The GPS equipment that has been placed records the coordinates, which are then used to find potholes along the same route. A Fire Bird V Robot with a constant speed is employed for experimentation. It is fitted with a servo motor that rotates 0-180 degrees and an IR Sharp sensor that detects variations in steady speed. If variance is found, there is probably a pothole there. The robot stops moving. When the GPS gadget records the pothole's coordinates, the camera snaps a photo of it.

A model developed (Sharma et al., 2022) by Kongyang Chen, et al. proposes the use of a 3-axis accelerometer and a GPS sensor for the detection of potholes. A data cleaning technique receives input from the GPS sensor and the outputs from the 3-hub accelerometer. The inputs for the method are analysed for Power Spectra Density and then divided into levels in the next section to determine the roughness of the potholes (Chen et al., 2011).

PROPOSED SYSTEM

The proposed system involves detection of potholes, controlling the steering (for driverless cars), extracting the location of pothole using Global positioning System (GPS) and storing the pothole data on database. Figure 1 shows the process.

None of the above system presented working of system during bad weather or rainy weather. Using the computer vision, our approach employs a two-dimensional picture of the roadways. The dashboard camera captures real time video, which is further processed by simulink model and based on realtime video input, the potholes can be detected.

For pothole detection, The suggested work conducts bilateral filtering and edge identification after converting the RGB input video to intensity. The highway area is chosen by the subsystem Trapezoidal-

Figure 1. Proposed system

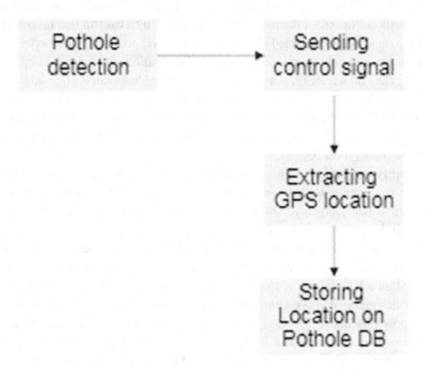

Figure 2. Simulink model

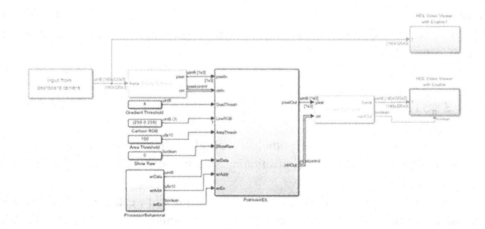

Mask. Following that, the design does a morphological approach and determines the centroid coordinates for every probable pothole. Each frame's greatest pothole is chosen by the detector, and its centre coordinates are stored. The input stream and the coordinates' time are synchronised using the pixel stream aligner. The pothole centre marker and text label are added to the frame using alpha channel overlays by the Fiducial31x31 and Overlay32x32 subsystems. Figure 2. shows Simulink model

Figure 3. Pothole detection algorithm steps

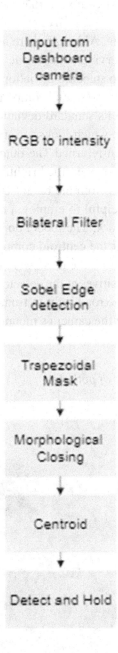

When the subsystem is in operation, its four input parameters can be altered. The intensity gradient parameter. Gradient Threshold influences the method's edge detection. When the Cartoon RGB option is selected, the overlays, including the text and the fiducially marker, have a unique colour. According to the Area Threshold option, how many highlighted pixel must be available in the target object for it to be classed as a pothole. If this number is too low, linear cracks and other non-hazardous potholes will be seen. Only the most dangerous hazards will be displayed if the pothole is too high. The detection algorithm performs following tasks for detection of pothole which is shown by figure 3.

The model separates the input RGB pixel stream such that a copy may be sent in the direction of the overlay blocks. The detector starts by converting RGB to intensity. The system then filters out high visual frequency noise and minute road defects. Although there are many methods for doing this, using a bilateral filter has the advantage of preserving edges while reducing noise in smaller areas. The settings for the neighbourhood size and the two standard deviations in the bilateral filter block, one for the intensity component of the filter and one for the spatial component. For this application, a relatively large neighbourhood of works well. The model's standard deviations are 0.75 & 3.The filtered image is delivered to the Sobel edge-detection block, which looks for any edges.Any edges that are stronger than the gradient threshold parameter are then returned.The outcome is a binary picture.Depending on factors like the condition of the roads, the weather, the brightness of the image, etc., this threshold may be set in your final application. The edges from the binary edge image that are not necessary for identifying potholes are then removed. It is helpful to employ a mask that selects a polygonal region of interest and renders the surrounding area dark. The model does not use a normal ROI block since it would remove the spatial context needed for the centroid computation and labelling thereafter. The order of operations is crucial in this case because if the mask were used before edge detection, its edges would become strong lines and lead to false positives at the detector. The only spots in the input footage where the automobile may hit a pothole are the road right in front of it and a trapezoidal portion of it up ahead. The exact locations are impacted by the camera's mounting and lens. The top and bottom of

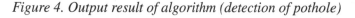

Figure 4. Output result of algorithm (detection of pothole)

Figure 5. Output result of algorithm (detection of pothole)

Figure 6. Output result of algorithm (detection of pothole)

the trapezoidal section in this movie are not parallel, hence it is not a true trapezoid. The corners on the left and right, top, and bottom of the mask are connected by straight lines. The centroid computation is used to determine where an active area's centre is. The centroid of the designated region is continuously determined for each pixel sector in the design. It only saves the centre coordinates when the detected region exceeds an input value.

The experimental work is done by dashboard camera SYSTENE Dasboard Camera (VGA Resolution) during rainy season. The results are shown in figure 4,5 and 6.

Figure 7. Pothole database

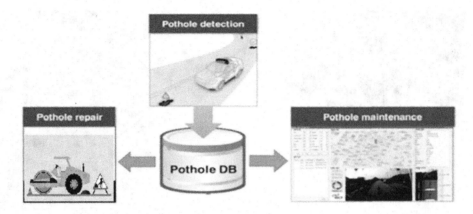

It can be observed the algorithm is able to detect the potholes in rainy season effectively. After detection using Global Positioning System (GPS), the location of pothole can be stored in database and can be further sent to authorities about potholes. The data can also be used for ambulances to avoid routes which are having more potholes in case of emergency or in case of pregnant ladies. The route may also be stored in database for driverless cars so that next time the alternate route can be taken or sudden steering is not done while car is approaching at same location. The database and method is shown in figure 7.

CONCLUSION

Due to irregular maintenance and other weather conditions, potholes are formed on roads. Potholes are health hazardous as it can cause severe accidents. One of the most crucial tasks in identifying suitable pavement maintenance and restoration plans is accurately recognizing potholes. In this paper, a model is propsed which takes real time input from dashboard camera, processes it, detects potholes and send the control signal. The model is capable for detection of potholes in rainy weather as well. The system can extract the location of pothole and can store for further processes like sending data to authorizes, rerouting for driverless cars etc. The present approach makes use of manual detection, which is done by people who want to help improve the road. So, it's crucial to avoid using too much human effort and to convert to an automatic technique instead.

REFERENCES

Bharadwaj, S., Murthy, S., & Varaprasad, G. (2013). Detection of potholes in autonomous vehicle. *IET Intelligent Transport Systems*, *8*(6), 543–549. doi:10.1049/iet-its.2013.0138

Chen, K., Lu, M., Fan, X., Wei, M., & Wu, J. (2011). Road Condition Monitoring Using On-board Three-axis Accelerometer and GPS Sensor. In *Proceedings of International ICST conference on Communication and Networking in China,* (pp.1032- 1037). IEEE.

Dhiman, A., & Klette, R. (2019). Pothole detection using computer vision and learning. *IEEE Transactions on Intelligent Transportation Systems, 21*(8), 3536–3550. doi:10.1109/TITS.2019.2931297

He, Y., Jian, W., Qiu, H., Wei, Z., & Xie, J. (2011). A Research of Pavement Potholes Detection Based on Three-Dimensional Project Transformation. In *Proceedings of International Congress on Image and Signal Processing,* (pp.1805-1808). IEEE.

Hegde, S., Mekali, H., & Varaprasad, G. (2019). Pothole Detection and Inter vehicular Communication. *Technical Report of Wireless Communications Laboratory.* BMS College of Engineering, Bangalore.

Hsu, C.-Y., Yang, C.-S., Yu, L.-C., Lin, C.-F., Yao, H.-H., Chen, D.-Y., Lai, K. R., & Chang, P.-C. (2015). Development of a cloud-based service framework for energy conservation in a sustainable intelligent transportation system. *International Journal of Production Economics, 164*, 454–461. doi:10.1016/j.ijpe.2014.08.014

Jog, G. M., Koch, C., Golparvar-Fard, M., & Brilakis, I. (2021). Pothole properties measurement through visual 2D recognition and 3D reconstruction. In Computing in Civil Engineering (pp. 553-560). Semantic Scholar.

Kaur, S. P., & Sharma, M. (2015). Radially optimized zone-divided energy-aware wireless sensor networks (WSN) protocol using BA (bat algorithm). *Journal of the Institution of Electronics and Telecommunication Engineers, 61*(2), 170–179. doi:10.1080/03772063.2014.999833

Kim, T., & Ryu, S.-K. (2014). Review and analysis of pothole detection methods. *Journal of Emerging Trends in Computing and Information Sciences, 5*(8), 603–608.

Kim, Y.-M., Kim, Y.-G., Son, S.-Y., Lim, S.-Y., Choi, B.-Y., & Choi, D.-H. (2022). Review of Recent Automated Pothole-Detection Methods. *Applied Sciences (Basel, Switzerland), 12*(11), 5320. doi:10.3390/app12115320

Koch, C., & Brilakis, I. (2011). Pothole detection in asphalt pavement images. *Advanced Engineering Informatics, 25*(3), 507–515. doi:10.1016/j.aei.2011.01.002

Lin, J., & Liu, Y. (2020). Potholes Detection Based on SVM in the Pavement Distress Image. In *Proceedings of International Symposium on Distributed Computing and Applications to Business, Engineering and Science,* (pp. 544-547). IEEE.

Mednis, A., Strazdins, G., Zviedris, R., Kanonirs, G., & Selavo, L. (2011). Real Time Pothole Detection using Android Smartphones with Accelerometers. In *Proceedings of Distributed Computing in Sensor Systems Workshop,* (pp. 1-6). IEEE. 10.1109/DCOSS.2011.5982206

Moazzam, K., Kamal, S., Mathavan, S., Usman, M., & Rahman (2013). Metrology and Visualization of Potholes using the Microsoft Kinect Sensor. In *Proceedings of IEEE Conference on Intelligent Transport System,* (pp. 1284- 1291). IEEE.

More, P., Surendran, S., Mahajan, S., & Dubey, S. K. (2014). Potholes and pitfalls spotter. *IMPACT: IJRET, 4*, 69–74.

Orhan, F., & Eren, P. E. (2013). Road Hazard Detection and Sharing with Multimodal Sensor Analysis on Smartphones. In *Proceedings of International Conference on Next Generation Mobile Apps, Services and Technologies*, (pp. 56-61). IEEE. 10.1109/NGMAST.2013.19

Press Trust of India. (2019). Over 5000 killed in road accidents caused by potholes in 2018. *NDTV.* https://www.ndtv.com/india-news/over-5-000-killed-in-road-accidents-caused-by-potholes-in-2018-20-transport-ministry-3276432

Rode, S. S., Vijay, S., Goyal, P., Kulkarni, P., & Arya, K. (2009). Pothole Detection and Warning System. In *Proceedings of International Conference on Electronic Computer Technology*, (pp. 286- 290). IEEE.

Sharma, M., & Gupta, A. K. (2021). An algorithm for target detection, identification, tracking and estimation of motion for passive homing missile autopilot guidance. In *Mobile Radio Communications and 5G Networks: Proceedings of MRCN 2020*, (pp. 57-71). Springer. 10.1007/978-981-15-7130-5_5

Sharma, M., Pandey, D., Khosla, D., Goyal, S., Pandey, B. K., & Gupta, A. K. (2022). Design of a GaN-Based Flip Chip Light Emitting Diode (FC-LED) with Au Bumps & Thermal Analysis with Different Sizes and Adhesive Materials for Performance Considerations. *Silicon*, *14*(12), 7109–7120. doi:10.100712633-021-01457-x

Sharma, M., & Singh, H. (2022). Contactless Methods for Respiration Monitoring and Design of SIW-LWA for Real-Time Respiratory Rate Monitoring. *Journal of the Institution of Electronics and Telecommunication Engineers*, 1–11. doi:10.1080/03772063.2022.2069167

Strutu, M., Stamatescu, G., & Popescu, D. (2013). A Mobile Sensor Network Based Road Surface Monitoring System. In *Proceedings of IEEE Conference on System Theory, Control and Computing*, (pp. 630–634). IEEE. 10.1109/ICSTCC.2013.6689030

Venkatesh, S., Abhiram E, Rajarajeswari S, Kumar, K. M., & Balakuntala, S. (2014). An Intelligent System to Detect, Avoid and Maintain Potholes: A Graph Theoretic Approach. In *Proceedings of International Conference on Mobile Computing and Ubiquitous Networking*, (pp. 80). IEEE.

World Bank. (2019). *India: Safe, Clean, Affordable, and Smart Transport*. World Bank. https://www.worldbank.org/en/country/india/brief/india-safe-clean-affordable-smart-transport

Xu, X., Liu, Y., Wang, W., Zhao, X., Sheng, Q. Z., Wang, Z., & Shi, B. (2018). ITS-frame: A framework for multi-aspect analysis in the field of intelligent transportation systems. *IEEE Transactions on Intelligent Transportation Systems*, *20*(8), 2893–2902. doi:10.1109/TITS.2018.2868840

Yu, X., & Salari, E. (2011). Pavement pothole detection and severity measurement using laser imaging. In *2011 IEEE International Conference on Electro/Information Technology*, (pp. 1-5). IEEE. 10.1109/EIT.2011.5978573

Zhang, Z., Ai, X., Chan C., & Dahnoun, N. (2021). An Efficient Algorithm for Pothole Detection using Stereo Vision. In *Proceedings of IEEE Conference on Acoustic, Speech and Signal Processing*, (pp. 564-568). IEEE.

Zichichi, M., Ferretti, S., & D'angelo, G. (2020). A framework based on distributed ledger technologies for data management and services in intelligent transportation systems. *IEEE Access : Practical Innovations, Open Solutions*, *8*, 100384–100402. doi:10.1109/ACCESS.2020.2998012

Chapter 24
Recent Trends of Addressing COVID–19 Disease by AI/ML

Shawni Dutta

https://orcid.org/0000-0001-8557-0376

Department of Computer Science, The Bhawanipur Education Society College, Kolkata, India

Utsab Mukherjee

Department of Computer Science, The Bhawanipur Education Society College, Kolkata, India

Digvijay Pandey

https://orcid.org/0000-0003-0353-174X

Department of Technical Education, Institute of Engineering and Technology, Lucknow, India

ABSTRACT

A new hype known as the novel coronavirus has consumed many human lives over the past few years. Consequently, the continued pandemic crisis will necessitate the use of an automated system. The computerised system should be able to provide constant monitoring of different domains of the COVID-19 disease. This study has concentrated on heterogeneous fields of COVID-19 including suspected-infected-recovered-deceased count analysis, impact of lockdown, different health habits responsible for this disease, analysis perforation patterns of lungs due to COVID-19, vaccination intake, and progress investigation. The literature included in this study has been investigated in terms of their prediction efficiency and possible improvements. Due to the exhaustive discourse of current COVID-19 based literature, the study is able to provide a comprehensive knowledge of the ongoing research trends. A concrete future perspective regarding each of the aforementioned domains has been included in the conclusion section which can effectively assist in finding the shortcomings of the existing research.

1. INTRODUCTION

The life-threatening disease, COVID-19 has turned into an epidemic which was initiated in China's Wuhan province in December 2019 (Shereen, M. A., et al 2020). Coughing, sneezing are the primary reasons that

DOI: 10.4018/978-1-6684-8618-4.ch024

can create a chain for this virus propagation among humans (Moghadas, S. M., et al 2020) . The World Health Organization (WHO) has designated the 30th of January, 2020 as a significant milestone; where COVID-19 was declared as a global public hazard (Gentile, I., & Abenavoli, L. 2020). The virus that produces COVID-19 is clinically known as Severe Acute Respiratory Syndrome Coronavirus-2 or SARS-CoV-2 because its genetic structure is almost similar to its predecessor SARS-CoV that broke down a few years back on a much smaller scale. Corona is a family of viruses that causes simple coughs and colds and it mostly affects animals. Few corona viruses have affected human beings in the recent past; they are Middle East Respiratory Syndrome CoronaVirus (MERS-CoV) and Severe Acute Respiratory Syndrome CoronaVirus (SARS-CoV).(Song, Z., et al 2019). The disease was first uncovered in December 2019 hence the name COVID-19. Based on the reports of W.H.O., it is assumed that the virus is zoonotic in nature that is because the virus appeared due to contagion from animals to humans (Contini, C et al 2020[5]).

An important direction has been provided by these works (Andersen, K. G et al 2020 and Paraskevis, D., et al 2020) regarding the origin of the virus. The contamination started from bats and it jumped to the human body. Some theories suggest that the virus mutated from musk cats to the human body. It has been estimated by Day et al. that about 80% of the cases of the victims are asymptomatic where the sample size is 30. (Day, M. 2020). The spreading rate is quite alarming since these people can further spread the pathogen when exposed to gatherings. The lungs of some victims of low immunity are affected so badly that even death may occur. The epidemic is growing almost exponentially across the globe since the virus spreads by interaction between individuals through respiratory droplets from an individual if the person coughs. Some experts suggested that physical distancing is highly necessary since these droplets cannot travel more than 6 feet. (Kissler, S. M., et al 2020)

COVID-19 is characterized by some symptoms like loss of smell and taste, sore throat, headache, cough and cold, fever, fatigue, diarrhoea, respiratory problems like breathing difficulties, chest pain, and chronic cough and in some severe cases pneumonia may occur making some irreversible damage in lungs leading to multi-organ dysfunction syndrome leading to death (Daniel, J. 2020). It has been observed that so far the mortality rate of this pandemic is around 3% world-wide, but since the virus spreads so rapidly covering the face in public gatherings is highly necessary (Baud, D., et al 2020).

Coronaviruses are a wide group of retroviruses that often result in moderate to severe upper-respiratory tract inflammations, such as the cold or flu. Table 1 shows the family of corona viruses that affected human beings in the recent past. The genetic information of SARS-CoV-2 is transmitted by its RNA. The protein structure of the virus is such that it undergoes metamorphosis which creates a handful of strains. Usually, metals, UV radiation, and endogenous components of organisms influence updation. Each and every variant has a specific rate of transmission capability, severity, and even mortality based on the immune response and effectiveness of vaccines. It is highly important to gather data and predict the strains that are evolving. (Roy, B et al 2021). Another variant, popularly known as Omicron, replicated more slowly than the delta variant as analysed by Zhao, H and et al 2021. This statistical study has revealed that the omicron variant has lesser fusion activity and inefficient replication as compared with the delta variant.

The research primarily focuses on the detailed study regarding COVID-19 disease. An automated approach to improve the health care sector is addressed in this study. The study's objective is to identify AI and ML-based techniques while evaluating the COVID-19 and related parameters in order to facilitate easier automation. As opposed to merely focusing on a single location, this research examines a wide range of COVID-19. The different areas addressed in the paper are outlined as follows:

Table 1. Family of coronavirus (Rabaan, A. A., et al 2020)

CoronaVirus	Emergence	Timeframe (in year)	Mortality (in %)
SARS	Guangdong Province, China	2002	10
MERS	Saudi Arabia	2013	34
SARS-Cov-2	Wuhan, China	2019	2-3

- Different human health habits such as tobacco consumption, alcohol consumption can be analysed to identify how the human is vulnerable to this disease.
- The spreading of the disease can be monitored by implementing an automated Suspected-Infected-Recovered-Deceased (SIRD) model. An effective discussion is carried out on how the application of ML based methods has been utilized by existing research articles.
- Detection of COVID-19 based on perforation patterns present in the lungs are also addressed in the study. For the detection scheme, both traditional and AI based methods have been discussed along with their efficiency. The prospective enhancement for relevant research is also directed to encourage unmanned testing schemes.
- The vaccination process to combat COVID-19 disease is also highlighted in this study. How existing research articles have utilized the concept of AI and ML in this process are incorporated with necessary details.

All the above mentioned areas are discussed in detail by presenting comparative analysis among numerous research articles and thereby addressing the possible improvements that might guide the medical practitioners and the researchers to work in this domain helping different nations to deal with this infection by uplifting the entire healthcare system. The domains addressed by the study have been depicted in Figure 1.

Figure 1. Workflow to survey recent trends in COVID-19

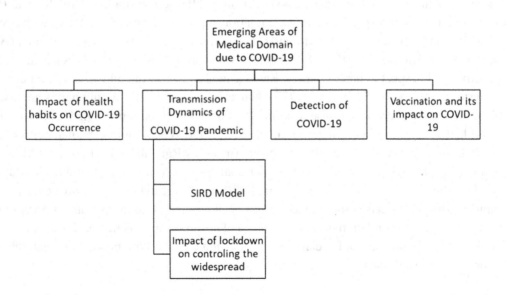

2. LITERATURE SURVEY

This section mostly encompasses the recent literature articles devoted to COVID-19. A thorough discourse analysis of the extant literature was performed. This analysis may be beneficial in advancing ongoing studies towards pandemic preparedness. We reviewed current literature using the keywords "COVID-19", "Vaccines", "Health Habits", "Lockdown", "Mortality", and "detection technique". Each of these works is described in full in the text. Numerous scientific article archives, including Web of Science, Scopus, and other Google Scholar papers, have been searched in order to get a general understanding of Covid-19 management strategies. ML is useful in predicting any event through regression or classification. Depending on the problem and the dataset, various models can be used to obtain the necessary analysis. Several publications were analysed in this study that used ML-based models to speculate on COVID-19's relationship with the above stated issues.

It is noteworthy to mention that several health habits like smoking cigarettes or consumption of alcoholic beverages hampers the immunity system of an individual which indirectly affects if the person is exposed to the virus. Section 2.1 shows some of such papers that depict the correlation between health habits and covid-19. In order to study any epidemic, the count of suspected, infected, recovered people and causalities must be analysed. In section 2.2, several research articles on the SIRD models have been investigated. Different countries have imposed lockdowns strictly or partially to curb the rate of spreading, the impact of lockdown was directed in Section 2.3. The disease spreads at an alarming rate. Besides this there are many individuals with no symptoms; so detection and isolation is highly recommended. Traditional RT-PCR methods can assess the existence of the virus; however image processing from chest X ray output can perform an alternate role. Traditional and AI based detection schemes have been studied in section 2.4. In section 2.5, several literatures on the role of vaccines have been shown.

2.1. Health Habits and COVID-19

The extremity of the viral attack depends on some health practices of an individual. This section highlights how the correlation between the health habits and COVID-19 severity has been established by current investigation.

It is obvious that the mortality rate increases significantly if the person smokes (Doll, R., et al 1994[15]). Some works have been surveyed which show the relationship of severity of COVID 19 with respect to smoking and drinking habits. It is needless to say that smoking tobacco compromises immunity (Arnson, Y., Shoenfeld, Y., & Amital, H. 2010[16]). It has been found that the lungs of smokers are more vulnerable to the virus with respect to healthy lungs. Regular intake of alcoholic beverages also hampers the immunity system of the body (Szabo, G. 1997[17]); hence the people with drinking habits are also more vulnerable to the virus. There was a misconception that drinking alcohol prevents COVID-19 and the myth was broken since alcohol consumption largely affects the WBC count in human beings hence it renders the immunity system (Chick, J. 2020[18]). As confirmed by Ramalho R in 2020[19], drinking alcohol can even affect the psychology of an individual, thus can assist deteriorating mental health during the pandemic. (Farsalinos, K., Barbouni, A., & Niaura, R. 2020 [20]) E-cigarettes vaping are equally harmful, the immunity of the person gets compromised. It has been observed that the people who vape are also vulnerable to the virus. A correlation between vaping and hospitalization is made. (Javanmard, S. H., & Toghyani, A. 2021)[21] Javanmard, S. H., came to a conclusion that smoking hookah or cigarettes are the prime factors of increase in the risk factors in pandemic.

Using an ML-based methodology, (Banoei, M. M., Dinparastisaleh, R., Zadeh, A. V., & Mirsaeidi, M. 2021[22]) predicted the probability of COVID-19-related mortality among smokers. The goal of their study is to examine the patients who had a low chance of passing away from COVID-19. They made use of information from 400 patients who were admitted to the University of Miami Hospital and underwent PCR tests. The Statistically Inspired Modification of Partial Least Square (SIMPLS) technique was used in their data set to estimate the findings. According to study, a number of variables affect mortality rates, and those with a history of smoking have more toxins in their bodies than non-smokers, increasing their risk of passing away. The study can be verified by employing more robust information from a multicenter sample.

(Yang H and et al. 2020[23]) discuss the changes in smoking behavior over the pandemic period. In October 2020, the participants who completed the questionnaire were from China. Statistical analysis (SAS 9.4) of the questionnaire data found that male smokers were less likely to abandon smoking as compared to the female; nevertheless the people with prolonged smoking history or the residents of the urban region are no different. It is needless to mention that the overall health and immunity gets affected by the smoking habits. Those who cut back on smoking more expressed greater physical and mental well-being, as well as greater contentment with their current state of physical health.

It has been found by (Neira, D. P. and et al 2020[24]) that patients who smoke are more likely to be hospitalized than those who don't. A person's smoking history is taken into consideration if they are found to be infected with SARS-COV2 at an academic medical center in the United States. SARS-COV2 patients with a history of smoking were studied between March 1, 2020, and January 31, 2021, in order to establish the risk of major health complications for COVID-19. Former smokers had a higher death and hospitalization rate from COVID-19 than current or never smokers. Ex-smokers' age and comorbidities have a role in this effect.

2.2. Suspected-Infected-Recovered-Deceased (SIRD)

The tracking and prediction of the spread of infectious diseases and viruses can be assessed by the concept of forecasting epidemics. There is a mathematical correlation between the disease spread as a function of time or death count with respect to time in any epidemic. It was back in 1766 when Daniel Bernoulli predicted the mortality rate of 'Smallpox' by his famous 'Bernoulli Epidemic Model'. (Bernoulli, D., & Blower, S. 2004[25]) This section provides an insight of different forecasting methods used to forecast the proliferation of Coronavirus illness. The SIRD model is centered on the concept of suspected rate, infected rate, recovery rate and death rate estimation. This SIRD model can be beneficial as the pattern of the spreading can be monitored and the healthcare workers can get an idea of how to combat the outbreak. An automated system construction mechanism employed by different articles for SIRD detection has been discussed in this section. ML or DL based methods can be utilized as a tool to construct the automated system.

Shahid, et al in their work focused on establishing the role of machine learning based models in detecting, monitoring, predicting spread count for the medical assistance. For this purpose datasets from X-RAY (CXR) and CT-Scans were used and the application of ML models like Convoluted Neural Networks based on DL for feature extraction was deployed. Besides this, Bayesian DL Classifiers, Capsule Network-based framework -COVID-CAPS, etc were also used. With the aid of these models, researchers found that ML algorithms play an important role in determining the widespread of the coronavirus and can aid in the discovery of a treatment by suggesting the appropriate vaccines. by being familiar with the virus's protein structure and sequencing. (Shahid, et al 2021[26])

It was (Gambhir. E and et al 2020[27]) who made a comprehensive study on the analysis of the pattern of COVID-19 transmission in India using regression based ML algorithms that includes Support vector ML algorithm, Polynomial regression. They have used the data of the family welfare of India and the Ministry of health as their data set. Using these algorithms they concluded that the methods that they had used to forecast the rise in covid 19 is 93% accurate and it can forecast the growth of Covid-19 affected people for the next 60 days.

The work of (Sarkar O, et al 2020[28]) emphasized on analyzing the effects of COVID-19. For this purpose, the dataset extracted from the human information association as well as certain data from the World Health Organization (WHO) has been collected and fed into ML models. The employed models include the ARIMA model analysis, the Clustering Algorithm, Polynomial Regression algorithm, and most importantly the Facebook prophet time series forecasting algorithm. An extensive comparison among these models was conducted and finally, the authors have concluded that the 'Facebook's Prophet model' can outperform as compared to the other implemented models. And the increasing count of confirmed cases in the whole world is quite impossible to control unless there is proper public awareness. It is noted that among different algorithms, the prophet model provides best analysis; however the research could also be carried out for other models for a better confirmation of the above mentioned problem.

The research (Khan, M. H. R., & Hossain, A. 2020[29]) aimed to determine whether the number of tests has any bearing on the overall prognosis of COVID-19 cases. Worldometer's website was used to gather the data along with ten other variables ranging from the number of confirmed fatalities to the number of recovered patients to the number of active cases, summative severely sick patients to the number of infections to the number of tests completed. To forecast the association between the quantity of tests and the COVID instances, the authors employed the Classification and Regression Tree (CART) (Lewis, R. J. 2000, May[30]) and Random Forest algorithms. Only characteristics such as total active cases, total number of healed patients, total fatalities, new cases, and total severe cases are significant to anticipate the cumulative number of COVID-19 confirmed cases worldwide, according to the research. Regression utilizing voting methods is superior to CART if the data contains uncorrelated variables. As a result of this, the CART algorithm is prone to overfitting. (Abu-Nimeh, S., Nappa, D., Wang, X., & Nair, S. 2007, October)[31]

Salam M. A. and et al[32]. Attempted to find which algorithm is better in terms of accuracy prediction and training time. They have used the datasets from COVID-19 Patients' Chest X-ray radiography. It is noteworthy to mention that federated ML algorithms and traditional ML algorithms were used in this research and have come across that federated ML algorithms are better in terms of accuracy prediction and training. And as federated machine-learning algorithms use individual machines to predict the outcome, data privacy of machines is also maintained, which is not possible in case of the traditional ML algorithm. They also concluded that increasing the number of rounds and rising data size does not influence the model accuracy or model loss. The primary drawback of this work is that the Federated learning algorithm takes longer time to get executed as compared to traditional ML.

Using ML algorithms, (Ardabili S.H. and et al 2020[33]) intended to anticipate the outbreak of the pandemic. This research aims to give a comparative comparison of ML and soft computing models to speculate the outbreak of COVID-19. They have acquired COVID-19 patient data from the Worldometer website from some nations namely, Italy, Germany, Iran, the United States of America, and China. On this data, they utilized two approaches to anticipate the outcome: multilayer perceptron (MLP) and

Adaptive Network-based Fuzzy Inference System (ANFIS). They found that traditional epidemiological methods have exhibited coarse accuracy for long-term speculation because of the significant degree of uncertainty and the absence of critical data. As far as long-term forecasting is concerned, the MLP and ANFIS ML models stand out for their ability to generalize. The observations of this study suggest that ML is a good approach for simulating the time series of the COVID-19 spread due to the extremely convoluted structure of the epidemic and the inequalities between nations.

Use of a variety of ML models to anticipate and quantify COVID-19 instances in India was done by (Jakka, A. 2020, October[34]). The purpose of this article is to investigate the efficacy of various learning models in estimating the number of COVID-19 confirmed cases across the nation, as well as the consequences for the future. In order to forecast the number of COVID-19 confirmed cases in India, they employed Sigmoid modelling, ARIMA, the SEIR model, and LSTM ML models using data acquired from John Hopkins University. They discovered that these models can forecast COVID-19 values up to 60 days in advance. In addition, they determined that the SEIR model has a solid foundation in pandemic analysis and can detect COVID-19 spikes, and the LSTM model also performed better than other models. Decision-makers would benefit from these models because they would be able to see how the pandemic would develop in their nation and take the appropriate measures to mitigate its effects.

(Capuano, A and et. al. 2020 [35]) have observed a high death rate in male patients with respect to females. It has been observed that men are more vulnerable to the virus, which can lead to undiagnosed cases of pulmonary embolism, pulmonary thrombosis, or other cardiovascular disorders. The research focuses on analysing factors that are responsible for the gender differences with respect to immune system modulation with sex hormones and health habits as well. Another study (Punn, N. S et al 2020[36]) predicted the transmission characteristics and identified possible measures to take necessary precautions to stop the transmission at a faster rate by means of ML and DL based methods. This paper tells us how ML and DL can be used in epidemic analysis so we can predict the transmission and able response faster to take necessary action to stop or reduce the transmission. The dataset of the paper uses the data from the Johns Hopkins dashboard, which comprises daily cases. In this paper the methods used are SVR, DNN, LSTM and PR. The result observed that the Polynomial Regression (PR) method best fits for the growing trend. PR method has exhibited the lowest RMSE value of 117.94 for recovered cases. Further incorporation of more data into the ML models may optimize the RMSE and provide insight to zero-error predictive analysis.

(Sujath, R et al 2020[37]) implemented a framework that predicts the spread of the pandemic. The primary objective was to estimate the pandemic outbreak in India using the datasets from Kaggle. The research was carried out by using LR,MLP and VAR. Beside these, it was analysed by (Yang, P. U., and et al 2020[38]) that the children (below 10 years old) are very much vulnerable towards the infection.

2.3. Impact of Lockdown to Restrict the Transmission of COVID-19

Since the disease spreads by transmission of respiratory droplets; it is advised to maintain physical distancing as far as practicable. Besides this it has been found that traveling from one place to the other largely affects the wide spread. Since the outbreak, the number of the affected people rose to such an extent that it became hard to accommodate all the patients in the hospitals. If such growth continued the entire healthcare system would fail. Hence, according to the epidemiologists, complete lockdown or partial lockdowns have been implemented by the governments of different nations, in order to curb the growth rate of the infection.

(Cauchemez, S., et al 2020 [39])have established how lockdown influences the widespread use of SAR-CoV-2 in France. The research indicated the success of the lockdown in France. They have shown that lockdown reduced the count of affected people; thereby reducing the 'burden' in the ICU and ITU. Also the growth of the epidemic was controlled in the first wave of the epidemic.

Nevertheless, (Cole, M. A., et al 2020[40]) have made an ML based framework that not only explained the need for lockdown in controlling the widespread, but also the research focused on the fact how air quality got improved due to less auto-emission during the lockdown. The research was carried out based on the data from 30 cities in China. Supervised learning models like Decision Tree and Random Forest algorithms were used to classify Air Quality Parameters based on lockdown and regular time from a time frame between 2013 to 2020. It was observed that lockdown inWuhan resulted in lowering of air pollutants like SO_2, NO_2, CO and Lead.

Besides this, it was stated by (Ntakolia, C., and et al 2022) [41]that the first cycle of lockdown has largely affected the mental wellbeing among children and youngsters in Greece. The model was implemented using ML. The ReliefF algorithm (Spolaôr, N., et al 2013[42]) was used for feature selection for the fact it shows good results in the medical field with very low impact of noise. (Ntakolia, C., and et al 2022) (Pasayat A and et al 2020[43]) have shown that using an exponential model and linear regression model, the impact of lockdown was studied as a function of the count of the infected patients. The data was taken from February 2020 to May 2020. (Moraliyage, H., and et al 2021[44]) have studied that during the lockdown, several cancer patients were also denied treatment, which resulted in a large collateral damage.

The research of (Saba, T et al, 2021[45]) shows a framework using ML based framework to forecast the daily count of the cumulative covid-19 affected people, also gave an insight of the fact how lockdown shapes the spreading of the disease. The authors have made a prediction that imposing lockdowns would actually reduce the count of the affected people significantly and thereby reduce the risks of death. The spreading of the epidemic is also controlled by imposing lockdowns. The authors have carried out the research based on three countries. Every lockdown type was studied by different supervised models like random forest, KNN, SVM, decision trees, Holt winter, ARIMA, SARIMA to forecast the confirmed affected cases per day. The data was extracted from the github repository from the month of January - September 2020 to train the models. The accuracy of the model was analysed by three performance criteria. The study ensured that herd lockdowns are the best lockdown strategy to combat the virus, to reduce the casualties of the pandemic.

It is needless to say that lockdowns would affect the economy, but at the same time, besides the vaccines; lockdowns are necessary to retard wide spreading of the virus. So for the regions that are densely populated but having poor infrastructure or poor economy, they must optimize the lockdowns so that a balance is there without. Hence a robust lockdown policy was stated by (Bhardwaj, A et al 2020[46]) based on ML based models (reinforcement learning tools were used). The research aimed to manage the spreading of the disease without severe impact in the economy. The possible improvement of the work can also be done by increasing the dataset in terms of time as well as number of persons affected and the analysis could also be done on how vaccines exhibited a prime contribution in shaping the pandemic.

2.4 COVID-19 Detection Schemes

It has been observed that the epidemic spreads at an alarming rate. Besides this, the disease is extremely contagious. In majority cases the victims of the virus don't have noticeable symptoms. However, the asymptomatic patients are capable of transmitting the infection. This makes it more harmful. Hence detection of the infection at the early stage is very important. Traditional RT-PCR (Tahamtan, A., & Ardebili, A. 2020) [47]exerted for the detection of the disease, apart from that alternate AI based detection schemes are also studied. The pros and cons of each work are stated in the following section.

2.4.1. Traditional RT-PCR Based Detection

Reverse Transcription Polymerase Chain Reaction (RT-PCR) is the traditional process by which SARS CoV-2 can be identified. It is a laboratory based chemical reaction where the respiratory samples are collected; if there is presence of the pathogen it gives positive results. RT is a technique in which complementary DNA is synthesized from an RNA template by means of an enzyme. The virus SARS CoV-2 has got an RNA which can replicate within the lungs of the host person. The RNA gets replicated and it multiplies very fast and even it can break the immune system of the host body. RT-PCR follows a nuclear derived mechanism which has the capability of detecting any sort of genetic material from any pathogen. By doing a series or 'chain' of chemical reactions using an enzyme called RT or reverse transcriptase a small part of RNA is extracted from the sample. The DNA is extracted, then a small part is amplified. This method is widely used for the detection of HIV in AIDS affected people by replicating the genome. The upper along with the lower respiratory specimens from the suspected individuals can be identified as SARS CoV-2 genetic code using the RT-PCR testing (Gibson, U. E., Heid, C. A., & Williams, P. M.

Figure 2. Traditional RTPCR technique workflow

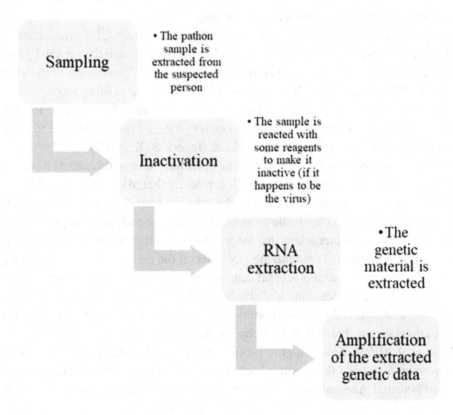

1996[48]). Now traditional testing is classified into two types; they are viral tests and antibody tests. Viral test says whether the individual is affected with COVID-19 or not, antibody test means whether the person was affected by the virus or not (Tahamtan, A., & Ardebili, A. 2020[49]).

The effectiveness of the RT-PCR technique for the detection of the presence of SARS-CoV-2 in a respiratory droplet was studied by Alsharif, W., & Qurashi, A. (2021). [50]

The basic workflow in the traditional RTPCR is stated in figure 2:

2.4.2 AI Based Detection Schemes

RT-PCR is the most accepted technology for the detection of presence of the coronavirus in an individual; however this method has certain drawbacks as stated by (Ai, T., 2020[51]). These are listed as follows:

- Even if a small DNA sample error happens during the amplification process, the system will give wrong or misleading results so testing must be performed repeatedly. This takes a lot of time as well as cost.
- The pathogen (SARS CoV-2) is highly contagious; so the medical staff performing the testing may get contaminated with the virus.

Hence an alternate method must be there; since not every nation has got sufficient infrastructure to conduct RT-PCR test, at the same time distant places lack a proper medical system so an unmanned system could be a better alternative as pointed by (Yang, Z., et al 2020[52]). It has been stated by the WHO (He, L. et al 2020[53]) that a person who gets affected with the virus will have certain perforations in lungs . This could be detected if we study digital images of lungs.

Therefore, several researches have been done using chest X-Ray images, CT scan images or MRI images of lungs to detect the presence of SARS CoV-2. AI based models train the system by some existing data, based on these data the system responds to any unknown data. The design of the system is very important to get significant accuracy. ML is a subset of AI; in all the existing works researchers have used ML algorithms to assess the presence of the virus from different lung images. Researchers have focused on making a framework which is capable enough to forecast the presence of 'SARS CoV-2' in an individual with significant accuracy. (Sethy, P. K., & Behera, S. K. 2020.).[54]

Since the past few months from the outbreak of the epidemic, several researches have been done on CNN based models to detect the novel coronavirus. It is relevant that MRI or CT scan images give much more clarity or 3D picture of the lungs but most of the scholars have deployed Chest X-Ray images to study this because X-Ray is widely available to most of the places even in rural places as well as it is affordable to the mass. The computer learns just the way human beings learn anything from past experience. The human brain is capable of recognizing any object if the person has experienced it previously, this is because the human brain contains several neurons, and with such a neural network human beings are capable of making decisions, detecting any object, etc. Therefore, some algorithms are made which makes such a network of artificial neurons (commonly called artificial neural networks) in computers which makes the computer capable of detecting objects (Maturana, D., & Scherer, S. 2015, September[55]) and (Zhao, Z. Q., et al 2019[56]). This is highly significant for the identification of coronavirus in chest images. It has been evident from the existing literature that the Deep Convolutional Neural Networks (CNN) has a great potential in automating the segregation of chest X-Ray images to expose the pathogen

(Anwar, S. M., et al 2018[57]). Additionally, the system ought to be able to discriminate between typical pneumonia and COVID pneumonia. Therefore, in-depth research in this particular field is strongly advised.

The main benefit of using a convolutional neural network (CNN) is it can perceive any object or image with very impressive accuracy without any human supervision (Zhang, K., et al 2018[58]) . This technique can be used as a reliable screening and very fast methodology to detect COVID-19 .Several model architectures in CNN have been explored recently to perform efficient image classification based on lung radiology images originating from X-Ray and CT-Scan. The CNN based framework has the power to extract hidden features from radiology images that can accurately identify the disease affecting the patient. Architecture differs in the number of parameters, number of layers and type of layer. Some popular architecture of CNN are AlexNet, DenseNet, GoogleNet, InceptionV2, InceptionV3, ResNet50, ResNet18, ResNet101, VGG16, VGG19, Inception ResNetV2, DeTraC-ResNet and Xception which differ in number of parameter, numbers of layer and type of layers. AlexNet was designed by the Supervision group that triumphed in the ImageNet Large Scale Visual Recognition Competition (ILSVRC) 2012 contest with error rates half that of its nearest competitors (from 26% to 15%) (S Lovelyn Rose et al 2019). [59]

Wang S. et al in 2020 [60]had developed a DL algorithm to monitor SARS-CoV-2 from CT scan images. The authors have collected around 1065 Computed Topographic Images that had 325 confirmed COVID-19 images and 740 images of normal viral pneumonia. The authors have implemented inception transfer learning to form the algorithm. In their project; the experiment resulted quite promisingly with efficiency of 89.5% by internal validation (sets used during training of model) and 79.3% by external validation (sets used while executing the model).So far we have got only one framework using CT scan. CT scan gives very good quality images; in spite of that, the majority of the researchers are working by considering the chest X-ray images as input since the CT scan is not available in the remote rural hospitals.

Narin A. and et. al. in 2020 [61]has presented a framework which can assess SARS-CoV-2 infection by using DL methodologies in chest X-Ray images. In the research, different convoluted neural network models like InceptionV3, ResNet50 and InceptionResNetV2 were executed to detect the presence of SARS-CoV-2 pathogen. The authors have taken the data from the chest X-Ray of corona virus affected people and implemented the above mentioned three models for learning approach. They have used the dataset from 16th February 2020 to 21st March 2020 shared by Dr. Joseph Cohen in the GitHub data set. It was concluded by the authors that DL methods in detection of COVID-19 disease would be an alternative to traditional test kits and early detection would help the physicians to treat the patients with ease.

In another paper, (Sethy P.K. and et. al 2020) made an investigation where DL-based image processing is performed from chest X ray images. The SVM classifier was used by the researchers in the model. The authors have taken the data from GitHub, Kaggle and Open-I repository datasets for the X-Ray Images of affected persons and some other relevant data was taken from WHO website and other official government sites. The authors have done a prolonged study of different classifier models and observed different efficiencies and some other parameters. The authors have done a prolonged study of different classifier models and observed different efficiencies and some other parameters. The result section observed that the ResNet with SVM shows best accuracy (95.38%). The authors have used a dataset where 25 were infected with 25 normal people in Kaggle. Zhang J and et. Al in 2020 [62]have preferred to perform the detection process of coronavirus. In their project they have used chest X-Ray and analyzed using DL tools. In their work, the authors developed a framework for fast as well as reliable monitoring of chest images. 100 chest X-Ray images were accumulated by the researchers in this project where 70 people were COVID-19 positive from GitHub Dataset. But in order to smooth the process of 'DL' more data were required and hence additional 1431 chest X-Ray images were taken that had 1008 pneumonia patients from the Chest X-ray 14 dataset that is open source. The authors have used the ResNet deep anomaly detection model which had detected COVID-19 positive with 96% efficiency and 70.65% for non covid-19 cases.

Apostopoulos ID and et al in 2020 [63]developed a framework to detect SARS-CoV-2 in chest X-ray images using transfer learning and CNN. Transfer learning (as stated by Pan, S. J., & Yang, Q. 2009[64]) is an ML method where a trained framework is reused on a similar job. It's an optimization strategy that speeds up or improves performance during the second task. Transfer learning is connected to multi-task learning and isn't a DL specialty. Transfer learning is well recognised in deep learning because of the massive resources needed to train DL models or the large, demanding datasets. DL only works if the first task's model features are generic. Transfer learning has several efficiencies. Class 2 refers to the model's first-task efficiency, while class 3 refers to the next-task efficiency. The authors gathered X-rays from people suffering from pneumonia, COVID 19, and normal subjects. 1427 X-rays were collected, including 224 from COVID-19-positive persons, 700 from pneumonia, and 500 from normal people. The researchers hoped to improve coronavirus identification using CNN over existing methods.

Abbas A and et.al. in 2020 [65]classified COVID-19 chest X-rays using Deep CNN. The authors lacked enough data, therefore they applied transfer learning to reduce errors. The authors used a CNN model dubbed DeTraC to identify and recognise coronavirus-affected chest X-ray pictures. Authors found that by exploring class boundaries using class decomposition, DeTraC can handle any picture dataset abnormality. In their paper, they built a framework that could classify acute or normal respiratory problems by implementing the DeTraC-ResNet18 model in chest X-ray pictures with 95.12% accuracy. 70% of the dataset was used to train the model and for experimental analysis.

It has been created by Wang L and et al that COVID-Net is a deep CNN framework to identify CO-VID-19 from public domain chest X-ray pictures. According to (Wang L and et al 2020[66]), a Chest X-Ray dataset with pictures of 13725 individuals was used to train the COVID-Net algorithm. The authors have studied how COVID-Net can be used to make certain predictions. Wang L et al have investigated their framework and evaluated the accuracy about 92.6% in deep neural network models.

Elaziz, et al in 2020 [67]have presented an ML based model to classify covid patient and non covid patient by analyzing the chest x-rays. This model is trained using the data from various sources. This model at first extracts the feature from the chest x-ray images using Fractional Multichannel Exponent Moments or FrMEMs (Hosny, Khalid & Darwish, Mohamed. 2018[68]) on Multicore CPU, after that by using optimization algorithm feature selection take place which is followed by training KNN classifier and evaluating KNN classifier at last the extracted features are compared and are bifurcated into two section covid positive and covid negative.The proposed model outperformed in terms of resource requirement along with the performance by extracting the most outstanding features.

Based on all the neural network models like inception net, resnet50, alexnet, resnet100, etc it is hard to detect whether the patient is suffering from pneumonia due to COVID-19 or any other pathogens. So researches have been performed on multi-classification that would predict whether the individual has been infected by SARS CoV-2 or the person is suffering from pneumonia due to any other reasons.

Ozturk T and et al[69]. in 2020 has implemented a multi-classifier model that uses deep neural networks on chest X-Ray images to predict the presence of SARS CoV-2 or not in an unmanned way. The authors have implemented both binary and multi classifiers. In the binary classification the authors have studied whether the person is infected to the pathogen or not and in the multi classifier model the authors have included the concept of pneumonia caused without COVID-19. They have used a darknet model in the YOLO system with 17 different convolutional layers introducing different filters in each layer.

Figure 3. Chest X Ray images showing perforated lungs for COVID affected individual

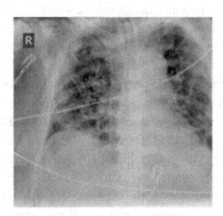

Chest X ray Image of a COVID-19 affected patient

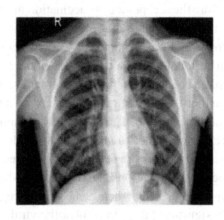

Chest X ray image of a healthy human being

For binary cases the best accuracy noted was 98.08% and for the multi classifier case the accuracy was significantly good, about 87.02%.

Jain, R., Gupta, M., Taneja, S., & Hemanth, D. J. (2021). [70]Analysed images obtained from chest X Ray by deep learning based model using inception V3, Xception Net and ResNeXt based models to identify the differences between a healthy and an infected lungs and obtained an accurate result that can also identify lungs affected by pneumonia caused by other pathogens. The following figure 3 shows the findings from the above mentioned research article.

2.5. Vaccinations to Combat Covid-19

Vaccines are chemical substances often created artificially that stimulate the production of antibodies in an individual from any particular disease. Fleming, A. in 1921 [71]stated that vaccines are proven to be the most efficient preventive measure against any pathogens, reducing the probability of death even if the person is affected by the pathogen. At first a very inactive dose of the virus is taken, then it is injected. Since the virus is inactive, it cannot multiply in the host body; rather the antibodies are generated. This makes the person more immune if he or she gets affected by the virus. The vaccine for COVID-19 has been in a mass testing phase since 2021. It has been proven that the vaccinated people are less vulnerable to the virus; even if they get affected it is less likely the person dies.

An automated intelligent regression model has been developed by Dutta et. al. 2021[72] for tracking the vaccination progress for the entire globe. The progress monitoring has been carried out by implementing ensemble ML based paradigms using an existing dataset available at Kaggle. The dataset lists the vaccination intake statistics information from the time period of 14th December, 2020 to 24th April, 2021. Among several existing employed models, Extra Trees method has exhibited the minimized Mean Absolute error (MAE) and Root Mean Squared Error (RMSE) of 6.465 and 8.127 respectively. However, the time period needs to be enlarged to obtain better monitoring of vaccination status. This work can be prolonged if the indication of the vaccination supply vs vaccination intake statistics could be provided.

In this research, Keshavarzi Arshadi, A., et al in 2020 [73]have made a review on some AI based frameworks to explore the acceptance of vaccination in Jordan. An online questionnaire was distributed among 3100 adults in Jordan to check the efficacy of the vaccination on them. Based on the analysis drawn from logistic regression, the acceptance of COVID-19 vaccines were found to be significantly low (37.4%). Hence it can be concluded that the attitude of the people towards vaccination in Jordan is not convincing.

S Mohapatra et al in 2020 [74]have implemented a framework using ML that takes some existing drugs and tests whether the clinical recovery is fast or not. In other words, repurposing of the drugs has been made to treat the epidemic. The dataset for training the model was taken from BioAssay Dataset in the PubChem repository. The data of the existing drug was extracted from the Drug Bank. It was a classification problem, where the research was carried out by classifying the data by Naive Bayse classifier using Balanced Classification Rate (BCR), the Matthews Correlation Coefficient (MCC). Based on the model, it was concluded that there can be three drugs that satisfies all the necessary conditions to become a potentially significant drug to combat the viral disease. The drug 'Amprenavir' was proven to be the most effective drug for the above mentioned reason.

The impact of vaccinations on the disease outbreak in the US was explained by (Moghadas and et al. 2021[75]) an agent based model of SARS-CoV-2 was developed based on the healthcare workers of the USA from a github data repository. It was found that the efficacy of the vaccine was 95% when double dosage has been taken. The notable outcome that was observed was the attack rate of the virus gone significantly down after the advent of vaccination. Nevertheless, the hospitalization rate also went down after vaccination by 54-62% among the senior citizens. Besides this the vaccination also reduced the fatality of the epidemic by reducing the mortality rate by more than 60% for the severe cases of CO-VID-19. The observations were taken based on age, and in every age group the result for hospitalization or mortality went down. The study was only confined to high risk individuals like healthcare workers. Hence the framework might not work for the entire population.

The attitude of the US and the UK citizens towards vaccination was studied by Hussain A and et al.in 2021[76] based on DL based models. 300,000 posts from facebook and twitter. Including 23,571 facebook posts from the UK and 144864 from the US. Besides this, there were 40268 twitter posts from the UK and 98358 from the US during the time frame of 1st March 2021 to 22nd November 2021. The NLP based framework was used to forecast average sentiments towards vaccinations. As a whole, positive, negative, neutral sentiments were found to be 58%, 22% and 17% respectively in the UK and 56%, 24% and 18% in the UK.

The impact of mutation of coronavirus and vaccination on spread was explained by (Zawbaa, H. M and et al. 2022[77]) Different waves were analyzed with interfering properties. Besides this the mortality and the severity of the disease spread is also monitored. Italy, Brazil, Japan, Germany, Spain, India, USA, UAE, Poland, Colombia, Turkey, and Switzerland were the countries where different waves were analyzed. This study confirmed that wave 2 affected more people's lives with respect to wave 1 in the aforementioned countries. The confirmed case count was decreased due to the appropriate application of vaccination and treatment.

3. RESULT ANALYSIS

This section investigates numerous well established publications on COVID-19. The association between several health habits and the epidemic has been stated in table 2. The forecast of the SIRD model, the impact

Table 2. Health habits and Covid-19

Reference	Findings of the research	Dataset Used	Models Used	Possible Improvement of the paper
Banoei, M. M, et. al. 2021.	This study analyzes whether the person is having any coronary diseases or having diabetes or dementia for the people older than 65 are more prone to die in the epidemic.	400 patient instances Miami University Hospital, Miller School of Medicine, Miami, Florida, in the United States.	SIMPLS model, AUC > 0.85	1.Incorporation of more patient instances can be provided to ensure better predictive analysis. 2. Instead of using SIMPLS algorithm as predictor, application of other ML or DL based models can be utilized. Moreover, the predictive model's performance may be justified based on other efficiency metrics such as Accuracy, f1-score etc rather than relying on AUC only.
Yang, H., & Ma, J. 2021	This study analyses the impact of tobacco consumption on the respiratory disease COVID-19. The analysis also considers the reasons for smoke reduction during pandemic. The analysis also prevails that different types of smokers should be facilitated with different medical policies and treatments.	Total 13484 patient instances were collected in October 2020, China.	Statistical Analysis using SAS 9.4	A promising correlation among smokers and respiratory disease has been established in this study. However, this study can be even prolonged by applying ML based analysis based on collected dataset. The study could analyse CT-scan based lung images to identify the patients who are smokers. To carry out such analysis, how the smoking pattern hampers the internal structure of lungs could be investigated. Hence, customized treatment and healthcare policies can be added with the study's outcome.
Neira, D. P., et al 2021	A comparative analysis between the recent and former smoker has been drawn to assess the COVID-19 severity; the focus has been made on the threat of rehabilitation due to COVID-19 if the person is a smoker.	The data was retrieved from the covid affected victims during the time frame: March - January 2021.	From the dataset, the mean and SD were summarized; coupled with that the Fisher's exact tests and the 'chi-squared' tests were deployed for the estimation of the dataset.	1. The study can be extended to understand the smoking impact on the severity level. How much the patient is vulnerable to death due to former smoking habits. 2. Along with statistical analysis, ML based predictive modeling can be implemented. This predictive analysis can alert a former smoker to control his tobacco consumption to avoid any health related complications. This prediction will even assist the medical experts regarding the current health status of former smokers before hospitalization

of lockdown, and the vaccination process have been critically discussed in table 3, 4 and 5 respectively. The carried out analysis is further supported by a few potential additions in the near or distant future.

4. DISCUSSION

Outbreak analysis is highly recommended for assessing any disease spreading nature. This analysis eventually provides an insight if the outbreak can lead to pandemic or not. Every epidemic hits globally in periodic nature, as observed in the recent past, where each period is termed a 'wave' (Tarrataca, L., Dias, C. M., Haddad, D. B., & De Arruda, E. F. 2021[78]). Covid-19 is essentially a pandemic having many waves. Most of the world wide countries have faced different waves such as the first wave, second wave and third wave of this deadly disease in different time periods. The severity of each wave turns out to be different for each country based on the virus mutation and proper medication. The peak counts of

Table 3. Suspected-infected-recovered-deceased (SIRD)

Reference	Findings of the research	Dataset Used	Models Used	Possible Improvement of the paper
Shahid, O, et al 2021	Detection and spreading of the virus was studied to predict the spreading of the virus	Data was extracted from the computed tomographic images and the X-RAY Images of the chest	DL - CNN, Feature Extraction, Bayesian DL Classifiers, Capsule Network-based classifier.	1. The research might have been carried out by including the impact of vaccines in spreading. 2. If larger data was used, reliability would have improved.
Gambhir, E., et al, 2020.	This study analyses the pattern of COVID-19 transmission across India, the authors have obtained an accuracy of 93% in predicting the count of COVID positive cases for 60 days.	Ministry of health and family welfare of India	Regression study, SVM, polynomial regression	1. This research could have been carried out using other datasets to train the model to predict the trend for more than 60 days. 2. The random forest algorithm could have produced more reliable results.
Sarkar, O., et al, 2020	Severity analysis of covid-19 was predicted using ML algorithms; prophet time series model showed best results.	The data was taken from the website of World Health Organization (WHO) and besides that, human information association has been collected	The Polynomial Regression algorithm, Clustering Algorithm, ARIMA model analysis, and Facebook prophet time series forecasting algorithms were used.	1. The research could also be carried out for other models for a better confirmation of the above mentioned problem.
Lewis, R. J., 2020	The primary finding was to check whether the test count and the confirmed instances of COVID-19 are dependent or not.	Data was extracted from wordometer website	CART model was used to perform regression	1. If the problem of overfitting comes, the CART algorithm would fail to solve that. 2. Voting algorithms might produce better results for larger datasets 3. If the dataset contains uncorrelated variables then the CART model may fail.
Abdul Salam, et al, 2021	The recovery rate and infection rate of the disease was predicted keeping data privacy in mind using a decentralized model.	The datasets were taken from COVID-19 sufferers' Chest X-ray radiography	Federated learning model	1. Slower as compared to traditional ML algorithms.
Ardabili, S. F et al, 2020	The nature of the outbreak was predicted	The data was extracted from the Worldometer website for different demographic regions including Italy, Germany, Iran, the USA, and China.	MLP and ANFIS algorithms	1. More data would have been fruitful for MLP models. 2. The mortality rate might be incorporated and analyzed in the work.
Jakka, A., 2020	The authors have forecasted the status of the pandemic in India for upcoming 60 days	John Hopkins University - JHU CSSE	Sigmoid modeling, ARIMA, SEIR model, and LSTM ML models	1. The influence of vaccinations may be included in the work. 2. The testing set might have been larger. 3. A verification of larger set would have made the model even more reliable
Punn, N. S., et al, 2020.	Emphasized on forecasting the rise of the epidemic, thereby reducing the risks of any potential damage. Polynomial Regression proved to be the best model to predict this problem	Johns Hopkins dashboard	SVR, DNN, LSTM and PR.	1. Larger dataset is needed for confirmation or reliability 2. More models could have been tested
Sujath, R., et al, 2020	Predicted the spread of the epidemic	kaggle	LR, MLP, VAR models	1. More data would have been better for learning multi-layer perceptron

Table 4. Impact of lockdown to restrict the transmission of COVID-19

Reference	Findings of the research	Dataset Used	Models Used	Possible Improvement of the paper
Cole, M. A et al, 2020	How lockdowns in Wuhan affected the air quality of the province	Qingyue Open Environmental Data Center' during the time period from 18th January 2013 - 29th February 2020.	Supervised models like decision tree and random forests were used to classify the air pollutants in the mentioned cities	1. The influence of lockdown on air pollution was tested in the Wuhan province and the model was learned by the air quality data from the aforementioned cities. If the research was done by considering all relevant states and other climatic conditions it would have been much better.
Pasayat, A. K, et al, 2020	How lockdown can influence the count of COVID 19 cases.	Humanitarian (February 2020 to May 2020)	Linear regression model	1. For larger data the result would be more reliable 2. Influence of vaccinations and impact of partial lockdowns might have been included
Saba, T., et al, 2021	Prediction of daily count of covid-19 affected people due to lockdown. The study ensured that herd lockdowns are the best lockdown strategy to combat the virus, to reduce the casualties of the pandemic	Github repository, 9 nations India, Iran, Hubei (China), Iceland, Sweden, Netherland, Russia, Bulgaria, and Greece, between 22nd January 2020 to 30th September 2020	Supervised models like random forest, KNN, SVM, decision trees, Holt winter, ARIMA, SARIMA	1. If the time window of the data was larger, it would have been more reliable. 2. Influence of vaccines and partial lockdowns with respect to strict lockdown might be mentioned. 3. Voting based algorithms show best results, but for multiple data sets a hybrid model must be prepared.
Bhardwaj, A et al 2020	Robust lockdowns are needed to have a balance between epidemic spread and economic growth	Survey in Mumbai	Reinforcement learning	The work can also be done by increasing the dataset in terms of time as well as number of persons affected and the analysis could also be done on how vaccines played a vital role in shaping the pandemic.

Table 5. Vaccination to combat Covid-19

Reference	Findings of the research	Dataset Used	Models Used	Possible Improvement of the paper
Jain, R., et al 2021	Global vaccination process was tracked	Kaggle, 14th December, 2020 to 24th April, 2021	Ensemble based learning models	1. The time period needs to be enlarged to obtain better monitoring of vaccination status. 2. This work can be prolonged if the indication of the vaccination supply vs vaccination intake statistics could be provided.
Dutta, S, et al 2021	How drugs can be repurposed dependent on ML based tools	Antiviral data	Regression	More data will make the framework more reliable.

every wave happen to be different for the above mentioned reasons. Proper medication and lockdown should be imposed to flatten the infection rate (Vermund, S. H., & Pitzer, V. E. 2021[79]). Besides this it should be kept in mind that the mutation of the virus might lead us to a different direction in terms of the SIRD model. So a detailed correlation between the mutation, medication must be checked. Even before the discovery of the medicine, the mortality rate was much lower as compared to other deadly diseases; still it is regarded as a 'World-Wide-Threat' since the transmission rate is very high even if the person is asymptomatic (Nomura, Yushi, et al.). [80]So rapid detection and isolation of the affected people is highly recommended. Also it is to be noted that based on the research of Nomura, et al the smoking habits can slow down the efficacy of vaccines (Mandal, S., et al 2021[81]). Since the immunity system gets reduced the person may die. Also, the authors have explained mathematically how the efficacy of vaccines gets affected in a person if the individual is a smoker.

5. CONCLUSION

Any deadly pathogens can highly perturbed the existing world within a few amount of time. The Covid-19 disease actually indicated how the worldwide healthcare system is lagging from the benchmark. Hence it is needed to detect, alert, and as well as manage the entire pandemic by uplifting the global medical system. Proper investigation and research work should be carried out to assess this deadly disease and its effects. The review work exhibited in the current study has exhaustively searched for numerous promising research areas and assembled the following areas where the research work can be made further.

- The outbreak analysis of any pandemic is highly dependent on the dataset. Hence, a large amount of datasets should be analysed to forecast general trends of the corresponding disease. In fact, the outbreak analysis should be considered as a big data problem where enormous amounts of data from different countries across the world should be examined. This data should also include the variants of COVID-19 viruses along with its impact and spreading nature. A full-fledged analysis will be feasible if all these mentioned features are incorporated within a dataset. The outbreak analysis can even be extended to predict forthcoming waves by using a computerized system.
- The analysis can be done by a statistical or any automated procedure. Since, the data is highly stochastic and time-variant in nature, application of automated methods using any ML or DL models will be highly beneficial. These models should be robust in nature so that it can perceive and understand the hidden patterns present in the dataset. The models should be properly tuned in terms of different parameters so that it can exhibit promising prediction efficiency.
- All the aforementioned areas discussed in this paper may be extended by applying hybrid ML or DL models. The hybrid model can be constructed by taking two or more dissimilar models as its components. Proper hyper-parameter adjustment along with the hybridization procedure can ensure benchmark predictive outcome.
- In case of COVID-19 vaccination process, the demand-supply trade-off should be tracked using an automated process. Application of ML, or deep-learning models may be utilized for this purpose. In fact, zone-wise supply-demand prediction can benefit the overall distribution of the vaccine.

REFERENCES

Cole, M. A., Elliott, R. J., & Liu, B. (2020). The impact of the Wuhan Covid-19 lockdown on air pollution and health: a machine learning and augmented synthetic control approach. *Environmental and Resource Economics, 76*(4), 553-580

Abbas, A., Abdelsamea, M. M., & Gaber, M. M. (2020). Classification of COVID-19 in chest X-ray images using DeTraC deep convolutional neural network. *arXiv preprint arXiv:2003.13815* doi:10.1101/2020.03.30.20047456

Abdul Salam, M., Taha, S., & Ramadan, M. (2021). COVID-19 detection using federated machine learning. *PLoS One, 16*(6), e0252573. doi:10.1371/journal.pone.0252573 PMID:34101762

Abu-Nimeh, S., Nappa, D., Wang, X., & Nair, S. (2007, October). A comparison of machine learning techniques for phishing detection. In *Proceedings of the anti-phishing working groups 2nd annual eCrime researchers summit* (pp. 60-69). 10.1145/1299015.1299021

Ai, T., Yang, Z., Hou, H., Zhan, C., Chen, C., Lv, W., Tao, Q., Sun, Z., & Xia, L. (2020). Correlation of chest CT and RT-PCR testing for coronavirus disease 2019 (COVID-19) in China: A report of 1014 cases. *Radiology, 296*(2), E32–E40. doi:10.1148/radiol.2020200642 PMID:32101510

Alsharif, W., & Qurashi, A. (2021). Effectiveness of COVID-19 diagnosis and management tools: A review. *Radiography, 27*(2), 682–687. doi:10.1016/j.radi.2020.09.010 PMID:33008761

Andersen, K. G., Rambaut, A., Lipkin, W. I., Holmes, E. C., & Garry, R. F. (2020). The proximal origin of SARS-CoV-2. *Nature Medicine, 26*(4), 450–452. doi:10.103841591-020-0820-9 PMID:32284615

Anwar, S. M., Majid, M., Qayyum, A., Awais, M., Alnowami, M., & Khan, M. K. (2018). Medical image analysis using convolutional neural networks: A review. *Journal of Medical Systems, 42*(11), 226. doi:10.100710916-018-1088-1 PMID:30298337

Apostolopoulos, I. D., & Mpesiana, T. A. (2020). Covid-19: automatic detection from x-ray images utilizing transfer learning with convolutional neural networks. *Physical and Engineering Sciences in Medicine.*

Ardabili, S. F., Mosavi, A., Ghamisi, P., Ferdinand, F., Varkonyi-Koczy, A. R., Reuter, U., Rabczuk, T., & Atkinson, P. M. (2020). Covid-19 outbreak prediction with machine learning. *Algorithms, 13*(10), 249. doi:10.3390/a13100249

Arnson, Y., Shoenfeld, Y., & Amital, H. (2010). Effects of tobacco smoke on immunity, inflammation and autoimmunity. *Journal of Autoimmunity, 34*(3), J258–J265. doi:10.1016/j.jaut.2009.12.003 PMID:20042314

Banoei, M. M., Dinparastisaleh, R., Zadeh, A. V., & Mirsaeidi, M. (2021). Machine-learning-based CO-VID-19 mortality prediction model and identification of patients at low and high risk of dying. *Critical Care, 25*(1), 1–14. doi:10.118613054-021-03749-5 PMID:34496940

Baud, D., Qi, X., Nielsen-Saines, K., Musso, D., Pomar, L., & Favre, G. (2020). Real estimates of mortality following COVID-19 infection. *The Lancet. Infectious Diseases, 20*(7), 773. doi:10.1016/S1473-3099(20)30195-X PMID:32171390

Bernoulli, D., & Blower, S. (2004). An attempt at a new analysis of the mortality caused by smallpox and of the advantages of inoculation to prevent it. *Reviews in Medical Virology*, *14*(5), 275–288. doi:10.1002/rmv.443 PMID:15334536

Bhardwaj, A., Ou, H. C., Chen, H., Jabbari, S., Tambe, M., Panicker, R., & Raval, A. (2020). Robust lock-down optimization for COVID-19 policy guidance. In *AAAI Fall Symposium*.

Capuano, A., Rossi, F., & Paolisso, G. (2020). Covid-19 kills more men than women: An overview of possible reasons. *Frontiers in Cardiovascular Medicine*, *7*, 131. doi:10.3389/fcvm.2020.00131 PMID:32766284

Cauchemez, S., Kiem, C. T., Paireau, J., Rolland, P., & Fontanet, A. (2020). Lockdown impact on CO-VID-19 epidemics in regions across metropolitan France. *Lancet*, *396*(10257), 1068–1069. doi:10.1016/S0140-6736(20)32034-1 PMID:33007219

Chick, J. 2020. Alcohol and COVID-19. *Alcohol and Alcoholism (Oxford, Oxfordshire)*.

Contini, C., Di Nuzzo, M., Barp, N., Bonazza, A., De Giorgio, R., Tognon, M., & Rubino, S. (2020). The novel zoonotic COVID-19 pandemic: An expected global health concern. *Journal of Infection in Developing Countries*, *14*(03), 254–264. doi:10.3855/jidc.12671 PMID:32235085

Daniel, J. (2020). Education and the COVID-19 pandemic. *Prospects*, *49*(1), 91–96. doi:10.100711125-020-09464-3 PMID:32313309

Day, M. (2020). *Covid-19: four fifths of cases are asymptomatic, China figures indicate*. BMJ.

Doll, R., Peto, R., Wheatley, K., Gray, R., & Sutherland, I. (1994). Mortality in relation to smoking: 40 years' observations on male British doctors. *BMJ (Clinical Research Ed.)*, *309*(6959), 901–911. doi:10.1136/bmj.309.6959.901 PMID:7755693

Dutta, S., Mukherjee, U., & Bandyopadhyay, S. (2021). Pharmacy Impact on Covid-19 Vaccination Progress Using Machine Learning Approach. *Journal of Pharmaceutical Research International*, 202–217. doi:10.9734/jpri/2021/v33i38A32076

Elaziz, M. A., Hosny, K. M., Salah, A., Darwish, M. M., Lu, S., & Sahlol, A. T. (2020). New machine learning method for image-based diagnosis of COVID-19. *PLoS One*, *15*(6), e0235187. doi:10.1371/journal.pone.0235187 PMID:32589673

Farsalinos, K., Barbouni, A., & Niaura, R. (2020). *Smoking, vaping and hospitalization for COVID-19*. Qeios.

Fleming, A. (1921). A British Medical Association lecture on vaccine therapy in regard to general practice. *British Medical Journal*, *1*(3138), 255–259. doi:10.1136/bmj.1.3138.255 PMID:20770181

Gambhir, E., Jain, R., Gupta, A., & Tomer, U. 2020, September. Regression analysis of COVID-19 using machine learning algorithms. In *2020 International conference on smart electronics and communication (ICOSEC)* (pp. 65-71). IEEE. 10.1109/ICOSEC49089.2020.9215356

Gentile, I., & Abenavoli, L. (2020). COVID-19: Perspectives on the potential novel global threat. *Reviews on Recent Clinical Trials*, *15*(2), 84–86. PMID:32116200

Gibson, U. E., Heid, C. A., & Williams, P. M. (1996). A novel method for real time quantitative RT-PCR. *Genome Research*, *6*(10), 995–1001. doi:10.1101/gr.6.10.995 PMID:8908519

He, L., Zhao, W., Zhou, W., Pang, P., Liao, Y., & Liu, J. (2020). an emergency surgery in severe case infected by COVID-19 with perforated duodenal bulb ulcer. *Annals of Surgery*, *272*(1), e35–e37. doi:10.1097/SLA.0000000000003958 PMID:32433280

Hosny, K., & Darwish, M. (2018). New Set of Multi-Channel Orthogonal Moments for Color Image Representation and Recognition. *Pattern Recognition*, *88*, 153–173. doi:10.1016/j.patcog.2018.11.014

Hussain, A., Tahir, A., Hussain, Z., Sheikh, Z., Gogate, M., Dashtipour, K., Ali, A., & Sheikh, A. (2021). Sheikh AArtificial Intelligence–Enabled Analysis of Public Attitudes on Facebook and Twitter Toward COVID-19 Vaccines in the United Kingdom and the United States: Observational Study. *Journal of Medical Internet Research*, *23*(4), e26627. https://www.jmir.org/2021/4/e26627. doi:10.2196/26627 PMID:33724919

Jain, R., Gupta, M., Taneja, S., & Hemanth, D. J. (2021). Deep learning based detection and analysis of COVID-19 on chest X-ray images. *Applied Intelligence*, *51*(3), 1690–1700. doi:10.100710489-020-01902-1 PMID:34764553

Jakka, A. (2020, October). Forecasting COVID-19 cases in India Using Machine Learning Models. In *2020 International Conference on Smart Technologies in Computing, Electrical and Electronics (IC-STCEE)* (pp. 466-471). IEEE

Javanmard, S. H., & Toghyani, A. 2021. How hookah increases the risk of corona virus in younger people?. *Journal of Research in Medical Sciences: The Official Journal of Isfahan University of Medical Sciences, 26*.

Keshavarzi Arshadi, A., Webb, J., Salem, M., Cruz, E., Calad-Thomson, S., Ghadirian, N., Collins, J., Diez-Cecilia, E., Kelly, B., Goodarzi, H., & Yuan, J. S. (2020). Artificial intelligence for COVID-19 drug discovery and vaccine development. *Frontiers in Artificial Intelligence*, *3*, 65. doi:10.3389/frai.2020.00065 PMID:33733182

Khan, M. H. R., & Hossain, A. (2020). Machine Learning Approaches Reveal That the Number of Tests Do Not Matter to the Prediction of Global Confirmed COVID-19 Cases. *Frontiers in Artificial Intelligence*, *3*, 3. doi:10.3389/frai.2020.561801 PMID:33748745

Kissler, S. M., Tedijanto, C., Lipsitch, M., & Grad, Y. 2020. Social distancing strategies for curbing the COVID-19 epidemic. MedRxiv. doi:10.1101/2020.03.22.20041079

Lewis, R. J. (2000, May). An introduction to classification and regression tree (CART) analysis. In *Annual meeting of the society for academic emergency medicine in San Francisco, California* (Vol. 14). ACM.

Mandal, S., Arinaminpathy, N., Bhargava, B., & Panda, S. (2021). Plausibility of a third wave of COVID-19 in India: A mathematical modelling based analysis. *The Indian Journal of Medical Research*, *153*(5-6), 522. PMID:34643562

Maturana, D., & Scherer, S. (2015, September). Voxnet: A 3d convolutional neural network for real-time object recognition. In *2015 IEEE/RSJ International Conference on Intelligent Robots and Systems (IROS)* (pp. 922-928). IEEE 10.1109/IROS.2015.7353481

Moghadas, S. M., Fitzpatrick, M. C., Sah, P., Pandey, A., Shoukat, A., Singer, B. H., & Galvani, A. P. (2020). The implications of silent transmission for the control of COVID-19 outbreaks. *Proceedings of the National Academy of Sciences of the United States of America, 117*(30), 17513–17515. doi:10.1073/pnas.2008373117 PMID:32632012

Moghadas, S. M., Vilches, T. N., Zhang, K., Wells, C. R., Shoukat, A., Singer, B. H., & Galvani, A. P. (2021). The impact of vaccination on COVID-19 outbreaks in the United States. medRxiv.

Mohapatra, S., Nath, P., Chatterjee, M., Das, N., Kalita, D., Roy, P., & Satapathi, S. (2020). Repurposing therapeutics for COVID-19: Rapid prediction of commercially available drugs through machine learning and docking. *PLoS One, 15*(11), e0241543. doi:10.1371/journal.pone.0241543 PMID:33180803

Moraliyage, H., De Silva, D., Ranasinghe, W., Adikari, A., Alahakoon, D., Prasad, R., Lawrentschuk, N., & Bolton, D. (2021). Cancer in lockdown: Impact of the COVID-19 pandemic on patients with cancer. *The Oncologist, 26*(2), e342–e344. doi:10.1002/onco.13604 PMID:33210442

Narin, A., Kaya, C., & Pamuk, Z. (2020). Automatic detection of coronavirus disease (covid-19) using x-ray images and deep convolutional neural networks. *arXiv preprint arXiv:2003.10849*

Neira, D. P., Watts, A., Seashore, J., Polychronopoulou, E., Kuo, Y. F., & Sharma, G. (2021). Smoking and risk of COVID-19 hospitalization. *Respiratory Medicine, 182*, 106414. doi:10.1016/j.rmed.2021.106414 PMID:33915414

Nomura, Y. (2021). Age and smoking predict antibody titres at 3 months after the second dose of the BNT162b2 COVID-19 vaccine. *Vaccines.*

Ntakolia, C., Priftis, D., Charakopoulou-Travlou, M., Rannou, I., Magklara, K., Giannopoulou, I., & Lazaratou, E. (2022, January). An Explainable Machine Learning Approach for COVID-19's Impact on Mood States of Children and Adolescents during the First Lockdown in Greece. []. Multidisciplinary Digital Publishing Institute.]. *Health Care, 10*(1), 149. PMID:35052311

Ozturk, T., Talo, M., Yildirim, E. A., Baloglu, U. B., Yildirim, O., & Acharya, U. R. (2020). Automated detection of COVID-19 cases using deep neural networks with X-ray images. *Computers in Biology and Medicine, 121*, 103792. doi:10.1016/j.compbiomed.2020.103792 PMID:32568675

Pan, S. J., & Yang, Q. (2009). A survey on transfer learning. *IEEE Transactions on Knowledge and Data Engineering, 22*(10), 1345–1359. doi:10.1109/TKDE.2009.191

Paraskevis, D., Kostaki, E. G., Magiorkinis, G., Panayiotakopoulos, G., Sourvinos, G., & Tsiodras, S. (2020). Full-genome evolutionary analysis of the novel corona virus (2019-nCoV) rejects the hypothesis of emergence as a result of a recent recombination event. *Infection, Genetics and Evolution, 79*, 104212. doi:10.1016/j.meegid.2020.104212 PMID:32004758

Pasayat, A. K., Pati, S. N., & Maharana, A. (2020). Predicting the COVID-19 positive cases in India with concern to Lockdown by using Mathematical and Machine Learning based Models. medRxiv. doi:10.1101/2020.05.16.20104133

Punn, N. S., Sonbhadra, S. K., & Agarwal, S. (2020). COVID-19 epidemic analysis using machine learning and deep learning algorithms. MedRxiv. doi:10.1101/2020.04.08.20057679

Rabaan, A. A., Al-Ahmed, S. H., Haque, S., Sah, R., Tiwari, R., Malik, Y. S., & Rodriguez-Morales, A. J. (2020). SARS-CoV-2, SARS-CoV, and MERS-COV: A comparative overview. *Le Infezioni in Medicina*, *28*(2), 174–184. PMID:32275259

Ramalho, R. (2020). Alcohol consumption and alcohol-related problems during the COVID-19 pandemic: A narrative review. *Australasian Psychiatry*, *28*(5), 524–526. doi:10.1177/1039856220943024 PMID:32722961

Roy, B., Dhillon, J. K., Habib, N., & Pugazhandhi, B. (2021). Global variants of COVID-19: Current understanding. *Journal of Biomedical Science*, *8*(1), 8–11. doi:10.3126/jbs.v8i1.38453 PMID:33435938

Rose, S., Kumar A., & Renuka, K. (2019). Deep Learning using Python. Wiley India Pvt. Ltd.

Saba, T., Abunadi, I., Shahzad, M. N., & Khan, A. R. (2021). Machine learning techniques to detect and forecast the daily total COVID-19 infected and deaths cases under different lockdown types. *Microscopy Research and Technique*, *84*(7), 1462–1474. doi:10.1002/jemt.23702 PMID:33522669

Sarkar, O., Ahamed, M. F., & Chowdhury, P. (2020, December). Forecasting & Severity Analysis of COVID-19 Using Machine Learning Approach with Advanced Data Visualization. In *2020 23rd International Conference on Computer and Information Technology (ICCIT)* (pp. 1-6). IEEE. 10.1109/ICCIT51783.2020.9392704

Sethy, P. K., & Behera, S. K. (2020). Detection of coronavirus disease (covid-19) based on deep features. *International Journal of Mathematical, Engineering and Management Sciences*.

Shahid, O., Nasajpour, M., Pouriyeh, S., Parizi, R. M., Han, M., Valero, M., Li, F., Aledhari, M., & Sheng, Q. Z. (2021). Machine learning research towards combating COVID-19: Virus detection, spread prevention, and medical assistance. *Journal of Biomedical Informatics*, *117*, 103751. doi:10.1016/j.jbi.2021.103751 PMID:33771732

Shereen, M. A., Khan, S., Kazmi, A., Bashir, N., & Siddique, R. (2020). COVID-19 infection: Origin, transmission, and characteristics of human coronaviruses. *Journal of Advanced Research*, *24*, 91–98. doi:10.1016/j.jare.2020.03.005 PMID:32257431

Song, Z., Xu, Y., Bao, L., Zhang, L., Yu, P., Qu, Y., & Qin, C. (2019). From SARS to MERS, thrusting coronaviruses into the spotlight. *viruses, 11*(1), 59

Spolaôr, N., Cherman, E. A., Monard, M. C., & Lee, H. D. (2013, October). ReliefF for multi-label feature selection. In *2013 Brazilian Conference on Intelligent Systems* (pp. 6-11). IEEE 10.1109/BRACIS.2013.10

Sujath, R., Chatterjee, J. M., & Hassanien, A. E. (2020). A machine learning forecasting model for COVID-19 pandemic in India. *Stochastic Environmental Research and Risk Assessment*, *34*(7), 959–972. doi:10.100700477-020-01827-8 PMID:32837309

Szabo, G. (1997). Alcohol's contribution to compromised immunity. *Alcohol Health and Research World*, *21*(1), 30. PMID:15706761

Tahamtan, A., & Ardebili, A. (2020). Real-time RT-PCR in COVID-19 detection: Issues affecting the results. *Expert Review of Molecular Diagnostics*, *20*(5), 453–454. doi:10.1080/14737159.2020.1757437 PMID:32297805

Tahamtan, A., & Ardebili, A. (2020). Real-time RT-PCR in COVID-19 detection: Issues affecting the results. *Expert Review of Molecular Diagnostics*, *20*(5), 453–454. doi:10.1080/14737159.2020.1757437 PMID:32297805

Tarrataca, L., Dias, C. M., Haddad, D. B., & De Arruda, E. F. (2021). Flattening the curves: On-off lock-down strategies for COVID-19 with an application to Brazil. *Journal of Mathematics in Industry*, *11*(1), 1–18. doi:10.118613362-020-00098-w PMID:33432282

Vermund, S. H., & Pitzer, V. E. (2021). Asymptomatic transmission and the infection fatality risk for COVID-19: Implications for school reopening. *Clinical Infectious Diseases*, *72*(9), 1493–1496. doi:10.1093/cid/ciaa855 PMID:32584967

Wang, L., & Wong, A. (2020). COVID-Net: A Tailored Deep Convolutional Neural Network Design for Detection of COVID-19 Cases from Chest X-Ray Images. *arXiv preprint arXiv:2003.09871*.

Wang, S., Kang, B., Ma, J., Zeng, X., Xiao, M., Guo, J., & Xu, B. (2020). A deep learning algorithm using CT images to screen for Corona Virus Disease (COVID-19). MedRxiv. doi:10.1101/2020.02.14.20023028

Yang, H., & Ma, J. (2021). How the COVID-19 pandemic impacts tobacco addiction: Changes in smoking behavior and associations with well-being. *Addictive Behaviors*, *119*, 106917. doi:10.1016/j.addbeh.2021.106917 PMID:33862579

Yang, P. U., Liu, P., Li, D., & Zhao, D. (2020). Corona Virus Disease 2019, a growing threat to children? *The Journal of Infection*, *80*(6), 671–693. doi:10.1016/j.jinf.2020.02.024 PMID:32142929

Yang, Z., Zeng, Z., Wang, K., Wong, S. S., Liang, W., Zanin, M., Liu, P., Cao, X., Gao, Z., Mai, Z., Liang, J., Liu, X., Li, S., Li, Y., Ye, F., Guan, W., Yang, Y., Li, F., Luo, S., & He, J. (2020). Modified SEIR and AI prediction of the epidemics trend of COVID-19 in China under public health interventions. *Journal of Thoracic Disease*, *12*(3), 165–174. doi:10.21037/jtd.2020.02.64 PMID:32274081

Zawbaa, H. M., Osama, H., El-Gendy, A., Saeed, H., Harb, H. S., Madney, Y. M., Abdelrahman, M., Mohsen, M., Ali, A. M. A., Nicola, M., Elgendy, M. O., Ibrahim, I. A., & Abdelrahim, M. E. (2022). Effect of mutation and vaccination on spread, severity, and mortality of COVID-19 disease. *Journal of Medical Virology*, *94*(1), 197–204. doi:10.1002/jmv.27293 PMID:34427922

Zhang, J., Xie, Y., Li, Y., Shen, C., & Xia, Y. (2020). Covid-19 screening on chest x-ray images using deep learning based anomaly detection. *arXiv preprint arXiv:2003.12338*.

Zhang, K., Zuo, W., & Zhang, L. (2018). FFDNet: Toward a fast and flexible solution for CNN-based image denoising. *IEEE Transactions on Image Processing*, *27*(9), 4608–4622. doi:10.1109/TIP.2018.2839891 PMID:29993717

Zhao, H., Lu, L., Peng, Z., Chen, L. L., Meng, X., Zhang, C., & To, K. K. W. 2021. SARS-CoV-2 Omicron variant shows less efficient replication and fusion activity when compared with the delta variant in TMPRSS2-expressed cells: Omicron variant replication kinetics. *Emerging microbes & infections*, 1-18.

Zhao, Z. Q., Zheng, P., Xu, S. T., & Wu, X. (2019). Object detection with deep learning: A review. *IEEE Transactions on Neural Networks and Learning Systems*, *30*(11), 3212–3232. doi:10.1109/TNNLS.2018.2876865 PMID:30703038

Chapter 25
Revolutionizing Warehouse Management With Image Processing:
A Review of Current Trends and Future Directions

Anantha Subramanya Iyer K. N.
Jain University (Deemed), India

S. Mahalakshmi
Jain University (Deemed), India

Hemanth Kumar S.
Jain University (Deemed), India

Anitha Nallasivam
Jain University (Deemed), India

C. Selvaraj
Dhaanish Ahmed College of Engineering, Chennai, India

ABSTRACT

The future directions and current trends of warehouse management using image processing techniques are thoroughly reviewed in this chapter. The chapter starts off with a summary of warehouse management and the function of image processing methods in analyzing and deciphering images from warehouse environments. It also discusses the benefits and drawbacks of popular image processing methods. The following section of the essay looks at current developments in image processing-based warehouse management, including the methods employed and the advantages of this approach. The potential for combining image processing with other cutting-edge technologies is also investigated, including cloud computing and the internet of things (IoT). The conclusion of the chapter discusses the opportunities and challenges of applying image processing techniques to warehouse management.

DOI: 10.4018/978-1-6684-8618-4.ch025

1. INTRODUCTION

Warehouse management has become increasingly complex due to the growth of e-commerce and the demand for faster and more accurate order fulfilment (Godavarthi et al., 2017). In response to these challenges, image processing technology has emerged as a promising solution to enhance the efficiency and accuracy of warehouse management. Image processing involves the use of algorithms and techniques to extract useful information from digital images (Awan et al., 2021). These images can be captured by cameras or sensors installed in the warehouse. The application of image processing in warehouse management is not new, but recent advancements in technology have enabled more sophisticated and efficient methods. For example, object recognition and tracking algorithms can be used to identify and locate items in a warehouse, while augmented reality and virtual reality can be used to optimize warehouse layouts and improve employee training (Anuradha et al., 2021). Image processing can also be integrated with other technologies, such as the Internet of Things (IoT) and cloud computing, to enable real-time tracking and analysis of inventory and order data (Godavarthi et al., 2017).

Image processing can help automate several warehouse management tasks, which can save time and reduce errors. One such task is inventory management, which is critical for efficient warehouse operations. Traditional inventory management systems rely on manual data entry, which can be time-consuming and error-prone. Image processing technology can help automate this process by using cameras or sensors to capture images of products, which can then be processed using object recognition algorithms to identify and track inventory levels (Zhao et al., 2021). Another area where image processing can have a significant impact is order picking. Order picking involves selecting and retrieving items from the warehouse based on customer orders. This task can be time-consuming and error-prone, especially in large warehouses with a vast number of products. Image processing can help automate this process by using cameras or sensors to identify and locate products, which can then be used to guide workers to the correct locations within the warehouse (Xu et al., 2020).

Image processing can also help improve warehouse safety. For example, cameras can be used to monitor the movement of equipment, such as forklifts, and alert workers if they are in danger of colliding with one another. Cameras can also be used to monitor workers and identify potential safety hazards, such as workers not wearing the proper safety gear (Liu et al., 2021). Image processing technology has the potential to revolutionize warehouse management by improving efficiency, accuracy, and safety. Recent advancements in technology have enabled more sophisticated and efficient methods for using image processing in warehouse management. Integration with other technologies, such as IoT and cloud computing, can further enhance the benefits of image processing. As technology continues to advance, it is likely that image processing will become even more prevalent in warehouse management, leading to increased productivity and cost savings for businesses.

Digital image manipulation using mathematical algorithms is the focus of the computer science discipline known as image processing. To improve their quality and extract valuable information, it entails collecting, examining, and processing digital images. Numerous industries, including healthcare, logistics, and transportation, use image processing. Image processing can be used to automate a number of processes in warehouse management, including logistics, order fulfillment, and inventory management. Image processing, for example, can be used to monitor inventory levels in real-time and notify warehouse managers when stock levels are low. As a result, order fulfillment procedures are made more accurate and effective. It can also be used to track the movement of goods inside the warehouse. Moreover, warehouse layouts can be monitored and improved with image processing, resulting in a more effective use of resources and space. Improving accuracy and reducing errors are two of image processing's most important benefits for warehouse management. Error-prone manual inventory tracking and order fulfillment procedures cause delays and inefficiencies. Warehouse managers can drastically cut the number of errors that occur by automating these procedures using image processing techniques, which also increases the warehouse's overall effectiveness. Computer vision, machine learning, and deep learning are three image processing techniques that are frequently employed in warehouse management. With the aid of these techniques, images can be analyzed to glean important data, such as the location of items within a warehouse or their state during transit.

The use of computer vision to track inventory levels is one illustration of a successful image processing application in warehouse management. Barcodes or RFID tags are used in conventional inventory management systems to track inventory levels. These systems call for manual scanning of each item, which can take time. Utilizing cameras placed inside the warehouse, inventory levels can be monitored in real-time using computer vision. This method does away with manual scanning and drastically cuts down on the amount of time needed to monitor inventory levels. Utilizing machine learning to enhance order fulfillment procedures is another effective way that image processing is used in warehouse management. The analysis of historical order data by machine learning algorithms can reveal trends in the turnaround times for orders. In order to reduce processing times and delays, warehouse managers can use this data to optimize order fulfillment procedures. Although image processing has many benefits for warehouse management, there are some issues that must be resolved as well. The expense of putting in place image processing systems is one of the major obstacles. Some warehouses, especially smaller ones, may find the cost of the cameras, sensors, and other hardware needed for image processing to be prohibitively expensive. The requirement for extensive training and knowledge in image processing presents another difficulty. For warehouse managers and employees to effectively operate and maintain image processing systems, they may need extensive training and experience. Particularly for smaller warehouses with constrained resources, this can be a significant adoption barrier.

1.1 Overview of Warehouse Management

In the field of study known as "image processing," digital images are altered using algorithms on computers to raise their quality, highlight their features, or glean useful information from them. It has numerous uses in a variety of industries, including process manufacturing, healthcare, home automation, and agriculture. The study by Kapoor et al. Presents one instance of the use of image processing in agriculture. (2016), where crop growth and health were tracked using IoT devices and image processing methods. The study showed how image processing could be used to improve crop yields, find early signs of plant diseases, and use less water. Creating algorithms and techniques that enable computers to comprehend and interpret images and videos is the focus of the subfield of computer vision within the field of image processing. Object detection, image recognition, and face recognition are just a few of the uses for computer vision. Bharath et al. Discuss home automation and security in this context. (2019) suggested using computer vision and IoT to develop intelligent sockets that can recognize unauthorized entry into homes and turn off electrical appliances when the owner isn't home.

The creation of algorithms that enable computers to learn from data and make predictions or decisions without being explicitly programmed constitutes another area of image processing known as machine learning. Bolhasani et al. Describe the medical field in this context. In their systematic review of deep learning applications for IoT in healthcare, (2021) discovered that methods for machine learning like neural networks and support vector machines have shown promise in terms of identifying diseases and forecasting patient outcomes. Healthcare is another industry that has seen a rise in the use of IoT devices in conjunction with image processing and machine learning. Haghi Kashani and other people. A systematic review of the use of IoT in healthcare was conducted by (2021), which discovered that IoT gadgets like wearable sensors, cameras, and smart home gadgets can be used to monitor patients remotely, catch falls, and give healthcare professionals real-time feedback. IoT devices and image processing can be combined in the process industry to enhance safety management. "Gnoni et al.". (2020) suggested using IoT technologies to keep an eye on employees' activities and spot risky behavior in real-time. In order to stop accidents from happening and enhance safety procedures, the system can also produce alerts and recommendations. The development of intelligent systems that can automate procedures, find anomalies, and give users real-time feedback is made possible by the integration of these techniques with IoT devices. The studies cited in this essay offer some illustrations of the potential of these methods for dealing with actual issues. A key component of computer vision, a branch of artificial intelligence aimed at giving computers the ability to comprehend and interpret visual information from their environment, is image processing. In order to improve the quality of digital images or extract valuable information from them, image processing refers to the use of algorithms and techniques to manipulate and analyze the images. This may entail techniques like filtering, noise reduction, edge detection, segmentation, and feature extraction. The field of image processing has undergone a revolutionary change in recent years thanks to the development of machine learning techniques, which enable algorithms to be trained to recognize objects, patterns, and other visual features in images with increasing precision. The Internet of Things (IoT) is one industry that heavily utilizes image processing and computer vision. IoT stands for the Internet of Things, which is a network of interconnected physical objects and devices that are equipped with sensors and software to collect and share data. In smart agriculture, where sensors and cameras are used to monitor crop health, soil moisture, and other environmental factors, image processing is particularly common in IoT applications. Kapoor and co. (2016) describe a smart agriculture application of IoT and image processing, where images of crops are taken using drones and then analyzed using algorithms to look for symptoms of disease, pests, or other issues. The same is true for home automation and security, according to Bharath et al. Using a combination of IoT and image processing technologies, (2019) suggest the use of intelligent sockets that can recognize changes in the environment, including the presence of people or objects, and act accordingly.

The healthcare industry is another one where image processing and computer vision are making a big difference. Clinical professionals are now better able to identify and treat a variety of conditions, such as cancer, heart disease, and neurological disorders, thanks to the use of machine learning and deep learning algorithms in medical imaging. For IoT in healthcare, Bolhasani et al. Conducted a systematic review of deep learning applications. (2021) highlight how these methods could enhance diagnosis speed and accuracy while also enabling telemedicine and remote patient monitoring. The same goes for Haghi Kashani and co. Review the use of IoT in healthcare applications in 2021, taking into account how sensors and cameras are used to track medication compliance, monitor patients' vital signs, and identify emergencies like falls. In the process industry, efficiency and safety are also being increased by using image processing and computer vision. "Gnoni et al.". According to (2020), an "intelligent" safety management system is created using IoT technologies, and cameras and other sensors are used to monitor the production process and find any potential dangers or safety risks. The data from these sensors can be used to identify potential issues and take corrective action before they develop into serious safety incidents using machine learning algorithms that analyze the data in real-time.

1.2 Image Processing Techniques

Digital image manipulation and analysis techniques are referred to as image processing techniques. These methods are used to improve the quality of images, extract information that can be used later on, and automate a number of image analysis and manipulation-related tasks. Many different image processing methods are available, and they can be roughly divided into two groups: spatial domain methods and frequency domain methods.

Spatial domain techniques directly alter an image's pixel structure. These methods use morphological, thresholding, and filtering operations, among others. In order to smooth or sharpen an image, filtering involves applying a mathematical function to each pixel, whereas thresholding divides an image into regions based on pixel intensity values. Morphological operations entail changing a region's shape within an image, such as by dilating or eroding it. By examining an image's frequency content, frequency domain techniques can be used. The Fourier transform, the wavelet transform, and image compression are a few examples of these methods. A more sophisticated technique called wavelet transform enables the analysis of both the frequency and spatial content of an image. Fourier transform is used to analyze the frequency content of an image by breaking it down into its frequency components. By eliminating extra or unnecessary data, image compression can help reduce the size of an image.

Machine learning, computer vision, and deep learning are additional methods of image processing that are frequently used. Large datasets of images are analyzed using machine learning algorithms to uncover insightful data. Deep learning, a subset of machine learning, uses neural networks to process and analyze images, whereas computer vision uses algorithms and techniques to analyze and interpret visual data. The type of information that needs to be extracted from the image and the specific application determine which image processing methods should be used. As an illustration, image processing methods are used in surveillance applications to find and follow objects of interest in video feeds as well as in medical imaging to extract diagnostic data from medical images. For analyzing and modifying digital images, image processing techniques are a vital tool. They comprise many different algorithms and techniques, including deep learning, machine learning, computer vision, and techniques in the frequency and spatial domains. It is possible to automate various tasks related to image analysis and manipulation, extract useful information from images, and enhance the accuracy and efficiency of various applications by selecting the appropriate image processing techniques.

1.3 Image Processing Techniques to Analyze and Interpret Images From Warehouse Environments

Following are some examples of how image processing techniques can be used to analyze and interpret images from warehouse environments.

1. *Object detection and tracking*: Image processing algorithms can be used to find and follow products, pallets, and forklifts in warehouse settings. This could aid in better inventory control and warehouse layout optimization.
2. *Quality control*: Image processing techniques can be used to automatically sort products based on their defects, such as scratches or dents.

3. *Predictive maintenance:* Image processing algorithms can be used to track the health of a warehouse's machinery, such as packaging equipment or conveyor belts, and to foretell when maintenance is necessary.
4. *Inventory management*: By automating the counting and tracking of inventory, image processing techniques can decrease the need for manual labor and boost accuracy.
5. *Security and safety*: Image processing algorithms can be used to find and stop unauthorized access to warehouse facilities as well as to spot safety risks like spills or obstacles in high-traffic areas.

1.3 Advantages and Limitations of Common Image Processing Techniques

The key benefits and drawbacks of various image processing techniques are outlined in the table 1 above. In order to select the best strategy for a particular application, it is crucial to take into account the advantages and disadvantages of different techniques as the field of image processing continues to develop and advance. Thresholding is one of the most popular methods for segmenting images based on pixel intensity. It is straightforward and computationally effective. Thresholding functions well for pictures with good contrast and little noise, but it can be affected by lighting and lead to information loss. (Bolhasani, H. et al., 2021)

Another popular method that works well to cut down on noise and highlight specific features in images is filtering. Although filtering can sometimes blur or distort edges and minute details, this makes it less suitable for some applications. Edge detection is an effective method for locating borders and shapes in images, but it is noise-sensitive and prone to false positives and false negatives. Contrarily, segmentation can successfully distinguish objects from backgrounds in images, but it necessitates prior knowledge or presumptions regarding the image's content.

A potent method for identifying and categorizing particular objects or features in images is object recognition. However, this method can be computationally expensive and requires a lot of training data. The choice of image processing method ultimately depends on the particular needs of the application, including the kind and quality of the input data, the level of accuracy that is desired, and the computational resources that are available. Researchers and practitioners can choose the best strategy for their needs by carefully weighing the benefits and limitations of various techniques, which will result in more effective and efficient image processing in a variety of fields.

Table 1. Advantages and limitations of common image processing techniques

Technique	Advantages	Limitations
Thresholding	Simple and computationally efficient; works well for images with good contrast and low noise	Sensitivity to lighting conditions; can result in loss of information
Filtering	Effective for reducing noise and enhancing features	Can blur or distort edges and small details
Edge detection	Useful for identifying boundaries and shapes	Sensitive to noise and can produce false positives and negatives
Segmentation	Can accurately separate objects from the background	Requires prior knowledge or assumptions about the image content
Object recognition	Can identify and classify specific objects or features	Requires extensive training data and can be computationally expensive

2. CURRENT TRENDS IN WAREHOUSE MANAGEMENT WITH IMAGE PROCESSING

The ability to automate and optimize a variety of tasks, including inventory management, quality control, and order fulfilment, has made image processing an increasingly crucial tool in warehouse management in recent years. Here are a few of the most recent developments in image-based warehouse management.

1. Automated inventory tracking: This is one of the image processing technology's most promising uses in warehouse management. In order to identify and count products as they are brought into and taken out of the warehouse, image recognition algorithms are used. Warehouses can increase accuracy and efficiency while lowering the need for manual labor by automating this process. Food distribution centers are one setting where this strategy has been proven to be successful (Li et al., 2019).

2. Quality control and defect detection: Quality control and defect detection are two additional crucial applications of image processing in warehouse management. Warehouses are able to quickly and precisely identify product flaws and quality problems by using computer vision algorithms to examine images of the goods. This enables warehouses to take corrective action before goods are shipped to customers. This strategy has been proven successful in sectors like textiles (Kobayashi et al. Wang et al., 2017) and electronics., 2019).

3. Order fulfilment: By using image processing, order fulfilment procedures in warehouses can be made more efficient. Warehouses can locate and retrieve items quickly, cutting down on the time needed to fill orders, by using computer vision algorithms to identify and track products. According to research by Jiang et al., this strategy has been proven successful in e-commerce environments., 2020), where precision and quickness are essential.

4. Real-time monitoring: This is another development in image-processing-based warehouse management. Managers can quickly spot and address problems like bottlenecks, equipment failures, and safety hazards by using cameras and computer vision algorithms to continuously monitor warehouse operations. This strategy has been demonstrated to be successful in enhancing operational efficiency and decreasing downtime (Kusakabe et al., 2019).

5. Integration with other technologies: This is a final development in the field of warehouse management using image processing. Examples include robotics, artificial intelligence, and the Internet of Things (IoT). Combining these technologies enables warehouses to build highly automated, cost-effective systems that increase efficiency. For instance, IoT sensors can provide real-time data on inventory levels and environmental conditions, while robots outfitted with cameras and image processing algorithms can automatically locate and pick products from shelves (Ravi et al., 2020).

Finally, it should be noted that image processing is a rapidly developing field that is fundamentally altering warehouse management. The accuracy, efficiency, and customer satisfaction of warehouse operations can be increased by automating processes like inventory tracking, quality control, and order fulfillment. We can anticipate seeing even more cutting-edge and significant applications in the years to come as image processing technologies advance.

2.1 Techniques Used in Warehouse Management

The use of image processing techniques to optimize inventory management, enhance worker safety, and boost operational effectiveness has completely changed warehouse management. Here are a few instances of applications that were successful:

1. Inventory management: Image processing methods can be used to keep track of stock levels and the flow of goods inside a warehouse. While image processing techniques offer additional advantages like real-time tracking, fewer errors, and higher accuracy, RFID tags and barcode scanning have long been used to track inventory. In its warehouses, Amazon has been streamlining inventory management by using image recognition technology. The system uses robots with cameras mounted on them to take pictures of the items on shelves, which are then compared to a database to make sure the right item is chosen for shipping.

2. Picking and Packing: Image processing techniques can be used in the warehouse to automate the picking and packing procedures. To identify items on shelves and direct pickers to the right spot, for example, computer vision algorithms can be used. Pickers can locate and choose items more quickly with the aid of augmented reality (AR) and smart glasses. One of the biggest logistics firms in the world, DHL, has introduced AR technology to help with picking and packing in its warehouses.

3. Quality Control: Image processing techniques can be used to find product flaws and perform quality control. Computer vision algorithms can find flaws like cracks, scratches, or dents by examining product images. In addition to increasing customer satisfaction and lowering returns, this can help stop defective products from reaching customers. Walmart has implemented image processing technology to find produce flaws, enabling them to take damaged goods off the shelves before they are even delivered to customers.

4. Worker Safety: Image processing techniques can be used to enhance warehouse worker safety. For example, cameras and sensors can be used to track employee activity and spot potentially dangerous circumstances. Amazon has put in place a machine learning-based system that examines video feeds from cameras to spot potential safety hazards like workers not wearing safety gear or moving too quickly.

5. Logistics Optimization: Tracking of vehicles, containers, and packages using image processing techniques can help with warehouse logistics. This enables real-time adjustments by allowing for the identification of system bottlenecks and inefficiencies. FedEx has put in place a system that tracks packages using image processing technology to make sure they are correctly sorted and delivered to the right place.

Image processing techniques have many uses in warehouse management, such as inventory management, logistics optimization, and worker safety. Companies can increase productivity, decrease errors, and improve the overall customer experience by implementing these technologies.

2.2 Benefits of Image Processing Techniques in Warehouse Management.

1. Enhanced productivity: Inventory tracking, order picking, and quality control are just a few of the warehouse management tasks that can be automated thanks to image processing. As a result,

overall efficiency is increased and less time and effort is needed to carry out these tasks manually (Bolhasani, H. et al., 2021).

2. Accuracy is increased: Image processing algorithms can detect and identify objects in images with high accuracy, decreasing the likelihood of mistakes in inventory tracking and order fulfilment (Wang, K.; Chen, C.-M et al., 2020).
3. Improved security: Image processing can assist in identifying security risks in the warehouse, such as spilled liquids, obstructions in walkways, and malfunctioning equipment (Zhang et al., 2021).
4. Cost Savings: Image processing can significantly lower the cost of warehouse management operations by automating processes and reducing errors (Lee et al., 2019).
5. Increased customer satisfaction: Image processing can result in faster and more accurate product delivery, increasing overall customer satisfaction by increasing efficiency and accuracy in order fulfilment (Arunkumar, S, et al., 2020).

3. FUTURE DIRECTIONS

There are a number of potential future directions that can be pursued to further improve the effectiveness and efficiency of warehouse operations as the application of image processing techniques in warehouse management is rapidly developing. Some of these upcoming directions will be covered in this section. Using image processing in conjunction with other cutting-edge technologies like robotics and artificial intelligence is one possible future direction. Robots with image sensors, for instance, are able to move around a warehouse, recognize products, and retrieve them on demand. By doing so, the workload of human workers can be reduced, errors can be reduced, and overall productivity can rise. Machine learning algorithms can also be trained to spot patterns in warehouse data and improve operations like inventory control and order fulfillment. Image processing can also be used to boost warehouse security, which is a promising future direction. Image processing algorithms can identify and notify security personnel of potential threats, such as unauthorized access or theft, by analyzing real-time video feeds from surveillance cameras. In addition to ensuring the security of workers and guests, this can assist in preventing inventory loss. (Wang, K.; Chen, C.-M et al., 2020).

The use of image processing in conjunction with other cutting-edge technologies, such as the Internet of Things (IoT) and blockchain, is also a possibility. IoT sensors, for instance, can be used to gather information about the whereabouts and state of inventory and then transmit it to algorithms for image processing for analysis. This can minimize waste and improve inventory placement. Image processing can be added to a blockchain-based system to provide visual confirmation of product movements and authenticity, further enhancing its security and transparency for tracking inventory and supply chain activities. In the creation of augmented reality (AR) applications for warehouse management, image processing can also make a significant difference. Workers can receive real-time information on inventory locations, order picking instructions, and other crucial information by using AR technology to overlay information on actual warehouse environments. By providing real-time product and other warehouse feature recognition, image processing can be used to improve the accuracy and dependability of AR applications. And finally, further advancements in warehouse management will probably be made thanks to the continued development of sophisticated image processing hardware and algorithms. For instance, specialized image processing hardware, such as Graphics Processing Units (GPUs), and deep learning algorithms can significantly improve the speed and accuracy of image processing applications. (Arunkumar, S, et al., 2020)

4. DISCUSSION

Image processing techniques have the potential to completely change the warehouse management sector, which is a crucial part of logistics operations. Image processing techniques, as was mentioned, can offer a number of advantages, such as increased effectiveness, accuracy, and safety. Through real-time data analysis, they can also facilitate more intelligent decision-making. These methods could be improved upon or used in a number of different contexts, though. The use of 3D imaging for warehouse layout and planning is one area in which image processing techniques could be further developed. According to Zhang et al. In order to improve decision-making regarding inventory management and storage optimization, 3D imaging can offer a more accurate and detailed representation of a warehouse space (2019). Additionally, as autonomous robot adoption increases in warehouses, 3D imaging may be used to improve the navigation and path planning abilities of these robots (Alizadeh et al., 2020).

The automation of quality control procedures is another area in which image processing methods could be used. It would be possible to detect flaws or inconsistencies in products quickly and precisely by analyzing images of them using machine learning algorithms. This might result in less waste and higher client satisfaction (Bartoszek et al., 2019). The condition of machinery and equipment could also be monitored in real-time using image processing techniques. It is possible to schedule maintenance proactively by monitoring equipment through image analysis, which lowers costs and downtime (Wang et al., 2019). To enable more accurate localization of goods in warehouses, image processing techniques may also be developed. It would be possible to track the precise location of goods in real-time and precisely by combining image processing and RFID technology. In larger warehouses, in particular, this might result in shorter search times and higher productivity (Sakamoto et al., 2019).

The use of image processing methods in warehouse management is accompanied by a number of difficulties, though. One significant obstacle is the requirement for high-quality image data, which can be difficult to come by in actual warehouse settings. The use of these methods also prompts worries about data security and privacy. The integration of image processing technologies with current warehouse management systems and processes may also present problems (Kannan et al., 2019).

5. CONCLUSION

As a result of their many advantages, including improved efficiency, accuracy, and safety, image processing techniques have completely changed the way warehouse management is done. These methods have already been successfully used in a number of aspects of warehouse management, including automation, quality control, and inventory management. According to current trends, there is an increasing demand for image processing techniques to be used in warehouse management, and as big data becomes more widely available, these techniques are expected to advance and become more efficient. The creation of real-time image processing systems, the fusion of image processing with robotics and other emerging technologies like artificial intelligence, and the use of these methods in brand-new fields like predictive maintenance and energy management are some of the future directions for image processing techniques in warehouse management. Despite the many benefits of image processing methods, some restrictions still need to be resolved. The high cost of implementing these technologies, the requirement for specialized skills to use and maintain them, and the difficulties relating to data privacy and security are a few of these. Overall, there are enormous potential advantages to using image processing methods for warehouse management, and as technology advances, it is anticipated that these methods will become more widely used and more easily accessible. In the quick-paced and constantly changing world of logistics and supply chain management, warehouse managers can enhance their operations and gain a competitive advantage by utilizing these techniques.

REFERENCES

Abas, K., Obraczka, K., & Miller, L. (2018). Solar-powered, wireless smart camera network: An IoT solution for outdoor video monitoring. *Computer Communications*, *118*, 217–233. doi:10.1016/j.comcom.2018.01.007

Al-Dhief, F. T., Latiff, N. M. A., Malik, N. N. N. A., Salim, N. S., Baki, M. M., Albadr, M. A. A., & Mohammed, M. A. (2020). A Survey of Voice Pathology Surveillance Systems Based on Internet of Things and Machine Learning Algorithms. *IEEE Access : Practical Innovations, Open Solutions*, *8*, 64514–64533. doi:10.1109/ACCESS.2020.2984925

Anuradha, M., Jayasankar, T., Prakash, N. B., Sikkandar, M. Y., Hemalakshmi, G. R., Bharatiraja, C., & Britto, A. S. F. (2021). IoT enabled cancer prediction system to enhance the authentication and security using cloud computing. *Microprocessors and Microsystems*, *80*, 103301. doi:10.1016/j.micpro.2020.103301

Arunkumar, S., Vairavasundaram, S., Ravichandran, K. S., & Ravi, L. (2019). RIWT and QR factorization-based hybrid robust image steganography using block selection algorithm for IoT devices. *Journal of Intelligent & Fuzzy Systems*, *36*(5), 4265–4276. doi:10.3233/JIFS-169984

Awan, M. J., Bilal, M. H., Yasin, A., Nobanee, H., Khan, N. S., & Zain, A. M. (2021). Detection of CO-VID-19 in Chest X-ray Images: A Big Data Enabled Deep Learning Approach. *International Journal of Environmental Research and Public Health*, *18*(19), 10147. doi:10.3390/ijerph181910147 PMID:34639450

Aydin, I., & Othman, N. A. A new IoT combined face detection of people by using computer vision for security application. In *Proceedings of the 2017 International Artificial Intelligence and Data Processing Symposium (IDAP)*, (pp. 1–6). IEEE. 10.1109/IDAP.2017.8090171

Balla, P. B., & Jadhao, K. T. (2018). IoT Based Facial Recognition Security System. In *Proceedings of the 2018 International Conference on Smart City and Emerging Technology (ICSCET)*, (pp. 1–4). IEEE.

Bharadwaj, H. K., Agarwal, A., Chamola, V., Lakkaniga, N. R., Hassija, V., Guizani, M., & Sikdar, B. (2021). A Review on the Role of Machine Learning in Enabling IoT Based Healthcare Applications. *IEEE Access : Practical Innovations, Open Solutions*, *9*, 38859–38890. doi:10.1109/ACCESS.2021.3059858

Bharath, V., Adyanth, H., Shreekanth, T., Suresh, N., & Ananya, M. (2019). Intelligent sockets for home automation and security: An approach through IoT and image processing. In *The IoT and the Next Revolutions Automating the World* (pp. 252–279). IGI Global. doi:10.4018/978-1-5225-9246-4.ch016

Bolhasani, H., Mohseni, M., & Rahmani, A. M. (2021). Deep learning applications for IoT in health care: A systematic review. *Informatics in Medicine Unlocked*, 23, 100550. doi:10.1016/j.imu.2021.100550

Cui, F. (2020). Deployment and integration of smart sensors with IoT devices detecting fire disasters in huge forest environment. *Computer Communications*, *150*, 818–827. doi:10.1016/j.comcom.2019.11.051

Gnoni, M. G., Bragatto, P. A., Milazzo, M. F., & Setola, R. (2020). Integrating IoT technologies for an "intelligent" safety management in the process industry. *Procedia Manufacturing*, *42*, 511–515. doi:10.1016/j.promfg.2020.02.040

Godavarthi, B., Nalajala, P., & Ganapuram, V. (2017). Design and implementation of vehicle navigation system in urban environments using internet of things (IoT). In *IOP Conference Series: Materials Science and Engineering*, Hyderabad, India. 10.1088/1757-899X/225/1/012262

Haghi Kashani, M., Madanipour, M., Nikravan, M., Asghari, P., & Mahdipour, E. (2021). A systematic review of IoT in healthcare: Applications, techniques, and trends. *Journal of Network and Computer Applications*, *192*, 103164. doi:10.1016/j.jnca.2021.103164

Hossain, M. S., Muhammad, G., Rahman, S. M. M., Abdul, W., Alelaiwi, A., & Alamri, A. (2016). Toward end-to-end biomet rics-based security for IoT infrastructure. *IEEE Wireless Communications*, *23*(5), 44–51. doi:10.1109/MWC.2016.7721741

Jiang, Z., Wu, D., Zheng, L., Yao, Y., & Chen, Y. (2020). A Deep Learning-Based Visual Object Recognition System for Warehouse Robots. *Journal of Intelligent & Robotic Systems*, *98*(1), 157–173.

Kapoor, A., Bhat, S. I., Shidnal, S., & Mehra, A. Implementation of IoT (Internet of Things) and Image processing in smart agriculture. In *Proceedings of the 2016 International Conference on Computation System and Information Technology for Sustainable Solutions (CSITSS)*, (pp. 21–26). IEEE. 10.1109/CSITSS.2016.7779434

Kobayashi, K., Suzuki, K., & Arakawa, Y. (2017). Quality inspection of woven fabrics using image processing. *International Journal of Clothing Science and Technology*, *29*(4), 465–476.

Kusakabe, T., Okazaki, T., Iwamoto, K., & Ito, T. (2019). Real-time Monitoring of Warehouse Environment Using IoT Sensor and Video Image Processing. In *International Conference on Innovative Mobile and Internet Services in Ubiquitous Computing* (pp. 225-233). Springer, Cham.

Li, X., Li, J., Yiu, S., Gao, C., & Xiong, J. (2019). Privacy-preserving edge-assisted image retrieval and classification in IoT. *Frontiers of Computer Science*, *13*(5), 1136–1147. doi:10.100711704-018-8067-z

Muhammad, K., Hamza, R., Ahmad, J., Lloret, J., Wang, H., & Baik, S. W. (2018). Secure Surveillance Framework for IoT Systems Using Probabilistic Image Encryption. *IEEE Transactions on Industrial Informatics*, *14*(8), 3679–3689. doi:10.1109/TII.2018.2791944

Nag, A., Nikhilendra, J. N., & Kalmath, M. (2018). IOT Based Door Access Control Using Face Recognition. In *Proceedings of the 2018 3rd International Conference for Convergence in Technology (I2CT)*, (pp. 1–3). IEEE. 10.1109/I2CT.2018.8529749

Nauman, A., Qadri, Y. A., Amjad, M., Zikria, Y. B., Afzal, M. K., & Kim, S. W. (2020). Multimedia Internet of Things: A Comprehensive Survey. *IEEE Access : Practical Innovations, Open Solutions, 8,* 8202–8250. doi:10.1109/ACCESS.2020.2964280

Patil, N., Ambatkar, S., & Kakde, S. (2017). IoT based smart surveillance security system using raspberry Pi. In Proceedings of the 2017 International Conference on Communication and Signal Processing (ICCSP), (pp. 344–348). IEEE. 10.1109/ICCSP.2017.8286374

Punyavathi, G., Neeladri, M., & Singh, M. K. (2021). Vehicle tracking and detection techniques using IoT. *Materials Today: Proceedings, 51,* 909–913. doi:10.1016/j.matpr.2021.06.283

Roy, S., Rawat, U., Sareen, H. A., & Nayak, S. K. (2020). IECA: An efficient IoT friendly image encryption technique using programmable cellular automata. *Journal of Ambient Intelligence and Humanized Computing, 11*(11), 5083–5102. doi:10.100712652-020-01813-6

Roy, S., Shrivastava, M., Pandey, C. V., Nayak, S. K., & Rawat, U. (2021). IEVCA: An efficient image encryption technique for IoT applications using 2-D Von-Neumann cellular automata. *Multimedia Tools and Applications, 80*(21-23), 31529–31567. doi:10.100711042-020-09880-9

Santhanakrishnan, C., Annapurani, K., Singh, R., & Krishnaveni, C. (2021). An IOT based system for monitoring environmental and physiological conditions. *Materials Today: Proceedings, 46,* 3832–3840. doi:10.1016/j.matpr.2021.02.077

Sharmila, V., Rejin Paul, N. R., Ezhumalai, P., Reetha, S., & Naresh Kumar, S. (2020). IOT enabled smart assistance system using face detection and recognition for visually challenged people. *Materials Today: Proceedings.* Advance online publication. doi:10.1016/j.matpr.2020.10.198

Su, J., Vasconcellos, D. V., Prasad, S., Sgandurra, D., Feng, Y., & Sakurai, K. (2018). Lightweight Classification of IoT Malware Based on Image Recognition. In *Proceedings of the 2018 IEEE 42nd Annual Computer Software and Applications Conference (COMPSAC),* (pp. 664–669). IEEE. 10.1109/COMPSAC.2018.10315

Wang, K., Chen, C.-M., Hossain, M. S., Muhammad, G., Kumar, S., & Kumari, S. (2021). Transfer reinforcement learning-based road object detection in next generation IoT domain. *Computer Networks, 193,* 108078. doi:10.1016/j.comnet.2021.108078

Chapter 26
Use of Artificial Intelligence for Image Processing to Aid Digital Forensics:
Legislative Challenges

Rajesh Gupta
Sanskriti University, Mathura, India

Manashree Mane
School of Sciences, Jain University (Deemed), India

Shambhu Bhardwaj
College of Computing Sciences and I.T., Teerthanker Mahaveer University, Moradabad, India

Ujwal Nandekar
https://orcid.org/0000-0003-2545-6736
Symbiosis Law School, Symbiosis International University (Deemed), India

Ahmar Afaq
Symbiosis Law School, Symbiosis International University (Deemed), India

Dharmesh Dhabliya
Symbiosis Law School, Symbiosis International University (Deemed), India

Binay Kumar Pandey
https://orcid.org/0000-0002-4041-1213
Department of Information Technology, Govind Ballabh Pant University of Agriculture and Technology, Pantnagar, India

ABSTRACT

Use of artificial intelligence for image processing to aid digital forensics is a controversial topic. Some people believe that AI can be very helpful in this field, while others are concerned about the potential misuse of AI technology. There are a few key legislative challenges that need to be addressed before AI can be widely used for image processing in digital forensics. First, there is the issue of data privacy. If images processed by AI contain personal data, then there are risks that this data could be mishandled or misused. There are also concerns that AI could be used to create false or misleading evidence. Another key challenge is ensuring that AI systems are transparent and accountable. If an AI system makes a mistake, it should be possible to understand why it made that mistake and how to avoid similar mistakes in the future. AI has the potential to revolutionize digital forensics, but there are still some important challenges that need to be addressed before it can be widely used.

DOI: 10.4018/978-1-6684-8618-4.ch026

1. INTRODUCTION

1.1 Artificial Intelligence

The term AI refers to the practise of programming computers to mimic human intellect. Expert systems, NLP, voice recognition, and machine vision are all concrete examples of where AI has been put to use (Ahmed Alaa El-Din, E., 2022).

The basic objective of AI is to make enable to the computers to learn automatically. It is possible without human intervention. It provides the automatically learning efficiency to any. It improves the system from experience. The explicitly programming is not required by Machine learning. It is a process in which a device learns of observations. In machine learning, a machine observes the data, direct experience, and instruction. It has been done to create the patterns in data. After observation, the machine can formulate better decisions for future operation. This better decision is made on the base provided examples to the machine.

Figure 1. Artificial intelligence

All the researches which are related to artificial intelligence is practical and particular. One of the fundamental complications in artificial intelligence is that how computer programming has been done for some definite characteristic such as: understanding, analysis, Problem solving, awareness, education, Planning, Ability to manipulate and move objects. Knowledge engineering is considered as the fundamental part of AI research. Approaches involved arithmetic procedure, calculation cleverness and flexible calculation along with conventional representational AI. Some approach is exploited in AI, involved exploration along with arithmetical growth methods which enlighten prospect along with financial matters.

Figure 2. Machine learning in artificial intelligence

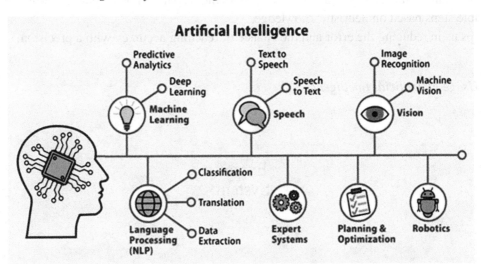

Artificial intelligence is defined as intelligence shown by the machines. These machines are moveable lucid mediator which perceives its surroundings. These take steps helpful in maximizing the chance of achievement at aim. AI is a research which is distributed into subfields that focus on specific problems, on approaches .It enables the use of a particular tool and give satisfaction with the use of that particular application. Problems came in AI research are reasoning, knowledge and planning. Where the term general intelligence is long-term field of goal. There are various methods like statistical method, computational intelligence, soft computing also known as machine learning. AI can be displayed on machines. In computer science, an ideal intelligent device has been referred as variable rational agent. It recognizes the environment and takes actions .It increases the chance of success at some aim. In this research is alienated into subarea meeting important issues along with the important approaches.

Main issues come across Artificial Intelligence research involves thinking, knowledge, natural language processing. It has acuity and ability to take step and manipulate system. Universal intelligence will be a big area to be aimed at. There are many methods like data analyzing method, computational intelligence, soft computing and traditional symbolic AI. Some approach is used in Artificial Intelligence. It involves the type of searches and mathematical development methods. It is helpful in explaining probability and economics. Artificial intelligence is used for upcoming purposes which are Speech Recognition, transcribing, transforming human speech into format useful for computer applications. Speech Recognition is a useful tool which is used in interactive voice calls and mobile applications. AI is a machine which is designed to do programming in such a way that they can think and act like a human. AI is an integral part of our life. It has changed our life by **as** it can be used in a wide area of routine services.

1.2 Usage of AI

1. It enables the devices to reduce the time cycle. It improves the proper use of resources.
2. Some tools are providing by machine learning. These tools are capable to improve the quality in huge and tough process system.
3. Able to communicate with the computers that understand human used natural language

4. It plays an important role in strategic games. Here the machine should be able to think of multiple possible steps based on heuristic knowledge.
5. It helps us in reducing the error and the chance of reaching accuracy with a precision.

Figure 3. Usage of Artificial Intelligence

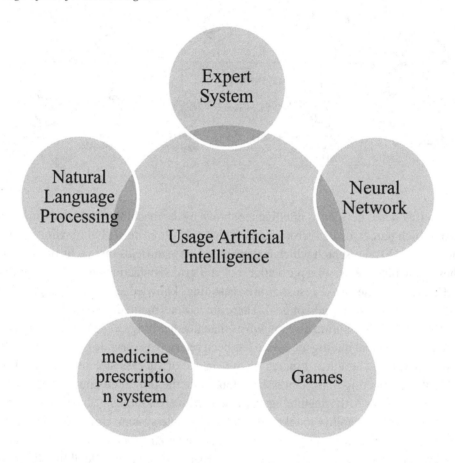

1.3 The Four Types of Artificial Intelligence

These are the several types:

- **Reactive machines.** These artificial intelligence systems are memory less and purpose-built. Deep Blue, IBM's chess software from the 1990s, is a good example. It defeated Garry Kasparov. Deep Blue can recognize chess pieces and make predictions, but it cannot learn from its previous mistakes or build on its successes since it lacks a memory. (Ali, M. R., 2020)
- **Limited memory.** These AIs are memory-enabled, allowing them to learn from their prior judgements. This is how some autonomous vehicle decision-making processes are set up. (Noori, Z. S., 2022).

- **Theory of mind.** "Theory of mind" is a psychological concept. In the context of artificial intelligence, this implies the programme can identify and react appropriately to human feelings. One of the key capabilities for AI systems to join human teams is the ability to discern intentions and forecast behaviour. (Kumar, B., 2023).
- **Self-awareness.** Self-aware artificial intelligences are a kind of AI that exhibits consciousness by virtue of their awareness of their own existence. Self-conscious machines are aware of their own existence. It's currently impossible to find AI of this kind. (Babu, S.Z.D. et al., 2022).

1.4 The Applications of AI

- **AI in healthcare:** More focus is being placed on bettering patient outcomes while simultaneously decreasing healthcare expenses. Machine learning is being used by businesses to improve upon and speed up human diagnosis. IBM Watson is one of the most well-known healthcare technologies available today. (Nassa V. K., 2021).
- **AI in business:** Analytics and CRM systems are using machine learning algorithms to learn more about how to better serve customers. Websites now use chatbots to respond to clients in real time. The topic of job-position automation has also gained traction among academics and IT experts. (Ouazzane, K., 2022).
- **AI in education:** Grading may be automated by AI, freeing up valuable time for teachers. It has the ability to analyse student performance and modify itself accordingly, allowing for flexible, individualised instruction. By giving pupils extra help, AI tutors can make sure they don't fall behind. And technology has the potential to alter where and how children study, maybe even making certain professors obsolete. (Pramanik, S., 2022)
- **AI in finance:** Personal finance apps using AI, such as Intuit Mint or TurboTax, are upending the banking industry. These apps help users manage their finances by gathering personal information. IBM Watson (Berner, S., 2022) is just one example of software that has found its way into the home-buying process. Most Wall Street trading is now executed by computer programmes using AI.
- **AI in law:** The discovery process in the law entails the exhaustive sorting through of documents, which is a task that might be too much for human beings to do (Correia, M. E., 2021).
- **AI in manufacturing:** The manufacturing industry has been in the front of adopting robots into the production process. One example is the rise of cobots, or collaborative robots, which are smaller, multitasking robots that work alongside people to complete more aspects of the job in settings such as warehouses, factories, and other workplaces (Gupta A., et. al, 2019).
- **AI in banking:** Chatbots are being used effectively by financial institutions to inform consumers about available services and to process routine transactions without the need for human participation. Compliance with banking laws is becomes easier and cheaper thanks to artificial intelligence virtual assistants. Financial institutions are also using AI to enhance loan approvals, reduce over-extensions, and spot promising investments (Gupta A., et. al, 2020).
- **AI in transportation:** The application of AI in transportation is not limited to its primary function of running autonomous cars; rather, it is also used to traffic management, aircraft delay prediction, and the improvement of ocean shipping safety and efficiency (Verma A., 2020).

- **AI in Security:** Today's security providers employ cutting-edge technologies like artificial intelligence and machine learning to set them apart from the competition. In addition, such expressions denote technologies that are both plausible and practical (Koti K., 2021).

1.5 Image Processing

The term "image processing" refers to a series of operations that are carried out on a picture in order to produce an improved version of the image or to derive some helpful information from it. It is a sort of signal processing in which the input is an image and the output might either be the picture itself or the characteristics or features that are connected with that image. When an algorithm analyses a picture, this is known as image processing. picture processing may be used to discover data insights or to assist automated operations in computer vision use cases. During the current phase of picture preprocessing research, researchers are thinking about hair removal and noise reduction mechanisms.

Image processing refers to any technique used to enhance a picture for the purpose of extracting data from it. It is possible to do image processing in two distinct ways:

- Photographs, prints, and other tangible reproductions of images may all benefit from analogue image processing (Crespo, R. G., 2020).
- Using sophisticated algorithms, digital image processing allows for the modification of digital pictures (Choo, K. R., 2022).

Main Purpose of Image Processing is to providing shape to intangibles by giving them a visual representation after processing data. Image sharpening and restoration is an effective method for enhancing the quality of a processed picture. The recovery of a picture is useful for a search. Classifying things in a picture, pinpointing their location, and gaining a broad grasp of the scene are all simplified by pattern recognition (Jeong, D., 2020).

When it comes to getting rid of undesirable noise and boosting the quality of the image as a whole, picture pre-processing is very important during the detecting phase. It was necessary to make use of it in order to limit the scope of the inquiry that was being done into possible confounding variables. Eliminating components of the backdrop that aren't essential in order to improve the quality of the melanoma image is the major objective of this procedure. By carefully choosing the most effective preprocessing techniques, it is possible to significantly improve the accuracy of the system.

Image processing is the process of transforming an image into a digital form and performing certain operations to get some useful information from it. The image processing system usually treats all images as 2D signals when applying certain predetermined signal processing methods.

Digital Image processing is the class of methods that deal with manipulating digital images through the use of computer algorithms. It is an essential preprocessing step in many applications, such as face recognition, object detection, and image compression.Image processing is done to enhance an existing image or to sift out important information from it. This is important in several Deep Learning-based Computer Vision applications, where such preprocessing can dramatically boost the performance of a model. Manipulating images, for example, adding or removing objects to images, is another application, especially in the entertainment industry.

Figure 4. Image processing

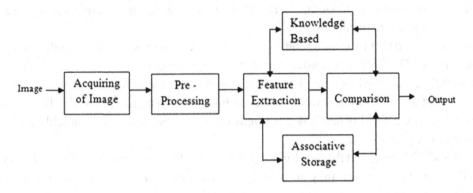

1.6 Types of Image Processing

There are five main types of image processing:

- Visualization - Find objects that are not visible in the image
- Recognition - Distinguish or detect objects in the image
- Sharpening and restoration - Create an enhanced image from the original image
- Pattern recognition - Measure the various patterns around the objects in the image
- Retrieval - Browse and search images from a large database of digital images that are similar to the original image

2. LITERATURE REVIEW

A. A. Solanke, et al.(2022) reviewed interpretable models in AI-based digital forensics investigation as a means of reducing scepticism. Courts, lawyers, and the general public all seem sceptical of current methods for extracting digital evidence that rely on AI, and this was completely understandable.

A. A. Solanke, et al.(2022) presented work on artificial intelligence in digital forensics: comparing, standardizing, and bettering data mining practices. In this study, they provide three important tools for building reliable machine-driven digital forensics approaches. Here, they discuss a variety of approaches for assessing, standardizing, and improving AI models used in digital forensics.

B. Lorch, et al.(2022) provided work on forensic picture analysis and the legislative barriers to AI-based compliance. In this article, they discuss the dangers of using machine learning for forensic picture analysis and provide several solutions.

D. Dunsin, et al.(2022) looked AI to DFIR in a limited setting. Lone Wolf data and picture files were used to evaluate the proposed system. The MADIK framework was able to complete the same integrity check on the Lone Wolf picture file in 16 minutes, whereas it took a digital forensics toolkit about 48 minutes (2,880 ms) (960 ms).

E. A. A E. Din, et al.(2022) did researched on artificial intelligence in forensic science. This review has offered an introduction to artificial intelligence and discussed its current and potential future uses in the field of forensic science. DNA evidence, pattern recognition, crime scene reconstruction, digital forensics, image processing, psycho- and narco-analysis, ballistics, and satellite surveillance were all areas where AI has found applications.

J. Fähndrich, et al.(2022) focused on the digital forensics the use of artificial intelligence in investigating cybercrimes . The field of forensics may benefit from several areas of AI study. Yet, this link is not yet sufficiently established for scientists to desire to do a comprehensive study.

J. M. Atiyah, et al.(2022) looked machine-based image analysis and forensics. The application of machine learning in the field of multimedia forensics is new because it can quickly and accurately identify instances of photo fraud.

M. A. L, et al.(2022) reviewed the development of a hybrid-learning-based model for digital forensics triage classification. In this paper, they provide a digital forensic model that might be used to create a robotic digital device classification tool for use in actual forensic investigations.

S. Ferreira, et al.(2021) reviewed the pictures and movies for use in machine learning analyses of digital forensics. CNN's F1-score for still images is 0.9968 while its F1-score for moving images was 0.8415. Using 5-fold cross-validation, SVM's accuracy for image and video processing was 0.9953 and 0.7955, respectively.

S. Raponi, et al.(2022) introduced AI meets digital forensics of gunfire audio samples. They provide a unique method that was mic- and shooter independent and does not need any prior information about the recording environment. Using a dataset made up of 3655 samples taken from YouTube films, our solution achieves over 90% accuracy when classifying the category, calibre, and model of the gun. The findings show that using a CNN to categories gunshots was both successful and efficient, since it does away with the requirement for ad hoc setup while greatly enhancing classification performance.

S. W. Hall, et al.(2022) reviewed the better understand digital forensics AI that can be explained. Used examples from the present state of the art, they want to investigate how XAI might be used to improve the triage and analysis of digital forensic evidence. This advisory will explore how XAI may be used to increase the efficiency of DF analysis and to extract forensically sound bits of evidence that can be utilized to aid investigations and possibly in a court of law.

Y. A. Balushi, et al. (2023) focused on the ML in digital forensics a literature survey. This study provides a comprehensive overview of the many machine learning approaches that may be used to investigate digital evidence.

3. DIGITAL FORENSICS

The term "Digital Forensics" refers to the practise of securing, identifying, extracting, and documenting digital evidence suitable for use in legal proceedings. Digital forensics is the study of recovering data from electronic devices including PCs, smart phones, servers, and networks. It equips the forensics team with cutting-edge methods and resources for handling complex digital investigations. Process of Digital forensics consists of Identification, Preservation, Analysis, Documentation, and Presentation. (Gupta, A., 2021).)

3.1 Types of Digital Forensics

The three subfields of digital forensics are:

Disk Forensics:

Information is retrieved from several types of files, including those that are open, edited, or deleted (Pramanik, S., 2021).

Network Forensics:

It is a specialization in computer science. It has to do with keeping tabs on and analysing the data flowing across a network to gather evidence in a court case (K, P., 2022).

Wireless Forensics:

Network forensics is a subfield of computer science. (Riess, C., 2022). Wireless forensics primarily aims to provide the means to gather and examine information gleaned from wireless network traffic (Dhabliya, D., 2022).

Database Forensics:

Database forensics is the study and analysis of databases and the information that describes them (Mattias Sjostrand, 2020).

Malware Forensics:

This subfield focuses on the detection of harmful code, such as viruses, worms, and their respective payloads (Qiao, W., 2020).

Email Forensics

Emails, calendars, and contacts, as well as other electronic messages, are the focus of this article, which analyses and recovers lost data (Ortega, M., 2020).

Memory Forensics:

The process involves obtaining a raw dump of information (Li, F., 2016) stored in various parts of the computer's memory (the system registers, cache, and RAM).

Mobile Phone Forensics:

It mainly deals with the examination and analysis of mobile devices. It helps to retrieve (K. K. R., 2021) phone and SIM contacts, call logs, incoming, and outgoing SMS/MMS, Audio, videos, etc.

3.2 Challenges Faced by Digital Forensics

These are some of the biggest problems that the Digital Forensics industry has to deal with:

- The proliferation of personal computers and ever-increasing internet use
- Easy access to hacking software (B.K. et al., 2022)
- It's hard to go to court when there's no tangible proof to back up the accusations.
- Because of the massive amounts of data (terabytes), this study is challenging.
- Advancement in technology necessitates a rethinking of current approaches.

3.3 AI Can Help Digital Forensics Investigations

Promptness is essential for reliable forensics investigations. There is a risk of losing or damaging evidence if it is not swiftly located and evaluated. Yet, the data is becoming more complicated and large, and the available forensic resources and human capacity are just not sufficient to deal with it. This is when AI comes into play. (Pathania, V. et al, 2022) Experts can swiftly filter through the unstructured forensics data they've acquired thanks to AI technology. With AI, we can better detect objects in images and videos, as well as find patterns in interactions across space and time. Digital forensics investigators may benefit from this knowledge discovery process in two ways: first, by identifying potential leads to a suspect, and second, by identifying potential leads to a future occurrence. Artificial intelligence is not designed to replace human digital forensic investigators. On the contrary, it enhances the precision of the data analysis and serves as a supplement to their existing talents. By doing so, fraudulent activity may be uncovered, criminals apprehended, and cyber threats mitigated or halted. (Varol, A., 2020)

3.4 Limits of AI in Digital Forensics

While artificial intelligence (AI) has the potential to advance digital forensics, the area is still in its infancy and faces certain unique obstacles. Most crucially, when dealing with massive volumes of data, pattern recognition methods may sometimes produce false positives and incorrect conclusions. To speed up the process, digital forensics teams need collaborate with AI technology. This might take some time. (Ali, I. M., 2022)

4. PROBLEM STATEMENT

One of the major issues with artificial intelligence for image processing to aid digital forensics is the lack of accuracy of results. AI-based systems are known to have errors and produce incorrect results, which can adversely affect the accuracy of the digital forensics process (Rughani, P. H., 2017). AI systems are also prone to bias, which can lead to incorrect conclusions. Additionally, AI-based image processing systems often require a large amount of data to be effective, which can be challenging to obtain in digital forensics investigations. Finally, AI-based image processing can be expensive to implement and maintain, which can be prohibitive for some digital forensics investigators. These issues must be addressed in order for AI-based image processing to be successfully integrated into digital forensics. (Author, C., 2020)

5. PROPOSED METHODOLOGY OF DIGITAL FORENSIC BASED IMAGE PROCESSING WITH AI

Forensic image are collected and resized then noise removal technique is applied to improve the image quality before training. Then parameters are initialized to perform RESNET based image classification.

6. IMPLEMENTATION

The layers and epochs are set for training and data is classified for training and testing. Training model provides accuracy then error rate is finding considering accuracy. Moreover time taken for simulation is also considered. Finally comparative analysis of proposed work is making to conventional in order to assure the reliability, performance and efficiency of model.

Forensic samples have been collected from kaggle.com. Link for dataset is https://www.kaggle.com/code/nageshsingh/recreating-fingerprints/input, where tif images are considered for training and testing.

Considering average of Table 1, Figure 7 has been generated to present the comparative analysis between conventional and proposed approach

Figure 5. Process flow of proposed image classification to aid digital forensics

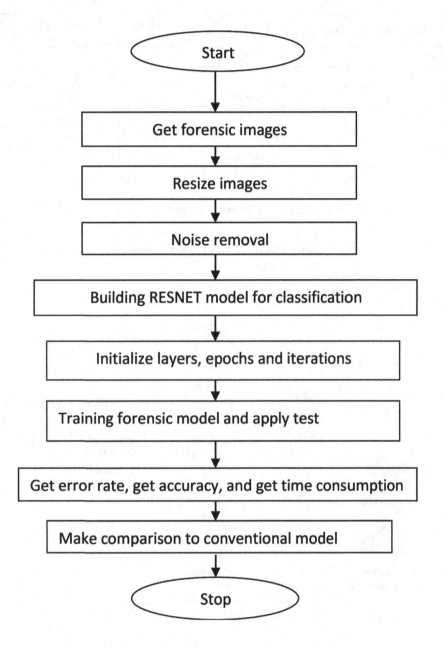

Figure 6. Forensic images

Table 1. Comparative analysis of accuracy

	Conventional CNN approach	**Conventional CNN approach with noise removal**	**Proposed RESNET approach with noise removal**
Case 1	87.26314807	88.86772272	90.78800734
Case 2	87.82630433	89.32872427	90.9842222
Case 3	87.6822461	89.62085815	90.63818549
Case 4	87.67355252	89.6352821	91.51678641
Case 5	87.19712733	88.63535249	90.23311614
Case 6	87.32768579	88.8787363	90.45322738

Figure 7. Comparative analysis of accuracy for proposed forensic model

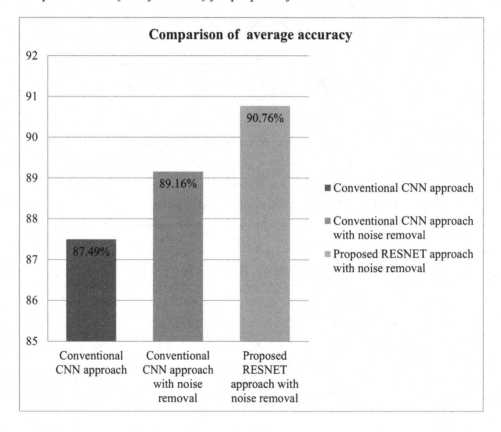

7. CONCLUSION

The purpose of this study is to provide suggestions on the use of artificial intelligence and image processing to digital forensics. During image processing, one of the challenges that might be encountered is poor picture quality, which can be improved by removing noise. Following that, a CNN-based deep learning strategy was used in order to categorize the picture collection. Simulation results conclude that proposed model is providing better accuracy and performance as compared to conventional model. And this model is reliable and efficient but there is need to do more work on real life implications.

8. FUTURE SCOPE

The development of Artificial Intelligence (AI) is revolutionizing digital forensics, creating far-reaching implications for the entire field. AI is impacting digital forensics in a number of ways, from providing new tools and techniques to completely rewriting the rules of digital forensics. AI-driven tools are helping investigators to process vast amounts of data more quickly and accurately, while AI-enabled analytics are providing deeper insights into digital evidence. AI is also helping to automate tedious and time-consuming tasks, such as the collection, preservation, and analysis of digital evidence. Furthermore, AI-driven algorithms are being used to identify patterns and anomalies in digital evidence, allowing investigators to quickly identify potential leads and suspects. The impact of AI is not limited to the technical aspects of digital forensics; it is also redefining the investigative process itself. AI is making it possible to automate the process of evidence gathering and analysis, allowing investigators to focus on the creative aspects of their work. By leveraging AI, digital forensics is becoming more efficient and effective, allowing investigators to solve cases more quickly and accurately. The future of digital forensics is increasingly reliant on AI, as the technology continues to evolve and revolutionize the field.

REFERENCES

Ahmed Alaa El-Din, E. (2022). Artificial Intelligence in Forensic Science : Invasion or Revolution? *Egyptian Society of Clinical Toxicology Journal, 10*(2), 20–32. doi:10.21608/esctj.2022.158178.1012

Ali, M. R. (2020). Digital Forensics and Artificial Intelligence A Study. *International Journal of Innovative Science and Research Technology, 5*(12), 651–654. www.ijisrt.com651

Atiyah, J. M., & Noori, Z. S. (2022). *Image Forensic and Analytics using Machine Learning.* Research Gate. https://www.researchgate.net/publication/358942562

B, Y. A. B., Shaker, H., & Kumar, B. (2023). *The Use of Machine Learning in Digital Forensics : Review Paper.* Atlantis Press International BV. doi:10.2991/978-94-6463-110-4

Dunsin, D., Ghanem, M. C., & Ouazzane, K. (2022). The Use of Artificial Intelligence in Digital Forensics and Incident Response in a Constrained Environment. *International Journal of Information and Communication Engineering, 16*(8), 280–285.

Dushyant, K., Muskan, G., Gupta, A., & Pramanik, S. (2022). Utilizing Machine Learning and Deep Learning in Cyber security: An Innovative Approach. In M. M. Ghonge, S. Pramanik, R. Mangrulkar, & D. N. Le (Eds.), *Cyber security and Digital Forensics.* Wiley. doi:10.1002/9781119795667.ch12

Fähndrich, J., Honekamp, W., Povalej, R., Rittelmeier, H., & Berner, S. (2022). Special Issue on Application of AI in Digital Forensics. KI -. *Kunstliche Intelligenz, 36*(2), 121–124. doi:10.100713218-022-00777-3

Ferreira, S., Antunes, M., & Correia, M. E. (2021). A dataset of photos and videos for digital forensics analysis using machine learning processing. *Data, 6*(8), 1–15. doi:10.3390/data6080087

Gupta A. (2020). *An Analysis of Digital Image Compression Technique in Image.* SERSC.

Gupta, N., Khosravy, M., Patel, N., Dey, N., Gupta, S., Darbari, H., & Crespo, R. G. (2020). Economic data analytic AI technique on IoT edge devices for health monitoring of agriculture machines. *Applied Intelligence*, *50*(11), 3990–4016. doi:10.100710489-020-01744-x

Hall, S. W., Sakzad, A., & Choo, K. R. (2022). Explainable artificial intelligence for digital forensics. *WIREs Forensic Science*, *4*(2), 1–11. doi:10.1002/wfs2.1434

Jain, V., Beram, S. M., Talukdar, V., Patil, T., Dhabliya, D., & Gupta, A. (2022). Accuracy Enhancement in Machine Learning During Blockchain Based Transaction Classification. *Seventh International Conference on Parallel, Distributed and Grid Computing (PDGC)*, Solan, Himachal Pradesh, India. 10.1109/PDGC56933.2022.10053213

Javed, A. R., Jalil, Z., Zehra, W., Gadekallu, T. R., Suh, D. Y., & Piran, M. J. (2021). A comprehensive survey on digital video forensics: Taxonomy, challenges, and future directions. *Engineering Applications of Artificial Intelligence*, *106*(September), 104456. doi:10.1016/j.engappai.2021.104456

Jeong, D. (2020). Artificial intelligence security threat, crime, and forensics: Taxonomy and open issues. *IEEE Access : Practical Innovations, Open Solutions*, *8*, 184560–184574. doi:10.1109/ACCESS.2020.3029280

L, M. A., & K, P. (2022). Digital Forensics Triage Classification Model using Hybrid Learning Approaches. *International Journal of Innovative Research in Computer Science & Technology, 3*, 29–39. doi:10.55524/ijircst.2022.10.3.7

Lorch, B., Scheler, N., & Riess, C. (2022). Compliance Challenges in Forensic Image Analysis Under the Artificial Intelligence Act. *European Signal Processing Conference*, (pp. 613–617). IEEE. 10.23919/EUSIPCO55093.2022.9909723

Meng, X., Meng, K., & Qiao, W. (2020). A Survey of Research on Image Data Sources Forensics. *ACM International Conference Proceeding Series*, (pp. 174–179). ACM. 10.1145/3430199.3430241

Mesejo, P., Martos, R., Ibáñez, Ó., Novo, J., & Ortega, M. (2020). A Survey on artificial intelligence techniques for biomedical image analysis in skeleton-based forensic human identification. *Applied Sciences (Basel, Switzerland)*, *10*(14), 4703. doi:10.3390/app10144703

Mohammed, H., Clarke, N., & Li, F. (2016). An Automated Approach for Digital Forensic Analysis of Heterogeneous Big Data. Journal of Digital Forensics. *Security and Law*, *11*(2). doi:10.15394/jdfsl.2016.1384

Nowroozi, E., Dehghantanha, A., Parizi, R. M., & Choo, K. K. R. (2021). A survey of machine learning techniques in adversarial image forensics. *Computers & Security*, *100*(June), 1–37. doi:10.1016/j.cose.2020.102092

Pandey, B. K., Pandey, D., Wariya, S., Aggarwal, G., & Rastogi, R. (2021). Deep learning and particle swarm optimisation-based techniques for visually impaired humans' text recognition and identification. *Augmented Human Research*, *6*(1), 1–14. doi:10.100741133-021-00051-5

Pandey, D., Wairya, S., Sharma, M., Gupta, A. K., Kakkar, R., & Pandey, B. K. (2022). An approach for object tracking, categorization, and autopilot guidance for passive homing missiles. *Aerospace Systems*, 1-14.

Pathania, V. (2022). A Database Application of Monitoring COVID-19 in India. In M. Gupta, S. Ghatak, A. Gupta, & A. L. Mukherjee (Eds.), *Artificial Intelligence on Medical Data. Lecture Notes in Computational Vision and Biomechanics* (Vol. 37). Springer. doi:10.1007/978-981-19-0151-5_23

Qadir, A. M., & Varol, A. (2020). The Role of Machine Learning in Digital Forensics. *8th International Symposium on Digital Forensics and Security, ISDFS 2020.* IEEE. 10.1109/ISDFS49300.2020.9116298

Raponi, S., Oligeri, G., & Ali, I. M. (2022). Sound of guns: Digital forensics of gun audio samples meets artificial intelligence. *Multimedia Tools and Applications*, *81*(21), 30387–30412. doi:10.100711042-022-12612-w

Rughani, P. H. (2017). Artificial Intelligence Based Digital Forensics Framework. *International Journal of Advanced Research in Computer Science*, *8*(8), 10–14. doi:10.26483/ijarcs.v8i8.4571

Shivan Othman, P., Rebar Ihsan, R., Marqas, R. B., Almufti, S. M., & Author, C. (2020). Image Processing Techniques for Identifying Impostor Documents Through Digital Forensic Examination. *Region*, *62*(04), 1781–1794.

Solanke, A. A. (2022). Explainable digital forensics AI: Towards mitigating distrust in AI-based digital forensics analysis using interpretable models. *Forensic Science International: Digital Investigation*, *42*, 301403. doi:10.1016/j.fsidi.2022.301403

Solanke, A. A., & Biasiotti, M. A. (2022). Digital Forensics AI: Evaluating, Standardizing and Optimizing Digital Evidence Mining Techniques. KI -. *Kunstliche Intelligenz*, *36*(2), 143–161. doi:10.100713218-022-00763-9

Talukdar, V., Dhabliya, D., Kumar, B., Talukdar, S. B., Ahamad, S., & Gupta, A. (2022) Suspicious Activity Detection and Classification in IoT Environment Using Machine Learning Approach. *Seventh International Conference on Parallel, Distributed and Grid Computing (PDGC)*, Solan, Himachal Pradesh, India. 10.1109/PDGC56933.2022.10053312

Ullal, M. S., Hawaldar, I. T., Soni, R., & Nadeem, M. (2021). The Role of Machine Learning in Digital Marketing. *SAGE Open*, *11*(4), 1–5. doi:10.1177/21582440211050394

Veeraiah, V., Rajaboina, N. B., Rao, G. N., Ahamad, S., Gupta, A., & Suri, C. S. (2022).Securing Online Web Application for IoT Management. *2022 2nd International Conference on Advance Computing and Innovative Technologies in Engineering (ICACITE)*, (pp. 1499-1504). IEEE. 10.1109/ICACITE53722.2022.9823733

Chapter 27
Visual Cryptographic Shares Using Color Components

Sabyasachi Samanta
Haldia Institute of Technology, India

Priyatosh Jana
Haldia Institute of Technology, India

Abhijit Sarkar
Haldia Institute of Technology, India

Soumen Ghosh
Haldia Institute of Technology, India

ABSTRACT

Visual cryptography is an excellent cryptographic method by which the visual information is encrypted and decrypted with or without using of computer systems depending on the human visual system. In visual cryptography techniques, the carrier (with secret information) is divided into multiple shares, in particular any one of which does not reveal any knowledge about the secret information. In this chapter, a newly color component-based visual cryptographic technique, i.e., image share formation for image and video, has been introduced. As video is a sequential amalgamation of image frames, the same has also been implemented for video. In this time, the method supports the {k, n} threshold framework. Out of n transparencies, using k number of shares, the reformation is possible. Using the image, shares data may be embedded to different shares using steganography or watermarking techniques. Furthermore, some suitable comparisons also have been performed to measure the newly developed technique.

1. INTRODUCTION

Hiding information is a strategy for preventing unwanted access to material or for making information unavailable over a communication channel. Steganography is a method that extracts information via the use of appropriate cover carriers or media such as images, texts, audio recordings, and videos. Digital

DOI: 10.4018/978-1-6684-8618-4.ch027

watermarking may be thought of as a kind of embedding that is either obvious or covert inside the cover signal. In most cases, the ownership of the copyright may be determined based on the apparent basis. The process of transforming plaintext into cypher text is referred to as cryptography. Another kind of cryptographic technique is known as visual cryptography. This form of cryptography allows the encryption process to be dependent on the human visual system. The translated visual information is then used to execute the decryption process in a manner that does not need the usage of a mathematical computer system. Visual cryptography has the potential to become one of the most superior levels of security module in the field of information security. This would allow for encrypted communication via digital cover medium. (P. S. Revenkar et al., 2010, Ankita Maheshwari, 2015).

Another kind of emerging cryptographic technology is known as visual cryptography. In visual encryption, a secret message is encoded as a collection of "shares" that can be graphically merged to disclose the original secret message. Different people receive the shares, and they can use them to decrypt the communication without having to figure out a complicated encryption method or find a hidden key. Originally suggested in 1994 by Moni Naor and Adi Shamir, the method has since found use in digital watermarking, private picture transfer, and identification systems among other places. You can classify visual encryption as either "basic" or "extended," the former being the more common of the two. To divide a hidden communication into two or more parts, visual cryptography's rudimentary technique of using one-time tokens is used. These tokens are then printed on transparency sheets, and the hidden message is revealed upon superimposing the sheets.

In contrast, extended visual encryption permits the generation of more than two shares, and these shares may be organized in such a way that the secret message is obscured without the knowledge of the proper combination of shares. Without the need for complicated encryption methods or passwords, visual cryptography is a helpful technique for securely and efficiently exchanging secrets. However, there are restrictions, such as the need for actual distribution of the shares, which may be problematic in some cases. Decryption of encrypted pictures is often accomplished by the use of Human Visual Intelligence (HVI) elements. Understanding cryptography or performing difficult mathematical computations is never required in order to share the carrier (Kimmo Halunen et al. 2021, Feng Liu et al. 2011). During the process of encryption, it will never attempt to conceal any information to itself. On occasion, though, it will make use of the method of breaking a covert picture down into a series of binary or patchy images or shares, which will make the covert image look to us as random noise. During the process of decryption, parts of the hidden picture files are pieced together, and thereafter they may at last be seen by the human visual system (In Koo Kang et al. 2011, Annalisa De Bonis et al. 2004).

The visual cryptography approach uses statistical techniques to practice the secret sharing algorithm that is developed on a backdrop of (k, n) distribution. Where "n" refers for the number of transparency copies, indicating that the hidden picture will be covered up using n copies of the transparency. And 'k' is the value by which, at the very least by using that many or more transparencies, we are able to reconstruct the hidden picture (Ching-Nung Yang et al. 2012, Xiuhao Ma et al. 2022). Figuratively speaking, a number of hidden sharing from the original picture have been generated here in Figure 1. The first picture creation is also displayed in the figure, and it was created utilizing just k of the n shares available.

The image that is shared here has been constructed with several color components in mind, as seen in this work. It is possible to build a variety of distinct picture shares by combining various RGB color components in a variety of different ways. In the event that any one of the components is missing, there are only three potential shares. In the event that one or more of the components are missing, combination eight is feasible. Both of these methods are appropriate for use with color images and videos. In

Figure 1. Secret sharing scheme for visual cryptography

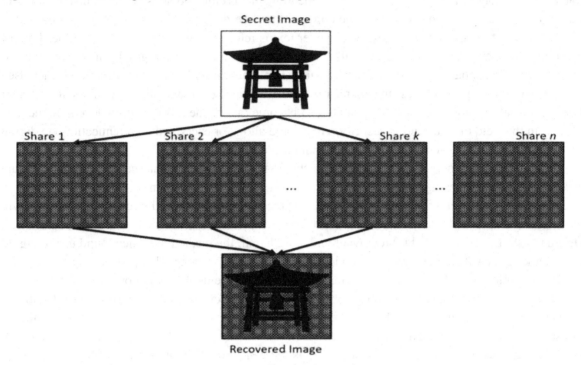

accordance with the protocol of cryptography, it is also feasible to reconstruct the final picture or video from the sharing. The techniques of steganography and watermarking may be used to implant data into separate picture sharing. This can be done via the image shares. It is recommended that additional data be implanted via the shares as well as at the receiving end, and that this data be reformed using the reversing procedure. The color component-based approach has been proposed here as a means of securing communication using steganography. This is done without focusing on the bitwise image sharing.

The most recent developments in visual cryptography are covered in Section 2. Implementing a component-based visual cryptography approach for images and videos is the focus of Section 3, which outlines the process. In the fourth section, we conduct an analysis of the results of the newly devised technique. The component based visual cryptography system is broken down and its implications are discussed in Section 5.

2. RELATED WORKS

M. Manisha et al. (2021) came up with an alternative kind of visual cryptography strategy for color pictures that were in CMY format. In addition to this, it safeguards the identity of the image's creator by encrypting the data so that it cannot be read by any other method besides the one we use to retrieve it. M. G. Devi Tiwari et al. (2021) suggested a secure online polling system based on visual cryptography. Their system is effectively developed with Python and produces improved performance on systems with minimal software and hardware configurations. L. Ren et al. (2021) suggested an innovative expanded visual encryption method for safely encoding a raster map as a combination of two interpretable halftone maps. The method avoids the insecure and difficult-to-manage visual cryptography's random-looking shares. We start by converting a color secret map into halftone pictures using the halftone and color decomposition techniques. After that, the hidden map is encoded into blocks, one at a time, to prevent the growth of the map's pixels. Finally, we accomplish a high-quality secret retrieval from produced numerous equal-sized shares by maximizing the selection of encrypted blocks. It is accomplished through the use of a safe and flexible vector image sharing. The experimental findings demonstrate that the suggested method greatly boosts the performance of restored raster maps in comparison to the prior work. A novel VC method based on binary amplitude-only holograms (AOHs) produced by a tweaked version of the Gerchberg-Saxton algorithm was suggested by Lina Zhou et al. 2022. Using the MGSA, an encrypted picture is first partitioned into a collection of random, unconnected pieces called "shares," and then those "shares" are transformed into binary AOHs. In order to reveal the hidden picture, the binary AOHs are first rationally combined to create a piled hologram. The suggested VC strategy is distinct from other VC methods because it uses binary AOHs to represent a hidden picture. Because of the produced binary AOHs' duplication, the suggested technique is both mathematically and empirically proven to be viable and effective, and it holds high resilience against interference assaults. The visible encryption for facial pictures used in a fingerprint application was implemented by J. Mohan et al. (2020). It is impossible to handle one-shot learning problems without the Siamese network, which uses a model of learning features to perform comparisons with verifying tasks. Finding the facial picture among n raw images is an important step toward achieving consistency in this study. In this study, we investigate whether or not it is possible to use visible encryption to protect the confidentiality of biological information. When compared to the methods currently being used, the suggested method's 93% precision stands out as the clear winner. To safely send multiple grayscale secret images to the receiver, A. John Blesswin et al. (2022) suggested a novel method called Multiple grayscale Secret Image Sharing (MSIS). Color overlay pictures are used to increase protection in MSIS. To further simplify things, it limits things like the amount of likes and header pictures used. A visual cryptography approach was presented by L. J. Chmielewski et al. (2021), and it was based on the unpredictability of shares. They changed the composition of the shares and made sure that each share had the same amount of black and red, green, and blue (RGB) pixels. M. Wafy et al. (2022) proposed a method of visual cryptography that is based on video identification. They conceal a number of pictures in the film by dividing it up into considerable parts using binary, grayscale, or colour images. This method was proposed by Th. R. Singh et al. (2013) as a video watermarking system employing visual cryptography. They did this by incorporating the many components of a single watermark picture into the several segments of a film to create confidential information. R. Munir et al. (2012) suggested employing Wang's approach for a video-based visual cryptography. In this case, Wang's (n, n) onset method was used so that the encoded video may be distributed to an unlimited number of contributors. The original video was recreated using all of the shares that were available. Tripathi, J. et al. (2022) proposed a Visual Cryptography using (3, 3) shares by utilizing the concept of keys to secure information. They also introduced a (2, 3) - visual cryptographic scheme.

M. Karolin et al. (2022) proposed a Secret Share scheme using Several Image Encryption and Decryption method and Elliptic Curve Cryptography technique. They used the encryption technique by using public key cryptography generator and secret key arbitrarily generators of the Elliptic Curve Cryptography method. Ling Fu Wang et al. (2021) proposed a progressive visual cryptography scheme by using scalable basis matrices and random Gaussian noise. They used the optimization techniques like PSNR, MSE, NPCR and UACI.

Table 1. Formation of image shares using 3-shares

Image Shares	Color Components		
	Red(R_c)	Green(G_c)	Blue(B_c)
I_0	Ab	Pr	Pr
I_1	Pr	Ab	Pr
I_2	Pr	Pr	Ab

3. IMPLEMENTATION OF THE ALGORITHM FOR IMAGE

3.1 3-Shares Method

As shown in Table 1, three different image shares have been produced depending on the absence (Ab) of one of the color components. Every time we notice that any one of the three is missing or that any two of them are present, we do so. At the completion of the decryption process, the original picture may be reformed by joining two image shares (k=2) into a single one. In light of this, the visual cryptography rubrics, which were also satisfied, given that the value of k is lower than the total number of components.

3.2 8-Shares Method

Depending on Absence (Ab) of one or more color components here the eight image shares are formed. Using 8-shares method eight image shares (I_0-I_7) have been formed on presence or absence of basic color components. Absence and presence of color components are summarized in Table 2. Here also using only two or more shares (k>=2) original image formation is possible and thus the rubrics of visual cryptography also gratified as the value of k is less than the number of total components. Only using the precise unification of image shares the original image (I) formation is possible (as in Table 3). In case of I_0 and I_7 mistake the threshold framework of visual cryptography.

In that case the value of n may be consider as 6 but the value of k remains as earlier. By combining I_0 and I_7 shares the reformation of original is possible as I_7 contains the similar to it. Presence of share

Table 2. Formation of image shares using 8-shares

Image Shares	Color Components		
	Red(R_c)	Green(G_c)	Blue(B_c)
I_0	Ab	Ab	Ab
I_1	Ab	Ab	Pr
I_2	Ab	Pr	Ab
I_3	Ab	Pr	Pr
I_4	Pr	Ab	Ab
I_5	Pr	Ab	Pr
I_6	Pr	Pr	Ab
I7	Pr	Pr	Pr

I_7 may produce more six combination. Such as $\{I_{1+}\ I_7\}$, $\{I_{2+}\ I_7\}$.............$\{I_{6+}\ I_7\}$ make possible to create the original one. The share I_0 forms a total black image and I_7 contain all of the RGB components. So, for the presence of I_7 does not follow the visual cryptography regulation. So for in place of eight only six shares have been formed with the visual cryptographic rules.

By using only two shares:

Table 3. Possible combination to reform image

Image Formation	Image Shares Combinations
I_{21}	$\{I_0, I_7\}$
I_{22}	$\{I_1, I_6\}$
I_{23}	$\{I_2, I_5\}$
I_{24}	$\{I_3, I_4\}$
I_{25}	$\{I_3, I_5\}$
I_{26}	$\{I_5, I_6\}$
I_{27}	$\{I_3, I_6\}$

4. EXPERIMENTAL RESULT AND ANALYSIS

4.1 Image Analysis

In this section, we brought the investigation to a successful conclusion to demonstrate that the recommended steganography method is effective. Two different measurements have been used to determine how good the quality of a steganographic photograph is. The first measurement is referred to as the peak signal-to-noise ratio (PSNR), and the second measurement is referred to as the structural similarity index measure. (SSIM). The PSNR is utilized to determine the degree to which there is a disparity between the picture on the label and the steganographic image. The following is a possible definition for the algorithm for PSNR:

$$PSNR = \frac{10.log_{10}\left(255\times255\right)}{MSE}\ db\ ....$$ (1)

$$MSE = \frac{1}{MN}\sum_{i=1}^{M}\sum_{j=1}^{N}\left(img_{i,j}-C_{i,j}\right)^2 ....$$ (2)

A higher PSNR value indicates that the proposed algorithm has the greatest quality, and an MSE value that is as low as possible indicates that the method has a low error rate. Both of these values should be as close to one another as possible. The steganographic photograph is represented by the symbol $C(i, j)$ in MSE, while the original image is represented by the symbol $img.(i, j)$.

With the help of a method known as the structural similarity index measure, it is possible to make educated guesses about the content of pictures, other digital photos, and videos. (SSIM). Utilize the Similarity Coefficient between Images if you are interested in determining the degree to which two photographs are comparable to one another. (SSIM). The SSIM index is a comprehensive reference measure because it bases its assessments and predictions on a picture of the baseline that has not been compressed or otherwise distorted.

The SSIM index is calculated using a number of different segments from within a picture. SSIM is defined as the following when given two windows x and y of the same dimension N x N:

$$SSIM(x, y) = \frac{\left(2\mu_x\mu_y + c_1\right)\left(2\sigma_{xy} + c_2\right)}{\left(\mu_x^2 + \mu_y^2 + c_1\right)\left(\sigma_x^2 + \sigma_y^2 + c_2\right)} \tag{3}$$

As input, it requires the mean, variance, and correlation of image samples across two windows (x and y).

Both the 3-shares approach and the 8-shares method have their performance analyzed and explained in this section. The formation of image shares using the 3-shares approach is shown in Figure 2, which provides a general concept of how the process works. Figure 3 illustrates how the combined picture shares lead to the formation of the original image. The first picture creation of MONALISA is seen below, and it was constructed with the help of image sharing IS0 and IS1.

Here the performance of 8-shares method has been presented. Figure 4 represents the original image of LENA and image shares using 8-shares method. Figure 5 shows the process of original image formation by combining two shares as in Table 3.

Table 4 is with a comparison of 3-shares and 8-shares method by different measures related to visual cryptography. Table 5 represents the superiority of proposed methodologies over existing one.

Figure 2. Image shares using 3-shares

(I₁)　　　　　　　(I₂)　　　　　　　(I₃)

Figure 3. Original image formation

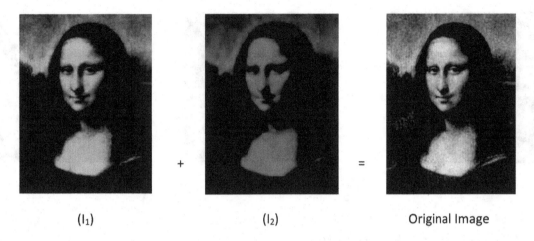

(I₁)   +   (I₂)   =   Original Image

Figure 4. Original image and its shares (LENA) using 8-shares

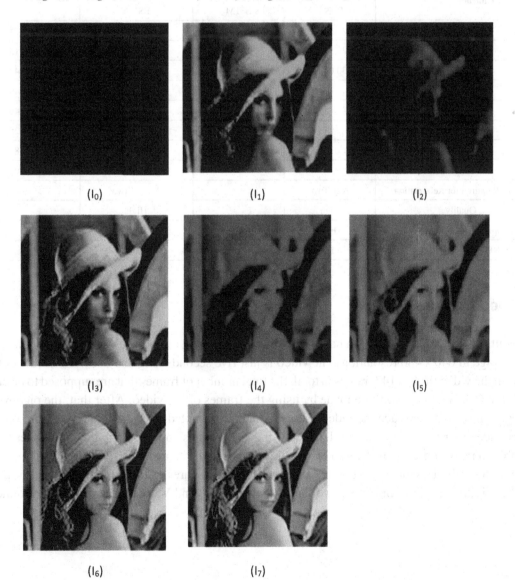

(I₀)   (I₁)   (I₂)

(I₃)   (I₄)   (I₅)

(I₆)   (I₇)

Figure 5. Original image formation (LENA)

| (I₄) | (I₅) | Original Image |

Table 4. Comparison of 3-shares and 8-shares

Characteristics	3-Shares		8-Shares	
	PSNR	SSIM	PSNR	SSIM
I_0	27.8866	0.1191	26.6274	0.2141
I_1	28.5859	0.1316	27.1404	0.1813
I_2	30.0579	0.1484	27.2427	0.1342
I_3			27.8866	0.1749
I_4			28.5859	0.1946
I_5			30.0579	0.1125
I_6			30.2734	0.1387
I_7			Infinity	NA
Shares Required for Reformation	Any Two		At least two	
Quality	High		High	
Computational Complexity	High		High	
PSNR after Reformation	Infinity		Infinity	

4.2 Video Analysis

The results of the 3-shares approach have been shared below for your perusal. Also captured here is the same footage in 640 x 480 resolution. The video is just five seconds long and has a frame rate of thirty. Although the video file has 147 frames in total, the total number of frames that are supposed to be created is 150. First, the picture shares are made by using the frames of the video. After that, the picture share is merged in order to produce the video shares, which are denoted with the letter V. Figure 6 depicts the first video along with the shares calculated using the 3-shares approach. Figure 7 illustrates how we were able to recover the original video by merging two separate shares.

Figure 8 symbolizes the original video and shares using 8-shares method. Figure 9 shows how to get back the original video by combining two shares. As earlier V_0 and V_7 mistake the threshold framework

Table 5. Comparative analysis of visual cryptographic characteristics for image

Characteristics	Pradeep Kumar Sharma et al.	Proposed Method for Image	
		3-Shares	8-Shares
Types of Distribution	{2,2}	{1,3}	{1,8}
Image Type	Halftone (black & white)	RGB	RGB
Dimension	(512 x 512)	Any	Any
Pixel Development	X	X	X
Intensity Division	X	X	X
Dissimilarity	X	X	X
Additional Information Requirement	Yes	X	X
Code Requirement	Yes	X	X
Shares Based on	Blocks	Color Component	Color Component

**X=NO

Figure 6. (a) Original video and its shares using 3-shares

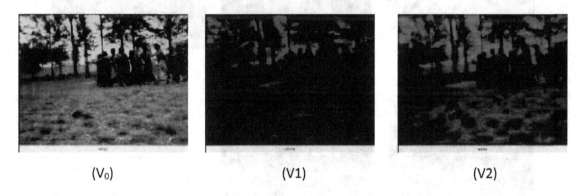

(V₀)   (V1)   (V2)

Figure 7. Original video formation using 3-shares

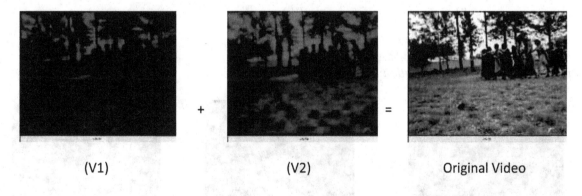

(V1)   +   (V2)   =   Original Video

Figure 8. Original video and its shares using 8-shares

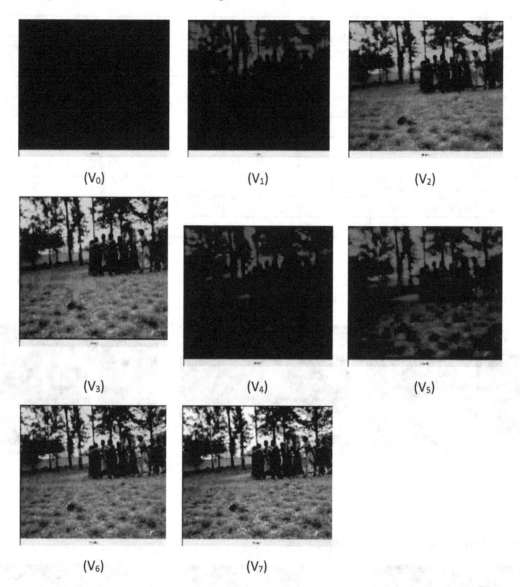

(V₀)   (V₁)   (V₂)

(V₃)   (V₄)   (V₅)

(V₆)   (V₇)

Figure 9. Original video formation using 8-shares

Table 6. Comparison of 3-shares and 8-shares

Characteristics	3-Shares		8-Shares	
	PSNR	SSIM	PSNR	SSIM
V_0	40.3304	0.7692	34.9145	0.3412
V_1	34.3557	0.5314	33.1837	0.3492
V_2	NA	NA	NA	NA
V_3			40.3303	0.5716
V_4			NA	NA
V_5			34.3557	0.6172
V_6			NA	NA
V_7			Infinity	NA
Shares Required for Reformation	Any Two		At least two	
Quality	High		High	
Computational Complexity	High		High	
PSNR after Reformation	Infinity		Infinity	

Table 7. Comparative analysis of visual cryptographic characteristics

Characteristics	Pradeep Kumar Sharma et al.	Proposed Method for Video	
		3-Shares	8-Shares
Types of Distribution	(1,3)	(1,3)	(1,8)
Image Type	Color video	Color video	Color video
Dimension	Video File	Any	Any
Pixel Development	X	X	X
Intensity Division	X	X	X
Dissimilarity	X	X	X
Additional Information Requirement	Yes	X	X
Code Requirement	Yes	X	X
Shares Based on	Color Component	Color Component	Color Component

of visual cryptography. But by combining that two shares the reformation of original is possible as I_7 contains the similar to it.

The methods of three shares and eight shares are compared in Table 6, which bears the phrase "terms with." The comparative study of our suggested procedure may be seen in Table 7. The PSNR and SSIM measures, respectively, are shown for image and video sharing in figures 10 and 11, respectively. Both of the graphs show the nonlinear increasing in a saw tooth-like pattern dissimilarities.

Figure 10. PSNR measure for image and video shares

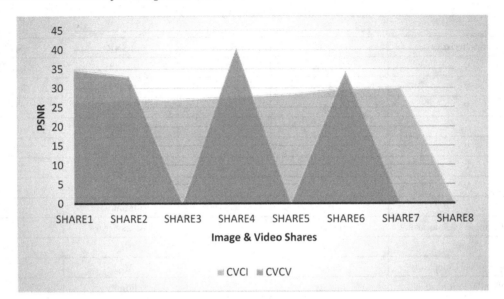

Figure 11. SSIM measure for image and video shares

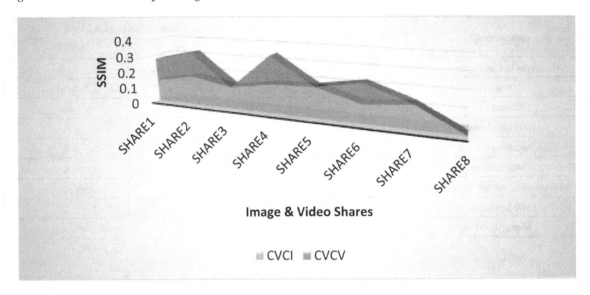

5. CONCLUSION

The component-based visual cryptography algorithms for both still images and moving videos have been dissected and analyzed in this body of work. By making use of the color component of the picture, it is feasible to build shares for both the image and the video. In addition, the reconstruction of the original picture is achievable for the eight shares approach when only acceptable combinations are used. A contrast has been drawn between this method and other approaches already in use. Better results may be obtained in the field of information concealment via the use of visual cryptography in the process of invisible watermarking or keyed steganography. It has been determined, based on findings from a variety of analyses, that the suggested schemes provide a higher level of security and safety for the image and video secret sharing communication system.

REFERENCES

Chmielewski, L. J., Nieniewski, M., & Orłowski, A. (2021). Testing the randomness of shares in color visual cryptography. In Pattern Analysis and Applications (Vol. 24, Issue 4, pp. 1475–1487). Springer Science and Business Media LLC. doi:10.100710044-021-00999-5

De Bonis, A., & De Santis, A. (2004). Randomness in secret sharing and visual cryptography schemes. In Theoretical Computer Science (Vol. 314, Issue 3, pp. 351–374). Elsevier BV. doi:10.1016/j.tcs.2003.12.018

Halunen, K., & Latvala, O.-M. (2021). Review of the use of human senses and capabilities in cryptography. In *Computer Science Review* (Vol. 39, p. 100340). Elsevier BV. doi:10.1016/j.cosrev.2020.100340

John Blesswin, A., Selva Mary, G., & Manoj Kumar, S. (2021). Multiple Secret Image Communication Using Visual Cryptography. In Wireless Personal Communications (Vol. 122, Issue 4, pp. 3085–3103). Springer Science and Business Media LLC. doi:10.100711277-021-09041-7

Kang, I. K., Arce, G. R., & Lee, H.-K. (2011). Color Extended Visual Cryptography Using Error Diffusion. *IEEE Transactions on Image Processing*, *20*(1), 132–145. doi:10.1109/TIP.2010.2056376 PMID:20615812

Karolin, M., & Meyyappan, T. (2022). Visual Cryptography Secret Share Creation Techniques with Multiple Image Encryption and Decryption Using Elliptic Curve Cryptography. In IETE Journal of Research (pp. 1–8). Informa UK Limited. doi:10.1080/03772063.2022.2142684

Liu, F., & Wu, C. (2011). Embedded Extended Visual Cryptography Schemes. In IEEE Transactions on Information Forensics and Security (Vol. 6, Issue 2, pp. 307–322). Institute of Electrical and Electronics Engineers (IEEE). doi:10.1109/TIFS.2011.2116782

Ma, X., Song, B., Lin, W., Wu, J., Huang, W., & Liu, B. (2022). High-fidelity decryption technology of Visual Cryptography based on optical coherence operation. In *Results in Physics* (Vol. 43, p. 106065). Elsevier BV. doi:10.1016/j.rinp.2022.106065

Maheshwari, A. (2015). A New Image Encryption Algorithm Based Slicing and Displacement Followed By Symmetric and Asymmetric Cryptography Technique. *International Journal on Recent and Innovation Trends in Computing and Communication, 3*(5), 2679 – 2684.

Manisha & Rao. (2021). Colour Visual Cryptography (3,3) Scheme. *Turkish Journal of Computer and Mathematics Education, 12*(2), 3189–3198.

Mohan, J., & R, D. R. (2021). Enhancing home security through visual cryptography. In *Microprocessors and Microsystems* (Vol. 80, p. 103355). Elsevier BV. doi:10.1016/j.micpro.2020.103355

Munir, R., & Harlili. (2018). Video Encryption by Using Visual Cryptography Based on Wang's Scheme. In *2018 4th International Conference on Electrical, Electronics and System Engineering (ICEESE).* *2018 4th International Conference on Electrical, Electronics and System Engineering (ICEESE).* IEEE. doi:10.1109/ICEESE.2018.8703567

Ren, L. (2021). A Novel Raster Map Exchange Scheme Based on Visual Cryptography. In R. Kaluri (Ed.), *Advances in Multimedia* (Vol. 2021, pp. 1–7). Hindawi Limited. doi:10.1155/2021/3287774

Revenkar, P. S., & Anisa Anjum, W. Z. (2010). Secure Iris Authentication Using Visual Cryptography. *International Journal of Computer Science and Information Security, 7*(3), 217-221.

Reyad, O., & Karar, M. E. (2021). Secure CT-Image Encryption for COVID-19 Infections Using HBBS-Based Multiple Key-Streams. In Arabian Journal for Science and Engineering (Vol. 46, Issue 4, pp. 3581–3593). Springer Science and Business Media LLC. doi:10.100713369-020-05196-w

Sharma & Singh. (2014). Visual Cryptography Scheme for Gray Scale Images based on Intensity Division. *International Journal of Current Engineering and Technology, 4*(1), 211-215.

Shrivas & Yadav. (2015). Visual Cryptography in the Video using Halftone Technique. *International Journal of Computer Applications, 117*(14).

Singh, T. R., Singh, Kh. M., & Roy, S. (2013). Video watermarking scheme based on visual cryptography and scene change detection. In AEU - International Journal of Electronics and Communications (Vol. 67, Issue 8, pp. 645–651). Elsevier BV. doi:10.1016/j.aeue.2013.01.008

Tiwari & Kakelli. (2021). Secure Online Voting System using Visual Cryptography. *Walailak J Sci & Tech, 18*(15), 1-14.

Tripathi, J., & Saini, A. (2020). Enhanced Visual Cryptography: An Augmented Model for Image Security. In Procedia Computer Science (Vol. 167, pp. 323–333). Elsevier BV. doi:10.1016/j.procs.2020.03.232

Wafy, M., Gamal Zanaty, S., & Elkhouly, M. (2022). Video Identification Based on Watermarking Schemes and Visual Cryptography. In Computer Systems Science and Engineering (Vol. 40, Issue 2, pp. 441–453). Computers, Materials and Continua (Tech Science Press). doi:10.32604/csse.2022.018597

Wang, L., Wang, J., & Huang, W. (2021). A scalable ideal progressive visual cryptography scheme. In *2021 10th International Conference on Internet Computing for Science and Engineering. ICICSE 2021: 2021 10th International Conference on Internet Computing for Science and Engineering.* ACM. 10.1145/3485314.3485320

Yang, C.-N., Shih, H.-W., Wu, C.-C., & Harn, L. (2012). k Out of n Region Incrementing Scheme in Visual Cryptography. In IEEE Transactions on Circuits and Systems for Video Technology (Vol. 22, Issue 5, pp. 799–810). Institute of Electrical and Electronics Engineers (IEEE). doi:10.1109/TC-SVT.2011.2180952

Zhou, L., Xiao, Y., Pan, Z., Cao, Y., & Chen, W. (2022). Visual Cryptography Using Binary Amplitude-Only Holograms. In Frontiers in Photonics (Vol. 2). Frontiers Media SA. doi:10.3389/fphot.2021.821304

Chapter 28
Visualizing the Future of Marketing:
A Review of Image Processing Techniques and Their Implications for Marketing Management

Ganesh Waghmare
Lexicon Management Institute of Leadership and Excellence, India

Nishant Tyagi
Lexicon Management Institute of Leadership and Excellence, India

Anshuman Vijay Magar
Lexicon Management institute of Leadership and Excellence, India

ABSTRACT

The integration of image processing techniques in marketing has rapidly increased in recent years, and their implications for marketing management are becoming more significant. The chapter highlights the various types of image processing techniques used in marketing, including image segmentation, image filtering, and image recognition. The review also discusses the applications of these techniques in marketing, including product classification, branding, advertising, and customer experience management. Additionally, the review identifies the implications of image processing techniques for marketing management. The chapter also examines the limitations of image processing techniques in marketing. Finally, the chapter concludes by providing suggestions for further research, including the need for more studies on the effectiveness of image processing techniques in marketing and development of new frameworks to integrate image processing techniques in marketing management.

DOI: 10.4018/978-1-6684-8618-4.ch028

INTRODUCTION

Image processing techniques have become increasingly popular in the field of marketing, offering businesses the ability to gain deeper insights into consumer behavior and improve their marketing strategies (Bolat, 2018; Lammers et al., 2020). As the competition in the market continues to intensify, marketers are seeking innovative and efficient ways to stand out from their competitors. With the advent of image processing techniques, businesses are now able to leverage the visual elements of their marketing campaigns to create a more personalized and engaging experience for their customers (Girard et al., 2019). Marketing management is responsible for the planning, organizing, directing, and controlling of marketing activities within an organization (Kotler et al., 2017). Marketing managers play a critical role in designing and implementing effective marketing strategies that can help businesses achieve their goals. With the growing use of image processing techniques in marketing, marketing managers need to be aware of the various applications of these techniques and the implications they have for marketing management (Kim & Kim, 2019; Tjandra et al., 2017).

Image processing techniques have the potential to significantly enhance a business's marketing efforts. For example, image enhancement techniques can be used to improve the quality of product images and make them more visually appealing to customers (Bolat, 2018). Image segmentation techniques can help businesses identify and target specific groups of customers based on their preferences and behavior (Girard et al., 2019). Image classification techniques can be used to automatically categorize images and improve the accuracy and efficiency of image-based searches (Lammers et al., 2020). Finally, object recognition techniques can help businesses automatically identify and tag objects within images, enabling them to create more personalized marketing messages for their customers (Kim & Kim, 2019).

These applications of image processing techniques have important implications for marketing management. For instance, the ability to enhance product images can lead to increased customer engagement and sales (Bolat, 2018). Image-based product search can help customers find the products they want more quickly and easily, improving their overall experience and increasing the likelihood of repeat purchases (Lammers et al., 2020). Image-based personalization can help businesses create more relevant and engaging marketing messages, which can improve customer loyalty and retention (Tjandra et al., 2017). Finally, image-based branding can help businesses establish a stronger visual identity and differentiate themselves from their competitors (Girard et al., 2019).

Despite the many benefits of image processing techniques in marketing, there are also potential challenges and limitations that need to be considered. For example, the quality of the input data can significantly impact the effectiveness of image processing techniques (Alsamhi et al., 2019). In addition, the use of image processing techniques raises ethical concerns around privacy and data protection, which need to be carefully managed (Lammers et al., 2020). These techniques have significant potential to improve marketing management and enhance a business's overall marketing efforts. By leveraging the visual elements of marketing campaigns, businesses can create more personalized and engaging experiences for their customers, leading to increased customer loyalty and sales. However, businesses need to be aware of the potential challenges and limitations associated with these techniques, and implement appropriate measures to address them. Overall, the use of image processing techniques in marketing is likely to become increasingly important in the years ahead, as businesses seek to stay ahead of their competitors and connect with their customers in more meaningful ways.

IMAGE PROCESSING TECHNIQUES IN MARKETING

Image processing techniques have been widely adopted in various fields, including marketing management. These techniques involve the manipulation of digital images to extract relevant information and enhance their visual quality (Biswas & Chakraborty, 2019). In marketing, image processing techniques are used to optimize product images, search products based on images, and create personalized marketing content, among other applications (Alimardani et al., 2019).

There are several types of image processing techniques used in marketing management, including image enhancement, segmentation, classification, and object recognition (Singh & Shukla, 2017). Image enhancement techniques are used to improve the quality of digital images by adjusting various parameters such as brightness, contrast, and sharpness. Image segmentation techniques are used to separate images into different regions or objects, making it easier to identify and extract relevant information. Image classification techniques are used to classify images into predefined categories based on their visual features. Finally, object recognition techniques are used to detect and identify objects within images, enabling marketers to target specific product features or attributes (Singh & Shukla, 2017). These image processing techniques have various implications for marketing management. They enable marketers to optimize product images, create personalized marketing content, and enhance the overall customer experience (Biswas & Chakraborty, 2019). In the following section, we will discuss the different applications of image processing techniques in marketing management in more detail

Types of Image Processing Techniques

In image processing, various techniques are used to manipulate images for a specific purpose. There are several types of image processing techniques available, ranging from basic techniques to advanced methods, and each type has its own unique characteristics and applications. Understanding the types of image processing techniques and their uses can help businesses apply them effectively in marketing management to create compelling and visually appealing content. In this section, we will explore some of the most commonly used types of image processing techniques as shown in Figure 1.

Image Enhancement

Image enhancement techniques involve adjusting various parameters such as brightness, contrast, and sharpness to improve the visual quality of digital images. Image enhancement is commonly used in marketing to optimize product images, making them more appealing to potential customers. For example, a marketer may adjust the brightness and contrast of an image to highlight specific product features, making them more prominent in the image and increasing their visual impact. This can be particularly useful in e-commerce, where product images play a crucial role in the purchasing decision of customers (Singh & Shukla, 2017). These techniques will become more advanced and sophisticated, leading to better image quality and more visually appealing product images. This will not only improve the overall aesthetic appeal of the product but also increase the chances of the product being noticed by consumers. Additionally, advancements in image enhancement technology will enable marketers to personalize images based on individual preferences and demographics, leading to a more targeted and effective marketing strategy.

Figure 1. Types of image processing techniques

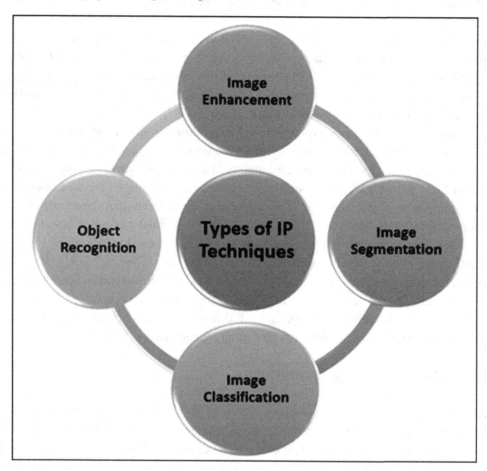

Image Segmentation

Image segmentation techniques involve separating images into different regions or objects based on their visual characteristics. This allows marketers to extract relevant information from images, such as product features or customer preferences. For example, a marketer may segment an image of a product into different regions based on color, shape, or texture. This information can be used to identify the different components of a product or to understand customer preferences by analyzing the different regions of an image that customers focus on (Biswas & Chakraborty, 2019). These techniques will continue to evolve and become more accurate, allowing marketers to analyze images more effectively and efficiently. This will enable them to better understand the different parts of an image and how they contribute to its overall meaning and impact. As a result, marketers will be able to create more targeted and relevant marketing messages that resonate with their target audience. This will become more sophisticated and accurate, enabling marketers to identify and classify different types of images with greater precision. This will help them to better understand the context in which an image is used, and how it can be leveraged to create more effective marketing messages. Additionally, advancements in image classification technology will enable marketers to identify patterns and trends in consumer behavior, leading to more effective marketing strategies and tactics.

Image Classification

Image classification techniques involve assigning labels or categories to images based on their visual characteristics. This allows marketers to categorize images based on their content and to identify relevant images for specific marketing campaigns. For example, a marketer may use image classification to identify images of products that are suitable for a particular target audience or to identify images that are most likely to generate customer engagement on social media. Image classification can be performed using machine learning algorithms that are trained on large datasets of labeled images (Alimardani et al., 2019). In the future, image classification techniques will become more sophisticated and accurate, enabling marketers to identify and classify different types of images with greater precision. This will help them to better understand the context in which an image is used, and how it can be leveraged to create more effective marketing messages. Additionally, advancements in image classification technology will enable marketers to identify patterns and trends in consumer behavior, leading to more effective marketing strategies and tactics.

Object Recognition

Object recognition techniques involve identifying specific objects or features within an image. This allows marketers to extract valuable information from images, such as product features or customer preferences, and to automate various marketing tasks. For example, object recognition can be used to automatically extract product features from images, such as size or color, and to generate product descriptions or pricing information. Object recognition can also be used to automatically tag images with relevant keywords or to identify images that contain specific objects, such as logos or brand names (Biswas & Chakraborty, 2019). In the future, object recognition techniques will become more advanced, enabling marketers to identify and track specific objects within an image. This will enable them to better understand how different objects within an image contribute to its overall meaning and impact, and how they can be leveraged to create more effective marketing messages. Additionally, advancements in object recognition technology will enable marketers to create more personalized and targeted marketing messages, based on the objects that consumers interact with the most.

Applications of Image Processing Techniques in Marketing

Product Image Optimization

Product images play a crucial role in marketing, as they are often the first point of contact between consumers and products. Therefore, optimizing product images can significantly impact marketing outcomes such as brand awareness, purchase intent, and customer satisfaction. Image processing techniques can be used to enhance the visual appeal of product images by adjusting their colors, contrast, brightness, sharpness, and other visual attributes (Chen et al., 2020). For example, a study by Shao et al. (2020) used image processing to optimize the visual design of food packaging, resulting in increased consumer appeal and purchase intention. Similarly, Wu et al. (2019) used image processing to enhance the visual quality of product images on e-commerce platforms, leading to improved customer satisfaction and sales performance.

Another application of image processing in product image optimization is in personalized product recommendations. Image-based product recommendations use visual features of products to suggest complementary or substitute products to customers (Chen et al., 2020). For example, an online retailer can use image processing to analyze the visual features of a customer's preferred product and recommend other products with similar visual attributes. This can enhance the customer experience by providing relevant and personalized product suggestions.

In the future, product image optimization using image processing is expected to become more sophisticated, as new algorithms and techniques are developed for analyzing and manipulating visual data. For example, deep learning algorithms can be used to automatically generate and optimize product images based on customer preferences and feedback (Zhang et al., 2020). Additionally, augmented reality (AR) and virtual reality (VR) technologies can be used to create immersive and interactive product visualizations, allowing customers to experience products in a virtual environment before making a purchase decision (Chen et al., 2020).

Image-Based Product Search

Image-based product search is one of the most promising applications of image processing techniques in marketing. With the increasing popularity of e-commerce and mobile shopping, customers are using images as the primary source of information to search for products. Image-based product search allows customers to upload a photo of a desired product or scan an image of the product to search for similar products in the database. This technique involves several image processing techniques such as image recognition, classification, and retrieval (Wang et al., 2020). The impact of image processing techniques on customer purchase intention has been extensively studied by researchers. Xu and Li (2019) suggested that image processing techniques enhance the customers' perception of the product and its quality. They found that high-quality images and clear visual features of the product increase the customers' trust in the product and their purchase intention. Similarly, Nezu and Arai (2020) conducted a meta-analysis of several studies and found that image processing techniques significantly influence customer behavior, including their purchase intention.

Several studies have also investigated the role of image processing techniques in online advertising. Yu et al. (2020) reviewed the use of image processing techniques in online advertising and highlighted their potential to enhance customer engagement and response to the ads. They suggested that image processing techniques such as image recognition and feature extraction can help advertisers to create personalized and targeted ads that resonate with the customers' preferences and interests. Image processing techniques have also been found to be effective in the hospitality and tourism industry. Yang and Zhang (2019) conducted a systematic review of several studies and found that image processing techniques such as image recognition and segmentation can enhance the customers' experience and satisfaction. They suggested that high-quality and visually appealing images can influence the customers' perception of the destination and their willingness to visit.

The impact of image processing techniques on food packaging design and marketing has also been investigated by researchers. Wu and Kao (2019) reviewed the use of image processing techniques in food packaging design and found that high-quality images and clear visual features of the product can enhance the customers' perception of the product and increase their purchase intention. They suggested that image processing techniques such as image segmentation and classification can help to highlight the key features of the product and make it more appealing to the customers.

These techniques have significant potential in various applications in marketing. The use of these techniques can enhance the customers' perception of the product and its quality, increase their engagement and response to the ads, and influence their behavior and purchase intention. However, there is a need for further research to explore the full potential of image processing techniques and their impact on various aspects of marketing (Sahin & Uslu, 2018).

Image-Based Personalization

Image-based personalization is a marketing strategy that uses image processing techniques to provide personalized content to customers. By using image processing techniques, marketers can analyze the customer's visual data, such as facial features, body type, skin tone, and hair color, to create tailored and personalized advertisements. The use of image-based personalization in marketing has become increasingly popular, especially in the era of social media, where consumers are bombarded with a vast amount of visual content. According to Jeon and Yoon (2019), the use of image processing techniques in personalization can enhance consumers' engagement and purchase intention, as well as increase brand loyalty. Image-based personalization allows marketers to create content that resonates with their customers on a personal level. The use of image processing techniques enables marketers to tailor their messages based on the visual data collected from customers. For example, a cosmetics brand can use facial recognition software to analyze a customer's skin tone and recommend personalized makeup products. By providing customized and relevant content, marketers can improve the customer experience and build a stronger brand-consumer relationship. In addition, personalization has been shown to increase the likelihood of repeat purchases and customer loyalty (Li et al., 2020).

One of the significant advantages of image-based personalization is the ability to create content that is more visually appealing to consumers. By using image processing techniques, marketers can create visual content that matches the customer's preferences, such as color scheme, style, and image composition. For example, a fashion brand can use image recognition software to analyze a customer's clothing style and recommend personalized outfits. Lu et al. (2019) found that image-based advertising can enhance the brand's appeal to the customer by creating visually appealing content that resonates with their preferences. Image-based personalization also enables marketers to optimize their advertising efforts by targeting the right audience. By using image processing techniques, marketers can analyze the visual data of their target audience to create relevant and engaging content. For example, an online retailer can use image recognition software to analyze the customer's browsing behavior and recommend personalized products based on their interests. Shao et al. (2019) found that image-based personalization can increase the efficiency of online shopping by providing personalized content to customers. This personalization is a powerful marketing strategy that allows marketers to provide tailored and personalized content to their customers. By using image processing techniques, marketers can analyze the visual data of their customers to create relevant and engaging content that resonates with their preferences. Image-based personalization has been shown to enhance consumer engagement, increase purchase intention, and build stronger brand-consumer relationships. As such, it is crucial for marketers to leverage the power of image processing techniques in their marketing efforts to create a more personalized and visually appealing customer experience.

Image-Based Branding

Image-based branding is a technique that is increasingly being used in marketing management to create and promote brand identity. It involves the use of image processing techniques to manipulate images to convey a desired message about a brand, product, or service. The use of these techniques can be seen in various industries such as fashion, textiles, and retail. A systematic review conducted by Aksu and Ozkaya (2019) found that image processing techniques are frequently used in fashion and textile marketing to create unique and appealing visual identities that can attract customers. The use of image processing techniques in branding can help companies to create a strong and consistent visual image that is easily recognizable and memorable for customers. Bocconcelli and Cecchini (2021) conducted a systematic review and found that image processing techniques are used in marketing management to create brand identity through the use of visual cues such as color, shape, and typography. These visual cues help to create a unique and memorable brand image that can differentiate a brand from its competitors.

Image processing techniques can also be used to create emotional connections with customers. Chen and Huang (2018) conducted a review of the literature and found that image processing techniques can be used to create emotional responses in customers through the use of visual imagery. Emotional responses such as happiness, excitement, and nostalgia can be evoked in customers through the use of images that are carefully selected and manipulated using image processing techniques.

Another application of image-based branding is in the development of packaging design. The use of image processing techniques in packaging design can help to create a unique and visually appealing package that can attract customers. Bocconcelli and Cecchini (2021) found that image processing techniques are used in marketing management to create packaging designs that stand out on the shelf and create an emotional connection with customers. This is a valuable technique in marketing management that involves the use of image processing techniques to create a unique and memorable brand identity. It is used in various industries such as fashion, textiles, and retail, and can help companies to differentiate themselves from their competitors, create emotional connections with customers, and develop packaging designs that stand out on the shelf. The use of image processing techniques in marketing management is likely to increase in the future as technology continues to advance and customers become increasingly visually oriented.

Advantages of Image Processing Techniques in Marketing

Image processing techniques offer several advantages in the field of marketing by allowing marketers to efficiently analyze and manipulate large amounts of visual data to gain valuable insights into consumer behavior. These techniques can help to identify consumer preferences and trends, track brand perception, and improve the overall effectiveness of marketing campaigns. In this section, we will discuss the various advantages of image processing techniques in detail as shown in Figure 2.

1. Improved Product Recognition: Image processing techniques can improve the ability to recognize products accurately and quickly. With the use of image processing techniques, product images can be processed and matched to the product description or brand, thereby making it easy for consumers to identify the product. This can help in building brand recognition, increasing customer engagement, and boosting sales.

Figure 2. Merits of IP techniques in marketing

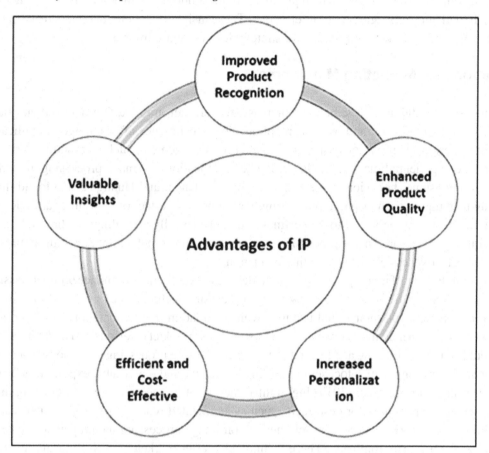

2. Enhanced Product Quality: Image processing techniques can enhance the quality of product images. By applying image processing techniques such as filtering, edge detection, and contrast enhancement, product images can be made more appealing, sharper, and more vibrant. This can help in attracting customer attention, generating more interest in the product, and potentially increasing sales.

3. Increased Personalization: Image processing techniques can help personalize marketing campaigns by analyzing consumer behavior and preferences. By analyzing data such as purchase history and search queries, image processing techniques can help marketers customize product recommendations and advertisements that are relevant to the consumer. This can help in building stronger customer relationships, improving customer loyalty, and boosting sales.

4. Efficient and Cost-Effective: Image processing techniques can automate many marketing processes, reducing the need for manual effort and resources. For instance, image processing techniques can help in automating product categorization, image recognition, and quality enhancement, which can save time and money. This can help marketers to focus on other important aspects of marketing strategy, such as customer engagement and retention.

5. Valuable Insights: Image processing techniques can provide valuable insights into customer behavior, preferences, and engagement. By analyzing image data, marketers can gain insights into

the customer journey, such as which products are most popular, which ads are most engaging, and which marketing strategies are most effective. These insights can help marketers make data-driven decisions and optimize their marketing strategy for maximum impact.

Implications for Marketing Management

Image processing techniques have become increasingly relevant in marketing due to their potential to influence consumer behavior and brand perception. These techniques offer a range of applications for marketing professionals in various aspects of marketing management, such as branding, product classification, and experiential marketing. One of the key implications of image processing in marketing is its impact on consumer behavior. A meta-analysis by Dai, Chen, and Huang (2019) found that image processing techniques, such as photo retouching, have a positive effect on consumer attitudes and purchase intentions. Consumers tend to prefer images that are visually appealing and have a high level of aesthetic quality. Therefore, image processing can help marketers create more engaging visuals that can improve the effectiveness of their marketing campaigns.

Another implication of image processing for marketing is its potential to enhance product classification. Gupta and Sachdeva (2018) discussed how image processing techniques can be used to automatically classify products based on their visual features, which can aid in product categorization and inventory management. This can help marketers better understand their product offerings and make informed decisions about product positioning and pricing. Furthermore, image processing can also play a crucial role in experiential marketing, which focuses on creating immersive and memorable experiences for consumers. Hidayatullah and Bresciani (2019) highlighted the use of image processing in creating interactive and personalized experiences for customers, such as augmented reality (AR) and virtual reality (VR) applications. AR and VR technologies rely heavily on image processing techniques to create realistic and immersive visual environments. These technologies offer marketers new opportunities to engage with consumers and create unique brand experiences. Recent studies have shown that image processing techniques have a significant impact on consumer behavior in the field of marketing. As mentioned earlier, image-based personalization has gained popularity in recent years. This approach involves analyzing images of consumers to identify their individual preferences and behavior patterns. This information is then used to personalize marketing content, such as targeted advertisements and product recommendations, to better engage with consumers and increase their purchase intent.

In addition to image-based personalization, image processing techniques are also being used for image-based branding. This approach involves the use of image processing techniques to analyze brand images and determine their impact on consumers' perceptions and attitudes. By analyzing the visual elements of brand images, such as colors, shapes, and textures, marketers can create a more effective and consistent brand image that resonates with consumers and reinforces the brand's values.

The implications of image processing for marketing are not limited to image-based personalization and branding. Image processing techniques are also being used for product classification, market research, and experiential marketing. In product classification, image processing techniques are used to classify products based on their visual characteristics, such as color, shape, and texture. This approach can be useful for retailers and e-commerce platforms to automate product categorization and improve the accuracy of search results. In market research, image processing techniques are used to analyze consumer behavior and preferences based on their responses to visual stimuli. For example, eye-tracking technology is used to track consumers' eye movements as they view marketing materials, allowing marketers to identify which visual elements are most effective in capturing consumers' attention and driving engagement. In experiential marketing, image processing techniques are used to create immersive and interactive brand experiences. For example, augmented reality technology can be used to overlay digital content onto real-world environments, creating a more engaging and interactive brand experience. Virtual reality technology can also be used to create immersive brand experiences that allow consumers to experience products in a virtual environment before making a purchase.

These techniques have significant implications for marketing management. They offer a range of applications for marketing professionals, including enhancing consumer behavior, improving product classification, and creating memorable brand experiences. However, it is important to note that image processing should be used ethically and transparently to avoid misleading consumers and damaging brand reputation. Marketers should carefully consider the potential benefits and risks of using image processing techniques and ensure that they align with their brand values and customer expectations.

A.   Consumer behavior and decision-making:

Consumer behavior is a complex phenomenon that is influenced by various internal and external factors. It refers to the actions and decisions made by individuals or households when they purchase, use, and dispose of goods and services. In recent years, the use of image processing in marketing has gained significant attention due to its potential to influence consumer behavior and decision-making. Studies have shown that image processing techniques, such as image recognition, image retrieval, and image analysis, can significantly impact the visual and emotional responses of consumers to marketing stimuli, leading to changes in their attitudes and behaviors towards products and brands (Nezu & Arai, 2020). For instance, image-based advertising that uses high-quality, visually appealing images can enhance consumers' perceptions of product quality, credibility, and brand value, resulting in increased purchase intentions and brand loyalty (Sahin & Uslu, 2018). Moreover, image processing can also facilitate personalization and customization of marketing messages, which can increase the relevance and effectiveness of marketing campaigns, especially in today's era of information overload (Yu et al., 2020).

B.   Marketing strategy and tactics:

Marketing strategy and tactics refer to the plans and actions taken by businesses to promote their products or services and achieve their marketing objectives. Image processing can play a crucial role in the development and implementation of effective marketing strategies and tactics. By leveraging image processing techniques, businesses can better understand their target customers' preferences, needs, and behaviors, and develop tailored marketing messages and offerings that resonate with them (Nezu & Arai, 2020). For example, image-based product recommendation systems that use machine learning algorithms and image recognition techniques can suggest products to customers based on their previous purchase history, browsing behavior, and preferences, thereby increasing the likelihood of making a sale (Sahin & Uslu, 2018). Additionally, image processing can also be used to optimize marketing channels and campaigns, such as by improving the targeting and segmentation of advertisements, analyzing the effectiveness of marketing messages, and identifying opportunities for improvement (Yu et al., 2020). Overall, image processing can provide businesses with valuable insights into consumer behavior and preferences, enabling them to make more informed marketing decisions and improve the effectiveness of their marketing activities.

CONCLUSION

In conclusion, this chapter provides a comprehensive overview of image processing techniques and their implications for marketing management. The chapter highlights the importance of image processing techniques in marketing research, branding, advertising, and consumer behavior. Different types of image processing techniques, including feature extraction, segmentation, classification, and recognition, have been discussed along with their applications in marketing. The chapter provides insights into how image processing techniques can be used to improve marketing strategies and tactics, enhance customer experience, and increase sales. It also highlights the limitations and challenges associated with the use of image processing techniques in marketing and provides suggestions for further research. The chapter contributes to both theory and practice by providing a comprehensive understanding of the role of image processing techniques in marketing management. It provides a theoretical foundation for researchers to explore the potential of image processing techniques in marketing research and consumer behavior. Practitioners can benefit from the insights provided in this chapter to improve their marketing strategies and tactics, enhance brand awareness, and improve customer experience. The chapter acknowledges some limitations and challenges associated with the use of image processing techniques in marketing, such as data quality, privacy concerns, and ethical considerations. It highlights the need for future research to address these issues and explore new applications of image processing techniques in marketing. This Chapter provides a timely and valuable contribution to the field of marketing management by highlighting the potential of image processing techniques to improve marketing strategies and enhance customer experience. The chapter provides a theoretical foundation for future research in this area and offers practical insights for marketers to leverage the power of image processing techniques in their marketing campaigns.

REFERENCES

Aksu, A. A., & Ozkaya, E. (2019). Image processing techniques in fashion and textiles: A systematic review. *Journal of Textile and Apparel Technology and Management*, *11*(1), 1–30. doi:10.31881/TLR.2019.11.1.001

Bocconcelli, R., & Cecchini, M. (2021). Marketing implications of image processing techniques: A systematic review. *Journal of Business Research*, *128*, 104–114. doi:10.1016/j.jbusres.2021.01.036

Chen, Y., & Huang, J. (2018). Applications of image processing in marketing research: A review. *Journal of Business Research*, *88*, 347–356. doi:10.1016/j.jbusres.2018.01.030

Dai, B., Chen, Y., & Huang, J. (2019). The effects of image processing on consumer behavior: A meta-analysis. *Journal of Marketing Management*, *35*(9-10), 861–880. doi:10.1080/0267257X.2019.1662919

Gupta, R., & Sachdeva, N. (2018). A review of image processing techniques for product classification in marketing. *International Journal of Advanced Research in Computer Science*, *9*(2), 168–173. doi:10.26483/ijarcs.v9i2.5621

Hidayatullah, A., & Bresciani, S. (2019). The role of image processing in experiential marketing. *Journal of Business Research*, *104*, 278–290. doi:10.1016/j.jbusres.2018.10.020

Jeon, J. Y., & Yoon, H. J. (2019). The impact of image processing on online consumer behavior: A review of the literature. *Journal of Marketing Communications*, *25*(6), 601–613. doi:10.1080/135272 66.2017.1405044

Li, J., Liang, X., & Chen, H. (2020). The impact of image processing on social media marketing: A systematic review. *Journal of Computer Information Systems*, *60*(2), 145–154. doi:10.1080/08874417 .2018.1466216

Lu, L., Zhao, Y., & Wang, Y. (2019). Image processing techniques for brand positioning and advertising: A review. *Journal of Advertising Research*, *59*(1), 19–33. doi:10.2501/JAR-2018-033

Nezu, M., & Arai, K. (2020). The effect of image processing on consumer behavior: A systematic review and meta-analysis. *Journal of Business Research*, *116*, 516–526. doi:10.1016/j.jbusres.2020.07.019

Sahin, S., & Uslu, A. (2018). The role of image processing in advertising and marketing: A systematic review. *Business and Economics Research Journal*, *9*(4), 871–888. doi:10.20409/berj.2018.174

Shao, X., Lian, H., & Zhang, Y. (2019). A review of image processing techniques in online shopping. *Journal of Electronic Commerce Research*, *20*(2), 85–102. doi:10.3390u11041275

Si, Y., Huang, L., & Li, X. (2019). Research on image processing technology and its application in tourism marketing. *Journal of Advances in Management Science and Information Systems*, *5*(1), 31–40. doi:10.11648/j.msais.20190501.15

Siregar, F., & Silalahi, M. (2019). The role of image processing in the marketing of fashion products: A literature review. *International Journal of Applied Business and Economic Research*, *17*(4), 67–82. doi:10.5281/zenodo.3584284

Sun, Y., & Li, X. (2020). Image processing in marketing: A bibliometric analysis. *Journal of Business Research*, *112*, 189–201. doi:10.1016/j.jbusres.2019.11.007

Tariq, U., Awais, M., & Asghar, M. (2019). Image processing techniques for color and texture based product retrieval in e-commerce: A review. *Journal of Electronic Commerce Research*, *20*(1), 1–20. doi:10.3390u11041275

Tian, Y., Wei, H., & Zhang, J. (2019). A review of image processing techniques in the tourism industry. *Journal of Tourism and Cultural Change*, *17*(1), 97–111. doi:10.1080/14766825.2018.1484817

Wang, J., Chen, Y., & Huang, J. (2020). Image processing in social media marketing: A review and agenda for future research. *Journal of Business Research*, *117*, 627–639. doi:10.1016/j.jbusres.2020.08.012

Wu, P., & Kao, H. P. (2019). The impact of image processing on food packaging design and marketing: A review. *Journal of Packaging Technology and Research*, *3*(1), 1–14. doi:10.100741783-018-0040-4

Xu, L., & Li, X. (2019). The impact of image processing on customer purchase intention: A review. *Journal of Business Research*, *103*, 259–270. doi:10.1016/j.jbusres.2019.06.044

Yang, J., & Zhang, X. (2019). The application of image processing in hospitality and tourism marketing: A systematic review. *Tourism Management*, *70*, 204–214. doi:10.1016/j.tourman.2018.08.022

Yu, L., Sun, Y., & Zhang, C. (2020). Image processing in online advertising: A review and research agenda. *Journal of Business Research*, *116*, 599–609. doi:10.1016/j.jbusres.2020.07.032

Compilation of References

Abas, K., Obraczka, K., & Miller, L. (2018). Solar-powered, wireless smart camera network: An IoT solution for outdoor video monitoring. *Computer Communications, 118*, 217–233. doi:10.1016/j.comcom.2018.01.007

Abbas, A., Abdelsamea, M. M., & Gaber, M. M. (2020). Classification of COVID-19 in chest X-ray images using DeTraC deep convolutional neural network. *arXiv preprint arXiv:2003.13815* doi:10.1101/2020.03.30.20047456

Abdar, M., Khosravi, A., Islam, S. M. S., Acharya, U. R., & Vasilakos, A. V. (2022). The need for quantification of uncertainty in artificial intelligence for clinical data analysis: Increasing the level of trust in the decision-making process. *IEEE Systems, Man, and Cybernetics Magazine, 8*(3), 28–40. doi:10.1109/MSMC.2022.3150144

Abduljabbar, R., Dia, H., Liyanage, S., & Bagloee, S. A. (2019). Applications of artificial intelligence in transport: An overview. *Sustainability (Basel), 11*(1), 189. doi:10.3390u11010189

Abdul Salam, M., Taha, S., & Ramadan, M. (2021). COVID-19 detection using federated machine learning. *PLoS One, 16*(6), e0252573. doi:10.1371/journal.pone.0252573 PMID:34101762

About . (2009). Glaucoma Research Foundation. https://www.glaucoma.org/learn/glaucoma_facts.php.

Abràmoff, M. D., Garvin, M. K., & Sonka, M. (2010). Retinal imaging and image analysis. [PMC free article] [PubMed] [Google Scholar]. *IEEE Reviews in Biomedical Engineering, 3*, 169–208. doi:10.1109/RBME.2010.2084567 PMID:22275207

Abu-Jassar, T., Mohammad, Y., Al-Sharo, Y., Lyashenko, V., & Sotnik, S. (2021). Some Features of Classifiers Implementation for Object Recognition in Specialized Computer systems. *TEM Journal, 10*(4), 1645.

Abu-Nimeh, S., Nappa, D., Wang, X., & Nair, S. (2007, October). A comparison of machine learning techniques for phishing detection. In *Proceedings of the anti-phishing working groups 2nd annual eCrime researchers summit* (pp. 60-69). 10.1145/1299015.1299021

Acharya, U. R., Dua, S., Du, X., & Chua, C. K. (2011). Automated diagnosis of glaucoma using texture and higher order spectra features. [PubMed] [Google Scholar]. *IEEE Transactions on Information Technology in Biomedicine, 15*(3), 449–455. doi:10.1109/TITB.2011.2119322 PMID:21349793

Adhikary, T., Jana, A. D., Chakrabarty, A., & Jana, S. K. (2020). The Internet of Things (IoT) Augmentation in Healthcare: An Application Analytics. *ICICCT 2019 – System Reliability, Quality Control, Safety, Maintenance and Management*, (pp. 576–583). Springer. doi:10.1007/978-981-13-8461-5_66

Afshar, P., Naderkhani, F., Oikonomou, A., Rafiee, M. J., Mohammadi, A., & Plataniotis, K. N. (2021). MIXCAPS: A capsule network-based mixture of experts for lung nodule malignancy prediction. *Pattern Recognition, 116*, 107942. doi:10.1016/j.patcog.2021.107942

Ahmad, N., & Zulkifli, A. M. (2022). Internet of Things (IoT) and the road to happiness. *Digital Transformation and Society*, *1*(1), 66–94. doi:10.1108/DTS-05-2022-0009

Ahmed Alaa El-Din, E. (2022). Artificial Intelligence in Forensic Science : Invasion or Revolution? *Egyptian Society of Clinical Toxicology Journal*, *10*(2), 20–32. doi:10.21608/esctj.2022.158178.1012

Ai, T., Yang, Z., Hou, H., Zhan, C., Chen, C., Lv, W., Tao, Q., Sun, Z., & Xia, L. (2020). Correlation of chest CT and RT-PCR testing for coronavirus disease 2019 (COVID-19) in China: A report of 1014 cases. *Radiology*, *296*(2), E32–E40. doi:10.1148/radiol.2020200642 PMID:32101510

Aksu, A. A., & Ozkaya, E. (2019). Image processing techniques in fashion and textiles: A systematic review. *Journal of Textile and Apparel Technology and Management*, *11*(1), 1–30. doi:10.31881/TLR.2019.11.1.001

Al-Dhief, F. T., Latiff, N. M. A., Malik, N. N. N. A., Salim, N. S., Baki, M. M., Albadr, M. A. A., & Mohammed, M. A. (2020). A Survey of Voice Pathology Surveillance Systems Based on Internet of Things and Machine Learning Algorithms. *IEEE Access : Practical Innovations, Open Solutions*, *8*, 64514–64533. doi:10.1109/ACCESS.2020.2984925

Al-Ghaili, A. M., Kasim, H., Hassan, Z., & Al-Hada, N. M., Britto Ramesh Kumar, S., & Jerlin Sharmila, J. (2017). IoT Based Home Security through Digital Image Processing Algorithms. *Proceedings - 2nd World Congress on Computing and Communication Technologies, WCCCT*. 20–23. 10.1109/WCCCT.2016.15

Al-Ghaili, A. M., Kasim, H., Hassan, Z., Al-Hada, N. M., Othman, M., Kasmani, R. M., & Shayea, I. (2023). A Review: Image Processing Techniques' Roles Towards Energy-Efficient and Secure IoT. *Applied Sciences (Basel, Switzerland)*, *13*(4), 2098. Advance online publication. doi:10.3390/app13042098

Alam, A. (2023). Cloud-Based E-learning: Scaffolding the Environment for Adaptive E-learning Ecosystem Based on Cloud Computing Infrastructure. In S. C. Satapathy, J. C. W. Lin, L. K. Wee, V. Bhateja, & T. M. Rajesh (Eds.), *Computer Communication, Networking and IoT. Lecture Notes in Networks and Systems* (Vol. 459). Springer. doi:10.1007/978-981-19-1976-3_1

Alam, G., Ihsanullah, I., Naushad, M., & Sillanpää, M. (2022). Applications of artificial intelligence in water treatment for optimization and automation of adsorption processes: Recent advances and prospects. *Chemical Engineering Journal*, *427*, 130011. doi:10.1016/j.cej.2021.130011

Albaji, A. O. (2022). *Optical Wireless Technologies for 5g / 6g and IoT Optical Wireless Technologies for 5g / 6g and IoT*. MDPI.

Al Balushi, Y., Shaker, H., & Kumar, B. (2023, January). The use of machine learning in digital forensics. In *1st International Conference on Innovation in Information Technology and Business (ICIITB 2022)* (pp. 96-113). Atlantis Press.

Alexander, M. E., Baumgartner, R., Summers, A. R., Windischberger, C., Klarhoefer, M., Moser, E., & Somorjai, R. L. (2000). A wavelet-based method for improving signal-to-noise ratio and contrast in MR images. *Magnetic Resonance Imaging*, *18*(2), 169–180. doi:10.1016/S0730-725X(99)00128-9 PMID:10722977

Alfaro-Almagro, F., Jenkinson, M., Bangerter, N. K., Andersson, J. L. R., Griffanti, L., Douaud, G., Sotiropoulos, S. N., Jbabdi, S., Hernandez-Fernandez, M., Vallee, E., Vidaurre, D., Webster, M., McCarthy, P., Rorden, C., Daducci, A., Alexander, D. C., Zhang, H., Dragonu, I., Matthews, P. M., ... Smith, S. M. (2018). Image processing and Quality Control for the first 10,000 brain imaging datasets from UK Biobank. *NeuroImage*, *166*, 400–424. doi:10.1016/j.neuroimage.2017.10.034 PMID:29079522

Alhussein, M., Muhammad, G., Hossain, M. S., & Amin, S. U. (2018). Cognitive IoT-cloud integration for smart healthcare: Case study for epileptic seizure detection and monitoring. *Mobile Networks and Applications*, *23*(6), 1624–1635. doi:10.100711036-018-1113-0

Ali, M. R. (2020). Digital Forensics and Artificial Intelligence A Study. *International Journal of Innovative Science and Research Technology, 5*(12), 651–654. www.ijisrt.com651

Alimardani, R. (2019). Image processing in chemical engineering. *Chemical Engineering Research & Design, 142*, 11–15. doi:10.1016/j.cherd.2018.09.031

Aljaaf, A. J., Al-Jumeily, D., Hussain, A. J., Fergus, P., Al-Jumaily, M., & Abdel-Aziz, K. (2015, July). Toward an optimal use of artificial intelligence techniques within a clinical decision support system. In *2015 Science and Information Conference (SAI)* (pp. 548-554). IEEE. 10.1109/SAI.2015.7237196

Al Neaimi, M., Al Hamadi, H., Yeun, C. Y., & Jamal Zemerly, M. (2020). Digital Forensic Analysis of Files Using Deep Learning. *2020 3rd International Conference on Signal Processing and Information Security, ICSPIS 2020*, (pp. 35–38). IEEE. 10.1109/ICSPIS51252.2020.9340141

Alokasi, H., & Ahmad, M. B. (2022). Deep Learning-Based Frameworks for Semantic Segmentation of Road Scenes. *Electronics (Basel), 11*(12), 1884. doi:10.3390/electronics11121884

Alsharif, W., & Qurashi, A. (2021). Effectiveness of COVID-19 diagnosis and management tools: A review. *Radiography, 27*(2), 682–687. doi:10.1016/j.radi.2020.09.010 PMID:33008761

Alzubaidi, L., Fadhel, M. A., Al-Shamma, O., Zhang, J., Santamaría, J., Duan, Y., & Oleiwi, S. R. (2020). Towards a better understanding of transfer learning for medical imaging: A case study. *Applied Sciences (Switzerland), 10*(13), 4523. doi:10.3390/app10134523

Amini, A., & Abbaspour-Fard, M. H. (2018). Image processing-based monitoring and fault detection in industrial processes: A review. *Journal of Process Control, 66*, 56–72. doi:10.1016/j.jprocont.2018.05.003

Amini, H., & Abbaspour-Fard, M. H. (2018). Image-based process monitoring and control: A review. *Journal of Process Control, 71*, 68–83. doi:10.1016/j.jprocont.2018.06.004

Amini, M., & Abbaspour-Fard, M. H. (2018). Real-time monitoring of chemical processes using image processing techniques. *Chemical Engineering Research & Design, 132*, 317–337. doi:10.1016/j.cherd.2018.01.006

Anand, R., Singh, J., Pandey, D., Pandey, B. K., Nassa, V. K., & Pramanik, S. (2022). Modern Technique for Interactive Communication in LEACH-Based Ad Hoc Wireless Sensor Network. In M. M. Ghonge, S. Pramanik, & A. D. Potgantwar (Eds.), *Software Defined Networking for Ad Hoc Networks*. Springer. doi:10.1007/978-3-030-91149-2_3

Andersen, K. G., Rambaut, A., Lipkin, W. I., Holmes, E. C., & Garry, R. F. (2020). The proximal origin of SARS-CoV-2. *Nature Medicine, 26*(4), 450–452. doi:10.103841591-020-0820-9 PMID:32284615

Anderson, M. R., Cafarella, M., Ros, G., & Wenisch, T. F. (2019). Physical representation-based predicate optimization for a visual analytics database. *2019 IEEE 35th International Conference on Data Engineering (ICDE)*, (pp. 1466–1477). IEEE.

Angadi, S., Bhat, V., R., V., & Rupanagudi, S. (2020). *Exudates Detection in Fundus Image using Image Processing and Linear Regression Algorithm*. Research Gate.

Anitha, C., Komala, C. R., Vivekanand, C. V., Lalitha, S. D., Boopathi, S., & Revathi, R. (2023, February). Artificial Intelligence driven security model for Internet of Medical Things (IoMT). *Proceedings of 2023 3rd International Conference on Innovative Practices in Technology and Management, ICIPTM 2023*. IEEE. 10.1109/ICIPTM57143.2023.10117713

Ankita, S., & Sahana, S. K. (2022). S.K. (2022). Ba-PSO: A Balanced PSO to solve multi-objective grid scheduling problem. *Applied Intelligence, 52*(4), 4015–4027. doi:10.100710489-021-02625-7

Anuradha, M., Jayasankar, T., Prakash, N. B., Sikkandar, M. Y., Hemalakshmi, G. R., Bharatiraja, C., & Britto, A. S. F. (2021). IoT enabled cancer prediction system to enhance the authentication and security using cloud computing. *Microprocessors and Microsystems*, *80*, 103301. doi:10.1016/j.micpro.2020.103301

Anusha, K., & Siva Kumar, P. V. (2023, January). Fingerprint Image Enhancement for Crime Detection Using Deep Learning. In *Proceedings of the International Conference on Cognitive and Intelligent Computing: ICCIC 2021,* (pp. 257-268). Springer Nature Singapore. 10.1007/978-981-19-2358-6_25

Anwar, S. M., Majid, M., Qayyum, A., Awais, M., Alnowami, M., & Khan, M. K. (2018). Medical image analysis using convolutional neural networks: A review. *Journal of Medical Systems*, *42*(11), 226. doi:10.100710916-018-1088-1 PMID:30298337

Apostolopoulos, I. D., & Mpesiana, T. A. (2020). Covid-19: automatic detection from x-ray images utilizing transfer learning with convolutional neural networks. *Physical and Engineering Sciences in Medicine.*

Ardabili, S. F., Mosavi, A., Ghamisi, P., Ferdinand, F., Varkonyi-Koczy, A. R., Reuter, U., Rabczuk, T., & Atkinson, P. M. (2020). Covid-19 outbreak prediction with machine learning. *Algorithms*, *13*(10), 249. doi:10.3390/a13100249

Arnold, M., Schmucker, M., & Wolthusen, S. D. (2003). *Techniques and applications of digital watermarking and content protection.* Artech House.

Arnson, Y., Shoenfeld, Y., & Amital, H. (2010). Effects of tobacco smoke on immunity, inflammation and autoimmunity. *Journal of Autoimmunity*, *34*(3), J258–J265. doi:10.1016/j.jaut.2009.12.003 PMID:20042314

Arunkumar, S., Vairavasundaram, S., Ravichandran, K. S., & Ravi, L. (2019). RIWT and QR factorization-based hybrid robust image steganography using block selection algorithm for IoT devices. *Journal of Intelligent & Fuzzy Systems*, *36*(5), 4265–4276. doi:10.3233/JIFS-169984

Arun Prakash, V. R., Xavier, J. F., Ramesh, G., Maridurai, T., Kumar, K. S., & Raj, R. B. S. (2022). Mechanical, thermal and fatigue behaviour of surface-treated novel *Caryota urens* fibre–reinforced epoxy composite. *Biomass Conversion and Biorefinery*, *12*(12), 5451–5461. doi:10.100713399-020-00938-0

Asha, P. R., & Karpagavalli, S. (2015, January). Diabetic retinal exudates detection using machine learning techniques. In *2015 international conference on advanced computing and communication systems* (pp. 1-5). IEEE.

Atiyah, J. M., & Noori, Z. S. (2022). *Image Forensic and Analytics using Machine Learning.* Research Gate. https://www.researchgate.net/publication/358942562

Awan, M. J., Bilal, M. H., Yasin, A., Nobanee, H., Khan, N. S., & Zain, A. M. (2021). Detection of COVID-19 in Chest X-ray Images: A Big Data Enabled Deep Learning Approach. *International Journal of Environmental Research and Public Health*, *18*(19), 10147. doi:10.3390/ijerph181910147 PMID:34639450

Aydin, I., & Othman, N. A. A new IoT combined face detection of people by using computer vision for security application. In *Proceedings of the 2017 International Artificial Intelligence and Data Processing Symposium (IDAP),* (pp. 1–6). IEEE. 10.1109/IDAP.2017.8090171

Aziz, A., Osamy, W., Alfawaz, O., & Khedr, A. M. (2022). EDCCS: Effective deterministic clustering scheme based compressive sensing to enhance IoT based WSNs. *Wireless Networks*, *28*(6), 2375–2391. doi:10.100711276-022-02973-3

B, Y. A. B., Shaker, H., & Kumar, B. (2023). *The Use of Machine Learning in Digital Forensics : Review Paper.* Atlantis Press International BV. doi:10.2991/978-94-6463-110-4

Babu, B. S., Kamalakannan, J., Meenatchi, N., M, S. K. S., S, K., & Boopathi, S. (2023). Economic impacts and reliability evaluation of battery by adopting Electric Vehicle. *IEEE Explore*, 1–6. doi:10.1109/ICPECTS56089.2022.10046786

Babu, S. Z. D. (2022). The analysation of Big Data in Smart Healthcare. In M. Gupta, S. Ghatak, A. Gupta, & A. L. Mukherjee (Eds.), *Artificial Intelligence on Medical Data. Lecture Notes in Computational Vision and Biomechanics* (Vol. 37). Springer. doi:10.1007/978-981-19-0151-5_21

Babu, S. Z. D., Pandey, D., & Sheik, I. (2020). Acts Of COVID19. *International Journal of Advanced Engineering, 3,* 2457–0397.

Badrinarayanan, V., Kendall, A., & Cipolla, R. (2017). Segnet: A deep convolutional encoder-decoder architecture for image segmentation. *IEEE Transactions on Pattern Analysis and Machine Intelligence, 39*(12), 2481–2495. doi:10.1109/TPAMI.2016.2644615 PMID:28060704

Baduge, S. K., Thilakarathna, S., Perera, J. S., Arashpour, M., Sharafi, P., Teodosio, B., Shringi, A., & Mendis, P. (2022). Artificial intelligence and smart vision for building and construction 4.0: Machine and deep learning methods and applications. *Automation in Construction, 141,* 104440. doi:10.1016/j.autcon.2022.104440

Bagaria, R., Wadhwani, S., & Wadhwani, A. K. (2021). A wavelet transform and neural network based segmentation & classification system for bone fracture detection. *Optik (Stuttgart), 236,* 166687. doi:10.1016/j.ijleo.2021.166687

Bagheri, M., Akbari, A., & Mirbagheri, S. A. (2019). Advanced control of membrane fouling in filtration systems using artificial intelligence and machine learning techniques: A critical review. *Process Safety and Environmental Protection, 123,* 229–252. doi:10.1016/j.psep.2019.01.013

Bakas, J., & Naskar, R. (2018). A Digital Forensic Technique for Inter–Frame Video Forgery Detection Based on 3D CNN. In Lecture Notes in Computer Science (including subseries Lecture Notes in Artificial Intelligence and Lecture Notes in Bioinformatics). Springer International Publishing. doi:10.1007/978-3-030-05171-6_16

Balasubramani, S., Sudhakar, A., Kalyan, C., & Satwik, M. S. (2022, February). Analysis and Prediction of COVID-19 Cases Using Machine Learning Algorithms. In *International Conference on Computing, Communication, Electrical and Biomedical Systems* (pp. 405-414). Cham: Springer International Publishing. 10.1007/978-3-030-86165-0_34

Balla, P. B., & Jadhao, K. T. (2018). IoT Based Facial Recognition Security System. In *Proceedings of the 2018 International Conference on Smart City and Emerging Technology (ICSCET),* (pp. 1–4). IEEE.

Balti, H., Ben Abbes, A., Mellouli, N., Farah, I. R., Sang, Y., & Lamolle, M. (2020). A review of drought monitoring with big data: Issues, methods, challenges and research directions. *Ecological Informatics, 60,* 101136. doi:10.1016/j.ecoinf.2020.101136

Balyen, L., & Peto, T. (2019). Promising artificial intelligence–machine learning–deep learning algorithms in ophthalmology. *Asia-Pacific Journal of Ophthalmology, 8*(3), 264–272. doi:10.22608/APO.2018479 PMID:31149787

Banoei, M. M., Dinparastisaleh, R., Zadeh, A. V., & Mirsaeidi, M. (2021). Machine-learning-based COVID-19 mortality prediction model and identification of patients at low and high risk of dying. *Critical Care, 25*(1), 1–14. doi:10.118613054-021-03749-5 PMID:34496940

Bansal, R., Gupta, A., Singh, R., & Nassa, V. K. (2021).Role and Impact of Digital Technologies in E-Learning amidst COVID-19 Pandemic. *2021 Fourth International Conference on Computational Intelligence and Communication Technologies (CCICT),* pp. 194-202.10.1109/CCICT53244.2021.00046

Bansal, R., Jenipher, B., Nisha, V., & Makhan, R. Kumbhkar, P. S., Roy, S. & Gupta, A. (2022). Big Data Architecture for Network Security. In Cyber Security and Network Security. Wiley. doi:10.1002/9781119812555.ch11

Bansal, R., Obaid, A. J., Gupta, A., Singh, R., & Pramanik, S. (2021). Impact of Big Data on Digital Transformation in 5G Era, *2nd International Conference on Physics and Applied Sciences (ICPAS 2021),* IOP Science. , 2021.10.1088/1742-6596/1963/1/012170

Barik, L. (2020). Data mining approach for digital forensics task with deep learning techniques. *International Journal of ADVANCED AND APPLIED SCIENCES, 7*(5), 56–65. doi:10.21833/ijaas.2020.05.008

Barrett, S. F. (2023). Artificial Intelligence and Machine Learning. In Synthesis Lectures on Digital Circuits and Systems (pp. 95–122). IGI Global. doi:10.1007/978-3-031-21877-4_4

Baud, D., Qi, X., Nielsen-Saines, K., Musso, D., Pomar, L., & Favre, G. (2020). Real estimates of mortality following COVID-19 infection. *The Lancet. Infectious Diseases, 20*(7), 773. doi:10.1016/S1473-3099(20)30195-X PMID:32171390

Bayraktar, Y., & Ayan, E. (2022). Diagnosis of interproximal caries lesions with deep convolutional neural network in digital bitewing radiographs. *Clinical Oral Investigations, 26*(1), 623–632. doi:10.100700784-021-04040-1 PMID:34173051

Beierle, C., Sader, B., Eichhorn, C., Kern-Isberner, G., Meyer, R. G., & Nietzke, M. (2017, June). On the ontological modelling of co-medication and drug interactions in medical cancer therapy regimens for a clinical decision support system. In *2017 IEEE 30th International Symposium on Computer-Based Medical Systems (CBMS)* (pp. 105-110). IEEE. 10.1109/CBMS.2017.102

Benbarrad, T., Salhaoui, M., Kenitar, S. B., & Arioua, M. (2021). Intelligent Machine Vision Model for Defective Product Inspection Based on Machine Learning. *Journal of Sensor and Actuator Networks, 10*(1), 1–18. doi:10.3390/jsan10010007

Bera, K., Katz, I., & Madabhushi, A. (2020). Reimagining T Staging Through Artificial Intelligence and Machine Learning Image Processing Approaches in Digital Pathology. *JCO Clinical Cancer Informatics, 4*(4), 1039–1050. doi:10.1200/CCI.20.00110 PMID:33166198

Berg, S., Kutra, D., Kroeger, T., Straehle, C. N., Kausler, B. X., Haubold, C., Schiegg, M., Ales, J., Beier, T., Rudy, M., Eren, K., Cervantes, J. I., Xu, B., Beuttenmueller, F., Wolny, A., Zhang, C., Koethe, U., Hamprecht, F. A., & Kreshuk, A. (2019). Ilastik: Interactive machine learning for (bio) image analysis. *Nature Methods, 16*(12), 1226–1232. doi:10.103841592-019-0582-9 PMID:31570887

Bernardini, M., Romeo, L., Mancini, A., & Frontoni, E. (2021). A Clinical Decision Support System to Stratify the Temporal Risk of Diabetic Retinopathy. *IEEE Access : Practical Innovations, Open Solutions, 9,* 151864–151872. doi:10.1109/ACCESS.2021.3127274

Bernoulli, D., & Blower, S. (2004). An attempt at a new analysis of the mortality caused by smallpox and of the advantages of inoculation to prevent it. *Reviews in Medical Virology, 14*(5), 275–288. doi:10.1002/rmv.443 PMID:15334536

Bharadwaj, H. K., Agarwal, A., Chamola, V., Lakkaniga, N. R., Hassija, V., Guizani, M., & Sikdar, B. (2021). A Review on the Role of Machine Learning in Enabling IoT Based Healthcare Applications. *IEEE Access : Practical Innovations, Open Solutions, 9,* 38859–38890. doi:10.1109/ACCESS.2021.3059858

Bharadwaj, S., Murthy, S., & Varaprasad, G. (2013). Detection of potholes in autonomous vehicle. *IET Intelligent Transport Systems, 8*(6), 543–549. doi:10.1049/iet-its.2013.0138

Bharath, V., Adyanth, H., Shreekanth, T., Suresh, N., & Ananya, M. (2019). Intelligent sockets for home automation and security: An approach through IoT and image processing. In *The IoT and the Next Revolutions Automating the World* (pp. 252–279). IGI Global. doi:10.4018/978-1-5225-9246-4.ch016

Bhardwaj, A., Ou, H. C., Chen, H., Jabbari, S., Tambe, M., Panicker, R., & Raval, A. (2020). Robust lock-down optimization for COVID-19 policy guidance. In *AAAI Fall Symposium.*

Bhatia, A., Kedia, V., Shroff, A., Kumar, M., Shah, B. K., & Aryan. (2021). Fake currency detection with machine learning algorithm and image processing. *Proceedings - 5th International Conference on Intelligent Computing and Control Systems, ICICCS 2021*, (pp. 755–760). IEEE. doi:10.1109/ICICCS51141.2021.9432274

Bhatia, S., Mallikarjuna, B., Gautam, D., Gupta, U., Kumar, S., & Verma, S. (2023). The Future IoT: The Current Generation 5G and Next Generation 6G and 7G Technologies. *Proceedings - IEEE International Conference on Device Intelligence, Computing and Communication Technologies, DICCT 2023*, (pp. 212–217). IEEE. 10.1109/DICCT56244.2023.10110066

Bhattacharya, S., Reddy Maddikunta, P. K., Pham, Q. V., Gadekallu, T. R., & Krishnan, S. (2020, November). Deep learning and medical image processing for coronavirus (COVID-19) pandemic: A survey. *Sustainable Cities and Society*, *65*, 102589. doi:10.1016/j.scs.2020.102589 PMID:33169099

Biswas, A., & Islam, M. S. "ANN-Based Brain Tumor Classification: Performance Analysis Using K-Means and FCM Clustering With Various Training Functions." In Explainable Artificial Intelligence for Smart Cities, pp. 83-102. CRC Press, 2021. doi:10.1201/9781003172772-6

Biyani, R. S., & Patre, B. M. (2016, October). A clustering approach for exudates detection in screening of diabetic retinopathy. In *2016 International Conference on Signal and Information Processing (IConSIP)* (pp. 1-5). IEEE. 10.1109/ICONSIP.2016.7857495

Bocconcelli, R., & Cecchini, M. (2021). Marketing implications of image processing techniques: A systematic review. *Journal of Business Research*, *128*, 104–114. doi:10.1016/j.jbusres.2021.01.036

Bock, R., Meier, J., Nyúl, L. G., Hornegger, J., & Michelson, G. (2010). Glaucoma risk index: Automated glaucoma detection from color fundus images. [PubMed] [Google Scholar]. *Medical Image Analysis*, *14*(3), 471–481. doi:10.1016/j.media.2009.12.006 PMID:20117959

Bolhasani, H., Mohseni, M., & Rahmani, A. M. (2021). Deep learning applications for IoT in health care: A systematic review. *Informatics in Medicine Unlocked*, *23*, 100550. doi:10.1016/j.imu.2021.100550

Boomija, M. D., & Raja, S. V. K. (2023). Securing medical data by role-based user policy with partially homomorphic encryption in AWS cloud. *Soft Computing*, *27*(1), 559–568. doi:10.100700500-022-06950-y

Boopathi, S. (2019). Experimental investigation and parameter analysis of LPG refrigeration system using Taguchi method. *SN Applied Sciences*, *1*(8), 892. doi:10.100742452-019-0925-2

Boopathi, S. (2021). Improving of Green Sand-Mould Quality using Taguchi Technique. *Journal of Engineering Research*. doi:10.36909/jer.14079

Boopathi, S. (2022a). An experimental investigation of Quench Polish Quench (QPQ) coating on AISI 4150 steel. *Engineering Research Express*, *4*(4), 45009. doi:10.1088/2631-8695/ac9ddd

Boopathi, S. (2022a). An investigation on gas emission concentration and relative emission rate of the near-dry wire-cut electrical discharge machining process. *Environmental Science and Pollution Research International*, *29*(57), 86237–86246. doi:10.100711356-021-17658-1 PMID:34837614

Boopathi, S. (2022b). An Extensive Review on Sustainable Developments of Dry and Near-Dry Electrical Discharge Machining Processes. *Journal of Manufacturing Science and Engineering*, *144*(5), 50801. doi:10.1115/1.4052527

Boopathi, S. (2022b). Cryogenically treated and untreated stainless steel grade 317 in sustainable wire electrical discharge machining process: A comparative study. *Environmental Science and Pollution Research International*, 1–10. doi:10.100711356-022-22843-x PMID:36057706

Boopathi, S. (2022c). Experimental investigation and multi-objective optimization of cryogenic Friction-stir-welding of AA2014 and AZ31B alloys using MOORA technique. *Materials Today. Communications*, *33*, 104937. doi:10.1016/j.mtcomm.2022.104937

Boopathi, S. (2022d). Performance Improvement of Eco-Friendly Near-Dry Wire-Cut Electrical Discharge Machining Process Using Coconut Oil-Mist Dielectric Fluid. *Journal of Advanced Manufacturing Systems*. doi:10.1142/S0219686723500178

Boopathi, S. (2023a). An Investigation on Friction Stir Processing of Aluminum Alloy-Boron Carbide Surface Composite. In *Materials Horizons: From Nature to Nanomaterials* (pp. 249–257). Springer. doi:10.1007/978-981-19-7146-4_14

Boopathi, S. (2023b). *Impact analysis of ceramic tile powder aggregates on self-compacting concrete*. Engineering Research Express.

Boopathi, S. (n.d.). Deep Learning Techniques Applied for Automatic Sentence Generation. IGI Global. doi:10.4018/978-1-6684-3632-5.ch016

Boopathi, S., Arigela, S. H., Raman, R., Indhumathi, C., Kavitha, V., & Bhatt, B. C. (2023). Prominent Rule Control-based Internet of Things: Poultry Farm Management System. *IEEE Explore*, 1–6. doi:10.1109/ICPECTS56089.2022.10047039

Boopathi, S., Balasubramani, V., & Sanjeev Kumar, R. (2023). Influences of various natural fibers on the mechanical and drilling characteristics of coir-fiber-based hybrid epoxy composites. *Engineering Research Express*, *5*(1), 15002. doi:10.1088/2631-8695/acb132

Boopathi, S., Haribalaji, V., Mageswari, M., & Asif, M. M. (2022). Influences of Boron Carbide Particles on the Wear Rate and Tensile Strength of Aa2014 Surface Composite Fabricated By Friction-Stir Processing. *Materiali in Tehnologije*, *56*(3), 263–270. doi:10.17222/mit.2022.409

Boopathi, S., Khare, R., Jaya Christiyan, K. G., Muni, T. V., & Khare, S. (2023). Additive Manufacturing Developments in the Medical Engineering Field. In Development, Properties, and Industrial Applications of 3D Printed Polymer Composites (pp. 86–106). IGI Global. doi:10.4018/978-1-6684-6009-2.ch006

Boopathi, S., Siva Kumar, P. K., & Meena, R. S. J., S. I., P., S. K., & Sudhakar, M. (2023). Sustainable Developments of Modern Soil-Less Agro-Cultivation Systems. In Human Agro-Energy Optimization for Business and Industry (pp. 69–87). IGI Global. doi:10.4018/978-1-6684-4118-3.ch004

Boopathi, S., Thillaivanan, A., Azeem, M. A., Shanmugam, P., & Pramod, V. R. (2022). Experimental investigation on abrasive water jet machining of neem wood plastic composite. *Functional Composites and Structures*, *4*(2), 25001. doi:10.1088/2631-6331/ac6152

Boopathi, S., Venkatesan, G., & Anton Savio Lewise, K. (2023). Mechanical Properties Analysis of Kenaf–Grewia–Hair Fiber-Reinforced Composite. In *Lecture Notes in Mechanical Engineering* (pp. 101–110). Springer. doi:10.1007/978-981-16-9057-0_11

Bora, D. J. (2017). Importance Of Image Enhancement Techniques In Color Image Segmentation: A Comprehensive And Comparative Study. *Indian Journal of Scientific Research*, 115–131.

Borsos, B., Nagy, L., Iclănzan, D., & Szilágyi, L. (2019). Automatic detection of hard and soft exudates from retinal fundus images. Acta Universitatis Sapientiae. *Informatica (Vilnius)*, *11*(1), 65–79.

Boukabous, M., & Azizi, M. (2023). Image and video-based crime prediction using object detection and deep learning. *Bulletin of Electrical Engineering and Informatics*, *12*(3), 1630–1638. doi:10.11591/eei.v12i3.5157

Boukerch, A., & Belaroussi, R. (2019). Lane detection and tracking for autonomous driving applications: A comprehensive review. *Journal of Intelligent Transport Systems*, *23*(5), 441–462.

Bouti, A., Mahraz, M. A., Riffi, J., & Tairi, H. (2020). Med AdnaneMahraz, Jamal Riffi, and Hamid Tairi. "A robust system for road sign detection and classification using LeNet architecture based on convolutional neural network.". *Soft Computing*, *24*(9), 6721–6733. doi:10.100700500-019-04307-6

Brasil, L. M., Gomes, M. M. F., Miosso, C. J., da Silva, M. M., & Amvame-Nze, G. D. (2015). Web platform using digital image processing and geographic information system tools: A Brazilian case study on dengue. *Biomedical Engineering Online*, *14*(1), 1–14. doi:10.118612938-015-0052-2 PMID:26178732

Brosnan, T., & Sun, D.-W. (2004). Improving quality inspection of food products by computer vision—A review. *Journal of Food Engineering*, *61*(1), 3–16. doi:10.1016/S0260-8774(03)00183-3

Bruntha, P. M., Dhanasekar, S., Hepsiba, D., Sagayam, K. M., Neebha, T. M., Pandey, D., & Pandey, B. K. (2022). Application of switching median filter with L 2 norm-based auto-tuning function for removing random valued impulse noise. *Aerospace Systems*, 1-7.

Cai, Y., Zhou, W., Zhang, L., Yu, L., & Luo, T. (2023). DHFNet: Dual-decoding hierarchical fusion network for RGB-thermal semantic segmentation. *The Visual Computer*. doi:10.100700371-023-02773-6

Cai, Z., Tan, C., Zhang, J., Xiao, T., & Feng, Y. (2022). An Unhealthy Webpage Discovery System Based on Convolutional Neural Network. *International Journal of Digital Crime and Forensics*, *14*(3), 1–15. doi:10.4018/IJDCF.315614

Caldwell, M., Andrews, J. T. A., Tanay, T., & Griffin, L. D. (2020). AI-enabled future crime. *Crime Science*, *9*(1), 1–13. doi:10.118640163-020-00123-8

Cao, C. F., Yu, B., Chen, Z. Y., Qu, Y.-X., Li, Y.-T., Shi, Y.-Q., Ma, Z.-W., Sun, F.-N., Pan, Q.-H., Tang, L.-C., Song, P., & Wang, H. (2022). Fire Intumescent, High-Temperature Resistant, Mechanically Flexible Graphene Oxide Network for Exceptional Fire Shielding and Ultra-Fast Fire Warning. *Nano-Micro Letters*, *14*(1), 92. doi:10.100740820-022-00837-1 PMID:35384618

Capuano, A., Rossi, F., & Paolisso, G. (2020). Covid-19 kills more men than women: An overview of possible reasons. *Frontiers in Cardiovascular Medicine*, *7*, 131. doi:10.3389/fcvm.2020.00131 PMID:32766284

Caramihale, T., Popescu, D., & Ichim, L. (2017, March). A neural-network based approach for exudates evaluation in retinal images. In *2017 10th International Symposium on Advanced Topics in Electrical Engineering (ATEE)* (pp. 268-273). IEEE. 10.1109/ATEE.2017.7905107

Cauchemez, S., Kiem, C. T., Paireau, J., Rolland, P., & Fontanet, A. (2020). Lockdown impact on COVID-19 epidemics in regions across metropolitan France. *Lancet*, *396*(10257), 1068–1069. doi:10.1016/S0140-6736(20)32034-1 PMID:33007219

Cebrián-Lloret, V., Martínez-Abad, A., López-Rubio, A., & Martínez-Sanz, M. (2023). Sustainable Bio-Based Materials from Minimally Processed Red Seaweeds: Effect of Composition and Cell Wall Structure. *Journal of Polymers and the Environment*, *31*(3), 886–899. doi:10.100710924-022-02648-2

Cengil, E., & Cinar, A. (2018). A deep learning based approach to lung cancer identification. In *2018 International Conference on Artificial Intelligence and Data Processing (IDAP)*, (pp. 1-5). IEEE. 10.1109/IDAP.2018.8620723

Chakravarthi, P. K., Yuvaraj, D., & Venkataramanan, V. (2022). IoT-based smart energy meter for smart grids. *ICDCS 2022 - 2022 6th International Conference on Devices, Circuits and Systems*, (pp. 360–363). IEEE. 10.1109/ICDCS54290.2022.9780714

Chamola, V., Goyal, A., & Sharma, P. (2022). *Artificial intelligence-assisted blockchain-based framework for smart and secure EMR management.* Neural Comput & Applic., doi:10.100700521-022-07087-7

Chand, C. R., & Dheeba, J. (2015). Automatic detection of exudates in color fundus retinopathy images. *Indian Journal of Science and Technology*, *8*(26), 1–6.

Chandan, G. (2018). Ayush Jain, and Harsh Jain. "Real time object detection and tracking using Deep Learning and OpenCV. In *2018 International Conference on inventive research in computing applications (ICIRCA)*, (pp. 1305-1308). IEEE. 10.1109/ICIRCA.2018.8597266

Chandan, R. R., Soni, S., Raj, A., Veeraiah, V., Dhabliya, D., Pramanik, S., & Gupta, A. (2023). Genetic Algorithm and Machine Learning. Advanced Bioinspiration Methods for Healthcare Standards, Policies, and Reform. IGI Global, doi:10.4018/978-1-6684-5656-9

Chandrasegaran, K., Tran, N. T., Binder, A., & Cheung, N. M. (2022).Discovering Transferable Forensic Features for CNN-Generated Images Detection. Lecture Notes in Computer Science (Including Subseries Lecture Notes in Artificial Intelligence and Lecture Notes in Bioinformatics), 13675 LNCS, 671–689. Springer. doi:10.1007/978-3-031-19784-0_39

Chang, K. C., Huang, J. W., & Wu, Y. F. (2021, September). Design of e-health system for heart rate and lung sound monitoring with AI-based analysis. In *2021 IEEE International Conference on Consumer Electronics-Taiwan (ICCE-TW)* (pp. 1-2). IEEE.

Chaudhari, A., & Walke, R. (2022). Role of artificial intelligence and Machine learning in musculoskeletal physiotherapy. *Journal of Pharmaceutical Negative Results*, *13*(36), 2868–2870. doi:10.47750/pnr.2022.13.S06.369

Chen, B., Yan, Z., & Nahrstedt, K. (2022). Context-aware image compression optimization for visual analytics offloading. *Proceedings of the 13th ACM Multimedia Systems Conference*, (pp. 27–38). ACM. 10.1145/3524273.3528178

Chen, K., Lu, M., Fan, X., Wei, M., & Wu, J. (2011). Road Condition Monitoring Using On-board Three-axis Accelerometer and GPS Sensor. In *Proceedings of International ICST conference on Communication and Networking in China*, (pp.1032- 1037). IEEE.

Chen, M., Hao, Y., Hwang, K., Wang, L., & Wang, L. (2017). Disease prediction by machine learning over big data from healthcare communities. *IEEE Access : Practical Innovations, Open Solutions*, *5*, 8869–8879. doi:10.1109/AC-CESS.2017.2694446

Chen, Q., & Liu, W. (2021). Image processing and machine learning techniques for corrosion evaluation and prediction: A review. *Measurement*, *177*, 109272. doi:10.1016/j.measurement.2021.109272

Chen, Y., & Huang, J. (2018). Applications of image processing in marketing research: A review. *Journal of Business Research*, *88*, 347–356. doi:10.1016/j.jbusres.2018.01.030

Cheng, D., Luo, J., & Li, Y. (2017). Image processing application in chemical engineering: A review. *Chemical Engineering Science*, *170*, 1–15. doi:10.1016/j.ces.2017.04.007

Cheng, J., Liu, J., Xu, Y., Yin, F., Wong, D. W. K., Tan, N.-M., Tao, D., Cheng, C.-Y., Aung, T., & Wong, T. Y. (2013). Superpixel classification based optic disc and optic cup segmentation for glaucoma screening. *IEEE Transactions on Medical Imaging*, *32*(6), 1019–1032. doi:10.1109/TMI.2013.2247770 PMID:23434609

Cheng, P., Liang, M., Yun, X., & Dong, T. (2022). Biodegradable blend films of poly(ε-caprolactone)/poly(propylene carbonate) for shelf life extension of whole white button mushrooms. *Journal of Food Science and Technology*, *59*(1), 144–156. doi:10.100713197-021-04995-9 PMID:35068559

Chick, J. 2020. Alcohol and COVID-19. *Alcohol and Alcoholism (Oxford, Oxfordshire)*.

Chidambaram, N., & Vijayan, D. (2018, September). Detection of exudates in diabetic retinopathy. In *2018 International Conference on Advances in Computing, Communications and Informatics (ICACCI)* (pp. 660-664). IEEE. 10.1109/ICACCI.2018.8554923

Chiuchisan, I., & Dimian, M. (2015). Internet of Things for e-Health: An approach to medical applications. *2015 International Workshop on Computational Intelligence for Multimedia Understanding, IWCIM 2015*, (pp. 1–5). IEEE. 10.1109/IWCIM.2015.7347091

Chmielewski, L. J., Nieniewski, M., & Orłowski, A. (2021). Testing the randomness of shares in color visual cryptography. In Pattern Analysis and Applications (Vol. 24, Issue 4, pp. 1475–1487). Springer Science and Business Media LLC. doi:10.100710044-021-00999-5

Choi, Y. H., Liu, P., Shang, Z., Wang, H., Wang, Z., Zhang, L., Zhou, J., & Zou, Q. (2020). Using deep learning to solve computer security challenges: A survey. *Cybersecurity*, *3*(1), 15. doi:10.118642400-020-00055-5

Choudhary, S., Narayan, V., Faiz, M., & Pramanik, S. (2022). Fuzzy Approach-Based Stable Energy-Efficient AODV Routing Protocol in Mobile Ad hoc Networks. In M. M. Ghonge, S. Pramanik, & A. D. Potgantwar (Eds.), *Software Defined Networking for Ad Hoc Networks*. Springer. doi:10.1007/978-3-030-91149-2_6

Cole, M. A., Elliott, R. J., & Liu, B. (2020). The impact of the Wuhan Covid-19 lockdown on air pollution and health: a machine learning and augmented synthetic control approach. *Environmental and Resource Economics*, *76*(4), 553-580

Contini, C., Di Nuzzo, M., Barp, N., Bonazza, A., De Giorgio, R., Tognon, M., & Rubino, S. (2020). The novel zoonotic COVID-19 pandemic: An expected global health concern. *Journal of Infection in Developing Countries*, *14*(03), 254–264. doi:10.3855/jidc.12671 PMID:32235085

Cui, F. (2020). Deployment and integration of smart sensors with IoT devices detecting fire disasters in huge forest environment. *Computer Communications*, *150*, 818–827. doi:10.1016/j.comcom.2019.11.051

Cui, J., Feng, Y., Zhang, G., & Yu, Z. (2019). Image processing-based quality control in plastic injection molding. *Measurement*, *131*, 559–568. doi:10.1016/j.measurement.2018.08.030

Cui, J., Zheng, B., & Yin, Z. (2019). Real-time monitoring and quality control system for plastic injection molding based on machine vision and machine learning. *Measurement*, *133*, 482–491. doi:10.1016/j.measurement.2018.09.065

Dai, B., Chen, Y., & Huang, J. (2019). The effects of image processing on consumer behavior: A meta-analysis. *Journal of Marketing Management*, *35*(9-10), 861–880. doi:10.1080/0267257X.2019.1662919

Dakalbab, F., Abu Talib, M., Abu Waraga, O., Bou Nassif, A., Abbas, S., & Nasir, Q. (2022). Artificial intelligence & crime prediction: A systematic literature review. *Social Sciences & Humanities Open*, *6*(1), 100342. doi:10.1016/j.ssaho.2022.100342

Dalal, N., & Triggs, B. (2005). Histograms of oriented gradients for human detection. In *Proceedings of the IEEE conference on computer vision and pattern recognition* (pp. 886-893). IEEE. 10.1109/CVPR.2005.177

Daniel, J. (2020). Education and the COVID-19 pandemic. *Prospects*, *49*(1), 91–96. doi:10.100711125-020-09464-3 PMID:32313309

Dash, S., Senapati, M. R., & Jena, U. R. (2018). K-NN based automated reasoning using Bilateral Filter Based Texture Descriptor for computing Texture Classification. *Egyptian Informatics Journal*, *19*(2), 133–144. doi:10.1016/j.eij.2018.01.003

Dash, S., Verma, S., Bevinakoppa, M., Wozniak, J. H., & Ijaz, M. (2022). Guidance image-based enhanced matched filter with modified thresholding for blood vessel extraction. *Symmetry 14*(2), 194.

Day, M. (2020). *Covid-19: four fifths of cases are asymptomatic, China figures indicate*. BMJ.

De Bonis, A., & De Santis, A. (2004). Randomness in secret sharing and visual cryptography schemes. In Theoretical Computer Science (Vol. 314, Issue 3, pp. 351–374). Elsevier BV. doi:10.1016/j.tcs.2003.12.018

de Cassan, D., Hoheisel, A. L., Glasmacher, B., & Menzel, H. (2019). Impact of sterilization by electron beam, gamma radiation and X-rays on electrospun poly-(ε-caprolactone) fiber mats. *Journal of Materials Science. Materials in Medicine*, *30*(4), 42. doi:10.100710856-019-6245-7 PMID:30919082

Deepa, R., Anand, R., Pandey, D., Pandey, B. K., & Karki, B. (2022). Comprehensive performance analysis of classifiers in diagnosis of epilepsy. *Mathematical Problems in Engineering*, *2022*, 2022. doi:10.1155/2022/1559312

Deepak, K. S., Jain, M., Joshi, G. D., & Sivaswamy, J. (2012, December). Motion pattern-based image features for glaucoma detection from retinal images. In *Proceedings of the Eighth Indian Conference on Computer Vision, Graphics and Image Processing* (pp. 1-8). Google Scholar. 10.1145/2425333.2425380

De la Escalera, A., Armingol, J. M., & Mata, M. (2003). Traffic sign recognition and analysis for intelligent vehicles. *Image and Vision Computing*, *21*(3), 247–258. doi:10.1016/S0262-8856(02)00156-7

de Venâncio, P. V. A. B., Lisboa, A. C., & Barbosa, A. V. (2022). An automatic fire detection system based on deep convolutional neural networks for low-power, resource-constrained devices. *Neural Computing & Applications*, *34*(18), 15349–15368. doi:10.100700521-022-07467-z

Dhiman, A., & Klette, R. (2019). Pothole detection using computer vision and learning. *IEEE Transactions on Intelligent Transportation Systems*, *21*(8), 3536–3550. doi:10.1109/TITS.2019.2931297

Dhiman, P., Kaur, A., Iwendi, C., & Mohan, S. K. (2023). A scientometric analysis of deep learning approaches for detecting fake news. *Electronics (Basel)*, *12*(4), 948. doi:10.3390/electronics12040948

Diallo, B., Urruty, T., Bourdon, P., & Fernandez-Maloigne, C. (2020). Robust forgery detection for compressed images using CNN supervision. *Forensic Science International: Reports*, *2*(June), 100112. doi:10.1016/j.fsir.2020.100112

Dik, G., Bogdanov, A., Shchegoleva, N., Dik, A., & Kiyamov, J. (2022). Challenges of IoT Identification and Multi-Level Protection in Integrated Data Transmission Networks Based on 5G/6G Technologies. *Computers*, *11*(12), 178. doi:10.3390/computers11120178

Dikici, E., Bigelow, M., Prevedello, L. M., White, R. D., & Erdal, B. S. (2020). Integrating AI into radiology workflow: Levels of research, production, and feedback maturity. *Journal of Medical Imaging (Bellingham, Wash.)*, *7*(01), 1. doi:10.1117/1.JMI.7.1.016502 PMID:32064302

DJ. B. J., Rajan, S. S., Vibinanth, R., Pamela, D., & Manimegalai, P. (2022, April). I-Doc–A Cloud Based Data Management System For Health Care. In *2022 6th International Conference on Devices, Circuits and Systems (ICDCS)* (pp. 85-88). IEEE.

Dol, M., & Geetha, A. (2021, August). A learning transition from machine learning to deep learning: A survey. In *2021 International Conference on Emerging Techniques in Computational Intelligence (ICETCI)* (pp. 89-94). IEEE. 10.1109/ICETCI51973.2021.9574066

Doll, R., Peto, R., Wheatley, K., Gray, R., & Sutherland, I. (1994). Mortality in relation to smoking: 40 years' observations on male British doctors. *BMJ (Clinical Research Ed.)*, *309*(6959), 901–911. doi:10.1136/bmj.309.6959.901 PMID:7755693

Domakonda, V. K., Farooq, S., Chinthamreddy, S., Puviarasi, R., Sudhakar, M., & Boopathi, S. (2023). Sustainable Developments of Hybrid Floating Solar Power Plants. In *Human Agro-Energy Optimization for Business and Industry* (pp. 148–167). IGI Global. doi:10.4018/978-1-6684-4118-3.ch008

Doğan, K., Özgün, M. İ., Sübütay, H., Salur, E., Eker, Y., Kuntoğlu, M., Aslan, A., Gupta, M. K., & Acarer, M. (2022). Dispersion mechanism-induced variations in microstructural and mechanical behavior of CNT-reinforced aluminum nanocomposites. *Archives of Civil and Mechanical Engineering*, *22*(1), 55. doi:10.100743452-022-00374-z

Dubey, S. R., Singh, S. K., & Chaudhuri, B. B. (2022). Activation functions in deep learning: A comprehensive survey and benchmark. *Neurocomputing*, *503*, 92–108. doi:10.1016/j.neucom.2022.06.111

Duncan, J. S., Insana, M. F., & Ayache, N. (2019). Biomedical imaging and analysis in the age of big data and deep learning [scanning the issue]. *Proceedings of the IEEE*, *108*(1), 3–10. doi:10.1109/JPROC.2019.2956422

Dunsin, D., Ghanem, M. C., & Ouazzane, K. (2022). The Use of Artificial Intelligence in Digital Forensics and Incident Response in a Constrained Environment. *International Journal of Information and Communication Engineering*, *16*(8), 280–285.

Dushyant, K., Muskan, G., Gupta, A., & Pramanik, S. (2022). Utilizing Machine Learning and Deep Learning in Cyber security: An Innovative Approach. In M. M. Ghonge, S. Pramanik, R. Mangrulkar, & D. N. Le (Eds.), *Cyber security and Digital Forensics*. Wiley. doi:10.1002/9781119795667.ch12

Dutta, M. K., Srivastava, K., Ganguly, S., Ganguly, S., Parthasarathi, M., Burget, R., & Prinosil, J. (2015, July). Exudates detection in digital fundus image using edge based method & strategic thresholding. In *2015 38th International Conference on Telecommunications and Signal Processing (TSP)* (pp. 748-752). IEEE. 10.1109/TSP.2015.7296364

Dutta, S., Mukherjee, U., & Bandyopadhyay, S. (2021). Pharmacy Impact on Covid-19 Vaccination Progress Using Machine Learning Approach. *Journal of Pharmaceutical Research International*, 202–217. doi:10.9734/jpri/2021/v33i38A32076

Díaz, M., Martín, C., & Rubio, B. (2016). State-of-the-art, challenges, and open issues in the integration of Internet of things and cloud computing. *Journal of Network and Computer Applications*, *67*, 99–117. doi:10.1016/j.jnca.2016.01.010

Egmont-Petersen, M., de Ridder, D., & Handels, H. (2002). Image processing with neural networks—A review. *Pattern Recognition*, *35*(10), 2279–2301. doi:10.1016/S0031-3203(01)00178-9

Elaziz, M. A., Hosny, K. M., Salah, A., Darwish, M. M., Lu, S., & Sahlol, A. T. (2020). New machine learning method for image-based diagnosis of COVID-19. *PLoS One*, *15*(6), e0235187. doi:10.1371/journal.pone.0235187 PMID:32589673

Elgendy, M. Y., Abdelsalam, M., Mohamed, S. A., & Ali, S. E. (2022). Molecular characterization, virulence profiling, antibiotic susceptibility, and scanning electron microscopy of *Flavobacterium columnare* isolates retrieved from Nile tilapia (*Oreochromis niloticus*). *Aquaculture International*, *30*(2), 845–862. doi:10.100710499-021-00819-x

Erickson, B. J. (2021). Basic Artificial Intelligence Techniques: Machine Learning and Deep Learning. *Radiologic Clinics of North America*, *59*(6), 933–940. doi:10.1016/j.rcl.2021.06.004 PMID:34689878

Esenogho, E., Djouani, K., & Kurien, A. M. (2022). Integrating Artificial Intelligence Internet of Things and 5G for Next-Generation Smartgrid: A Survey of Trends Challenges and Prospect. *IEEE Access : Practical Innovations, Open Solutions*, *10*, 4794–4831. doi:10.1109/ACCESS.2022.3140595

Esquivel, N., Nicolis, O., Peralta, B., & Mateu, J. (2020). Spatio-Temporal Prediction of Baltimore Crime Events Using CLSTM Neural Networks. *IEEE Access : Practical Innovations, Open Solutions*, *8*, 209101–209112. doi:10.1109/ACCESS.2020.3036715

Fan, C., & Ren, Y. (2010). Study on the edge detection algorithms of road image. In *2010 Third International Symposium on Information Processing*, (pp. 217-220). IEEE.

Fan, E. (2004). Extended tanh-function method and its applications to nonlinear equations. *Physics Letters A*, *4*(5), 212-218.

Fan, Y. (2021). Criminal psychology trend prediction based on deep learning algorithm and three-dimensional convolutional neural network. *Journal of Psychology in Africa, 31*(3), 292–297. doi:10.1080/14330237.2021.1927317

Farooq, F., Govindaraju, V., & Perrone, M. (2005). Pre-processing methods for handwritten Arabic documents. *Proceedings of the International Conference on Document Analysis and Recognition, ICDAR, 2005*, (pp. 267–271). IEEE. 10.1109/ICDAR.2005.191

Farsalinos, K., Barbouni, A., & Niaura, R. (2020). *Smoking, vaping and hospitalization for COVID-19.* Qeios.

Ferreira, S., Antunes, M., & Correia, M. E. (2021). A dataset of photos and videos for digital forensics analysis using machine learning processing. *Data, 6*(8), 1–15. doi:10.3390/data6080087

Ferreira, S., Antunes, M., & Correia, M. E. (2021). Exposing manipulated photos and videos in digital forensics analysis. *Journal of Imaging, 7*(7), 102. doi:10.3390/jimaging7070102

Ferzli, R., & Khalife, I. (2011). Mobile cloud computing educational tool for image/video processing algorithms. *2011 Digital Signal Processing and Signal Processing Education Meeting (DSP/SPE)*, (pp. 529–533). IEEE.

Firouzi, F., Farahani, B., Daneshmand, M., Grise, K., Song, J., Saracco, R., Wang, L. L., Lo, K., Angelov, P., Soares, E., Loh, P.-S., Talebpour, Z., Moradi, R., Goodarzi, M., Ashraf, H., Talebpour, M., Talebpour, A., Romeo, L., Das, R., & Luo, A. (2021). Harnessing the power of smart and connected health to tackle COVID-19: IoT, AI, robotics, and blockchain for a better world. *IEEE Internet of Things Journal, 8*(16), 12826–12846. doi:10.1109/JIOT.2021.3073904 PMID:35782886

Fitriyani, N. L., Syafrudin, M., Alfian, G., & Rhee, J. (2020). HDPM: An effective heart disease prediction model for a clinical decision support system. *IEEE Access : Practical Innovations, Open Solutions, 8*, 133034–133050. doi:10.1109/ACCESS.2020.3010511

Fleming, A. (1921). A British Medical Association lecture on vaccine therapy in regard to general practice. *British Medical Journal, 1*(3138), 255–259. doi:10.1136/bmj.1.3138.255 PMID:20770181

Franklin, S. W., & Rajan, S. E. (2014). Diagnosis of diabetic retinopathy by employing image processing technique to detect exudates in retinal images. *IET Image processing, 8*(10), 601-609. 20.

Fu, H., Cheng, J., Xu, Y., Zhang, C., Wong, D. W. K., Liu, J., & Cao, X. (2018). Disc-aware ensemble nework for glaucoma screening from fundus image. *IEEE Transactions on Medical Imaging, 37*(11), 2493–2501. doi:10.1109/TMI.2018.2837012 PMID:29994764

Fähndrich, J., Honekamp, W., Povalej, R., Rittelmeier, H., & Berner, S. (2022). Special Issue on Application of AI in Digital Forensics. KI -. *Kunstliche Intelligenz, 36*(2), 121–124. doi:10.100713218-022-00777-3

Gambhir, E., Jain, R., Gupta, A., & Tomer, U. 2020, September. Regression analysis of COVID-19 using machine learning algorithms. In *2020 International conference on smart electronics and communication (ICOSEC)* (pp. 65-71). IEEE. 10.1109/ICOSEC49089.2020.9215356

Gao, H., Cheng, B., Wang, J., Li, K., Zhao, J., & Li, D. (2018). Object classification using CNN-based fusion of vision and LIDAR in autonomous vehicle environment. *IEEE Transactions on Industrial Informatics, 14*(9), 4224–4231. doi:10.1109/TII.2018.2822828

Garcia-Pérez, J. S., Ortiz-Boyer, D., Montejano-Carrizales, J. M., Mota-Babiloni, A., & Barrientos-Reyes, G. (2021). A review of image processing techniques for non-destructive testing in metal manufacturing. *Journal of Manufacturing Processes, 68*, 441–452. doi:10.1016/j.jmapro.2021.08.026

Garg, R., Maheshwari, S., & Shukla, A. (2021). Decision support system for detection and classification of skin cancer using CNN. In *Innovations in Computational Intelligence and Computer Vision: Proceedings of ICICV 2020*, (pp. 578-586). Springer Singapore. 10.1007/978-981-15-6067-5_65

Geetha, A., & Prakash, N. B. (2022). Classification of glaucoma in retinal images using efficient B4 deep learning model. *Computer Systems Science and Engineering*, *43*(3), 1041–1055. doi:10.32604/csse.2022.023680

Gentile, I., & Abenavoli, L. (2020). COVID-19: Perspectives on the potential novel global threat. *Reviews on Recent Clinical Trials*, *15*(2), 84–86. PMID:32116200

Ghassemi, N., Shoeibi, A., & Rouhani, M. (2020). Deep neural network with generative adversarial networks pre-training for brain tumor classification based on MR images. *Biomedical Signal Processing and Control*, *57*, 101678. doi:10.1016/j.bspc.2019.101678

Ghimire, A., Thapa, S., Jha, A. K., Kumar, A., Kumar, A., & Adhikari, S. (2020, November). AI and IoT solutions for tackling COVID-19 pandemic. In *2020 4th International Conference on Electronics, Communication and Aerospace Technology (ICECA)* (pp. 1083-1092). IEEE.

Ghosh, R., & Kumar, A. (2022). A hybrid deep learning model by combining convolutional neural network and recurrent neural network to detect forest fire. *Multimedia Tools and Applications*, *81*(27), 38643–38660. doi:10.100711042-022-13068-8

Gibson, U. E., Heid, C. A., & Williams, P. M. (1996). A novel method for real time quantitative RT-PCR. *Genome Research*, *6*(10), 995–1001. doi:10.1101/gr.6.10.995 PMID:8908519

Gillani, I. S., Shahzad, M., Mobin, A., Munawar, M. R., Awan, M. U., & Asif, M. (2022, September). Explainable AI in Drug Sensitivity Prediction on Cancer Cell Lines. In *2022 International Conference on Emerging Trends in Smart Technologies (ICETST)* (pp. 1-5). IEEE. 10.1109/ICETST55735.2022.9922931

Gnoni, M. G., Bragatto, P. A., Milazzo, M. F., & Setola, R. (2020). Integrating IoT technologies for an "intelligent" safety management in the process industry. *Procedia Manufacturing*, *42*, 511–515. doi:10.1016/j.promfg.2020.02.040

Godavarthi, B., Nalajala, P., & Ganapuram, V. (2017). Design and implementation of vehicle navigation system in urban environments using internet of things (IoT). In *IOP Conference Series: Materials Science and Engineering*, Hyderabad, India. 10.1088/1757-899X/225/1/012262

Goel, M., Mohan, A., Patkar, S., Gala, K., Shetty, N., Kulkarni, S., & Dhareshwar, J. (2022). Leiomyosarcoma of inferior vena cava (IVC): Do we really need to reconstruct IVC post resection? Single institution experience. *Langenbeck's Archives of Surgery*, *407*(3), 1209–1216. doi:10.100700423-021-02408-1 PMID:35022833

Goodyear, O. M., Shamsolmaali, A., Hobsley, M., & Scurr, J. (1990, April). Decision support and the medical data environment: an example from breast surgery. In *IET Colloquium on AI in Medical Decision Making* (pp. 6-1). IET.

Gowri, N. V., Dwivedi, J. N., Krishnaveni, K., Boopathi, S., Palaniappan, M., & Medikondu, N. R. (2023). Experimental investigation and multi-objective optimization of eco-friendly near-dry electrical discharge machining of shape memory alloy using Cu/SiC/Gr composite electrode. *Environmental Science and Pollution Research International*, *0123456789*. doi:10.100711356-023-26983-6 PMID:37126160

Gowri, V., & Baranidharan, B. (2023). Dynamic Energy Efficient Load Balancing Approach in Fog Computing Environment. In G. Rajakumar, K. L. Du, C. Vuppalapati, & G. N. Beligiannis (Eds.), *Intelligent Communication Technologies and Virtual Mobile Networks. Lecture Notes on Data Engineering and Communications Technologies* (Vol. 131). Springer., doi:10.1007/978-981-19-1844-5_13

Goyal, S. (2022). Handling Class-Imbalance with KNN (Neighbourhood) Under-Sampling for Software Defect Prediction. *Artificial Intelligence Review*, *55*(3), 2023–2064. doi:10.100710462-021-10044-w

Gross, H. (2008). *Fritz Blechinger, Bertram Achtner. Handbook of Optical Systems: Survey of Optical Instruments* (Vol. 4). Human Eye. doi:10.1002/9783527699247

Grupac, M. (2022). Image processing computational algorithms, sensory data mining techniques, and predictive customer analytics in the metaverse economy. *Review of Contemporary Philosophy*, *21*(0), 205–222. doi:10.22381/RCP21202213

Gull, S., & Akbar, S. (2021). *Artificial intelligence in brain tumor detection through MRI scans: Advancements and challenges*. Artificial Intelligence and Internet of Things. doi:10.1201/9781003097204-10

Guo, W., Gong, J., Jiang, W., Liu, Y., & She, B. (2010). OpenRS-Cloud: A remote sensing image processing platform based on cloud computing environment. *Science China. Technological Sciences*, *53*(S1), 221–230. doi:10.100711431-010-3234-y

Guorui, F., & Jian, W. (2020). Image Forgery Detection Based on the Convolutional Neural Network. *ACM International Conference Proceeding Series*, (pp. 266–270). ACM. 10.1145/3383972.3384023

Gupta, A. (2019). Script classification at the word level for a Multilingual Document. *International Journal of Advanced Science and Technology*, *28*(20), 1247–1252. http://sersc.org/journals/index.php/IJAST/article/view/3835

Gupta, A. (2019). Script classification at word level for a Multilingual Document. *International Journal of Advanced Science and Technology*, *28*(20), 1247–1252. http://sersc.org/journals/index.php/IJAST/article/view/3835

Gupta, A., Anand, R., Pandey, D., Sindhwani, N., Wairya, S., Pandey, B. K., & Sharma, M. (2021). Prediction of breast cancer using extremely randomized clustering forests (ERCF) technique: Prediction of breast cancer. [IJDST]. *International Journal of Distributed Systems and Technologies*, *12*(4), 1–15. doi:10.4018/IJDST.287859

Gupta, A., Asad, A., Meena, L., & Anand, R. (2023). IoT and RFID-Based Smart Card System Integrated with Health Care, Electricity, QR and Banking Sectors. In M. Gupta, S. Ghatak, A. Gupta, & A. L. Mukherjee (Eds.), *Artificial Intelligence on Medical Data. Lecture Notes in Computational Vision and Biomechanics* (Vol. 37). Springer. doi:10.1007/978-981-19-0151-5_22

Gupta, A., Kaushik, D., Garg, M., & Verma, A. (2020). Machine Learning model for Breast Cancer Prediction. *2020 Fourth International Conference on I-SMAC (IoT in Social, Mobile, Analytics and Cloud) (I-SMAC)*, (pp. 472–477). IEEE. 10.1109/I-SMAC49090.2020.9243323

Gupta, A., Singh, R., Nassa, V. K., Bansal, R., Sharma, P., & Koti, K. (2021) Investigating Application and Challenges of Big Data Analytics with Clustering. *2021 International Conference on Advancements in Electrical, Electronics, Communication, Computing and Automation (ICAECA)*, (pp. 1-6). IEEE.10.1109/ICAECA52838.2021.9675483

Gupta, A., Verma, A., & Pramanik, S. (2022). Advanced Security System in Video Surveillance for COVID-19. In *An Interdisciplinary Approach to Modern Network Security, S. Pramanik, A. Sharma, S. Bhatia and D. N. Le*. CRC Press. doi:10.1201/9781003147176-8

Gupta, A., Verma, A., & Pramanik, S. (2022). Advanced Security System in Video Surveillance for COVID-19. In S. Pramanik, A. Sharma, S. Bhatia, & D. N. Le. (eds.) An Interdisciplinary Approach to Modern Network Security. CRC Press.

Gupta, A. K., Sharma, M., Sharma, A., & Menon, V. (2022). A study on SARS-CoV-2 (COVID-19) and machine learning based approach to detect COVID-19 through X-ray images. *International Journal of Image and Graphics*, *22*(03), 2140010. doi:10.1142/S0219467821400106

Gupta, A. K., Sharma, M., Singh, S., & Palta, P. (2020). *A Modified Blind Deconvolution Algorithm for Deblurring of Colored Images.* Advances in Computational Intelligence Techniques. doi:10.1007/978-981-15-2620-6_10

Gupta, N., Khosravy, M., Patel, N., Dey, N., Gupta, S., Darbari, H., & Crespo, R. G. (2020). Economic data analytic AI technique on IoT edge devices for health monitoring of agriculture machines. *Applied Intelligence, 50*(11), 3990–4016. doi:10.100710489-020-01744-x

Gupta, P., & Yadav, S. (2022). A TAM-based Study on the ICT Usage by the Academicians in Higher Educational Institutions of Delhi NCR. In M. Saraswat, H. Sharma, K. Balachandran, J. H. Kim, & J. C. Bansal (Eds.), *Congress on Intelligent Systems. Lecture Notes on Data Engineering and Communications Technologies* (Vol. 111). Springer. doi:10.1007/978-981-16-9113-3_25

Gupta, R., & Sachdeva, N. (2018). A review of image processing techniques for product classification in marketing. *International Journal of Advanced Research in Computer Science, 9*(2), 168–173. doi:10.26483/ijarcs.v9i2.5621

Gupta A. (2020). *An Analysis of Digital Image Compression Technique in Image.* SERSC.

Haghi Kashani, M., Madanipour, M., Nikravan, M., Asghari, P., & Mahdipour, E. (2021). A systematic review of IoT in healthcare: Applications, techniques, and trends. *Journal of Network and Computer Applications, 192*, 103164. doi:10.1016/j.jnca.2021.103164

Hague, T., Marchant, J. A., & Tillett, N. D. (2000). Ground based sensing systems for autonomous agricultural vehicles. *Computers and Electronics in Agriculture, 25*(1-2), 11–28. doi:10.1016/S0168-1699(99)00053-8

Hai, J., Xuan, Z., Yang, R., Hao, Y., Zou, F., Lin, F., & Han, S. (2023). R2rnet: Low-light image enhancement via real-low to real-normal network. *Journal of Visual Communication and Image Representation, 90*, 103712. doi:10.1016/j.jvcir.2022.103712

Hall, S. W., Sakzad, A., & Choo, K. R. (2022). Explainable artificial intelligence for digital forensics. *WIREs Forensic Science, 4*(2), 1–11. doi:10.1002/wfs2.1434

Halunen, K., & Latvala, O.-M. (2021). Review of the use of human senses and capabilities in cryptography. In *Computer Science Review* (Vol. 39, p. 100340). Elsevier BV. doi:10.1016/j.cosrev.2020.100340

Han, X., & Fischl, B. (2007). Atlas renormalization for improved brain MR image segmentation across scanner platforms. *IEEE Transactions on Medical Imaging, 26*(4), 479–486. doi:10.1109/TMI.2007.893282 PMID:17427735

Han, X., Ma, H., & Chen, G. (2020). Machine vision-based automatic detection system for ceramic tile quality. *Measurement, 163*, 108143. doi:10.1016/j.measurement.2020.108143

Han, X., Wang, Z., Liu, X., & Li, G. (2020). Ceramic tile defect detection based on machine vision and image processing. *Measurement, 167*, 108225. doi:10.1016/j.measurement.2020.108225

Han, Z., Liu, K., Li, Z., & Luo, P. (2022). A pre-check operator for reducing algorithmic optimisation time in image processing applications. *Enterprise Information Systems, 16*(10–11), 1543–1555. doi:10.1080/17517575.2020.1864022

Harikaran, M., & Boopathi, S. (2023). Impact analysis of ceramic tile powder aggregates on self-compacting concrete. Engineering Research Express. 5(3), https://iopscience.iop.org/article/10.1088/2631-8695/acde48/meta

Harikaran, M., Boopathi, S., Gokulakannan, S., & Poonguzhali, M. (2023). Study on the Source of E-Waste Management and Disposal Methods. In *Sustainable Approaches and Strategies for E-Waste Management and Utilization* (pp. 39–60). IGI Global. doi:10.4018/978-1-6684-7573-7.ch003

Hasan, A., Pandey, D., & Khan, A. (2021). Application of EEG Time-Varying Networks in the Evaluation of Dynamic Functional Brain Networks. *Augmented Human Research*, 6(1), 1–8. doi:10.100741133-021-00046-2

Hasan, M., Islam, I., & Hasan, K. A. (2019, February). Sentiment analysis using out of core learning. In *2019 International Conference on Electrical, Computer and Communication Engineering (ECCE)* (pp. 1-6). IEEE. 10.1109/ECACE.2019.8679298

Hasan, M., Islam, M. M., Zarif, M. I. I., & Hashem, M. M. A. (2019). Attack and anomaly detection in IoT sensors in IoT sites using machine learning approaches. *Internet of Things*, 7, 100059. doi:10.1016/j.iot.2019.100059

Hashemi, M., & Hall, M. (2020). Criminal tendency detection from facial images and the gender bias effect. *Journal of Big Data*, 7(1), 2. doi:10.118640537-019-0282-4

Hashemi, S. M. A., Nikoo, M. R., & Mozafari, M. (2019). Review of image processing techniques for the detection of welding defects. *Journal of Materials Engineering and Performance*, 28(5), 2905–2923. doi:10.100711665-019-03906-9

Hassan, N. M., Hamad, S., & Mahar, K. (2022). Mammogram breast cancer CAD systems for mass detection and classification: A review. *Multimedia Tools and Applications*, 81(14), 20043–20075. doi:10.100711042-022-12332-1

Hassanien, R. H., Elhoseny, M., Mohamed, E. M., El-Sappagh, S., & Riad, A. M. (2019). Image processing applications in industry 4.0: A review. *Proceedings of the Institution of Mechanical Engineers. Part C, Journal of Mechanical Engineering Science*, 233(17), 5967–5984. doi:10.1177/0954406219865447

Haug, C. J., & Drazen, J. M. (2022). *Artificial intelligence and machine learning in clinical medicine, 2023* (Vol. 388, Issue 13). Mathworks.

He, L., Zhao, W., Zhou, W., Pang, P., Liao, Y., & Liu, J. (2020). an emergency surgery in severe case infected by COVID-19 with perforated duodenal bulb ulcer. *Annals of Surgery*, 272(1), e35–e37. doi:10.1097/SLA.0000000000003958 PMID:32433280

He, Y., Jian, W., Qiu, H., Wei, Z., & Xie, J. (2011). A Research of Pavement Potholes Detection Based on Three-Dimensional Project Transformation. In *Proceedings of International Congress on Image and Signal Processing,* (pp. 1805-1808). IEEE.

He, Y., Luo, C., Camacho, R. S., Wang, K., & Zhang, H. (2020, September). AI-Based Security Attack Pathway for Cardiac Medical Diagnosis Systems (CMDS). In 2020 [IEEE.]. *Computers in Cardiology*, 1–4.

Hegde, S., Mekali, H., & Varaprasad, G. (2019). Pothole Detection and Inter vehicular Communication. *Technical Report of Wireless Communications Laboratory*. BMS College of Engineering, Bangalore.

Hidayatullah, A., & Bresciani, S. (2019). The role of image processing in experiential marketing. *Journal of Business Research*, 104, 278–290. doi:10.1016/j.jbusres.2018.10.020

Hilmizen, N., Bustamam, A., & Sarwinda, D. (2020, December). The multimodal deep learning for diagnosing COVID-19 pneumonia from chest CT-scan and X-ray images. In *2020 3rd international seminar on research of information technology and intelligent systems (ISRITI)* (pp. 26-31). IEEE.

Ho, C. W. L., Soon, D., Caals, K., & Kapur, J. (2019). Governance of automated image analysis and artificial intelligence analytics in healthcare. *Clinical Radiology*, 74(5), 329–337. doi:10.1016/j.crad.2019.02.005 PMID:30898383

Hollywood, J. S., Vermeer, M. J. D., Woods, D., Goodison, S. E., & Jackson, B. A. (2018). Using Video Analytics and Sensor Fusion in Law Enforcement. 1–35.

Hosny, K., & Darwish, M. (2018). New Set of Multi-Channel Orthogonal Moments for Color Image Representation and Recognition. *Pattern Recognition*, 88, 153–173. doi:10.1016/j.patcog.2018.11.014

Hossain, M. S., Muhammad, G., Rahman, S. M. M., Abdul, W., Alelaiwi, A., & Alamri, A. (2016). Toward end-to-end biomet rics-based security for IoT infrastructure. *IEEE Wireless Communications*, *23*(5), 44–51. doi:10.1109/MWC.2016.7721741

Hsu, C.-Y., Yang, C.-S., Yu, L.-C., Lin, C.-F., Yao, H.-H., Chen, D.-Y., Lai, K. R., & Chang, P.-C. (2015). Development of a cloud-based service framework for energy conservation in a sustainable intelligent transportation system. *International Journal of Production Economics*, *164*, 454–461. doi:10.1016/j.ijpe.2014.08.014

Huang, B., Ye, Y., Xu, Z., Cai, Z., He, Y., Zhong, Z., Liu, L., Chen, X., Chen, H., & Huang, B. (2021). 3D lightweight network for simultaneous registration and segmentation of organs-at-risk in CT images of head and neck cancer. *IEEE Transactions on Medical Imaging*, *41*(4), 951–964. doi:10.1109/TMI.2021.3128408 PMID:34784272

Huang, T., Zhang, Q., Tang, X., Zhao, S., & Lu, X. (2022). A novel fault diagnosis method based on CNN and LSTM and its application in fault diagnosis for complex systems. *Artificial Intelligence Review*, *55*(2), 1289–1315. doi:10.100710462-021-09993-z

Huang, X., & Chen, J. (2021). A comprehensive review of image processing techniques for quality inspection in the food industry. *Food Control*, *124*, 107901. doi:10.1016/j.foodcont.2020.107901

Huda, S., Yearwood, J., Jelinek, H. F., Hassan, M. M., Fortino, G., & Buckland, M. (2016). A Hybrid Feature Selection with Ensemble Classification for Imbalanced Healthcare Data: A Case Study for Brain Tumor Diagnosis. *IEEE Access : Practical Innovations, Open Solutions*, *4*, 9145–9154. doi:10.1109/ACCESS.2016.2647238

Hussain, A., Tahir, A., Hussain, Z., Sheikh, Z., Gogate, M., Dashtipour, K., Ali, A., & Sheikh, A. (2021). Sheikh AArtificial Intelligence–Enabled Analysis of Public Attitudes on Facebook and Twitter Toward COVID-19 Vaccines in the United Kingdom and the United States: Observational Study. *Journal of Medical Internet Research*, *23*(4), e26627. https://www.jmir.org/2021/4/e26627. doi:10.2196/26627 PMID:33724919

Iester, M., & Zingirian, M. (2002). Quality of life in patients with early, moderate and advanced glaucoma. *Eye (London, England)*, *16*(1), 44–49. doi:10.1038j.eye.6700036 PMID:11913887

Iftikhar, S., Zhang, Z., Asim, M., Muthanna, A., Koucheryavy, A., & Abd El-Latif, A. A. (2022). Deep Learning-Based Pedestrian Detection in Autonomous Vehicles: Substantial Issues and Challenges. *Electronics (Basel)*, *11*(21), 3551. doi:10.3390/electronics11213551

Iftikhar, U., Anwer, M., Butt, R., & Ahmed, G. (2023). Towards 5G, 6G and 7G Sustainable and Potential Applications Using Blockchain: Comparative Analysis and Prospective Challenges*. *2023 4th International Conference on Computing, Mathematics and Engineering Technologies: Sustainable Technologies for Socio-Economic Development, ICoMET 2023*, (pp. 1–7). IEEE. 10.1109/iCoMET57998.2023.10099241

Ikram, S. T., Chambial, S., & Sood, D. (2023). A performance enhancement of deepfake video detection through the use of a hybrid CNN Deep learning model. *International journal of electrical and computer engineering systems, 14*(2), 169-178.

Ikuesan, R. A., Ganiyu, S. O., Majigi, M. U., Opaluwa, Y. D., & Venter, H. S. (2020). Practical Approach to Urban Crime Prevention in Developing Nations. *ACM International Conference Proceeding Series*, (pp. 0–7). ACM. https://doi.org/10.1145/3386723.3387867

Iliev, A., Kyurkchiev, N., & Markov, S. (2017). On the Approximation of the step function by some sigmoid functions. *Mathematics and Computers in Simulation*, *133*, 223–234. doi:10.1016/j.matcom.2015.11.005

Imaizumi, H., Watanabe, A., Hirano, H., Takemura, M., Kashiwagi, H., & Monobe, S. (2017, June). Hippocra: Doctor-to-doctor teledermatology consultation service towards future ai-based diagnosis system in japan. In *2017 IEEE International Conference on Consumer Electronics-Taiwan (ICCE-TW)* (pp. 51-52). IEEE. 10.1109/ICCE-China.2017.7990990

Inibhunu, C., McGregor, C., & Pugh, J. E. V. (2021, December). An alert notification subsystem for ai based clinical decision support: A protoype in nicu. In *2021 IEEE International Conference on Big Data (Big Data)* (pp. 3511-3518). IEEE. 10.1109/BigData52589.2021.9671579

Iosup, A., Ostermann, S., Yigitbasi, N., Prodan, R., Fahringer, T., & Epema, D. (2011). Performance Analysis of Cloud Computing Services for MTC-Based Scientific Computing. *IEEE Transactions on Parallel and Distributed Systems*, *22*(6), 931–945. doi:10.1109/TPDS.2011.66

Jain, R., Gupta, M., Taneja, S., & Hemanth, D. J. (2021). Deep learning based detection and analysis of COVID-19 on chest X-ray images. *Applied Intelligence*, *51*(3), 1690–1700. doi:10.100710489-020-01902-1 PMID:34764553

Jain, S., Gupta, S., Sreelakshmi, K. K., & Rodrigues, J. J. P. C. (2022). Fog computing in enabling 5G-driven emerging technologies for development of sustainable smart city infrastructures. *Cluster Computing*, *25*(2), 1111–1154. doi:10.100710586-021-03496-w

Jain, V., Beram, S. M., Talukdar, V., Patil, T., Dhabliya, D., & Gupta, A. (2022). Accuracy Enhancement in Machine Learning During Blockchain-Based Transaction Classification. *Seventh International Conference on Parallel, Distributed and Grid Computing (PDGC)*. IEEE. 10.1109/PDGC56933.2022.10053213

Jakka, A. (2020, October). Forecasting COVID-19 cases in India Using Machine Learning Models. In *2020 International Conference on Smart Technologies in Computing, Electrical and Electronics (ICSTCEE)* (pp. 466-471). IEEE

Janardhana, K., Anushkannan, N. K., Dinakaran, K. P., Puse, R. K., & Boopathi, S. (2023). *Experimental Investigation on Microhardness, Surface Roughness, and White Layer Thickness of Dry EDM*. Engineering Research Express. doi:10.1088/2631-8695/acce8f

Janardhana, K., Singh, V., Singh, S. N., Babu, T. S. R., Bano, S., & Boopathi, S. (2023). Utilization Process for Electronic Waste in Eco-Friendly Concrete: Experimental Study. In Sustainable Approaches and Strategies for E-Waste Management and Utilization (pp. 204–223). IGI Global.

Janz, N. K., Wren, P. A., Guire, K. E., Musch, D. C., Gillespie, B. W., & Lichter, P. R. (1998). Collaborative Initial Glaucoma Treatment Study. Fear of blindness in the Collaborative Initial Glaucoma Treatment Study: Patterns and correlates over time. *Ophthalmology*, *114*(12), 2213–2220. doi:10.1016/j.ophtha.2007.02.014 PMID:17490746

Javaid, M., & Khan, I. H. (2021). Internet of Things (IoT) enabled healthcare helps to take the challenges of COVID-19 Pandemic. *Journal of Oral Biology and Craniofacial Research*, *11*(2), 209–214. doi:10.1016/j.jobcr.2021.01.015 PMID:33665069

Javanmard, S. H., & Toghyani, A. 2021. How hookah increases the risk of corona virus in younger people?. *Journal of Research in Medical Sciences: The Official Journal of Isfahan University of Medical Sciences, 26*.

Javed, A. R., & Jalil, Z. (2020). Byte-Level Object Identification for Forensic Investigation of Digital Images. *1st Annual International Conference on Cyber Warfare and Security, ICCWS 2020 - Proceedings*, (pp. 12–15). IEEE. 10.1109/ICCWS48432.2020.9292387

Javed, A. R., Jalil, Z., Zehra, W., Gadekallu, T. R., Suh, D. Y., & Piran, M. J. (2021). A comprehensive survey on digital video forensics: Taxonomy, challenges, and future directions. *Engineering Applications of Artificial Intelligence*, *106*(September), 104456. doi:10.1016/j.engappai.2021.104456

Javidi, M., Saboohi, H., & Mehran, M. (2019). Image processing in chemical engineering: An overview of recent developments and future prospects. *Chemical Engineering Research & Design*, *143*, 1–20. doi:10.1016/j.cherd.2019.01.022

Jayapoorani, S., Pandey, D., Sasirekha, N. S., Anand, R., & Pandey, B. K. (2023). Systolic optimized adaptive filter architecture designs for ECG noise cancellation by Vertex-5. *Aerospace Systems*, *6*(1), 163–173. doi:10.100742401-022-00177-3

Jayaraman, G., & Dhulipala, V. R. S. (2022). FEECS: Fuzzy-Based Energy-Efficient Cluster Head Selection Algorithm for Lifetime Enhancement of Wireless Sensor Networks. *Arabian Journal for Science and Engineering*, *47*(2), 1631–1641. doi:10.100713369-021-06030-7

Jayasingh, R. (2022). Speckle noise removal by SORAMA segmentation in Digital Image Processing to facilitate precise robotic surgery. *International Journal of Reliable and Quality E-Healthcare*, *11*(1), 1–19. doi:10.4018/IJRQEH.295083

Jeevanantham, Y. A., A, S., V, V., J, S. I., Boopathi, S., & Kumar, D. P. (2023). Implementation of Internet-of Things (IoT) in Soil Irrigation System. *IEEE Explore*, 1–5. doi:10.1109/ICPECTS56089.2022.10047185

Jenga, K., Catal, C., & Kar, G. (2023). Machine learning in crime prediction. *Journal of Ambient Intelligence and Humanized Computing*, *14*(3), 2887–2913. doi:10.100712652-023-04530-y

Jeon, J. Y., & Yoon, H. J. (2019). The impact of image processing on online consumer behavior: A review of the literature. *Journal of Marketing Communications*, *25*(6), 601–613. doi:10.1080/13527266.2017.1405044

Jeong, D. (2020). Artificial intelligence security threat, crime, and forensics: Taxonomy and open issues. *IEEE Access : Practical Innovations, Open Solutions*, *8*, 184560–184574. doi:10.1109/ACCESS.2020.3029280

Jeyaboopathiraja, J., & Priscilla, D. G. M. (2021). Binning and Improved Deep. *IT in Industry*, *9*(2), 1428–1436.

Jiang, B. C., Szu-Lang Tasi, & Chien-Chih Wang. (2002). Machine vision-based gray relational theory applied to IC marking inspection. *IEEE Transactions on Semiconductor Manufacturing*, *15*(1), 531–539. doi:10.1109/TSM.2002.804906

Jiang, X., Xu, C., Guo, Q., & Zhu, H. (2021, October). AI-aided Data Mining in Gut Microbiome: The Road to Precision Medicine. In *2021 14th International Congress on Image and Signal Processing, BioMedical Engineering and Informatics (CISP-BMEI).* (pp. 1-5). IEEE.

Jiang, Z., Wu, D., Zheng, L., Yao, Y., & Chen, Y. (2020). A Deep Learning-Based Visual Object Recognition System for Warehouse Robots. *Journal of Intelligent & Robotic Systems*, *98*(1), 157–173.

Jin, L., & Liu, G., (2021). An approach to image processing of deep learning based on improved SSD.

Jog, G. M., Koch, C., Golparvar-Fard, M., & Brilakis, I. (2021). Pothole properties measurement through visual 2D recognition and 3D reconstruction. In Computing in Civil Engineering (pp. 553-560). Semantic Scholar.

John Blesswin, A., Selva Mary, G., & Manoj Kumar, S. (2021). Multiple Secret Image Communication Using Visual Cryptography. In Wireless Personal Communications (Vol. 122, Issue 4, pp. 3085–3103). Springer Science and Business Media LLC. doi:10.100711277-021-09041-7

Ju, L., Wang, X., Wang, L., Mahapatra, D., Zhao, X., Zhou, Q., Liu, T., & Ge, Z. (2022). Improving medical images classification with label noise using dual-uncertainty estimation. *IEEE Transactions on Medical Imaging*, *41*(6), 1533–1546. doi:10.1109/TMI.2022.3141425 PMID:34995185

Juang, L.-H., & Wu, M.-N. (2011). Psoriasis image identification using k-means clustering with morphological processing. *Measurement*, *44*(5), 895–905. doi:10.1016/j.measurement.2011.02.006

Jyotika, P., Kavita, K., & Arora, S. (2020). Optic cup segmentation from retinal fundus images using glow swarm optimization for glaucoma detection. *Biomedical Signal Processing and Control*, *60*, 1–12.

Kadiyam, P. (2021). *Crime rate prediction from street view images using convolutional neural networks and transfer learning*. UTWENTE.

Kagadis, G. C., Kloukinas, C., Moore, K., Philbin, J., Papadimitroulas, P., Alexakos, C., Nagy, P. G., Visvikis, D., & Hendee, W. R. (2013). Cloud computing in medical imaging. *Medical Physics*, *40*(7), 70901. doi:10.1118/1.4811272 PMID:23822402

Kan, A. (2017). Machine learning applications in cell image analysis. *Immunology and Cell Biology*, *95*(6), 525–530. doi:10.1038/icb.2017.16 PMID:28294138

Kanavati, F., Ichihara, S., & Tsuneki, M. (2022). A deep learning model for breast ductal carcinoma in situ classification in whole slide images. *Virchows Archiv*, *480*(5), 1009–1022. doi:10.100700428-021-03241-z PMID:35076741

Kang, I. K., Arce, G. R., & Lee, H.-K. (2011). Color Extended Visual Cryptography Using Error Diffusion. *IEEE Transactions on Image Processing*, *20*(1), 132–145. doi:10.1109/TIP.2010.2056376 PMID:20615812

Kannan, E., Trabelsi, Y., Boopathi, S., & Alagesan, S. (2022). Influences of cryogenically treated work material on near-dry wire-cut electrical discharge machining process. *Surface Topography: Metrology and Properties*, *10*(1), 15027. doi:10.1088/2051-672X/ac53e1

Kanwal, A., Zhang, M., Sharaf, F., & Li, C. (2022). Enzymatic degradation of poly (butylene adipate co-terephthalate) (PBAT) copolymer using lipase B from Candida antarctica (CALB) and effect of PBAT on plant growth. *Polymer Bulletin*, *79*(10), 9059–9073. doi:10.100700289-021-03946-w

Kapoor, A., Bhat, S. I., Shidnal, S., & Mehra, A. Implementation of IoT (Internet of Things) and Image processing in smart agriculture. In *Proceedings of the 2016 International Conference on Computation System and Information Technology for Sustainable Solutions (CSITSS)*, (pp. 21–26). IEEE. 10.1109/CSITSS.2016.7779434

Karatekin, T., Sancak, S., Celik, G., Topcuoglu, S., Karatekin, G., Kirci, P., & Okatan, A. (2019, August). Interpretable machine learning in healthcare through generalized additive model with pairwise interactions (GA2M): Predicting severe retinopathy of prematurity. In *2019 International Conference on Deep Learning and Machine Learning in Emerging Applications (Deep-ML)* (pp. 61-66). IEEE.

Karbuz, P., & Tugrul, N. (2021). Microwave and ultrasound assisted extraction of pectin from various fruits peel. *Journal of Food Science and Technology*, *58*(2), 641–650. doi:10.100713197-020-04578-0 PMID:33568858

Karolin, M., & Meyyappan, T. (2022). Visual Cryptography Secret Share Creation Techniques with Multiple Image Encryption and Decryption Using Elliptic Curve Cryptography. In IETE Journal of Research (pp. 1–8). Informa UK Limited. doi:10.1080/03772063.2022.2142684

Kaur, K., Bharany, S., Badotra, S., Aggarwal, K., Nayyar, A., & Sharma, S. (2023). Energy-efficient polyglot persistence database live migration among heterogeneous clouds. *The Journal of Supercomputing*, *79*(1), 265–294. doi:10.100711227-022-04662-6

Kaur, N., & Sharma, M. (2017). Brain tumor detection using self-adaptive K-means clustering. In *2017 International Conference on Energy, Communication, Data Analytics and Soft Computing (ICECDS)*, (pp. 1861-1865). IEEE. 10.1109/ICECDS.2017.8389771

Kaur, S. P., & Sharma, M. (2015). Radially optimized zone-divided energy-aware wireless sensor networks (WSN) protocol using BA (bat algorithm). *Journal of the Institution of Electronics and Telecommunication Engineers*, *61*(2), 170–179. doi:10.1080/03772063.2014.999833

Kaushik, D., & Gupta, A. (2021). Ultra-secure transmissions for 5G-V2X communications. *Materials Today: Proceedings*. doi:10.1016/j.matpr.2020.12.130

Kaushik, K., & Garg, M. Annu, Gupta, A. & Pramanik, S. (2021). Application of Machine Learning and Deep Learning in Cyber security: An Innovative Approach, in Cybersecurity and Digital Forensics: Challenges and Future Trends, M. Ghonge, S. Pramanik, R. Mangrulkar and D. N. Le, Eds, Wiley.

Kaushik, K., & Garg, M. Annu, Gupta, A. & Pramanik, S. (2021). Application of Machine Learning and Deep Learning in Cyber security: An Innovative Approach. In Ghonge, S. Pramanik, R. Mangrulkar and D. N. Le, (eds.), Cybersecurity and Digital Forensics: Challenges and Future Trends, Wiley.

Kaushik, K., Garg, M., Gupta, A., & Pramanik, S. (2021). Application of Machine Learning and Deep Learning in Cyber security: An Innovative Approach. in M. Ghonge, S. Pramanik, R. Mangrulkar and D. N. Le, (eds.) Cybersecurity and Digital Forensics: Challenges and Future Trends. Wiley.

Kaushik, K., Garg, M. Annu, G., & Pramanik, S. (2021). Application of Machine Learning and Deep Learning in Cyber security: An Innovative Approach, in Cybersecurity and Digital Forensics. In M. Ghonge, S. Pramanik, R. Mangrulkar & D. N. Le (eds). Challenges and Future Trends. Wiley.

Kavitha, C., Geetha Malini, P. S., Charan Kantumuchu, V., Manoj Kumar, N., Verma, A., & Boopathi, S. (2023). An experimental study on the hardness and wear rate of carbonitride coated stainless steel. *Materials Today: Proceedings*, *74*, 595–601. doi:10.1016/j.matpr.2022.09.524

Kavitha, M., & Palani, S. (2014). Hierarchical classifier for soft and hard exudates detection of retinal fundus images. *Journal of Intelligent & Fuzzy Systems*, *27*(5), 2511–2528. doi:10.3233/IFS-141224

Kernbach, J. M., & Staartjes, V. E. (2022). Foundations of Machine Learning-Based Clinical Prediction Modeling: Part II—Generalization and Overfitting. In V. E. Staartjes, L. Regli, & C. Serra (Eds.), *Machine Learning in Clinical Neuroscience. Acta Neurochirurgica Supplement* (Vol. 134). Springer. doi:10.1007/978-3-030-85292-4_3

Keshani, M., Azimifar, Z., Tajeripour, F., & Boostani, R. (2013). Lung nodule segmentation and recognition using SVM classifier and active contour modeling: A complete intelligent system. *Computers in Biology and Medicine*, *43*(4), 287–300. doi:10.1016/j.compbiomed.2012.12.004 PMID:23369568

Keshavarzi Arshadi, A., Webb, J., Salem, M., Cruz, E., Calad-Thomson, S., Ghadirian, N., Collins, J., Diez-Cecilia, E., Kelly, B., Goodarzi, H., & Yuan, J. S. (2020). Artificial intelligence for COVID-19 drug discovery and vaccine development. *Frontiers in Artificial Intelligence*, *3*, 65. doi:10.3389/frai.2020.00065 PMID:33733182

Khaddar, M. A. El, & Boulmalf, M. (2017). Smartphone: The Ultimate IoT and IoE Device. *Smartphones from an Applied Research Perspective*. doi:10.5772/intechopen.69734

Khan, M. A.-M., Haque, M. F., Hasan, K. R., Alajmani, S. H., Baz, M., Masud, M., & Nahid, A.-A. (2022). LLDNet: A Lightweight Lane Detection Approach for Autonomous Cars Using Deep Learning. *Sensors (Basel)*, *22*(15), 5595. doi:10.339022155595 PMID:35898103

Khan, M. H. R., & Hossain, A. (2020). Machine Learning Approaches Reveal That the Number of Tests Do Not Matter to the Prediction of Global Confirmed COVID-19 Cases. *Frontiers in Artificial Intelligence*, *3*, 3. doi:10.3389/frai.2020.561801 PMID:33748745

Khan, R. A., Hussain, A., Bajwa, U. I., Raza, R. H., & Anwar, M. W. (2023). Fire and Smoke Detection Using Capsule Network. *Fire Technology*, *59*(2), 581–594. doi:10.100710694-022-01352-w

Khine, E. E., Koncz-Horvath, D., Kristaly, F., Ferenczi, T., Karacs, G., Baumli, P., & Kaptay, G. (2022). Synthesis and characterization of calcium oxide nanoparticles for CO_2 capture. *Journal of Nanoparticle Research*, *24*(7), 139. doi:10.100711051-022-05518-z

Khokhar, S., Zin, A. A. B. M., Mokhtar, A. S. B., & Pesaran, M. (2015). A comprehensive overview on signal processing and artificial intelligence techniques applications in classification of power quality disturbances. *Renewable & Sustainable Energy Reviews*, *51*, 1650–1663. doi:10.1016/j.rser.2015.07.068

Khurana, D., Koli, A., Khatter, K., & Singh, S. (2023). Natural language processing: State of the art, current trends and challenges. *Multimedia Tools and Applications*, *82*(3), 3713–3744. doi:10.100711042-022-13428-4 PMID:35855771

Kim, B., & Lee, E. (2022, October). Medical artificial intelligence framework for the development of medical imaging artificial intelligence devices. In *2022 13th International Conference on Information and Communication Technology Convergence (ICTC)* (pp. 2210-2212). IEEE. 10.1109/ICTC55196.2022.9952625

Kim, T., & Ryu, S.-K. (2014). Review and analysis of pothole detection methods. *Journal of Emerging Trends in Computing and Information Sciences*, *5*(8), 603–608.

Kim, Y.-M., Kim, Y.-G., Son, S.-Y., Lim, S.-Y., Choi, B.-Y., & Choi, D.-H. (2022). Review of Recent Automated Pothole-Detection Methods. *Applied Sciences (Basel, Switzerland)*, *12*(11), 5320. doi:10.3390/app12115320

Kirpichnikov, D., Pavlyuk, A., Grebneva, Y., & Okagbue, H. (2020). Criminal Liability of the Artificial Intelligence. *E3S Web of Conferences, 159*, 1–10. https://doi.org/ doi:10.1051/e3sconf/202015904025

Kiruba Shankar, R., Indra, J., Oviya, R., Heeraj, A., & Ragunathan, R. (2020). Machine Vision Based Quality Inspection for Automotive Parts using Edge Detection Technique. *IOP Conference Series: Material Science and Engineering*, (pp. 1-10). IOP Science. 10.1088/1757-899X/1055/1/012029

Kissler, S. M., Tedijanto, C., Lipsitch, M., & Grad, Y. 2020. Social distancing strategies for curbing the COVID-19 epidemic. MedRxiv. doi:10.1101/2020.03.22.20041079

Kobayashi, K., Suzuki, K., & Arakawa, Y. (2017). Quality inspection of woven fabrics using image processing. *International Journal of Clothing Science and Technology*, *29*(4), 465–476.

Koch, C., & Brilakis, I. (2011). Pothole detection in asphalt pavement images. *Advanced Engineering Informatics*, *25*(3), 507–515. doi:10.1016/j.aei.2011.01.002

Koshariya, A. K. (2023). *AI-Enabled IoT and WSN-Integrated Smart.*, doi:10.4018/978-1-6684-8516-3.ch011

Koshariya, A. K., Khatoon, S., Marathe, A. M., Suba, G. M., Baral, D., & Boopathi, S. (2023). Agricultural Waste Management Systems Using Artificial Intelligence Techniques. In *AI-Enabled Social Robotics in Human Care Services* (pp. 236–258). IGI Global. doi:10.4018/978-1-6684-8171-4.ch009

Kotenko, I., Izrailov, K., & Buinevich, M. (2022). Static Analysis of Information Systems for IoT Cyber Security: A Survey of Machine Learning Approaches. *Sensors (Basel)*, *22*(4), 1335. doi:10.339022041335 PMID:35214237

Krishnan, M. M. R., & Faust, O. (2013). Automated glaucoma detection using hybrid feature extraction in retinal fundus images. [Google Scholar]. *Journal of Mechanics in Medicine and Biology*, *13*(01), 1350011. doi:10.1142/S0219519413500115

Kulvir Singh, E. N. (2016). A Review on Image Fusion Techniques and Proposal of New Hybrid Technique. *International Research Journal of Engineering and Technology*, (03), 1321-1324.

Kumar, A. (2019). SS Sai Satyanarayana Reddy, and Vivek Kulkarni. "An object detection technique for blind people in real-time using deep neural network. In *2019 Fifth International Conference on Image Information Processing (ICIIP)*, (pp. 292-297). IEEE. 10.1109/ICIIP47207.2019.8985965

Kumar, D., Mohan, R., & Samant, A. (2017). Image processing techniques for automatic process control: A review. *Journal of Process Control*, *54*, 1–23. doi:10.1016/j.jprocont.2017.06.004

Kumar, M. S., Sankar, S., Nassa, V. K., Pandey, D., Pandey, B. K., & Enbeyle, W. (2021). Innovation and creativity for data mining using computational statistics. In *Methodologies and Applications of Computational Statistics for Machine Intelligence* (pp. 223–240). IGI Global. doi:10.4018/978-1-7998-7701-1.ch012

Kumar, P. S., Kumar, R. R., Sathar, A., & Sahasranamam, V. (2013, December). Automatic detection of exudates in retinal images using histogram analysis. In *2013 IEEE Recent Advances in Intelligent Computational Systems (RAICS)* (pp. 277-281). IEEE..

Kumar, R., Narayanan, S., & Kaur, G. (2021). Future of the Internet of Everything. *International Research Journal of Computer Science*, *8*(4), 84–92. doi:10.26562/irjcs.2021.v0804.003

Kumar, S., Tiwari, P., & Zymbler, M. (2019). Internet of Things is a revolutionary approach for future technology enhancement: A review. *Journal of Big Data*, *6*(1), 111. doi:10.118640537-019-0268-2

Kumar, S. A. (2009). *A modified statistical approach for image fusion using wavelet transform*. Springer.

Kumar, Y., Gupta, S., & Gupta, A. (2021, November). Study of machine and deep learning classifications for IOT enabled healthcare devices. In *2021 International Conference on Technological Advancements and Innovations (ICTAI)* (pp. 212-217). IEEE. 10.1109/ICTAI53825.2021.9673437

Kumara, V., Mohanaprakash, T. A., Fairooz, S., Jamal, K., Babu, T., & B., S. (2023). Experimental Study on a Reliable Smart Hydroponics System. In *Human Agro-Energy Optimization for Business and Industry* (pp. 27–45). IGI Global. doi:10.4018/978-1-6684-4118-3.ch002

Kumar Pandey, B., Pandey, D., Nassa, V. K., Ahmad, T., Singh, C., George, A. S., & Wakchaure, M. A. (2021). Encryption and steganography-based text extraction in IoT using the EWCTS optimizer. *Imaging Science Journal*, *69*(1-4), 38–56. doi:10.1080/13682199.2022.2146885

Kusakabe, T., Okazaki, T., Iwamoto, K., & Ito, T. (2019). Real-time Monitoring of Warehouse Environment Using IoT Sensor and Video Image Processing. In *International Conference on Innovative Mobile and Internet Services in Ubiquitous Computing* (pp. 225-233). Springer, Cham.

Kuthadi, V. M., Selvaraj, R., Baskar, S., Shakeel, P. M., & Ranjan, A. (2022). Optimized Energy Management Model on Data Distributing Framework of Wireless Sensor Network in IoT System. *Wireless Personal Communications*, *127*(2), 1377–1403. doi:10.100711277-021-08583-0

L, M. A., & K, P. (2022). Digital Forensics Triage Classification Model using Hybrid Learning Approaches. *International Journal of Innovative Research in Computer Science & Technology, 3*, 29–39. doi:10.55524/ijircst.2022.10.3.7

Lanjewar, M. G., Parab, J. S., & Shaikh, A. Y. (2022). Development of framework by combining CNN with KNN to detect Alzheimer's disease using MRI images. *Multimedia Tools and Applications*, *82*(8), 12699–12717. doi:10.100711042-022-13935-4

Latif, G., Iskandar, D. N. F. A., Alghazo, J., & Jaffar, A. (2018). Improving brain MR image classification for tumor segmentation using phase congruency. *Current Medical Imaging*, *14*(6), 914–922. doi:10.2174/157340561466618040 2150218

Law, S., Seresinhe, C. I., Shen, Y., & Gutierrez-Roig, M. (2020). Street-Frontage-Net: Urban image classification using deep convolutional neural networks. *International Journal of Geographical Information Science, 34*(4), 681–707. doi: 10.1080/13658816.2018.1555832

Lelisho, M. E., Pandey, D., Alemu, B. D., Pandey, B. K., & Tareke, S. A. (2023). The negative impact of social media during COVID-19 pandemic. *Trends in Psychology, 31*(1), 123–142. doi:10.100743076-022-00192-5

Letourneau-Guillon, L., Camirand, D., Guilbert, F., & Forghani, R. (2020). Artificial intelligence applications for workflow, process optimization and predictive analytics. *Neuroimaging Clinics of North America, 30*(4), e1–e15. doi:10.1016/j.nic.2020.08.008 PMID:33039002

Lewis, R. J. (2000, May). An introduction to classification and regression tree (CART) analysis. In *Annual meeting of the society for academic emergency medicine in San Francisco, California* (Vol. 14). ACM.

Li, C., Cui, Z., Zhao, M., & Zhao, Z. (2020). Real-time process monitoring and optimization based on machine vision and image processing in chemical industry. *Journal of Cleaner Production, 245*, 118861. doi:10.1016/j.jclepro.2019.118861

Li, J., & Zhang, Y. (2013). Learning surf cascade for fast and accurate object detection. In *Proceedings of the IEEE conference on computer vision and pattern recognition*, (pp. 3468-3475). IEEE. 10.1109/CVPR.2013.445

Li, J., Liang, X., & Chen, H. (2020). The impact of image processing on social media marketing: A systematic review. *Journal of Computer Information Systems, 60*(2), 145–154. doi:10.1080/08874417.2018.1466216

Li, L., Cheng, Z., Zhang, X., & Gu, Y. (2020). Radiomics analysis of CT images for prediction of chemotherapy response and survival in patients with advanced non-small cell lung cancer. *Medical Science Monitor, 26*, e922451.

Li, Q., & Li, X. (2021). A review of pedestrian detection for autonomous vehicles. *IEEE Access : Practical Innovations, Open Solutions, 9*, 54332–54350.

Li, S., Kang, X., & Hu, J. (2013). Image fusion with guided filtering [J]. *IEEE Transactions on Image Processing, 22*(7), 2864–2875. doi:10.1109/TIP.2013.2244222 PMID:23372084

Li, S., Kwok, J., Tsang, I., & Wang, Y. (2004, November). Fusing images with different focuses using support vector machines. *IEEE Transactions on Neural Networks, 15*(6), 1555–1561. doi:10.1109/TNN.2004.837780 PMID:15565781

Li, X., Li, J., Yiu, S., Gao, C., & Xiong, J. (2019). Privacy-preserving edge-assisted image retrieval and classification in IoT. *Frontiers of Computer Science, 13*(5), 1136–1147. doi:10.100711704-018-8067-z

Li, Y., Zhang, W., Liu, Y., & Jin, Y. (2022). A visualized fire detection method based on convolutional neural network beyond anchor. *Applied Intelligence, 52*(11), 13280–13295. doi:10.100710489-022-03243-7

Li, Z., Zhang, X., Müller, H., & Zhang, S. (2018). Large-scale retrieval for medical image analytics: A comprehensive review. *Medical Image Analysis, 43*, 66–84. doi:10.1016/j.media.2017.09.007 PMID:29031831

Li, Z., Zhang, Y., & Fu, Y. (2020). Recent advances in machine vision-based quality inspection of fruit and vegetables: A review. *Food Control, 108*, 106835. doi:10.1016/j.foodcont.2019.106835

Liang, L. L., Chu, S. C., Du, Z. G., & Pan, J.-S. (2023). Surrogate-assisted Phasmatodea population evolution algorithm applied to wireless sensor networks. *Wireless Networks, 29*(2), 637–655. doi:10.100711276-022-03168-6

Liang, Z., Zhang, G., Huang, J. X., & Hu, Q. V. (2014, November). Deep learning for healthcare decision making with EMRs. In *2014 IEEE International Conference on Bioinformatics and Biomedicine (BIBM)* (pp. 556-559). IEEE. 10.1109/BIBM.2014.6999219

Liberati, A., Altman, D. G., Tetzlaff, J., Mulrow, C., Gøtzsche, P. C., Ioannidis, J. P., & Moher, D. (2009). The PRISMA statement for reporting systematic reviews and meta-analyses of studies that evaluate health care interventions: Explanation and elaboration. *Annals of Internal Medicine*, *151*(4), W-65. doi:10.7326/0003-4819-151-4-200908180-00136 PMID:19622512

Lin, C.-S., & Lin, Y.-C. (2020). Applications of image processing in automated visual inspection of semiconductor devices: A review. *Journal of Intelligent Manufacturing*, *31*, 53–65. doi:10.100710845-019-01517-2

Lin, J., & Liu, Y. (2020). Potholes Detection Based on SVM in the Pavement Distress Image. In *Proceedings of International Symposium on Distributed Computing and Applications to Business, Engineering and Science*, (pp. 544-547). IEEE.

Lin, L., Li, M., Huang, Y., Cheng, P., Xia, H., Wang, K., Yuan, J., & Tang, X. (2020). The SUSTech-SYSU dataset for automated exudate detection and diabetic retinopathy grading. *Scientific Data*, *7*(1), 1–10. doi:10.103841597-020-00755-0 PMID:33219237

Lingxin, Z., Junkai, S., & Baijie, Z. (2022). A review of the research and application of deep learning-based computer vision in structural damage detection. *Earthquake Engineering and Engineering Vibration*, *21*(1), 1–21. doi:10.100711803-022-2074-7

Liu, F., & Wu, C. (2011). Embedded Extended Visual Cryptography Schemes. In IEEE Transactions on Information Forensics and Security (Vol. 6, Issue 2, pp. 307–322). Institute of Electrical and Electronics Engineers (IEEE). doi:10.1109/TIFS.2011.2116782

Liu, J., Dian, R., Li, S., & Liu, H. (2023). SGFusion: A saliency guided deep-learning framework for pixel-level image fusion. *Information Fusion*, *91*, 205–214. doi:10.1016/j.inffus.2022.09.030

Liu, Q., Cao, L., Zhang, X., Yang, W., & Zhang, X. (2019). A review of image processing techniques for road surface distress detection. [English Edition]. *Journal of Traffic and Transportation Engineering*, *6*(1), 70–79. doi:10.1016/j.jtte.2018.10.004

Liu, Q., Zou, B., Chen, J., Ke, W., Yue, K., Chen, Z., & Zhao, G. (2017). A location-to-segmentation strategy for automatic exudate segmentation in colour retinal fundus images. *Computerized Medical Imaging and Graphics*, *55*, 78–86. doi:10.1016/j.compmedimag.2016.09.001 PMID:27665058

Liu, X., Li, Y., Zhang, R., Huangfu, L., Du, G., & Xiang, Q. (2021). Inactivation effects and mechanisms of plasma-activated water combined with sodium laureth sulfate (SLES) against *Saccharomyces cerevisiae*. *Applied Microbiology and Biotechnology*, *105*(7), 2855–2865. doi:10.100700253-021-11227-9 PMID:33738554

Liu, X., Ma, W., Ma, X., & Wang, J. (2023). LAE-Net: A locally-adaptive embedding network for low-light image enhancement. *Pattern Recognition*, *133*, 109039. doi:10.1016/j.patcog.2022.109039

Liu, Y. Y., Chen, M., Ishikawa, H., Wollstein, G., Schuman, J. S., & Rehg, J. M. (2011). Automated macular pathology diagnosis in retinal OCT images using multi-scale spatial pyramid and local binary patterns in texture and shape encoding. [PMC free article] [PubMed] [Google Scholar]. *Medical Image Analysis*, *15*(5), 748–759. doi:10.1016/j.media.2011.06.005 PMID:21737338

Liu, Z. G., Yang, Y., & Ji, X. H. (2016). Flame detection algorithm based on a saliency detection technique and the uniform local binary pattern in the YCbCr color space. *Signal, Image and Video Processing*, *10*(2), 277–284. doi:10.100711760-014-0738-0

Lokuarachchi, D., Gunarathna, K., Muthumal, L., & Gamage, T. (2019, March). Automated detection of exudates in retinal images. In *2019 IEEE 15th International Colloquium on Signal Processing & Its Applications (CSPA)* (pp. 43-47). IEEE. 10.1109/CSPA.2019.8696052

Long, J., Shelhamer, E., & Darrell, T. (2015). Fully convolutional networks for semantic segmentation. In *Proceedings of the IEEE conference on computer vision and pattern recognition* (pp. 3431-3440). IEEE.

Lorch, B., Scheler, N., & Riess, C. (2022). Compliance Challenges in Forensic Image Analysis Under the Artificial Intelligence Act. *European Signal Processing Conference*, (pp. 613–617). IEEE. 10.23919/EUSIPCO55093.2022.9909723

Lu, L., Zhao, Y., & Wang, Y. (2019). Image processing techniques for brand positioning and advertising: A review. *Journal of Advertising Research*, *59*(1), 19–33. doi:10.2501/JAR-2018-033

Ma, J., Tang, L., Fan, F., Huang, J., Mei, X., & Ma, Y. (2022). SwinFusion: Cross-domain long-range learning for general image fusion via swin transformer. *IEEE/CAA Journal of Automatica Sinica*, *9*(7), 1200-1217.

Ma, X., Song, B., Lin, W., Wu, J., Huang, W., & Liu, B. (2022). High-fidelity decryption technology of Visual Cryptography based on optical coherence operation. In *Results in Physics* (Vol. 43, p. 106065). Elsevier BV. doi:10.1016/j. rinp.2022.106065

Macyszyn, L., Akbari, H., Pisapia, J. M., Da, X., Attiah, M., Pigrish, V., Bi, Y., Pal, S., Davuluri, R. V., Roccograndi, L., Dahmane, N., Martinez-Lage, M., Biros, G., Wolf, R. L., Bilello, M., O'Rourke, D. M., & Davatzikos, C. (2015). Imaging patterns predict patient survival and molecular subtype in glioblastoma via machine learning techniques. *Neuro-Oncology*, *18*(3), 417–425. doi:10.1093/neuonc/nov127 PMID:26188015

Madabhushi, A., & Lee, G. (2016). Image analysis and machine learning in digital pathology: Challenges and opportunities. *Medical Image Analysis*, *33*, 170–175. doi:10.1016/j.media.2016.06.037 PMID:27423409

Madhumathy, P., & Pandey, D. (2022). Deep learning based photo acoustic imaging for non-invasive imaging. *Multimedia Tools and Applications*, *81*(5), 7501–7518. doi:10.100711042-022-11903-6

Maglietta, R., Carlucci, R., Fanizza, C., & Dimauro, G. (2022). Machine Learning and Image Processing Methods for Cetacean Photo Identification: A Systematic Review. *IEEE Access : Practical Innovations, Open Solutions*, *10*(July), 80195–80207. doi:10.1109/ACCESS.2022.3195218

Maheshwari, A. (2015). A New Image Encryption Algorithm Based Slicing and Displacement Followed By Symmetric and Asymmetric Cryptography Technique. *International Journal on Recent and Innovation Trends in Computing and Communication, 3*(5), 2679 – 2684.

Malamas, E. N., Petrakis, E. G. M., Zervakis, M., Petit, L., & Legat, J.-D. (2003). A survey on industrial vision systems, applications and tools. *Image and Vision Computing*, *21*(2), 171–188. doi:10.1016/S0262-8856(02)00152-X

Malathi, M., Sinthia, P., Farzana, F., & Aloy Anuja Mary, G. (2021). Breast cancer detection using active contour and classification by deep belief network. *Materials Today: Proceedings*, *45*, 2721–2724. doi:10.1016/j.matpr.2020.11.551

Malik, H., Srivastava, S., Sood, Y. R., & Ahmad, A. (2018). Applications of artificial intelligence techniques in engineering. *Sigma, 1*.

Malinovskiy, Y., Wu, Y.-J., & Wang, Y. (2009). Video-based vehicle detection and tracking using spatiotemporal maps. *Transportation Research Record: Journal of the Transportation Research Board*, *2121*(1), 81–89. doi:10.3141/2121-09

Mall, P. K., Pramanik, S., Srivastava, S., Faiz, M., Sriramulu, S., & Kumar, M. N. (2023). FuzztNet-Based Modelling Smart Traffic System in Smart Cities Using Deep Learning Models. In *Data-Driven Mathematical Modeling in Smart Cities*. IGI Global., doi:10.4018/978-1-6684-6408-3.ch005

Malmir, S., & Shalchian, M. (2019). Design and FPGA implementation of dual-stage lane detection, based on Hough transform and localized stripe features. *Microprocessors and Microsystems*, *64*, 12–22. doi:10.1016/j.micpro.2018.10.003

Mamun, M., Farjana, A., Al Mamun, M., & Ahammed, M. S. (2022, June). Lung cancer prediction model using ensemble learning techniques and a systematic review analysis. In *2022 IEEE World AI IoT Congress (AIIoT)* (pp. 187-193). IEEE. 10.1109/AIIoT54504.2022.9817326

Mandal, A., Dutta, S., & Pramanik, S. (2021). Machine Intelligence of Pi from Geometrical Figures with Variable Parameters using SCILab. In D. Samanta, R. R. Althar, S. Pramanik, & S. Dutta (Eds.), *Methodologies and Applications of Computational Statistics for Machine Learning* (pp. 38–63). IGI Global. doi:10.4018/978-1-7998-7701-1.ch003

Mandal, S., Arinaminpathy, N., Bhargava, B., & Panda, S. (2021). Plausibility of a third wave of COVID-19 in India: A mathematical modelling based analysis. *The Indian Journal of Medical Research*, *153*(5-6), 522. PMID:34643562

Manikandan, V., & Amirtharajan, R. (2022). A simple embed over encryption scheme for DICOM images using Bülban Map. *Medical & Biological Engineering & Computing*, *60*(3), 701–717. doi:10.100711517-021-02499-4 PMID:35040082

Manisha & Rao. (2021). Colour Visual Cryptography (3,3) Scheme. *Turkish Journal of Computer and Mathematics Education*, *12*(2), 3189–3198.

Manju, K., & Sabeenian, R. S. (2018). Robust CDR calculation for glaucoma identification. *Biomedical Research* (0970-938X).

Manju, K., & Sabeenian, R. S. (2019). Cup and Disc Ratio and Inferior, Superior, Temporal and Nasal Calculation for Glaucoma Identification. *Journal of Medical Imaging and Health Informatics*, *9*(6), 1316–1319. doi:10.1166/jmihi.2019.2720

Manju, K., Sabeenian, R. S., & Surendar, A. (2017). A review on optic disc and cup segmentation. *Biomedical & Pharmacology Journal*, *10*(1), 373–379. doi:10.13005/bpj/1118

Manjunath, S., Hosmane, S., Punyashree, M., Ladia, A., & Malpani, A. (2022). *Study on Deep Learning Based Techniques for Image Tamper Detection.*, *8*(11), 368–376.

Marias, K. (2021). The constantly evolving role of medical image processing in oncology: From traditional medical image processing to imaging biomarkers and radiomics. *Journal of Imaging*, *7*(8), 124. doi:10.3390/jimaging7080124 PMID:34460760

Marks, B., & Thomas, J. (2022). Adoption of virtual reality technology in higher education: An evaluation of five teaching semesters in a purpose-designed laboratory. *Education and Information Technologies*, *27*(1), 1287–1305. doi:10.100710639-021-10653-6 PMID:34257511

Martínez-Mascorro, G. A., Abreu-Pederzini, J. R., Ortiz-Bayliss, J. C., Garcia-Collantes, A., & Terashima-Marín, H. (2021). Criminal intention detection at early stages of shoplifting cases by using 3D convolutional neural networks. *Computation (Basel, Switzerland)*, *9*(2), 1–25. doi:10.3390/computation9020024

Mateen, M., Wen, J., Nasrullah, N., Sun, S., & Hayat, S. (2020). Exudate detection for diabetic retinopathy using pretrained convolutional neural networks. *Complexity*, *2020*, 2020. doi:10.1155/2020/5801870

Mathur, N., Meena, Y. K., Mathur, S., & Mathur, D. (2018). *Detection of brain tumor in MRI image through fuzzy-based approach*. High-Resolution Neuroimaging-Basic Physical Principles and Clinical Applications. doi:10.5772/intechopen.71485

Maturana, D., & Scherer, S. (2015, September). Voxnet: A 3d convolutional neural network for real-time object recognition. In *2015 IEEE/RSJ International Conference on Intelligent Robots and Systems (IROS)* (pp. 922-928). IEEE 10.1109/IROS.2015.7353481

Mavandadi, S., Dimitrov, S., Feng, S., Yu, F., Sikora, U., Yaglidere, O., Padmanabhan, S., Nielsen, K., & Ozcan, A. (2012). Distributed medical image analysis and diagnosis through crowd-sourced games: A malaria case study. *PLoS One*, 7(5), e37245. doi:10.1371/journal.pone.0037245 PMID:22606353

McCall, J. C., & Trivedi, M. M. (2006). Video-based lane estimation and tracking for driver assistance: Survey, system, and evaluation. *IEEE Transactions on Intelligent Transportation Systems*, 7(1), 20–37. doi:10.1109/TITS.2006.869595

Mednis, A., Strazdins, G., Zviedris, R., Kanonirs, G., & Selavo, L. (2011). Real Time Pothole Detection using Android Smartphones with Accelerometers. In *Proceedings of Distributed Computing in Sensor Systems Workshop*, (pp. 1-6). IEEE. 10.1109/DCOSS.2011.5982206

Mehdy, M. M., Ng, P. Y., Shair, E. F., Saleh, N. I., & Gomes, C. (2017). Artificial neural networks in image processing for early detection of breast cancer. *Computational and Mathematical Methods in Medicine*, 2017, 2017. doi:10.1155/2017/2610628 PMID:28473865

Meng, X., Meng, K., & Qiao, W. (2020). A Survey of Research on Image Data Sources Forensics. *ACM International Conference Proceeding Series*, (pp. 174–179). ACM. 10.1145/3430199.3430241

Mesejo, P., Martos, R., Ibáñez, Ó., Novo, J., & Ortega, M. (2020). A Survey on artificial intelligence techniques for biomedical image analysis in skeleton-based forensic human identification. *Applied Sciences (Basel, Switzerland)*, 10(14), 4703. doi:10.3390/app10144703

Meslie, Y., Enbeyle, W., Pandey, B. K., Pramanik, S., Pandey, D., Dadeech, P., & Saini, A. (2021). Machine intelligence-based trend analysis of COVID-19 for total daily confirmed cases in Asia and Africa. In *Methodologies and Applications of Computational Statistics for Machine Intelligence* (pp. 164–185). IGI Global. doi:10.4018/978-1-7998-7701-1.ch009

Mhatre, A., & Sharma, P. (2023). Deep Learning Approach for Vehicle Number Plate Recognition System with Image Enhancement Technique. *International Journal of Intelligent Systems and Applications in Engineering*, 11(1s), 251–262.

Mikołajczyk, T., Nowicki, K., Bustillo, A., & Pimenov, D. Y. (2018). Predicting tool life in turning operations using neural networks and image processing. *Mechanical Systems and Signal Processing*, 104, 503–513. doi:10.1016/j.ymssp.2017.11.022

Minh, T. N., Sinn, M., Lam, H. T., & Wistuba, M. (2018). *Automated image data preprocessing with deep reinforcement learning*. ArXiv Preprint ArXiv:1806.05886.

Mishra, M., Nath, M. K., & Dandapat, S. (2011). Glaucoma detection from color fundus images. [IJCCT]. *International Journal of Computer & Communication Technology*, 2(6), 7–10.

Mishra, S., Mishra, B. K., Tripathy, H. K., & Dutta, A. (2019). Analysis of the role and scope of big data analytics with IoT in health care domain. In *Handbook of Data Science Approaches for Biomedical Engineering* (pp. 1–23). Elsevier. doi:10.1016/B978-0-12-818318-2.00001-5

Mittal, P. (2023). Fusion of Machine Learning and Blockchain Techniques in IoT-based Smart Healthcare Systems. In *Deep Learning for Healthcare Decision Making* (pp. 245–266). River Publishers.

Moazzam, K., Kamal, S., Mathavan, S., Usman, M., & Rahman (2013). Metrology and Visualization of Potholes using the Microsoft Kinect Sensor. In *Proceedings of IEEE Conference on Intelligent Transport System,* (pp. 1284- 1291). IEEE.

Modwi, A., Daoush, W. M., El-Eteaby, M., Aissa, M. A. B., Ghoniem, M. G., & Khairy, M. (2022). Fabrication and adsorption studies of paste/TiO_2 nanocomposites through recycling of spent dry batteries. *Journal of Materials Science Materials in Electronics*, 33(32), 24869–24883. doi:10.100710854-022-09197-3

Moghadam, P. Wijesoma, W., & Feng, D. (2008). Improving path planning and mapping based on stereo vision and lidar. In *2008 10th International Conference on Control, Automation, Robotics and Vision*, (pp. 384-389). IEEE.

Moghadas, S. M., Fitzpatrick, M. C., Sah, P., Pandey, A., Shoukat, A., Singer, B. H., & Galvani, A. P. (2020). The implications of silent transmission for the control of COVID-19 outbreaks. *Proceedings of the National Academy of Sciences of the United States of America*, *117*(30), 17513–17515. doi:10.1073/pnas.2008373117 PMID:32632012

Moghadas, S. M., Vilches, T. N., Zhang, K., Wells, C. R., Shoukat, A., Singer, B. H., & Galvani, A. P. (2021). The impact of vaccination on COVID-19 outbreaks in the United States. medRxiv.

Mohamad Zamri, N. F., Md Tahir, N., Megat Amin, M. S., & Khirul Ashar, N. D., & Abd Al-misreb, A. (. (2021). Mini-review of Street Crime Prediction and Classification Methods. *Jurnal Kejuruteraan*, *33*(3), 391–401. doi:10.17576/jkukm-2021-33(3)-02

Mohammed, H., Clarke, N., & Li, F. (2016). An Automated Approach for Digital Forensic Analysis of Heterogeneous Big Data. Journal of Digital Forensics. *Security and Law*, *11*(2). doi:10.15394/jdfsl.2016.1384

Mohan, J., & R, D. R. (2021). Enhancing home security through visual cryptography. In *Microprocessors and Microsystems* (Vol. 80, p. 103355). Elsevier BV. doi:10.1016/j.micpro.2020.103355

Mohanarathinam, A., Kamalraj, S., Prasanna Venkatesan, G. K. D., Ravi, R. V., & Manikandababu, C. S. (2020). Digital watermarking techniques for image security: A review. *Journal of Ambient Intelligence and Humanized Computing*, *11*(8), 3221–3229. doi:10.100712652-019-01500-1

Mohanty, A., Jothi, B., Jeyasudha, J., Ranjit, P. S., Isaac, J. S., & Boopathi, S. (2023). Additive Manufacturing Using Robotic Programming. In *AI-Enabled Social Robotics in Human Care Services* (pp. 259–282). IGI Global. doi:10.4018/978-1-6684-8171-4.ch010

Mohanty, A., Venkateswaran, N., Ranjit, P. S., Tripathi, M. A., & Boopathi, S. (2023). Innovative Strategy for Profitable Automobile Industries: Working Capital Management. In Handbook of Research on Designing Sustainable Supply Chains to Achieve a Circular Economy (pp. 412–428). IGI Global.

Mohanty, S. P. (1999). Digital watermarking: A tutorial review. CSEE. Http://Www. Csee. Usf. Edu/\~{} Smohanty/Research/Reports/WMSurvey1999Mohanty. Pdf.

Mohapatra, S., Nath, P., Chatterjee, M., Das, N., Kalita, D., Roy, P., & Satapathy, S. (2020). Repurposing therapeutics for COVID-19: Rapid prediction of commercially available drugs through machine learning and docking. *PLoS One*, *15*(11), e0241543. doi:10.1371/journal.pone.0241543 PMID:33180803

Mondal, D., Ratnaparkhi, A., Deshpande, A., Deshpande, V., Kshirsagar, A. P., & Pramanik, S. (2023). Applications, Modern Trends and Challenges of Multiscale Modelling in Smart Cities. In *Data-Driven Mathematical Modeling in Smart Cities*. IGI Global. doi:10.4018/978-1-6684-6408-3.ch001

Monga, V., Li, Y., & Eldar, Y. C. (2021). Algorithm Unrolling. *IEEE Signal Processing Magazine*, *38*(March), 18–44. doi:10.1109/MSP.2020.3016905

Mookiah, M. R. K., Acharya, U. R., Lim, C. M., Petznick, A., & Suri, J. S. (2012). Data mining technique for automated diagnosis of glaucoma using higher order spectra and wavelet energy features. *Knowledge-Based Systems*, *33*, 73–82. doi:10.1016/j.knosys.2012.02.010

Moraliyage, H., De Silva, D., Ranasinghe, W., Adikari, A., Alahakoon, D., Prasad, R., Lawrentschuk, N., & Bolton, D. (2021). Cancer in lockdown: Impact of the COVID-19 pandemic on patients with cancer. *The Oncologist*, *26*(2), e342–e344. doi:10.1002/onco.13604 PMID:33210442

More, P., Surendran, S., Mahajan, S., & Dubey, S. K. (2014). Potholes and pitfalls spotter. *IMPACT: IJRET*, *4*, 69–74.

Muhammad, G., Rahman, S. K. M. M., Alelaiwi, A., & Alamri, A. (2017). Smart health solution integrating IoT and cloud: A case study of voice pathology monitoring. *IEEE Communications Magazine*, *55*(1), 69–73. doi:10.1109/MCOM.2017.1600425CM

Muhammad, K., Hamza, R., Ahmad, J., Lloret, J., Wang, H., & Baik, S. W. (2018). Secure Surveillance Framework for IoT Systems Using Probabilistic Image Encryption. *IEEE Transactions on Industrial Informatics*, *14*(8), 3679–3689. doi:10.1109/TII.2018.2791944

Muhammad, K., Khan, S., Del Ser, J., & De Albuquerque, V. H. C. (2020). Deep learning for multigrade brain tumor classification in smart healthcare systems: A prospective survey. *IEEE Transactions on Neural Networks and Learning Systems*, *32*(2), 507–522. doi:10.1109/TNNLS.2020.2995800 PMID:32603291

Munawar, H. S., Hammad, A. W. A., & Waller, S. T. (2021). A review on flood management technologies related to image processing and machine learning. *Automation in Construction*, *132*, 103916. doi:10.1016/j.autcon.2021.103916

Munir, R., & Harlili. (2018). Video Encryption by Using Visual Cryptography Based on Wang's Scheme. In *2018 4th International Conference on Electrical, Electronics and System Engineering (ICEESE). 2018 4th International Conference on Electrical, Electronics and System Engineering (ICEESE)*. IEEE. doi:10.1109/ICEESE.2018.8703567

Murali, S., Govindan, V. K., & Kalady, S. (2022). Quaternion-based image shadow removal. *The Visual Computer*, *38*(5), 1527–1538. doi:10.100700371-021-02086-6

Muramatsu, C., Hayashi, Y., Sawada, A., Hatanaka, Y., Hara, T., Yamamoto, T., & Fujita, H. (2010). Detection of retinal nerve fiber layer defects on retinal fundus images for early diagnosis of glaucoma. *Journal of Biomedical Optics*, *15*(1), 016021. doi:10.1117/1.3322388 PMID:20210467

Murray, M., Macedo, M., & Glynn, C. (2019, November). Delivering health intelligence for healthcare services. In *2019 First International Conference on Digital Data Processing (DDP)* (pp. 88-91). IEEE. 10.1109/DDP.2019.00026

Nabati, R., & Qi, H. (2019). Rrpn: Radar region proposal network for object detection in autonomous vehicles. In *2019 IEEE International Conference on Image Processing (ICIP)*, (pp. 3093-3097). IEEE. 10.1109/ICIP.2019.8803392

Nag, A., Nikhilendra, J. N., & Kalmath, M. (2018). IOT Based Door Access Control Using Face Recognition. In *Proceedings of the 2018 3rd International Conference for Convergence in Technology (I2CT)*, (pp. 1–3). IEEE. 10.1109/I2CT.2018.8529749

Nagulan, S., Srinivasa Krishnan, A. N., Kiran Kumar, A., Vishnu Kumar, S., & Suchithra, M. (2023). An Efficient Real-Time Fire Detection Method Using Computer Vision and Neural Network-Based Video Analysis. In: Khanna, A., Gupta, D., Kansal, V., Fortino, G., Hassanien, A.E. (eds) *Proceedings of Third Doctoral Symposium on Computational Intelligence. Lecture Notes in Networks and Systems, (vol 479)*. Springer, Singapore. 10.1007/978-981-19-3148-2_55

Naranjo-Torres, J., Mora, M., Hernández-García, R., Barrientos, R. J., Fredes, C., & Valenzuela, A. (2020). A review of convolutional neural network applied to fruit image processing. *Applied Sciences (Basel, Switzerland)*, *10*(10), 3443. doi:10.3390/app10103443

Narin, A., Kaya, C., & Pamuk, Z. (2020). Automatic detection of coronavirus disease (covid-19) using x-ray images and deep convolutional neural networks. *arXiv preprint arXiv:2003.10849*

Nauman, A., Qadri, Y. A., Amjad, M., Zikria, Y. B., Afzal, M. K., & Kim, S. W. (2020). Multimedia Internet of Things: A Comprehensive Survey. *IEEE Access : Practical Innovations, Open Solutions*, *8*, 8202–8250. doi:10.1109/AC-CESS.2020.2964280

Nawaz, M., Hassan, M. U., Chattha, M. U., Mahmood, A., Shah, A. N., Hashem, M., Alamri, S., Batool, M., Rasheed, A., Thabit, M. A., Alhaithloul, H. A. S., & Qari, S. H. (2022). Trehalose: A promising osmo-protectant against salinity stress—physiological and molecular mechanisms and future prospective. *Molecular Biology Reports*, *49*(12), 11255–11271. doi:10.100711033-022-07681-x PMID:35802276

Nayak, N., Odhekar, S., Patwa, S., & Roychowdhury, S. (2022).. . *Real Time Crime Detection By Captioning Video Surveillance Using Deep Learning.*, *10*(7), 367–376.

Nayera Nahvi, O. C. (2014). Comparative Analysis of Various Image Fusion Techniques For Biomedical Images: A Review. *International Journal of Engineering Research and Applications*, *04*, 81–86.

Neira, D. P., Watts, A., Seashore, J., Polychronopoulou, E., Kuo, Y. F., & Sharma, G. (2021). Smoking and risk of COVID-19 hospitalization. *Respiratory Medicine*, *182*, 106414. doi:10.1016/j.rmed.2021.106414 PMID:33915414

Nezu, M., & Arai, K. (2020). The effect of image processing on consumer behavior: A systematic review and meta-analysis. *Journal of Business Research*, *116*, 516–526. doi:10.1016/j.jbusres.2020.07.019

Ni, J., Chen, Y., Chen, Y., Zhu, J., Ali, D., & Cao, W. (2020). A survey on theories and applications for self-driving cars based on deep learning methods. *Applied Sciences (Basel, Switzerland)*, *10*(8), 2749. doi:10.3390/app10082749

Niinimäki, M., Zhou, X., Depeursinge, A., Geissbuhler, A., & Müller, H. (2008). Building a Community Grid for Medical Image Analysis inside a Hospital, a Case Study. *Proceedings of the MICCAI-Grid Workshop*, (pp. 3–12). IEEE.

Nilashi, M., Ibrahim, O., Ahmadi, H., & Shahmoradi, L. (2017). A knowledge-based system for breast cancer classification using fuzzy logic method. *Telematics and Informatics*, *34*(4), 133–144. doi:10.1016/j.tele.2017.01.007

Niu, K., Chen, Y., & Shen, J. (2021). Dual-channel night vision image restoration method based on deep learning. Computer Applications, vol. 41, no. 6, p. 10, doi:10.339022186904

Nižetić, S., Šolić, P., López-de-Ipiña González-de-Artaza, D., & Patrono, L. (2020). Internet of Things (IoT): Opportunities, issues, and challenges towards a smart and sustainable future. *Journal of Cleaner Production*, *274*, 122877. doi:10.1016/j.jclepro.2020.122877 PMID:32834567

Nomura, Y. (2021). Age and smoking predict antibody titres at 3 months after the second dose of the BNT162b2 COVID-19 vaccine. *Vaccines*.

Nowroozi, E., Dehghantanha, A., Parizi, R. M., & Choo, K. K. R. (2021). A survey of machine learning techniques in adversarial image forensics. *Computers & Security*, *100*(June), 1–37. doi:10.1016/j.cose.2020.102092

Ntakolia, C., Priftis, D., Charakopoulou-Travlou, M., Rannou, I., Magklara, K., Giannopoulou, I., & Lazaratou, E. (2022, January). An Explainable Machine Learning Approach for COVID-19's Impact on Mood States of Children and Adolescents during the First Lockdown in Greece. []. Multidisciplinary Digital Publishing Institute.]. *Health Care*, *10*(1), 149. PMID:35052311

Oladipo, F., Ogbuju, E., Alayesanmi, F. S., & Musa, A. E. (2020).The State of the Art in Machine Learning-Based Digital Forensics. SSRN *Electronic Journal*. doi:10.2139/ssrn.3668687

Ono, K., Punt, A. E., & Rivot, E. (2012). Model performance analysis for Bayesian biomass dynamics models using bias, precision and reliability metrics. *Fisheries Research*, *125–126*, 173–183. doi:10.1016/j.fishres.2012.02.022

Orhan, F., & Eren, P. E. (2013). Road Hazard Detection and Sharing with Multimodal Sensor Analysis on Smartphones. In *Proceedings of International Conference on Next Generation Mobile Apps, Services and Technologies*, (pp. 56-61). IEEE. 10.1109/NGMAST.2013.19

Ozkan, O., & Kilic, S. (2023). UAV routing by simulation-based optimization approaches for forest fire risk mitigation. *Annals of Operations Research*, *320*(2), 937–973. doi:10.100710479-021-04393-6

Ozturk, T., Talo, M., Yildirim, E. A., Baloglu, U. B., Yildirim, O., & Acharya, U. R. (2020). Automated detection of COVID-19 cases using deep neural networks with X-ray images. *Computers in Biology and Medicine, 121*, 103792. doi:10.1016/j.compbiomed.2020.103792 PMID:32568675

O'Malley, P., & Smith, G. J. D. (2022). 'Smart' crime prevention? Digitization and racialized crime control in a Smart City. *Theoretical Criminology*, *26*(1), 40–56. doi:10.1177/1362480620972703

Pachiyappan, A., Das, U. N., Murthy, T. V., & Tatavarti, R. (2012). Automated diagnosis of diabetic retinopathy and glaucoma using fundus and OCT images. *Lipids in Health and Disease*, *11*(1), 1–10. doi:10.1186/1476-511X-11-73 PMID:22695250

Palaniappan, M., Tirlangi, S., Mohamed, M. J. S., Moorthy, R. M. S., Valeti, S. V., & Boopathi, S. (2023). Fused Deposition Modelling of Polylactic Acid (PLA)-Based Polymer Composites. In Development, Properties, and Industrial Applications of 3D Printed Polymer Composites (pp. 66–85). IGI Global. doi:10.4018/978-1-6684-6009-2.ch005

Pan, S. J., & Yang, Q. (2009). A survey on transfer learning. *IEEE Transactions on Knowledge and Data Engineering*, *22*(10), 1345–1359. doi:10.1109/TKDE.2009.191

Pandey, B., Kumar Pandey, D., Pratap Mishra, B., & Rhmann, W. (2022). A comprehensive survey of deep learning in the field of medical imaging and medical natural language processing: Challenges and research directions. *Journal of King Saud University - Computer and Information Sciences, 34*(8), 5083–5099. doi:10.1016/j.jksuci.2021.01.007

Pandey, B. K. (2022). Effective and Secure Transmission of Health Information Using Advanced Morphological Component Analysis and Image Hiding. In M. Gupta, S. Ghatak, A. Gupta, & A. L. Mukherjee (Eds.), *Artificial Intelligence on Medical Data. Lecture Notes in Computational Vision and Biomechanics* (Vol. 37). Springer. doi:10.1007/978-981-19-0151-5_19

Pandey, B. K., Pandey, D., & Agarwal, A. (2022). Encrypted Information Transmission by Enhanced Steganography and Image Transformation. [IJDAI]. *International Journal of Distributed Artificial Intelligence*, *14*(1), 1–14. doi:10.4018/IJDAI.297110

Pandey, B. K., Pandey, D., Gupta, A., Nassa, V. K., Dadheech, P., & George, A. S. (2023). Secret Data Transmission Using Advanced Morphological Component Analysis and Steganography. In *Role of Data-Intensive Distributed Computing Systems in Designing Data Solutions* (pp. 21–44). Springer International Publishing. doi:10.1007/978-3-031-15542-0_2

Pandey, B. K., Pandey, D., Wairya, S., & Agarwal, G. (2021). An advanced morphological component analysis, steganography, and deep learning-based system to transmit secure textual data. [IJDAI]. *International Journal of Distributed Artificial Intelligence*, *13*(2), 40–62. doi:10.4018/IJDAI.2021070104

Pandey, B. K., Pandey, D., Wairya, S., Agarwal, G., Dadeech, P., Dogiwal, S. R., & Pramanik, S. (2022). Application of integrated steganography and image compressing techniques for confidential information transmission. *Cyber Security and Network Security*, 169-191.

Pandey, B. K., Pandey, D., Wairya, S., Agarwal, G., Dadeech, P., Dogiwal, S. R., & Pramanik, S. (2022). Application of Integrated Steganography and Image Compressing Techniques for Confidential Information Transmission. *Cyber Security and Network Security,* 169-191.

Pandey, B. K., Pandey, D., Wariya, S., & Agarwal, G. (2021). A deep neural network-based approach for extracting textual images from deteriorate images. *EAI Endorsed Transactions on Industrial Networks and Intelligent Systems*, 8(28), e3–e3. doi:10.4108/eai.17-9-2021.170961

Pandey, B. K., Pandey, D., Wariya, S., Aggarwal, G., & Rastogi, R. (2021). Deep learning and particle swarm optimisation-based techniques for visually impaired humans' text recognition and identification. *Augmented Human Research*, *6*(1), 1–14. doi:10.100741133-021-00051-5

Pandey, D., & Pandey, B. K. (2022). An Efficient Deep Neural Network with Adaptive Galactic Swarm Optimization for Complex Image Text Extraction. In *Process Mining Techniques for Pattern Recognition* (pp. 121–137). CRC Press. doi:10.1201/9781003169550-10

Pandey, D., & Wairya, S. (2023). An optimization of target classification tracking and mathematical modelling for control of autopilot. *Imaging Science Journal*, ●●●, 1–16.

Pandey, D., Aswari, A., Taufiqurakman, M., Khalim, A., & Azahrah, F. F. (2021). System of education changes due to Covid-19 pandemic. *Asian Journal of Advances in Research*, 168-173.

Pandey, D., George, S., Aremu, B., Wariya, S., & Pandey, B. K. (2021). *Critical Review on Integration of Encryption*. Steganography, IOT and Artificial Intelligence for the Secure Transmission of Stego Images.

Pandey, D., Islam, T., & Malik, M. A. (2021). Novel coronavirus disease (SARS-COV-2): an overview. *Asian Journal of Advances in Medical Science*, 39-43.

Pandey, D., Islam, T., Magray, J. A., Gulzar, A., & Zargar, S. A. (2021). Use of statistical analysis to monitor novel coronavirus-19 cases in Jammu and Kashmir, India. *European Journal of Biological Research*, *11*(3), 274–282.

Pandey, D., Nassa, V. K., Jhamb, A., Mahto, D., Pandey, B. K., George, A. H., & Bandyopadhyay, S. K. (2021). An integration of keyless encryption, steganography, and artificial intelligence for the secure transmission of stego images. In *Multidisciplinary approach to modern digital steganography* (pp. 211–234). IGI Global. doi:10.4018/978-1-7998-7160-6.ch010

Pandey, D., Pandey, B. K., & Wariya, S. (2019). Study of various types noise and text extraction algorithms for degraded complex image. *Journal of Emerging Technologies and Innovative Research*, *6*(6), 234–247.

Pandey, D., Pandey, B. K., & Wariya, S. (2020). An approach to text extraction from complex degraded scene. *IJCBS*, *1*(2), 4–10.

Pandey, D., Pandey, B. K., Noibi, T. O., Babu, S., Patra, P. M., Kassaw, C., & Canete, J. J. O. (2020). Covid-19: Unlock 1.0 risk, test, transmission, incubation and infectious periods and reproduction of novel Covid-19 pandemic. *Asian Journal of Advances in Medical Science*, 23-28.

Pandey, D., Wairya, S., Pradhan, B., & Wangmo. (2022). Understanding COVID-19 response by twitter users: A text analysis approach. *Heliyon*, *8*(8), e09994. doi:10.1016/j.heliyon.2022.e09994 PMID:35873536

Pandey, D., Wairya, S., Sharma, M., Gupta, A. K., Kakkar, R., & Pandey, B. K. (2022). An approach for object tracking, categorization, and autopilot guidance for passive homing missiles. *Aerospace Systems*, 1-14.

Paraskevis, D., Kostaki, E. G., Magiorkinis, G., Panayiotakopoulos, G., Sourvinos, G., & Tsiodras, S. (2020). Full-genome evolutionary analysis of the novel corona virus (2019-nCoV) rejects the hypothesis of emergence as a result of a recent recombination event. *Infection, Genetics and Evolution*, *79*, 104212. doi:10.1016/j.meegid.2020.104212 PMID:32004758

Park, M., & Jeong, J. (2022). Design and Implementation of Machine Vision-Based Quality Inspection System in Mask Manufacturing Process. *Sustainability (Basel)*, *14*(10), 6009. doi:10.3390u14106009

Pasayat, A. K., Pati, S. N., & Maharana, A. (2020). Predicting the COVID-19 positive cases in India with concern to Lockdown by using Mathematical and Machine Learning based Models. medRxiv. doi:10.1101/2020.05.16.20104133

Patel, K., Kar, A., Jha, S., & Khan, M. (2012). Machine vision system: A tool for quality inspection of food and agricultural products. *Journal of Food Science and Technology*, *49*(2), 123–141. doi:10.100713197-011-0321-4 PMID:23572836

Pathania, V. (2022). A Database Application for Monitoring COVID-19 in India. In M. Gupta, S. Ghatak, A. Gupta, & A. L. Mukherjee (Eds.), *Artificial Intelligence on Medical Data. Lecture Notes in Computational Vision and Biomechanics* (Vol. 37). Springer. doi:10.1007/978-981-19-0151-5_23

Patil, N., Ambatkar, S., & Kakde, S. (2017). IoT based smart surveillance security system using raspberry Pi. In Proceedings of the 2017 International Conference on Communication and Signal Processing (ICCSP), (pp. 344–348). IEEE. 10.1109/ICCSP.2017.8286374

Paul, S., Sevcenco, I. S., & Agathoklis, P. (2016). Multi-Exposure and Multi-Focus Picture Fusion in Gradient Domain. *Journal of Circuits, Systems, and Computers, 25*, 1 - 18.

Pazhani, A. A. J., & Vasanthanayaki, C. (2022). Object detection in satellite images by faster R-CNN incorporated with enhanced ROI pooling (FrRNet-ERoI) framework. *Earth Science Informatics*, *15*(1), 553–561. doi:10.100712145-021-00746-8

Piza, E. L., Welsh, B. C., Farrington, D. P., & Thomas, A. L. (2019). CCTV surveillance for crime prevention: A 40-year systematic review with meta-analysis. *Criminology & Public Policy*, *18*(1), 135–159. doi:10.1111/1745-9133.12419

Podoletz, L. (2022). We have to talk about emotional AI and crime. *AI & Society, 0123456789*. doi:10.100700146-022-01435-w

Prabaharan, T., Periasamy, P., Mugendiran, V., & Ramanan. (2020). Studies on the application of image processing in various fields: An overview. *IOP Conference Series. Materials Science and Engineering*, *961*(1), 012006. doi:10.1088/1757-899X/961/1/012006

Pradhan, D., Sahu, P. K., Goje, N. S., Myo, H., Ghonge, M. M., Tun, M., Rajeswari, R., & Pramanik, S. (2022). Security, Privacy, Risk, and Safety Toward 5G Green Network (5G-GN). In Cyber Security and Network Security. Wiley. doi:10.1002/9781119812555.ch9

Pramanik, S. (2022). An Effective Secured Privacy-Protecting Data Aggregation Method in IoT. In M. O. Odhiambo, W. Mwashita, & I. G. I. Global (Eds.), *Achieving Full Realization and Mitigating the Challenges of the Internet of Things.*, doi:10.4018/978-1-7998-9312-7.ch008

Pramanik, S. (2022). Carpooling Solutions using Machine Learning Tools. In *Handbook of Research on Evolving Designs and Innovation in ICT and Intelligent Systems for Real-World Applications*. IGI Global. doi:10.4018/978-1-7998-9795-8.ch002

Pramanik, S. (2023). An Adaptive Image Steganography Approach depending on Integer Wavelet Transform and Genetic Algorithm. *Multimedia Tools and Applications*. doi:10.100711042-023-14505-y

Pramanik, S., & Bandyopadhyay, S. (2023). Analysis of Big Data. In I. G. I. John Wang (Ed.), *Encyclopedia of Data Science and Machine Learning*. IGI Global. doi:10.4018/978-1-7998-9220-5.ch006

Pramanik, S., & Ghosh, R. (2020). Techniques of Steganography and Cryptography in Digital Transformation. In K. Sandhu (Ed.), *Management and Strategies for Digital Enterprise Transformation* (pp. 24–44). IGI Global. doi:10.4018/978-1-7998-8587-0.ch002

Pramanik, S., & Suresh Raja, S. (2020). A Secured Image Steganography using Genetic Algorithm. *Advances in Mathematics: Scientific Journal*, *9*(7), 4533–4541. doi:10.37418/amsj.9.7.22

Pramanik, S., Galety, M. G., Samanta, D., & Joseph, N. P. (2022). Data Mining Approaches for Decision Support Systems. *3rd International Conference on Emerging Technologies in Data Mining and Information Security*. IEEE.

Pramanik, S., Sagayam, K. M., & Jena, O. P. (2021). Machine Learning Frameworks in Cancer Detection. ICCSRE 2021, Morocco. doi:10.1051/e3sconf/202129701073

Pramanik, S., Samanta, D., Ghosh, R., Bandyopadhyay, S. K. (2021). A New Combinational Technique in Image Steganography. *International Journal of Information Security and Privacy, 15*(3). IGI Global. doi:10.4018/IJISP.2021070104

Pramanik, S., Singh, R. P., Ghosh, R., & Bandyopadhyay, S. K. (2020). A Unique Way to Generate Password at Random Basis and Sending it Using a New Steganography Technique. *Indonesian Journal of Electrical Engineering and Informatics, 8*(3), 525–531.

Prem, S. S., & Umesh, A. C. (2020, October). Classification of exudates for diabetic retinopathy prediction using machine learning. In *2020 IEEE 5th International Conference on Computing Communication and Automation (ICCCA)* (pp. 357-362). IEEE. 10.1109/ICCCA49541.2020.9250858

Press Trust of India. (2019). Over 5000 killed in road accidents caused by potholes in 2018. *NDTV*. https://www.ndtv.com/india-news/over-5-000-killed-in-road-accidents-caused-by-potholes-in-2018-20-transport-ministry-3276432

Priya, E., & Rajinikanth, V. (2021). Signal and Image Processing Techniques for the Development of Intelligent Healthcare Systems. In *Signal and Image Processing Techniques for the Development of Intelligent Healthcare Systems*. Springer. doi:10.1007/978-981-15-6141-2

Protonotarios, N. E., Katsamenis, I., Sykiotis, S., Dikaios, N., Kastis, G. A., Chatziioannou, S. N., Metaxas, M., Doulamis, N., & Doulamis, A. (2022). A few-shot U-Net deep learning model for lung cancer lesion segmentation via PET/CT imaging. *Biomedical Physics & Engineering Express, 8*(2), 025019. doi:10.1088/2057-1976/ac53bd PMID:35144242

Punn, N. S., Sonbhadra, S. K., & Agarwal, S. (2020). COVID-19 epidemic analysis using machine learning and deep learning algorithms. MedRxiv. doi:10.1101/2020.04.08.20057679

Punyavathi, G., Neeladri, M., & Singh, M. K. (2021). Vehicle tracking and detection techniques using IoT. *Materials Today: Proceedings, 51*, 909–913. doi:10.1016/j.matpr.2021.06.283

Qadir, A. M., & Varol, A. (2020). The Role of Machine Learning in Digital Forensics. *8th International Symposium on Digital Forensics and Security, ISDFS 2020*. IEEE. 10.1109/ISDFS49300.2020.9116298

Qu, G., Zhang, D., & Yan, P. (2002, March). Information measure for performance of image fusion. *Electronics Letters, 38*(7), 313–315. doi:10.1049/el:20020212

Quan, W., Wang, K., Yan, D. M., Zhang, X., & Pellerin, D. (2020). Learn with diversity and from harder samples: Improving the generalization of CNN-Based detection of computer-generated images. *Forensic Science International: Digital Investigation, 35*, 301023. doi:10.1016/j.fsidi.2020.301023

Quigley, Harry A. (1993). Open-angle glaucoma. *New England Journal of Medicine, 15*, 1097-1106.

Rabaan, A. A., Al-Ahmed, S. H., Haque, S., Sah, R., Tiwari, R., Malik, Y. S., & Rodriguez-Morales, A. J. (2020). SARS-CoV-2, SARS-CoV, and MERS-COV: A comparative overview. *Le Infezioni in Medicina, 28*(2), 174–184. PMID:32275259

Radulov. (2019). Artificial intelligence and security. *Instructional Scientific Journal Security and Future, 3*(1), 3–5. http://www.springerlink.com/index/M1042VT3791654RK.pdf

Radulović, S., Sunkara, S., Rachel, R., & Leitinger, G. (2022). Three-dimensional SEM, TEM, and STEM for analysis of large-scale biological systems. *Histochemistry and Cell Biology*, *158*(3), 203–211. doi:10.100700418-022-02117-w PMID:35829815

Rafik, M. K. M. (2021). Quality Checking of Fruits using Image Processing. *International Journal for Research in Applied Science and Engineering Technology*, *9*(5), 1979–1980. doi:10.22214/ijraset.2021.34518

Rahamathunnisa, U. (2023). *Cloud Computing Principles for Optimizing Robot Task Offloading Processes.*, doi:10.4018/978-1-6684-8171-4.ch007

Rahman, T., & Muhammad, E. H. (2020). Transfer learning with deep convolutional neural network (CNN) for pneumonia detection using chest X-ray. *Applied Sciences (Basel, Switzerland)*, *10*(9), 3233. doi:10.3390/app10093233

Rajesh, A., & Asaad, M. (2023). Artificial Intelligence and Machine Learning in Surgery. *The American Surgeon*, *89*(1), 9–10. doi:10.1177/00031348221117024 PMID:35969467

Raju, G., & Madhu, S. (2014). A fast and efficient color image enhancement method based on fuzzy-logic and histogram. *AEÜ. International Journal of Electronics and Communications*, *68*(3), 237–243. doi:10.1016/j.aeue.2013.08.015

Ramachandran, P., Zoph, B., & Le, Q. V. (2017). *Searching for activation functions.*

Ramalho, R. (2020). Alcohol consumption and alcohol-related problems during the COVID-19 pandemic: A narrative review. *Australasian Psychiatry*, *28*(5), 524–526. doi:10.1177/1039856220943024 PMID:32722961

Ranganath, H. S., Kuntimad, G., & Johnson, J. L. (1995). Pulse coupled neural networks for image processing. *Proceedings IEEE Southeastcon'95. Visualize the Future*, (pp. 37–43). IEEE.

Rangel-Porras, G., Olivares-Peregrino, G., & Bocanegra-Mendoza, L. A. (2021). A review of image processing techniques for pavement crack detection. *Measurement*, *179*, 109321. doi:10.1016/j.measurement.2021.109321

Rani Roopha Devi, K. G., Mahendra Chozhan, R., & Murugesan, R. (2019). Cognitive IoT Integration for Smart Healthcare: Case Study for Heart Disease Detection and Monitoring. *2019 International Conference on Recent Advances in Energy-Efficient Computing and Communication, ICRAECC 2019*, (pp. 1–6). IEEE. 10.1109/ICRAECC43874.2019.8995049

Raponi, S., Oligeri, G., & Ali, I. M. (2022). Sound of guns: Digital forensics of gun audio samples meets artificial intelligence. *Multimedia Tools and Applications*, *81*(21), 30387–30412. doi:10.100711042-022-12612-w

Reddy, M. A., Reddy, B. M., Mukund, C. S., Venneti, K., Preethi, D. M. D., & Boopathi, S. (2023). Social Health Protection During the COVID-Pandemic Using IoT. In *The COVID-19 Pandemic and the Digitalization of Diplomacy* (pp. 204–235). IGI Global. doi:10.4018/978-1-7998-8394-4.ch009

Reddy, M. B., Pravalika, R., & Krishnaveni, R. (2020). A Journey From the Internet of Things (IoT) To the Internet of Everything. *International Journal of Scientific Research and Engineering Development*, *3*(5), 345–348. http://www.ijsred.com/volume3/issue5/IJSRED-V3I5P48.pdf

Redmon, J., Divvala, S., Girshick, R., & Farhadi, A. (2016). You only look once: Unified, real-time object detection. In *Proceedings of the IEEE conference on computer vision and pattern recognition* (pp. 779-788). 10.1109/CVPR.2016.91

Reepu, S. Kumar, M., Chaudhary, G., Gupta, K., Pramanik, S., & Gupta, A. (2023). Information Security and Privacy on IoT. J. Zhao, V. V. Kumar, R. Natarajan and T. R. Mahesh, (eds.) Handbook of Research in Advancements in AI and IoT Convergence Technologies. IGI Global.

Rehnström, F. (2021). *How Capable is Artificial Intelligence (AI) in Crime Prediction and Prevention?* doi:10.1109/ACCESS.2019.2941978

Reid, L. (2021). An Introduction to Biomedical Computational Fluid Dynamics. In P. M. Rea (Ed.), *Biomedical Visualisation. Advances in Experimental Medicine and Biology* (Vol. 1334). Springer., doi:10.1007/978-3-030-76951-2_10

Ren, L. (2021). A Novel Raster Map Exchange Scheme Based on Visual Cryptography. In R. Kaluri (Ed.), *Advances in Multimedia* (Vol. 2021, pp. 1–7). Hindawi Limited. doi:10.1155/2021/3287774

Ren, S., He, K., Girshick, R., & Sun, J. (2015). Faster R-CNN: Towards real-time object detection with region proposal networks. In Advances in neural information processing systems (pp. 91-99).

Revenkar, P. S., & Anisa Anjum, W. Z. (2010). Secure Iris Authentication Using Visual Cryptography. *International Journal of Computer Science and Information Security, 7*(3), 217-221.

Reyad, O., & Karar, M. E. (2021). Secure CT-Image Encryption for COVID-19 Infections Using HBBS-Based Multiple Key-Streams. In Arabian Journal for Science and Engineering (Vol. 46, Issue 4, pp. 3581–3593). Springer Science and Business Media LLC. doi:10.100713369-020-05196-w

Riyahi, R., Kleinn, C., & Fuchs, H. (2009). *Comparison of Different Image Fusion Techniques for Individual Tree Crown Identification Using Quick bird Images.* Research Gate.

Robertson, S., Azizpour, H., Smith, K., & Hartman, J. (2018). Digital image analysis in breast pathology—From image processing techniques to artificial intelligence. *Translational Research; the Journal of Laboratory and Clinical Medicine, 194*, 19–35. doi:10.1016/j.trsl.2017.10.010 PMID:29175265

Rode, S. S., Vijay, S., Goyal, P., Kulkarni, P., & Arya, K. (2009). Pothole Detection and Warning System. In *Proceedings of International Conference on Electronic Computer Technology*, (pp. 286- 290). IEEE.

Rong, G., Mendez, A., Bou Assi, E., Zhao, B., & Sawan, M. (2020). Artificial Intelligence in Healthcare: Review and Prediction Case Studies. *Engineering (Beijing), 6*(3), 291–301. doi:10.1016/j.eng.2019.08.015

Ronneberger, O., Fischer, P., & Brox, T. (2015). U-net: Convolutional networks for biomedical image segmentation. In *International Conference on Medical image computing and computer-assisted intervention* (pp. 234-241). Springer, Cham. 10.1007/978-3-319-24574-4_28

Rose, S., Kumar A., & Renuka, K. (2019). Deep Learning using Python. Wiley India Pvt. Ltd.

Roy, B., Dhillon, J. K., Habib, N., & Pugazhandhi, B. (2021). Global variants of COVID-19: Current understanding. *Journal of Biomedical Science, 8*(1), 8–11. doi:10.3126/jbs.v8i1.38453 PMID:33435938

Roy, S., Rawat, U., Sareen, H. A., & Nayak, S. K. (2020). IECA: An efficient IoT friendly image encryption technique using programmable cellular automata. *Journal of Ambient Intelligence and Humanized Computing, 11*(11), 5083–5102. doi:10.100712652-020-01813-6

Roy, S., Shrivastava, M., Pandey, C. V., Nayak, S. K., & Rawat, U. (2021). IEVCA: An efficient image encryption technique for IoT applications using 2-D Von-Neumann cellular automata. *Multimedia Tools and Applications, 80*(21-23), 31529–31567. doi:10.100711042-020-09880-9

Rughani, P. H. (2017). Artificial Intelligence Based Digital Forensics Framework. *International Journal of Advanced Research in Computer Science, 8*(8), 10–14. doi:10.26483/ijarcs.v8i8.4571

Ruta, A., Li, Y., & Liu, X. (2010). Real-time traffic sign recognition from video by class-specific discriminative features. *Pattern Recognition, 43*(1), 416–430. doi:10.1016/j.patcog.2009.05.018

S., P. K., Sampath, B., R., S. K., Babu, B. H., & N., A. (2022). Hydroponics, Aeroponics, and Aquaponics Technologies in Modern Agricultural Cultivation. In *Trends, Paradigms, and Advances in Mechatronics Engineering* (pp. 223–241). IGI Global. doi:10.4018/978-1-6684-5887-7.ch012

Saba, T., Abunadi, I., Shahzad, M. N., & Khan, A. R. (2021). Machine learning techniques to detect and forecast the daily total COVID-19 infected and deaths cases under different lockdown types. *Microscopy Research and Technique*, *84*(7), 1462–1474. doi:10.1002/jemt.23702 PMID:33522669

Sabeenian, R. S., & Surendar, A. (2017). An Automated Detection of Microaneursym to facilitate better Diagnosis of Diabetic Retinopathy. *Biosciences Biotechnology Research Asia*, *10*(1), 483–488.

Sachdev, R. (2020). Towards Security and Privacy for Edge AI in IoT/IoE based Digital Marketing Environments. *2020 5th International Conference on Fog and Mobile Edge Computing, FMEC 2020*, (pp. 341–346). IEEE. 10.1109/FMEC49853.2020.9144755

Sahin, M. E., Arslan, O., & Aydın, N. (2018). Application of image processing techniques for monitoring and control of industrial processes: A review. *Measurement*, *116*, 590–605. doi:10.1016/j.measurement.2017.11.023

Sahin, S., & Uslu, A. (2018). The role of image processing in advertising and marketing: A systematic review. *Business and Economics Research Journal*, *9*(4), 871–888. doi:10.20409/berj.2018.174

Samikannu, R., Koshariya, A. K., Poornima, E., Ramesh, S., Kumar, A., & Boopathi, S. (2023). Sustainable Development in Modern Aquaponics Cultivation Systems Using IoT Technologies. In *Human Agro-Energy Optimization for Business and Industry* (pp. 105–127). IGI Global. doi:10.4018/978-1-6684-4118-3.ch006

Sampath, B., & Haribalaji, V. (2021). Influences of welding parameters on friction stir welding of aluminum and magnesium: A review. *Materials Research Proceedings*, *19*(1), 222–230. doi:10.21741/9781644901618-28

Sampath, B. C. S., & Myilsamy, S. (2022). Application of TOPSIS Optimization Technique in the Micro-Machining Process. In Trends, Paradigms, and Advances in Mechatronics Engineering (pp. 162–187). IGI Global. doi:10.4018/978-1-6684-5887-7.ch009

Sang, X., Zhou, R., Li, Y., & Xiong, S. (2022). One-Dimensional Deep Convolutional Neural Network for Mineral Classification from Raman Spectroscopy. *Neural Processing Letters*, *54*(1), 677–690. doi:10.100711063-021-10652-1

Santhanakrishnan, C., Annapurani, K., Singh, R., & Krishnaveni, C. (2021). An IOT based system for monitoring environmental and physiological conditions. *Materials Today: Proceedings*, *46*, 3832–3840. doi:10.1016/j.matpr.2021.02.077

Santosh, K. C., Antani, S., Guru, D. S., & Dey, N. (2022). *Medical Imaging: Artificial Intelligence, Image Recognition, and Machine Learning Techniques*. CRC Press.

Saravanan, M., Vasanth, M., Boopathi, S., Sureshkumar, M., & Haribalaji, V. (2022). Optimization of Quench Polish Quench (QPQ) Coating Process Using Taguchi Method. *Key Engineering Materials*, *935*, 83–91. doi:10.4028/p-z569vy

Sarkar, O., Ahamed, M. F., & Chowdhury, P. (2020, December). Forecasting & Severity Analysis of COVID-19 Using Machine Learning Approach with Advanced Data Visualization. In *2020 23rd International Conference on Computer and Information Technology (ICCIT)* (pp. 1-6). IEEE. 10.1109/ICCIT51783.2020.9392704

Sathish, T., Sunagar, P., Singh, V., Boopathi, S., Al-Enizi, A. M., Pandit, B., Gupta, M., & Sehgal, S. S. (2023). Characteristics estimation of natural fibre reinforced plastic composites using deep multi-layer perceptron (MLP) technique. *Chemosphere*, *337*, 139346. doi:10.1016/j.chemosphere.2023.139346 PMID:37379988

Sathiyamoorthy, S. (2014). Industrial Application of Machine Vision. *International Journal of Research in Engineering and Technology*, *3*(1), 1–5. doi:10.15623/ijret.2014.0319120

Saxena, S., & Paul, S. (2022). *High-Performance Medical Image Processing.*

Schmidt-Hieber, J. (2004). Nonparametric regression using deep neural networks with ReLU activation function. The Annals of Statistics, 4, 1875-1897.

Seifert, R., Weber, M., Kocakavuk, E., Rischpler, C., & Kersting, D. (2021). Artificial Intelligence and Machine Learning in Nuclear Medicine: Future Perspectives. *Seminars in Nuclear Medicine, 51*(2), 170–177. doi:10.1053/j.semnuclmed.2020.08.003 PMID:33509373

Sekaran, R., Patan, R., Raveendran, A., Al-Turjman, F., Ramachandran, M., & Mostarda, L. (2020). Survival Study on Blockchain Based 6G-Enabled Mobile Edge Computation for IoT Automation. *IEEE Access : Practical Innovations, Open Solutions, 8,* 143453–143463. doi:10.1109/ACCESS.2020.3013946

Selvakumar, S., Adithe, S., Isaac, J. S., Pradhan, R., Venkatesh, V., & Sampath, B. (2023). A Study of the Printed Circuit Board (PCB) E-Waste Recycling Process. In Sustainable Approaches and Strategies for E-Waste Management and Utilization (pp. 159–184). IGI Global.

Sennan, S., Pandey, D., Alotaibi, Y., & Alghamdi, S. (2022). A Novel Convolutional Neural Networks Based Spinach Classification and Recognition System. *Computers, Materials & Continua, 73*(1), 343–361. doi:10.32604/cmc.2022.028334

Senthil, T. S. R. Ohmsakthi vel, Puviyarasan, M., Babu, S. R., Surakasi, R., & Sampath, B. (2023). Industrial Robot-Integrated Fused Deposition Modelling for the 3D Printing Process. In Development, Properties, and Industrial Applications of 3D Printed Polymer Composites (pp. 188–210). IGI Global. doi:10.4018/978-1-6684-6009-2.ch011

Sethy, P. K., & Behera, S. K. (2020). Detection of coronavirus disease (covid-19) based on deep features. *International Journal of Mathematical, Engineering and Management Sciences.*

Shah, N., Bhagat, N., & Shah, M. (2021). Crime forecasting: A machine learning and computer vision approach to crime prediction and prevention. *Visual Computing for Industry, Biomedicine, and Art, 4*(1), 9. doi:10.118642492-021-00075-z PMID:33913057

Shah, S. K., & Shah, P. D. (2014). Comparative Study of Image Fusion. *International Journal of Innovative Research in Science,* (p. 10168 to 10175).

Shahid, O., Nasajpour, M., Pouriyeh, S., Parizi, R. M., Han, M., Valero, M., Li, F., Aledhari, M., & Sheng, Q. Z. (2021). Machine learning research towards combating COVID-19: Virus detection, spread prevention, and medical assistance. *Journal of Biomedical Informatics, 117,* 103751. doi:10.1016/j.jbi.2021.103751 PMID:33771732

Shangzheng, L. (2019). A traffic sign image recognition and classification approach based on convolutional neural network. In *2019 11th International Conference on Measuring Technology and Mechatronics Automation (ICMTMA),* (pp. 408-411). IEEE. 10.1109/ICMTMA.2019.00096

Shanqing, G., Pednekar, M., & Slater, R. (2019). Improve Image Classification Using Data Augmentation and Neural Networks. *SMU Data Science Review, 2*(2), 1–43. https://scholar.smu.edu/datasciencereviewhttp://digitalrepository.smu.edu.Availableat:https://scholar.smu.edu/datasciencereview/vol2/iss2/1

Shanthi, T., & Sabeenian, R. S. (2019). Modified Alexnet architecture for classification of diabetic retinopathy images. *Computers & Electrical Engineering, 76,* 56–64. doi:10.1016/j.compeleceng.2019.03.004

Shanthi, T., Sabeenian, R. S., Manju, K., Paramasivam, M. E., Dinesh, P. M., & Anand, R. (2021). Fundus Image Classification using Hybridized GLCM Features and Wavelet Features. *ICTACT Journal on Image and Video Processing, 11*(3), 2372–2375.

Shao, X., Lian, H., & Zhang, Y. (2019). A review of image processing techniques in online shopping. *Journal of Electronic Commerce Research, 20*(2), 85–102. doi:10.3390u11041275

Sharma & Singh. (2014). Visual Cryptography Scheme for Gray Scale Images based on Intensity Division. *International Journal of Current Engineering and Technology, 4*(1), 211-215.

Sharma, A., Kulshrestha, S., & Daniel, S. (2017). Machine learning approaches for breast cancer diagnosis and prognosis. In *2017 International conference on soft computing and its engineering applications (icSoftComp)*, (pp. 1-5). IEEE. 10.1109/ICSOFTCOMP.2017.8280082

Sharma, M., & Gupta, A. K. (2021). An algorithm for target detection, identification, tracking and estimation of motion for passive homing missile autopilot guidance. In *Mobile Radio Communications and 5G Networks: Proceedings of MRCN 2020*, (pp. 57-71). Springer Singapore. 10.1007/978-981-15-7130-5_5

Sharma, M., & Singh, H. (2022). Contactless Methods for Respiration Monitoring and Design of SIW-LWA for Real-Time Respiratory Rate Monitoring. *Journal of the Institution of Electronics and Telecommunication Engineers*, 1–11. doi:10.1080/03772063.2022.2069167

Sharma, M., Pandey, D., Khosla, D., Goyal, S., Pandey, B. K., & Gupta, A. K. (2022). Design of a GaN-Based Flip Chip Light Emitting Diode (FC-LED) with Au Bumps & Thermal Analysis with Different Sizes and Adhesive Materials for Performance Considerations. *Silicon, 14*(12), 7109–7120. doi:10.100712633-021-01457-x

Sharma, M., Pandey, D., Palta, P., & Pandey, B. K. (2022). Design and power dissipation consideration of PFAL CMOS V/S conventional CMOS based 2: 1 multiplexer and full adder. *Silicon, 14*(8), 4401–4410. doi:10.100712633-021-01221-1

Sharma, M., Sharma, B., Gupta, A. K., & Pandey, D. (2023). Recent developments of image processing to improve explosive detection methodologies and spectroscopic imaging techniques for explosive and drug detection. *Multimedia Tools and Applications, 82*(5), 6849–6865. doi:10.100711042-022-13578-5

Sharma, M., Sharma, B., Gupta, A. K., Khosla, D., Goyal, S., & Pandey, D. (2021). A study and novel AI/ML-based framework to detect COVID-19 virus using smartphone embedded sensors. In *Sustainability Measures for COVID-19 Pandemic* (pp. 59–74). Springer Nature Singapore. doi:10.1007/978-981-16-3227-3_4

Sharma, M., Singh, H., & Pandey, D. (2022). Parametric Considerations and Dielectric Materials Impacts on the Performance of 10 GHzSIW-LWA for Respiration Monitoring. *Journal of Electronic Materials, 51*(5), 2131–2141. doi:10.100711664-022-09482-1

Sharma, M., Singh, H., Singh, S., & Gupta, A. (2020). A novel approach of object detection using point feature matching technique for colored images. In *Proceedings of ICRIC 2019: Recent Innovations in Computing*, (pp. 561-576). Springer International Publishing. 10.1007/978-3-030-29407-6_40

Sharma, P. K., Srivastava, A., & Perti, A. (2018). NOVEL IDEA FOR REAL-TIME HEALTH MONITORING USING WEARABLE DEVICES. [IJMET]. *International Journal of Mechanical Engineering and Technology, 9*(13), 213–216.

Sharmila, V., Rejin Paul, N. R., Ezhumalai, P., Reetha, S., & Naresh Kumar, S. (2020). IOT enabled smart assistance system using face detection and recognition for visually challenged people. *Materials Today: Proceedings*. Advance online publication. doi:10.1016/j.matpr.2020.10.198

Shereen, M. A., Khan, S., Kazmi, A., Bashir, N., & Siddique, R. (2020). COVID-19 infection: Origin, transmission, and characteristics of human coronaviruses. *Journal of Advanced Research, 24*, 91–98. doi:10.1016/j.jare.2020.03.005 PMID:32257431

Shi, F., Wang, J., Shi, J., Wu, Z., Wang, Q., Tang, Z., He, K., Shi, Y., & Shen, D. (2021). Review of Artificial Intelligence Techniques in Imaging Data Acquisition, Segmentation, and Diagnosis for COVID-19. *IEEE Reviews in Biomedical Engineering*, *14*, 4–15. doi:10.1109/RBME.2020.2987975 PMID:32305937

Shi, L., Guo, Y., Wang, J., Wu, J., & Zhang, H. (2018). Image processing for the extraction of relevant information in chemical engineering: A review. *Measurement*, *123*, 143–157. doi:10.1016/j.measurement.2018.02.020

Shi, W., Alawieh, M. B., Li, X., & Yu, H. (2017). Algorithm and hardware implementation for visual perception system in autonomous vehicle: A survey. *Integration (Amsterdam)*, *59*, 148–156. doi:10.1016/j.vlsi.2017.07.007

Shi, Y., & Karl, W. C. (2008). A real-time algorithm for the approximation of level-set-based curve evolution. *IEEE Transactions on Image Processing*, *17*(5), 645–656. doi:10.1109/TIP.2008.920737 PMID:18390371

Shilpa, A., Muneeswaran, V., Rathinam, D. K., Grace, S. A., & Sherin, J. (2019). Exploring the Benefits of Sensors in the Internet of Everything (IoE). *2019 5th International Conference on Advanced Computing and Communication Systems, ICACCS 2019*, (pp. 510–514). IEEE. 10.1109/ICACCS.2019.8728530

Shivan Othman, P., Rebar Ihsan, R., Marqas, R. B., Almufti, S. M., & Author, C. (2020). Image Processing Techniques for Identifying Impostor Documents Through Digital Forensic Examination. *Region*, *62*(04), 1781–1794.

Shivsubramani Krishnamoorthy, K. P. (2010). Implementation and Comparative Study of Image Fusion Algorithms. *International Journal of Computer Applications*, *09*, 0975 – 8887.

Shrivakshan, G. T., & Chandrasekar, C. (2012). A comparison of various edge detection techniques used in image processing. [IJCSI]. *International Journal of Computer Science Issues*, *9*(5), 269.

Shrivas & Yadav. (2015). Visual Cryptography in the Video using Halftone Technique. *International Journal of Computer Applications, 117*(14).

Si, Y., Huang, L., & Li, X. (2019). Research on image processing technology and its application in tourism marketing. *Journal of Advances in Management Science and Information Systems*, *5*(1), 31–40. doi:10.11648/j.msais.20190501.15

Sigit, R., Arief, Z., & Bachtiar, M. M. (2016). Development of Healthcare Kiosk for Checking Heart Health. *EMITTER International Journal of Engineering Technology*, *3*(2), 99–114. doi:10.24003/emitter.v3i2.49

Silva, R. L., Rudek, M., Szejka, A. L., & Junior, O. C. (2019). Machine Vision Systems for Industrial Quality Control Inspections. *IPIP International Conference on Product Lifecycle Management*, (pp. 631-641). IEEE. 10.1007/978-3-030-01614-2_58

Singh, A., & Singh, J. (2018). Image Processing and IoT-based Applications. *International Journal of Innovative Science and Research Technology*, *3*(11), 236–238. https://www.cognizant.com/InsightsWhitepapers/Designi

Singh, D., Dhar, S., & Gupta, S. (2020). Recent developments in machine vision and image processing techniques for online quality monitoring in pharmaceutical manufacturing. *Journal of Pharmaceutical Innovation*, *15*(3), 337–352. doi:10.100712247-019-09440-1

Singh, E., & Julka, E. N. (2016). A Review on Picture Fusion Techniques and Proposal of New Hybrid Technique. *International Research Journal of Engineering and Technology*, *03*(03), 1321–1324.

Singh, S., Kumar, R., & Kumar, R. (2021). Forged Image Identification with Digital Image Forensic Tools. *Journal of Biological Engineering Research & Review*, *8*(2), 162–168. www.biologicalengineering.in/Archive

Singh, S., Singla, B., Sharma, M., Goyal, S., & Sabo, A. (2020). Comprehensive Study on Internet of Things (IoT) and Design Considerations of Various Microstrip Patch Antennas for IoT Applications. In *Mobile Radio Communications and 5G Networks: Proceedings of MRCN 2020*, (pp. 19-30). Springer Singapore.

Singh, T. R., Singh, Kh. M., & Roy, S. (2013). Video watermarking scheme based on visual cryptography and scene change detection. In AEU - International Journal of Electronics and Communications (Vol. 67, Issue 8, pp. 645–651). Elsevier BV. doi:10.1016/j.aeue.2013.01.008

Sinha, M., Chacko, E., Makhija, P., & Pramanik, S. (2021). Energy Efficient Smart Cities with Green IoT. In C. Chakrabarty (Ed.), *Green Technological Innovation for Sustainable Smart Societies: Post Pandemic Era*. Springer. doi:10.1007/978-3-030-73295-0_16

Sinthanayothin, C., Boyce, J. F., Cook, H. L., & Williamson, T. H. (2004). Automated localisation of the optic disc, fovea, and retinal blood vessels from digital colour fundus images. British journal of ophthalmology, 8, 902-910.

Siregar, F., & Silalahi, M. (2019). The role of image processing in the marketing of fashion products: A literature review. *International Journal of Applied Business and Economic Research*, *17*(4), 67–82. doi:10.5281/zenodo.3584284

Sivaswamy, J., Krishnadas, S. R., Joshi, G. D., Jain, M., & Tabish, A. U. S. (2014, April). Drishti-gs: Retinal image dataset for optic nerve head (onh) segmentation. In 2014 *IEEE 11th international symposium on biomedical imaging* (ISBI), vol. 4, pp. 53-56, IEEE, 2014.

Sliwa, T., Martens, M., Plasson, R., & Godet-Bar, T. (2018). Image analysis applied to the study of coatings for high-temperature applications. *Surface and Coatings Technology*, *352*, 564–573.

Solanke, A. A. (2022). Explainable digital forensics AI: Towards mitigating distrust in AI-based digital forensics analysis using interpretable models. *Forensic Science International: Digital Investigation*, *42*, 301403. doi:10.1016/j.fsidi.2022.301403

Solanke, A. A., & Biasiotti, M. A. (2022). Digital Forensics AI: Evaluating, Standardizing and Optimizing Digital Evidence Mining Techniques. KI -. *Kunstliche Intelligenz*, *36*(2), 143–161. doi:10.100713218-022-00763-9

Sonali Dash, P. S. R. (2022). *Chowdary, Dr. C. V. Gopal Raju, Dr. Y. Umamaheswar, KJN Siva Charan, Optic Disc Segmentation based on Active Contour model for Detection and Evaluation of Glaucoma on Real Time Challenging Dataset, In proceedings of Theory and Applications (FICTA 2021)*. Springer.

Sonali Dash, P. S. R. Chowdary, VSSS Chakraborty, GupteswarSahu et al., Real Time Retinal Optic Disc Segmentation via Guided filter and Discrete Wavelet Transform, third international conference on emerging electrical energy, electronics and computing technologies 2021 (ice4ct 2021, 16th-17th December 2021, Malaysia.

Song, Z., Xu, Y., Bao, L., Zhang, L., Yu, P., Qu, Y., & Qin, C. (2019). From SARS to MERS, thrusting coronaviruses into the spotlight. *viruses, 11*(1), 59

Sonka, M., Hlavac, V., Boyle, R., Sonka, M., Hlavac, V., & Boyle, R. (n.d.). *Image pre-processing*. 56–111.

Spolaôr, N., Cherman, E. A., Monard, M. C., & Lee, H. D. (2013, October). ReliefF for multi-label feature selection. In *2013 Brazilian Conference on Intelligent Systems* (pp. 6-11). IEEE 10.1109/BRACIS.2013.10

Stalidis, P., Semertzidis, T., & Daras, P. (2021). Examining Deep Learning Architectures for Crime Classification and Prediction. *Forecasting*, *3*(4), 741–762. doi:10.3390/forecast3040046

Stec, A., & Klabjan, D. (2018). Forecasting Crime with Deep Learning. 1–20. https://arxiv.org/abs/1806.01486

Stoyanova, M., Nikoloudakis, Y., Panagiotakis, S., Pallis, E., & Markakis, E. K. (2020). A Survey on the Internet of Things (IoT) Forensics: Challenges, Approaches, and Open Issues. *IEEE Communications Surveys and Tutorials*, *22*(2), 1191–1221. doi:10.1109/COMST.2019.2962586

Strutu, M., Stamatescu, G., & Popescu, D. (2013). A Mobile Sensor Network Based Road Surface Monitoring System. In *Proceedings of IEEE Conference on System Theory, Control and Computing,* (pp. 630–634). IEEE. 10.1109/ICSTCC.2013.6689030

Su, J., Vasconcellos, D. V., Prasad, S., Sgandurra, D., Feng, Y., & Sakurai, K. (2018). Lightweight Classification of IoT Malware Based on Image Recognition. In *Proceedings of the 2018 IEEE 42nd Annual Computer Software and Applications Conference (COMPSAC),* (pp. 664–669). IEEE. 10.1109/COMPSAC.2018.10315

Subha, S., Inbamalar, T. M., Komala, C. R., Suresh, L. R., Boopathi, S., & Alaskar, K. (2023, February). A Remote Health Care Monitoring system using internet of medical things (IoMT). *Proceedings of 2023 3rd International Conference on Innovative Practices in Technology and Management, ICIPTM 2023*. IEEE. 10.1109/ICIPTM57143.2023.10118103

Subiksha, K. P. (2018, December). Improvement in analyzing healthcare systems using deep learning architecture. In *2018 4th International Conference on Computing Communication and Automation (ICCCA)* (pp. 1-4). IEEE. 10.1109/CCAA.2018.8777545

Sujath, R., Chatterjee, J. M., & Hassanien, A. E. (2020). A machine learning forecasting model for COVID-19 pandemic in India. *Stochastic Environmental Research and Risk Assessment*, *34*(7), 959–972. doi:10.100700477-020-01827-8 PMID:32837309

Sun, L., Sun, H., Wang, J., Wu, S., Zhao, Y., & Xu, Y. (2021). Breast mass detection in mammography based on image template matching and CNN. *Sensors (Basel)*, *21*(8), 2855. doi:10.339021082855 PMID:33919623

Sun, Q., Zhang, M., & Mujumdar, A. S. (2019). Recent developments of artificial intelligence in drying of fresh food: A review. *Critical Reviews in Food Science and Nutrition*, *59*(14), 2258–2275. doi:10.1080/10408398.2018.1446900 PMID:29493285

Sun, T., & Cao, J. (2022). Research on Machine Vision System Design Based on Deep Learning Neural Network. *Wireless Communications and Mobile Computing*, *2022*, 1–16. doi:10.1155/2022/4808652

Sun, X., Wang, J., Chen, R., Kong, L., & She, M. F. (2011). Directional Gaussian filter-based LBP descriptor for textural image classification. [Google Scholar]. *Procedia Engineering*, *15*, 1771–1779. doi:10.1016/j.proeng.2011.08.330

Sun, Y., & Li, X. (2020). Image processing in marketing: A bibliometric analysis. *Journal of Business Research*, *112*, 189–201. doi:10.1016/j.jbusres.2019.11.007

Sun, Y., Wu, N., Tateno, S., & Ogai, H. (2012). Development of driving support system for electric vehicle by using image processing technology. In *2012 12th International Conference on Control, Automation and Systems,* (pp. 1965-1968). IEEE.

Sung, C. S., & Park, J. Y. (2021). Design of an intelligent video surveillance system for crime prevention: Applying deep learning technology. *Multimedia Tools and Applications*, *80*(26–27), 34297–34309. doi:10.100711042-021-10809-z

Sungheetha, A. (2021). 3D Image Processing using Machine Learning based Input Processing for Man-Machine Interaction. *Journal of Innovative Image Processing*, *3*(1), 1–6. doi:10.36548/jiip.2021.1.001

Suzuki, K. (2017). Overview of deep learning in medical imaging. *Radiological Physics and Technology*, *10*(3), 257–273. doi:10.100712194-017-0406-5 PMID:28689314

Swaminathan, B., Rahul, R., Ragul, S., & Ramavel, M. (2018). Integration of IOT and Data Analytics : Performance Analysis System for Outdoor Sports using Electromyography and Image Data. *International Journal of Applied Engineering Research, 13*(8), 6158–6164.

Swapna, G., Vinayakumar, R., & Soman, K. P. (2018). Diabetes detection using deep learning algorithms. *ICT express, 4*(4), 243-246.

Szabo, G. (1997). Alcohol's contribution to compromised immunity. *Alcohol Health and Research World, 21*(1), 30. PMID:15706761

Tahamtan, A., & Ardebili, A. (2020). Real-time RT-PCR in COVID-19 detection: Issues affecting the results. *Expert Review of Molecular Diagnostics, 20*(5), 453–454. doi:10.1080/14737159.2020.1757437 PMID:32297805

Talukdar, V., Dhabliya, D., Kumar, B., Talukdar, S. B., Ahamad, S., & Gupta, A. (2022) Suspicious Activity Detection and Classification in IoT Environment Using Machine Learning Approach. *Seventh International Conference on Parallel, Distributed and Grid Computing (PDGC)*, Solan, Himachal Pradesh, India. 10.1109/PDGC56933.2022.10053312

Tang, L., Xiang, X., Zhang, H., Gong, M., & Ma, J. (2023). DIVFusion: Darkness-free infrared and visible image fusion. *Information Fusion, 91*, 477–493. doi:10.1016/j.inffus.2022.10.034

Tang, S., Yuan, S., & Zhu, Y. (2020). Data preprocessing techniques in convolutional neural network based on fault diagnosis towards rotating machinery. *IEEE Access: Practical Innovations, Open Solutions, 8*, 149487–149496. doi:10.1109/ACCESS.2020.3012182

Tarrataca, L., Dias, C. M., Haddad, D. B., & De Arruda, E. F. (2021). Flattening the curves: On-off lock-down strategies for COVID-19 with an application to Brazil. *Journal of Mathematics in Industry, 11*(1), 1–18. doi:10.118613362-020-00098-w PMID:33432282

Tasci, E., Uluturk, C., & Ugur, A. (2021). A voting-based ensemble deep learning method focusing on image augmentation and preprocessing variations for tuberculosis detection. *Neural Computing & Applications, 33*(22), 15541–15555. doi:10.100700521-021-06177-2 PMID:34121816

Taskin, O., Polat, A., Etemoglu, A. B., & Izli, N. (2022). Energy and exergy analysis, drying kinetics, modeling, microstructure and thermal properties of convective-dried banana slices. *Journal of Thermal Analysis and Calorimetry, 147*(3), 2343–2351. doi:10.100710973-021-10639-z

Teleron, J. I. (2022). The Implementation of IoT-Based Android App Vegetable Health Check Using Image Processing. *International Research Journal of Advanced Engineering and Science, 7*(1), 203–207.

Tian, Y., Wei, H., & Zhang, J. (2019). A review of image processing techniques in the tourism industry. *Journal of Tourism and Cultural Change, 17*(1), 97–111. doi:10.1080/14766825.2018.1484817

Tiwari & Kakelli. (2021). Secure Online Voting System using Visual Cryptography. *Walailak J Sci & Tech, 18*(15), 1-14.

Todan, L., Voicescu, M., Culita, D. C., Lincu, D., Ion, R. M., Călin, M., Răut, I., & Kuncser, A. C. (2022). A curcumin-loaded silica carrier with NH_3 sensitivity and antimicrobial properties. *Chemicke Zvesti, 76*(5), 3087–3096. doi:10.100711696-022-02090-7

Tran, N. D. T., Leung, C. K., Madill, E. W., & Binh, P. T. (2022, June). A deep learning based predictive model for healthcare analytics. In *2022 IEEE 10th International Conference on Healthcare Informatics (ICHI)* (pp. 547-549). IEEE.

Traverso, C. E., Walt, J. G., Kelly, S. P., Hommer, A. H., Bron, A. M., Denis, P., & … . (2005). Direct costs of glaucoma and severity of the disease: A multinational long term study of resource utilisation in Europe. *The British Journal of Ophthalmology, 89*(10), 1245–1249. doi:10.1136/bjo.2005.067355 PMID:16170109

Tripathi, J., & Saini, A. (2020). Enhanced Visual Cryptography: An Augmented Model for Image Security. In *Procedia Computer Science* (Vol. 167, pp. 323–333). Elsevier BV. doi:10.1016/j.procs.2020.03.232

Trojovský, P., Dhasarathan, V., & Boopathi, S. (2023). Experimental investigations on cryogenic friction-stir welding of similar ZE42 magnesium alloys. *Alexandria Engineering Journal*, *66*(1), 1–14. doi:10.1016/j.aej.2022.12.007

Tundis, A., Kaleem, H., & Mühlhäuser, M. (2020). Detecting and tracking criminals in the real world through an IoT-based system. *Sensors (Basel)*, *20*(13), 1–27. doi:10.339020133795 PMID:32645873

Turner, C. (2022). Augmented Reality, Augmented Epistemology, and the Real-World Web. *Philosophy & Technology*, *35*(1), 19. doi:10.100713347-022-00496-5

Tyagi, S. (2022). *Modern CNN-based Image Forgery Detection Network*. ForensicNet.

Ullal, M. S., Hawaldar, I. T., Soni, R., & Nadeem, M. (2021). The Role of Machine Learning in Digital Marketing. *SAGE Open*, *11*(4), 1–5. doi:10.1177/21582440211050394

Valdez-Rodriguez, J. E., Felipe-Riveron, E. M., & Calvo, H. (2021). Optic Disc preprocessing for reliable glaucoma detection in small dataset. *Mathematics*, *9*(2237), 1–14. doi:10.3390/math9182237

Valikhani, A., Jaberi Jahromi, A., Pouyanfar, S., Mantawy, I. M., & Azizinamini, A. (2021). Machine learning and image processing approaches for estimating concrete surface roughness using basic cameras. *Computer-Aided Civil and Infrastructure Engineering*, *36*(2), 213–226. doi:10.1111/mice.12605

Vanitha, S. K. R., & Boopathi, S. (2023). Artificial Intelligence Techniques in Water Purification and Utilization. In *Human Agro-Energy Optimization for Business and Industry* (pp. 202–218). IGI Global. doi:10.4018/978-1-6684-4118-3.ch010

Varghese, J. Z., & Boone, R. G. (2015). Overview of autonomous vehicle sensors and systems. In *International Conference on Operations Excellence and Service Engineering*, (pp. 178-191). IEEE.

Varuna Shree, N., & Kumar, T. N. R. (2018). Identification and classification of brain tumor MRI images with feature extraction using DWT and probabilistic neural network. *Brain Informatics*, *5*(1), 23–30. doi:10.100740708-017-0075-5 PMID:29313301

Vasan, D., Alazab, M., Wassan, S., Safaei, B., & Zheng, Q. (2020). Image-Based malware classification using ensemble of CNN architectures (IMCEC). *Computers & Security*, *92*, 101748. doi:10.1016/j.cose.2020.101748

Veeraiah, V., Ahamad, G. P. S., Talukdar, S. B., Gupta, A., & Talukdar, V. (2022) Enhancement of Meta Verse Capabilities by IoT Integration. *2022 2nd International Conference on Advance Computing and Innovative Technologies in Engineering (ICACITE)*, (pp. 1493-1498). 10.1109/ICACITE53722.2022.9823766

Veeraiah, V., Khan, H., Kumar, A., Ahamad, S., Mahajan, A., & Gupta, A. (2022). Integration of PSO and Deep Learning for Trend Analysis of Meta-Verse. *2022 2nd International Conference on Advance Computing and Innovative Technologies in Engineering (ICACITE)*, (pp. 713-718). IEEE. 10.1109/ICACITE53722.2022.9823883

Veeraiah, V., Rajaboina, N. B., Rao, G. N., Ahamad, S., Gupta, A., & Suri, C. S. (2022).Securing Online Web Application for IoT Management. *2022 2nd International Conference on Advance Computing and Innovative Technologies in Engineering (ICACITE)*, (pp. 1499-1504). IEEE. 10.1109/ICACITE53722.2022.9823733

Venkatesh, S., & Owens, R. "On the classification of image features." Pattern Recognition Letters 11, vol. 5, pp. 339-349, 2002.

Venkatesh, S., Abhiram E, Rajarajeswari S, Kumar, K. M., & Balakuntala, S. (2014). An Intelligent System to Detect, Avoid and Maintain Potholes: A Graph Theoretic Approach. In *Proceedings of International Conference on Mobile Computing and Ubiquitous Networking,* (pp. 80). IEEE.

Vennila, T., Karuna, M. S., Srivastava, B. K., Venugopal, J., Surakasi, R., & B., S. (2023). New Strategies in Treatment and Enzymatic Processes. In *Human Agro-Energy Optimization for Business and Industry* (pp. 219–240). IGI Global. doi:10.4018/978-1-6684-4118-3.ch011

Verma, H., Lotia, S., & Singh, A. (2020). Convolutional neural network based criminal detection. *IEEE Region 10 Annual International Conference, Proceedings/TENCON,* (pp. 1124–1129). 10.1109/TENCON50793.2020.9293926

Vermund, S. H., & Pitzer, V. E. (2021). Asymptomatic transmission and the infection fatality risk for COVID-19: Implications for school reopening. *Clinical Infectious Diseases*, 72(9), 1493–1496. doi:10.1093/cid/ciaa855 PMID:32584967

Vidal, M., & Amigo, J. M. (2012). Pre-processing of hyperspectral images. Essential steps before image analysis. *Chemometrics and Intelligent Laboratory Systems*, 117, 138–148. doi:10.1016/j.chemolab.2012.05.009

Vijayan, A., & Sreeram, S. (2015). Survey On Picture Fusion Techniques. *International Journal of Engineering Research and General Science*, 3(3), 744–748.

Vinh, T. Q., & Nguyen, T. N. A. (2020). Real-time face mask detector using YOLOv3 algorithm and Haar cascade classifier. In *2020 international conference on advanced computing and applications (ACOMP),* (pp. 146-149). IEEE. doi:10.1109/ACOMP50827.2020.00029

Viola, P., & Jones, M. J. (2004). Robust real-time face detection. *International Journal of Computer Vision*, 57(2), 137–154. doi:10.1023/B:VISI.0000013087.49260.fb

Vivek, S., Srinivasan, K., Sharmila, B., Dharshan, Y., Panchal, H., Suresh, M., Ashokkumar, R., Sadasivuni, K. K., Elkelawy, M., & Shrimali, N. (2022). An Improved Quality Inspection of Engine Bearings Using Machine Vision Systems. *Smart and Sustainable Manufacturing Systems*, 6(1), 20210012. doi:10.1520/SSMS20210012

Vivo Delgado, G., & Castro-Toledo, F. J. (2020). Urban security and crime prevention in smart cities: a systematic review. *International E-Journal of Criminal Sciences, 15*(6).

Vivone, G. (2023). Multispectral and hyperspectral image fusion in remote sensing: A survey. *Information Fusion, 89*, 405–417. doi:10.1016/j.inffus.2022.08.032

Voyatzis, G., Nikolaidis, N., & Pitas, I. (1998). Digital watermarking: An overview. *9Th European Signal Processing Conference (EUSIPCO 1998),* (pp. 1–4). IEEE.

Wafy, M., Gamal Zanaty, S., & Elkhouly, M. (2022). Video Identification Based on Watermarking Schemes and Visual Cryptography. In Computer Systems Science and Engineering (Vol. 40, Issue 2, pp. 441–453). Computers, Materials and Continua (Tech Science Press). doi:10.32604/csse.2022.018597

Waheed, S. R., Rahim, M. S. M., Suaib, N. M., & Salim, A. A. (2023). CNN deep learning-based image to vector depiction. *Multimedia Tools and Applications*, 82(13), 1–20. doi:10.100711042-023-14434-w

Wang, C., Lin, Z., Yang, X., Sun, J., Yue, M., & Shahabi, C. (2022). HAGEN: Homophily-Aware Graph Convolutional Recurrent Network for Crime Forecasting. *Proceedings of the AAAI Conference on Artificial Intelligence*, 36(4), 4193–4200. doi:10.1609/aaai.v36i4.20338

Wang, C.-X., Di Renzo, M., Stanczak, S., Wang, S., & Larsson, E. G. (2020). Artificial intelligence enabled wireless networking for 5G and beyond: Recent advances and future challenges. *IEEE Wireless Communications*, 27(1), 16–23. doi:10.1109/MWC.001.1900292

Wang, J., & Zhang, Y. (2020). Median filtering forensics scheme for color images based on quaternion magnitude-phase CNN. *Computers, Materials & Continua*, *62*(1), 99–112. doi:10.32604/cmc.2020.04373

Wang, J., Chen, Y., & Huang, J. (2020). Image processing in social media marketing: A review and agenda for future research. *Journal of Business Research*, *117*, 627–639. doi:10.1016/j.jbusres.2020.08.012

Wang, K., Chen, C.-M., Hossain, M. S., Muhammad, G., Kumar, S., & Kumari, S. (2021). Transfer reinforcement learning-based road object detection in next generation IoT domain. *Computer Networks*, *193*, 108078. doi:10.1016/j.comnet.2021.108078

Wang, L., & Wong, A. (2020). COVID-Net: A Tailored Deep Convolutional Neural Network Design for Detection of COVID-19 Cases from Chest X-Ray Images. *arXiv preprint arXiv:2003.09871.*

Wang, L., Wang, J., & Huang, W. (2021). A scalable ideal progressive visual cryptography scheme. In *2021 10th International Conference on Internet Computing for Science and Engineering. ICICSE 2021: 2021 10th International Conference on Internet Computing for Science and Engineering.* ACM. 10.1145/3485314.3485320

Wang, Q., Jin, G., Zhao, X., Feng, Y., & Huang, J. (2020). CSAN: A neural network benchmark model for crime forecasting in spatio-temporal scale. *Knowledge-Based Systems, 189*, 105120. doi:10.1016/j.knosys.2019.105120

Wang, S., Kang, B., Ma, J., Zeng, X., Xiao, M., Guo, J., & Xu, B. (2020). A deep learning algorithm using CT images to screen for Corona Virus Disease (COVID-19). MedRxiv. doi:10.1101/2020.02.14.20023028

Wang, W., Chen, S., Chen, L., & Chang, W. (2017). A Machine Vision Based Automatic Optical Inspection System for Measuring Drilling Quality of Printed Circuit Boards. *IEEE Access : Practical Innovations, Open Solutions*, *5*, 10817–10833. doi:10.1109/ACCESS.2016.2631658

Wang, X., Chen, H., Gan, C., Lin, H., Dou, Q., Tsougenis, E., Huang, Q., Cai, M., & Heng, P. A. (2019). Weakly supervised deep learning for whole slide lung cancer image analysis. *IEEE Transactions on Cybernetics*, *50*(9), 3950–3962. doi:10.1109/TCYB.2019.2935141 PMID:31484154

Wang, X., Wang, H., & Niu, S. (2020). An Intelligent Forensics Approach for Detecting Patch-Based Image Inpainting. *Mathematical Problems in Engineering*, *2020*, 1–10. doi:10.1155/2020/8892989

Wang, Z., Sun, X., Zhang, X., Han, T., & Gao, F. (2020). Algorithm Improvement of Pedestrians' Red-Light Running Snapshot System Based on Image Recognition. In Q. Liang, W. Wang, X. Liu, Z. Na, M. Jia, & B. Zhang (Eds.), *Communications, Signal Processing, and Systems. CSPS 2019. Lecture Notes in Electrical Engineering* (Vol. 571). Springer. doi:10.1007/978-981-13-9409-6_207

Weigand, K., Witte, R., Moukabary, T., Chinyere, I., Lancaster, J., Pierce, M. K., Goldman, S., & Juneman, E. (2016). In vivo electrophysiological study of induced ventricular tachycardia in intact rat model of chronic ischemic heart failure. *IEEE Transactions on Biomedical Engineering*, *64*(6), 1393–1399. doi:10.1109/TBME.2016.2605578 PMID:27608446

Williams, A., Corner, E., & Taylor, H. (2022). Vehicular Ramming Attacks: Assessing the Effectiveness of Situational Crime Prevention Using Crime Script Analysis. *Terrorism and Political Violence*, *34*(8), 1549–1563. doi:10.1080/09546553.2020.1810025

Wirayasa, I. K. A. (2021). Comparison of Convolutional Neural Networks Model Using Different Optimizers for Image Classification International Journal of Sciences. *Comparison of Convolutional Neural Networks Model Using Different Optimizers for Image Classification.*, *4531*(September), 116–126.

Wong, D. W. K., Liu, J., Lim, J. H., Jia, X., Yin, F., Li, H., & Wong, T. Y. (2008). Level-set based automatic cup-to-disc ratio determination using retinal fundus images in ARGALI. In *2008 30th annual international conference of the IEEE engineering in medicine and biology society*, (pp. 2266-2269). IEEE. 10.1109/IEMBS.2008.4649648

World Bank. (2019). *India: Safe, Clean, Affordable, and Smart Transport*. World Bank. https://www.worldbank.org/en/country/india/brief/india-safe-clean-affordable-smart-transport

Wu, C. T., Wang, S. M., Su, Y. E., Hsieh, T. T., Chen, P. C., Cheng, Y. C., Tseng, T.-W., Chang, W.-S., Su, C.-S., Kuo, L.-C., Chien, J.-Y., & Lai, F. (2022). A Precision Health Service for Chronic Diseases: Development and Cohort Study Using Wearable Device, Machine Learning, and Deep Learning. *IEEE Journal of Translational Engineering in Health and Medicine*, *10*, 1–14. doi:10.1109/JTEHM.2022.3207825 PMID:36199984

Wu, J., Wang, Y., Wu, T., Zhao, W., & Zhu, H. (2020). A review of image processing techniques for gas turbine blade manufacturing. *Journal of Manufacturing Systems*, *57*, 37–50. doi:10.1016/j.jmsy.2020.03.011

Wu, P., & Kao, H. P. (2019). The impact of image processing on food packaging design and marketing: A review. *Journal of Packaging Technology and Research*, *3*(1), 1–14. doi:10.100741783-018-0040-4

Wu, Y., & Francis, L. F. (2017). Effect of particle size distribution on stress development and microstructure of particulate coatings. *Journal of Coatings Technology and Research*, *14*(2), 455–465. doi:10.100711998-016-9866-5

Wu, Z., Xue, R., & Li, H. (2022). Real-Time Video Fire Detection via Modified YOLOv5 Network Model. *Fire Technology*, *58*(4), 2377–2403. doi:10.100710694-022-01260-z

Xiao, H., Xinzhi, T., Liu, C., Li, T., Ren, G., Yang, R., Shen, D., & Cai, J. (2021). A review of deep learning-based three-dimensional medical image registration methods. *Quantitative Imaging in Medicine and Surgery*, *11*(12), 11. doi:10.21037/qims-21-175 PMID:34888197

Xu, L., & Li, X. (2019). The impact of image processing on customer purchase intention: A review. *Journal of Business Research*, *103*, 259–270. doi:10.1016/j.jbusres.2019.06.044

Xu, X., Liu, Y., Wang, W., Zhao, X., Sheng, Q. Z., Wang, Z., & Shi, B. (2018). ITS-frame: A framework for multi-aspect analysis in the field of intelligent transportation systems. *IEEE Transactions on Intelligent Transportation Systems*, *20*(8), 2893–2902. doi:10.1109/TITS.2018.2868840

Xu, Y., Li, D., Xie, Q., Wu, Q., & Wang, J. (2021). Automatic defect detection and segmentation of tunnel surface using modified Mask R-CNN. *Measurement*, *178*, 109316. doi:10.1016/j.measurement.2021.109316

Xu, Y., Xu, D., Lin, S., Liu, J., Cheng, J., Cheung, C. Y., & Wong, T. Y. (2011, September). Sliding window and regression based cup detection in digital fundus images for glaucoma diagnosis. *In International Conference on Medical Image Computing and Computer-Assisted Intervention* (pp. 1-8). Springer. [10.1007/978-3-642-23626-6_1

Xu, Z., Cheng, C., & Sugumaran, V. (2020). Big data analytics of crime prevention and control based on image processing upon cloud computing. *J Surveill Secur Saf*, *1*, 16–33. doi:10.20517/jsss.2020.04

Xuehua, J. (2010). Digital watermarking and its application in image copyright protection. *2010 International Conference on Intelligent Computation Technology and Automation*, (vol. 2, 114–117). IEEE. 10.1109/ICICTA.2010.625

Yamada, Y., & Beltran, H. (2021). Clinical and Biological Features of Neuroendocrine Prostate Cancer. *Current Oncology Reports*, *23*(2), 15. doi:10.100711912-020-01003-9 PMID:33433737

Yan, H., Lu, H., Ye, M., Yan, K., Xu, Y., & Jin, Q. (2019). Improved mask R-CNN for lung nodule segmentation. In *2019 10th International Conference on Information Technology in Medicine and Education (ITME)*, (pp. 137-141). IEEE. 10.1109/ITME.2019.00041

Yan, L., Fu, J., Wang, C., Ye, Z., Chen, H., & Ling, H. (2021). Enhanced network optimized generative adversarial network for image enhancement. *Multimedia Tools and Applications*, *80*(9), 14363–14381. doi:10.100711042-020-10310-z

Yan, Y., & Huang, L. (2014). Large-scale image processing research cloud. *Cloud Computing*, 88–93.

Yang, C.-N., Shih, H.-W., Wu, C.-C., & Harn, L. (2012). k Out of n Region Incrementing Scheme in Visual Cryptography. In IEEE Transactions on Circuits and Systems for Video Technology (Vol. 22, Issue 5, pp. 799–810). Institute of Electrical and Electronics Engineers (IEEE). doi:10.1109/TCSVT.2011.2180952

Yang, E., Ene, I. C., Arabi Belaghi, R., Koff, D., Stein, N., & Santaguida, P. (2022). Stakeholders' perspectives on the future of artificial intelligence in radiology: A scoping review. *European Radiology*, *32*(3), 1477–1495. doi:10.100700330-021-08214-z PMID:34545445

Yang, H., & Ma, J. (2021). How the COVID-19 pandemic impacts tobacco addiction: Changes in smoking behavior and associations with well-being. *Addictive Behaviors*, *119*, 106917. doi:10.1016/j.addbeh.2021.106917 PMID:33862579

Yang, J., & Zhang, X. (2019). The application of image processing in hospitality and tourism marketing: A systematic review. *Tourism Management*, *70*, 204–214. doi:10.1016/j.tourman.2018.08.022

Yang, J., Ge, H., Yang, J., Tong, Y., & Su, S. (2022). Online multi-object tracking using multi-function integration and tracking simulation training. *Applied Intelligence*, *52*(2), 1268–1288. doi:10.100710489-021-02457-5

Yang, P., Baracchi, D., Ni, R., Zhao, Y., Argenti, F., & Piva, A. (2020). A survey of deep learning-based source image forensics. *Journal of Imaging*, *6*(3), 9. doi:10.3390/jimaging6030009 PMID:34460606

Yang, P. U., Liu, P., Li, D., & Zhao, D. (2020). Corona Virus Disease 2019, a growing threat to children? *The Journal of Infection*, *80*(6), 671–693. doi:10.1016/j.jinf.2020.02.024 PMID:32142929

Yang, Z., Zeng, Z., Wang, K., Wong, S. S., Liang, W., Zanin, M., Liu, P., Cao, X., Gao, Z., Mai, Z., Liang, J., Liu, X., Li, S., Li, Y., Ye, F., Guan, W., Yang, Y., Li, F., Luo, S., & He, J. (2020). Modified SEIR and AI prediction of the epidemics trend of COVID-19 in China under public health interventions. *Journal of Thoracic Disease*, *12*(3), 165–174. doi:10.21037/jtd.2020.02.64 PMID:32274081

Yap, M. H., Pons, G., Marti, J., & Ganau, S. (2015). Automated detection of breast cancer in mammograms using cascaded deep learning neural networks. In *International Conference on Medical Image Computing and Computer-Assisted Intervention* (pp. 632-640). Springer.

Yaqoob, M., Sharma, S., & Aggarwal, P. (2021). Imaging techniques in Agro-industry and their applications, a review. *Journal of Food Measurement and Characterization*, *15*(3), 2329–2343. doi:10.100711694-021-00809-w

Ying, L., Qian Nan, Z., Fu Ping, W., Tuan Kiang, C., Keng Pang, L., Heng Chang, Z., Lu, C., Jun, L. G., & Nam, L. (2021). Adaptive weights learning in CNN feature fusion for crime scene investigation image classification. *Connection Science*, *33*(3), 719–734. doi:10.1080/09540091.2021.1875987

Yoshinaga, T., Fukuda, Y., Watanabe, Y., & Hiroike, A. (2019). *Video Analytics AI for Public Safety and Security.*, *71*(2), 131–137.

Yu, L., Sun, Y., & Zhang, C. (2020). Image processing in online advertising: A review and research agenda. *Journal of Business Research*, *116*, 599–609. doi:10.1016/j.jbusres.2020.07.032

Yu, S., Xiao, D., & Kanagasingam, Y. (2017, July). Exudate detection for diabetic retinopathy with convolutional neural networks. In *2017 39th Annual International Conference of the IEEE Engineering in Medicine and Biology Society (EMBC)* (pp. 1744-1747). IEEE. 10.1109/EMBC.2017.8037180

Yu, X., & Salari, E. (2011). Pavement pothole detection and severity measurement using laser imaging. In *2011 IEEE International Conference on Electro/Information Technology*, (pp. 1-5). IEEE. 10.1109/EIT.2011.5978573

Yuan, G., & Hao, Q. (2020). Digital watermarking secure scheme for remote sensing image protection. *China Communications*, *17*(4), 88–98. doi:10.23919/JCC.2020.04.009

Yue, X., Li, H., Shimizu, M., Kawamura, S., & Meng, L. (2022). Deep learning-based real-time object detection for empty-dish recycling robot. In *2022 13th Asian Control Conference (ASCC)*, (pp. 2177-2182). IEEE. 10.23919/ASCC56756.2022.9828060

Yue, X., Li, H., Shimizu, M., Kawamura, S., & Meng, L. (2022). YOLO-GD: A deep learning-based object detection algorithm for empty-dish recycling robots. *Machines*, *10*(5), 294. doi:10.3390/machines10050294

Yupapin, P., Trabelsi, Y., Nattappan, A., & Boopathi, S. (2023). Performance Improvement of Wire-Cut Electrical Discharge Machining Process Using Cryogenically Treated Super-Conductive State of Monel-K500 Alloy. *Iranian Journal of Science and Technology. Transaction of Mechanical Engineering*, *47*(1), 267–283. doi:10.100740997-022-00513-0

Zargar, S. A., Islam, T., Rehman, I. U., & Pandey, D. (2021). Use of cluster analysis to monitor novel corona virus (Covid-19) infections In India. *Asian Journal of Advances in Medical Science*, 32-38.

Završnik, A. (2020). Criminal justice, artificial intelligence systems, and human rights. *ERA Forum, 20*(4), 567–583. 10.100712027-020-00602-0

Zawbaa, H. M., Osama, H., El-Gendy, A., Saeed, H., Harb, H. S., Madney, Y. M., Abdelrahman, M., Mohsen, M., Ali, A. M. A., Nicola, M., Elgendy, M. O., Ibrahim, I. A., & Abdelrahim, M. E. (2022). Effect of mutation and vaccination on spread, severity, and mortality of COVID-19 disease. *Journal of Medical Virology*, *94*(1), 197–204. doi:10.1002/jmv.27293 PMID:34427922

Zhang, D., Yuan, Z., Hu, P., & Yang, Y. (2022). Automatic treatment planning for cervical cancer radiation therapy using direct three-dimensional patient anatomy match. *Journal of Applied Clinical Medical Physics*, *23*(8), e13649. doi:10.1002/acm2.13649 PMID:35635799

Zhang, J., Xie, Y., Li, Y., Shen, C., & Xia, Y. (2020). Covid-19 screening on chest x-ray images using deep learning based anomaly detection. *arXiv preprint arXiv:2003.12338.*

Zhang, J., Yu, Z., Cheng, Y., Sha, X., & Zhang, H. (2022). A novel hierarchical framework to evaluate residential exposure to green spaces. *Landscape Ecology*, *37*(3), 895–911. doi:10.100710980-021-01378-5

Zhang, K., Zuo, W., & Zhang, L. (2018). FFDNet: Toward a fast and flexible solution for CNN-based image denoising. *IEEE Transactions on Image Processing*, *27*(9), 4608–4622. doi:10.1109/TIP.2018.2839891 PMID:29993717

Zhang, N., Zhang, N., Zheng, Q., & Xu, Y.-S. (2022). Real-time prediction of shield moving trajectory during tunnelling using GRU deep neural network. *Acta Geotechnica*, *17*(4), 1167–1182. doi:10.100711440-021-01319-1

Zhang, P. (2022). Image Enhancement Method Based on Deep Learning. *Mathematical Problems in Engineering*, *2022*, 1–9. Advance online publication. doi:10.1155/2022/6797367 PMID:35781947

Zhang, R., Guo, L., Huang, S., & Wen, B. (2021)ReLLIE: Deep reinforcement learning for customized low-light image enhancement. In *Proceedings of the 29th ACM international conference on multimedia*, (pp. 2429-2437). IEEE. 10.1145/3474085.3475410

Zhang, S., Zhao, Y., & Bai, P. (2018). Object localization improved grabcut for lung parenchyma segmentation. *Procedia Computer Science*, *131*, 1311–1317. doi:10.1016/j.procs.2018.04.330

Zhang, T., Aftab, W., Mihaylova, L., Langran-Wheeler, C., Rigby, S., Fletcher, D., Maddock, S., & Bosworth, G. (2022). Recent Advances in Video Analytics for Rail Network Surveillance for Security, Trespass and Suicide Prevention—A Survey. *Sensors (Basel)*, *22*(12), 4324. doi:10.339022124324 PMID:35746103

Zhang, X., & Zhu, X. (2019). Autonomous path tracking control of intelligent electric vehicles based on lane detection and optimal preview method. *Expert Systems with Applications*, *121*, 38–48. doi:10.1016/j.eswa.2018.12.005

Zhang, X., Zhu, S., & Tann, J. (2016). A review of recent advances in lane detection and departure warning system. In *International Conference on Intelligent Transportation* (pp. 107-118). Springer, Cham.

Zhang, Z., Ai, X., Chan C., & Dahnoun, N. (2021). An Efficient Algorithm for Pothole Detection using Stereo Vision. In *Proceedings of IEEE Conference on Acoustic, Speech and Signal Processing*, (pp. 564-568). IEEE.

Zhao, G., Ge, W., & Yu, Y. (2021). GraphFPN: Graph feature pyramid network for object detection." In *Proceedings of the IEEE/CVF international conference on computer vision*, (pp. 2763-2772). IEEE. 10.1109/ICCV48922.2021.00276

Zhao, H., Gallo, O., Frosio, I., & Kautz, J. (2015). Loss functions for neural networks for image processing. *ArXiv Preprint ArXiv:1511.08861*.

Zhao, H., Lu, L., Peng, Z., Chen, L. L., Meng, X., Zhang, C., & To, K. K. W. 2021. SARS-CoV-2 Omicron variant shows less efficient replication and fusion activity when compared with the delta variant in TMPRSS2-expressed cells: Omicron variant replication kinetics. *Emerging microbes & infections*, 1-18.

Zhao, K., Kang, J., Jung, J., & Sohn, G. (2018). Building extraction from satellite images using mask R-CNN with building boundary regularization. In *Proceedings of the IEEE conference on computer vision and pattern recognition workshops*, (pp. 247-251).

Zhao, Z. Q., Zheng, P., Xu, S. T., & Wu, X. (2019). Object detection with deep learning: A review. *IEEE Transactions on Neural Networks and Learning Systems*, *30*(11), 3212–3232. doi:10.1109/TNNLS.2018.2876865 PMID:30703038

Zheng, L., Guo, S., & Kawanishi, M. (2022). Magnetically Controlled Multifunctional Capsule Robot for Dual-Drug Delivery. *IEEE Systems Journal*, *16*(4), 6413–6424. doi:10.1109/JSYST.2022.3145869

Zheng, X., & Cloutier, R. S. (2022). A Review of Image Classification Algorithms in IoT. *EAI Endorsed Transactions on Internet of Things*, *7*(28), 1–11. doi:10.4108/eetiot.v7i28.562

Zhijun Wang, D. Z. (june 2005). *A Comparative Analysis of Image Fusion Methods*. IEEE.

Zhou, L., Xiao, Y., Pan, Z., Cao, Y., & Chen, W. (2022). Visual Cryptography Using Binary Amplitude-Only Holograms. In Frontiers in Photonics (Vol. 2). Frontiers Media SA. doi:10.3389/fphot.2021.821304

Zhou, S. K., Greenspan, H., Davatzikos, C., Duncan, J. S., Van Ginneken, B., Madabhushi, A., Prince, J. L., Rueckert, D., & Summers, R. M. (2021). A Review of Deep Learning in Medical Imaging: Imaging Traits, Technology Trends, Case Studies with Progress Highlights, and Future Promises. *Proceedings of the IEEE*, *109*(5), 820–838. doi:10.1109/JPROC.2021.3054390

Zhu, H., Crabb, D. P., Schlottmann, P. G., Wollstein, G., & Garway-Heath, D. F. (2011). Aligning scan acquisition circles in optical coherence tomography images of the retinal nerve fibre layer. *IEEE Transactions on Medical Imaging*, *30*(6), 1228–1238. doi:10.1109/TMI.2011.2109962 PMID:21296706

Zichichi, M., Ferretti, S., & D'angelo, G. (2020). A framework based on distributed ledger technologies for data management and services in intelligent transportation systems. *IEEE Access : Practical Innovations, Open Solutions*, 8, 100384–100402. doi:10.1109/ACCESS.2020.2998012

Zohora, S. E., Chakraborty, S., Khan, A. M., & Dey, N. (2016, March). Detection of exudates in diabetic retinopathy: a review. In *2016 International Conference on Electrical, Electronics, and Optimization Techniques (ICEEOT)* (pp. 2063-2068). IEEE. 10.1109/ICEEOT.2016.7755052

(1950). Monika, &Passi, A. (2021). Digital Image Forensic based on Machine Learning approach for Forgery Detection and Localization. *Journal of Physics: Conference Series*, (1). doi:10.1088/1742-6596/1950/1/012035

About the Contributors

Binay Kumar Pandey is currently working as an Assistant Professor in Department of Information Technology of Govind Ballabh Pant University of Agriculture and Technology Pantnagar Uttrakhand, India. He obtained his M. Tech with Specialization in Bioinformatics from Maulana Azad National Institute of Technology Bhopal M. P. India, in 2008 . He obtained his First Degree B. Tech at the IET Lucknow (Uttar Pradesh Technical University, Uttar Pradesh and Lucknow) India, in 2005. In 2010, he joined Department of Information Technology of College of Technology in Govind Ballabh Pant University of Agriculture and Technology Pantnagar as an Assistant Professor and worked for various UG and PG projects till date. He has more than ten years of experience in the field of teaching and research. He has more than 40 publications in reputed peer journal reputed journal Springer, Inderscience (sci and socopus indexed journal and others) and 3 patents. He has many awards such PM Scholarship etc . He session chair in IEEE International Conference on Advent Trends in Multidisciplinary Research and Innovation (ICATMRI-2020) on December 30, 2020 organized by Pankaj Laddhad Institute of Technology and Management Studies Buldhana, Maharashtra, India.

Digvijay Pandey is a Lecturer, Department of Technical Education, Research Scholar, IET Lucknow, India.

Rohit Anand is currently working as an Assistant Professor in the Department of Electronics and Communication Engineering at G.B. Pant Engineering College (Government of NCT of Delhi), New Delhi, India. He has teaching experience of more than 18 years including UG and PG Courses. He is a Life Member of Indian Society for Technical Education (ISTE). He has published 6 book chapters in reputed books and 8 papers in Scopus/SCI Indexed Journals. He has chaired a Session in AICTE-Sponsored International Conference. His research areas include Electromagnetic Field Theory, Antenna Theory and Design, Wireless Communication, Image Processing, Optical Fiber Communication, Machine Learning, etc.

* * *

Ahmar Afaq is presently working as an Assistant Professor at Symbiosis Law School, Nagpur. He has over 6 years of teaching experience at some of the premium law colleges such as Symbiosis Law School, Hyderabad, and Aligarh Muslim University. He was the former head and founder of the Centre for Human Rights, Symbiosis Law School, Hyderabad. His areas of interest are Family Law, Muslim Law, and Human Rights apart from various gender-related issues. He is presently pursuing his PhD.

from Symbiosis International (Deemed University), Pune. He has been training budding lawyers for competitive exams such as the judiciary and civil services. Apart from teaching his passion spills into the areas of research. He has over half a decade of experience in research and he has contributed his research articles in papers in some of the well-known and established journals and books apart from presenting papers at international conferences. He is also working as an editor in various reputed journals and has conducted numerous lectures and seminars on varied topics. His day-to-day efforts towards the environmental cause were recognized by the KPR Foundation which awarded him with the Global Sustainable Leader Award in February 2020.

Sharmila B. received her Ph.D. Degree in Electrical Engineering under Anna University, Chennai in the year of 2013. She completed her Post Graduate in Applied Electronics in 2004 and her Under Graduate in Electronics and Instrumentation Engineering in the year 2000. She has secured Bharathiar University Second Rank during her Under Graduate Programme. She began her career as a Software Engineer at Vigil Software Pvt. Ltd., Bangalore in 2000. Then started her teaching profession in the year 2001. She is now working as Professor in the Department of Electronics and Instrumentation Engineering at Sri Ramakrishna Engineering College, Coimbatore. She has a total experience of 18 years in teaching. She holds on additional responsibility of Chief Officer (Operations) in SREC SPARK Incubation Foundation. She is the NISP Convenor, MoE of the institution. She is a active member of MHRD IIC, MoE; CoIN and Innovation Ambassador for mentoring the Stakeholders for Projects, Startups and Incubation. She is a recognized Research Supervisor under Anna University, Chennai. Currently she guides One Full Time Research Scholar and 4 Part Time Research Scholars. Her area of interest includes Control Systems, Sensor Technology, Networked Control System and Automation.

Kallol Bhaumik received his Bachelor's degree in Electrical Engineering from the West Bengal University of Technology, West Bengal, India, in2011, his Post-Graduate degree in Power Systems from the West Bengal University of Technology, West Bengal, India, in 2013, and his Ph.D.(Engineering) degrees in electrical engineering from Indian Institute of Technology (Indian School of Mines), Dhanbad, India in 2023, respectively. He was appointed to the Department of Electrical Engineering at Saroj Mohan Institute of Technology under Techno India Group in 2014 as an Assistant Professor. Currently, he is working as an Assistant Professor in the Electrical and Electronics Engineering Department of Malla Reddy Engineering College & Management Science, affiliated with JNTU, Hyderabad. Telangana, India. He has a total experience of 10years in teaching. He has two Patents. He has several journal and conference publications at the national and international levels. His current areas of interest are wireless Power Transfer, Power Electronics Applications, Application of High-Frequency Converter, Resonant power conversion, mainly applied to contactless energy transfer, high-frequency induction heating systems, and Multi-zone Multi-output Inverters.

Sampath Boopathi completed his undergraduate in Mechanical Engineering and postgraduate in the field of Computer-Aided Design. He completed his Ph.D. from Anna University and his field of research includes Manufacturing and optimization. He published 100 more research articles in Internationally Peer-reviewed journals, one Patent grant, and three published patents.He has 16 more years of academic and research experiences in the various Engineering Colleges in Tamilnadu, India.

Pankaj Dadheech received his Ph.D. degree in Computer Science & Engineering from Suresh Gyan Vihar University (Accredited by NAAC with 'A' Grade), Jaipur, Rajasthan, India. He received his M.Tech. degree in Computer Science & Engineering from Rajasthan Technical University, Kota and he has received his B.E. in Computer Science & Engineering from University of Rajasthan, Jaipur. He has more than 18 years of experience in teaching. He is currently working as an Associate Professor & Dy. HOD in the Department of Computer Science & Engineering (NBA Accredited), Swami Keshvanand Institute of Technology, Management & Gramothan (SKIT), Jaipur, Rajasthan, India. He has published 25 Patents at Intellectual Property India, Office of the Controller General of Patents, Design and Trade Marks, Department of Industrial Policy and Promotion, Ministry of Commerce and Industry, Government of India. He has published 8 International Patents (USA, South African, Australian, Germany) & 2 Copyrights. He has 72 publications in various International & National Journals, 62 papers in various National & International conferences. He has published 9 Books & 22 Book Chapters.

Sonali Dash received the B.Tech. degree in 1992 from Utkal University, Bhubaneswar, Odisha, India, M.Tech. degree in 2005 from KIIT Bhubaneswar, Odisha, India, and the Ph.D. degree in 2019 from VSSUT, Burla, Odisha, India. She is currently working an Associate Professor in the department of Electronics and Communication Engineering, Raghu Institute of Technology (A), Visakhapatnam, India. Her research interests include Image processing, Pattern recognition, Biomedical image processing, and Communication Engineering. She has published more than 30 high-quality journal and conference papers. She is a recognised reviewer in reputed journals like Elsevier, Springer, Willey, and SPIE.

S. Dhamodaran is currently working as Assistant Professor of Department of Computer Science and Engineering in Sathyabama University, Chennai. Myself more than 12 years in Teaching and working in Sathyabama University from 2011 holding different positions. Completed My My Ph.D. in Sathyabama Institute of Science and Technology in the area of Spatial Data Mining Myself published 33 Papers in International Journals, Conference and national Conferences. In that 7 Papers are In web of science publication. Published patent. Co-ordinate and Organized National conferences, Faculty development programs and many workshops to students, faculty and Research scholars.

Shawni Dutta is a lecturer in the Computer Science department of Bhawanipur Education Society College, Kolkata. Her research areas are Machine Learning, Deep Learning, Medical Data Analysis and Recommended systems. Currently she is engaged as a reviewer in many reputed journals. She has also published certain research articles in Scopus and Web-Of-Science Indexed International Journals and Conferences.

Ankur Gupta has received the B.Tech and M.Tech in Computer Science and Engineering from Ganga Institute of Technology and Management, Kablana affiliated with Maharshi Dayanand University, Rohtak in 2015 and 2017. He is an Assistant Professor in the Department of Computer Science and Engineering at Vaish College of Engineering, Rohtak, and has been working there since January 2019. He has many publications in various reputed national/ international conferences, journals, and online book chapter contributions (Indexed by SCIE, Scopus, ESCI, ACM, DBLP, etc). He is doing research in the field of cloud computing, data security & machine learning. His research work in M.Tech was based on biometric security in cloud computing.

Anuj Kumar Gupta is an attentive teacher with excellent communication skills and intelligence. Organized and driven with the innate ability to stay on task. Uses effective and efficient methods of teaching while focusing on the individual needs of each student. More than 19 years of academic & research experience. Currently associated with Chandigarh Group of Colleges, Punjab as Officiating Director Principal cum Professor & Head (CSED). Published 100+ research papers in reputed journals and attended & presented more than 25 papers in National/International Conferences. Has guided 20+ PG scholars and 7 Ph.D. scholars. Also published 5 books and has also filed 6 patents to date.

Shashikala Gurpur has 23 plus years of teaching and research experience with 80 publications with 20 scopus and Web of science articles, 14 PhDs guided, 4 European projects, 6 Indian projects, Fulbright and AHRB fellow, Former Law commission Member with Govt of India, currently resource person and curriculum advisor to national judicial academy, many national law universities, state universities, phd referee to many, global evaluation and accreditation team member of IALS, among others.

Priyatosh Jana is Assistant Professor at the Department of Computer Science and Engineering (Cyber Security) in Haldia Institute of Technology, West Bengal, India.

R. Jayanthi is working as a Professor at Jain University Bangalore, India. She has completed her Ph.D. from Bharathiyar University. Her research area is Artifical Intellingence, Machine Learning, Data Mining, Software Engineering and Neural Networks.

Huma Khan is a committed teacher with over 13+ years of experience, teaching students from various social and cultural backgrounds. Published many research articles in various renowned journal international and national level. Many Patent published.

Deepti Khubalkar is an Assistant Professor at Symbiosis Law School, Nagpur. She has a rich experience of more than 15yrs in teaching graduate and post-graduate students, as well as guiding them in their research projects. She has written many papers in national and international journals including SCOPUS and WOS. Besides this, she also has authored few books. She is an editor in Indian Law Institute Law journal, an UGC online journal and editor in editorial board of International Bi-annual Refereed/ Peer Reviewed Research Journal, Indian Journal of Social Legal Studies and Chhattisgarh Law Journal.

Sunil Kumar obtained his Bachelor of Technology degree in 2008 from the Institute of Engineering and Technology (IET), CSJM University, Kanpur, India, and his Master of Technology degree in 2010 from the YMCA Institute of Engineering, Faridabad, India. He is a doctoral candidate at J.C. Bose University of Science and Technology, YMCA, Faridabad, Haryana, India. His research focuses on the identification of pulmonary diseases using machine learning and imaging techniques. He is an Assistant Professor in the Department of Computer Science Engineering at UIET, CSJM University, Kanpur, India. He has more than twelve years of experience teaching computer science and engineering.

Gabriela Michael is a Teaching Assistant in Symbiosis Law School, Nagpur.

D. Devasena Mohan completed her Ph.D Degree in Information and Communication Engineering under Anna University, Chennai in the year 2020. She completed her post Graduate degree in Communication Systems in the year 2010 under Anna University, Coimbatore. She secured university rank during her post Graduate Programme. She completed her under graduate degree in B.E. Electronics and Instrumentation Engineering from Maharaja Engineering College, Avinashi, Coimbatore under Anna University Chennai. She began her career as a Lecturer in the Department of Electronics and Instrumentation Engineering, Sri Ramakrishna Engineering College, Coimbatore in the year 2007. She is now currently working as Assistant Professor (Sl.Gr) in the Department of Electronics and Instrumentation Engineering, Sri Ramakrishna Engineering College, Coimbatore. She has 15 years of experience in teaching. Her research interests are in Image Processing, VLSI Implementation. Sensors, Instrumentation, waste management. She has presented papers 9 papers in National and International Conferences. She published 15 technical papers in international Journals and published three book chapters. She received 3 IPR copyrights for laboratory manuals and granted 2 patents. She acted as organizing secretary for conducting various seminars, Faculty Development Programmes, Short Term Training Programmes and National Conference sponsored by AICTE, ICMR and CSIR. Her research work had received fund from AICTE under Research Promotion Scheme (RPS) for Rs.14,17,647/-. She acted as Resource person for various events. She guided various innovative projects and the projects has been presented in various forum and secured cash prizes. She holds membership in professional bodies like ISTE and ISOI.

Aparajita Mohanty is an Associate Professor at Symbiosis Law School, Pune, Symbiosis International (Deemed University) India. She has 26 years of teaching experience. She has a Master's Degree in Political Science with an M. Phil on Public Administration. Her area of Doctoral thesis is on higher education policy. At the law school, she teaches varied courses ranging from Political Theory to International Relations, Public Administration, Law and Governance and Comparative Constitution. She is a resource person for the Certificate Programme for EU Legal Studies. She has been a part of DAAD Passage to India and Eurasia project. As the co-faculty-in-charge of international cell of the law school, she looks into the Eurasia and other project related activities. She has several publications in peer-reviewed journals and some are published in journals indexed in SCOPUS and WoS. She is a guide to Ph. D. students supervisor to LLM Dissertations.

Utsab Mukherjee is a lecturer in the Computer Science department of Bhawanipur Education Society College, Kolkata. His research areas are Machine Learning, IoT and Blockchain.

Priyadarsan Parida is an Associate Professor at GIET University, where Dr. Parida is involved in academic activities (including teaching various UG/PG courses related to electronics & communication engineering) and research. Dr. Parida has 10 years of teaching and 5 years of research experience. The research activities are reflected in different international journals and conferences of repute. His research interests mainly focuses in different computer vision applications to biomedical images.

Pawan Kumar Patidar is working as an Assistant Professor in SKIT, Jaipur in Computer Science and Engineering Department .He has done his BE(Honors) from Govt Engineering College, Bikaner in Computer Science & Engineering in 2008.He has done his MTech from Rajasthan Technical University, Kota in 2012.He has published many National and International papers in Conferences and Journals. His research areas are Image Processing and Cloud Computing.

Sabyasachi Pramanik is a professional IEEE member. He obtained a PhD in Computer Science and Engineering from Sri Satya Sai University of Technology and Medical Sciences, Bhopal, India. Presently, he is an Associate Professor, Department of Computer Science and Engineering, Haldia Institute of Technology, India. He has many publications in various reputed international conferences, journals, and book chapters (Indexed by SCIE, Scopus, ESCI, etc). He is doing research in the fields of Artificial Intelligence, Data Privacy, Cybersecurity, Network Security, and Machine Learning. He also serves on the editorial boards of several international journals. He is a reviewer of journal articles from IEEE, Springer, Elsevier, Inderscience, IET and IGI Global. He has reviewed many conference papers, has been a keynote speaker, session chair, and technical program committee member at many international conferences. He has authored a book on Wireless Sensor Network. He has edited 8 books from IGI Global, CRC Press, Springer and Wiley Publications.

Ganesh Kumar R. is an Associate Professor in the Department Computer Science and Engineering at CHRIST (Deemed to be University), Bangalore, India. He received his Master of Engineering (Computer Science and Engineering) and Ph.D., from Sathyabama University, Chennai, India. Dr. Ganesh Kumar's areas of interest in teaching and research are Data Science, Cloud Computing, Data Mining, Signal Processing, Computer Networks, High Performance Computing and Modelling and Simulation. He has over 20 papers to his credit and also supervising Doctoral students. He has served on program committees of various International and National Conferences. He is a Senior Member - IEEE, Fellow - Institute of Engineers (FIE), Member of ISTE (India).

Rupal Rautdesai, B.Sc. (Chemistry), LL.B., LL.M., Ph.D. (Law), NET, Patent Attorney, currently is a Visiting Professor and Research Advisor at Symbiosis Law School, Pune (SLS-P), Symbiosis International (Deemed University), (SIU). She also is an independent practitioner and consultant in the field of Intellectual Property Rights. She practiced as a lawyer in Goa's Local Courts under the guidance of Adv. Mahendra Khandeparkar in the initial years of her career after completing her graduation in Law. She later completed successfully National Lectureship Exams (National Eligibility Test, NET) and Patent Agent Exams in the year 2005 and decided to pursue full time teaching in law. Thus, in the past she taught law full time, from 2005 to 2007 at V. M. Salgaocar College of Law, Miramar, Goa, 2008 to 2010 at Faculty of Law, M. S. University of Baroda, and from 2010 to 2021 at Symbiosis Law School, Pune (SLS P). She has published several research papers especially in the field of Intellectual Property Rights, Data Protection Law, Big Data, Artificial Intelligence and Taxation Law. Many of her papers are SCOPUS and WoS indexed. She has been the reviewer for the Journal of Intellectual Property Rights, published by NISCAIR-CSIR, which is a SCOPUS Indexed Journal since 2008. She has guided several LL.M. and Ph.D. Students. She has been the been involved as a member of Erasmus+ Capacity Building Higher Education (International Research Projects) such as EURASIA and 21st Teach Skills which are carried out under the leadership of Dr. Shashikala Gurpur at SLS P. She visited Bulgaria and Poland under the EURASIA Project, as a part of the team that carried out important tasks. She also was part of the team that visited Greece and Cambodia while making important contributions in the 21st Teach Skills Project. She has delivered several invited sessions and workshops in the field of Intellectual Property Rights and provided consultancy to students and faculty on protection of their creativity and innovations. She visited and delivered symposium and invited sessions at Leibniz University, Hannover, Germany under the DAAD Programme in 2011 and Chuo University, Tokyo, Japan under the SIU Faculty Exchange Programme in 2015.

Saripalli Sudhakara Reddy is a visionary and a dynamic leader. Dr S. Sudhakara Reddy, Principal, has rich teaching and industrial experience for over three and half decades. As an administrator, he has been instrumental in acquiring accreditation status for most of the institutions that he has worked with. He has spearheaded the transformation of the institution from an ordinary engineering college to a 'Centre of Excellence' to produce globally competent engineers. A distinguished scholar with lofty ideas, Dr S.Sudhakara Reddy has played a significant role in revamping, restructuring and reorganising the systems at the previous colleges. He obtained his B.Tech Degree in Mechanical Engineering (Production) from Kakatiya University, Warangal, M.Tech Degree in Design and Production Engineering (Machine Tools) from NIT, Warangal and M.B.A (Human Resource Management) from Dr. B.R. Ambedkar Open University, Hyderabad. He obtained his Ph.D. in Mechanical Engineering from Sri Venkateswara University Tirupati, Andhra Pradesh. The research work related to his Ph.D was carried out at Defence Metallurgical Research Laboratory (DMRL) and Advanced Research Center for Powder Metallurgy and New Materials (ARCI) at Hyderabad. His area of research includes Tribology, CAD/CAM& Advanced Manufacturing Technology. He has authored four text books and published 56 technical papers in national, international conferences and journals. He is a life member of various Professional bodies. He is fellow of Institution of Engineers.

Abhijit Sarkar is an Assistant Professor in the Department of CSE(Cyber Security) of Haldia Institute of Technology with more than 11 years of teaching experience. He is presently pursuing research work in the domain of Steganography. His research interests include Steganography, Cryptography, Machine Learning, Deep Learning, Cloud Computing etc. He has published several research papers in different Journals, International Conference Proceedings.

Manvinder Sharma is working as Professor and Head in department of ECE, Malla Reddy Engineering College and Management Sciences, Hyderabad. He has done his Ph.D from Punjabi University Patiala. He has Published 7 SCIE papers, 6 ESCI, 16 Scopus and 10 UGC & Others. He has published 7 patents. His areas of interest are antennas, biomedical, and computer vision.

Harjinder Singh is Assistant Professor in Department of Electronics and Communication at Punjabi University.

Rajneesh Talwar is presently working as DEAN, DICE (Department of Interdisciplinary courses in Engineering at Chitkara University). He is taking care of Projects such as E-Cycle, E-Bike, Robotics, Drones, etc. Was earlier Director, Chandigarh Engineering College, Jhanjeri, Mohali. Worked as Principal, CGC Technical Campus, Jhanjeri, Mohali, Punjab, India. He has more than 21 Years of Professional Experience of Teaching, Research and Administration. Did his PhD. in 2010 and M.Tech in 2002 from Thapar University, Patiala, Punjab, India. Has more than 10 patents filed till date and the first one was a U.S Patent Granted "Fiber Optic Point Temperature Sensor" to his credit filed in 2005, More than SIXTY international Journal Publications, presented papers /participated in more than ten International conferences and many national level conference participations. He has been Delivering Expert talks on Wireless Communication, IOT, Communication Systems, etc. at various national level FDP's and Invited Talks. Has been guest of Honour at STTP. Chaired many International Conferences. He was Editorial board member of International Journal of Engg. Science and Technology, Nigeria, was Reviewer of MAEJO International Journal of Engineering Science and Technology, Thailand and is reviewer of "Materials and Design", an Elsevier International Journal. He is on TPC of various IEEE ongoing and Upcoming Conferences. GUIDED 10 candidates for their PhD. Work. Guided TEN M.Tech. thesis. Worked as principal CGC-COE Landran and Swift Technical Campus, Rajpura, Punjab, India. He has worked at various positions such as Professor and Vice Principal RIMT-MAEC, MandiGobindgarh, Professor and Head, Electronics and communication Engineering department at RIMT-IET, Mandigobindgarh, Punjab India. Was Coordinator ECE Department at Chitkara Institute of Engineering, Rajpura, Punjab India. Has been an active member in organizing national level seminars, workshops, conferences at various institutes he has worked. Has been mentor to students for various national level events such as Hackathon 2017, 2018, 2019, 2020, 2021,2022 Efficycle competition by SAE, go carts competition. Dr. Talwar has been instrumental in Signing MOU with various industries (Bosch, AWS, Red Hat, Palo Alto) and ensuring regular Seminars, Workshops, Industrial visits for providing practical exposure to the Students and for students placements. Organized Asia's Biggest Electrical Vehicle Championship at CEC Jhanjeri in Dec.2021 Organized Punjab Skill competition at CEC Jhanjeri Campus in 2021 Was Nodal Center Head for conducting Toycathon 2021 by AICTE Govt. of India. Guided various Projects which have won at National Level such as HACKATHON 2017, where the team got Three Lakh, Fifty Thousand from Govt. of India and handed over the project to Govt. He was President of Institute Innovation Council of CEC Jhanjeri, ensuring regular sessions on Innovation, entrepreneurship and Startups. Got 3.5 star out of four for 2020-21 Has been the Judge and into core organizing committee of India International Science festival held in 2020, 2021,2022. Every year on 15th September more than 20 technical events are organized under his Guidance and Mentorship on Engineer's day where students from all over India participate. He is BOG Member of ASHRE Chandigarh Chapter. A professional body for HVAC industry. He is Member of BOS of IKGPTU, Member of CDC IKGPTU and also approved PhD. Guide of IKGPTU. Organized International Conference on "Latest Trends in Engineering and Technology" on 15th July 2022.

Raj Varma is an Assistant Professor of Law at Symbiosis International (Deemed University). He is an expert in Innovation Law, Criminal Law, and AI Law. Besides that, he has a keen interest EU Law, International Law, Human Rights Law, and Constitutional Law among others. Prof. Raj is a key member of the International Cell at Symbiosis Law School, Pune; Symbiosis International (Deemed University) India where he is actively involved in four Erasmus+ CBHE projects that are being executed by his institution. These projects are: - European Studies Revitalized Across Asian Universities (EURASIA) - Teacher training with specialization on life and information technology skills (21st TS) - Curricula development on Climate Change Policy and Law - International Law and Forced Migration He has been involved in these projects right from the inception to ensuring key deliverables. As a part of these project's, he has visited the EU on multiple occasions for receiving specialized training for developing course curricula as per best practices and implementing 21st Century Training Skills within the curriculum. He has also assisted in developing niche courses in EU Legal Studies that are now taught at his institute. Besides the above, he was a core member of the team that received the prestigious Shastri Indo-Canadian Institute grant for organizing a conference on "Right to Breathe Clean Air: Health and Environment-related SDGs" Prof. Raj Varma has also presented his research at prestigious international conferences and has also been invited to various events as a judge, speaker, and resource person. He has published multiple research papers in peer-reviewed journals and his work was also referenced in a UN Sustainable Development Report.

Dharshan Y. has received his Master's degree in Control and Instrumentation Engineering from Regional centre of Anna University, Coimbatore in the year 2015 and Bachelor's degree in Instrumentation and Control Engineering from Tamilnadu College of Engineering, Coimbatore in the year 2011. Currently he is pursuing his Doctoral Degree in the Faculty of Electrical Engineering from Anna University. He has 11 years of experience in the field of teaching. His areas of interest are Control Systems, Sensors and Automation. He has published 10 technical papers in International Journals in which 35 journals are indexed in Scopus and 2 journal is indexed in Web of Science. He has attended and presented his technical papers in 5 International Conferences and 2 National Conferences. He has published a book on the title Fuzzy Logic Controller for Real Time Networked Control System by Lambert Academic Publishing. He has published 5 Patents in the Indian Patent Journal and has received 1 Copyright for the laboratory manual on Microprocessor and Microcontroller. He has attended workshops and seminars held in various colleges in and around Tamilnadu. He has been certified on Business English by Cambridge University. He has been a part of various consultancy projects undertaken by the institution to provide solution to the industries on the area of Machine Vision System for with the total fund of Rs.49,29,000/- from various industries. He has been a part of the research project funded by AICTE, New Delhi under Research Promotion Scheme for the cost of Rs.8,23,421/-. Also, he has received fund of USD 2,210 from IEEE Headquarters, New York for R&D activities on environment and social welfare of the society. Also he holds the membership of many professional bodies such as IEEE, IAENG, ISOI, and ISTE.

Index

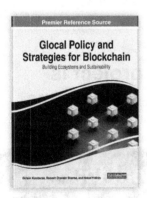

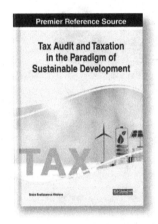

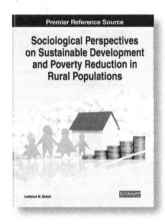

Printed in the United States
by Baker & Taylor Publisher Services